CONTEMPORARY ENGLISH VERSION

New Life

New Testament

Unless otherwise indicated, all Scripture quotations are taken from the
Contemporary English Version.

THE NEW LIFE
NEW TESTAMENT

INCLUDING:

THE NEW LIFE...THE START OF SOMETHING WONDERFUL
Copyright ©2005 by Dr. David R. Williams

and

THE CONTEMPORARY ENGLISH VERSION
of the NEW TESTAMENT
Copyright ©1995, American Bible Society

Second Printing 2007
ISBN   0-938020-81-1
Cover by: Gerard R. Jones

Published by

DECAPOLIS
PUBLISHING

In Partnership with

AMERICAN BIBLE SOCIETY
WWW.BIBLES.COM

Printed in the United States of America

WELCOME TO THE NEW LIFE

I want to congratulate you on your commitment to follow Jesus. Right now, angels are rejoicing over your decision, and the devil is trembling. You see, when you took a stand for God, the devil knew he lost — permanently — in your life. **You are a child of God today with much greater power than all of hell's forces. You have a New Life!**

God said, "But as many as received Him (Jesus), to them gave He *Power* to become the sons [and daughters] of God, even to them that believe on His name" (John 1:12 KJV).

Even the most wicked person on earth, the very instant he or she receives Jesus Christ, becomes a precious and powerful child of God. You have a call and a destiny now, regardless of how "bad" you were, or how "good" you were. We all come to God in the same way...

Jesus said, "I am the Way, the Truth, and the Life!, without me, no one can go to the Father (God) (John 14:6 *pg 82*).

You are a new person today. You have a brand New Life! All your sins have been forgiven.

USE YOUR NEW POWER

Now, I know the devil will whisper in your mind that it didn't work for you. Then he'll remind you of all the wrong you've ever done. But today, you can use your new power from God to tell Satan to **"Scram! Get out and** stay out!" Tell the devil, "I'm a new person. My past is forgiven and I'm a powerful child of God. In the authority of Jesus, I command you, devil, to go!"

And, he must go! Look at this Scripture, and think about the magnitude of His promise to YOU:

"Surrender to God! Resist the devil, and he will run from you" (James 4:7 *pg 167*).

I want to encourage you to grow strong in your faith and in your *New Life*. You have a destiny to make a difference in this world for God. And, just as your physical body has certain needs, so does your soul and spirit.

LEARNING TO GROW IN GOD WILL HELP YOU

1. A Proper Diet. In order to grow strong, you need good nutrition. Your spirit (the part of you God communicates with) needs good nutrition too. Where do you find spiritual food? You find it in the Bible. Jesus said, "learn of Me" (Matthew 11:29 KJV). And He also said, "The words that I speak to you, they are *Spirit*, and they are *Life*" (John 6:63 KJV). The Bible is "spiritual food." That's why I'm so excited about the *New Life New Testament*; it's "spiritual food."

Read Matthew, Mark, Luke and John. Learn about Jesus. Read as much as you can every day and God will open fresh truths to your heart that will help you become successful in every area of your life. Then, go on and read the rest of the *New Life New Testament*. Read a portion of it every day. Just as your body needs daily food, so does your spirit. God will show you, by the Holy Spirit, important things you'll need to know every day.

Also, be sure you find a church that teaches and preaches from the Bible, God's Word. You'll need positive, encouraging messages of faith every week.

A nutritious diet is very important.

2. Exercise. Yes, just as you need to exercise a muscle to make it grow, you need to exercise — or practice — being a Christian in order to grow spiritually.

It helps to be involved with other solid believers. They will help you learn how to share your faith, how to walk in victory, how to pray for others, and even how to cast out demons! If you have no church yet, and you want one that believes the Bible and believes in the miracle-working power of God, I'd be thrilled to see you here at Mount Hope Church regularly. (See listing on page 94.)

You'll need to exercise your faith if you want it to grow. When you do, be prepared — because genuine *miracles will begin to happen in your life.* Proper spiritual exercise is a critical stage of spiritual growth.

3. Proper Rest. Yes, I said, "rest." What do I mean by rest? Simply this: There comes a time when we must leave our future in the hands of the Lord. We cannot rest if we are filled with fear, worry, and anxiety about tomorrow.

Talk to God. Tell Him your cares, then cast them all on Him. Watch how He works things out in your life.

"God cares for you, so turn all your worries over to him" (1 Peter 5:7 *pg 171*).

"There remaineth therefore a rest to the people of God" (Hebrew 4:9 KJV).

YOU ARE A WINNER!

God called you to be a winner. You are more than a conqueror through Jesus Christ. You are a person with a destiny.

Now, let me share one other thing. God knows it takes a while to practice being a champion believer. Sometimes we "stumble" or "slip." I sure did. But God, in His kindness, gave us several promises just in case we slip in our walk with Him. First, He assures us that He doesn't condemn us.

"There is therefore now no condemnation to them which are in Christ Jesus" (Romans 8:1a KJV).

Second, He's promised to forgive us, if we tell Him about our sin, and He'll help us to go on from there. This way the devil can't succeed when he whispers, "You've sinned...you're mine now." No! You belong to God now.

"But if we confess our sins to God, he can always be trusted to forgive us and take our sins away" (1 John 1:9 *pg 173*).

If you ever need help, please feel free to call us at (517)321-CARE or 327-PRAY. We have ministers, prayer partners, and caring leaders that can offer the encouragement you need to be a *winner* for Christ.

HOW THIS BOOK WILL HELP YOU

This book will help you learn more about Jesus. It will teach you how to talk with Him, how to read His Word, how to introduce Him to your friends, and much more! You will want to look up all the suggested Scripture meditations in your Bible. We've even added the Bible page numbers for you, to make it easier to look up the Scriptures. Doing this will help you learn where the various books of the Bible are located, and will teach you the importance of referring to "the Word" in all situations of life. Studying God's Word will be a thrilling, heart-stirring experience for you.

The American Bible Society and I have partnered together to bring you the *New Life New Testament*. The Bible pages are taken from one of the world's most understandable Bibles — The Contemporary English Version. You are going to love reading it, and as you do, your faith will grow strong.

God bless you now as you "... study to show yourself approved unto God, a workman that doesn't need to be ashamed." (2 Timothy 2:15 KJV)

And, thanks for letting me share these thoughts with you. I care about you. **God cares about you.**

God's richest blessings on your life.

Your friend in Jesus,

Dave Williams

Dr. Dave Williams
Pastor, Mount Hope Church

FOR EASY REFERENCE:

Throughout **Part One** of *The New Life New Testament*, we have placed next to each Scripture reference the page number on which it appears in **Part Two**, *The Contemporary English Version of the New Testament*.

— **The Editors**

CONTENTS

Part One: The New Life

**Part Two: The Contemporary English
    Version New Testament**

PART 1

THE NEW LIFE...
THE START OF SOMETHING
WONDERFUL

DAVE WILLIAMS

MOUNT HOPE CHURCH

202 S. Creyts Road • Lansing, MI 48917

(517) 321-CARE • (517) 321-2780

www.mounthopechurch.org

(See page 93 for a listing of Mount Hope churches)

FIRST WORD

A young man named Reggie had the dream of becoming a famous rock musician. As the months went by, up the ladder of success he went to fame and fortune, working with several well-known rock groups.

With several gold records to his credit, Reggie had reached the top. He saw his dreams coming true, yet there still remained an unexplainable emptiness in his life. There was no genuine peace, no joy, and no love.

Surrounding this successful writer of rock music were all the things he had always dreamed about: fame, money, travel, women, popularity, and excitement. But something was drastically wrong. Reggie saw many of his so-called "successful" friends dying from drug overdoses. Some were committing suicide. Others were turning to other forms of sexual debasement in order to experience some strange "kicks."

What was wrong?

Disillusioned with life, unfulfilled by success, running away from reality, Reggie turned on the television set in his hotel room one night after returning from a concert, and there was Billy Graham!

"You've run far enough," Billy's voice rang out, "You've come to the end of the road. It's time to turn your life over to Jesus Christ — completely and wholeheartedly!"

Tears swelled up in Reggie's eyes as he experienced God's call to his heart. He knelt by the television and prayed, "Oh, God, please be merciful to me, a sinner. I'm sorry for the wrong I have done. I believe you died on the cross for me and I believe you were raised from the dead. Please come into my heart, Jesus, and change me."

That night Reggie became a new creation. He began a *New Life*. Now instead of having selfish desires, carnal dreams and plans, *he wanted* to give all his dreams and plans to Jesus Christ. In return, the Lord gave Reggie a new dream, a new vision, a new desire, and a *New Life!*

Now Reggie travels the country telling people about Jesus. He has written a book, made Gospel music albums, and has appeared on national television programs, giving his testimony of how Jesus Christ changed his life and made him brand new.

You see Reggie made the decision to follow Jesus 100% — not 75% or 80% — *but 100%*. And Jesus gave him new desires. Now the desire to sin is gone. Oh yes, there are still temptations, but the root desire to sin is gone. Now his greatest desire is to please the Master. He has found that the only true success — eternal success — is found in a Man named **Jesus Christ, the Son of God**.

Today Reggie has real peace, real joy, real love, real fulfillment ... not some phony thing. Why? Because he has been given a *New Life!* The old things are passed away!

And when you prayed and asked Jesus to come into your life, He gave you a new life too...and a brand new start.

Are you ready? Let's get started on our journey to becoming a rock-solid disciple of Jesus Christ.

Anyone who belongs to Christ is a NEW PERSON. The past is forgotten, and EVERYTHING IS NEW.

—2 Corinthians 5:17 (pg 133)

In order to truly make Jesus Christ the Lord of your life as Reggie did there are certain things you will *want* to do after receiving the *New Life*. These things will help you become a victorious, successful Christian — a "hundred-percenter!"

CHAPTER
1

TAKE A PUBLIC STAND
FOR CHRIST

Scripture Meditations

❏ *Matthew 10:32-33* (pg 8)   ❏ *Luke 12:8-9* (pg 56)
❏ *2 Timothy 2:12* (pg 155)

Let others know *immediately* that you have determined to follow Jesus. The longer you wait, the more difficult it will become. People may persecute you, ridicule you and criticize you. Be prepared for it!

Scripture Meditations

❏ *2 Timothy 3:12* (pg 155)   ❏ *Matthew 5:10-12* (pg 3)

The reason for this is because you have become a prime target for the devil. He wants to rob you of your victory in Christ. He hates to see people happily rejoicing in Jesus, so he stirs up trouble to try to rob you.

Scripture Meditations

❏ *John 10:10* (pg 78)   ❏ *1 Peter 5:8* (pg 171)
❏ *Ephesians 6:10-11* (pg 142)

As a Christian you should pray for the people who criticize you. Ask God to bless them and help them see the "light." Ask God to convict them of their sins that they too will come to know the joy of following Christ.

Scripture Meditations

❑ *Matthew 5:44-47* (pg 4)   ❑ *Romans 12:14* (pg 119)

2
CHAPTER

NEVER LOOK BACK TO
THE OLD LIFE

Keep your eyes on Jesus, not on people, projects, programs, or things. People will fail. They are not perfect. We all have certain weaknesses and cannot live up to our expectations all the time. That's why you must always look to Jesus.

You will probably go through a faultfinding period in your Christian experience. Most Christians do. This is where the devil shows you everything wrong in everybody else. He will show you the pastor's shortcomings. He will show you other people's faults and weaknesses. If you listen to him, you might even quit your church and go somewhere else, only to discover the same cycle all over again. Or you may try to grow spiritual by watching religious shows on television or by listening to audio teachings; not realizing that, though most of these programs are good, they cannot substitute God's plan for your growth which is to be in the Church. (Ephesians 4:11-16 *pg 141*) Sad to say, some Christians have never grown beyond this faultfinding stage of development.

Keep your eyes on Christ. Don't ever look back to the old life. You are in a race now according to the Bible. Run the race to win, not to come in second or third place

— **Run To Win!** Don't be satisfied with a mediocre, luke-warm life. Go all out — victory or death! Burn all the bridges behind you and move ahead with Jesus Christ!

Scripture Meditations

❏ *Revelation 3:15, 16* (pg 180)   ❏ *Luke 9:62* (pg 53)
❏ *1 Corinthians 9:24* (pg 126)

CHAPTER 3

BE BAPTIZED IN WATER

This should be done at the *first* opportunity. Don't put it off. If you were baptized as a baby or before you were genuinely converted to Christ, it doesn't count. Being baptized in water is a sign of true belief. It means you are openly confessing that you are now dead to the old life and alive to the *New Life* through Jesus Christ.

Scripture Meditations

- ❏ *Mark 16:16* (pg 42)
- ❏ *Matthew 3:6* (pg 2)
- ❏ *Acts 8:12* (pg 94)
- ❏ *Acts 9:18* (pg 95)
- ❏ *Acts 16:33* (pg 101)
- ❏ *Acts 22:16* (pg 106)

- ❏ *Matthew 28:19* (pg 26)
- ❏ *Acts 2:38* (pg 89)
- ❏ *Acts 8:36-39* (pg 94)
- ❏ *Acts 16:15* (pg 101)
- ❏ *Acts 18:8* (pg 103)
- ❏ *Romans 6:3-9* (pg 115)

CHAPTER 4

BEGIN A REGULAR PRAYER LIFE

This is perhaps one of the most exciting areas of our Christian walk. We have the unique privilege of communicating with our Creator. That's really what prayer is — communion with God. Prayer will help you find the perfect will of God for your life as you begin to seek Him on a daily basis.

Prayer is one area that Satan will try to attack you the hardest. It's because he knows that through faith-filled prayer, great advances are wrought in the Kingdom of God and great wreckage is brought to his own miserable kingdom of darkness.

Prayer is a source of the Christian's power. It should be a **daily habit.** Start out by setting aside 15 minutes regularly each day for prayer. As you grow in the Lord, you will have more to pray about and will want to spend even more time talking with your Heavenly Father. Some Christians spend one or two hours a day in prayer. Of course, the amount of time isn't nearly as important as the quality of the time you spend. Some people can pray for 15 minutes in faith and accomplish more than a person who spends five hours in prayer with no faith. Make sure your prayers are filled with faith based upon God's promises.

DIFFERENT KINDS OF PRAYER

There are different kinds of prayer for different situations and circumstances. Let's look at some of them.

1. Prayer Of Confession. This is the kind of prayer you pray when you have sinned under a sudden temptation. Simply tell the Lord what it is you have done and ask Him to forgive you for it. He will forgive you and it will be as though you had never sinned at all! (See 1 John 1:9 *pg 173*)

The lord will see his people righted and will have compassion on them when they slip.

—Deuteronomy 32:36 (TLB)

2. Prayer Of Petition. This is the type of prayer you pray when you desire something from the Lord. It can be just a simple request. Use your own words and talk to the Lord like He is your best friend, right there in the room with you (He is!). (See Mark 11:24 *pg 36* and Matthew 21:22 *pg 18*)

3. Prayer Of Worship And Praise. This is the kind of prayer when you simply praise and thank the Lord. You don't ask Him for anything, only tell Him how much you love Him and appreciate Him. Thank Him and adore Him for who He is and all He has done for you. Thank Him in advance for answering your prayers. This is one of the most powerful forms of prayer! (See Luke 24:50-53 *pg 68* and Acts 16:22-25 *pg 101*)

4. Intercessory Prayer. This is the kind of prayer you pray when you are approaching God on behalf of another person. For example, you may intercede for your family members, your friends, your pastor, the president, the governor, the mayor, etc. (See 1 Timothy 2:1 *pg 151*)

5. United Prayer. This is when two or more believers pray together. This also is a dynamic form of prayer. (See Matthew 18:19 *pg 16* and Acts 4:23-30 *pg 91*)

There are other types of prayer, and you will learn them as you continue in your Christian walk.

Scripture Meditations

❑ *Matthew 7:7-8* (pg 5)

❑ *John 16:23-24* (pg 83)

❑ *Romans 8:26* (pg 116)

❑ *Acts 13:1-4* (pg 98)

❑ *2 Chronicles 20:17-22*

❑ *Psalm 37:5*

❑ *Luke 11:5-13* (pg 54)

❑ *1 Peter 3:12* (pg 170)

❑ *1 John 5:14* (pg 175)

❑ *John 15:7* (pg 82)

❑ *Matthew 18:18-20* (pg 16)

❑ *Jude 1:20* (pg 177)

❑ *Luke 24:52-53* (pg 68)

❑ *Acts 1: 14* (pg 88)

❑ *Matthew 7:7-11* (pg 5)

❑ *James 5:17-18* (pg 168)

❑ *1 Timothy 2:1-2* (pg 151)

❑ *1 Corinthians 14:14-15* (pg 129)

❑ *1 Thessalonians 5:16-18* (pg 149)

❑ *Philippians 4:6* (pg 145)

❑ *John 14:14* (pg 82)

❑ *Matthew 21:22* (pg 18)

❑ *Acts 16:22-25* (pg 101)

❑ *Acts 4:31* (pg 91)

❑ *1 Peter 5:7* (pg 171)

❑ *James 5:13-16* (pg 168)

❑ *Jeremiah 29:12-13*

❑ *Mark 11:23-26* (pg 36)

❑ *Ephesians 5:20* (pg 142)

❑ *Ephesians 6:18* (pg 143)

❑ *Luke 22:42* (pg 66)

❑ *2 Chronicles 20:15*

❑ *Matthew 6:5-13* (pg 4)

❑ *1 Timothy 2:8* (pg 151)

❑ *Mark 13:33* (pg 39)

You won't even have to fight. Just take your position and watch the LORD rescue you from your enemy. Don't be afraid. Just do as you're told. And as you march out tomorrow, the LORD will be there with you.

Jehoshaphat bowed low to the ground and everyone worshiped the LORD. Then some Levites from the Kohath and Korah clans stood up and shouted praises to the LORD God of Israel.

Early the next morning, as everyone got ready to leave for the desert near Tekoa, Jehoshaphat stood up and said, "Listen my friends, if we trust the LORD God and believe what these prophets have told us, the LORD will help us, and we will be successful." Then he explained his plan and appointed men to march in front of the army and praise the LORD for his holy power by singing: "Praise the LORD! His love never ends." As soon as they began singing, the LORD confused the enemy camp.

—2 Chronicles 20:17-22

Let the LORD lead you and trust him to help.

—Psalm 37:5

You will turn back to me and ask for help, and I will answer your prayers. You will worship me with all your heart, and I will be with you.

—Jeremiah 29:12-13

Then Jahaziel said: Your Majesty and everyone from Judah and Jerusalem, the LORD says that you don't need to be afraid or let this powerful army discourage you. God will fight on your side!

—2 Chronicles 20:15

You will never be able to *find* the time to pray. *You must make the time to pray.* Almost immediately the enemy attacks the new believer's prayer life. He may try to inject obscene thoughts into your mind and make you think they were yours, in hopes of causing you to feel guilty and ashamed and unable to pray effectively. Or he will try to get you thinking about all the work around the house that needs to be done so you can't concentrate on praying. But remember this: *More can be accomplished in three minutes of prayer than in three hours of hard work!* Of course there must be a good balance, but prayer — your time of conversation with God — is extremely important to your own spiritual health, growth, and stability. Make prayer a way of life. Jesus did!

ENEMIES OF ANSWERED PRAYER

The devil doesn't want your prayers to be answered. He knows that when they are answered, God's kingdom moves forward while damage is brought to his kingdom of darkness. Therefore, he sends out many enemies to hinder your prayers. It is important to recognize these enemies in order to eliminate them.

1. An Impure Heart. The Lord said He will not listen to you if you regard iniquity (sin) in your heart. The solution to this problem is to put Jesus Christ first place in your life. Let His Word become your authority. A Christian who has confessed his sin to God and is sorry for that sin has been cleansed of all unrighteousness and his heart is made pure by the Blood of Jesus. God then listens because the Blood of His Son has made your heart pure.

2. Wrong Motives. A young man prayed, "Oh, Lord, please send me a new Corvette sports car. The only reason I want it, Lord, is so I can pick up kids and take them to Sunday school." Oh yes! Check your motives carefully when asking God for something.

3. Failing To Praise God. Learn the secret of praising God in all situations and many of the prayer enemies will automatically be eliminated.

4. Poor Human Relations. You must forgive others if you want to receive answers to your prayers.

5. Praying Out Of The Will Of God.

6. Negative Praying. Don't tell God how rotten you are. He knows everything! He considered you worthy enough to die for you. Confess your sins quickly, then forget about them! Center your attention upon Jesus Christ and His strength, *not* upon your weaknesses. Negative prayers equal negative results.

7. Failing To Be Honest With God. You must worship God in Spirit and *in truth*. Be honest with God. He knows your heart anyway.

8. Failing To Get Quiet Before The Lord. There are many spiritual motor mouths today. They can talk for six hours about nothing! They say, "Listen, Lord, I'm talking now." The Lord can't even get a word in edgewise! Learn the secret of getting still before the Lord and say, "Speak, Lord, your servant is listening." Listen for God to speak to you through a still, small voice or through a Scripture verse. Perhaps He wants to tell you *how* He wants to answer your prayer and what you should be doing about it.

9. Lack Of Persistence. You must keep claiming the promises found in God's Word if you are to be successful.

10. Lack Of Honest Desires. You must really *desire* the answer to your prayer. For example, some people pray for healing, but deep down in their hearts they really *desire* to be sick so that they can get sympathy from others.

11. Failing To See The Answer In Your Mind And Heart. When you pray, make sure you are picturing the answer through your "eye of faith."

12. Failing To Believe The Answer Is On The Way. God hears and answers *every prayer* as we abide in Him and His Word abides in us.

Resist these prayer enemies, submit yourself to God, and watch your prayer life perk up!

Scripture Meditations

- ❏ *1 John 5:14* (pg 175)
- ❏ *James 4:3* (pg 167)
- ❏ *John 4:24* (pg 72)
- ❏ *Isaiah 30:15*
- ❏ *Psalm 81:13*
- ❏ *Hebrews 10:23* (pg 163)
- ❏ *Matthew 18:19* (pg 16)
- ❏ *John 15:7* (pg 82)
- ❏ *Psalm 66:18*
- ❏ *Psalm 150:6*
- ❏ *Mark 11:26* (pg 37)
- ❏ *1 Peter 3:7* (pg 169)
- ❏ *Psalm 46:10*
- ❏ *Mark 11:24* (pg 36)
- ❏ *Psalm 37:4*

The holy LORD God of Israel had told all of you, "I will keep you safe if you turn back to me and calm down. I will make you strong if you quietly trust me."

—Isaiah 30:15

"My people, Israel, if only you would listen and do as I say!

—Psalm 81:13

If my thoughts had been sinful, he would have refused to hear me.

—Psalm 66:18

Let every living creature praise the LORD. Shout praises to the LORD!

—Psalm 150:6

Our God says, "Calm down, and learn that I am God! All nations on earth will honor me."

—Psalm 46:10

Do what the LORD wants, and he will give you your heart's desire.

—Psalm 37:4

CHAPTER 5

BEGIN A PROGRAM OF DAILY BIBLE READING

The Bible is God's letter to you. When you receive a letter in the mail, you read it, don't you? Well, God has sent you a letter. The Bible is a list of all your assets in Christ. When you accepted Christ into your heart and life, you became a joint heir with Him. Read the Bible to find out all you inherited when you started the *New Life*.

WHY READ THE BIBLE?

(See 2 Timothy 3:16 pg 155)

1. It Teaches You Doctrine. It gives you guidance and shows you the right path to walk.

2. It Gives You Reproof. This means that it shows when you are getting off the right path.

3. It Gives You Correction. It tells you how to correct your course; how to get back on the right path.

4. It Gives You God's Instructions. This means that it shows you how to stay on the right path.

28

Scripture Meditations

❑ *Acts 20:32* (pg 105)   ❑ *Ezra 7:10*
❑ *Joshua 1:8*   ❑ *Isaiah 55:10-11*
❑ *Hebrews 4:12* (pg 160) ❑ *John 8:31-32* (pg 76)
❑ *John 15:7* (pg 82)
❑ *1 Thessalonians 2:13* (pg 148)

Ezra had spent his entire life studying and obeying the Law of the LORD and teaching it to others.

—Ezra 7:10

"Rain and snow fall from the sky. But they don't return without watering the earth that produces seeds to plant and grain to eat. That's how it is with my words. They don't return to me without doing everything I send them to do."

—Isaiah 55:10-11

This Book of the Law shall not depart from your mouth, but you shall meditate in it day and night, that you may observe to do according to all that is written in it. For then you will make your way prosperous, and then you will have good success.

—Joshua 1:8 (NKJV)

The Word of God will provide genuine guidance for your life. It is the primary way that God guides His people.

Your word is a lamp that gives light wherever I walk.

—Psalm 119:105

The Word of God is to be used in your spiritual warfare against the devil. (See Matthew 4:1-11 *pg 2* and Ephesians 6:17 *pg 143*)

Get to know God better in His Word. Read it and study it daily. Let's discuss this some more.

How To Read The Bible

1. Find A Quiet Place. This may be difficult but it can be done. You may have to get up an hour earlier or find yourself a spot in the basement or in the attic, but you can do it...if you really want to!

2. Set A Regular Time. Human beings are creatures of habit. If you work various shifts you'll not be able to have a definite time, but you could set aside the first hour of each day for Bible reading and prayer.

3. Read It Prayerfully. Ask God questions as you read. Ask the Holy Spirit to give you understanding of the Word and to teach you some great, practical truths that you can apply to your life personally.

4. Read It Expecting God To Show You Something Wonderful! It's easier to read your Bible when you really *expect* God to speak to you through it.

5. Read It As If God Were Speaking Directly To You. God's Word cannot lie. The prophets wrote it as the Holy Spirit moved upon them. (See 2 Peter 1:21 *pg 171*) Read the Bible as if it were written especially for you. Remember that the Bible is God's letter to you.

6. Have A Notebook Handy. You will want to write down the things God reveals to you as you read His Word.

7. Use Colored Pencils Or Special Markers. You will want to make notes in your Bible and mark certain passages that really speak to you.

Satan's Attacks

Satan is God's enemy. He is also your enemy. He will subtly attack the Scriptures to make you doubt the integrity of your Heavenly Father. On television and in the movies, Satan has used ungodly producers and comedians to attack the Bible. You should be very selective in your entertainment so that seeds of doubt are not sown in your mind regarding God's Word.

SOME EXCUSES SATAN WILL HELP YOU THINK OF FOR NOT READING THE BIBLE:

1. *I don't have the time.*

2. *I'm too tired.*

3. *I can't fit it into my tight schedule.*

4. *Every time I read it I get sleepy.*

5. *I can't remember what I read anyway.*

6. *I don't get anything out of it.*

7. *I don't understand it.*

8. *People call me a fanatic when I read it.*

9. *It offends people.*

10. *People will say I'm crazy if I read that Book.*

11. *I'm ashamed of it.*

12. *It's boring.*

Oh yes, and there is a whole host of other excuses for not reading the Bible. But *you* be strong! *You* be aware of Satan's tactics. He is the author of all these flimsy excuses. Be wise to his cunning devices. The more Bible you can get into you, the more genuine faith you will have, and the more accomplishments you will experience.

Scripture Meditations

❑ *Romans 10: 17* (pg 118)   ❑ *John 6:63* (pg 74)
❑ *Psalm 1:1-3*   ❑ *Luke 4:4* (pg 46)
❑ *Acts 17:10-11* (pg 102)

God blesses those people who refuse evil advice and won't follow sinners or join in sneering at God. Instead, the Law of the LORD makes them happy, and they think about it day and night. They are like trees growing beside a stream, trees that produce fruit in season and always have leaves. Those people succeed in everything they do.

—Psalm 1:1-3

And remember: **After Reading The Word, Always Apply It To Your Life.**

CHAPTER 6

RENOUNCE YOUR OLD LIFE OF SIN

WHAT IS SIN?

1. *To miss the mark of the standard.*

2. *A lapse or deviation from truth and uprightness.*

3. *A transgression.*

4. *Disobedience.*

5. *Falling short of one's duty.*

6. *Doing wrong, even though done in ignorance.*

7. *Actions contrary to the law.*

Humans are sinners for two reasons. First, we are sinners by nature, inherited from Adam. Secondly, humans are sinners by deliberate choice.

Sin loves to get a grip on people and hold them in bondage. Sin doesn't like to let go of a person it has in its grips. If it weren't for a Holy God who provided a remedy for sin, we'd all be lost, on a journey to hell.

Scripture Meditations

❑ *Romans 3:23* (pg 113) ❑ *Psalm 51:5*
❑ *Romans 5:15-20* (pg.114) ❑ *Romans 6:23* (pg 115)
❑ *Matthew 6:14-15* (pg 5) ❑ *Ephesians 1:7* (pg 140)
❑ *Colossians 2:13* (pg 146) ❑ *Galatians 6:1* (pg 139)
❑ *James 5:16* (pg 168) ❑ *Romans 11:11* (pg 118)
❑ *Galatians 3:19* (pg 138) ❑ *Romans 3:9-20* (pg 113)
❑ *2 Corinthians 5:19* (pg 133) ❑ *Isaiah 64:6*
❑ *Matthew 18:15, 21-35* (pg 15,16)

We are unfit to worship you; each of our good deeds is merely a filthy rag. We dry up like leaves; our sins are storm winds sweeping us away.

—Isaiah 64:6

I have sinned and done wrong since the day I was born.

—Psalm 51:5

JUMPING THE CHASM

It is not how many sins we have committed that separates us from God. It is the fact that we have sinned and continue to sin. Regardless of how good we try to be, we cannot be good enough. We cannot earn salvation or be saved by our own merits.

For example, suppose three men try to jump across a chasm fifteen feet wide. To fail would be sure death. The first man tries hard but jumps only six feet and falls. The second man is more successful. He jumps ten feet, but he also falls. The third man jumps fourteen feet! However, he suffers the same end as the first two. It makes no difference how close they came to jumping the chasm, the end result was the same.

It is the same in dealing with our sins. Salvation is offered to us as a free gift. The only forgiveness is in Jesus Christ, and no one is too great a sinner to be saved.

Scripture Meditations

❑ *Romans 6:23* (pg 115)   ❑ *Isaiah 1:18*

I, the LORD, invite you to come and talk it over. Your sins are scarlet red, but they will be whiter than snow or wool.

—Isaiah 1:18

CHAPTER 7

SHARE CHRIST WITH OTHERS

Witnessing means to tell others what you know about Christ. You don't have to be a Bible scholar or expert to share Christ with others. But you must know Him in order to introduce Him to people.

How To Witness

1. **Prepare Your Heart By Prayer.** The more you pray and commune with the Father, the more effective you will become and the more power you will have.

2. **Do Not Argue With People.** Present Christ as a person, not as a religion.

3. **Scriptures For The Presentation:**

    a. Romans 3:23 describes the problem.

    b. Romans 6:23 tells the penalty.

    c. Acts 3:19 gives the solution.

    d. John 1:12 tells that Christ must be received personally.

e. Revelation 3:20 tells that Christ is waiting and knocking, ready to come into a person's life.

4. **Pray With The Person A Simple Prayer Of Repentance And Ask Jesus To Come Into His Or Her Heart.**

Scripture Meditations

- ❏ *Acts 1:8* (pg 88)
- ❏ *Acts chapter 4* (pg 90)
- ❏ *Matthew 28:19-20* (pg 26)
- ❏ *Mark 16:15-18* (pg 42)
- ❏ *1 Peter 3:15* (pg 170)

List at least one person you can witness to:

How do you plan to do this?

Questions

1. **What must you do before leading others to Christ?** (See Matthew 4:19 *pg 3*)

2. **What did God want Paul to do since he was to be His witness?** (See Acts 22:14-15 *pg 106*)

3. **How does a person acknowledge Christ as Lord in his life?** (See Romans 12:1-2 *pg 119*)

4. **What may cause people to ask about your relationship to Christ?** (See Matthew 5:16 *pg 3*)

5. **What should you tell others?** (See Acts 4:20 *pg 90*)

6. **What should characterize your conversation?** (See Colossians 4:5-6 *pg 147*)

CHAPTER 8

BE FILLED WITH THE HOLY SPIRIT

Now that you are a born-again Christian, there is another experience you may have with God. It is called the baptism in the Holy Spirit. It is an experience that is promised to all who will believe. The Holy Spirit will give you the power to do unusual things such as speaking in other languages you have not learned. It may sound strange but this experience will give you the ability to be a powerful witness for Christ.

Jesus taught us to *ask* for the Spirit. He didn't say to merely assume that the Holy Spirit has filled us upon conversion, but He said to *ask*. (Read Luke 11:13 *pg 54*) Some people are afraid to ask God for the Holy Spirit baptism with the evidence of speaking in other tongues because they are afraid they will receive a demon. But Jesus explained carefully in the eleventh chapter of St. Luke that God, being a good God, would *never* allow such a thing to happen. If you ask for the Holy Spirit, do you honestly believe that a good God would allow an *unclean* spirit to come upon you? Of course not!

Jesus described baptism in the Holy Spirit as "rivers of living water flowing out of your belly." Strange as it may seem, people who ask God for the Holy Spirit baptism often experience a surge of excitement through their belly area as they begin to speak in other languages of praise unto God. It's not necessary to feel this sensation before speaking in tongues, but it comes often when the Holy Spirit fills a person.

Scripture Meditations

- ❑ *Matthew 3:16* (pg 2)
- ❑ *Acts 2:1-4* (pg 88)
- ❑ *Romans 8:26* (pg 116)
- ❑ *John 14:17* (pg 82)
- ❑ *Acts 8:17-18* (pg 94)
- ❑ *John 4:23-24* (pg 72)
- ❑ *Luke 11:13* (pg 54)
- ❑ *Acts 2:4* (pg 88)
- ❑ *Acts 19:6* (pg 103)
- ❑ *1 Corinthians 12-14* (pg 127)

- ❑ *Acts 1:4-5* (pg 88)
- ❑ *John 14:16-17* (pg 82)
- ❑ *John 7:37-39* (pg 75)
- ❑ *Acts 10:46* (pg 96)
- ❑ *Mark 16:15-17* (pg 42)
- ❑ *John 16:12-13* (pg 83)
- ❑ *Acts 8:14-17* (pg 94)
- ❑ *Acts 9:17* (pg 95)
- ❑ *Luke 3:16* (pg 45)

CHAPTER

USE YOUR PRAYER LANGUAGE DAILY

When you receive the baptism in the Holy Spirit, you will have the ability to pray in another language. Have you ever wanted to thank God for all He has done, but couldn't seem to find the right words? Well, the Holy Spirit will give you the right words through a language known as "tongues." Some call it the "prayer language."

When you use your prayer language, you are bypassing your intellect and speaking right out of your spirit. We don't always know how to pray as we ought. That's why we need the help of the Holy Spirit and the prayer language.

Sometimes you may feel depressed or worried and not know why or how to deal with it. Begin to use your prayer language. You may not "feel" like using it, but do it anyway. You will be energized by the Spirit of God. It may sound foolish, but God has taken the foolish things to confound the wise. (See 1 Corinthians 2:14 *pg 123* and 1 Corinthians 1:27 *pg 122*)

> **"He that speaketh in an unknown tongue edifieth himself."**
>
> **—1 Corinthians 14:4a (KJV)**

The word "edify," in the Greek, means to "charge up, like electricity." When you use your prayer language, you are being edified, or charged up with power. Use it every day whether you feel like it or not and you will experience the ever-increasing joy of watching your prayers being answered supernaturally.

Sometimes it seems as though obstacles remain in the way of answered prayer. The answer seems just out of reach. What could it be? Secret sin? Secret habit? Some chronic affliction? What is the answer? There is a deep dimension of prayer that we can use when we don't know how to pray as we should or what we should pray.

As we begin to yield to the Spirit of God in our prayer life, we will begin to achieve victories that seem quite beyond us.

Scripture Meditations

❑ *1 Corinthians 14:15* (pg 129) ❑ *Romans 8:26* (pg 116)
❑ *1 Corinthians 14:2* (pg 128) ❑ *Ephesians 6:18* (pg 143)

CHAPTER

GET RID OF ALL REMINDERS OF THE OLD LIFE

This is very important although some do not recognize it as such. Have you ever heard an old record and immediately were reminded of exactly what you were doing when it was popular? And have you ever experienced a depression after listening to a song that brought back old memories? It is not a good practice to keep remnants of the old life around.

Some Christians report throwing out such things as:

1. Pot smoking pipes and accessories.

2. Photographs (*old boyfriends, girlfriends, etc.*).

3. Liquor.

4. Tobacco products.

5. Record albums.

6. Astrology books and other occult artifacts.

7. Pornography and other suggestive material contrary to Christianity.

8. Books of philosophy and other religions.

9. Party tapes and CDs.

10. Other unwholesome materials.

Scripture Meditations

❏ *2 Corinthians 5:17* (pg 133)   ❏ *Acts 19:18-19* (pg 103)

CHAPTER 11

SELECT THE RIGHT FRIENDS AND COMPANIONS

Don't fool yourselves. Bad friends will destroy you.

— 1 Corinthians 15:33 *(pg 130)*

A mirror reflects a man's face, but what he is really like is shown by the kind of friends he chooses.

— Proverbs 27:19 (TLB)

When you really become a Christian, you will no longer desire to go to the old hang outs and associate with the people you once did. Of course this doesn't mean you should shun them or treat them with disrespect, it's just that you simply no longer need to chum with them. In fact, when you start witnessing to them about how Jesus transformed your life, your old friends will either get saved or decide they don't want you around anymore. You are now a "holy Joe" or a "holy roller" to them. They can't understand why you say, "Praise the Lord," at the strangest times. They can't figure out why you want to go to church and talk about Jesus all the time.

In the Old Testament, there is a story about King Jehoshaphat that vividly illustrates the importance of selecting good associates. Jehoshaphat was a godly king that went into a business alliance with an ungodly, unconverted king named Ahaziah. They built ships together and God allowed all of the ships to be sunk before ever being put to use because Jehoshaphat went into this unwholesome partnership.

> While Jehoshaphat was king, he signed a peace treaty with Ahaziah the wicked king of Israel. They agreed to build several seagoing ships at Ezion-Geber. But the prophet Eliezer warned Jehoshaphat, "The LORD will destroy these ships because you have supported Ahaziah." The ships were wrecked and never sailed.
>
> —2 Chronicles 20:35-37

You cannot drink from the cup of the Lord and demons too.

I knew a young lady who said she had accepted Christ, but refused to quit going to her card parties. She deliberately threw herself into a place of compromise and temptation. As a result, her experience was frozen in a matter of just a few weeks. The last time I saw her, she was back to drinking and running around with no interest in the Lord at all. She claims that the "dirty devil" made her do it, but it wasn't the "dirty devil" that made her do it — it was *her* choice; she made herself do it!

When you become a genuine Christian, you will have an intense desire to associate with other Christians. You will want to be around people who can help you grow in the faith and come closer to Christ. You don't want to be around someone who serves the devil in dragging you back to the old life. That's why church fellowship is so vitally important.

Scripture Meditations

Don't be tempted by sinners...

—Proverbs 1:10

Don't be jealous of crooks or want to be their friend.

—Proverbs 24:1

Silver must be purified before it can be used to make something of value. Evil people must be removed before anyone can rule with justice.

—Proverbs 25:4-5

Giving an honest answer is a sign of true friendship.

—Proverbs 24:26

I don't spend my time with worthless liars or go with evil crowds.

—Psalm 26:4-5

Stay away from fools, or you won't learn a thing.

—Proverbs 14:7

You are better off to do right, than to lose your way by doing wrong.

—Proverbs 12:26

If you choose the wrong friends and associates, they will become a snare to you; a thorn in your side. Make sure you are very selective in your friendships. Find faith-filled people who love Jesus and who love to pray; people you know to be spiritual and will be a positive influence upon your life. Your eternity is too important to take a chance on making friends with people who will be open to satanic suggestions and cause you to stumble.

Don't misunderstand. You cannot isolate yourself. You must still rub shoulders with people and tell them about Jesus — just don't make a habit of "running" with them.

CHAPTER 12

DEAL PROPERLY WITH TEMPTATION

Just because you are now a born-again Christian, it doesn't mean that you will no longer be tempted. The reverse is true. Satan wants to win you back. He already controls, more or less, the person who doesn't love the Lord, so he concentrates his efforts on trying to trip up Christians.

You will at times be tempted with certain sins of the flesh. Then there are times you will be tempted with sins of the mind such as worry and fear. You will be tempted in subtle ways. You must learn to live one day at a time without worrying about tomorrow. Discipline yourself to stay away from tempting situations. Some ex-drunkards go back to the bars just "to witness to their old friends." That's what *they* think, but actually it is a temptation from the enemy to get them back on his territory and into the old habits again. You be wiser than that! Get yourself out of tempting situations immediately.

Sometimes a young person will continue to go on dates with the unsaved. They compromise their principles, guilt sets in, fellowship with God is broken, and they go back to the same old rut...and the devil has succeeded in his mission.

You are a child of God. You have a New Life now. You do not have to let Satan make you a failure. You do not have to give in to temptation. Remember, though, you cannot resist the devil in your own strength; you must do it in Christ's strength, claiming His Blood over your life and His strength over your whole being.

HOW TO GET VICTORY OVER TEMPTATION

1. Claim Your Position In Christ. When you received Christ, you received authority over the devil. He doesn't have authority over you, although he'd like you to think so.

2. Decide Firmly, Without Wavering, To Walk In Obedience To God And His Word. This is where many new Christians go wrong. They try to hang on to some secret sin instead of making the quality decision to "put off the old man" and let the fullness of the new life begin! Holding onto a secret sin will open the door to greater and more powerful temptations. (Read Hebrews 12:1-4 *pg 164*)

3. Actively Resist The Devil!

4. Trust In God's Keeping Power.

Scripture Meditations

❑ *John 1: 12* (pg 69)   ❑ *Luke 10: 19* (pg 54)
❑ *Mark 16:17* (pg 42)   ❑ *James 1:5-8* (pg 166)
❑ *Ephesians 6:11-17* (pg 142)   ❑ *Genesis chapter 39*
❑ *Ephesians 1:1-23* (pg 140)   ❑ *1 John 4:4* (pg 174)
❑ *Jude 1:24* (pg 177)   ❑ *1 John 5:1-5* (pg 175)
❑ *1 Corinthians 10:13* (pg 126)   ❑ *James 4:7* (pg 167)
❑ *1 Samuel 15:22*

The Ishmaelites took Joseph to Egypt and sold him to Potiphar, the king's official in charge of the palace guard. So Joseph lived in the home of Potiphar, his Egyptian owner. Soon Potiphar realized that the LORD was helping Joseph to be successful in whatever he did. Potiphar liked Joseph and made him his personal assistant, putting him in charge of his house and all of his property. Because of Joseph, the LORD began to bless Potiphar's family and fields. Potiphar left everything up to Joseph, and with Joseph there, the only decision he had to make was what he wanted to eat.

Joseph was well-built and handsome, and Potiphar's wife soon noticed him. She asked him to make love to her, but he refused and said, "My master isn't worried about anything in his house, because he has placed me in charge of everything he owns. No one in my master's house is more important than I am. The only thing he hasn't given me is you, and that's because you are his wife. I won't sin against God by doing such a terrible thing as this." She kept begging Joseph day after day, but he refused to do what she wanted or even to go near her.

One day, Joseph went to Potiphar's house to do his work, and none of the other servants were there. Potiphar's wife grabbed hold of his coat and said, "Make love to me!" Joseph ran out of the house, leaving her hanging onto his coat.

When this happened, she called in her servants and said, "Look! This Hebrew has come just to make fools of us. He tried to rape me, but I screamed for help. And when he heard me scream, he ran out of the house, leaving his coat with me."

Potiphar's wife kept Joseph's coat until her husband came home. Then she said, "That Hebrew slave of yours tried to rape me! But when I screamed for help, he left his coat and ran out of the house."

Potiphar became very angry and threw Joseph in the same prison where the king's prisoners were kept.

While Joseph was in prison, the LORD helped him and was good to him. He even made the jailer like Joseph so much that he put him in charge of the other prisoners and of everything that was done in the jail. The jailer did not worry about anything, because the LORD was with Joseph and made him successful in all that he did.

—Genesis 39:1-23

"Tell me," Samuel said. "Does the LORD really want sacrifices and offerings? No! He doesn't want your sacrifices. He wants you to obey him.

—1 Samuel 15:22

13

CHAPTER

MAKE YOUR FAITH GROW

What is faith anyway? "It is the confident assurance that something we want is going to happen. It is the certainty that what we hope for is waiting for us, even though we cannot see it up ahead."

> **What is faith? It is the confident assurance that something we want is going to happen. It is the certainty that what we hope for is waiting for us, even though we cannot see it up ahead.**
>
> **— Hebrews 11:1 (TLB)**

There is one impossibility. That is: You can never please God without faith. All of God's work must be done by faith. You need to stand firm when the trials come. Your faith will always be tested to prove its genuineness.

The universe is expanding at the rate of 128,000 miles per second. Just as there is no limit to this ever-expanding universe, there is no limit to God's power for the person who is operating by faith.

There are different degrees, or measures, of faith. God gave to every person a measure of faith to start them off. But after that, it's up to us to make our faith grow. In the

Bible we read about "weak faith," "little faith," "strong faith," and "growing faith."

Faith is claiming and laying hold of the unreality of hope and bringing it out of the realm of the invisible and into the realm of the visible.

Faith is not hope. Hope is good, but it focuses upon the future. Faith takes what is hoped for and begins claiming it *Now*. "Now faith is…" the Bible says.

How Does Faith Grow?

1. **You Must Desire It To Grow.**

2. **You Must Believe It Can Grow.**

3. **Let The Word Of God Be Your Authority.** Read it, study it, and meditate upon it daily. Develop a craving for the Word of God.

4. **Put Action To The Word.** If it tells you to do something — do it!

5. **Speak The Word With Your Mouth.** Learn to speak the Word no matter what the conditions look like. Walk by faith, not by sight. Say what the Word says.

6. **Be Willing To Pass Through The "Waiting Period" Or "Testing Period."** This is the period of time between the time you start believing a promise, and the time it actually becomes a reality in the visible realm.

7. **Exercise Your Faith And It Will Grow.** It's just like a muscle; it grows with the proper exercise.

Scripture Meditations

❑ *Mark 11:23-24* (pg 36) ❑ *Matthew 17:20* (pg 15)
❑ *2 Corinthians 1:24* (pg 131) ❑ *Luke 7:50* (pg 50)
❑ *2 Thessalonians 1:3* (pg 150) ❑ *Romans 3:3-4* (pg 113)
❑ *2 Corinthians 5:7* (pg 133) ❑ *Luke 5:17-26* (pg 47)

❑ *Romans 1:5-31* (pg 112)   ❑ *1 Peter 1:7* (pg 168)
❑ *Romans 3:22-31* (pg 113) ❑ *Psalm 37:7*
❑ *Hebrews 11:1-40* (pg 163) ❑ *Luke 7:1-10* (pg 49)
❑ *Romans 12:3* (pg 119)   ❑ *James 1:1-4* (pg 166)
❑ *Ephesians 3:12* (pg 141) ❑ *Mark 6:4-6* (pg 31)
❑ *Mark 10:46-52* (pg 36)

Be patient and trust the LORD. Don't let it bother you when all goes well for those who do sinful things.

—**Psalm 37:7**

14
CHAPTER

GROW UP SPIRITUALLY AND PRODUCE FRUIT IN YOUR LIFE

Nothing in life is stagnate. Nothing remains as it is. Everything from the tiniest cell to the highest man has an urge for a fuller, more mature life. If a person does not want to grow — to mature — it is indeed a sad picture. Yet we see Christians who have been saved for several years but have never developed beyond spiritual babyhood. This ought not to be.

God gave us His Word and the ability to communicate with Him in order that we might grow into maturity. The only thing that will prevent us from growing up spiritually is our refusal to yield to the Holy Spirit in us. If we refuse to read the Bible, or refuse to pray, or refuse to fellowship with other Christians regularly, we will not grow, but will remain spiritually immature. (Remember, it's not difficult to recognize a twenty-year-old "baby.")

You can grow as quickly or as slowly as you desire. You can go as far with God as you want. God is willing to bring you into a deep, fruitful, meaningful relationship with Himself, but you must be willing to **crave** spiritual things. You *must* **want** *spiritual things more than your very breath.*

A time will come when the excitement of the *New Life* will wear off. You will not feel as full of enthusiasm as you did at the start. That's the time to make the decision to seek God through His Word and prayer regardless of how you feel. Feelings have nothing to do with your walk with God. You will know you are growing when you begin to pray because you *want* to, and not because you *feel* like it.

Let's look at three basic stages of growth in the believer's life:

1. Babyhood. Babies can't do things for themselves very well. They must depend upon others. They have to be spoon-fed.

Their diapers need changing once in a while. You can't get too angry with them over the little fusses they make. After all, they are just babies; they don't know any better. In the spiritual sense, it's okay to "spoon feed" a new Christian for a couple of months, and change his "diapers" when he has an accident, but if it continues, something is wrong.

There comes a time when Christians must grow out of the stage where they have to call the pastor every day and request other people to pray for them all the time. There comes a time when a baby should learn to feed himself and change his own clothes. Babies should learn to do things for themselves and grow up into a child.

Babies are easily spoiled. They are easily irritated. They are easily distracted, easily frustrated, easily hurt. Nobody minds helping a little baby, but when it comes to spiritual things, we don't like to see babies that are satisfied with being babies forever!

2. Childhood Stage. Children are unsteady, curious and talkative. A child doesn't know any better so he's always talking - always blabbing about something (but usually nothing). A person in the childhood stage of spiritual development will most likely be a talker. He will talk usually about himself, his petty accomplishments, his plans, his projects, his interests, etc. His conversations are generally self-centered.

Another characteristic of children is they haven't learned good discipline yet. They are unreliable and spasmodic. In the spiritual sense, a "child" hasn't learned the discipline of budgeting his time and money. He hasn't learned to get his life organized. Like in the natural, a spiritual child is unreliable; he's up and down, in and out, on and off. He reminds you of a roller coaster.

3. Adulthood Stage. Here are some signs of spiritual maturity from Evangelist Charles Finney's writings:

a. *More implicit and universal trust in God.*

b. *A separation from the world and an increasing deadness to all the world has to offer.*

c. *Less temptation to sins of omission. (example: neglect of prayer, Bible reading, etc.)*

d. *A growing steadiness and intensity of zeal in promoting the cause of Christ.*

e. *Less self-consciousness and more Jesus-consciousness.*

f. *A growing deadness to the praise of men.*

g. *A growing warmth and sincere acceptance of the whole will of God.*

h. *A growing calmness and quietness under great afflictions.*

i. *A growing patience under much provocation.*

j. *Joyfulness even when disappointments come.*

k. *Less temptation to gripe, complain, criticize, and murmur.*

l. *Less temptation to resentment and the attitude of retaliation when insulted, criticized, or abused.*

m. *Less temptation to dwell upon and magnify our trials and troubles.*

n. *Less anxiety about the future.*

o. *Less inclination to speak uncharitably about another individual.*

p. *A growing readiness to forgive others and forget old injuries.*

q. *An increasing naturalness in treating people kindly and praying for them.*

r. *Finding it easier and easier to make whole hearted sacrifices.*

s. *We find ourselves more and more impressed with revelations of Bible truths.*

t. *A growing jealousy for the honor of God, and for the honor and purity of His Church.*

HOW TO GROW UP SPIRITUALLY

1. Proper Diet. The Word of God and prayer feed the human spiritual life.

2. Exercise. Practice faith, hope and love. Reach out to others in practical ways. Look for opportunities to reach out to others and to share your testimony.

Just as a baby cannot grow without the proper nourishment and adequate exercise, neither can the spiritual baby grow without the proper spiritual food and practical exercise.

Scripture Meditations

❑ *1 Corinthians 3:1-3* (pg 123)   ❑ *1 Peter 2:2* (pg 169)
❑ *Ephesians 4:8-15* (pg 141)   ❑ *1 John 2:15-17* (pg 173)
❑ *1 Corinthians 2:6* (pg 123)   ❑ *John 3:1-7* (pg 70)

15

CHAPTER

JOIN A
CHRIST-CENTERED,
SPIRIT-FILLED CHURCH

The Church is the foundation of the Christian ministry. Jesus founded and endorsed the Church when He said, "I will build my Church." It is in the heart of every believer to have the feeling of "belonging." And church membership is a scripturally-sound approach to meeting that need to "belong." Acts 5:12-14 indicates a very definite membership in the Early Church days.

Scripture Meditations

❑ *Titus 3:10-11* (pg 157)   ❑ *Acts 1:15* (pg 88)
❑ *Hebrews 10:25* (pg 163)   ❑ *Acts 4:4* (pg 90)
❑ *1 Corinthians 5:2-13* (pg 124) ❑ *Acts 2:41* (pg 89)

Also, by joining a church, you will become a voting member of that body, and will be able to prayerfully help plan the programs offered by the church. For example, you will have a voice in business decisions the church must make, etc. If you see something wrong in your church, and you are not a voting member, it will be difficult to change it.

You will grow spiritually as you fellowship with believers of like precious faith. You will be a contribution to the health, growth and stability of the church. To illustrate the importance of fellowship with other Christians, let us look at this example: When working with charcoal briquettes, you gather them together. Once started, you can spread them out and cook a very large meal. But, you cannot cook much with one little coal. As a member of a larger body of believers, you will have a greater impact.

Church membership is extremely important to your growth. Make the selection of a church a matter of much prayer. Although we are all members of one Church (God's heavenly Church), God puts us in a local assembly where we can do the most good for Him. Pray and discover which local assembly you should attend.

Interesting Note: Did you know that the military services get their chaplains based upon church membership? It's true. The armed forces get so many chaplains per so many church members. If your church has more members, the military is entitled to more chaplains of your particular faith. The more members a denomination has the more military preachers they qualify for.

THINGS TO LOOK FOR IN A CHURCH:

1. **Salvation is by faith in the shed Blood of Jesus Christ.** It is a work of grace, not human effort.

2. **The Bible is the Inspired Word of God, from Genesis to Revelation.**

3. **God is eternally existent in three Persons: God the Father, God the Son, and God the Holy Spirit.** This is known as the Trinity; the Triune God.

4. **The Holy Spirit baptism.**

5. **Divine healing.**

6. **Mission-mindedness.** (Make sure your church supports missionary projects.)

7. **Evangelism.** (Make sure your church believes in and practices soul winning.)

8. **The imminent return of the Lord Jesus Christ.**

BEWARE OF SO-CALLED MINISTERS WHO DENY:

1. **The Virgin Birth of Christ.**

2. **The Deity of Christ.** (Deity means that Jesus Christ is actually God, the Second Person of the Trinity.)

3. **The Blood Atonement.**

4. **The Death, Burial, and Resurrection of Jesus Christ.**

5. **Christ's miracle-working power today.**

6. **The imminent return of Jesus Christ.**

7. **The Inspired, Infallible Word of God.**

8. **Everlasting punishment for the unsaved.**

Ministers who deny any of these cardinal doctrines of the Christian faith are not ministers of God, but of Satan!

Scripture Meditations

❑ *2 Corinthians 11:14* (pg 135) ❑ *Galatians 1:7-9* (pg 137)
❑ *Philippians 3:18* (pg 144) ❑ *1 Timothy 4:1-2* (pg 152)
❑ *2 Peter chapter 2* (pg 172) ❑ *Mark 12:29* (pg 37)
❑ *Philippians 2:5-11* (pg 144) ❑ *John 3:3* (pg 70)
❑ *Romans 10:8-13* (pg 117) ❑ *Acts 2:4* (pg 88)
❑ *Matthew 8:16-17* (pg 6) ❑ *Titus 2:13* (pg 157)
❑ *Matthew 25:46* (pg 23) ❑ *2 Peter 1:21* (pg 171)
❑ *Revelation 20:11-15* (pg 189) ❑ *Deuteronomy 6:4*

❑ *Matthew 28:19* (pg 26) ❑ *John 17:5* (pg 84)

❑ *Hebrews 1:2* (pg 158) ❑ *John 3:16-17* (pg 71)

❑ *2 Timothy 3:15-17* (pg 155) ❑ *Acts 1:5* (pg 88)

❑ *Revelation 19:20* (pg 188) ❑ *Acts 19:1-7* (pg 103)

❑ *James 5:13-16* (pg 168) ❑ *Romans 8:2* (pg 116)

❑ *1 Thessalonians 4:13-18* (pg 149)

❑*1 Corinthians 15:51-52* (pg 130)

Listen, Israel! The LORD our God is the only true God!

—Deuteronomy 6:4

16
CHAPTER

BE FAITHFUL IN GIVING TO GOD

Some Christians wonder why they can never get ahead. They always seem to be in debt. They are uncertain as to why they can't seem to make ends meet. With things continually breaking down, clothes wearing out too fast, grocery prices soaring like a skyrocket, and bills becoming "past due," they just can't find any money left over to give to God's work.

They don't seem to realize that *this* is the real root of their problem. God didn't ask us for the "leftovers." He said that if we would give to Him *first,* He would see to it that our "barns would be filled to overflowing...."

Scripture Meditations

❏ *Proverbs 3:9-10* ❏ *Matthew 6:33* (pg 5)
❏ *Malachi 3:8-11* ❏ *Deuteronomy 14:23*

Honor the LORD by giving him your money and the first part of all your crops. Then you will have more grain and grapes than you will ever need.

—Proverbs 3:9-10

You people are robbing me, your God. And, here you are, asking, "How are we robbing you?" You are robbing me of the offerings and of the ten percent that belongs to me. That's why your whole nation is under a curse. I am the LORD All-Powerful, and I challenge you to put me to the test. Bring the entire ten percent into the storehouse, so there will be food in my house. Then I will open the windows of heaven and flood you with blessing after blessing. I will also stop locusts from destroying your crops and keeping your vineyards from producing.

—Malachi 3:8-11

Also set aside ten percent of your wine and olive oil, and the first-born of every cow, sheep, and goat. Take these to the place where the LORD chooses to be worshiped, and eat them there. This will teach you to always respect the LORD your God.

—Deuteronomy 14:23

TYPES OF GIVING

1. The Tithe. This is 10% of your gross income, which is to be given to God's work.

The purpose of tithing is to teach you always to put God first in your lives.

—Deuteronomy 14:23 (TLB)

If a person does not put God first in his financial affairs, it is certain that he does not put God first in other areas of his life.

Some do not pay tithes because they contend that tithing was under the Old Testament Law and not meant for the age of grace. It must be pointed out that grace is grace, but willful disobedience is not grace — it is *dis*-grace. The principle of tithing was instituted **before** the Old Testament Law was given.

> King Melchizedek of Salem was a priest of God
> Most High. He brought out some bread and wine
> and said to Abram: "I bless you in the name of
> God Most High, Creator of heaven and earth. All
> praise belongs to God Most High for helping you
> defeat your enemies." Then Abram gave
> Melchizedek a tenth of everything.
>
> —Genesis 14:18-20

> This rock will be your house, and I will give back
> to you a tenth of everything you give me."
>
> —Genesis 28:22

Moreover, Jesus Himself, in the New Testament, placed His endorsement on the practice of tithing. When the tithe is withheld, the law of prosperity is violated, the law of blessing cancelled, and it becomes increasingly difficult for a person to balance his books.

2. The Offering. This is anything above and beyond the initial 10%. Christians who dedicate themselves to Christ will soon give beyond the tithe. As God blesses them, they will increase their giving. Some now give 20%, 30%, and even more of their income to God's work. And the more they increase their giving, the more God blesses them.

3. The Special Offering. This is the offering you give *beyond* your ability to give. With the special offering, you ask God what you should give, you commit yourself to giving it, and then you trust God to supply it supernaturally as He uses you as a channel for the special offering to flow. Some people call this a *Faith Promise* and many churches use this method of giving for missionary projects. (See 2 Corinthians 8:1-4 *pg 134*)

Some people give only what they can afford. Others give beyond what they can afford and learn to experience God's supernatural blessings of supply!

Principles Of Giving

1. You Must Purpose In Your Heart To Give. Don't wait for a bolt of lightning from heaven to strike you and a thundering voice to tell you to start giving. YOU must purpose in your heart to do it.

2. Giving Must Be Regular. It must become a habit; a way of life with you. The enemy will give you a great number of excuses for not giving. They will seem reasonable and logical, but don't listen to him. "... At the proper time we will reap a harvest **if we do not give up**," (Galatians 6:9 *pg 139*). Don't be discouraged when the times of testing come. Continue to give regularly and you will see God work miracles on your behalf.

3. Giving Must Be Done Cheerfully. (See 2 Corinthians 9:7 *pg 135*)

4. Giving Should Be Sacrificial. (See Philippians 4:18 *pg 145*, Mark 12:41-44 *pg 38*)

> But David answered, "No! I have to pay you what they're worth. I can't offer the LORD my God a sacrifice that I got for nothing." So David bought the threshing place and the oxen for fifty pieces of silver.
>
> —2 Samuel 24:24

5. Giving Must Be Generous. (See 2 Corinthians 8:7 *pg 134* and 2 Corinthians 9:5 *pg 134*)

> Don't be selfish and eager to get rich— you will end up worse off than you can imagine.
>
> — Proverbs 28:22

> A generous man will himself be blessed.
>
> — Proverbs 22:9 (NIV)

> ...a good person is generous and never stops giving.
>
> —Psalm 37:21b

> One man gives freely, yet gains even more; another man withholds unduly, but comes to poverty. A generous man will prosper . . .
>
> —Proverbs 11:24-25 (NIV)

6. Giving Must Be Done In Faith And In Obedience To God's Word. (See 2 Corinthians 9:13 *pg 135*)

> You people are robbing me, your God. And, here you are, asking, "How are we robbing you?" You are robbing me of the offerings and of the ten percent that belongs to me. That's why your whole nation is under a curse. I am the LORD All-Powerful, and I challenge you to put me to the test. Bring the entire ten percent into the storehouse, so there will be food in my house. Then I will open the windows of heaven and flood you with blessing after blessing. I will also stop locusts from destroying your crops and keeping your vineyards from producing.
>
> —Malachi 3:8-11

7. Giving Must Be Done For Jesus And For The Gospel's Sake.

Scripture Meditations

❑ *2 Corinthians 9:7* (pg 135)   ❑ *James 1:5-8* (pg 166)
❑ *Matthew 6:1* (pg 4)   ❑ *Mark 10:29-30* (pg 35)
❑ *2 Corinthians 8:8* (pg 134)

PROMISES TO THE PERSON WHO GIVES IN FAITH

1. Prosperity For The Generous Remember: "whoever sows sparingly will also reap sparingly, and whoever sows generously will also reap generously." (Luke 6:38 *pg 49*, 2 Corinthians 9:6 *pg 134*)

> Shout praises to the LORD! The LORD blesses everyone who worships him and gladly obeys his

teachings. Their descendants will have great power in the land, because the LORD blesses all who do right. They will get rich and prosper and will always be remembered for their fairness. They will be so kind and merciful and good, that they will be a light in the dark for others who do the right thing. Life will go well for those who freely lend and are honest in business. They won't ever be troubled, and the kind things they do will never be forgotten.

—Psalm 112:1-6

2. A 30, 60, Or 100-Fold Return Now, In This Life! Where else can you find such a tremendous yield of interest on your investment? (See Luke 18:29-30 *pg 62*, Mark 10:30 *pg 35*)

3. Treasure In Your Heavenly Bank Account! You have a bank account in heaven that is gaining interest every day. It's an account that no depression or recession can touch; no thief can steal from it; no corruption can destroy it. You can draw from this account by faith when you have a need. (See Matthew 6:20 *pg 5*, Philippians 4:17-19 *pg 145*, Luke 12:32-34 *pg 56*)

4. You Will "Eat" From The Best Of The Land! God promises you His best when you give Him your best.

If you willingly obey me, the best crops in the land will be yours. But if you turn against me, your enemies will kill you. I, the LORD, have spoken.

—Isaiah 1:19-20

I lifted the burden from your shoulder and took the heavy basket from your hands.

—Psalm 81:6

Our LORD and our God, you are like the sun and also like a shield. You treat us with kindness and

> with honor, never denying any good thing to those
> who live right.
>
> —Psalm 84:11

5. You Will Be Blessed Beyond Human Understanding!

> I am the LORD All-Powerful, and I challenge you
> to put me to the test. Bring the entire ten percent
> into the storehouse, so there will be food in my
> house. Then I will open the windows of heaven
> and flood you with blessing after blessing.
>
> —Malachi 3:10

> Honor the LORD by giving him your money and
> the first part of all your crops. Then you will have
> more grain and grapes than you will ever need.
>
> —Proverb 3:9-10

6. God Will Rebuke The Devourer For Your Sake!
Things you own will for "some strange reason" seem to last longer. For example, while others are getting only 40,000 miles on a set of tires, you may be getting 80,000!

> I will also stop locusts from destroying your crops
> and keeping your vineyards from producing.
>
> —Malachi 3:11

7. Your Needs Will Always Be Met.
After the Philippians had given so that St. Paul was amply supplied to carry on his work of promoting the Gospel, he told them, "And my God shall supply all your needs according to his riches in glory by Christ Jesus." Even during times of trouble, famine, and despair, the faithful, obedient giver will have plenty to eat!

> Those who obey the LORD are daily in his care,
> and what he has given them will be theirs forever.
> They won't be in trouble when times are bad, and
> they will have plenty when food is scarce.
>
> —Psalm 37:18-19

As long as I can remember, good people have never been left helpless, and their children have never gone begging for food. They gladly give and lend, and their children turn out good.

—Psalm 37:25-26

CHAPTER 17

USE YOUR TALENTS FOR GOD

You are unique — one of a kind. When God made you He threw away the blueprint. There is not another person on earth quite like you. You have special gifts and talents from God which He wants you to use for His glory.

It may be a gift of singing, or teaching, or being able to play a musical instrument. It may be the capacity to preach or even mow lawns, wash windows, paint ...whatever! But you can be sure of this: God has given you a special talent.

When a person comes to know Jesus Christ in a real way, he will not have much desire to use his talents to glorify himself. Instead he will want to glorify Jesus with the talents God has given.

Scripture Meditations

❏ *Matthew 25:14-30* (pg 22)   ❏ *Exodus chapter 35*

> Moses called together the people of Israel and told them that the LORD had said: You have six days in which to do your work. But the seventh day must be dedicated to me, your LORD, as a day of rest. Whoever works on the Sabbath will be put

to death. Don't even build a cooking fire at home on the Sabbath.

Moses told the people of Israel that the LORD had said: I would welcome an offering from anyone who wants to give something. You may bring gold, silver, or bronze; blue, purple, or red wool; fine linen; goat hair; tanned ram skin or fine leather; acacia wood; olive oil for the lamp; sweet-smelling spices for the oil of dedication and for the incense; or onyx stones or other gems for the sacred vest and breastpiece. If you have any skills, you should use them to help make what I have commanded: the sacred tent with its covering and hooks, its framework and crossbars, and its post and stands; the sacred chest with its carrying poles, its place of mercy, and the curtain in front of it; the table with all that goes on it, including the sacred bread; the lamp with its equipment and oil; the incense altar with its carrying poles and sweet-smelling incense; the ordination oil; the curtain for the entrance to the sacred tent; the altar for sacrifices with its bronze grating, its carrying poles, and its equipment; the large bronze bowl with its stand; the curtains with the posts and stands that go around the courtyard; the pegs and ropes for the tent and the courtyard; and the finely woven priestly clothes for Aaron and his sons.

Moses finished speaking, and everyone left. Then those who wanted to bring gifts to the LORD, brought them to be used for the sacred tent, the worship services, and the priestly clothes. Men and women came willingly and gave all kinds of gold jewelry such as pins, earrings, rings, and necklaces. Everyone brought their blue, purple, and red wool, their fine linen, and their cloth made of goat hair, as well as their ram skins dyed red and their fine leather. Anyone who had silver or bronze or acacia wood brought it as a gift to the LORD. The women who were good at weaving cloth brought the blue, purple, and red wool and the fine linen they had made. And the women who knew how to make cloth from goat hair were glad to do so. The leaders brought different kinds of jewels to be sewn on the special clothes and the breastpiece for the high priest. They also brought sweet-smelling spices to be mixed with the incense and olive oil that were for the lamps and for ordaining the priests. Moses had told the people what the LORD wanted them to do, and many of them decided to bring their gifts.

Moses said to the people of Israel: The LORD has chosen Bezalel of the Judah tribe. Not only has the LORD filled him with his Spirit, but he has given him wisdom and made him a skilled craftsman who can create objects of art with gold, silver, bronze, stone, and wood. The LORD is urging him and Oholiab from the tribe of Dan to teach others. And he has given them all kinds of artistic skills, including the ability to design and embroider with blue, purple, and red wool and to weave fine linen.

—Exodus 35:1-35

18
CHAPTER

PREPARE FOR THE SECOND COMING OF CHRIST

Jesus Christ promised to return to the earth. By all indications, His return could take place any day now. Many discerning Bible scholars believe that we are now in the final hours of history. The stage is set; the conditions are right; the scriptures are being fulfilled concerning the "last days," and Jesus could appear at any moment to evacuate His people from the earth just prior to the world's deepest hour of agony.

Many people do not understand that the Second Coming of Christ will occur in two distinct phases:

Phase 1 - *Christ comes* **FOR** *the Christians.*

Phase 2 - *Christ comes* **WITH** *the Christians.*

I believe that some of the people who are reading this book will never see death, but will be translated to meet the Lord in the air at His coming. That's how close I believe we are to that day of the "Blessed Hope." (See Titus 2:13 *pg 157*)

How To Prepare To Meet Jesus

1. **Receive Him Personally Into Your Heart By Faith.**

2. **Be Walking In All The Light That You Have.** In other words, do what you know is right, do the best you know how.

3. **Be Developing Your Faith.** It was by faith that Enoch was translated without ever tasting death. He went directly to Heaven without dying!

4. **Be Looking For His Second Coming Any Day Now.**

5. **Be Evangelistic — Be A Soul Winner.**

6. **Be Missionary-Minded.**

7. **Develop A Genuine Love For People.**

8. **Don't Be A Hypocrite.**

9. **Stay Close To Jesus And To Fellow Believers.**

10. **Be Doing The Lord's Work Patiently And Unselfishly.**

11. **Watch And Pray Always That You Will Be Counted Worthy To Escape The Coming Time Of Trouble And To Stand Before Jesus.**

Scripture Meditations

- ❑ *2 Corinthians 5:10* (pg 133)
- ❑ *Luke chapter 21* (pg 64)
- ❑ *1 Timothy 4:1-2* (pg 152)
- ❑ *Matthew chapter 24* (pg 21)
- ❑ *Romans 8:23* (pg 116)
- ❑ *John 14:1-3* (pg 82)
- ❑ *Acts 1:10-11* (pg 88)
- ❑ *Luke 18:8* (pg 61)
- ❑ *Titus 2:11-13* (pg 156)
- ❑ *Luke 17:26-30* (pg 61)

❑ *2 Timothy 3:1-5* (pg 155)   ❑ *1 John 3:3* (pg 174)
❑ *1 Thessalonians 4:13-18* (pg 149)
❑ *1 Corinthians 15:51-52* (pg 130)

CHAPTER 19

BE A GOOD CITIZEN

You are now a representative of Jesus Christ. It is important that you represent Him accurately. This means that we pay our bills on time, we keep our word, we pray for our governmental officials instead of complaining about them. In other words, we decide to become good citizens. Although this earth is not our final home, we are here now and have certain responsibilities to our country and to our fellow man.

Scripture Meditations

❏ *Romans 13:1-7* (pg 119)　　　❏ *1 Timothy 2:1-2* (pg 151)

As God's people, we have the duty to pray for our leaders, both spiritual and political. Daily we need to take authority over the powers of darkness that would seek to destroy our nation. (See Ephesians 6:12 *pg 142*) We must bind them in the Name of Jesus. (See Matthew 18:18 *pg 16*) The devil will do his best to ruin our country and our leaders if we don't use our God-given authority over him.

CHAPTER 20

GET ALONG WITH PEOPLE

It's no easy task to get along with others because we are all so different. We have different backgrounds, different schooling, different upbringing, and different past experiences. Our opinions vary on certain issues and we have different ideas on different subjects. It's not easy to be at peace with someone who disagrees with you even on the minor issues.

Nonetheless, the Holy Spirit, through the writings of St. Paul, said to "… live peaceably with all men." We don't have to agree with everyone about everything, and we don't even have to respect their opinions, but we must respect them as human beings, having been created in the image and likeness of God.

GENERAL RULES FOR GETTING ALONG WITH PEOPLE

1. **Take a genuine interest in other people.**
   (See Philippians 2:20-21 *pg 144*)

2. **Never resort to cheap flattery to win a person's favor.** (See 1 Thessalonians 2:5 *pg 148*)

Watch out for anyone who tells lies and flatters— they are out to get you.

—Proverbs 26:28

3. **Never rebuke an older person harshly.** (See 1 Timothy 5:1 *pg 152*)

4. **Avoid foolish and stupid arguments.** (See 2 Timothy 2:23 *pg 155*)

5. **Always offer hospitality without grumbling.** (See 1 Peter 4:9 *pg 170*)

6. **Never embarrass another human being for any reason.**

Hanun arrested David's officials and had their beards shaved off on one side of their faces. He had their robes cut off just below the waist, and then he sent them away. They were terribly ashamed. When David found out what had happened to his officials, he sent a message and told them, "Stay in Jericho until your beards grow back. Then you can come home."

—2 Samuel 10:4-5

7. **Let your conversation always be full of grace.** (See Colossians 4:6 *pg 147*)

8. **Always say "thanks" to anyone who has helped you.** (See Luke 17:15 *pg 61*)

9. **Appreciate other people.**

10. **Don't praise yourself or brag about yourself.**

Don't brag about yourself— let others praise you.

—Proverbs 27:2

11. **Always be sincere, not phoney.**
    (See Romans 12:9 *pg 119*)

12. **Speak words to encourage and strengthen others.** (See Acts 15:32 *pg 101*)

13. **Don't be unjustly critical of others.**
    (See Luke 6:41-42 *pg 49*)

    When rulers decide cases, they weigh the evidence...Two things the LORD hates are dishonest scales and dishonest measures.

    —Proverbs 20:8,10

14. **Don't talk too much.**

    Stay away from gossips— they tell everything.

    —Proverbs 20: 19

21
CHAPTER

WATCH OUT FOR COMMON CAUSES OF FAILURE IN THE CHRISTIAN WALK

Here is a list of the most common causes of failure in the Christian's life:

1. Lack of confidence in God and in His word.

2. Not plunging ahead wholeheartedly, but dragging your feet.

3. A contrary desire.

4. Beginning to think about what you don't have instead of all you do have.

5. Failing to think in terms of God's supply house, which is unlimited.

6. Lack of perseverance during the trials.

7. Wasting time on silly magazines, television shows, etc., instead of using the extra time to get into God's word and good gospel books.

8. Selfishness.

9. Not desiring the will of God above all else in your life.

10. Flirting with the world and its amusements.

11. Pride.

12. Compromising your principles.

13. Lack of prayer, fellowship and Bible reading.

14. Lack of witnessing.

15. Fear and uncertainty.

16. Poor choice of associates.

17. Laziness.

18. Materialism.

19. Looking for a shortcut to spirituality.

20. Becoming negative minded.

21. Allowing Satan to distort your concept of God.

22. Putting anything ahead of Jesus.

23. Conforming to the world and its system and philosophies.

24. Lack of vision and having no goals in your Christian life.

25. Lack of Bible knowledge with the Holy Spirit revealing the truths to your heart.

26. Resentment of authority.

27. Security hang-up.

28. Not expecting the return of Jesus for His Church.

29. Shunning responsibility — not becoming involved in Church activities, etc.

30. Continuing in sin after Christ has set you free.

31. Unbelief in your thoughts, words, and actions.

32. Being self deceived by: A.) not being a doer of the Word; and B.) not talking like God talks. In other words, not speaking as though the Word of God were really true.

33. Criticizing or downgrading a man of God.

34. Being unconcerned with people; particularly people who are hurting in some way.

35. Instead of being a diligent seeker of God, being only a "casual inquirer."

Whenever you notice the victory being squeezed out of your Christian experience, check this list over. You will most likely see where you have been missing the mark.

CHAPTER 22

BEWARE OF FALSE PROPHETS AND FALSE TEACHERS

Scripture Meditations

❑ *Matthew 7:15-23* (pg 6) ❑ *Matthew 24:4-5* (pg 21)
❑ *Romans 16:17-19* (pg 121) ❑ *Acts 13:6-12* (pg 98)
❑ *Philippians 3:18-19* (pg 144) ❑ *Acts 20:28-31* (pg 105)
❑ *2 Peter chapter 2* (pg 172) ❑ *Galatians 1:8-9* (pg 137)
❑ *Colossians 2:18-19* (pg 146) ❑ *John 10:12-13* (pg 78)
❑ *1 Timothy 4:1-5* (pg 152) ❑ *Colossians 2:8* (pg 146)
❑ *2 Corinthians 11:3-4* (pg 135)
❑ *2 Corinthians 11:12-25* (pg 135)

The Bible instructs us to test the spirits to see if they are of God.

Jesus said to *beware* of false prophets. The word *"beware"* actually means (from the Greek) to shun, avoid, and stay away from. *Don't dabble in things you know to be false because little by little the thoughts will begin to penetrate your resistance if you keep toying with them.*

Stop listening to teaching that contradicts what you know is right.

— Proverbs 19:27 (TLB)

CHAPTER

TAKE CARE OF YOUR BODY

God created man as a trichotomy. That means that man is a little trinity, so to speak. He is:

1. Spirit

2. Soul

3. Body

The spirit of man is fed by the Word of God. The soul is the area of the mind and emotions. It too must be fed a healthy diet in order to be kept in tip-top shape. We human beings are interrelated with ourselves. In other words, our spiritual life will affect our mental life and possibly our physical life. In the same way, our mental life, if it is poor, can adversely affect our spiritual lives as well as our physical bodies.

Preachers always tell people to take care of their spiritual lives, but sometimes we forget that taking care of our physical bodies is also a part of genuine Christianity. If you are born again, your physical body not only houses your personal spirit, but also has become the abode of the Holy Spirit. God Himself is actually living inside your body!

Therefore, you will want to take care of your body. Watch your diet! In America it has been discovered that we eat way too much sugar and salt. Some doctors believe this could be the cause for the high cancer rate. Learn to regulate your diet. Stay away from foods you know are bad for you.

If you smoke or chew tobacco, ask God to deliver you from it. Believe Him for the full, complete victory over these damaging habits.

Take care of the body you are living in. Get a proper diet and adequate exercise. You will feel better, look better, think better, and most likely live longer!

Scripture Meditations

❑ *1 Corinthians 6:19* (pg 124)   ❑ *Romans 12:1-3* (pg 119)
❑ *1 Corinthians 3:16-17* (pg 123)

24

CHAPTER

PRESS TOWARD THE FOLLOWING GENERAL GOALS

1. Become A Mature Christian.
2. Develop A Christ-Like Character.
3. Be Trained As A Leader/Worker.

CHAPTER

DEVELOP THE FOLLOWING TRAITS

1. A Life Of Prayer.

2. Love For The Bible.

3. Dependability.

4. Loyalty To Church And Faithful In Attendance.

5. Respect For Leadership.

6. Continual Deepening Of Your Spiritual Life.

7. An Active Life Of Christian Service.

8. Yieldedness To The Will Of God.

9. A Vision For World Evangelism.

10. A Heart For Worship And Praise.

11. A Growing Love For All People.

CHAPTER 26

READ GOOD MATERIAL

The Bible tells us to "renew our minds." We have been programmed to think like the world and it may take a while to reprogram our thinking. But we can speed the process by reading good, well-balanced Christian material. You can ask your pastor for a list of good reading material. He'll be able to help you in selecting some good books and magazines.

TOOLS THAT WILL HELP YOU STUDY THE BIBLE

1. **Dictionary**

2. **Bible Dictionary**

3. **Parallel Bible**

4. **Concordance**

5. **Various Bible translations.** You will love the Contemporary English Version New Testament.

6. **Study tapes** (ask your pastor or his assistant for a listing.)

SPECIAL PROJECTS

Get a dictionary, or call an older Christian and find out the meaning of these words:

1. Atonement
2. Conversion
3. Doctrine
4. Faith
5. Meditation
6. Prayer
7. Repentance
8. Salvation
9. Sin
10. Satan
11. Temptation
12. Worldly

Take a piece of paper and list the 26 things you will WANT to do now that you are a Christian.

CONCLUSION

There you have them! Twenty-six powerful things that will help catapult you to growth and success now that you've been given a fresh *New Life*. I cannot possibly emphasize enough the importance of daily reading God's Word.

The Contemporary English Version of the New Testament follows in Part Two of the *New Life New Testament*. I have chosen this version in a partnership with the American Bible Society because it is "user friendly." In other words, it is readable, understandable, shareable, and is an *actual* translation, true to the original languages.

You're going to have fun reading through the *New Life New Testament* over and over again. And as you do, your faith will grow and you'll find yourself coming into a deeper, more fruitful fellowship with God Himself. You discover yourself talking to others about what you've read and learned, and they too will, sooner or later, want the *New Life* you've discovered.

Now a word of encouragement. Don't get discouraged if there are portions of the *New Life New Testament* that you don't quite understand. Trust the Holy Spirit to reveal to your heart whatever He sees fit at the time. When you're ready, He'll give you more revelation and light. Simply read the *New Life New Testament* every day and apply the issues that speak to your heart on any given day. Everyday, the Holy Spirit will reveal something important to you. It's your task to read. As you read, you'll think of things to pray about also. Read and talk to God as you go. Ask Him questions, trusting that He will answer you in time. Ask Him to help you in certain areas as the Holy Spirit speaks to your heart.

Are you ready to start reading the New Testament? Are you willing to read some portion each day as you can? Are you going to place this as a high priority in your life? If you answered "Yes" to these questions, then I know you are destined to be very fruitful in this precious *New Life*.

Now, let's read the New Testament ...

NOTES

NOTES

NOTES

THE NEW TESTAMENT —

CONTEMPORARY ENGLISH VERSION

PART 2

THE NEW TESTAMENT —

CONTEMPORARY ENGLISH VERSION

AMERICAN BIBLE SOCIETY
WWW.BIBLES.COM

NEW TESTAMENT

CONTEMPORARY ENGLISH VERSION

Quotation Rights for the *Contemporary English Version*

The American Bible Society is glad to grant authors and publishers the right to use up to five hundred (500) verses from the *Contemporary English Version* text in church, religious and other publications without the need to seek and receive written permission. However, the extent of quotation must not comprise a complete book nor should it amount to more than 25% of the work. The proper copyright notice must appear on the title or copyright page.

When quotations from the *CEV* are used in non-saleable media such as church bulletins, orders of service, posters, transparencies or similar media, a complete copyright notice is not required, but the initials *(CEV)* must appear at the end of each quotation.

Requests for quotations in excess of five hundred (500) verses in any publication must be directed to, and written approval received from, the American Bible Society, 1865 Broadway, New York, NY 10023.

The work of the American Bible Society is made possible by contributions from supporters. If you would like to help spread the Gospel through Scripture distribution and engagement in the USA and around the world, we would be grateful for your donation.

You can mail your gift to the American Bible Society at the address below. Credit card contributions can be made at our secure website, www.americanbible.org. or through our toll-free number 1-866-895-4448.

American Bible Society/1865 Broadway/New York, NY 10025

ISBN 1-58516-533-6

Printed in the United States of America
Eng. NT CEV250-111434
ABS-9/05-10,000-467,200-DP4(7)

WELCOME TO THE CONTEMPORARY ENGLISH VERSION

Languages are spoken before they are written. And far more communication is done through the spoken word than through the written word. In fact, more people *hear* the Bible read than read it for themselves. Traditional translations of the Bible count on the *reader's* ability to understand a *written* text. But the *Contempoary English Version* differs from all other English Bibles—past and present—in that it takes into consideration the needs of the *hearer*, as well as those of the *reader*, who may not be familiar with traditional biblical language.

The *Contemporary English Version* has been described as a "user-friendly"and a "mission- driven" translation that can be *read aloud* without stumbling, *heard* without misunderstanding, and *listened to* with enjoyment and appreciation, because the language is contemporary and the style is lucid and lyrical.

The *Contemporary English Version* invites you to *read*, to *hear*, to *understand* and to *share*

the Word of God now
as never before!

In order to assure a text that is faithful to the *meaning* of the original, the *Contemporary English Version* New Testament was translated directly from the Greek text published by the United Bible Societies (third edition corrected and compared with the fourth revised edition). The drafts in their earliest stages were sent for review and comment to all English-speaking Bible Societies and to more than forty United Bible translation consultants around the world. Final approval of the text was given by the American Bible Society Board of Trustees on the recommendation of its Translations Subcommittee.

CONTENTS

OTHER ABBREVIATIONS

CIRCA (around)	c.
New Testament	NT
Septuagint	LXX

MATTHEW

The Ancestors of Jesus

1 Jesus Christ came from the family of King David and also from the family of Abraham. And this is a list of his ancestors. 2-6a From Abraham to King David, his ancestors were:

Abraham, Isaac, Jacob, Judah and his brothers (Judah's sons were Perez and Zerah, and their mother was Tamar), Hezron;

Ram, Amminadab, Nahshon, Salmon, Boaz (his mother was Rahab), Obed (his mother was Ruth), Jesse, and King David.

6b-11 From David to the time of the exile in Babylonia, the ancestors of Jesus were:

David, Solomon (his mother had been Uriah's wife), Rehoboam, Abijah, Asa, Jehoshaphat, Jehoram;

Uzziah, Jotham, Ahaz, Hezekiah, Manasseh, Amon, Josiah, and Jehoiachin and his brothers.

12-16 From the exile to the birth of Jesus, his ancestors were:

Jehoiachin, Shealtiel, Zerubbabel, Abiud, Eliakim, Azor, Zadok, Achim;

Eliud, Eleazar, Matthan, Jacob, and Joseph, the husband of Mary, the mother of Jesus, who is called the Messiah.

17 There were fourteen generations from Abraham to David. There were also fourteen from David to the exile in Babylonia and fourteen more to the birth of the Messiah.

The Birth of Jesus

18 This is how Jesus Christ was born. A young woman named Mary was engaged to Joseph from King David's family. But before they were married, she learned that she was going to have a baby by God's Holy Spirit. 19 Joseph was a good man[a] and did not want to embarrass Mary in front of everyone. So he decided to quietly call off the wedding.

20 While Joseph was thinking about this, an angel from the Lord came to him in a dream. The angel said, "Joseph, the baby that Mary will have is from the Holy Spirit. Go ahead and marry her. 21 Then after her baby is born, name him Jesus, because he will save his people from their sins."

22 So the Lord's promise came true, just as the prophet had said, 23 "A virgin will have a baby boy, and he will be called Immanuel," which means "God is with us."

24 After Joseph woke up, he and Mary were soon married, just as the Lord's angel had told him to do. 25 But they did not sleep together before her baby was born. Then Joseph named him Jesus.

The Wise Men

2 When Jesus was born in the village of Bethlehem in Judea, Herod was king. During this time some wise men from the east came to Jerusalem 2 and said, "Where is the child born to be king of the Jews? We saw his star in the east[b] and have come to worship him."

3 When King Herod heard about this, he was worried, and so was everyone else in Jerusalem. 4 Herod brought together the chief priests and the teachers of the Law of Moses and asked them, "Where will the Messiah be born?"

5 They told him, "He will be born in Bethlehem, just as the prophet wrote,

6 'Bethlehem in the land
    of Judea,
you are very important
    among the towns of Judea.
From your town
    will come a leader,
who will be like a shepherd
    for my people Israel.' "

7 Herod secretly called in the wise men and asked them when they had first seen the star. 8 He told them, "Go to Bethlehem and search carefully for the child. As soon as you find him, let me know. I want to go and worship him too."

9 The wise men listened to what the king said and then left. And the star they had seen in the east went on ahead of them until it stopped over the place where the child was. 10 They were thrilled and excited to see the star.

11 When the men went into the house and saw the child with Mary, his mother, they knelt down and worshiped him. They took out their gifts of gold, frankincense, and myrrh and gave them to him. 12 Later they were warned in a dream not to return to Herod, and they went back home by another road.

The Escape to Egypt

13 After the wise men had gone, an angel from the Lord appeared to Joseph in a dream and said, "Get up! Hurry and take the child and his mother to Egypt! Stay there until I tell you to return, because Herod is looking for the child and wants to kill him."

14 That night, Joseph got up and took his wife and the child to Egypt, 15 where they stayed until Herod died. So the Lord's promise came true, just as the prophet had said, "I called my son out of Egypt."

The Killing of the Children

16 When Herod found out that the wise men from the east had tricked him, he was very angry. He gave orders for his men to kill all the boys who lived in or near Bethlehem and were two years old and younger. This was based on what he had learned from the wise men.

17 So the Lord's promise came true, just as the prophet Jeremiah had said,

18 "In Ramah a voice was heard
    crying and weeping loudly.

---

a **1.19** *good man*: Or "kind man," or "man who always did the right thing."   *b* **2.2** *his star in the east*: Or "his star rise."

1

Rachel was mourning
      for her children,
and she refused
to be comforted,
      because they were dead."

The Return from Egypt

¹⁹ After King Herod died, an angel from the Lord appeared in a dream to Joseph while he was still in Egypt. ²⁰ The angel said, "Get up and take the child and his mother back to Israel. The people who wanted to kill him are now dead."

²¹ Joseph got up and left with them for Israel. ²² But when he heard that Herod's son Archelaus was now ruler of Judea, he was afraid to go there. Then in a dream he was told to go to Galilee, ²³ and they went to live there in the town of Nazareth. So the Lord's promise came true, just as the prophet had said, "He will be called a Nazarene."

The Preaching of John the Baptist

3 Years later, John the Baptist started preaching in the desert of Judea. ² He said, "Turn back to God! The kingdom of heaven will soon be here."ᶜ

³ John was the one the prophet Isaiah was talking about, when he said,

"In the desert someone
      is shouting,
'Get the road ready
      for the Lord!
Make a straight path
      for him.' "

⁴ John wore clothes made of camel's hair. He had a leather strap around his waist and ate grasshoppers and wild honey.

⁵ From Jerusalem and all Judea and from the Jordan River Valley crowds of people went to John. ⁶ They told how sorry they were for their sins, and he baptized them in the river.

⁷ Many Pharisees and Sadducees also came to be baptized. But John said to them:

You bunch of snakes! Who warned you to run from the coming judgment? ⁸ Do something to show that you have really given up your sins. ⁹ And don't start telling yourselves that you belong to Abraham's family. I tell you that God can turn these stones into children for Abraham. ¹⁰ An ax is ready to cut the trees down at their roots. Any tree that doesn't produce good fruit will be chopped down and thrown into a fire.

¹¹ I baptize you with water so that you will give up your sins.ᵈ But someone more powerful is going to come, and I am not good enough even to carry his sandals. He will baptize you with the Holy Spirit and with fire. ¹² His threshing fork is in his hand, and he is ready to separate the wheat from the husks. He will store the wheat in a barn and burn the husks in a fire that never goes out.

The Baptism of Jesus

¹³ Jesus left Galilee and went to the Jordan River to be baptized by John. ¹⁴ But John kept objecting and said, "I ought to be baptized by you. Why have you come to me?"

¹⁵ Jesus answered, "For now this is how it should be, because we must do all that God wants us to do." Then John agreed.

¹⁶ So Jesus was baptized. And as soon as he came out of the water, the sky opened, and he saw the Spirit of God coming down on him like a dove. ¹⁷ Then a voice from heaven said, "This is my own dear Son, and I am pleased with him."

Jesus and the Devil

4 The Holy Spirit led Jesus into the desert, so that the devil could test him. ² After Jesus had gone without eating for forty days and nights, he was very hungry. ³ Then the devil came to him and said, "If you are God's Son, tell these stones to turn into bread."

⁴ Jesus answered, "The Scriptures say:

'No one can live only on food.
People need every word
      that God has spoken.' "

⁵ Next, the devil took Jesus to the holy city and had him stand on the highest part of the temple. ⁶ The devil said, "If you are God's Son, jump off. The Scriptures say:

'God will give his angels
      orders about you.
They will catch you
      in their arms,
and you won't hurt
      your feet on the stones.' "

⁷ Jesus answered, "The Scriptures also say, 'Don't try to test the Lord your God!' "

⁸ Finally, the devil took Jesus up on a very high mountain and showed him all the kingdoms on earth and their power. ⁹ The devil said to him, "I will give all this to you, if you will bow down and worship me."

¹⁰ Jesus answered, "Go away Satan! The Scriptures say:

'Worship the Lord your God
      and serve only him.' "

¹¹ Then the devil left Jesus, and angels came to help him.

Jesus Begins His Work

¹² When Jesus heard that John had been put in prison, he went to Galilee. ¹³ But instead of staying in Nazareth, Jesus moved to Capernaum. This town was beside Lake Galilee in the territory of Zebulun and Naphtali. ¹⁴ So God's promise came true, just as the prophet Isaiah had said,

¹⁵ "Listen, lands of Zebulun
      and Naphtali,

ᶜ **3.2** *will soon be here*: Or "is already here."   ᵈ **3.11** *so that you will give up your sins*: Or "because you have given up your sins."

lands along the road
to the sea and east
of the Jordan!
Listen Galilee,
land of the Gentiles!
16 Although your people
live in darkness,
they will see
a bright light.
Although they live
in the shadow of death,
a light will shine
on them."

17 Then Jesus started preaching, "Turn back to God! The kingdom of heaven will soon be here."*e*

Jesus Chooses Four Fishermen

18 While Jesus was walking along the shore of Lake Galilee, he saw two brothers. One was Simon, also known as Peter, and the other was Andrew. They were fishermen, and they were casting their net into the lake. 19 Jesus said to them, "Come with me! I will teach you how to bring in people instead of fish." 20 Right then the two brothers dropped their nets and went with him.

21 Jesus walked on until he saw James and John, the sons of Zebedee. They were in a boat with their father, mending their nets. Jesus asked them to come with him too. 22 Right away they left the boat and their father and went with Jesus.

Jesus Teaches, Preaches, and Heals

23 Jesus went all over Galilee, teaching in the Jewish meeting places and preaching the good news about God's kingdom. He also healed every kind of disease and sickness. 24 News about him spread all over Syria, and people with every kind of sickness or disease were brought to him. Some of them had a lot of demons in them, others were thought to be crazy, and still others could not walk. But Jesus healed them all.

25 Large crowds followed Jesus from Galilee and the region around the ten cities known as Decapolis. They also came from Jerusalem, Judea, and from across the Jordan River.

The Sermon on the Mount

5 When Jesus saw the crowds, he went up on the side of a mountain and sat down.

Blessings

Jesus' disciples gathered around him, 2 and he taught them:

3 God blesses those people
who depend only on him.
They belong to the kingdom
of heaven!*f*
4 God blesses those people

who grieve.
They will find comfort!
5 God blesses those people
who are humble.
The earth will belong
to them!
6 God blesses those people
who want to obey him*g*
more than to eat or drink.
They will be given
what they want!
7 God blesses those people
who are merciful.
They will be treated
with mercy!
8 God blesses those people
whose hearts are pure.
They will see him!
9 God blesses those people
who make peace.
They will be called
his children!
10 God blesses those people
who are treated badly
for doing right.
They belong to the kingdom
of heaven.

11 God will bless you when people insult you, mistreat you, and tell all kinds of evil lies about you because of me. 12 Be happy and excited! You will have a great reward in heaven. People did these same things to the prophets who lived long ago.

Salt and Light

13 You are like salt for everyone on earth. But if salt no longer tastes like salt, how can it make food salty? All it is good for is to be thrown out and walked on.

14 You are like light for the whole world. A city built on top of a hill cannot be hidden, 15 and no one would light a lamp and put it under a clay pot. A lamp is placed on a lampstand, where it can give light to everyone in the house. 16 Make your light shine, so that others will see the good that you do and will praise your Father in heaven.

The Law of Moses

17 Don't suppose that I came to do away with the Law and the Prophets. I did not come to do away with them, but to give them their full meaning. 18 Heaven and earth may disappear. But I promise you that not even a period or comma will ever disappear from the Law. Everything written in it must happen.

19 If you reject even the least important command in the Law and teach others to do the same, you will be the least important person in the kingdom of heaven. But if you obey and teach others its

---

e **4.17** *will soon be here:* See the note at 3.2.   *f* **5.3** *They belong to the kingdom of heaven:* Or "The kingdom of heaven belongs to them."
g **5.6** *who want to obey him:* Or "who want to do right" or "who want everyone to be treated right."

commands, you will have an important place in the kingdom. 20 You must obey God's commands better than the Pharisees and the teachers of the Law obey them. If you don't, I promise you that you will never get into the kingdom of heaven.

Anger

21 You know that our ancestors were told, "Do not murder" and "A murderer must be brought to trial." 22 But I promise you that if you are angry with someone,*h* you will have to stand trial. If you call someone a fool, you will be taken to court. And if you say that someone is worthless, you will be in danger of the fires of hell.

23 So if you are about to place your gift on the altar and remember that someone is angry with you, 24 leave your gift there in front of the altar. Make peace with that person, then come back and offer your gift to God.

25 Before you are dragged into court, make friends with the person who has accused you of doing wrong. If you don't, you will be handed over to the judge and then to the officer who will put you in jail. 26 I promise you that you will not get out until you have paid the last cent you owe.

Marriage

27 You know the commandment which says, "Be faithful in marriage." 28 But I tell you that if you look at another woman and want her, you are already unfaithful in your thoughts. 29 If your right eye causes you to sin, poke it out and throw it away. It is better to lose one part of your body, than for your whole body to end up in hell. 30 If your right hand causes you to sin, chop it off and throw it away! It is better to lose one part of your body, than for your whole body to be thrown into hell.

Divorce

31 You have been taught that a man who divorces his wife must write out divorce papers for her. 32 But I tell you not to divorce your wife unless she has committed some terrible sexual sin. If you divorce her, you will cause her to be unfaithful, just as any man who marries her is guilty of taking another man's wife.

Promises

33 You know that our ancestors were told, "Don't use the Lord's name to make a promise unless you are going to keep it." 34 But I tell you not to swear by anything when you make a promise! Heaven is God's throne, so don't swear by heaven. 35 The earth is God's footstool, so don't swear by the earth. Jerusalem is the city of the great king, so don't swear by it. 36 Don't swear by your own head. You cannot make one hair white or black. 37 When you make a promise, say only "Yes" or "No." Anything else comes from the devil.

Revenge

38 You know that you have been taught, "An eye for an eye and a tooth for a tooth." 39 But I tell you not to try to get even with a person who has done something to you. When someone slaps your right cheek, turn and let that person slap your other cheek. 40 If someone sues you for your shirt, give up your coat as well. 41 If a soldier forces you to carry his pack one mile, carry it two miles. 42 When people ask you for something, give it to them. When they want to borrow money, lend it to them.

Love

43 You have heard people say, "Love your neighbors and hate your enemies." 44 But I tell you to love your enemies and pray for anyone who mistreats you. 45 Then you will be acting like your Father in heaven. He makes the sun rise on both good and bad people. And he sends rain for the ones who do right and for the ones who do wrong. 46 If you love only those people who love you, will God reward you for that? Even tax collectors love their friends. 47 If you greet only your friends, what's so great about that? Don't even unbelievers do that? 48 But you must always act like your Father in heaven.

Giving

6 When you do good deeds, don't try to show off. If you do, you won't get a reward from your Father in heaven.

2 When you give to the poor, don't blow a loud horn. That's what show-offs do in the meeting places and on the street corners, because they are always looking for praise. I can assure you that they already have their reward.

3 When you give to the poor, don't let anyone know about it.*i* 4 Then your gift will be given in secret. Your Father knows what is done in secret, and he will reward you.

Prayer

5 When you pray, don't be like those show-offs who love to stand up and pray in the meeting places and on the street corners. They do this just to look good. I can assure you that they already have their reward.

6 When you pray, go into a room alone and close the door. Pray to your Father in private. He knows what is done in private, and he will reward you.

7 When you pray, don't talk on and on as people do who don't know God. They think God likes to hear long prayers. 8 Don't be like them. Your Father knows what you need before you ask.

9 You should pray like this:

Our Father in heaven,

---

h **5.22** *someone*: In verses 22-24 the Greek text has "brother," which may refer to people in general or to other followers.
i **6.3** *don't let anyone know about it*: The Greek text has, "Don't let your left hand know what your right hand is doing."

help us to honor
your name.
10 Come and set up
your kingdom,
so that everyone on earth
will obey you,
as you are obeyed
in heaven.
11 Give us our food for today.*j*
12 Forgive us for doing wrong,
as we forgive others.
13 Keep us from being tempted
and protect us from evil.*k*

14 If you forgive others for the wrongs they do to you, your Father in heaven will forgive you. 15 But if you don't forgive others, your Father will not forgive your sins.

Worshiping God by Going without Eating

16 When you go without eating, don't try to look gloomy as those show-offs do when they go without eating. I can assure you that they already have their reward. 17 Instead, comb your hair and wash your face. 18 Then others won't know that you are going without eating. But your Father sees what is done in private, and he will reward you.

Treasures in Heaven

19 Don't store up treasures on earth! Moths and rust can destroy them, and thieves can break in and steal them. 20 Instead, store up your treasures in heaven, where moths and rust cannot destroy them, and thieves cannot break in and steal them. 21 Your heart will always be where your treasure is.

Light

22 Your eyes are like a window for your body. When they are good, you have all the light you need. 23 But when your eyes are bad, everything is dark. If the light inside you is dark, you surely are in the dark.

Money

24 You cannot be the slave of two masters! You will like one more than the other or be more loyal to one than the other. You cannot serve both God and money.

Worry

25 I tell you not to worry about your life. Don't worry about having something to eat, drink, or wear. Isn't life more than food or clothing? 26 Look at the birds in the sky! They don't plant or harvest. They don't even store grain in barns. Yet your Father in heaven takes care of them. Aren't you worth more than birds? 27 Can worry make you live longer?*l* 28 Why

worry about clothes? Look how the wild flowers grow. They don't work hard to make their clothes. 29 But I tell you that Solomon with all his wealth wasn't as well clothed as one of them. 30 God gives such beauty to everything that grows in the fields, even though it is here today and thrown into a fire tomorrow. He will surely do even more for you! Why do you have such little faith?

31 Don't worry and ask yourselves, "Will we have anything to eat? Will we have anything to drink? Will we have any clothes to wear?" 32 Only people who don't know God are always worrying about such things. Your Father in heaven knows that you need all of these. 33 But more than anything else, put God's work first and do what he wants. Then the other things will be yours as well.

34 Don't worry about tomorrow. It will take care of itself. You have enough to worry about today.

Judging Others

7 Don't condemn others, and God won't condemn you. 2 God will be as hard on you as you are on others! He will treat you exactly as you treat them.

3 You can see the speck in your friend's eye, but you don't notice the log in your own eye. 4 How can you say, "My friend, let me take the speck out of your eye," when you don't see the log in your own eye? 5 You're nothing but show-offs! First, take the log out of your own eye. Then you can see how to take the speck out of your friend's eye.

6 Don't give to dogs what belongs to God. They will only turn and attack you. Don't throw pearls down in front of pigs. They will trample all over them.

Ask, Search, Knock

7 Ask, and you will receive. Search, and you will find. Knock, and the door will be opened for you. 8 Everyone who asks will receive. Everyone who searches will find. And the door will be opened for everyone who knocks. 9 Would any of you give your hungry child a stone, if the child asked for some bread? 10 Would you give your child a snake if the child asked for a fish? 11 As bad as you are, you still know how to give good gifts to your children. But your heavenly Father is even more ready to give good things to people who ask.

12 Treat others as you want them to treat you. This is what the Law and the Prophets are all about.

The Narrow Gate

13 Go in through the narrow gate. The gate to destruction is wide, and the road that leads there is easy to follow. A lot of people go through that gate. 14 But the gate to life is very narrow. The road that leads there is so hard to follow that only a few people find it.

---

j **6.11** *our food for today*: Or "the food that we need" or "our food for the coming day." *k* **6.13** *evil*: Or "the evil one," that is, the devil. Some manuscripts add, "The kingdom, the power, and the glory are yours forever. Amen." *l* **6.27** *live longer*: Or "grow taller."

A Tree and Its Fruit

15 Watch out for false prophets! They dress up like sheep, but inside they are wolves who have come to attack you. **16** You can tell what they are by what they do. No one picks grapes or figs from thornbushes. **17** A good tree produces good fruit, and a bad tree produces bad fruit. **18** A good tree cannot produce good fruit, and a bad tree cannot produce good fruit. **19** Every tree that produces bad fruit will be chopped down and burned. **20** You can tell who the false prophets are by their deeds.

A Warning

21 Not everyone who calls me their Lord will get into the kingdom of heaven. Only the ones who obey my Father in heaven will get in. **22** On the day of judgment many will call me their Lord. They will say, "We preached in your name, and in your name we forced out demons and worked many miracles." **23** But I will tell them, "I will have nothing to do with you! Get out of my sight, you evil people!"

Two Builders

24 Anyone who hears and obeys these teachings of mine is like a wise person who built a house on solid rock. **25** Rain poured down, rivers flooded, and winds beat against that house. But it did not fall, because it was built on solid rock. **26** Anyone who hears my teachings and doesn't obey them is like a foolish person who built a house on sand. **27** The rain poured down, the rivers flooded, and the winds blew and beat against that house. Finally, it fell with a crash.

28 When Jesus finished speaking, the crowds were surprised at his teaching. **29** He taught them like someone with authority, and not like their teachers of the Law of Moses.

Jesus Heals a Man

8 As Jesus came down the mountain, he was followed by large crowds. **2** Suddenly a man with leprosy came and knelt in front of Jesus. He said, "Lord, you have the power to make me well, if only you wanted to."

3 Jesus put his hand on the man and said, "I want to! Now you are well." At once the man's leprosy disappeared. **4** Jesus told him, "Don't tell anyone about this, but go and show the priest that you are well. Then take a gift to the temple just as Moses commanded, and everyone will know that you have been healed."

Jesus Heals an Army Officer's Servant

5 When Jesus was going into the town of Capernaum, an army officer came up to him and said, **6** "Lord, my servant is at home in such terrible pain that he can't even move."

7 "I will go and heal him," Jesus replied.

8 But the officer said, "Lord, I'm not good enough for you to come into my house. Just give the order, and my servant will get well. **9** I have officers who give orders to me, and I have soldiers who take orders from me. I can say to one of them, 'Go!' and he goes. I can say to another, 'Come!' and he comes. I can say to my servant, 'Do this!' and he will do it."

10 When Jesus heard this, he was so surprised that he turned and said to the crowd following him, "I tell you that in all of Israel I've never found anyone with this much faith! **11** Many people will come from everywhere to enjoy the feast in the kingdom of heaven with Abraham, Isaac, and Jacob. **12** But the ones who should have been in the kingdom will be thrown out into the dark. They will cry and grit their teeth in pain."

13 Then Jesus said to the officer, "You may go home now. Your faith has made it happen."

Right then his servant was healed.

Jesus Heals Many People

14 Jesus went to the home of Peter, where he found that Peter's mother-in-law was sick in bed with fever. **15** He took her by the hand, and the fever left her. Then she got up and served Jesus a meal.

16 That evening many people with demons in them were brought to Jesus. And with only a word he forced out the evil spirits and healed everyone who was sick. **17** So God's promise came true, just as the prophet Isaiah had said,

> "He healed our diseases
> and made us well."

Some Who Wanted To Go with Jesus

18 When Jesus saw the crowd,*m* he went across Lake Galilee. **19** A teacher of the Law of Moses came up to him and said, "Teacher, I'll go anywhere with you!"

20 Jesus replied, "Foxes have dens, and birds have nests. But the Son of Man doesn't have a place to call his own."

21 Another disciple said to Jesus, "Lord, let me wait till I bury my father."

22 Jesus answered, "Come with me, and let the dead bury their dead."

A Storm

23 After Jesus left in a boat with his disciples, **24** a terrible storm suddenly struck the lake, and waves started splashing into their boat.

Jesus was sound asleep, **25** so the disciples went over to him and woke him up. They said, "Lord, save us! We're going to drown!"

26 But Jesus replied, "Why are you so afraid? You surely don't have much faith." Then he got up and ordered the wind and the waves to calm down. And everything was calm.

27 The men in the boat were amazed and said, "Who is this? Even the wind and the waves obey him."

Two Men with Demons in Them

28 After Jesus had crossed the lake, he came to shore near the town of Gadara*n* and started down the road. Two men with demons in them came to him from the tombs. They were so fierce that no one could travel that way.

---

m **8.18** *saw the crowd:* Some manuscripts have "large crowd." Others have "large crowds." *n* **8.28** *Gadara:* Some manuscripts have "Gergesa." Others have "Gerasa."

²⁹ Suddenly they shouted, "Jesus, Son of God, what do you want with us? Have you come to punish us before our time?"

³⁰ Not far from there a large herd of pigs was feeding. ³¹ So the demons begged Jesus, "If you force us out, please send us into those pigs!" ³² Jesus told them to go, and they went out of the men and into the pigs. All at once the pigs rushed down the steep bank into the lake and drowned.

³³ The people taking care of the pigs ran to the town and told everything, especially what had happened to the two men. ³⁴ Everyone in town came out to meet Jesus. When they saw him, they begged him to leave their part of the country.

Jesus Heals a Crippled Man

9 Jesus got into a boat and crossed back over to the town where he lived. ² Some people soon brought to him a crippled man lying on a mat. When Jesus saw how much faith they had, he said to the crippled man, "My friend, don't worry! Your sins are forgiven."

³ Some teachers of the Law of Moses said to themselves, "Jesus must think he is God!"

⁴ But Jesus knew what was in their minds, and he said, "Why are you thinking such evil things? ⁵ Is it easier for me to tell this crippled man that his sins are forgiven or to tell him to get up and walk? ⁶ But I will show you that the Son of Man has the right to forgive sins here on earth." So Jesus said to the man, "Get up! Pick up your mat and go on home." ⁷ The man got up and went home. ⁸ When the crowds saw this, they were afraid° and praised God for giving such authority to people.

Jesus Chooses Matthew

⁹ As Jesus was leaving, he saw a tax collector named Matthew sitting at the place for paying taxes. Jesus said to him, "Come with me." Matthew got up and went with him.

¹⁰ Later, Jesus and his disciples were having dinner at Matthew's house.ᵖ Many tax collectors and other sinners were also there. ¹¹ Some Pharisees asked Jesus' disciples, "Why does your teacher eat with tax collectors and other sinners?"

¹² Jesus heard them and answered, "Healthy people don't need a doctor, but sick people do. ¹³ Go and learn what the Scriptures mean when they say, 'Instead of offering sacrifices to me, I want you to be merciful to others.' I didn't come to invite good people to be my followers. I came to invite sinners."

People Ask about Going without Eating

¹⁴ One day some followers of John the Baptist came and asked Jesus, "Why do we and the Pharisees often go without eating, while your disciples never do?"

¹⁵ Jesus answered:

The friends of a bridegroom don't go without eating while he is still with them. But the time will come when he will be taken from them. Then they will go without eating.

¹⁶ No one uses a new piece of cloth to patch old clothes. The patch would shrink and tear a bigger hole.

¹⁷ No one pours new wine into old wineskins. The wine would swell and burst the old skins. Then the wine would be lost, and the skins would be ruined. New wine must be put into new wineskins. Both the skins and the wine will then be safe.

A Dying Girl and a Sick Woman

¹⁸ While Jesus was still speaking, an official came and knelt in front of him. The man said, "My daughter has just now died! Please come and place your hand on her. Then she will live again."

¹⁹ Jesus and his disciples got up and went with the man.

²⁰ A woman who had been bleeding for twelve years came up behind Jesus and barely touched his clothes. ²¹ She had said to herself, "If I can just touch his clothes, I will get well."

²² Jesus turned. He saw the woman and said, "Don't worry! You are now well because of your faith." At that moment she was healed.

²³ When Jesus went into the home of the official and saw the musicians and the crowd of mourners, ²⁴ he said, "Get out of here! The little girl isn't dead. She is just asleep." Everyone started laughing at Jesus. ²⁵ But after the crowd had been sent out of the house, Jesus went to the girl's bedside. He took her by the hand and helped her up. ²⁶ News about this spread all over that part of the country.

Jesus Heals Two Blind Men

²⁷ As Jesus was walking along, two blind men began following him and shouting, "Son of David, have pity on us!"

²⁸ After Jesus had gone indoors, the two blind men came up to him. He asked them, "Do you believe I can make you well?"

"Yes, Lord," they answered.

²⁹ Jesus touched their eyes and said, "Because of your faith, you will be healed." ³⁰ They were able to see, and Jesus strictly warned them not to tell anyone about him. ³¹ But they left and talked about him to everyone in that part of the country.

Jesus Heals a Man Who Could Not Talk

³² As Jesus and his disciples were on their way, some people brought to him a man who could not talk because a demon was in him. ³³ After Jesus had forced the demon out, the man started talking. The crowds were so amazed that they began saying, "Nothing like this has ever happened in Israel!"

³⁴ But the Pharisees said, "The leader of the demons gives him the power to force out demons."

Jesus Has Pity on People

³⁵ Jesus went to every town and village. He taught in their meeting places and preached the good news about God's kingdom. Jesus also healed every kind of disease and sickness. ³⁶ When he saw the crowds, he felt sorry for them. They were confused and helpless, like sheep without a shepherd. ³⁷ He said to his disciples, "A large crop is in

---

°9.8 *afraid*: Some manuscripts have "amazed."   ᵖ9.10 *Matthew's house*: Or "Jesus' house."

the fields, but there are only a few workers. [38] Ask the Lord in charge of the harvest to send out workers to bring it in."

Jesus Chooses His Twelve Apostles

10 Jesus called together his twelve disciples. He gave them the power to force out evil spirits and to heal every kind of disease and sickness. [2] The first of the twelve apostles was Simon, better known as Peter. His brother Andrew was an apostle, and so were James and John, the two sons of Zebedee. [3] Philip, Bartholomew, Thomas, Matthew the tax collector, James the son of Alphaeus, and Thaddaeus were also apostles. [4] The others were Simon, known as the Eager One,[q] and Judas Iscariot who later betrayed Jesus.

Instructions for the Twelve Apostles

[5] Jesus sent out the twelve apostles with these instructions:

Stay away from the Gentiles and don't go to any Samaritan town. [6] Go only to the people of Israel, because they are like a flock of lost sheep. [7] As you go, announce that the kingdom of heaven will soon be here.[r] [8] Heal the sick, raise the dead to life, heal people who have leprosy, and force out demons. You received without paying, now give without being paid. [9] Don't take along any gold, silver, or copper coins. [10] And don't carry[s] a traveling bag or an extra shirt or sandals or a walking stick.

Workers deserve their food. [11] So when you go to a town or a village, find someone worthy enough to have you as their guest and stay with them until you leave. [12] When you go to a home, give it your blessing of peace. [13] If the home is deserving, let your blessing remain with them. But if the home isn't deserving, take back your blessing of peace. [14] If someone won't welcome you or listen to your message, leave their home or town. And shake the dust from your feet at them. [15] I promise you that the day of judgment will be easier for the towns of Sodom and Gomorrah than for that town.

Warning about Trouble

[16] I am sending you like lambs into a pack of wolves. So be as wise as snakes and as innocent as doves. [17] Watch out for people who will take you to court and have you beaten in their meeting places. [18] Because of me, you will be dragged before rulers and kings to tell them and the Gentiles about your faith. [19] But when someone arrests you, don't worry about what you will say or how you will say it. At that time you will be given the words to say. [20] But you will not really be the one speaking. The Spirit from your Father will tell you what to say.

[21] Brothers and sisters will betray one another and have each other put to death. Parents will betray their own children, and children will turn against their parents and have them killed. [22] Everyone will hate you because of me. But if you remain faithful until the end, you will be saved. [23] When people mistreat you in one town, hurry to another one. I promise you that before you have gone to all the towns of Israel, the Son of Man will come.

[24] Disciples are not better than their teacher, and slaves are not better than their master. [25] It is enough for disciples to be like their teacher and for slaves to be like their master. If people call the head of the family Satan, what will they say about the rest of the family?

The One To Fear

[26] Don't be afraid of anyone! Everything that is hidden will be found out, and every secret will be known. [27] Whatever I say to you in the dark, you must tell in the light. And you must announce from the housetops whatever I have whispered to you. [28] Don't be afraid of people. They can kill you, but they cannot harm your soul. Instead, you should fear God who can destroy both your body and your soul in hell. [29] Aren't two sparrows sold for only a penny? But your Father knows when any one of them falls to the ground. [30] Even the hairs on your head are counted. [31] So don't be afraid! You are worth much more than many sparrows.

Telling Others about Christ

[32] If you tell others that you belong to me, I will tell my Father in heaven that you are my followers. [33] But if you reject me, I will tell my Father in heaven that you don't belong to me.

Not Peace, but Trouble

[34] Don't think that I came to bring peace to the earth! I came to bring trouble, not peace. [35] I came to turn sons against their fathers, daughters against their mothers, and daughters-in-law against their mothers-in-law. [36] Your worst enemies will be in your own family.

[37] If you love your father or mother or even your sons and daughters more than me, you are not fit to be my disciples. [38] And unless you are willing to take up your cross and come with me, you are not fit to be my disciples. [39] If you try to save your life, you will lose it. But if you give it up for me, you will surely find it.

Rewards

[40] Anyone who welcomes you welcomes me. And anyone who welcomes me also welcomes the one who sent me. [41] Anyone who welcomes a prophet, just because that person is a prophet, will be given the same reward as a prophet. Anyone who welcomes a good person, just because that person is good, will be given the same reward as a good person. [42] And anyone who gives one of my most humble followers a cup of cool water, just because that person is my follower, will surely be rewarded.

---

[q] **10.4** *known as the Eager One*: The Greek text has "Cananaean," which probably comes from a Hebrew word meaning "zealous" (see Luke 6.15). "Zealot" was the name later given to the members of a Jewish group that resisted and fought against the Romans.
[r] **10.7** *will soon be here*: Or "is already here."   [s] **10.9,10** *Don't take along . . . don't carry*: Or "Don't accept . . . don't accept."

John the Baptist

11 After Jesus had finished instructing his twelve disciples, he left and began teaching and preaching in the towns.[t]

2 John was in prison when he heard what Christ was doing. So John sent some of his followers 3 to ask Jesus, "Are you the one we should be looking for? Or must we wait for someone else?"

4 Jesus answered, "Go and tell John what you have heard and seen. 5 The blind are now able to see, and the lame can walk. People with leprosy are being healed, and the deaf can hear. The dead are raised to life, and the poor are hearing the good news. 6 God will bless everyone who doesn't reject me because of what I do."

7 As John's followers were going away, Jesus spoke to the crowds about John:

What sort of person did you go out into the desert to see? Was he like tall grass blown about by the wind? 8 What kind of man did you go out to see? Was he someone dressed in fine clothes? People who dress like that live in the king's palace. 9 What did you really go out to see? Was he a prophet? He certainly was. I tell you that he was more than a prophet. 10 In the Scriptures God says about him, "I am sending my messenger ahead of you to get things ready for you." 11 I tell you that no one ever born on this earth is greater than John the Baptist. But whoever is least in the kingdom of heaven is greater than John.

12 From the time of John the Baptist until now, violent people have been trying to take over the kingdom of heaven by force. 13 All the Books of the Prophets and the Law of Moses told what was going to happen up to the time of John. 14 And if you believe them, John is Elijah, the prophet you are waiting for. 15 If you have ears, pay attention!

16 You people are like children sitting in the market and shouting to each other,

17 "We played the flute,
　　but you would not dance!
We sang a funeral song,
　　but you would not mourn!"

18 John the Baptist did not go around eating and drinking, and you said, "That man has a demon in him!" 19 But the Son of Man goes around eating and drinking, and you say, "That man eats and drinks too much! He is even a friend of tax collectors and sinners." Yet Wisdom is shown to be right by what it does.

The Unbelieving Towns

20 In the towns where Jesus had worked most of his miracles, the people refused to turn to God. So Jesus was upset with them and said:

21 You people of Chorazin are in for trouble! You people of Bethsaida are in for trouble too! If the miracles that took place in your towns had happened in Tyre and Sidon, the people there would have turned to God long ago. They would have dressed in sackcloth and put ashes on their heads. 22 I tell you that on the day of judgment the people of Tyre and Sidon will get off easier than you will.

23 People of Capernaum, do you think you will be honored in heaven? You will go down to hell! If the miracles that took place in your town had happened in Sodom, that town would still be standing. 24 So I tell you that on the day of judgment the people of Sodom will get off easier than you.

Come to Me and Rest

25 At that moment Jesus said:

My Father, Lord of heaven and earth, I am grateful that you hid all this from wise and educated people and showed it to ordinary people. 26 Yes, Father, that is what pleased you.

27 My Father has given me everything, and he is the only one who knows the Son. The only one who truly knows the Father is the Son. But the Son wants to tell others about the Father, so that they can know him too.

28 If you are tired from carrying heavy burdens, come to me and I will give you rest. 29 Take the yoke I give you. Put it on your shoulders and learn from me. I am gentle and humble, and you will find rest. 30 This yoke is easy to bear, and this burden is light.

A Question about the Sabbath

12 One Sabbath, Jesus and his disciples were walking through some wheat fields. His disciples were hungry and began picking and eating grains of wheat. 2 Some Pharisees noticed this and said to Jesus, "Why are your disciples picking grain on the Sabbath? They are not supposed to do that!"

3 Jesus answered:

You surely must have read what David did when he and his followers were hungry. 4 He went into the house of God, and then they ate the sacred loaves of bread that only priests are supposed to eat. 5 Haven't you read in the Law of Moses that the priests are allowed to work in the temple on the Sabbath? But no one says that they are guilty of breaking the law of the Sabbath. 6 I tell you that there is something here greater than the temple. 7 Don't you know what the Scriptures mean when they say, "Instead of offering sacrifices to me, I want you to be merciful to others?" If you knew what this means, you would not condemn these innocent disciples of mine. 8 So the Son of Man is Lord over the Sabbath.

A Man with a Crippled Hand

9 Jesus left and went into one of the Jewish meeting places, 10 where there was a man whose hand was crippled. Some Pharisees wanted to accuse Jesus of doing something wrong, and they asked him, "Is it right to heal someone on the Sabbath?"

11 Jesus answered, "If you had a sheep that fell into a

---

[t] 11.1 *the towns:* The Greek text has "their towns," which may refer to the towns of Galilee or to the towns where Jesus' disciples had lived.

ditch on the Sabbath, wouldn't you lift it out? ¹² People are worth much more than sheep, and so it is right to do good on the Sabbath." ¹³ Then Jesus told the man, "Hold out your hand." The man did, and it became as healthy as the other one.

¹⁴ The Pharisees left and started making plans to kill Jesus.

God's Chosen Servant

¹⁵ When Jesus found out what was happening, he left there and large crowds followed him. He healed all of their sick, ¹⁶ but warned them not to tell anyone about him. ¹⁷ So God's promise came true, just as Isaiah the prophet had said,

¹⁸ "Here is my chosen servant!
I love him,
   and he pleases me.
I will give him my Spirit,
and he will bring justice
   to the nations.
¹⁹ He won't shout or yell
   or call out in the streets.
²⁰ He won't break off a bent reed
   or put out a dying flame,
but he will make sure
   that justice is done.
²¹ All nations will place
   their hope in him."

Jesus and the Ruler of the Demons

²² Some people brought to Jesus a man who was blind and could not talk because he had a demon in him. Jesus healed the man, and then he was able to talk and see. ²³ The crowds were so amazed that they asked, "Could Jesus be the Son of David?"ᵘ

²⁴ When the Pharisees heard this, they said, "He forces out demons by the power of Beelzebul, the ruler of the demons!"

²⁵ Jesus knew what they were thinking, and he said to them:

Any kingdom where people fight each other will end up ruined. And a town or family that fights will soon destroy itself. ²⁶ So if Satan fights against himself, how can his kingdom last? ²⁷ If I use the power of Beelzebul to force out demons, whose power do your own followers use to force them out? Your followers are the ones who will judge you. ²⁸ But when I force out demons by the power of God's Spirit, it proves that God's kingdom has already come to you. ²⁹ How can anyone break into a strong man's house and steal his things, unless he first ties up the strong man? Then he can take everything.

³⁰ If you are not on my side, you are against me. If you don't gather in the harvest with me, you scatter it. ³¹⁻³² I tell you that any sinful thing you do or say can be forgiven. Even if you speak against the Son of Man, you can be forgiven. But if you speak against the Holy Spirit, you can never be forgiven, either in this life or in the life to come.

A Tree and Its Fruit

³³ A good tree produces only good fruit, and a bad tree produces bad fruit. You can tell what a tree is like by the fruit it produces. ³⁴ You are a bunch of evil snakes, so how can you say anything good? Your words show what is in your hearts. ³⁵ Good people bring good things out of their hearts, but evil people bring evil things out of their hearts. ³⁶ I promise you that on the day of judgment, everyone will have to account for every careless word they have spoken. ³⁷ On that day they will be told that they are either innocent or guilty because of the things they have said.

A Sign from Heaven

³⁸ Some Pharisees and teachers of the Law of Moses said, "Teacher, we want you to show us a sign from heaven."

³⁹ But Jesus replied:

You want a sign because you are evil and won't believe! But the only sign you will get is the sign of the prophet Jonah. ⁴⁰ He was in the stomach of a big fish for three days and nights, just as the Son of Man will be deep in the earth for three days and nights. ⁴¹ On the day of judgment the people of Nineveh will stand there with you and condemn you. They turned to God when Jonah preached, and yet here is something far greater than Jonah. ⁴² The Queen of the South will also stand there with you and condemn you. She traveled a long way to hear Solomon's wisdom, and yet here is something much greater than Solomon.

Return of an Evil Spirit

⁴³ When an evil spirit leaves a person, it travels through the desert, looking for a place to rest. But when the demon doesn't find a place, ⁴⁴ it says, "I will go back to the home I left." When it gets there and finds the place empty, clean, and fixed up, ⁴⁵ it goes off and finds seven other evil spirits even worse than itself. They all come and make their home there, and the person ends up in worse shape than before. That's how it will be with you evil people of today.

Jesus' Mother and Brothers

⁴⁶ While Jesus was still speaking to the crowds, his mother and brothers came and stood outside because they wanted to talk with him. ⁴⁷ Someone told Jesus, "Your mother and brothers are standing outside and want to talk with you."ᵛ

⁴⁸ Jesus answered, "Who is my mother and who are my brothers?" ⁴⁹ Then he pointed to his disciples and said, "These are my mother and my brothers! ⁵⁰ Anyone who obeys my Father in heaven is my brother or sister or mother."

ᵘ **12.23** *Could Jesus be the Son of David*: Or "Does Jesus think he is the Son of David?".   ᵛ **12.47** *with you*: Some manuscripts do not have verse 47.

A Story about a Farmer

13 That same day Jesus left the house and went out beside Lake Galilee, where he sat down to teach. [2] Such large crowds gathered around him that he had to sit in a boat, while the people stood on the shore. [3] Then he taught them many things by using stories. He said:

A farmer went out to scatter seed in a field. [4] While the farmer was scattering the seed, some of it fell along the road and was eaten by birds. [5] Other seeds fell on thin, rocky ground and quickly started growing because the soil wasn't very deep. [6] But when the sun came up, the plants were scorched and dried up, because they did not have enough roots. [7] Some other seeds fell where thornbushes grew up and choked the plants. [8] But a few seeds did fall on good ground where the plants produced a hundred or sixty or thirty times as much as was scattered. [9] If you have ears, pay attention!

Why Jesus Used Stories

[10] Jesus' disciples came to him and asked, "Why do you use nothing but stories when you speak to the people?"

[11] Jesus answered:

I have explained the secrets about the kingdom of heaven to you, but not to others. [12] Everyone who has something will be given more. But people who don't have anything will lose even what little they have. [13] I use stories when I speak to them because when they look, they cannot see, and when they listen, they cannot hear or understand. [14] So God's promise came true, just as the prophet Isaiah had said,

"These people will listen
and listen,
   but never understand.
They will look and look,
   but never see.
[15] All of them have
   stubborn minds!
Their ears are stopped up,
   and their eyes are covered.
They cannot see or hear
   or understand.
If they could,
   they would turn to me,
   and I would heal them."

[16] But God has blessed you, because your eyes can see and your ears can hear! [17] Many prophets and good people were eager to see what you see and to hear what you hear. But I tell you that they did not see or hear.

Jesus Explains the Story about the Farmer

[18] Now listen to the meaning of the story about the farmer:

[19] The seeds that fell along the road are the people who hear the message about the kingdom, but don't understand it. Then the evil one comes and snatches the message from their hearts. [20] The seeds that fell on rocky ground are the people who gladly hear the message and accept it right away. [21] But they don't have deep roots, and they don't last very long. As soon as life gets hard or the message gets them in trouble, they give up.

[22] The seeds that fell among the thornbushes are also people who hear the message. But they start worrying about the needs of this life and are fooled by the desire to get rich. So the message gets choked out, and they never produce anything. [23] The seeds that fell on good ground are the people who hear and understand the message. They produce as much as a hundred or sixty or thirty times what was planted.

Weeds among the Wheat

[24] Jesus then told them this story:

The kingdom of heaven is like what happened when a farmer scattered good seed in a field. [25] But while everyone was sleeping, an enemy came and scattered weed seeds in the field and then left.

[26] When the plants came up and began to ripen, the farmer's servants could see the weeds. [27] The servants came and asked, "Sir, didn't you scatter good seed in your field? Where did these weeds come from?"

[28] "An enemy did this," he replied.

His servants then asked, "Do you want us to go out and pull up the weeds?"

[29] "No!" he answered. "You might also pull up the wheat. [30] Leave the weeds alone until harvest time. Then I'll tell my workers to gather the weeds and tie them up and burn them. But I'll have them store the wheat in my barn."

Stories about a Mustard Seed and Yeast

[31] Jesus told them another story:

The kingdom of heaven is like what happens when a farmer plants a mustard seed in a field. [32] Although it is the smallest of all seeds, it grows larger than any garden plant and becomes a tree. Birds even come and nest on its branches.

[33] Jesus also said:

The kingdom of heaven is like what happens when a woman mixes a little yeast into three big batches of flour. Finally, all the dough rises.

The Reason for Teaching with Stories

[34] Jesus used stories when he spoke to the people. In fact, he did not tell them anything without using stories. [35] So God's promise came true, just as the prophet[w] had said,

"I will use stories
   to speak my message
and to explain things
   that have been hidden
since the creation
   of the world."

---

[w] **13.35** *the prophet*: Some manuscripts have "the prophet Isaiah."

Jesus Explains the Story about the Weeds

36 After Jesus left the crowd and went inside,[x] his disciples came to him and said, "Explain to us the story about the weeds in the wheat field."

37 Jesus answered:

The one who scattered the good seed is the Son of Man. **38** The field is the world, and the good seeds are the people who belong to the kingdom. The weed seeds are those who belong to the evil one, **39** and the one who scattered them is the devil. The harvest is the end of time, and angels are the ones who bring in the harvest.

40 Weeds are gathered and burned. That's how it will be at the end of time. **41** The Son of Man will send out his angels, and they will gather from his kingdom everyone who does wrong or causes others to sin. **42** Then he will throw them into a flaming furnace, where people will cry and grit their teeth in pain. **43** But everyone who has done right will shine like the sun in their Father's kingdom. If you have ears, pay attention!

A Hidden Treasure

44 The kingdom of heaven is like what happens when someone finds a treasure hidden in a field and buries it again. A person like that is happy and goes and sells everything in order to buy that field.

A Valuable Pearl

45 The kingdom of heaven is like what happens when a shop owner is looking for fine pearls. **46** After finding a very valuable one, the owner goes and sells everything in order to buy that pearl.

A Fish Net

47 The kingdom of heaven is like what happens when a net is thrown into a lake and catches all kinds of fish. **48** When the net is full, it is dragged to the shore, and the fishermen sit down to separate the fish. They keep the good ones, but throw the bad ones away. **49** That's how it will be at the end of time. Angels will come and separate the evil people from the ones who have done right. **50** Then those evil people will be thrown into a flaming furnace, where they will cry and grit their teeth in pain.

New and Old Treasures

51 Jesus asked his disciples if they understood all these things. They said, "Yes, we do."

52 So he told them, "Every student of the Scriptures who becomes a disciple in the kingdom of heaven is like someone who brings out new and old treasures from the storeroom."

The People of Nazareth Turn against Jesus

53 When Jesus had finished telling these stories, he left **54** and went to his hometown. He taught in their meeting place, and the people were so amazed that they asked, "Where does he get all this wisdom and the power to work these miracles? **55** Isn't he the son of the carpenter? Isn't Mary his mother, and aren't James, Joseph, Simon, and Judas his brothers? **56** Don't his sisters still live here in our town? How can he do all this?" **57** So the people were very unhappy because of what he was doing.

But Jesus said, "Prophets are honored by everyone, except the people of their hometown and their own family." **58** And because the people did not have any faith, Jesus did not work many miracles there.

The Death of John the Baptist

14 About this time Herod the ruler heard the news about Jesus **2** and told his officials, "This is John the Baptist! He has come back from death, and that's why he has the power to work these miracles."

3-4 Herod had earlier arrested John and had him chained and put in prison. He did this because John had told him, "It isn't right for you to take Herodias, the wife of your brother Philip." **5** Herod wanted to kill John. But the people thought John was a prophet, and Herod was afraid of what they might do.

6 When Herod's birthday came, the daughter of Herodias danced for the guests. She pleased Herod **7** so much that he swore to give her whatever she wanted. **8** But the girl's mother told her to say, "Here on a platter I want the head of John the Baptist!"

9 The king was sorry for what he had said. But he did not want to break the promise he had made in front of his guests. So he ordered a guard **10** to go to the prison and cut off John's head. **11** It was taken on a platter to the girl, and she gave it to her mother. **12** John's followers took his body and buried it. Then they told Jesus what had happened.

Jesus Feeds Five Thousand

13 After Jesus heard about John, he crossed Lake Galilee to go to some place where he could be alone. But the crowds found out and followed him on foot from the towns. **14** When Jesus got out of the boat, he saw the large crowd. He felt sorry for them and healed everyone who was sick.

15 That evening the disciples came to Jesus and said, "This place is like a desert, and it is already late. Let the crowds leave, so they can go to the villages and buy some food."

16 Jesus replied, "They don't have to leave. Why don't you give them something to eat?"

17 But they said, "We have only five small loaves of bread and two fish." **18** Jesus asked his disciples to bring the food to him, **19** and he told the crowd to sit down on the grass. Jesus took the five loaves and the two fish. He looked up toward heaven and blessed the food. Then he broke the bread and handed it to his disciples, and they gave it to the people.

20 After everyone had eaten all they wanted, Jesus' disciples picked up twelve large baskets of leftovers. **21** There were about five thousand men who ate, not counting the women and children.

Jesus Walks on the Water

22 Right away, Jesus made his disciples get into a boat and start back across the lake. But he stayed until he had

---

[x] **13.36** *went inside*: Or "went home."

sent the crowds away. 23 Then he went up on a mountain where he could be alone and pray. Later that evening, he was still there.

24 By this time the boat was a long way from the shore. It was going against the wind and was being tossed around by the waves. 25 A little while before morning, Jesus came walking on the water toward his disciples. 26 When they saw him, they thought he was a ghost. They were terrified and started screaming.

27 At once, Jesus said to them, "Don't worry! I am Jesus. Don't be afraid."

28 Peter replied, "Lord, if it is really you, tell me to come to you on the water."

29 "Come on!" Jesus said. Peter then got out of the boat and started walking on the water toward him.

30 But when Peter saw how strong the wind was, he was afraid and started sinking. "Save me, Lord!" he shouted.

31 Right away, Jesus reached out his hand. He helped Peter up and said, "You surely don't have much faith. Why do you doubt?"

32 When Jesus and Peter got into the boat, the wind died down. 33 The men in the boat worshiped Jesus and said, "You really are the Son of God!"

Jesus Heals Sick People in Gennesaret

34 Jesus and his disciples crossed the lake and came to shore near the town of Gennesaret. 35 The people found out that he was there, and they sent word to everyone who lived in that part of the country. So they brought all the sick people to Jesus. 36 They begged him just to let them touch his clothes, and everyone who did was healed.

The Teaching of the Ancestors

15 About this time some Pharisees and teachers of the Law of Moses came from Jerusalem. They asked Jesus, 2 "Why don't your disciples obey what our ancestors taught us to do? They don't even wash their hands before they eat."

3 Jesus answered:

Why do you disobey God and follow your own teaching? 4 Didn't God command you to respect your father and mother? Didn't he tell you to put to death all who curse their parents? 5 But you let people get by without helping their parents when they should. You let them say that what they have has been offered to God. 6 Is this any way to show respect to your parents? You ignore God's commands in order to follow your own teaching. 7 And you are nothing but show-offs! Isaiah the prophet was right when he wrote that God had said,

8 "All of you praise me
    with your words,
but you never really
    think about me.
9 It is useless for you
    to worship me,
when you teach rules
    made up by humans."

What Really Makes People Unclean

10 Jesus called the crowd together and said, "Pay attention and try to understand what I mean. 11 The food that you put into your mouth doesn't make you unclean and unfit to worship God. The bad words that come out of your mouth are what make you unclean."

12 Then his disciples came over to him and asked, "Do you know that you insulted the Pharisees by what you said?"

13 Jesus answered, "Every plant that my Father in heaven did not plant will be pulled up by the roots. 14 Stay away from those Pharisees! They are like blind people leading other blind people, and all of them will fall into a ditch."

15 Peter replied, "What did you mean when you talked about the things that make people unclean?"

16 Jesus then said:

Don't any of you know what I am talking about by now? 17 Don't you know that the food you put into your mouth goes into your stomach and then out of your body? 18 But the words that come out of your mouth come from your heart. And they are what make you unfit to worship God. 19 Out of your heart come evil thoughts, murder, unfaithfulness in marriage, vulgar deeds, stealing, telling lies, and insulting others. 20 These are what make you unclean. Eating without washing your hands will not make you unfit to worship God.

A Woman's Faith

21 Jesus left and went to the territory near the cities of Tyre and Sidon. 22 Suddenly a Canaanite woman from there came out shouting, "Lord and Son of David, have pity on me! My daughter is full of demons." 23 Jesus did not say a word. But the woman kept following along and shouting, so his disciples came up and asked him to send her away.

24 Jesus said, "I was sent only to the people of Israel! They are like a flock of lost sheep."

25 The woman came closer. Then she knelt down and begged, "Please help me, Lord!"

26 Jesus replied, "It isn't right to take food away from children and feed it to dogs."

27 "Lord, that's true," the woman said, "but even dogs get the crumbs that fall from their owner's table."

28 Jesus answered, "Dear woman, you really do have a lot of faith, and you will be given what you want." At that moment her daughter was healed.

Jesus Heals Many People

29 From there, Jesus went along Lake Galilee. Then he climbed a hill and sat down. 30 Large crowds came and brought many people who were crippled or blind or lame or unable to talk. They placed them, and many others, in front of Jesus, and he healed them all. 31 Everyone was amazed at what they saw and heard. People who had never spoken could now speak. The lame were healed, the crippled could walk, and the blind were able to see. Everyone was praising the God of Israel.

Jesus Feeds Four Thousand

32 Jesus called his disciples together and told them, "I feel sorry for these people. They have been with me for three days, and they don't have anything to eat. I don't

want to send them away hungry. They might faint on their way home."

³³ His disciples said, "This place is like a desert. Where can we find enough food to feed such a crowd?"

³⁴ Jesus asked them how much food they had. They replied, "Seven small loaves of bread and a few little fish."

³⁵ After Jesus had told the people to sit down, ³⁶ he took the seven loaves of bread and the fish and gave thanks. He then broke them and handed them to his disciples, who passed them around to the crowds.

³⁷ Everyone ate all they wanted, and the leftovers filled seven large baskets.

³⁸ There were four thousand men who ate, not counting the women and children.

³⁹ After Jesus had sent the crowds away, he got into a boat and sailed across the lake. He came to shore near the town of Magadan.

A Demand for a Sign from Heaven

16 The Pharisees and Sadducees came to Jesus and tried to test him by asking for a sign from heaven. ² He told them:

If the sky is red in the evening, you say the weather will be good. ³ But if the sky is red and gloomy in the morning, you say it is going to rain. You can tell what the weather will be like by looking at the sky. But you don't understand what is happening now.ʸ ⁴ You want a sign because you are evil and won't believe! But the only sign you will be given is what happened to Jonah.
Then Jesus left.

The Yeast of the Pharisees and Sadducees

⁵ The disciples had forgotten to bring any bread when they crossed the lake. ⁶ Jesus then warned them, "Watch out! Guard against the yeast of the Pharisees and Sadducees."

⁷ The disciples talked this over and said to each other, "He must be saying this because we didn't bring along any bread."

⁸ Jesus knew what they were thinking and said:

You surely don't have much faith! Why are you talking about not having any bread? ⁹ Don't you understand? Have you forgotten about the five thousand people and all those baskets of leftovers from just five loaves of bread? ¹⁰ And what about the four thousand people and all those baskets of leftovers from only seven loaves of bread? ¹¹ Don't you know by now that I am not talking to you about bread? Watch out for the yeast of the Pharisees and Sadducees!

¹² Finally, the disciples understood that Jesus wasn't talking about the yeast used to make bread, but about the teaching of the Pharisees and Sadducees.

Who Is Jesus?

¹³ When Jesus and his disciples were near the town of Caesarea Philippi, he asked them, "What do people say about the Son of Man?"

¹⁴ The disciples answered, "Some people say you are

John the Baptist or maybe Elijah or Jeremiah or some other prophet."

¹⁵ Then Jesus asked them, "But who do you say I am?"

¹⁶ Simon Peter spoke up, "You are the Messiah, the Son of the living God."

¹⁷ Jesus told him:

Simon, son of Jonah, you are blessed! You didn't discover this on your own. It was shown to you by my Father in heaven. ¹⁸ So I will call you Peter, which means "a rock." On this rock I will build my church, and death itself will not have any power over it. ¹⁹ I will give you the keys to the kingdom of heaven, and God in heaven will allow whatever you allow on earth. But he will not allow anything that you don't allow.

²⁰ Jesus told his disciples not to tell anyone that he was the Messiah.

Jesus Speaks about His Suffering and Death

²¹ From then on, Jesus began telling his disciples what would happen to him. He said, "I must go to Jerusalem. There the nation's leaders, the chief priests, and the teachers of the Law of Moses will make me suffer terribly. I will be killed, but three days later I will rise to life."

²² Peter took Jesus aside and told him to stop talking like that. He said, "God would never let this happen to you, Lord!"

²³ Jesus turned to Peter and said, "Satan, get away from me! You're in my way because you think like everyone else and not like God."

²⁴ Then Jesus said to his disciples:

If any of you want to be my followers, you must forget about yourself. You must take up your cross and follow me. ²⁵ If you want to save your life, you will destroy it. But if you give up your life for me, you will find it. ²⁶ What will you gain, if you own the whole world but destroy yourself? What would you give to get back your soul?

²⁷ The Son of Man will soon come in the glory of his Father and with his angels to reward all people for what they have done. ²⁸ I promise you that some of those standing here will not die before they see the Son of Man coming with his kingdom.

The True Glory of Jesus

17 Six days later Jesus took Peter and the brothers James and John with him. They went up on a very high mountain where they could be alone. ² There in front of the disciples, Jesus was completely changed. His face was shining like the sun, and his clothes became white as light.

³ All at once Moses and Elijah were there talking with Jesus. ⁴ So Peter said to him, "Lord, it is good for us to be here! Let us make three shelters, one for you, one for Moses, and one for Elijah."

⁵ While Peter was still speaking, the shadow of a bright cloud passed over them. From the cloud a voice said, "This is my own dear Son, and I am pleased with him. Listen to what he says!" ⁶ When the disciples heard the voice, they were so afraid that they fell flat on the ground. ⁷ But Jesus

---

ʸ **16.2,3** *If the sky is red . . . what is happening now*: The words of Jesus in verses 2 and 3 are not in some manuscripts.

came over and touched them. He said, "Get up and don't be afraid!" 8 When they opened their eyes, they saw only Jesus.

9 On their way down from the mountain, Jesus warned his disciples not to tell anyone what they had seen until after the Son of Man had been raised from death.

10 The disciples asked Jesus, "Don't the teachers of the Law of Moses say that Elijah must come before the Messiah does?"

11 Jesus told them, "Elijah certainly will come and get everything ready. 12 In fact, he has already come. But the people did not recognize him and treated him just as they wanted to. They will soon make the Son of Man suffer in the same way." 13 Then the disciples understood that Jesus was talking to them about John the Baptist.

Jesus Heals a Boy

14 Jesus and his disciples returned to the crowd. A man knelt in front of him 15 and said, "Lord, have pity on my son! He has a bad case of epilepsy and often falls into a fire or into water. 16 I brought him to your disciples, but none of them could heal him."

17 Jesus said, "You people are too stubborn to have any faith! How much longer must I be with you? Why do I have to put up with you? Bring the boy here." 18 Then Jesus spoke sternly to the demon. It went out of the boy, and right then he was healed.

19 Later the disciples went to Jesus in private and asked him, "Why couldn't we force out the demon?" .

20-21 Jesus replied:

It is because you don't have enough faith! But I can promise you this. If you had faith no larger than a mustard seed, you could tell this mountain to move from here to there. And it would. Everything would be possible for you.z

Jesus Again Speaks about His Death

22 While Jesus and his disciples were going from place to place in Galilee, he told them, "The Son of Man will be handed over to people 23 who will kill him. But three days later he will rise to life." All of this made the disciples very sad.

Paying the Temple Tax

24 When Jesus and the others arrived in Capernaum, the collectors for the temple tax came to Peter and asked, "Does your teacher pay the temple tax?"

25 "Yes, he does," Peter answered.

After they had returned home, Jesus went up to Peter and asked him, "Simon, what do you think? Do the kings of this earth collect taxes and fees from their own people or from foreigners?" a

26 Peter answered, "From foreigners."

Jesus replied, "Then their own people b don't have to pay. 27 But we don't want to cause trouble. So go cast a line into the lake and pull out the first fish you hook. Open its mouth, and you will find a coin. Use it to pay your taxes and mine."

Who Is the Greatest?

18 About this time the disciples came to Jesus and asked him who would be the greatest in the kingdom of heaven. 2 Jesus called a child over and had the child stand near him. 3 Then he said:

I promise you this. If you don't change and become like a child, you will never get into the kingdom of heaven. 4 But if you are as humble as this child, you are the greatest in the kingdom of heaven. 5 And when you welcome one of these children because of me, you welcome me.

Temptations To Sin

6 It will be terrible for people who cause even one of my little followers to sin. Those people would be better off thrown into the deepest part of the ocean with a heavy stone tied around their necks! 7 The world is in for trouble because of the way it causes people to sin. There will always be something to cause people to sin, but anyone who does this will be in for trouble.

8 If your hand or foot causes you to sin, chop it off and throw it away! You would be better off to go into life crippled or lame than to have two hands or two feet and be thrown into the fire that never goes out. 9 If your eye causes you to sin, poke it out and get rid of it. You would be better off to go into life with only one eye than to have two eyes and be thrown into the fires of hell.

The Lost Sheep

10-11 Don't be cruel to any of these little ones! I promise you that their angels are always with my Father in heaven.c 12 Let me ask you this. What would you do if you had a hundred sheep and one of them wandered off? Wouldn't you leave the ninety-nine on the hillside and go look for the one that had wandered away? 13 I am sure that finding it would make you happier than having the ninety-nine that never wandered off. 14 That's how it is with your Father in heaven. He doesn't want any of these little ones to be lost.

When Someone Sins

15 If one of my followersd sins against you, go and point out what was wrong. But do it in private, just between the two of you. If that person listens, you have won back a follower. 16 But if that one refuses to listen, take along one or two others. The Scriptures teach that every complaint must be proven true by two or more witnesses. 17 If the follower refuses to listen to them, report the matter to the church. Anyone who refuses to listen to the church must be treated like an unbeliever or a tax collector.

---

z **17.20,21** *for you:* Some manuscripts add, "But the only way to force out that kind of demon is by praying and going without eating." a **17.25** *from their own people or from foreigners:* Or "from their children or from others." b **17.26** *From foreigners . . . their own people:* Or "From other people . . . their children." c **18.10,11** *in heaven:* Some manuscripts add, "The Son of Man came to save people who are lost." d **18.15** *followers:* The Greek text has "brother," which is used here and elsewhere in this chapter to refer to a follower of Christ.

Allowing and Not Allowing

18 I promise you that God in heaven will allow whatever you allow on earth, but he will not allow anything you don't allow. **19** I promise that when any two of you on earth agree about something you are praying for, my Father in heaven will do it for you. **20** Whenever two or three of you come together in my name,*e* I am there with you.

An Official Who Refused To Forgive

21 Peter came up to the Lord and asked, "How many times should I forgive someone*f* who does something wrong to me? Is seven times enough?"

22 Jesus answered:

Not just seven times, but seventy-seven times!*g* **23** This story will show you what the kingdom of heaven is like:

One day a king decided to call in his officials and ask them to give an account of what they owed him. **24** As he was doing this, one official was brought in who owed him fifty million silver coins. **25** But he didn't have any money to pay what he owed. The king ordered him to be sold, along with his wife and children and all he owned, in order to pay the debt.

26 The official got down on his knees and began begging, "Have pity on me, and I will pay you every cent I owe!" **27** The king felt sorry for him and let him go free. He even told the official that he did not have to pay back the money.

28 As the official was leaving, he happened to meet another official, who owed him a hundred silver coins. So he grabbed the man by the throat. He started choking him and said, "Pay me what you owe!"

29 The man got down on his knees and began begging, "Have pity on me, and I will pay you back." **30** But the first official refused to have pity. Instead, he went and had the other official put in jail until he could pay what he owed.

31 When some other officials found out what had happened, they felt sorry for the man who had been put in jail. Then they told the king what had happened. **32** The king called the first official back in and said, "You're an evil man! When you begged for mercy, I said you did not have to pay back a cent. **33** Don't you think you should show pity to someone else, as I did to you?" **34** The king was so angry that he ordered the official to be tortured until he could pay back everything he owed. **35** That is how my Father in heaven will treat you, if you don't forgive each of my followers with all your heart.

Teaching about Divorce

19 When Jesus finished teaching, he left Galilee and went to the part of Judea that is east of the Jordan River. **2** Large crowds followed him, and he healed their sick people.

3 Some Pharisees wanted to test Jesus. They came up to him and asked, "Is it right for a man to divorce his wife for just any reason?"

4 Jesus answered, "Don't you know that in the beginning the Creator made a man and a woman? **5** That's why a man leaves his father and mother and gets married. He becomes like one person with his wife. **6** Then they are no longer two people, but one. And no one should separate a couple that God has joined together."

7 The Pharisees asked Jesus, "Why did Moses say that a man could write out divorce papers and send his wife away?"

8 Jesus replied, "You are so heartless! That's why Moses allowed you to divorce your wife. But from the beginning God did not intend it to be that way. **9** I say that if your wife has not committed some terrible sexual sin, you must not divorce her to marry someone else. If you do, you are unfaithful."

10 The disciples said, "If that's how it is between a man and a woman, it's better not to get married."

11 Jesus told them, "Only those people who have been given the gift of staying single can accept this teaching. **12** Some people are unable to marry because of birth defects or because of what someone has done to their bodies. Others stay single for the sake of the kingdom of heaven. Anyone who can accept this teaching should do so."

Jesus Blesses Little Children

13 Some people brought their children to Jesus, so that he could place his hands on them and pray for them. His disciples told the people to stop bothering him. **14** But Jesus said, "Let the children come to me, and don't try to stop them! People who are like these children belong to God's kingdom."*h* **15** After Jesus had placed his hands on the children, he left.

A Rich Young Man

16 A man came to Jesus and asked, "Teacher, what good thing must I do to have eternal life?"

17 Jesus said to him, "Why do you ask me about what is good? Only God is good. If you want to have eternal life, you must obey his commandments."

18 "Which ones?" the man asked.

Jesus answered, "Do not murder. Be faithful in marriage. Do not steal. Do not tell lies about others. **19** Respect your father and mother. And love others as much as you love yourself." **20** The young man said, "I have obeyed all of these. What else must I do?"

21 Jesus replied, "If you want to be perfect, go sell everything you own! Give the money to the poor, and you will have riches in heaven. Then come and be my follower." **22** When the young man heard this, he was sad, because he was very rich.

23 Jesus said to his disciples, "It's terribly hard for rich people to get into the kingdom of heaven! **24** In fact, it's easier for a camel to go through the eye of a needle than for a rich person to get into God's kingdom."

25 When the disciples heard this, they were greatly surprised and asked, "How can anyone ever be saved?"

---

e **18.20** *in my name*: Or "as my followers." *f* **18.21** *someone*: Or "a follower." See the note at 18.15. *g* **18.22** *seventy-seven times*: Or "seventy times seven." The large number means that one follower should never stop forgiving another. *h* **19.14** *People who are like these children belong to God's kingdom*: Or "God's kingdom belongs to people who are like these children."

26 Jesus looked straight at them and said, "There are some things that people cannot do, but God can do anything."

27 Peter replied, "Remember, we have left everything to be your followers! What will we get?"

28 Jesus answered:

Yes, all of you have become my followers. And so in the future world, when the Son of Man sits on his glorious throne, I promise that you will sit on twelve thrones to judge the twelve tribes of Israel. 29 All who have given up home or brothers and sisters or father and mother or children or land for me will be given a hundred times as much. They will also have eternal life. 30 But many who are now first will be last, and many who are last will be first.

Workers in a Vineyard

20 As Jesus was telling what the kingdom of heaven would be like, he said:

Early one morning a man went out to hire some workers for his vineyard. 2 After he had agreed to pay them the usual amount for a day's work, he sent them off to his vineyard.

3 About nine that morning, the man saw some other people standing in the market with nothing to do. 4 He said he would pay them what was fair, if they would work in his vineyard. 5 So they went.

At noon and again about three in the afternoon he returned to the market. And each time he made the same agreement with others who were loafing around with nothing to do.

6 Finally, about five in the afternoon the man went back and found some others standing there. He asked them, "Why have you been standing here all day long doing nothing?"

7 "Because no one has hired us," they answered. Then he told them to go work in his vineyard.

8 That evening the owner of the vineyard told the man in charge of the workers to call them in and give them their money. He also told the man to begin with the ones who were hired last. 9 When the workers arrived, the ones who had been hired at five in the afternoon were given a full day's pay.

10 The workers who had been hired first thought they would be given more than the others. But when they were given the same, 11 they began complaining to the owner of the vineyard. 12 They said, "The ones who were hired last worked for only one hour. But you paid them the same that you did us. And we worked in the hot sun all day long!"

13 The owner answered one of them, "Friend, I didn't cheat you. I paid you exactly what we agreed on. 14 Take your money now and go! What business is it of yours if I want to pay them the same that I paid you? 15 Don't I have the right to do what I want with my own money? Why should you be jealous, if I want to be generous?"

16 Jesus then said, "So it is. Everyone who is now first will be last, and everyone who is last will be first."

Jesus Again Tells about His Death

17 As Jesus was on his way to Jerusalem, he took his twelve disciples aside and told them in private:

18 We are now on our way to Jerusalem, where the Son of Man will be handed over to the chief priests and the teachers of the Law of Moses. They will sentence him to death, 19 and then they will hand him over to foreigners who will make fun of him. They will beat him and nail him to a cross. But on the third day he will rise from death.

A Mother's Request

20 The mother of James and John[i] came to Jesus with her two sons. She knelt down and started begging him to do something for her. 21 Jesus asked her what she wanted, and she said, "When you come into your kingdom, please let one of my sons sit at your right side and the other at your left."

22 Jesus answered, "Not one of you knows what you are asking. Are you able to drink from the cup that I must soon drink from?"

James and John said, "Yes, we are!"

23 Jesus replied, "You certainly will drink from my cup! But it isn't for me to say who will sit at my right side and at my left. That is for my Father to say."

24 When the ten other disciples heard this, they were angry with the two brothers. 25 But Jesus called the disciples together and said:

You know that foreign rulers like to order their people around. And their great leaders have full power over everyone they rule. 26 But don't act like them. If you want to be great, you must be the servant of all the others. 27 And if you want to be first, you must be the slave of the rest. 28 The Son of Man did not come to be a slave master, but a slave who will give his life to rescue[j] many people.

Jesus Heals Two Blind Men

29 Jesus was followed by a large crowd as he and his disciples were leaving Jericho. 30 Two blind men were sitting beside the road. And when they heard that Jesus was coming their way, they shouted, "Lord and Son of David, have pity on us!"

31 The crowd told them to be quiet, but they shouted even louder, "Lord and Son of David, have pity on us!"

32 When Jesus heard them, he stopped and asked, "What do you want me to do for you?"

33 They answered, "Lord, we want to see!"

34 Jesus felt sorry for them and touched their eyes. Right away they could see, and they became his followers.

Jesus Enters Jerusalem

21 When Jesus and his disciples came near Jerusalem, he went to Bethphage on the Mount of Olives and sent two of them on ahead. 2 He told them, "Go into the next village, where you will at once find a donkey and her

---

[i]20.20 *mother of James and John*: The Greek text has "mother of the sons of Zebedee" (see 26.37). [j]20.28 *rescue*: The Greek word often, though not always, means the payment of a price to free a slave or a prisoner.

colt. Untie the two donkeys and bring them to me. ³ If any-one asks why you are doing that, just say, 'The Lord[k] needs them.' Right away he will let you have the donkeys."

⁴ So God's promise came true, just as the prophet had said,

⁵ "Announce to the people
    of Jerusalem:
'Your king is coming to you!
He is humble
    and rides on a donkey.
He comes on the colt
    of a donkey.' "

⁶ The disciples left and did what Jesus had told them to do. ⁷ They brought the donkey and its colt and laid some clothes on their backs. Then Jesus got on.

⁸ Many people spread clothes in the road, while others put down branches which they had cut from trees. ⁹ Some people walked ahead of Jesus and others followed behind. They were all shouting,

"Hooray for the Son of David!
God bless the one who comes
    in the name of the Lord.
Hooray for God
    in heaven above!"

¹⁰ When Jesus came to Jerusalem, everyone in the city was excited and asked, "Who can this be?"

¹¹ The crowd answered, "This is Jesus, the prophet from Nazareth in Galilee."

Jesus in the Temple

¹² Jesus went into the temple and chased out everyone who was selling or buying. He turned over the tables of the moneychangers and the benches of the ones who were sell-ing doves. ¹³ He told them, "The Scriptures say, 'My house should be called a place of worship.' But you have turned it into a place where robbers hide."

¹⁴ Blind and lame people came to Jesus in the temple, and he healed them. ¹⁵ But the chief priests and the teach-ers of the Law of Moses were angry when they saw his mir-acles and heard the children shouting praises to the Son of David. ¹⁶ The men said to Jesus, "Don't you hear what those children are saying?"

"Yes, I do!" Jesus answered. "Don't you know that the Scriptures say, 'Children and infants will sing praises'?" ¹⁷ Then Jesus left the city and went out to the village of Bethany, where he spent the night.

Jesus Puts a Curse on a Fig Tree

¹⁸ When Jesus got up the next morning, he was hun-gry. He started out for the city, ¹⁹ and along the way he saw a fig tree. But when he came to it, he found only leaves and no figs. So he told the tree, "You will never again grow any fruit!" Right then the fig tree dried up.

²⁰ The disciples were shocked when they saw how quickly the tree had dried up. ²¹ But Jesus said to them, "If you have faith and don't doubt, I promise that you can do what I did to this tree. And you will be able to do even

more. You can tell this mountain to get up and jump into the sea, and it will. ²² If you have faith when you pray, you will be given whatever you ask for."

A Question about Jesus' Authority

²³ Jesus had gone into the temple and was teaching when the chief priests and the leaders of the people came up to him. They asked, "What right do you have to do these things? Who gave you this authority?"

²⁴ Jesus answered, "I have just one question to ask you. If you answer it, I will tell you where I got the right to do these things. ²⁵ Who gave John the right to baptize? Was it God in heaven or merely some human being?"

They thought it over and said to each other, "We can't say that God gave John this right. Jesus will ask us why we didn't believe John. ²⁶ On the other hand, these people think that John was a prophet, and we are afraid of what they might do to us. That's why we can't say that it was merely some human who gave John the right to baptize." ²⁷ So they told Jesus, "We don't know."

Jesus said, "Then I won't tell you who gave me the right to do what I do."

A Story about Two Sons

²⁸ Jesus said:

I will tell you a story about a man who had two sons. Then you can tell me what you think. The fa-ther went to the older son and said, "Go work in the vineyard today!" ²⁹ His son told him that he would not do it, but later he changed his mind and went. ³⁰ The man then told his younger son to go work in the vineyard. The boy said he would, but he didn't go. ³¹ Which one of the sons obeyed his father?

"The older one," the chief priests and leaders an-swered.

Then Jesus told them:

You can be sure that tax collectors and prosti-tutes will get into the kingdom of God before you ever will! ³² When John the Baptist showed you how to do right, you would not believe him. But these evil people did believe. And even when you saw what they did, you still would not change your minds and believe.

Renters of a Vineyard

³³ Jesus told the chief priests and leaders to listen to this story:

A land owner once planted a vineyard. He built a wall around it and dug a pit to crush the grapes in. He also built a lookout tower. Then he rented out his vineyard and left the country.

³⁴ When it was harvest time, the owner sent some servants to get his share of the grapes. ³⁵ But the renters grabbed those servants. They beat up one, killed one, and stoned one of them to death. ³⁶ He then sent more servants than he did the first time. But the renters treated them in the same way.

³⁷ Finally, the owner sent his own son to the renters, because he thought they would respect him. ³⁸ But when they saw the man's son, they said, "Someday he will own the vineyard. Let's kill

---

[k]**21.3** *The Lord*: Or "The master of the donkeys."

him! Then we can have it all for ourselves." ³⁹ So they grabbed him, threw him out of the vineyard, and killed him.

⁴⁰ Jesus asked, "When the owner of that vineyard comes, what do you suppose he will do to those renters?"

⁴¹ The chief priests and leaders answered, "He will kill them in some horrible way. Then he will rent out his vineyard to people who will give him his share of grapes at harvest time."

⁴² Jesus replied, "You surely know that the Scriptures say,

'The stone that the builders
    tossed aside
is now the most important
    stone of all.
This is something
the Lord has done,
    and it is amazing to us.'

⁴³ I tell you that God's kingdom will be taken from you and given to people who will do what he demands. ⁴⁴ Anyone who stumbles over this stone will be crushed, and anyone it falls on will be smashed to pieces."

⁴⁵ When the chief priests and the Pharisees heard these stories, they knew that Jesus was talking about them. ⁴⁶ So they looked for a way to arrest Jesus. But they were afraid to, because the people thought he was a prophet.

The Great Banquet

22 Once again Jesus used stories to teach the people: ² The kingdom of heaven is like what happened when a king gave a wedding banquet for his son. ³ The king sent some servants to tell the invited guests to come to the banquet, but the guests refused. ⁴ He sent other servants to say to the guests, "The banquet is ready! My cattle and prize calves have all been prepared. Everything is ready. Come to the banquet!"

⁵ But the guests did not pay any attention. Some of them left for their farms, and some went to their places of business. ⁶ Others grabbed the servants, then beat them up and killed them.

⁷ This made the king so furious that he sent an army to kill those murderers and burn down their city. ⁸ Then he said to the servants, "It is time for the wedding banquet, and the invited guests don't deserve to come. ⁹ Go out to the street corners and tell everyone you meet to come to the banquet." ¹⁰ They went out on the streets and brought in everyone they could find, good and bad alike. And the banquet room was filled with guests.

¹¹ When the king went in to meet the guests, he found that one of them wasn't wearing the right kind of clothes for the wedding. ¹² The king asked, "Friend, why didn't you wear proper clothes for the wedding?" But the guest had no excuse. ¹³ So the king gave orders for that person to be tied hand and foot and to be thrown outside into the dark. That's where people will cry and grit their teeth in pain. ¹⁴ Many are invited, but only a few are chosen.

Paying Taxes

¹⁵ The Pharisees got together and planned how they could trick Jesus into saying something wrong. ¹⁶ They sent some of their followers and some of Herod's followers to say to him, "Teacher, we know that you are honest. You teach the truth about what God wants people to do. And you treat everyone with the same respect, no matter who they are. ¹⁷ Tell us what you think! Should we pay taxes to the Emperor or not?"

¹⁸ Jesus knew their evil thoughts and said, "Why are you trying to test me? You show-offs! ¹⁹ Let me see one of the coins used for paying taxes." They brought him a silver coin, ²⁰ and he asked, "Whose picture and name are on it?"

²¹ "The Emperor's," they answered.

Then Jesus told them, "Give the Emperor what belongs to him and give God what belongs to God." ²² His answer surprised them so much that they walked away.

Life in the Future World

²³ The Sadducees did not believe that people would rise to life after death. So that same day some of the Sadducees came to Jesus and said:

²⁴ Teacher, Moses wrote that if a married man dies and has no children, his brother should marry the widow. Their first son would then be thought of as the son of the dead brother.

²⁵ Once there were seven brothers who lived here. The first one married, but died without having any children. So his wife was left to his brother. ²⁶ The same thing happened to the second and third brothers and finally to all seven of them. ²⁷ At last the woman died. ²⁸ When God raises people from death, whose wife will this woman be? She had been married to all seven brothers.

²⁹ Jesus answered:

You are completely wrong! You don't know what the Scriptures teach. And you don't know anything about the power of God. ³⁰ When God raises people to life, they won't marry. They will be like the angels in heaven. ³¹ And as for people being raised to life, God was speaking to you when he said, ³² "I am the God worshiped by Abraham, Isaac, and Jacob." He isn't the God of the dead, but of the living.

³³ The crowds were surprised to hear what Jesus was teaching.

The Most Important Commandment

³⁴ After Jesus had made the Sadducees look foolish, the Pharisees heard about it and got together. ³⁵ One of them was an expert in the Jewish Law. So he tried to test Jesus by asking, ³⁶ "Teacher, what is the most important commandment in the Law?"

³⁷ Jesus answered:

Love the Lord your God with all your heart, soul, and mind. ³⁸ This is the first and most important commandment. ³⁹ The second most important commandment is like this one. And it is, "Love others as much as you love yourself." ⁴⁰ All the Law of Moses and the Books of the Prophets are based on these two commandments.

About David's Son

41 While the Pharisees were still there, Jesus asked them, **42** "What do you think about the Messiah? Whose family will he come from?"

They answered, "He will be a son of King David."

43 Jesus replied, "How then could the Spirit lead David to call the Messiah his Lord? David said,

44 'The Lord said to my Lord:
Sit at my right side
until I make your enemies
into a footstool for you.'

45 If David called the Messiah his Lord, how can the Messiah be a son of King David?" **46** No one was able to give Jesus an answer, and from that day on, no one dared ask him any more questions.

Jesus Condemns the Pharisees and the Teachers of the Law of Moses

23 Jesus said to the crowds and to his disciples: **2** The Pharisees and the teachers of the Law are experts in the Law of Moses. **3** So obey everything they teach you, but don't do as they do. After all, they say one thing and do something else.

4 They pile heavy burdens on people's shoulders and won't lift a finger to help. **5** Everything they do is just to show off in front of others. They even make a big show of wearing Scripture verses on their foreheads and arms, and they wear big tassels for everyone to see. **6** They love the best seats at banquets and the front seats in the meeting places. **7** And when they are in the market, they like to have people greet them as their teachers.

8 But none of you should be called a teacher. You have only one teacher, and all of you are like brothers and sisters. **9** Don't call anyone on earth your father. All of you have the same Father in heaven. **10** None of you should be called the leader. The Messiah is your only leader. **11** Whoever is the greatest should be the servant of the others. **12** If you put yourself above others, you will be put down. But if you humble yourself, you will be honored.

13-14 You Pharisees and teachers of the Law of Moses are in for trouble! You're nothing but show-offs. You lock people out of the kingdom of heaven. You won't go in yourselves, and you keep others from going in.*

15 You Pharisees and teachers of the Law of Moses are in for trouble! You're nothing but show-offs. You travel over land and sea to win one follower. And when you have done so, you make that person twice as fit for hell as you are.

16 You are in for trouble! You are supposed to lead others, but you are blind. You teach that it doesn't matter if a person swears by the temple. But you say that it does matter if someone swears by the gold in the temple. **17** You blind fools! Which is greater, the gold or the temple that makes the gold sacred?

18 You also teach that it doesn't matter if a person swears by the altar. But you say that it does matter if someone swears by the gift on the altar. **19** Are you blind? Which is more important, the gift or the altar that makes the gift sacred? **20** Anyone who swears by the altar also swears by everything on it. **21** And anyone who swears by the temple also swears by God, who lives there. **22** To swear by heaven is the same as swearing by God's throne and by the one who sits on that throne.

23 You Pharisees and teachers are show-offs, and you're in for trouble! You give God a tenth of the spices from your garden, such as mint, dill, and cumin. Yet you neglect the more important matters of the Law, such as justice, mercy, and faithfulness. These are the important things you should have done, though you should not have left the others undone either. **24** You blind leaders! You strain out a small fly but swallow a camel.

25 You Pharisees and teachers are show-offs, and you're in for trouble! You wash the outside of your cups and dishes, while inside there is nothing but greed and selfishness. **26** You blind Pharisee! First clean the inside of a cup, and then the outside will also be clean.

27 You Pharisees and teachers are in for trouble! You're nothing but show-offs. You're like tombs that have been whitewashed. On the outside they are beautiful, but inside they are full of bones and filth. **28** That's what you are like. Outside you look good, but inside you are evil and only pretend to be good.

29 You Pharisees and teachers are nothing but show-offs, and you're in for trouble! You build monuments for the prophets and decorate the tombs of good people. **30** And you claim that you would not have taken part with your ancestors in killing the prophets. **31** But you prove that you really are the relatives of the ones who killed the prophets. **32** So keep on doing everything they did. **33** You are nothing but snakes and the children of snakes! How can you escape going to hell?

34 I will send prophets and wise people and experts in the Law of Moses to you. But you will kill them or nail them to a cross or beat them in your meeting places or chase them from town to town. **35** That's why you will be held guilty for the murder of every good person, beginning with the good man Abel. This also includes Barachiah's son Zechariah, the man you murdered between the temple and the altar. **36** I can promise that you people living today will be punished for all these things!

Jesus Loves Jerusalem

37 Jerusalem, Jerusalem! Your people have killed the prophets and have stoned the messengers who were sent to you. I have often wanted to

---

*23.13,14 *from going in*: Some manuscripts add, "You Pharisees and teachers are in for trouble! And you're nothing but show-offs! You cheat widows out of their homes and then pray long prayers just to show off. So you will be punished most of all."

gather your people, as a hen gathers her chicks under her wings. But you wouldn't let me. [38] And now your temple will be deserted. [39] You won't see me again until you say,

> "Blessed is the one who comes
> in the name of the Lord."

The Temple Will Be Destroyed

24 After Jesus left the temple, his disciples came over and said, "Look at all these buildings!"

[2] Jesus replied, "Do you see these buildings? They will certainly be torn down! Not one stone will be left in place."

Warning about Trouble

[3] Later, as Jesus was sitting on the Mount of Olives, his disciples came to him in private and asked, "When will this happen? What will be the sign of your coming and of the end of the world?"

[4] Jesus answered:

Don't let anyone fool you. [5] Many will come and claim to be me. They will say that they are the Messiah, and they will fool many people.

[6] You will soon hear about wars and threats of wars, but don't be afraid. These things will have to happen first, but that isn't the end. [7] Nations and kingdoms will go to war against each other. People will starve to death, and in some places there will be earthquakes. [8] But this is just the beginning of troubles.

[9] You will be arrested, punished, and even killed. Because of me, you will be hated by people of all nations. [10] Many will give up and will betray and hate each other. [11] Many false prophets will come and fool a lot of people. [12] Evil will spread and cause many people to stop loving others. [13] But if you keep on being faithful right to the end, you will be saved. [14] When the good news about the kingdom has been preached all over the world and told to all nations, the end will come.

The Horrible Thing

[15] Someday you will see that "Horrible Thing" in the holy place, just as the prophet Daniel said. Everyone who reads this must try to understand! [16] If you are living in Judea at that time, run to the mountains. [17] If you are on the roof of your house, don't go inside to get anything. [18] If you are out in the field, don't go back for your coat. [19] It will be a terrible time for women who are expecting babies or nursing young children. [20] And pray that you won't have to escape in winter or on a Sabbath. [21] This will be the worst time of suffering since the beginning of the world, and nothing this terrible will ever happen again. [22] If God doesn't make the time shorter, no one will be left alive. But because of God's chosen ones, he will make the time shorter.

[23] Someone may say, "Here is the Messiah!" or "There he is!" But don't believe it. [24] False messiahs and false prophets will come and work great miracles and signs. They will even try to fool God's chosen ones. [25] But I have warned you ahead of time. [26] If you are told that the Messiah is out in the desert, don't go there! And if you are told that he is in some secret place, don't believe it! [27] The coming of the Son of Man will be like lightning that can be seen from east to west. [28] Where there is a corpse, there will always be buzzards.

When the Son of Man Appears

[29] Right after those days of suffering,

> "The sun will become dark,
> and the moon
>   will no longer shine.
> The stars will fall,
> and the powers in the sky
>   will be shaken."

[30] Then a sign will appear in the sky. And there will be the Son of Man.[m] All nations on earth will weep when they see the Son of Man coming on the clouds of heaven with power and great glory. [31] At the sound of a loud trumpet, he will send his angels to bring his chosen ones together from all over the earth.

A Lesson from a Fig Tree

[32] Learn a lesson from a fig tree. When its branches sprout and start putting out leaves, you know that summer is near. [33] So when you see all these things happening, you will know that the time has almost come.[n] [34] I can promise you that some of the people of this generation will still be alive when all this happens. [35] The sky and the earth won't last forever, but my words will.

No One Knows the Day or Time

[36] No one knows the day or hour. The angels in heaven don't know, and the Son himself doesn't know.[o] Only the Father knows. [37] When the Son of Man appears, things will be just as they were when Noah lived. [38] People were eating, drinking, and getting married right up to the day that the flood came and Noah went into the big boat. [39] They didn't know anything was happening until the flood came and swept them all away. That is how it will be when the Son of Man appears.

[40] Two men will be in the same field, but only one will be taken. The other will be left. [41] Two women will be together grinding grain, but only one will be taken. The other will be left. [42] So be on your guard! You don't know when your Lord will come. [43] Homeowners never know when a thief is coming, and they are always on guard to keep one from breaking in. [44] Always be ready! You don't know when the Son of Man will come.

---

[m] **24.30** *And there will be the Son of Man:* Or "And it will be the Son of Man."   [n] **24.33** *the time has almost come:* Or "he (that is, the Son of Man) will soon be here."   [o] **24.36** *and the Son himself doesn't know:* These words are not in some manuscripts.

Faithful and Unfaithful Servants

45 Who are faithful and wise servants? Who are the ones the master will put in charge of giving the other servants their food supplies at the proper time? **46** Servants are fortunate if their master comes and finds them doing their job. **47** You may be sure that a servant who is always faithful will be put in charge of everything the master owns. **48** But suppose one of the servants thinks that the master won't return until late. **49** Suppose that evil servant starts beating the other servants and eats and drinks with people who are drunk. **50** If that happens, the master will surely come on a day and at a time when the servant least expects him. **51** That servant will then be punished and thrown out with the ones who only pretended to serve their master. There they will cry and grit their teeth in pain.

A Story about Ten Girls

25 The kingdom of heaven is like what happened one night when ten girls took their oil lamps and went to a wedding to meet the groom.*ᵖ* **2** Five of the girls were foolish and five were wise. **3** The foolish ones took their lamps, but no extra oil. **4** The ones who were wise took along extra oil for their lamps.

5 The groom was late arriving, and the girls became drowsy and fell asleep. **6** Then in the middle of the night someone shouted, "Here's the groom! Come to meet him!"

7 When the girls got up and started getting their lamps ready, **8** the foolish ones said to the others, "Let us have some of your oil! Our lamps are going out."

9 The girls who were wise answered, "There's not enough oil for all of us! Go and buy some for yourselves."

10 While the foolish girls were on their way to get some oil, the groom arrived. The girls who were ready went into the wedding, and the doors were closed. **11** Later the other girls returned and shouted, "Sir, sir! Open the door for us!"

12 But the groom replied, "I don't even know you!"

13 So, my disciples, always be ready! You don't know the day or the time when all this will happen.

A Story about Three Servants

14 The kingdom is also like what happened when a man went away and put his three servants in charge of all he owned. **15** The man knew what each servant could do. So he handed five thousand coins to the first servant, two thousand to the second, and one thousand to the third. Then he left the country.

16 As soon as the man had gone, the servant with the five thousand coins used them to earn five thousand more. **17** The servant who had two thousand coins did the same with his money and earned two thousand more. **18** But the servant with one thousand coins dug a hole and hid his master's money in the ground.

19 Some time later the master of those servants returned. He called them in and asked what they had done with his money. **20** The servant who had been given five thousand coins brought them in with the five thousand that he had earned. He said, "Sir, you gave me five thousand coins, and I have earned five thousand more."

21 "Wonderful!" his master replied. "You are a good and faithful servant. I left you in charge of only a little, but now I will put you in charge of much more. Come and share in my happiness!"

22 Next, the servant who had been given two thousand coins came in and said, "Sir, you gave me two thousand coins, and I have earned two thousand more."

23 "Wonderful!" his master replied. "You are a good and faithful servant. I left you in charge of only a little, but now I will put you in charge of much more. Come and share in my happiness!"

24 The servant who had been given one thousand coins then came in and said, "Sir, I know that you are hard to get along with. You harvest what you don't plant and gather crops where you haven't scattered seed. **25** I was frightened and went out and hid your money in the ground. Here is every single coin!"

26 The master of the servant told him, "You are lazy and good-for-nothing! You know that I harvest what I don't plant and gather crops where I haven't scattered seed. **27** You could have at least put my money in the bank, so that I could have earned interest on it."

28 Then the master said, "Now your money will be taken away and given to the servant with ten thousand coins! **29** Everyone who has something will be given more, and they will have more than enough. But everything will be taken from those who don't have anything. **30** You are a worthless servant, and you will be thrown out into the dark where people will cry and grit their teeth in pain."

The Final Judgment

31 When the Son of Man comes in his glory with all of his angels, he will sit on his royal throne. **32** The people of all nations will be brought before him, and he will separate them, as shepherds separate their sheep from their goats.

33 He will place the sheep on his right and the goats on his left. **34** Then the king will say to those on his right, "My father has blessed you! Come and receive the kingdom that was prepared for you before the world was created. **35** When I was hungry, you gave me something to eat, and when I was thirsty, you gave me something to drink. When I was a

---

ᵖ **25.1** *to meet the groom*: Some manuscripts add "and the bride." It was the custom for the groom to go to the home of the bride's parents to get his bride. Young girls and other guests would then go with them to the home of the groom's parents, where the wedding feast would take place.

stranger, you welcomed me, 36 and when I was na-ked, you gave me clothes to wear. When I was sick, you took care of me, and when I was in jail, you visited me."

37 Then the ones who pleased the Lord will ask, "When did we give you something to eat or drink? 38 When did we welcome you as a stranger or give you clothes to wear 39 or visit you while you were sick or in jail?"

40 The king will answer, "Whenever you did it for any of my people, no matter how unimportant they seemed, you did it for me."

41 Then the king will say to those on his left, "Get away from me! You are under God's curse. Go into the everlasting fire prepared for the devil and his angels! 42 I was hungry, but you did not give me anything to eat, and I was thirsty, but you did not give me anything to drink. 43 I was a stranger, but you did not welcome me, and I was naked, but you did not give me any clothes to wear. I was sick and in jail, but you did not take care of me."

44 Then the people will ask, "Lord, when did we fail to help you when you were hungry or thirsty or a stranger or naked or sick or in jail?"

45 The king will say to them, "Whenever you failed to help any of my people, no matter how un-important they seemed, you failed to do it for me."

46 Then Jesus said, "Those people will be punished for-ever. But the ones who pleased God will have eternal life."

The Plot To Kill Jesus

26 When Jesus had finished teaching, he told his disci-ples, 2 "You know that two days from now will be Passover. That is when the Son of Man will be handed over to his enemies and nailed to a cross."

3 At that time the chief priests and the nation's leaders were meeting at the home of Caiaphas the high priest. 4 They planned how they could sneak around and have Jesus arrested and put to death. 5 But they said, "We must not do it during Passover, because the people will riot."

At Bethany

6 Jesus was in the town of Bethany, eating at the home of Simon, who had leprosy. 7 A woman came in with a bot-tle of expensive perfume and poured it on Jesus' head. 8 But when his disciples saw this, they became angry and com-plained, "Why such a waste? 9 We could have sold this per-fume for a lot of money and given it to the poor."

10 Jesus knew what they were thinking, and he said:
Why are you bothering this woman? She has done a beautiful thing for me. 11 You will always have the poor with you, but you won't always have me. 12 She has poured perfume on my body to prepare it for burial. 13 You may be sure that wher-ever the good news is told all over the world, peo-ple will remember what she has done. And they will tell others.

Judas and the Chief Priests

14 Judas Iscariot was one of the twelve disciples. He went to the chief priests 15 and asked, "How much will you give me if I help you arrest Jesus?" They paid Judas thirty silver coins, 16 and from then on he started looking for a good chance to betray Jesus.

Jesus Eats the Passover Meal with His Disciples

17 On the first day of the Festival of Thin Bread, Jesus' disciples came to him and asked, "Where do you want us to prepare the Passover meal?"

18 Jesus told them to go to a certain man in the city and tell him, "Our teacher says, 'My time has come! I want to eat the Passover meal with my disciples in your home.'" 19 They did as Jesus told them and prepared the meal.

20-21 When Jesus was eating with his twelve disciples that evening, he said, "One of you will surely hand me over to my enemies."

22 The disciples were very sad, and each one said to Jesus, "Lord, you can't mean me!"

23 He answered, "One of you men who has eaten with me from this dish will betray me. 24 The Son of Man will die, as the Scriptures say. But it's going to be terrible for the one who betrays me! That man would be better off if he had never been born."

25 Judas said, "Teacher, you surely don't mean me!"

"That's what you say!" Jesus replied. But later, Judas did betray him.

The Lord's Supper

26 During the meal Jesus took some bread in his hands. He blessed the bread and broke it. Then he gave it to his dis-ciples and said, "Take this and eat it. This is my body."

27 Jesus picked up a cup of wine and gave thanks to God. He then gave it to his disciples and said, "Take this and drink it. 28 This is my blood, and with it God makes his agreement with you. It will be poured out, so that many people will have their sins forgiven. 29 From now on I am not going to drink any wine, until I drink new wine with you in my Father's kingdom." 30 Then they sang a hymn and went out to the Mount of Olives.

Peter's Promise

31 Jesus said to his disciples, "During this very night, all of you will reject me, as the Scriptures say,

'I will strike down
    the shepherd,
  and the sheep
    will be scattered.'

32 But after I am raised to life, I will go to Galilee ahead of you."

33 Peter spoke up, "Even if all the others reject you, I never will!"

34 Jesus replied, "I promise you that before a rooster crows tonight, you will say three times that you don't know me." 35 But Peter said, "Even if I have to die with you, I will never say I don't know you."

All the others said the same thing.

Jesus Prays

36 Jesus went with his disciples to a place called Geth-semane. When they got there, he told them, "Sit here while I go over there and pray."

37 Jesus took along Peter and the two brothers, James and John.*q* He was very sad and troubled, **38** and he said to them, "I am so sad that I feel as if I am dying. Stay here and keep awake with me."

39 Jesus walked on a little way. Then he knelt with his face to the ground and prayed, "My Father, if it is possible, don't make me suffer by having me drink from this cup. But do what you want, and not what I want."

40 He came back and found his disciples sleeping. So he said to Peter, "Can't any of you stay awake with me for just one hour? **41** Stay awake and pray that you won't be tested. You want to do what is right, but you are weak."

42 Again Jesus went to pray and said, "My Father, if there is no other way, and I must suffer, I will still do what you want."

43 Jesus came back and found them sleeping again. They simply could not keep their eyes open. **44** He left them and prayed the same prayer once more.

45 Finally, Jesus returned to his disciples and said, "Are you still sleeping and resting?*r* The time has come for the Son of Man to be handed over to sinners. **46** Get up! Let's go. The one who will betray me is already here."

Jesus Is Arrested

47 Jesus was still speaking, when Judas the betrayer came up. He was one of the twelve disciples, and a large mob armed with swords and clubs was with him. They had been sent by the chief priests and the nation's leaders. **48** Judas had told them ahead of time, "Arrest the man I greet with a kiss."

49 Judas walked right up to Jesus and said, "Hello, teacher." Then Judas kissed him.

50 Jesus replied, "My friend, why are you here?"*s*

The men grabbed Jesus and arrested him. **51** One of Jesus' followers pulled out a sword. He struck the servant of the high priest and cut off his ear.

52 But Jesus told him, "Put your sword away. Anyone who lives by fighting will die by fighting. **53** Don't you know that I could ask my Father, and right away he would send me more than twelve armies of angels? **54** But then, how could the words of the Scriptures come true, which say that this must happen?"

55 Jesus said to the mob, "Why do you come with swords and clubs to arrest me like a criminal? Day after day I sat and taught in the temple, and you didn't arrest me. **56** But all this happened, so that what the prophets wrote would come true."

All of Jesus' disciples left him and ran away.

Jesus Is Questioned by the Council

57 After Jesus had been arrested, he was led off to the house of Caiaphas the high priest. The nation's leaders and the teachers of the Law of Moses were meeting there. **58** But Peter followed along at a distance and came to the courtyard of the high priest's palace. He went in and sat down with the guards to see what was going to happen.

59 The chief priests and the whole council wanted to put Jesus to death. So they tried to find some people who would tell lies about him in court. **60** But they could not find any, even though many did come and tell lies. At last, two men came forward **61** and said, "This man claimed that he would tear down God's temple and build it again in three days."

62 The high priest stood up and asked Jesus, "Why don't you say something in your own defense? Don't you hear the charges they are making against you?" **63** But Jesus did not answer. So the high priest said, "With the living God looking on, you must tell the truth. Tell us, are you the Messiah, the Son of God?"

64 "That is what you say!" Jesus answered. "But I tell all of you,

> 'Soon you will see
>   the Son of Man
> sitting at the right side
>   of God All-Powerful
> and coming on the clouds
>   of heaven.' "

65 The high priest then tore his robe and said, "This man claims to be God! We don't need any more witnesses! You have heard what he said. **66** What do you think?"

They answered, "He is guilty and deserves to die!" **67** Then they spit in his face and hit him with their fists. Others slapped him **68** and said, "You think you are the Messiah! So tell us who hit you!"

Peter Says He Doesn't Know Jesus

69 While Peter was sitting out in the courtyard, a servant girl came up to him and said, "You were with Jesus from Galilee."

70 But in front of everyone Peter said, "That isn't so! I don't know what you are talking about!"

71 When Peter had gone out to the gate, another servant girl saw him and said to some people there, "This man was with Jesus from Nazareth."

72 Again Peter denied it, and this time he swore, "I don't even know that man!"

73 A little while later some people standing there walked over to Peter and said, "We know that you are one of them. We can tell it because you talk like someone from Galilee."

74 Peter began to curse and swear, "I don't know that man!"

Right then a rooster crowed, **75** and Peter remembered that Jesus had said, "Before a rooster crows, you will say three times that you don't know me." Then Peter went out and cried hard.

Jesus Is Taken to Pilate

27 Early the next morning all the chief priests and the nation's leaders met and decided that Jesus should be put to death. **2** They tied him up and led him away to Pilate the governor.

The Death of Judas

3 Judas had betrayed Jesus, but when he learned that Jesus had been sentenced to death, he was sorry for what he had done. He returned the thirty silver coins to the chief priests and leaders **4** and said, "I have sinned by betraying a man who has never done anything wrong."

---

q **26.37** *the two brothers, James and John*: The Greek text has "the two sons of Zebedee" (see 27.56).   *r* **26.45** *Are you still sleeping and resting*: Or "You may as well keep on sleeping and resting."   *s* **26.50** *why are you here*: Or "do what you came for."

"So what? That's your problem," they replied. 5 Judas threw the money into the temple and then went out and hanged himself.

6 The chief priests picked up the money and said, "This money was paid to have a man killed. We can't put it in the temple treasury." 7 Then they had a meeting and decided to buy a field that belonged to someone who made clay pots. They wanted to use it as a graveyard for foreigners. 8 That's why people still call that place "Field of Blood." 9 So the words of the prophet Jeremiah came true,

"They took
        the thirty silver coins,
the price of a person
        among the people of Israel.
10 They paid it
        for a potter's field,
as the Lord
        had commanded me."

Pilate Questions Jesus

11 Jesus was brought before Pilate the governor, who asked him, "Are you the king of the Jews?"

"Those are your words!" Jesus answered. 12 And when the chief priests and leaders brought their charges against him, he did not say a thing.

13 Pilate asked him, "Don't you hear what crimes they say you have done?" 14 But Jesus did not say anything, and the governor was greatly amazed.

The Death Sentence

15 During Passover the governor always freed a prisoner chosen by the people. 16 At that time a well-known terrorist named Jesus Barabbas* was in jail. 17 So when the crowd came together, Pilate asked them, "Which prisoner do you want me to set free? Do you want Jesus Barabbas or Jesus who is called the Messiah?" 18 Pilate knew that the leaders had brought Jesus to him because they were jealous.

19 While Pilate was judging the case, his wife sent him a message. It said, "Don't have anything to do with that innocent man. I have had nightmares because of him."

20 But the chief priests and the leaders convinced the crowds to ask for Barabbas to be set free and for Jesus to be killed. 21 Pilate asked the crowd again, "Which of these two men do you want me to set free?"

"Barabbas!" they replied.

22 Pilate asked them, "What am I to do with Jesus, who is called the Messiah?"

They all yelled, "Nail him to a cross!"

23 Pilate answered, "But what crime has he done?"

"Nail him to a cross!" they yelled even louder.

24 Pilate saw that there was nothing he could do and that the people were starting to riot. So he took some water and washed his hands in front of them and said, "I won't have anything to do with killing this man. You are the ones doing it!"

25 Everyone answered, "We and our own families will take the blame for his death!"

26 Pilate set Barabbas free. Then he ordered his soldiers to beat Jesus with a whip and nail him to a cross.

Soldiers Make Fun of Jesus

27 The governor's soldiers led Jesus into the fortress and brought together the rest of the troops. 28 They stripped off Jesus' clothes and put a scarlet robe on him. 29 They made a crown out of thorn branches and placed it on his head, and they put a stick in his right hand. The soldiers knelt down and pretended to worship him. They made fun of him and shouted, "Hey, you king of the Jews!" 30 Then they spit on him. They took the stick from him and beat him on the head with it.

Jesus Is Nailed to a Cross

31 When the soldiers had finished making fun of Jesus, they took off the robe. They put his own clothes back on him and led him off to be nailed to a cross. 32 On the way they met a man from Cyrene named Simon, and they forced him to carry Jesus' cross.

33 They came to a place named Golgotha, which means "Place of a Skull." 34 There they gave Jesus some wine mixed with a drug to ease the pain. But when Jesus tasted what it was, he refused to drink it.

35 The soldiers nailed Jesus to a cross and gambled to see who would get his clothes. 36 Then they sat down to guard him. 37 Above his head they put a sign that told why he was nailed there. It read, "This is Jesus, the King of the Jews." 38 The soldiers also nailed two criminals on crosses, one to the right of Jesus and the other to his left.

39 People who passed by said terrible things about Jesus. They shook their heads and 40 shouted, "So you're the one who claimed you could tear down the temple and build it again in three days! If you are God's Son, save yourself and come down from the cross!"

41 The chief priests, the leaders, and the teachers of the Law of Moses also made fun of Jesus. They said, 42 "He saved others, but he can't save himself. If he is the king of Israel, he should come down from the cross! Then we will believe him. 43 He trusted God, so let God save him, if he wants to. He even said he was God's Son." 44 The two criminals also said cruel things to Jesus.

The Death of Jesus

45 At noon the sky turned dark and stayed that way until three o'clock. 46 Then about that time Jesus shouted, "Eli, Eli, lema sabachthani?"u which means, "My God, my God, why have you deserted me?"

47 Some of the people standing there heard Jesus and said, "He's calling for Elijah." 48 One of them at once ran and grabbed a sponge. He soaked it in wine, then put it on a stick and held it up to Jesus.

49 Others said, "Wait! Let's see if Elijah will come and save him." 50 Once again Jesus shouted, and then he died.

51 At once the curtain in the temple was torn in two from top to bottom. The earth shook, and rocks split apart. 52 Graves opened, and many of God's people were raised to life. 53 Then after Jesus had risen to life, they came out of

---

t **27.16** *Jesus Barabbas*: Here and in verse 17 many manuscripts have "Barabbas." u **27.46** *Eli . . . Sabachthani*: These words are in Hebrew.

their graves and went into the holy city, where they were seen by many people.

54 The officer and the soldiers guarding Jesus felt the earthquake and saw everything else that happened. They were frightened and said, "This man really was God's Son!"

55 Many women had come with Jesus from Galilee to be of help to him, and they were there, looking on at a distance. **56** Mary Magdalene, Mary the mother of James and Joseph, and the mother of James and John^v were some of these women.

Jesus Is Buried

57 That evening a rich disciple named Joseph from the town of Arimathea **58** went and asked for Jesus' body. Pilate gave orders for it to be given to Joseph, **59** who took the body and wrapped it in a clean linen cloth. **60** Then Joseph put the body in his own tomb that had been cut into solid rock and had never been used. He rolled a big stone against the entrance to the tomb and went away.

61 All this time Mary Magdalene and the other Mary were sitting across from the tomb.

62 On the next day, which was a Sabbath, the chief priests and the Pharisees went together to Pilate. **63** They said, "Sir, we remember what that liar said while he was still alive. He claimed that in three days he would come back from death. **64** So please order the tomb to be carefully guarded for three days. If you don't, his disciples may come and steal his body. They will tell the people that he has been raised to life, and this last lie will be worse than the first one."

65 Pilate said to them, "All right, take some of your soldiers and guard the tomb as well as you know how." **66** So they sealed it tight and placed soldiers there to guard it.

Jesus Is Alive

28 The Sabbath was over, and it was almost daybreak on Sunday when Mary Magdalene and the other Mary went to see the tomb. **2** Suddenly a strong earthquake struck, and the Lord's angel came down from heaven. He rolled away the stone and sat on it. **3** The angel looked as bright as lightning, and his clothes were white as snow.

4 The guards shook from fear and fell down, as though they were dead.

5 The angel said to the women, "Don't be afraid! I know you are looking for Jesus, who was nailed to a cross. **6** He isn't here! God has raised him to life, just as Jesus said he would. Come, see the place where his body was lying. **7** Now hurry! Tell his disciples that he has been raised to life and is on his way to Galilee. Go there, and you will see him. That is what I came to tell you."

8 The women were frightened and yet very happy, as they hurried from the tomb and ran to tell his disciples. **9** Suddenly Jesus met them and greeted them. They went near him, held on to his feet, and worshiped him. **10** Then Jesus said, "Don't be afraid! Tell my followers to go to Galilee. They will see me there."

Report of the Guard

11 While the women were on their way, some soldiers who had been guarding the tomb went into the city. They told the chief priests everything that had happened. **12** So the chief priests met with the leaders and decided to bribe the soldiers with a lot of money. **13** They said to the soldiers, "Tell everyone that Jesus' disciples came during the night and stole his body while you were asleep. **14** If the governor hears about this, we will talk to him. You won't have anything to worry about." **15** The soldiers took the money and did what they were told. The Jewish people still tell each other this story.

What Jesus' Followers Must Do

16 Jesus' eleven disciples went to a mountain in Galilee, where Jesus had told them to meet him. **17** They saw him and worshiped him, but some of them doubted. **18** Jesus came to them and said:

I have been given all authority in heaven and on earth! **19** Go to the people of all nations and make them my disciples. Baptize them in the name of the Father, the Son, and the Holy Spirit, **20** and teach them to do everything I have told you. I will be with you always, even until the end of the world.

---

^v**27.56** *of James and John*: The Greek text has "of Zebedee's sons" (see 26.37).

MARK

The Preaching of John the Baptist

1 This is the good news about Jesus Christ, the Son of God.[a] 2 It began just as God had said in the book written by Isaiah the prophet,

"I am sending my messenger
to get the way ready
for you.
3 In the desert
someone is shouting,
'Get the road ready
for the Lord!
Make a straight path
for him.'"

4 So John the Baptist showed up in the desert and told everyone, "Turn back to God and be baptized! Then your sins will be forgiven."

5 From all Judea and Jerusalem crowds of people went to John. They told how sorry they were for their sins, and he baptized them in the Jordan River.

6 John wore clothes made of camel's hair. He had a leather strap around his waist and ate grasshoppers and wild honey.

7 John also told the people, "Someone more powerful is going to come. And I am not good enough even to stoop down and untie his sandals. 8 I baptize you with water, but he will baptize you with the Holy Spirit!"

The Baptism of Jesus

9 About that time Jesus came from Nazareth in Galilee, and John baptized him in the Jordan River. 10 As soon as Jesus came out of the water, he saw the sky open and the Holy Spirit coming down to him like a dove. 11 A voice from heaven said, "You are my own dear Son, and I am pleased with you."

Jesus and Satan

12 Right away God's Spirit made Jesus go into the desert. 13 He stayed there for forty days while Satan tested him. Jesus was with the wild animals, but angels took care of him.

Jesus Begins His Work

14 After John was arrested, Jesus went to Galilee and told the good news that comes from God.[b] 15 He said, "The time has come! God's kingdom will soon be here.[c] Turn back to God and believe the good news!"

Jesus Chooses Four Fishermen

16 As Jesus was walking along the shore of Lake Galilee, he saw Simon and his brother Andrew. They were fishermen and were casting their nets into the lake. 17 Jesus said to them, "Come with me! I will teach you how to bring in people instead of fish." 18 Right then the two brothers dropped their nets and went with him.

19 Jesus walked on and soon saw James and John, the sons of Zebedee. They were in a boat, mending their nets. 20 At once Jesus asked them to come with him. They left their father in the boat with the hired workers and went with him.

A Man with an Evil Spirit

21 Jesus and his disciples went to the town of Capernaum. Then on the next Sabbath he went into the Jewish meeting place and started teaching. 22 Everyone was amazed at his teaching. He taught with authority, and not like the teachers of the Law of Moses. 23 Suddenly a man with an evil spirit in him entered the meeting place and yelled, 24 "Jesus from Nazareth, what do you want with us? Have you come to destroy us? I know who you are! You are God's Holy One."

25 Jesus told the evil spirit, "Be quiet and come out of the man!" 26 The spirit shook him. Then it gave a loud shout and left.

27 Everyone was completely surprised and kept saying to each other, "What is this? It must be some new kind of powerful teaching! Even the evil spirits obey him." 28 News about Jesus quickly spread all over Galilee.

Jesus Heals Many People

29 As soon as Jesus left the meeting place with James and John, they went home with Simon and Andrew. 30 When they got there, Jesus was told that Simon's mother-in-law was sick in bed with fever. 31 Jesus went to her. He took hold of her hand and helped her up. The fever left her, and she served them a meal.

32 That evening after sunset, all who were sick or had demons in them were brought to Jesus. 33 In fact, the whole town gathered around the door of the house. 34 Jesus healed all kinds of terrible diseases and forced out a lot of demons. But the demons knew who he was, and he did not let them speak.

35 Very early the next morning, Jesus got up and went to a place where he could be alone and pray. 36 Simon and the others started looking for him. 37 And when they found him, they said, "Everyone is looking for you!"

38 Jesus replied, "We must go to the nearby towns, so that I can tell the good news to those people. This is why I have come." 39 Then Jesus went to Jewish meeting places everywhere in Galilee, where he preached and forced out demons.

Jesus Heals a Man

40 A man with leprosy came to Jesus and knelt down.[d] He begged, "You have the power to make me well, if only you wanted to."

41 Jesus felt sorry for[e] the man. So he put his hand on him and said, "I want to! Now you are well." 42 At once the man's leprosy disappeared, and he was well.

---

[a] 1.1 the Son of God: These words are not in some manuscripts. [b] 1.14 that comes from God: Or "that is about God." [c] 1.15 will soon be here: Or "is already here." [d] 1.40 and knelt down: These words are not in some manuscripts. [e] 1.41 felt sorry for: Some manuscripts have "was angry with."

43 After Jesus strictly warned the man, he sent him on his way. 44 He said, "Don't tell anyone about this. Just go and show the priest that you are well. Then take a gift to the temple as Moses commanded, and everyone will know that you have been healed."

45 The man talked about it so much and told so many people, that Jesus could no longer go openly into a town. He had to stay away from the towns, but people still came to him from everywhere.

Jesus Heals a Crippled Man

2 Jesus went back to Capernaum, and a few days later people heard that he was at home.ʲ 2 Then so many of them came to the house that there wasn't even standing room left in front of the door.

Jesus was still teaching 3 when four people came up, carrying a crippled man on a mat. 4 But because of the crowd, they could not get him to Jesus. So they made a hole in the roof above him and let the man down in front of everyone.

5 When Jesus saw how much faith they had, he said to the crippled man, "My friend, your sins are forgiven."

6 Some of the teachers of the Law of Moses were sitting there. They started wondering, 7 "Why would he say such a thing? He must think he is God! Only God can forgive sins."

8 Right away, Jesus knew what they were thinking, and he said, "Why are you thinking such things? 9 Is it easier for me to tell this crippled man that his sins are forgiven or to tell him to get up and pick up his mat and go on home? 10 I will show you that the Son of Man has the right to forgive sins here on earth." So Jesus said to the man, 11 "Get up! Pick up your mat and go on home."

12 The man got right up. He picked up his mat and went out while everyone watched in amazement. They praised God and said, "We have never seen anything like this!"

Jesus Chooses Levi

13 Once again, Jesus went to the shore of Lake Galilee. A large crowd gathered around him, and he taught them. 14 As he walked along, he saw Levi, the son of Alphaeus. Levi was sitting at the place for paying taxes, and Jesus said to him, "Come with me!" So he got up and went with Jesus.

15 Later, Jesus and his disciples were having dinner at Levi's house.ᵍ Many tax collectors and other sinners had become followers of Jesus, and they were also guests at the dinner.

16 Some of the teachers of the Law of Moses were Pharisees, and they saw that Jesus was eating with sinners and tax collectors. So they asked his disciples, "Why does he eat with tax collectors and sinners?"

17 Jesus heard them and answered, "Healthy people don't need a doctor, but sick people do. I didn't come to invite good people to be my followers. I came to invite sinners."

People Ask about Going without Eating

18 The followers of John the Baptist and the Pharisees often went without eating. Some people came and asked Jesus, "Why do the followers of John and those of the Pharisees often go without eating, while your disciples never do?"

19 Jesus answered:

The friends of a bridegroom don't go without eating while he is still with them. 20 But the time will come when he will be taken from them. Then they will go without eating.

21 No one patches old clothes by sewing on a piece of new cloth. The new piece would shrink and tear a bigger hole.

22 No one pours new wine into old wineskins. The wine would swell and burst the old skins. Then the wine would be lost, and the skins would be ruined. New wine must be put into new wineskins.

A Question about the Sabbath

23 One Sabbath Jesus and his disciples were walking through some wheat fields. His disciples were picking grains of wheat as they went along. 24 Some Pharisees asked Jesus, "Why are your disciples picking grain on the Sabbath? They are not supposed to do that!"

25 Jesus answered, "Haven't you read what David did when he and his followers were hungry and in need? 26 It was during the time of Abiathar the high priest. David went into the house of God and ate the sacred loaves of bread that only priests are allowed to eat. He also gave some to his followers."

27 Jesus finished by saying, "People were not made for the good of the Sabbath. The Sabbath was made for the good of people. 28 So the Son of Man is Lord over the Sabbath."

A Man with a Crippled Hand

3 The next time that Jesus went into the meeting place, a man with a crippled hand was there. 2 The Phariseesʰ wanted to accuse Jesus of doing something wrong, and they kept watching to see if Jesus would heal him on the Sabbath.

3 Jesus told the man to stand up where everyone could see him. 4 Then he asked, "On the Sabbath should we do good deeds or evil deeds? Should we save someone's life or destroy it?" But no one said a word.

5 Jesus was angry as he looked around at the people. Yet he felt sorry for them because they were so stubborn. Then he told the man, "Stretch out your hand." He did, and his bad hand was healed.

6 The Pharisees left. And right away they started making plans with Herod's followers to kill Jesus.

Large Crowds Come to Jesus

7 Jesus led his disciples down to the shore of the lake. Large crowds followed him from Galilee, Judea, 8 and Jerusalem. People came from Idumea, as well as other places east of the Jordan River. They also came from the region around the cities of Tyre and Sidon. All of these crowds came because they had heard what Jesus was doing. 9 He even had to tell his disciples to get a boat ready to keep him from being crushed by the crowds.

10 After Jesus had healed many people, the other sick people begged him to let them touch him. 11 And whenever any evil spirits saw Jesus, they would fall to the ground

---

ʲ2.1 *at home*: Or "in the house" (perhaps Simon Peter's home).   ᵍ2.15 *Levi's house*: Or "Jesus' house."   ʰ3.2 *Pharisees*: The Greek text has "they" (but see verse 6).

and shout, "You are the Son of God!" [12] But Jesus warned the spirits not to tell who he was.

Jesus Chooses His Twelve Apostles

[13] Jesus decided to ask some of his disciples to go up on a mountain with him, and they went. [14] Then he chose twelve of them to be his apostles,[i] so that they could be with him. He also wanted to send them out to preach [15] and to force out demons. [16] Simon was one of the twelve, and Jesus named him Peter. [17] There were also James and John, the two sons of Zebedee. Jesus called them Boanerges, which means "Thunderbolts." [18] Andrew, Philip, Bartholomew, Matthew, Thomas, James son of Alphaeus, and Thaddaeus were also apostles. The others were Simon, known as the Eager One,[j] [19] and Judas Iscariot, who later betrayed Jesus.

Jesus and the Ruler of Demons

[20] Jesus went back home,[k] and once again such a large crowd gathered that there was no chance even to eat. [21] When Jesus' family heard what he was doing, they thought he was crazy and went to get him under control.

[22] Some teachers of the Law of Moses came from Jerusalem and said, "This man is under the power of Beelzebul, the ruler of demons! He is even forcing out demons with the help of Beelzebul."

[23] Jesus told the people to gather around him. Then he spoke to them in riddles and said:

How can Satan force himself out? [24] A nation whose people fight each other won't last very long. [25] And a family that fights won't last long either. [26] So if Satan fights against himself, that will be the end of him.

[27] How can anyone break into the house of a strong man and steal his things, unless he first ties up the strong man? Then he can take everything.

[28] I promise you that any of the sinful things you say or do can be forgiven, no matter how terrible those things are. [29] But if you speak against the Holy Spirit, you can never be forgiven. That sin will be held against you forever.

[30] Jesus said this because the people were saying that he had an evil spirit in him.

Jesus' Mother and Brothers

[31] Jesus' mother and brothers came and stood outside. Then they sent someone with a message for him to come out to them. [32] The crowd that was sitting around Jesus told him, "Your mother and your brothers and sisters[l] are outside and want to see you."

[33] Jesus asked, "Who is my mother and who are my brothers?" [34] Then he looked at the people sitting around him and said, "Here are my mother and my brothers. [35] Anyone who obeys God is my brother or sister or mother."

A Story about a Farmer

4 The next time Jesus taught beside Lake Galilee, a big crowd gathered. It was so large that he had to sit in a boat out on the lake, while the people stood on the shore.

[2] He used stories to teach them many things, and this is part of what he taught:

[3] Now listen! A farmer went out to scatter seed in a field. [4] While the farmer was scattering the seed, some of it fell along the road and was eaten by birds. [5] Other seeds fell on thin, rocky ground and quickly started growing because the soil wasn't very deep. [6] But when the sun came up, the plants were scorched and dried up, because they did not have enough roots. [7] Some other seeds fell where thornbushes grew up and choked out the plants. So they did not produce any grain. [8] But a few seeds did fall on good ground where the plants grew and produced thirty or sixty or even a hundred times as much as was scattered.

[9] Then Jesus said, "If you have ears, pay attention."

Why Jesus Used Stories

[10] When Jesus was alone with the twelve apostles and some others, they asked him about these stories. [11] He answered:

I have explained the secret about God's kingdom to you, but for others I can use only stories. [12] The reason is,

"These people will look
    and look, but never see.
They will listen and listen,
    but never understand.
If they did,
they would turn to God,
    and he would forgive them."

Jesus Explains the Story about the Farmer

[13] Jesus told them:

If you don't understand this story, you won't understand any others. [14] What the farmer is spreading is really the message about the kingdom. [15] The seeds that fell along the road are the people who hear the message. But Satan soon comes and snatches it away from them. [16] The seeds that fell on rocky ground are the people who gladly hear the message and accept it right away. [17] But they don't have any roots, and they don't last very long. As soon as life gets hard or the message gets them in trouble, they give up.

[18] The seeds that fell among the thornbushes are also people who hear the message. [19] But they start worrying about the needs of this life. They are fooled by the desire to get rich and to have all kinds of other things. So the message gets choked out, and they never produce anything. [20] The seeds that fell on good ground are the people who hear and welcome the message. They produce thirty or sixty or even a hundred times as much as was planted.

Light

[21] Jesus also said:

---

*i*3.14 *to be his apostles*: These words are not in some manuscripts.   *j*3.18 *known as the Eager One*: The Greek text has "Cananaean," which probably comes from a Hebrew word meaning "zealous" (see Luke 6.15). "Zealot" was the name later given to the members of a Jewish group that resisted and fought against the Romans.   *k*3.20 *went back home*: Or "entered a house" (perhaps the home of Simon Peter).   *l*3.32 *and sisters*: These words are not in some manuscripts.

You don't light a lamp and put it under a clay pot or under a bed. Don't you put a lamp on a lampstand? [22] There is nothing hidden that will not be made public. There is no secret that will not be well known. [23] If you have ears, pay attention!

[24] Listen carefully to what you hear! The way you treat others will be the way you will be treated—and even worse. [25] Everyone who has something will be given more. But people who don't have anything will lose what little they have.

Another Story about Seeds

[26] Again Jesus said:

God's kingdom is like what happens when a farmer scatters seed in a field. [27] The farmer sleeps at night and is up and around during the day. Yet the seeds keep sprouting and growing, and he doesn't understand how. [28] It is the ground that makes the seeds sprout and grow into plants that produce grain. [29] Then when harvest season comes and the grain is ripe, the farmer cuts it with a sickle.

A Mustard Seed

[30] Finally, Jesus said:

What is God's kingdom like? What story can I use to explain it? [31] It is like what happens when a mustard seed is planted in the ground. It is the smallest seed in all the world. [32] But once it is planted, it grows larger than any garden plant. It even puts out branches that are big enough for birds to nest in its shade.

The Reason for Teaching with Stories

[33] Jesus used many other stories when he spoke to the people, and he taught them as much as they could understand. [34] He did not tell them anything without using stories. But when he was alone with his disciples, he explained everything to them.

A Storm

[35] That evening, Jesus said to his disciples, "Let's cross to the east side." [36] So they left the crowd, and his disciples started across the lake with him in the boat. Some other boats followed along. [37] Suddenly a windstorm struck the lake. Waves started splashing into the boat, and it was about to sink.

[38] Jesus was in the back of the boat with his head on a pillow, and he was asleep. His disciples woke him and said, "Teacher, don't you care that we're about to drown?"

[39] Jesus got up and ordered the wind and the waves to be quiet. The wind stopped, and everything was calm. [40] Jesus asked his disciples, "Why were you afraid? Don't you have any faith?"

[41] Now they were more afraid than ever and said to each other, "Who is this? Even the wind and the waves obey him!"

A Man with Evil Spirits

5 Jesus and his disciples crossed Lake Galilee and came to shore near the town of Gerasa.[m] [2] When he was getting out of the boat, a man with an evil spirit quickly ran to him [3] from the graveyard where he had been living. No one was able to tie the man up anymore, not even with a chain. [4] He had often been put in chains and leg irons, but he broke the chains and smashed the leg irons. No one could control him. [5] Night and day he was in the graveyard or on the hills, yelling and cutting himself with stones.

[6] When the man saw Jesus in the distance, he ran up to him and knelt down. [7] He shouted, "Jesus, Son of God in heaven, what do you want with me? Promise me in God's name that you won't torture me!" [8] The man said this because Jesus had already told the evil spirit to come out of him.

[9] Jesus asked, "What is your name?"

The man answered, "My name is Lots, because I have 'lots' of evil spirits." [10] He then begged Jesus not to send them away.

[11] Over on the hillside a large herd of pigs was feeding. [12] So the evil spirits begged Jesus, "Send us into those pigs! Let us go into them." [13] Jesus let them go, and they went out of the man and into the pigs. The whole herd of about two thousand pigs rushed down the steep bank into the lake and drowned.

[14] The men taking care of the pigs ran to the town and the farms to spread the news. Then the people came out to see what had happened. [15] When they came to Jesus, they saw the man who had once been full of demons. He was sitting there with his clothes on and in his right mind, and they were terrified.

[16] Everyone who had seen what had happened told about the man and the pigs. [17] Then the people started begging Jesus to leave their part of the country.

[18] When Jesus was getting into the boat, the man begged to go with him. [19] But Jesus would not let him. Instead, he said, "Go home to your family and tell them how much the Lord has done for you and how good he has been to you."

[20] The man went away into the region near the ten cities known as Decapolis and began telling everyone how much Jesus had done for him. Everyone who heard what had happened was amazed.

A Dying Girl and a Sick Woman

[21] Once again Jesus got into the boat and crossed Lake Galilee. Then as he stood on the shore, a large crowd gathered around him. [22] The person in charge of the Jewish meeting place was also there. His name was Jairus, and when he saw Jesus, he went over to him. He knelt at Jesus' feet [23] and started begging him for help. He said, "My daughter is about to die! Please come and touch her, so she will get well and live." [24] Jesus went with Jairus. Many people followed along and kept crowding around.

[25] In the crowd was a woman who had been bleeding for twelve years. [26] She had gone to many doctors, and they had not done anything except cause her a lot of pain. She had paid them all the money she had. But instead of getting better, she only got worse.

[27] The woman had heard about Jesus, so she came up behind him in the crowd and barely touched his clothes. [28] She had said to herself, "If I can just touch his clothes, I will get well." [29] As soon as she touched them, her bleeding stopped, and she knew she was well.

---

[m] 5.1 Gerasa: Some manuscripts have "Gadara," and others have "Gergesa."

[30] At that moment Jesus felt power go out from him. He turned to the crowd and asked, "Who touched my clothes?"

[31] His disciples said to him, "Look at all these people crowding around you! How can you ask who touched you?" [32] But Jesus turned to see who had touched him.

[33] The woman knew what had happened to her. She came shaking with fear and knelt down in front of Jesus. Then she told him the whole story.

[34] Jesus said to the woman, "You are now well because of your faith. May God give you peace! You are healed, and you will no longer be in pain."

[35] While Jesus was still speaking, some men came from Jairus' home and said, "Your daughter has died! Why bother the teacher anymore?"

[36] Jesus heard[n] what they said, and he said to Jairus, "Don't worry. Just have faith!"

[37] Jesus did not let anyone go with him except Peter and the two brothers, James and John. [38] They went home with Jairus and saw the people crying and making a lot of noise. [39] Then Jesus went inside and said to them, "Why are you crying and carrying on like this? The child isn't dead. She is just asleep." [40] But the people laughed at him.

After Jesus had sent them all out of the house, he took the girl's father and mother and his three disciples and went to where she was. [41-42] He took the twelve-year-old girl by the hand and said, "Talitha, koum!" which means, "Little girl, get up!" The girl got right up and started walking around. Everyone was greatly surprised. [43] But Jesus ordered them not to tell anyone what had happened. Then he said, "Give her something to eat."

The People of Nazareth Turn against Jesus

6 Jesus left and returned to his hometown with his disciples. [2] The next Sabbath he taught in the Jewish meeting place. Many of the people who heard him were amazed and asked, "How can he do all this? Where did he get such wisdom and the power to work these miracles? [3] Isn't he the carpenter, the son of Mary? Aren't James, Joseph, Judas, and Simon his brothers? Don't his sisters still live here in our town?" The people were very unhappy because of what he was doing.

[4] But Jesus said, "Prophets are honored by everyone, except the people of their hometown and their relatives and their own family." [5] Jesus could not work any miracles there, except to heal a few sick people by placing his hands on them. [6] He was surprised that the people did not have any faith.

Instructions for the Twelve Apostles

Jesus taught in all the neighboring villages. [7] Then he called together his twelve apostles and sent them out two by two with power over evil spirits. [8] He told them, "You may take along a walking stick. But don't carry food or a traveling bag or any money. [9] It's all right to wear sandals, but don't take along a change of clothes. [10] When you are welcomed into a home, stay there until you leave that town. [11] If any place won't welcome you or listen to your message, leave and shake the dust from your feet as a warning to them."

[12] The apostles left and started telling everyone to turn to God. [13] They forced out many demons and healed a lot of sick people by putting olive oil on them.

The Death of John the Baptist

[14] Jesus became so well-known that Herod the ruler heard about him. Some people thought he was John the Baptist, who had come back to life with the power to work miracles. [15] Others thought he was Elijah or some other prophet who had lived long ago. [16] But when Herod heard about Jesus, he said, "This must be John! I had his head cut off, and now he has come back to life."

[17-18] Herod had earlier married Herodias, the wife of his brother Philip. But John had told him, "It isn't right for you to take your brother's wife!" So, in order to please Herodias, Herod arrested John and put him in prison.

[19] Herodias had a grudge against John and wanted to kill him. But she could not do it [20] because Herod was afraid of John and protected him. He knew that John was a good and holy man. Even though Herod was confused by what John said,[o] he was glad to listen to him. And he often did.

[21] Finally, Herodias got her chance when Herod gave a great birthday celebration for himself and invited his officials, his army officers, and the leaders of Galilee. [22] The daughter of Herodias[p] came in and danced for Herod and his guests. She pleased them so much that Herod said, "Ask for anything, and it's yours! [23] I swear that I will give you as much as half of my kingdom, if you want it."

[24] The girl left and asked her mother, "What do you think I should ask for?"

Her mother answered, "The head of John the Baptist!"

[25] The girl hurried back and told Herod, "Right now on a platter I want the head of John the Baptist!"

[26] The king was very sorry for what he had said. But he did not want to break the promise he had made in front of his guests. [27] At once he ordered a guard to cut off John's head there in prison. The guard put the head on a platter and took it to the girl. Then she gave it to her mother.

[29] When John's followers learned that he had been killed, they took his body and put it in a tomb.

Jesus Feeds Five Thousand

[30] After the apostles returned to Jesus, they told him everything they had done and taught. [31] But so many people were coming and going that Jesus and the apostles did not even have a chance to eat. Then Jesus said, "Let's go to a place where we can be alone and get some rest." [32] They left in a boat for a place where they could be alone. [33] But many people saw them leave and figured out where they were going. So people from every town ran on ahead and got there first.

[34] When Jesus got out of the boat, he saw the large crowd that was like sheep without a shepherd. He felt sorry for the people and started teaching them many things.

[35] That evening the disciples came to Jesus and said, "This place is like a desert, and it is already late. [36] Let the crowds leave, so they can go to the farms and villages near here and buy something to eat."

[37] Jesus replied, "You give them something to eat."

---

[n] **5.36** *heard:* Or "ignored."   [o] **6.20** *was confused by what John said:* Some manuscripts have "did many things because of what John said."   [p] **6.22** *Herodias:* Some manuscripts have "Herod."

But they asked him, "Don't you know that it would take almost a year's wages[q] to buy all of these people something to eat?"

38 Then Jesus said, "How much bread do you have? Go and see!"

They found out and answered, "We have five small loaves of bread and two fish." 39 Jesus told his disciples to have the people sit down on the green grass. 40 They sat down in groups of a hundred and groups of fifty.

41 Jesus took the five loaves and the two fish. He looked up toward heaven and blessed the food. Then he broke the bread and handed it to his disciples to give to the people. He also divided the two fish, so that everyone could have some.

42 After everyone had eaten all they wanted, 43 Jesus' disciples picked up twelve large baskets of leftover bread and fish.

44 There were five thousand men who ate the food.

Jesus Walks on the Water

45 Right away, Jesus made his disciples get into the boat and start back across to Bethsaida. But he stayed until he had sent the crowds away. 46 Then he told them good-by and went up on the side of a mountain to pray.

47 Later that evening he was still there by himself, and the boat was somewhere in the middle of the lake. 48 He could see that the disciples were struggling hard, because they were rowing against the wind. Not long before morning, Jesus came toward them. He was walking on the water and was about to pass the boat.

49 When the disciples saw Jesus walking on the water, they thought he was a ghost, and they started screaming. 50 All of them saw him and were terrified. But at that same time he said, "Don't worry! I am Jesus. Don't be afraid." 51 He then got into the boat with them, and the wind died down. The disciples were completely confused. 52 Their minds were closed, and they could not understand the true meaning of the loaves of bread.

Jesus Heals Sick People in Gennesaret

53 Jesus and his disciples crossed the lake and brought the boat to shore near the town of Gennesaret. 54 As soon as they got out of the boat, the people recognized Jesus. 55 So they ran all over that part of the country to bring their sick people to him on mats. They brought them each time they heard where he was. 56 In every village or farm or marketplace where Jesus went, the people brought their sick to him. They begged him to let them just touch his clothes, and everyone who did was healed.

The Teaching of the Ancestors

7 Some Pharisees and several teachers of the Law of Moses from Jerusalem came and gathered around Jesus. 2 They noticed that some of his disciples ate without first washing their hands.

3 The Pharisees and many other Jewish people obey the teachings of their ancestors. They always wash their hands in the proper way[r] before eating. 4 None of them will eat anything they buy in the market until it is washed. They also follow a lot of other teachings, such as washing cups, pitchers, and bowls.[s]

5 The Pharisees and teachers asked Jesus, "Why don't your disciples obey what our ancestors taught us to do? Why do they eat without washing their hands?"

6 Jesus replied:

You are nothing but show-offs! The prophet Isaiah was right when he wrote that God had said,

"All of you praise me
    with your words,
but you never really
    think about me.
7 It is useless for you
    to worship me,
when you teach rules
    made up by humans."

8 You disobey God's commands in order to obey what humans have taught. 9 You are good at rejecting God's commands so that you can follow your own teachings! 10 Didn't Moses command you to respect your father and mother? Didn't he tell you to put to death all who curse their parents? 11 But you let people get by without helping their parents when they should. You let them say that what they own has been offered to God. 12 You won't let those people help their parents. 13 And you ignore God's commands in order to follow your own teaching. You do a lot of other things that are just as bad.

What Really Makes People Unclean

14 Jesus called the crowd together again and said, "Pay attention and try to understand what I mean. 15-16 The food that you put into your mouth doesn't make you unclean and unfit to worship God. The bad words that come out of your mouth are what make you unclean."[t]

17 After Jesus and his disciples had left the crowd and had gone into the house, they asked him what these sayings meant. 18 He answered, "Don't you know what I am talking about by now? You surely know that the food you put into your mouth cannot make you unclean. 19 It doesn't go into your heart, but into your stomach, and then out of your body." By saying this, Jesus meant that all foods were fit to eat.

20 Then Jesus said:

What comes from your heart is what makes you unclean. 21 Out of your heart come evil thoughts, vulgar deeds, stealing, murder, 22 unfaithfulness in marriage, greed, meanness, deceit, indecency, envy, insults, pride, and foolishness. 23 All of these come from your heart, and they are what make you unfit to worship God.

---

q 6.37 almost a year's wages: The Greek text has "two hundred silver coins." Each coin was the average day's wage for a worker. r 7.3 in the proper way: The Greek text has "with the fist," but the exact meaning is not clear. It could mean "to the wrist" or "to the elbow." s 7.4 bowls: Some manuscripts add "and sleeping mats." t 7.15,16 unclean: Some manuscripts add, "If you have ears, pay attention."

A Woman's Faith

24 Jesus left and went to the region near the city of Tyre, where he stayed in someone's home. He did not want people to know he was there, but they found out anyway. 25 A woman whose daughter had an evil spirit in her heard where Jesus was. And right away she came and knelt down at his feet. 26 The woman was Greek and had been born in the part of Syria known as Phoenicia. She begged Jesus to force the demon out of her daughter. 27 But Jesus said, "The children must first be fed! It isn't right to take away their food and feed it to dogs."

28 The woman replied, "Lord, even dogs eat the crumbs that children drop from the table."

29 Jesus answered, "That's true! You may go now. The demon has left your daughter." 30 When the woman got back home, she found her child lying on the bed. The demon had gone.

Jesus Heals a Man Who Was Deaf and Could Hardly Talk

31 Jesus left the region around Tyre and went by way of Sidon toward Lake Galilee. He went through the land near the ten cities known as Decapolis. 32 Some people brought to him a man who was deaf and could hardly talk. They begged Jesus just to touch him.

33 After Jesus had taken him aside from the crowd, he stuck his fingers in the man's ears. Then he spit and put it on the man's tongue. 34 Jesus looked up toward heaven, and with a groan he said, "Effatha!" which means "Open up!" 35 At once the man could hear, and he had no more trouble talking clearly.

36 Jesus told the people not to say anything about what he had done. But the more he told them, the more they talked about it. 37 They were completely amazed and said, "Everything he does is good! He even heals people who cannot hear or talk."

Jesus Feeds Four Thousand

8 One day another large crowd gathered around Jesus. They had not brought along anything to eat. So Jesus called his disciples together and said, 2 "I feel sorry for these people. They have been with me for three days, and they don't have anything to eat. 3 Some of them live a long way from here. If I send them away hungry, they might faint on their way home."

4 The disciples said, "This place is like a desert. Where can we find enough food to feed such a crowd?"

5 Jesus asked them how much food they had. They replied, "Seven small loaves of bread."

6 After Jesus told the crowd to sit down, he took the seven loaves and blessed them. He then broke the loaves and handed them to his disciples, who passed them out to the crowd. 7 They also had a few little fish, and after Jesus had blessed these, he told the disciples to pass them around.

8-9 The crowd of about four thousand people ate all they wanted, and the leftovers filled seven large baskets.

As soon as Jesus had sent the people away, 10 he got into the boat with the disciples and crossed to the territory near Dalmanutha.

A Sign from Heaven

11 The Pharisees came out and started an argument with Jesus. They wanted to test him by asking for a sign from heaven. 12 Jesus groaned and said, "Why are you always looking for a sign? I can promise you that you will not be given one!" 13 Then he left them. He again got into a boat and crossed over to the other side of the lake.

The Yeast of the Pharisees and of Herod

14 The disciples had forgotten to bring any bread, and they had only one loaf with them in the boat. 15 Jesus warned them, "Watch out! Guard against the yeast of the Pharisees and of Herod."

16 The disciples talked this over and said to each other, "He must be saying this because we don't have any bread."

17 Jesus knew what they were thinking and asked, "Why are you talking about not having any bread? Don't you understand? Are your minds still closed? 18 Are your eyes blind and your ears deaf? Don't you remember 19 how many baskets of leftovers you picked up when I fed those five thousand people with only five small loaves of bread?"

"Yes," the disciples answered. "There were twelve baskets."

20 Jesus then asked, "And how many baskets of leftovers did you pick up when I broke seven small loaves of bread for those four thousand people?"

"Seven," they answered.

21 "Don't you know what I am talking about by now?" Jesus asked.

Jesus Heals a Blind Man at Bethsaida

22 As Jesus and his disciples were going into Bethsaida, some people brought a blind man to him and begged him to touch the man. 23 Jesus took him by the hand and led him out of the village, where he spit into the man's eyes. He placed his hands on the blind man and asked him if he could see anything. 24 The man looked up and said, "I see people, but they look like trees walking around."

25 Once again Jesus placed his hands on the man's eyes, and this time the man stared. His eyes were healed, and he saw everything clearly. 26 Jesus said to him, "You may return home now, but don't go into the village."

Who Is Jesus?

27 Jesus and his disciples went to the villages near the town of Caesarea Philippi. As they were walking along, he asked them, "What do people say about me?"

28 The disciples answered, "Some say you are John the Baptist or maybe Elijah. Others say you are one of the prophets."

29 Then Jesus asked them, "But who do you say I am?"

"You are the Messiah!" Peter replied.

30 Jesus warned the disciples not to tell anyone about him.

Jesus Speaks about His Suffering and Death

31 Jesus began telling his disciples what would happen to him. He said, "The nation's leaders, the chief priests, and the teachers of the Law of Moses will make the Son of Man suffer terribly. He will be rejected and killed, but three days later he will rise to life." 32 Then Jesus explained clearly what he meant.

Peter took Jesus aside and told him to stop talking like that. 33 But when Jesus turned and saw the disciples, he corrected Peter. He said to him, "Satan, get away from me! You are thinking like everyone else and not like God."

34 Jesus then told the crowd and the disciples to come closer, and he said:

If any of you want to be my followers, you must forget about yourself. You must take up your cross and follow me. **35** If you want to save your life,*u* you will destroy it. But if you give up your life for me and for the good news, you will save it. **36** What will you gain, if you own the whole world but destroy yourself? **37** What could you give to get back your soul?

38 Don't be ashamed of me and my message among these unfaithful and sinful people! If you are, the Son of Man will be ashamed of you when he comes in the glory of his Father with the holy angels.

9 I can assure you that some of the people standing here will not die before they see God's kingdom come with power.

The True Glory of Jesus

2 Six days later Jesus took Peter, James, and John with him. They went up on a high mountain, where they could be alone. There in front of the disciples, Jesus was completely changed. **3** And his clothes became much whiter than any bleach on earth could make them. **4** Then Moses and Elijah were there talking with Jesus.

5 Peter said to Jesus, "Teacher, it is good for us to be here! Let us make three shelters, one for you, one for Moses, and one for Elijah." **6** But Peter and the others were terribly frightened, and he did not know what he was talking about.

7 The shadow of a cloud passed over and covered them. From the cloud a voice said, "This is my Son, and I love him. Listen to what he says!" **8** At once the disciples looked around, but they saw only Jesus.

9 As Jesus and his disciples were coming down the mountain, he told them not to say a word about what they had seen, until the Son of Man had been raised from death. **10** So they kept it to themselves. But they wondered what he meant by the words "raised from death."

11 The disciples asked Jesus, "Don't the teachers of the Law of Moses say that Elijah must come before the Messiah does?"

12 Jesus answered:

Elijah certainly will come to get everything ready. But don't the Scriptures also say that the Son of Man must suffer terribly and be rejected? **13** I can assure you that Elijah has already come. And people treated him just as they wanted to, as the Scriptures say they would.

Jesus Heals a Boy

14 When Jesus and his three disciples came back down, they saw a large crowd around the other disciples. The teachers of the Law of Moses were arguing with them.

15 The crowd was really surprised to see Jesus, and everyone hurried over to greet him.

16 Jesus asked, "What are you arguing about?"

17 Someone from the crowd answered, "Teacher, I brought my son to you. A demon keeps him from talking.

18 Whenever the demon attacks my son, it throws him to the ground and makes him foam at the mouth and grit his teeth in pain. Then he becomes stiff. I asked your disciples to force out the demon, but they couldn't do it."

19 Jesus said, "You people don't have any faith! How much longer must I be with you? Why do I have to put up with you? Bring the boy to me."

20 They brought the boy, and as soon as the demon saw Jesus, it made the boy shake all over. He fell down and began rolling on the ground and foaming at the mouth.

21 Jesus asked the boy's father, "How long has he been like this?"

The man answered, "Ever since he was a child. **22** The demon has often tried to kill him by throwing him into a fire or into water. Please have pity and help us if you can!"

23 Jesus replied, "Why do you say 'if you can'? Anything is possible for someone who has faith!"

24 Right away the boy's father shouted, "I do have faith! Please help me to have even more."

25 When Jesus saw that a crowd was gathering fast, he spoke sternly to the evil spirit that had kept the boy from speaking or hearing. He said, "I order you to come out of the boy! Don't ever bother him again."

26 The spirit screamed and made the boy shake all over. Then it went out of him. The boy looked dead, and almost everyone said he was. **27** But Jesus took hold of his hand and helped him stand up.

28 After Jesus and the disciples had gone back home and were alone, they asked him, "Why couldn't we force out that demon?"

29 Jesus answered, "Only prayer can force out that kind of demon."

Jesus Again Speaks about His Death

30 Jesus left with his disciples and started through Galilee. He did not want anyone to know about it, **31** because he was teaching the disciples that the Son of Man would be handed over to people who would kill him. But three days later he would rise to life. **32** The disciples did not understand what Jesus meant, and they were afraid to ask.

Who Is the Greatest?

33 Jesus and his disciples went to his home in Capernaum. After they were inside the house, Jesus asked them, "What were you arguing about along the way?" **34** They had been arguing about which one of them was the greatest, and so they did not answer.

35 After Jesus sat down and told the twelve disciples to gather around him, he said, "If you want the place of honor, you must become a slave and serve others!"

36 Then Jesus had a child stand near him. He put his arm around the child and said, **37** "When you welcome even a child because of me, you welcome me. And when you welcome me, you welcome the one who sent me."

For or against Jesus

38 John said, "Teacher, we saw a man using your name to force demons out of people. But he wasn't one of us, and we told him to stop."

39 Jesus said to his disciples:

---

u **8.35** *life*: In verses 35-37 the same Greek word is translated "life," "yourself," and "soul."

Don't stop him! No one who works miracles in my name will soon turn and say something bad about me. 40 Anyone who isn't against us is for us. 41 And anyone who gives you a cup of water in my name, just because you belong to me, will surely be rewarded.

Temptations To Sin

42 It will be terrible for people who cause even one of my little followers to sin. Those people would be better off thrown into the ocean with a heavy stone tied around their necks. 43-44 So if your hand causes you to sin, cut it off! You would be better off to go into life crippled than to have two hands and be thrown into the fires of hell that never go out.v 45-46 If your foot causes you to sin, chop it off. You would be better off to go into life lame than to have two feet and be thrown into hell.w 47 If your eye causes you to sin, get rid of it. You would be better off to go into God's kingdom with only one eye than to have two eyes and be thrown into hell. 48 The worms there never die, and the fire never stops burning.

49 Everyone must be salted with fire.x

50 Salt is good. But if it no longer tastes like salt, how can it be made salty again? Have salt among you and live at peace with each other.

Teaching about Divorce

10 After Jesus left, he went to Judea and then on to the other side of the Jordan River. Once again large crowds came to him, and as usual, he taught them.

2 Some Pharisees wanted to test Jesus. So they came up to him and asked if it was right for a man to divorce his wife. 3 Jesus asked them, "What does the Law of Moses say about that?"

4 They answered, "Moses allows a man to write out divorce papers and send his wife away."

5 Jesus replied, "Moses gave you this law because you are so heartless. 6 But in the beginning God made a man and a woman. 7 That's why a man leaves his father and mother and gets married. 8 He becomes like one person with his wife. Then they are no longer two people, but one. 9 And no one should separate a couple that God has joined together."

10 When Jesus and his disciples were back in the house, they asked him about what he had said. 11 He told them, "A man who divorces his wife and marries someone else is unfaithful to his wife. 12 A woman who divorces her husband and marries again is also unfaithful."

Jesus Blesses Little Children

13 Some people brought their children to Jesus so that he could bless them by placing his hands on them. But his disciples told the people to stop bothering him.

14 When Jesus saw this, he became angry and said, "Let the children come to me! Don't try to stop them. Peo-

ple who are like these little children belong to the kingdom of God.y 15 I promise you that you cannot get into God's kingdom, unless you accept it the way a child does." 16 Then Jesus took the children in his arms and blessed them by placing his hands on them.

A Rich Man

17 As Jesus was walking down a road, a man ran up to him. He knelt down, and asked, "Good teacher, what can I do to have eternal life?"

18 Jesus replied, "Why do you call me good? Only God is good. 19 You know the commandments. 'Do not murder. Be faithful in marriage. Do not steal. Do not tell lies about others. Do not cheat. Respect your father and mother.' "

20 The man answered, "Teacher, I have obeyed all these commandments since I was a young man."

21 Jesus looked closely at the man. He liked him and said, "There's one thing you still need to do. Go sell everything you own. Give the money to the poor, and you will have riches in heaven. Then come with me."

22 When the man heard Jesus say this, he went away gloomy and sad because he was very rich.

23 Jesus looked around and said to his disciples, "It's hard for rich people to get into God's kingdom!" 24 The disciples were shocked to hear this. So Jesus told them again, "It's terribly hardz to get into God's kingdom! 25 In fact, it's easier for a camel to go through the eye of a needle than for a rich person to get into God's kingdom."

26 Jesus' disciples were even more amazed. They asked each other, "How can anyone ever be saved?"

27 Jesus looked at them and said, "There are some things that people cannot do, but God can do anything."

28 Peter replied, "Remember, we left everything to be your followers!"

29 Jesus told him:

You can be sure that anyone who gives up home or brothers or sisters or mother or father or children or land for me and for the good news 30 will be rewarded. In this world they will be given a hundred times as many houses and brothers and sisters and mothers and children and pieces of land, though they will also be mistreated. And in the world to come, they will have eternal life. 31 But many who are now first will be last, and many who are now last will be first.

Jesus Again Tells about His Death

32 The disciples were confused as Jesus led them toward Jerusalem, and his other followers were afraid. Once again, Jesus took the twelve disciples aside and told them what was going to happen to him. He said:

33 We are now on our way to Jerusalem where the Son of Man will be handed over to the chief priests and the teachers of the Law of Moses. They will sentence him to death and hand him over to foreigners, 34 who will make fun of him and spit on

---

v 9.43,44 *never go out*: Some manuscripts add, "The worms there never die, and the fire never stops burning."   w 9.45,46 *thrown into hell*: Some manuscripts add, "The worms there never die, and the fire never stops burning."   x 9.49 *salted with fire*: Some manuscripts add "and every sacrifice will be seasoned with salt." The verse may mean that Christ's followers must suffer because of their faith.
y 10.14 *People who are like these little children belong to the kingdom of God*: Or "The kingdom of God belongs to people who are like these little children."   z 10.24 *hard*: Some manuscripts add "for people who trust in their wealth." Others add "for the rich."

him. They will beat him and kill him. But three days later he will rise to life.

The Request of James and John

³⁵ James and John, the sons of Zebedee, came up to Jesus and asked, "Teacher, will you do us a favor?"

³⁶ Jesus asked them what they wanted, ³⁷ and they answered, "When you come into your glory, please let one of us sit at your right side and the other at your left."

³⁸ Jesus told them, "You don't really know what you're asking! Are you able to drink from the cup that I must soon drink from or be baptized as I must be baptized?"

³⁹ "Yes, we are!" James and John answered.

Then Jesus replied, "You certainly will drink from the cup from which I must drink. And you will be baptized just as I must! ⁴⁰ But it isn't for me to say who will sit at my right side and at my left. That is for God to decide."

⁴¹ When the ten other disciples heard this, they were angry with James and John. ⁴² But Jesus called the disciples together and said:

You know that those foreigners who call themselves kings like to order their people around. And their great leaders have full power over the people they rule. ⁴³ But don't act like them. If you want to be great, you must be the servant of all the others. ⁴⁴ And if you want to be first, you must be everyone's slave. ⁴⁵ The Son of Man did not come to be a slave master, but a slave who will give his life to rescue many people.

Jesus Heals Blind Bartimaeus

⁴⁶ Jesus and his disciples went to Jericho. And as they were leaving, they were followed by a large crowd. A blind beggar by the name of Bartimaeus son of Timaeus was sitting beside the road. ⁴⁷ When he heard that it was Jesus from Nazareth, he shouted, "Jesus, Son of David, have pity on me!" ⁴⁸ Many people told the man to stop, but he shouted even louder, "Son of David, have pity on me!"

⁴⁹ Jesus stopped and said, "Call him over!"

They called out to the blind man and said, "Don't be afraid! Come on! He is calling for you." ⁵⁰ The man threw off his coat as he jumped up and ran to Jesus.

⁵¹ Jesus asked, "What do you want me to do for you?"

The blind man answered, "Master,ᵃ I want to see!"

⁵² Jesus told him, "You may go. Your eyes are healed because of your faith."

Right away the man could see, and he went down the road with Jesus.

Jesus Enters Jerusalem

11 Jesus and his disciples reached Bethphage and Bethany near the Mount of Olives. When they were getting close to Jerusalem, Jesus sent two of them on ahead. ² He told them, "Go into the next village. As soon as you enter it, you will find a young donkey that has never been ridden. Untie the donkey and bring it here. ³ If anyone asks why you are doing that, say, 'The Lordᵇ needs it and will soon bring it back.' "

⁴ The disciples left and found the donkey tied near a door that faced the street. While they were untying it, ⁵ some of the people standing there asked, "Why are you untying the donkey?" ⁶ They told them what Jesus had said, and the people let them take it.

⁷ The disciples led the donkey to Jesus. They put some of their clothes on its back, and Jesus got on. ⁸ Many people spread clothes on the road, while others went to cut branches from the fields.

⁹ In front of Jesus and behind him, people went along shouting,

"Hooray!
God bless the one who comes
in the name of the Lord!
¹⁰ God bless the coming kingdom
of our ancestor David.
Hooray for God
in heaven above!"

¹¹ After Jesus had gone to Jerusalem, he went into the temple and looked around at everything. But since it was already late in the day, he went back to Bethany with the twelve disciples.

Jesus Puts a Curse on a Fig Tree

¹² When Jesus and his disciples left Bethany the next morning, he was hungry. ¹³ From a distance Jesus saw a fig tree covered with leaves, and he went to see if there were any figs on the tree. But there were not any, because it wasn't the season for figs. ¹⁴ So Jesus said to the tree, "Never again will anyone eat fruit from this tree!" The disciples heard him say this.

Jesus in the Temple

¹⁵ After Jesus and his disciples reached Jerusalem, he went into the temple and began chasing out everyone who was selling and buying. He turned over the tables of the moneychangers and the benches of those who were selling doves. ¹⁶ Jesus would not let anyone carry things through the temple. ¹⁷ Then he taught the people and said, "The Scriptures say, 'My house should be called a place of worship for all nations.' But you have made it a place where robbers hide!"

¹⁸ The chief priests and the teachers of the Law of Moses heard what Jesus said, and they started looking for a way to kill him. They were afraid of him, because the crowds were completely amazed at his teaching.

¹⁹ That evening, Jesus and the disciples went outside the city.

A Lesson from the Fig Tree

²⁰ As the disciples walked past the fig tree the next morning, they noticed that it was completely dried up, roots and all. ²¹ Peter remembered what Jesus had said to the tree. Then Peter said, "Teacher, look! The tree you put a curse on has dried up."

²² Jesus told his disciples:

Have faith in God! ²³ If you have faith in God and don't doubt, you can tell this mountain to get up and jump into the sea, and it will. ²⁴ Everything you ask for in prayer will be yours, if you only have faith.

ᵃ **10.51** *Master*: A Hebrew word that may also mean "Teacher."   ᵇ **11.3** *The Lord*: Or "The master of the donkey."

25-26 Whenever you stand up to pray, you must forgive what others have done to you. Then your Father in heaven will forgive your sins.*c*

A Question about Jesus' Authority

27 Jesus and his disciples returned to Jerusalem. And as he was walking through the temple, the chief priests, the nation's leaders, and the teachers of the Law of Moses came over to him. **28** They asked, "What right do you have to do these things? Who gave you this authority?"

29 Jesus answered, "I have just one question to ask you. If you answer it, I will tell you where I got the right to do these things. **30** Who gave John the right to baptize? Was it God in heaven or merely some human being?"

31 They thought it over and said to each other, "We can't say that God gave John this right. Jesus will ask us why we didn't believe John. **32** On the other hand, these people think that John was a prophet. So we can't say that it was merely some human who gave John the right to baptize."

They were afraid of the crowd **33** and told Jesus, "We don't know."

Jesus replied, "Then I won't tell you who gave me the right to do what I do."

Renters of a Vineyard

12 Jesus then told them this story:
A farmer once planted a vineyard. He built a wall around it and dug a pit to crush the grapes in. He also built a lookout tower. Then he rented out his vineyard and left the country.

2 When it was harvest time, he sent a servant to get his share of the grapes. **3** The renters grabbed the servant. They beat him up and sent him away without a thing.

4 The owner sent another servant, but the renters beat him on the head and insulted him terribly. **5** Then the man sent another servant, and they killed him. He kept sending servant after servant. They beat some of them and killed others.

6 The owner had a son he loved very much. Finally, he sent his son to the renters because he thought they would respect him. **7** But they said to themselves, "Someday he will own this vineyard. Let's kill him! That way we can have it all for ourselves." **8** So they grabbed the owner's son and killed him. Then they threw his body out of the vineyard.

9 Jesus asked, "What do you think the owner of the vineyard will do? He will come and kill those renters and let someone else have his vineyard. **10** You surely know that the Scriptures say,

'The stone that the builders
    tossed aside
is now the most important
    stone of all.
11 This is something
    the Lord has done,
        and it is amazing to us.' "

12 The leaders knew that Jesus was really talking about

them, and they wanted to arrest him. But because they were afraid of the crowd, they let him alone and left.

Paying Taxes

13 The Pharisees got together with Herod's followers. Then they sent some men to trick Jesus into saying something wrong. **14** They went to him and said, "Teacher, we know that you are honest. You treat everyone with the same respect, no matter who they are. And you teach the truth about what God wants people to do. Tell us, should we pay taxes to the Emperor or not?"

15 Jesus knew what they were up to, and he said, "Why are you trying to test me? Show me a coin!"

16 They brought him a silver coin, and he asked, "Whose picture and name are on it?"

"The Emperor's," they answered.

17 Then Jesus told them, "Give the Emperor what belongs to him and give God what belongs to God." The men were amazed at Jesus.

Life in the Future World

18 The Sadducees did not believe that people would rise to life after death. So some of them came to Jesus and said:

19 Teacher, Moses wrote that if a married man dies and has no children, his brother should marry the widow. Their first son would then be thought of as the son of the dead brother. **20** There were once seven brothers. The first one married, but died without having any children. **21** The second brother married his brother's widow, and he also died without having children. The same thing happened to the third brother, **22** and finally to all seven brothers. At last the woman died. **23** When God raises people from death, whose wife will this woman be? After all, she had been married to all seven brothers.

24 Jesus answered:

You are completely wrong! You don't know what the Scriptures teach. And you don't know anything about the power of God. **25** When God raises people to life, they won't marry. They will be like the angels in heaven. **26** You surely know about people being raised to life. You know that in the story about Moses and the burning bush, God said, "I am the God worshiped by Abraham, Isaac, and Jacob." **27** He isn't the God of the dead, but of the living. You Sadducees are all wrong.

The Most Important Commandment

28 One of the teachers of the Law of Moses came up while Jesus and the Sadducees were arguing. When he heard Jesus give a good answer, he asked him, "What is the most important commandment?"

29 Jesus answered, "The most important one says: 'People of Israel, you have only one Lord and God. **30** You must love him with all your heart, soul, mind, and strength.' **31** The second most important commandment says: 'Love others as much as you love yourself.' No other commandment is more important than these."

32 The man replied, "Teacher, you are certainly right to

---

c **11.25,26** *your sins*: Some manuscripts add, "But if you do not forgive others, God will not forgive you."

say there is only one God. ³³ It is also true that we must love God with all our heart, mind, and strength, and that we must love others as much as we love ourselves. These commandments are more important than all the sacrifices and offerings that we could possibly make."

³⁴ When Jesus saw that the man had given a sensible answer, he told him, "You are not far from God's kingdom." After this, no one dared ask Jesus any more questions.

About David's Son

³⁵ As Jesus was teaching in the temple, he said, "How can the teachers of the Law of Moses say that the Messiah will come from the family of King David? ³⁶ The Holy Spirit led David to say,

'The Lord said to my Lord:
Sit at my right side
until I make your enemies
into a footstool for you.'

³⁷ If David called the Messiah his Lord, how can the Messiah be his son?"

The large crowd enjoyed listening to Jesus teach.

Jesus Condemns the Pharisees and the Teachers of the Law of Moses

³⁸ As Jesus was teaching, he said:

Guard against the teachers of the Law of Moses! They love to walk around in long robes and be greeted in the market. ³⁹ They like the front seats in the meeting places and the best seats at banquets. ⁴⁰ But they cheat widows out of their homes and pray long prayers just to show off. They will be punished most of all.

A Widow's Offering

⁴¹ Jesus was sitting in the temple near the offering box and watching people put in their gifts. He noticed that many rich people were giving a lot of money. ⁴² Finally, a poor widow came up and put in two coins that were worth only a few pennies. ⁴³ Jesus told his disciples to gather around him. Then he said:

I tell you that this poor widow has put in more than all the others. ⁴⁴ Everyone else gave what they didn't need. But she is very poor and gave everything she had. Now she doesn't have a cent to live on.

The Temple Will Be Destroyed

13 As Jesus was leaving the temple, one of his disciples said to him, "Teacher, look at these beautiful stones and wonderful buildings!"

² Jesus replied, "Do you see these huge buildings? They will certainly be torn down! Not one stone will be left in place."

Warning about Trouble

³ Later, as Jesus was sitting on the Mount of Olives across from the temple, Peter, James, John, and Andrew came to him in private. ⁴ They asked, "When will these things happen? What will be the sign that they are about to take place?"

⁵ Jesus answered:

Watch out and don't let anyone fool you! ⁶ Many will come and claim to be me. They will use my name and fool many people.

⁷ When you hear about wars and threats of wars, don't be afraid. These things will have to happen first, but that isn't the end. ⁸ Nations and kingdoms will go to war against each other. There will be earthquakes in many places, and people will starve to death. But this is just the beginning of troubles.

⁹ Be on your guard! You will be taken to courts and beaten with whips in their meeting places. And because of me, you will have to stand before rulers and kings to tell about your faith. ¹⁰ But before the end comes, the good news must be preached to all nations.

¹¹ When you are arrested, don't worry about what you will say. You will be given the right words when the time comes. But you will not really be the ones speaking. Your words will come from the Holy Spirit.

¹² Brothers and sisters will betray each other and have each other put to death. Parents will betray their own children, and children will turn against their parents and have them killed. ¹³ Everyone will hate you because of me. But if you keep on being faithful right to the end, you will be saved.

The Horrible Thing

¹⁴ Someday you will see that "Horrible Thing" where it should not be. Everyone who reads this must try to understand! If you are living in Judea at that time, run to the mountains. ¹⁵ If you are on the roof of your house, don't go inside to get anything. ¹⁶ If you are out in the field, don't go back for your coat. ¹⁷ It will be an awful time for women who are expecting babies or nursing young children. ¹⁸ Pray that it won't happen in winter. ¹⁹ This will be the worst time of suffering since God created the world, and nothing this terrible will ever happen again. ²⁰ If the Lord doesn't make the time shorter, no one will be left alive. But because of his chosen and special ones, he will make the time shorter.

²¹ If someone should say, "Here is the Messiah!" or "There he is!" don't believe it. ²² False messiahs and false prophets will come and work miracles and signs. They will even try to fool God's chosen ones. ²³ But be on your guard! That's why I am telling you these things now.

When the Son of Man Appears

²⁴ In those days, right after that time of suffering,

"The sun will become dark,
and the moon
will no longer shine.
²⁵ The stars will fall,
and the powers in the sky
will be shaken."

²⁶ Then the Son of Man will be seen coming in the clouds with great power and glory. ²⁷ He will send his angels to gather his chosen ones from all over the earth.

A Lesson from a Fig Tree

28 Learn a lesson from a fig tree. When its branches sprout and start putting out leaves, you know summer is near. **29** So when you see all these things happening, you will know that the time has almost come.[d] **30** You can be sure that some of the people of this generation will still be alive when all this happens. **31** The sky and the earth will not last forever, but my words will.

No One Knows the Day or Time

32 No one knows the day or the time. The angels in heaven don't know, and the Son himself doesn't know. Only the Father knows. **33** So watch out and be ready! You don't know when the time will come. **34** It is like what happens when a man goes away for a while and places his servants in charge of everything. He tells each of them what to do, and he orders the guard to keep alert. **35** So be alert! You don't know when the master of the house will come back. It could be in the evening or at midnight or before dawn or in the morning. **36** But if he comes suddenly, don't let him find you asleep. **37** I tell everyone just what I have told you. Be alert!

A Plot To Kill Jesus

14 It was now two days before Passover and the Festival of Thin Bread. The chief priests and the teachers of the Law of Moses were planning how they could sneak around and have Jesus arrested and put to death. **2** They were saying, "We must not do it during the festival, because the people will riot."

At Bethany

3 Jesus was eating in Bethany at the home of Simon, who once had leprosy,[e] when a woman came in with a very expensive bottle of sweet-smelling perfume. After breaking it open, she poured the perfume on Jesus' head. **4** This made some of the guests angry, and they complained, "Why such a waste? **5** We could have sold this perfume for more than three hundred silver coins and given the money to the poor!" So they started saying cruel things to the woman.

6 But Jesus said:

Leave her alone! Why are you bothering her? She has done a beautiful thing for me. **7** You will always have the poor with you. And whenever you want to, you can give to them. But you won't always have me here with you. **8** She has done all she could by pouring perfume on my body to prepare it for burial. **9** You may be sure that wherever the good news is told all over the world, people will remember what she has done. And they will tell others.

Judas and the Chief Priests

10 Judas Iscariot was one of the twelve disciples. He went to the chief priests and offered to help them arrest Jesus. **11** They were glad to hear this, and they promised to pay him. So Judas started looking for a good chance to betray Jesus.

Jesus Eats with His Disciples

12 It was the first day of the Festival of Thin Bread, and the Passover lambs were being killed. Jesus' disciples asked him, "Where do you want us to prepare the Passover meal?"

13 Jesus said to two of the disciples, "Go into the city, where you will meet a man carrying a jar of water. Follow him, **14** and when he goes into a house, say to the owner, 'Our teacher wants to know if you have a room where he can eat the Passover meal with his disciples.' **15** The owner will take you upstairs and show you a large room furnished and ready for you to use. Prepare the meal there."

16 The two disciples went into the city and found everything just as Jesus had told them. So they prepared the Passover meal.

17-18 While Jesus and the twelve disciples were eating together that evening, he said, "The one who will betray me is now eating with me."

19 This made the disciples sad, and one after another they said to Jesus, "You surely don't mean me!"

20 He answered, "It is one of you twelve men who is eating from this dish with me. **21** The Son of Man will die, just as the Scriptures say. But it is going to be terrible for the one who betrays me. That man would be better off if he had never been born."

The Lord's Supper

22 During the meal Jesus took some bread in his hands. He blessed the bread and broke it. Then he gave it to his disciples and said, "Take this. It is my body."

23 Jesus picked up a cup of wine and gave thanks to God. He gave it to his disciples, and they all drank some. **24** Then he said, "This is my blood, which is poured out for many people, and with it God makes his agreement. **25** From now on I will not drink any wine, until I drink new wine in God's kingdom." **26** Then they sang a hymn and went out to the Mount of Olives.

Peter's Promise

27 Jesus said to his disciples, "All of you will reject me, as the Scriptures say,

'I will strike down
     the shepherd,
   and the sheep
      will be scattered.'

28 But after I am raised to life, I will go ahead of you to Galilee."

29 Peter spoke up, "Even if all the others reject you, I never will!"

30 Jesus replied, "This very night before a rooster crows twice, you will say three times that you don't know me."

31 But Peter was so sure of himself that he said, "Even if I have to die with you, I will never say that I don't know you!"

All the others said the same thing.

Jesus Prays

32 Jesus went with his disciples to a place called Gethsemane, and he told them, "Sit here while I pray."

---

d 13.29 *the time has almost come*: Or "he (that is, the Son of Man) will soon be here."   **e 14.3** *leprosy*: In biblical times the word "leprosy" was used for many different skin diseases.

33 Jesus took along Peter, James, and John. He was sad and troubled and **34** told them, "I am so sad that I feel as if I am dying. Stay here and keep awake with me."

35-36 Jesus walked on a little way. Then he knelt down on the ground and prayed, "Father,/ if it is possible, don't let this happen to me! Father, you can do anything. Don't make me suffer by having me drink from this cup. But do what you want, and not what I want."

37 When Jesus came back and found the disciples sleeping, he said to Simon Peter, "Are you asleep? Can't you stay awake for just one hour? **38** Stay awake and pray that you won't be tested. You want to do what is right, but you are weak."

39 Jesus went back and prayed the same prayer. **40** But when he returned to the disciples, he found them sleeping again. They simply could not keep their eyes open, and they did not know what to say.

41 When Jesus returned to the disciples the third time, he said, "Are you still sleeping and resting?ᵍ Enough of that! The time has come for the Son of Man to be handed over to sinners. **42** Get up! Let's go. The one who will betray me is already here."

Jesus Is Arrested

43 Jesus was still speaking, when Judas the betrayer came up. He was one of the twelve disciples, and a mob of men armed with swords and clubs were with him. They had been sent by the chief priests, the nation's leaders, and the teachers of the Law of Moses. **44** Judas had told them ahead of time, "Arrest the man I greet with a kiss. Tie him up tight and lead him away."

45 Judas walked right up to Jesus and said, "Teacher!" Then Judas kissed him, **46** and the men grabbed Jesus and arrested him.

47 Someone standing there pulled out a sword. He struck the servant of the high priest and cut off his ear.

48 Jesus said to the mob, "Why do you come with swords and clubs to arrest me like a criminal? **49** Day after day I was with you and taught in the temple, and you didn't arrest me. But what the Scriptures say must come true."

50 All of Jesus' disciples ran off and left him. **51** One of them was a young man who was wearing only a linen cloth. And when the men grabbed him, **52** he left the cloth behind and ran away naked.

Jesus Is Questioned by the Council

53 Jesus was led off to the high priest. Then the chief priests, the nation's leaders, and the teachers of the Law of Moses all met together. **54** Peter had followed at a distance. And when he reached the courtyard of the high priest's house, he sat down with the guards to warm himself beside a fire.

55 The chief priests and the whole council tried to find someone to accuse Jesus of a crime, so they could put him to death. But they could not find anyone to accuse him. **56** Many people did tell lies against Jesus, but they did not agree on what they said. **57** Finally, some men stood up and lied about him. They said, **58** "We heard him say he would tear down this temple that we built. He also claimed that in three days he would build another one without any help." **59** But even then they did not agree on what they said.

60 The high priest stood up in the council and asked Jesus, "Why don't you say something in your own defense? Don't you hear the charges they are making against you?" **61** But Jesus kept quiet and did not say a word. The high priest asked him another question, "Are you the Messiah, the Son of the glorious God?"

62 "Yes, I am!" Jesus answered.

> "Soon you will see
> the Son of Man
> sitting at the right side
> of God All-Powerful,
> and coming with the clouds
> of heaven."

63 At once the high priest ripped his robe apart and shouted, "Why do we need more witnesses? **64** You heard him claim to be God! What is your decision?" They all agreed that he should be put to death.

65 Some of the people started spitting on Jesus. They blindfolded him, hit him with their fists, and said, "Tell us who hit you!" Then the guards took charge of Jesus and beat him.

Peter Says He Doesn't Know Jesus

66 While Peter was still in the courtyard, a servant girl of the high priest came up **67** and saw Peter warming himself by the fire. She stared at him and said, "You were with Jesus from Nazareth!"

68 Peter replied, "That isn't true! I don't know what you're talking about. I don't have any idea what you mean." He went out to the gate, and a rooster crowed.ʰ

69 The servant girl saw Peter again and said to the people standing there, "This man is one of them!"

70 "No, I'm not!" Peter replied.

A little while later some of the people said to Peter, "You certainly are one of them. You're a Galilean!"

71 This time Peter began to curse and swear, "I don't even know the man you're talking about!"

72 Right away the rooster crowed a second time. Then Peter remembered that Jesus had told him, "Before a rooster crows twice, you will say three times that you don't know me." So Peter started crying.

Pilate Questions Jesus

15 Early the next morning the chief priests, the nation's leaders, and the teachers of the Law of Moses met together with the whole Jewish council. They tied up Jesus and led him off to Pilate.

2 He asked Jesus, "Are you the king of the Jews?"

"Those are your words," Jesus answered.

3 The chief priests brought many charges against Jesus. **4** Then Pilate questioned him again, "Don't you have anything to say? Don't you hear what crimes they say you have done?" **5** But Jesus did not answer, and Pilate was amazed.

The Death Sentence

6 During Passover, Pilate always freed one prisoner chosen by the people. **7** And at that time there was a prisoner named Barabbas. He and some others had been ar-

---

ᶠ **14.35,36** *Father*: The Greek text has "Abba," which is an Aramaic word meaning "father."   ᵍ **14.41** *Are you still sleeping and resting*: Or "You may as well keep on sleeping and resting."   ʰ **14.68** *a rooster crowed*: These words are not in some manuscripts.

rested for murder during a riot. 8 The crowd now came and asked Pilate to set a prisoner free, just as he usually did.

9 Pilate asked them, "Do you want me to free the king of the Jews?" 10 Pilate knew that the chief priests had brought Jesus to him because they were jealous.

11 But the chief priests told the crowd to ask Pilate to free Barabbas.

12 Then Pilate asked the crowd, "What do you want me to do with this man you say is*i* the king of the Jews?"

13 They yelled, "Nail him to a cross!"

14 Pilate asked, "But what crime has he done?"

"Nail him to a cross!" they yelled even louder.

15 Pilate wanted to please the crowd. So he set Barabbas free. Then he ordered his soldiers to beat Jesus with a whip and nail him to a cross.

Soldiers Make Fun of Jesus

16 The soldiers led Jesus inside the courtyard of the fortress and called together the rest of the troops. 17 They put a purple robe on him, and on his head they placed a crown that they had made out of thorn branches. 18 They made fun of Jesus and shouted, "Hey, you king of the Jews!" 19 Then they beat him on the head with a stick. They spit on him and knelt down and pretended to worship him.

20 When the soldiers had finished making fun of Jesus, they took off the purple robe. They put his own clothes back on him and led him off to be nailed to a cross. 21 Simon from Cyrene happened to be coming in from a farm, and they forced him to carry Jesus' cross. Simon was the father of Alexander and Rufus.

Jesus Is Nailed to a Cross

22 The soldiers took Jesus to Golgotha, which means "Place of a Skull." 23 There they gave him some wine mixed with a drug to ease the pain, but he refused to drink it.

24 They nailed Jesus to a cross and gambled to see who would get his clothes. 25 It was about nine o'clock in the morning when they nailed him to the cross. 26 On it was a sign that told why he was nailed there. It read, "This is the King of the Jews." 27-28 The soldiers also nailed two criminals on crosses, one to the right of Jesus and the other to his left.*j*

29 People who passed by said terrible things about Jesus. They shook their heads and shouted, "Ha! So you're the one who claimed you could tear down the temple and build it again in three days. 30 Save yourself and come down from the cross!"

31 The chief priests and the teachers of the Law of Moses also made fun of Jesus. They said to each other, "He saved others, but he can't save himself. 32 If he is the Messiah, the king of Israel, let him come down from the cross! Then we will see and believe." The two criminals also said cruel things to Jesus.

The Death of Jesus

33 About noon the sky turned dark and stayed that way until around three o'clock. 34 Then about that time Jesus shouted, "Eloi, Eloi, lema sabachthani?"*k* which means, "My God, my God, why have you deserted me?"

35 Some of the people standing there heard Jesus and said, "He is calling for Elijah." 36 One of them ran and grabbed a sponge. After he had soaked it in wine, he put it on a stick and held it up to Jesus. He said, "Let's wait and see if Elijah will come and take him down!" 37 Jesus shouted and then died.

38 At once the curtain in the temple tore in two from top to bottom.

39 A Roman army officer was standing in front of Jesus. When the officer saw how Jesus died, he said, "This man really was the Son of God!"

40-41 Some women were looking on from a distance. They had come with Jesus to Jerusalem. But even before this they had been his followers and had helped him while he was in Galilee. Mary Magdalene and Mary the mother of the younger James and of Joseph were two of these women. Salome was also one of them.

Jesus Is Buried

42 It was now the evening before the Sabbath, and the Jewish people were getting ready for that sacred day. 43 A man named Joseph from Arimathea was brave enough to ask Pilate for the body of Jesus. Joseph was a highly respected member of the Jewish council, and he was also waiting for God's kingdom to come.

44 Pilate was surprised to hear that Jesus was already dead, and he called in the army officer to find out if Jesus had been dead very long. 45 After the officer told him, Pilate let Joseph have Jesus' body.

46 Joseph bought a linen cloth and took the body down from the cross. He had it wrapped in the cloth, and he put it in a tomb that had been cut into solid rock. Then he rolled a big stone against the entrance to the tomb.

47 Mary Magdalene and Mary the mother of Joseph were watching and saw where the body was placed.

Jesus Is Alive

16 After the Sabbath, Mary Magdalene, Salome, and Mary the mother of James bought some spices to put on Jesus' body. 2 Very early on Sunday morning, just as the sun was coming up, they went to the tomb. 3 On their way, they were asking one another, "Who will roll the stone away from the entrance for us?" 4 But when they looked, they saw that the stone had already been rolled away. And it was a huge stone!

5 The women went into the tomb, and on the right side they saw a young man in a white robe sitting there. They were alarmed.

6 The man said, "Don't be alarmed! You are looking for Jesus from Nazareth, who was nailed to a cross. God has raised him to life, and he isn't here. You can see the place where they put his body. 7 Now go and tell his disciples, and especially Peter, that he will go ahead of you to Galilee. You will see him there, just as he told you."

8 When the women ran from the tomb, they were confused and shaking all over. They were too afraid to tell anyone what had happened.

---

*i***15.12** *this man you say is*: These words are not in some manuscripts. *j***15.27-28** *left*: Some manuscripts add, "So the Scriptures came true which say, 'He was accused of being a criminal.' " *k***15.34** *Eloi ... sabachthani*: These words are in Aramaic, a language spoken in Palestine during the time of Jesus.

ONE OLD ENDING
TO MARK'S GOSPEL[l]

Jesus Appears to Mary Magdalene

⁹ Very early on the first day of the week, after Jesus had risen to life, he appeared to Mary Magdalene. Earlier he had forced seven demons out of her. ¹⁰ She left and told his friends, who were crying and mourning. ¹¹ Even though they heard that Jesus was alive and that Mary had seen him, they would not believe it.

Jesus Appears to Two Disciples

¹² Later, Jesus appeared in another form to two disciples, as they were on their way out of the city. ¹³ But when these disciples told what had happened, the others would not believe.

What Jesus' Followers Must Do

¹⁴ Afterwards, Jesus appeared to his eleven disciples as they were eating. He scolded them because they were too stubborn to believe the ones who had seen him after he had been raised to life. ¹⁵ Then he told them:

Go and preach the good news to everyone in the world. ¹⁶ Anyone who believes me and is baptized will be saved. But anyone who refuses to believe me will be condemned. ¹⁷ Everyone who believes me will be able to do wonderful things. By using my name they will force out demons, and they will speak new languages. ¹⁸ They will handle snakes and will drink poison and not be hurt. They will also heal sick people by placing their hands on them.

Jesus Returns to Heaven

¹⁹ After the Lord Jesus had said these things to the disciples, he was taken back up to heaven where he sat down at the right side of God. ²⁰ Then the disciples left and preached everywhere. The Lord was with them, and the miracles they worked proved that their message was true.

ANOTHER OLD ENDING
TO MARK'S GOSPEL[m]

⁹⁻¹⁰ The women quickly told Peter and his friends what had happened. Later, Jesus sent the disciples to the east and to the west with his sacred and everlasting message of how people can be saved forever.

---

[l]**16.9** *One Old Ending to Mark's Gospel*: Verses 9-20 are not in some manuscripts. [m]**16.9,10** *Another Old Ending to Mark's Gospel*: Some manuscripts and early translations have both this shorter ending and the longer one (verses 9-20).

LUKE

1 Many people have tried to tell the story of what God has done among us. ² They wrote what we had been told by the ones who were there in the beginning and saw what happened. ³ So I made a careful study[a] of everything and then decided to write and tell you exactly what took place. Honorable Theophilus, ⁴ I have done this to let you know the truth about what you have heard.

An Angel Tells about the Birth of John

⁵ When Herod was king of Judea, there was a priest by the name of Zechariah from the priestly group of Abijah. His wife Elizabeth was from the family of Aaron. ⁶ Both of them were good people and pleased the Lord God by obeying all that he had commanded. ⁷ But they did not have children. Elizabeth could not have any, and both Zechariah and Elizabeth were already old.

⁸ One day Zechariah's group of priests were on duty, and he was serving God as a priest. ⁹ According to the custom of the priests, he had been chosen to go into the Lord's temple that day and to burn incense, ¹⁰ while the people stood outside praying.

¹¹ All at once an angel from the Lord appeared to Zechariah at the right side of the altar. ¹² Zechariah was confused and afraid when he saw the angel. ¹³ But the angel told him:

Don't be afraid, Zechariah! God has heard your prayers. Your wife Elizabeth will have a son, and you must name him John. ¹⁴ His birth will make you very happy, and many people will be glad. ¹⁵ Your son will be a great servant of the Lord. He must never drink wine or beer, and the power of the Holy Spirit will be with him from the time he is born.

¹⁶ John will lead many people in Israel to turn back to the Lord their God. ¹⁷ He will go ahead of the Lord with the same power and spirit that Elijah had. And because of John, parents will be more thoughtful of their children. And people who now disobey God will begin to think as they ought to.

---

[a]**1.3** *a careful study*: Or "a study from the beginning."

That is how John will get people ready for the Lord.

18 Zechariah said to the angel, "How will I know this is going to happen? My wife and I are both very old."

19 The angel answered, "I am Gabriel, God's servant, and I was sent to tell you this good news. **20** You have not believed what I have said. So you will not be able to say a thing until all this happens. But everything will take place when it is supposed to."

21 The crowd was waiting for Zechariah and kept wondering why he was staying so long in the temple. **22** When he did come out, he could not speak, and they knew he had seen a vision. He motioned to them with his hands, but did not say a thing.

23 When Zechariah's time of service in the temple was over, he went home. **24** Soon after that, his wife was expecting a baby, and for five months she did not leave the house. She said to herself, **25** "What the Lord has done for me will keep people from looking down on me."

An Angel Tells about the Birth of Jesus

26 One month later God sent the angel Gabriel to the town of Nazareth in Galilee **27** with a message for a virgin named Mary. She was engaged to Joseph from the family of King David. **28** The angel greeted Mary and said, "You are truly blessed! The Lord is with you."

29 Mary was confused by the angel's words and wondered what they meant. **30** Then the angel told Mary, "Don't be afraid! God is pleased with you, **31** and you will have a son. His name will be Jesus. **32** He will be great and will be called the Son of God Most High. The Lord God will make him king, as his ancestor David was. **33** He will rule the people of Israel forever, and his kingdom will never end."

34 Mary asked the angel, "How can this happen? I am not married!"

35 The angel answered, "The Holy Spirit will come down to you, and God's power will come over you. So your child will be called the holy Son of God. **36** Your relative Elizabeth is also going to have a son, even though she is old. No one thought she could ever have a baby, but in three months she will have a son. **37** Nothing is impossible for God!"

38 Mary said, "I am the Lord's servant! Let it happen as you have said." And the angel left her.

Mary Visits Elizabeth

39 A short time later Mary hurried to a town in the hill country of Judea. **40** She went into Zechariah's home, where she greeted Elizabeth. **41** When Elizabeth heard Mary's greeting, her baby moved within her.

The Holy Spirit came upon Elizabeth. **42** Then in a loud voice she said to Mary:

God has blessed you more than any other woman! He has also blessed the child you will have. **43** Why should the mother of my Lord come to me? **44** As soon as I heard your greeting, my baby became happy and moved within me. **45** The Lord has blessed you because you believed that he will keep his promise.

Mary's Song of Praise

46 Mary said:

With all my heart
I praise the Lord,
47 and I am glad
because of God my Savior.
48 He cares for me,
his humble servant.
From now on,
all people will say
God has blessed me.
49 God All-Powerful has done
great things for me,
and his name is holy.
50 He always shows mercy
to everyone
who worships him.
51 The Lord has used
his powerful arm
to scatter those
who are proud.
52 He drags strong rulers
from their thrones
and puts humble people
in places of power.
53 God gives the hungry
good things to eat,
and sends the rich away
with nothing.
54 He helps his servant Israel
and is always merciful
to his people.
55 The Lord made this promise
to our ancestors,
to Abraham and his family
forever!

56 Mary stayed with Elizabeth about three months. Then she went back home.

The Birth of John the Baptist

57 When Elizabeth's son was born, **58** her neighbors and relatives heard how kind the Lord had been to her, and they too were glad.

59 Eight days later they did for the child what the Law of Moses commands. They were going to name him Zechariah, after his father. **60** But Elizabeth said, "No! His name is John."

61 The people argued, "No one in your family has ever been named John." **62** So they motioned to Zechariah to find out what he wanted to name his son.

63 Zechariah asked for a writing tablet. Then he wrote, "His name is John." Everyone was amazed. **64** Right away, Zechariah started speaking and praising God.

65 All the neighbors were frightened because of what had happened, and everywhere in the hill country people kept talking about these things. **66** Everyone who heard about this wondered what this child would grow up to be. They knew that the Lord was with him.

Zechariah Praises the Lord

67 The Holy Spirit came upon Zechariah, and he began to speak:

68 Praise the Lord,
the God of Israel!

He has come
    to save his people.
69 Our God has given us
    a mighty Savior*b*
from the family
    of David his servant.
70 Long ago the Lord promised
    by the words
    of his holy prophets
71 to save us from our enemies
    and from everyone
    who hates us.
72 God said he would be kind
    to our people and keep
    his sacred promise.
73 He told our ancestor Abraham
74 that he would rescue us
    from our enemies.
Then we could serve him
    without fear,
75 by being holy and good
    as long as we live.

76 You, my son, will be called
    a prophet of God
    in heaven above.
You will go ahead of the Lord
    to get everything ready
    for him.
77 You will tell his people
    that they can be saved
    when their sins
    are forgiven.
78 God's love and kindness
    will shine upon us
    like the sun that rises
    in the sky.*c*
79 On us who live
    in the dark shadow
    of death
this light will shine
    to guide us
    into a life of peace.

80 As John grew up, God's Spirit gave him great power. John lived in the desert until the time he was sent to the people of Israel.

The Birth of Jesus

2 About that time Emperor Augustus gave orders for the names of all the people to be listed in record books. 2 These first records were made when Quirinius was governor of Syria.

3 Everyone had to go to their own hometown to be listed. 4 So Joseph had to leave Nazareth in Galilee and go to Bethlehem in Judea. Long ago Bethlehem had been King David's hometown, and Joseph went there because he was from David's family.

5 Mary was engaged to Joseph and traveled with him to Bethlehem. She was soon going to have a baby, 6 and while they were there, 7 she gave birth to her first-born son. She dressed him in baby clothes*d* and laid him on a bed of hay, because there was no room for them in the inn.

The Shepherds

8 That night in the fields near Bethlehem some shepherds were guarding their sheep. 9 All at once an angel came down to them from the Lord, and the brightness of the Lord's glory flashed around them. The shepherds were frightened. 10 But the angel said, "Don't be afraid! I have good news for you, which will make everyone happy. 11 This very day in King David's hometown a Savior was born for you. He is Christ the Lord. 12 You will know who he is, because you will find him dressed in baby clothes and lying on a bed of hay."

13 Suddenly many other angels came down from heaven and joined in praising God. They said:

14 "Praise God in heaven!
    Peace on earth to everyone
    who pleases God."

15 After the angels had left and gone back to heaven, the shepherds said to each other, "Let's go to Bethlehem and see what the Lord has told us about." 16 They hurried off and found Mary and Joseph, and they saw the baby lying on a bed of hay.

17 When the shepherds saw Jesus, they told his parents what the angel had said about him. 18 Everyone listened and was surprised. 19 But Mary kept thinking about all this and wondering what it meant.

20 As the shepherds returned to their sheep, they were praising God and saying wonderful things about him. Everything they had seen and heard was just as the angel had said.

21 Eight days later Jesus' parents did for him what the Law of Moses commands. And they named him Jesus, just as the angel had told Mary when he promised she would have a baby.

Simeon Praises the Lord

22 The time came for Mary and Joseph to do what the Law of Moses says a mother is supposed to do after her baby is born.

They took Jesus to the temple in Jerusalem and presented him to the Lord, 23 just as the Law of the Lord says, "Each first-born baby boy belongs to the Lord." 24 The Law of the Lord also says that parents have to offer a sacrifice, giving at least a pair of doves or two young pigeons. So that is what Mary and Joseph did.

25 At this time a man named Simeon was living in Jerusalem. Simeon was a good man. He loved God and was waiting for God to save the people of Israel. God's Spirit came to him 26 and told him that he would not die until he had seen Christ the Lord.

27 When Mary and Joseph brought Jesus to the temple to do what the Law of Moses says should be done for a new

---

b **1.69** *a mighty Savior*: The Greek text has "a horn of salvation." In the Scriptures animal horns are often a symbol of great strength.
c **1.78** *like the sun that rises in the sky*: Or "like the Messiah coming from heaven."   *d* **2.7** *dressed him in baby clothes*: The Greek text has "wrapped him in wide strips of cloth," which was how young babies were dressed.

baby, the Spirit told Simeon to go into the temple. 28 Simeon took the baby Jesus in his arms and praised God,

> 29 "Lord, I am your servant,
>   and now I can die in peace,
>   because you have kept
>   your promise to me.
> 30 With my own eyes I have seen
>   what you have done
>   to save your people,
> 31 and foreign nations
>   will also see this.
> 32 Your mighty power is a light
>   for all nations,
>   and it will bring honor
>   to your people Israel."

33 Jesus' parents were surprised at what Simeon had said. 34 Then he blessed them and told Mary, "This child of yours will cause many people in Israel to fall and others to stand. The child will be like a warning sign. Many people will reject him, 35 and you, Mary, will suffer as though you had been stabbed by a dagger. But all this will show what people are really thinking."

Anna Speaks about the Child Jesus

36 The prophet Anna was also there in the temple. She was the daughter of Phanuel from the tribe of Asher, and she was very old. In her youth she had been married for seven years, but her husband died. 37 And now she was eighty-four years old.e Night and day she served God in the temple by praying and often going without eating. 38 At that time Anna came in and praised God. She spoke about the child Jesus to everyone who hoped for Jerusalem to be set free.

The Return to Nazareth

39 After Joseph and Mary had done everything that the Law of the Lord commands, they returned home to Nazareth in Galilee. 40 The child Jesus grew. He became strong and wise, and God blessed him.

The Boy Jesus in the Temple

41 Every year Jesus' parents went to Jerusalem for Passover. 42 And when Jesus was twelve years old, they all went there as usual for the celebration. 43 After Passover his parents left, but they did not know that Jesus had stayed on in the city. 44 They thought he was traveling with some other people, and they went a whole day before they started looking for him. 45 When they could not find him with their relatives and friends, they went back to Jerusalem and started looking for him there.

46 Three days later they found Jesus sitting in the temple, listening to the teachers and asking them questions. 47 Everyone who heard him was surprised at how much he knew and at the answers he gave.

48 When his parents found him, they were amazed. His mother said, "Son, why have you done this to us? Your father and I have been very worried, and we have been searching for you!"

49 Jesus answered, "Why did you have to look for me? Didn't you know that I would be in my Father's house?"f 50 But they did not understand what he meant.

51 Jesus went back to Nazareth with his parents and obeyed them. His mother kept on thinking about all that had happened.

52 Jesus became wise, and he grew strong. God was pleased with him and so were the people.

The Preaching of John the Baptist

3 For fifteen years Emperor Tiberius had ruled that part of the world. Pontius Pilate was governor of Judea, and Herod was the ruler of Galilee. Herod's brother, Philip, was the ruler in the countries of Iturea and Trachonitis, and Lysanias was the ruler of Abilene. 2 Annas and Caiaphas were the Jewish high priests.

At that time God spoke to Zechariah's son John, who was living in the desert. 3 So John went along the Jordan Valley, telling the people, "Turn back to God and be baptized! Then your sins will be forgiven." 4 Isaiah the prophet wrote about John when he said,

> "In the desert
>   someone is shouting,
>   'Get the road ready
>   for the Lord!
>   Make a straight path
>   for him.
> 5 Fill up every valley
>   and level every mountain
>   and hill.
>   Straighten the crooked paths
>   and smooth out
>   the rough roads.
> 6 Then everyone will see
>   the saving power of God.' "

7 Crowds of people came out to be baptized, but John said to them, "You bunch of snakes! Who warned you to run from the coming judgment? 8 Do something to show that you really have given up your sins. Don't start saying that you belong to Abraham's family. God can turn these stones into children for Abraham. 9 An ax is ready to cut the trees down at their roots. Any tree that doesn't produce good fruit will be cut down and thrown into a fire."

10 The crowds asked John, "What should we do?"

11 John told them, "If you have two coats, give one to someone who doesn't have any. If you have food, share it with someone else."

12 When tax collectors came to be baptized, they asked John, "Teacher, what should we do?"

13 John told them, "Don't make people pay more than they owe."

14 Some soldiers asked him, "And what about us? What do we have to do?"

John told them, "Don't force people to pay money to make you leave them alone. Be satisfied with your pay."

15 Everyone became excited and wondered, "Could John be the Messiah?"

16 John said, "I am just baptizing with water. But some-

---

e 2.37 And now she was eighty-four years old: Or "And now she had been a widow for eighty-four years."   f 2.49 in my Father's house: Or "doing my Father's work."

one more powerful is going to come, and I am not good enough even to untie his sandals. He will baptize you with the Holy Spirit and with fire. [17] His threshing fork is in his hand, and he is ready to separate the wheat from the husks. He will store the wheat in his barn and burn the husks with a fire that never goes out."

[18] In many different ways John preached the good news to the people. [19] But to Herod the ruler, he said, "It was wrong for you to take Herodias, your brother's wife." John also said that Herod had done many other bad things. [20] Finally, Herod put John in jail, and this was the worst thing he had done.

The Baptism of Jesus

[21] While everyone else was being baptized, Jesus himself was baptized. Then as he prayed, the sky opened up, [22] and the Holy Spirit came down upon him in the form of a dove. A voice from heaven said, "You are my own dear Son, and I am pleased with you."

The Ancestors of Jesus

[23] When Jesus began to preach, he was about thirty years old. Everyone thought he was the son of Joseph. But his family went back through Heli, [24] Matthat, Levi, Melchi, Jannai, Joseph, [25] Mattathias, Amos, Nahum, Esli, Naggai, [26] Maath, Mattathias, Semein, Josech, Joda;

[27] Joanan, Rhesa, Zerubbabel, Shealtiel, Neri, [28] Melchi, Addi, Cosam, Elmadam, Er, [29] Joshua, Eliezer, Jorim, Matthat, Levi;

[30] Simeon, Judah, Joseph, Jonam, Eliakim, [31] Melea, Menna, Mattatha, Nathan, David, [32] Jesse, Obed, Boaz, Salmon, Nahshon;

[33] Amminadab, Admin, Arni, Hezron, Perez, Judah, [34] Jacob, Isaac, Abraham, Terah, Nahor, [35] Serug, Reu, Peleg, Eber, Shelah;

[36] Cainan, Arphaxad, Shem, Noah, Lamech, [37] Methuselah, Enoch, Jared, Mahalaleel, Kenan, [38] Enosh, and Seth. The family of Jesus went all the way back to Adam and then to God.

Jesus and the Devil

4 When Jesus returned from the Jordan River, the power of the Holy Spirit was with him, and the Spirit led him into the desert. [2] For forty days Jesus was tested by the devil, and during that time he went without eating. When it was all over, he was hungry.

[3] The devil said to Jesus, "If you are God's Son, tell this stone to turn into bread."

[4] Jesus answered, "The Scriptures say, 'No one can live only on food.' "

[5] Then the devil led Jesus up to a high place and quickly showed him all the nations on earth. [6] The devil said, "I will give all this power and glory to you. It has been given to me, and I can give it to anyone I want to. [7] Just worship me, and you can have it all."

[8] Jesus answered, "The Scriptures say:

'Worship the Lord your God
     and serve only him!' "

[9] Finally, the devil took Jesus to Jerusalem and had him stand on top of the temple. The devil said, "If you are God's Son, jump off. [10-11] The Scriptures say:

'God will tell his angels
     to take care of you.
They will catch you
     in their arms,
and you will not hurt
     your feet on the stones.' "

[12] Jesus answered, "The Scriptures also say, 'Don't try to test the Lord your God!' "

[13] After the devil had finished testing Jesus in every way possible, he left him for a while.

Jesus Begins His Work

[14] Jesus returned to Galilee with the power of the Spirit. News about him spread everywhere. [15] He taught in the Jewish meeting places, and everyone praised him.

The People of Nazareth Turn against Jesus

[16] Jesus went back to Nazareth, where he had been brought up, and as usual he went to the meeting place on the Sabbath. When he stood up to read from the Scriptures, [17] he was given the book of Isaiah the prophet. He opened it and read,

[18] "The Lord's Spirit
     has come to me,
because he has chosen me
     to tell the good news
     to the poor.
The Lord has sent me
     to announce freedom
     for prisoners,
     to give sight to the blind,
     to free everyone
     who suffers,
[19] and to say, 'This is the year
     the Lord has chosen.' "

[20] Jesus closed the book, then handed it back to the man in charge and sat down. Everyone in the meeting place looked straight at Jesus.

[21] Then Jesus said to them, "What you have just heard me read has come true today."

[22] All the people started talking about Jesus and were amazed at the wonderful things he said. They kept on asking, "Isn't he the Joseph's son?"

[23] Jesus answered:

You will certainly want to tell me this saying, "Doctor, first make yourself well." You will tell me to do the same things here in my own hometown that you heard I did in Capernaum. [24] But you can be sure that no prophets are liked by the people of their own hometown.

[25] Once during the time of Elijah there was no rain for three and a half years, and people everywhere were starving. There were many widows in Israel, [26] but Elijah was sent only to a widow in the town of Zarephath near the city of Sidon. [27] During the time of the prophet Elisha, many men in Israel

had leprosy. But no one was healed, except Naaman who lived in Syria.

28 When the people in the meeting place heard Jesus say this, they became so angry 29 that they got up and threw him out of town. They dragged him to the edge of the cliff on which the town was built, because they wanted to throw him down from there. 30 But Jesus slipped through the crowd and got away.

A Man with an Evil Spirit

31 Jesus went to the town of Capernaum in Galilee and taught the people on the Sabbath. 32 His teaching amazed them because he spoke with power. 33 There in the Jewish meeting place was a man with an evil spirit. He yelled out, 34 "Hey, Jesus of Nazareth, what do you want with us? Are you here to get rid of us? I know who you are! You are God's Holy One."

35 Jesus ordered the evil spirit to be quiet and come out. The demon threw the man to the ground in front of everyone and left without harming him.

36 They all were amazed and kept saying to each other, "What kind of teaching is this? He has power to order evil spirits out of people!" 37 News about Jesus spread all over that part of the country.

Jesus Heals Many People

38 Jesus left the meeting place and went to Simon's home. When Jesus got there, he was told that Simon's mother-in-law was sick with a high fever. 39 So Jesus went over to her and ordered the fever to go away. Right then she was able to get up and serve them a meal.

40 After the sun had set, people with all kinds of diseases were brought to Jesus. He put his hands on each one of them and healed them. 41 Demons went out of many people and shouted, "You are the Son of God!" But Jesus ordered the demons not to speak because they knew he was the Messiah.

42 The next morning Jesus went out to a place where he could be alone, and crowds came looking for him. When they found him, they tried to stop him from leaving. 43 But Jesus said, "People in other towns must hear the good news about God's kingdom. That's why I was sent." 44 So he kept on preaching in the Jewish meeting places in Judea.*g*

Jesus Chooses His First Disciples

5 Jesus was standing on the shore of Lake Gennesaret, teaching the people as they crowded around him to hear God's message. 2 Near the shore he saw two boats left there by some fishermen who had gone to wash their nets. 3 Jesus got into the boat that belonged to Simon and asked him to row it out a little way from the shore. Then Jesus sat down in the boat to teach the crowd.

4 When Jesus had finished speaking, he told Simon, "Row the boat out into the deep water and let your nets down to catch some fish."

5 "Master," Simon answered, "we have worked hard all night long and have not caught a thing. But if you tell me to, I will let the nets down." 6 They did it and caught so many fish that their nets began ripping apart. 7 Then they signaled for their partners in the other boat to come and help them.

The men came, and together they filled the two boats so full that they both began to sink.

8 When Simon Peter saw this happen, he knelt down in front of Jesus and said, "Lord, don't come near me! I am a sinner." 9 Peter and everyone with him were completely surprised at all the fish they had caught. 10 His partners James and John, the sons of Zebedee, were surprised too.

Jesus told Simon, "Don't be afraid! From now on you will bring in people instead of fish." 11 The men pulled their boats up on the shore. Then they left everything and went with Jesus.

Jesus Heals a Man

12 Jesus came to a town where there was a man who had leprosy. When the man saw Jesus, he knelt down to the ground in front of Jesus and begged, "Lord, you have the power to make me well, if only you wanted to."

13 Jesus put his hand on him and said, "I want to! Now you are well." At once the man's leprosy disappeared. 14 Jesus told him, "Don't tell anyone about this, but go and show yourself to the priest. Offer a gift to the priest, just as Moses commanded, and everyone will know that you have been healed."

15 News about Jesus kept spreading. Large crowds came to listen to him teach and to be healed of their diseases. 16 But Jesus would often go to some place where he could be alone and pray.

Jesus Heals a Crippled Man

17 One day some Pharisees and experts in the Law of Moses sat listening to Jesus teach. They had come from every village in Galilee and Judea and from Jerusalem.

God had given Jesus the power to heal the sick, 18 and some people came carrying a crippled man on a mat. They tried to take him inside the house and put him in front of Jesus. 19 But because of the crowd, they could not get him to Jesus. So they went up on the roof, where they removed some tiles and let the mat down in the middle of the room.

20 When Jesus saw how much faith they had, he said to the crippled man, "My friend, your sins are forgiven."

21 The Pharisees and the experts began arguing, "Jesus must think he is God! Only God can forgive sins."

22 Jesus knew what they were thinking, and he said, "Why are you thinking that? 23 Is it easier for me to tell this crippled man that his sins are forgiven or to tell him to get up and walk? 24 But now you will see that the Son of Man has the right to forgive sins here on earth." Jesus then said to the man, "Get up! Pick up your mat and walk home."

25 At once the man stood up in front of everyone. He picked up his mat and went home, giving thanks to God. 26 Everyone was amazed and praised God. What they saw surprised them, and they said, "We have seen a great miracle today!"

Jesus Chooses Levi

27 Later, Jesus went out and saw a tax collector named Levi sitting at the place for paying taxes. Jesus said to him, "Come with me." 28 Levi left everything and went with Jesus.

29 In his home Levi gave a big dinner for Jesus. Many tax collectors and other guests were also there.

---

g **4.44** *Judea*: Some manuscripts have "Galilee."

30 The Pharisees and some of their teachers of the Law of Moses grumbled to Jesus' disciples, "Why do you eat and drink with those tax collectors and other sinners?"

31 Jesus answered, "Healthy people don't need a doctor, but sick people do. **32** I didn't come to invite good people to turn to God. I came to invite sinners."

People Ask about Going without Eating

33 Some people said to Jesus, "John's followers often pray and go without eating, and so do the followers of the Pharisees. But your disciples never go without eating or drinking."

34 Jesus told them, "The friends of a bridegroom don't go without eating while he is still with them. **35** But the time will come when he will be taken from them. Then they will go without eating."

36 Jesus then told them these sayings:

No one uses a new piece of cloth to patch old clothes. The patch would shrink and make the hole even bigger.

37 No one pours new wine into old wineskins. The new wine would swell and burst the old skins. Then the wine would be lost, and the skins would be ruined. **38** New wine must be put only into new wineskins.

39 No one wants new wine after drinking old wine. They say, "The old wine is better."

A Question about the Sabbath

6 One Sabbath when Jesus and his disciples were walking through some wheat fields, the disciples picked some wheat. They rubbed the husks off with their hands and started eating the grain.

2 Some Pharisees said, "Why are you picking grain on the Sabbath? You're not supposed to do that!"

3 Jesus answered, "You surely have read what David did when he and his followers were hungry. **4** He went into the house of God and took the sacred loaves of bread that only priests were supposed to eat. He not only ate some himself, but even gave some to his followers."

5 Jesus finished by saying, "The Son of Man is Lord over the Sabbath."

A Man with a Crippled Hand

6 On another Sabbath*h* Jesus was teaching in a Jewish meeting place, and a man with a crippled right hand was there. **7** Some Pharisees and teachers of the Law of Moses kept watching Jesus to see if he would heal the man. They did this because they wanted to accuse Jesus of doing something wrong.

8 Jesus knew what they were thinking. So he told the man to stand up where everyone could see him. And the man stood up. **9** Then Jesus asked, "On the Sabbath should we do good deeds or evil deeds? Should we save someone's life or destroy it?"

10 After he had looked around at everyone, he told the man, "Stretch out your hand." He did, and his bad hand became completely well.

11 The teachers and the Pharisees were furious and started saying to each other, "What can we do about Jesus?"

Jesus Chooses His Twelve Apostles

12 About that time Jesus went off to a mountain to pray, and he spent the whole night there. **13** The next morning he called his disciples together and chose twelve of them to be his apostles. **14** One was Simon, and Jesus named him Peter. Another was Andrew, Peter's brother. There were also James, John, Philip, Bartholomew, **15** Matthew, Thomas, and James the son of Alphaeus. The rest of the apostles were Simon, known as the Eager One,*i* **16** Jude, who was the son of James, and Judas Iscariot, who later betrayed Jesus.

Jesus Teaches, Preaches, and Heals

17 Jesus and his apostles went down from the mountain and came to some flat, level ground. Many other disciples were there to meet him. Large crowds of people from all over Judea, Jerusalem, and the coastal cities of Tyre and Sidon were there too. **18** These people had come to listen to Jesus and to be healed of their diseases. All who were troubled by evil spirits were also healed. **19** Everyone was trying to touch Jesus, because power was going out from him and healing them all.

Blessings and Troubles

20 Jesus looked at his disciples and said:

God will bless you people
who are poor.
His kingdom belongs to you!
21 God will bless
you hungry people.
You will have plenty
to eat!
God will bless you people
who are crying.
You will laugh!

22 God will bless you when others hate you and won't have anything to do with you. God will bless you when people insult you and say cruel things about you, all because you are a follower of the Son of Man. **23** Long ago your own people did these same things to the prophets. So when this happens to you, be happy and jump for joy! You will have a great reward in heaven.

24 But you rich people
are in for trouble.
You have already had
an easy life!
25 You well-fed people
are in for trouble.
You will go hungry!
You people
who are laughing now
are in for trouble.
You are going to cry
and weep!

26 You are in for trouble when everyone says

---

h **6.6** *On another Sabbath*: Some manuscripts have a reading which may mean "the Sabbath after the next." *i* **6.15** *known as the Eager One*: The word "eager" translates the Greek word "zealot," which was a name later given to the members of a Jewish group that resisted and fought against the Romans.

good things about you. That is what your own people said about those prophets who told lies.

Love for Enemies

27 This is what I say to all who will listen to me:

Love your enemies, and be good to everyone who hates you. 28 Ask God to bless anyone who curses you, and pray for everyone who is cruel to you. 29 If someone slaps you on one cheek, don't stop that person from slapping you on the other cheek. If someone wants to take your coat, don't try to keep back your shirt. 30 Give to everyone who asks and don't ask people to return what they have taken from you. 31 Treat others just as you want to be treated.

32 If you love only someone who loves you, will God praise you for that? Even sinners love people who love them. 33 If you are kind only to someone who is kind to you, will God be pleased with you for that? Even sinners are kind to people who are kind to them. 34 If you lend money only to someone you think will pay you back, will God be pleased with you for that? Even sinners lend to sinners because they think they will get it all back.

35 But love your enemies and be good to them. Lend without expecting to be paid back. Then you will get a great reward, and you will be the true children of God in heaven. He is good even to people who are unthankful and cruel. 36 Have pity on others, just as your Father has pity on you.

Judging Others

37 Jesus said:

Don't judge others, and God won't judge you. Don't be hard on others, and God won't be hard on you. Forgive others, and God will forgive you. 38 If you give to others, you will be given a full amount in return. It will be packed down, shaken together, and spilling over into your lap. The way you treat others is the way you will be treated.

39 Jesus also used some sayings as he spoke to the people. He said:

Can one blind person lead another blind person? Won't they both fall into a ditch? 40 Are students better than their teacher? But when they are fully trained, they will be like their teacher. 41 You can see the speck in your friend's eye. But you don't notice the log in your own eye. 42 How can you say, "My friend, let me take the speck out of your eye," when you don't see the log in your own eye? You show-offs! First, get the log out of your own eye. Then you can see how to take the speck out of your friend's eye.

A Tree and Its Fruit

43 A good tree cannot produce bad fruit, and a bad tree cannot produce good fruit. 44 You can tell what a tree is like by the fruit it produces. You cannot pick figs or grapes from thornbushes. 45 Good people do good things because of the good in their hearts. Bad people do bad things because of the evil in their hearts. Your words show what is in your heart.

Two Builders

46 Why do you keep on saying that I am your Lord, when you refuse to do what I say? 47 Anyone who comes and listens to me and obeys me 48 is like someone who dug down deep and built a house on solid rock. When the flood came and the river rushed against the house, it was built so well that it didn't even shake. 49 But anyone who hears what I say and doesn't obey me is like someone whose house wasn't built on solid rock. As soon as the river rushed against that house, it was smashed to pieces!

Jesus Heals an Army Officer's Servant

7 After Jesus had finished teaching the people, he went to Capernaum. 2 In that town an army officer's servant was sick and about to die. The officer liked this servant very much. 3 And when he heard about Jesus, he sent some Jewish leaders to ask him to come and heal the servant.

4 The leaders went to Jesus and begged him to do something. They said, "This man deserves your help! 5 He loves our nation and even built us a meeting place." 6 So Jesus went with them.

When Jesus wasn't far from the house, the officer sent some friends to tell him, "Lord, don't go to any trouble for me! I am not good enough for you to come into my house. 7 And I am certainly not worthy to come to you. Just say the word, and my servant will get well. 8 I have officers who give orders to me, and I have soldiers who take orders from me. I can say to one of them, 'Go!' and he goes. I can say to another, 'Come!' and he comes. I can say to my servant, 'Do this!' and he will do it."

9 When Jesus heard this, he was so surprised that he turned and said to the crowd following him, "In all of Israel I've never found anyone with this much faith!"

10 The officer's friends returned and found the servant well.

A Widow's Son

11 Soon Jesus and his disciples were on their way to the town of Nain, and a big crowd was going along with them. 12 As they came near the gate of the town, they saw people carrying out the body of a widow's only son. Many people from the town were walking along with her.

13 When the Lord saw the woman, he felt sorry for her and said, "Don't cry!"

14 Jesus went over and touched the stretcher on which the people were carrying the dead boy. They stopped, and Jesus said, "Young man, get up!" 15 The boy sat up and began to speak. Jesus then gave him back to his mother.

16 Everyone was frightened and praised God. They said, "A great prophet is here with us! God has come to his people."

17 News about Jesus spread all over Judea and everywhere else in that part of the country.

John the Baptist

18-19 John's followers told John everything that was being said about Jesus. So he sent two of them to ask the Lord, "Are you the one we should be looking for? Or must we wait for someone else?"

20 When these messengers came to Jesus, they said,

"John the Baptist sent us to ask, 'Are you the one we should be looking for? Or are we supposed to wait for someone else?' "

²¹ At that time Jesus was healing many people who were sick or in pain or were troubled by evil spirits, and he was giving sight to a lot of blind people. ²² Jesus said to the messengers sent by John, "Go and tell John what you have seen and heard. Blind people are now able to see, and the lame can walk. People who have leprosy are being healed, and the deaf can now hear. The dead are raised to life, and the poor are hearing the good news. ²³ God will bless everyone who doesn't reject me because of what I do."

²⁴ After John's messengers had gone, Jesus began speaking to the crowds about John:

What kind of person did you go out to the desert to see? Was he like tall grass blown about by the wind? ²⁵ What kind of man did you really go out to see? Was he someone dressed in fine clothes? People who wear expensive clothes and live in luxury are in the king's palace. ²⁶ What then did you go out to see? Was he a prophet? He certainly was! I tell you that he was more than a prophet. ²⁷ In the Scriptures, God calls John his messenger and says, "I am sending my messenger ahead of you to get things ready for you." ²⁸ No one ever born on this earth is greater than John. But whoever is least important in God's kingdom is greater than John.

²⁹ Everyone had been listening to John. Even the tax collectors had obeyed God and had done what was right by letting John baptize them. ³⁰ But the Pharisees and the experts in the Law of Moses refused to obey God and be baptized by John.

³¹ Jesus went on to say:

What are you people like? What kind of people are you? ³² You are like children sitting in the market and shouting to each other,

"We played the flute,
    but you would not dance!
We sang a funeral song,
    but you would not cry!"

³³ John the Baptist did not go around eating and drinking, and you said, "John has a demon in him!" ³⁴ But because the Son of Man goes around eating and drinking, you say, "Jesus eats and drinks too much! He is even a friend of tax collectors and sinners." ³⁵ Yet Wisdom is shown to be right by what its followers do.

Simon the Pharisee

³⁶ A Pharisee invited Jesus to have dinner with him. So Jesus went to the Pharisee's home and got ready to eat. ³⁷ When a sinful woman in that town found out that Jesus was there, she bought an expensive bottle of perfume. ³⁸ Then she came and stood behind Jesus. She cried and started washing his feet with her tears and drying them with her hair. The woman kissed his feet and poured the perfume on them.

³⁹ The Pharisee who had invited Jesus saw this and said to himself, "If this man really were a prophet, he would know what kind of woman is touching him! He would know that she is a sinner."

⁴⁰ Jesus said to the Pharisee, "Simon, I have something to say to you."

"Teacher, what is it?" Simon replied.

⁴¹ Jesus told him, "Two people were in debt to a moneylender. One of them owed him five hundred silver coins, and the other owed him fifty. ⁴² Since neither of them could pay him back, the moneylender said that they didn't have to pay him anything. Which one of them will like him more?"

⁴³ Simon answered, "I suppose it would be the one who had owed more and didn't have to pay it back."

"You are right," Jesus said.

⁴⁴ He turned toward the woman and said to Simon, "Have you noticed this woman? When I came into your home, you didn't give me any water so I could wash my feet. But she has washed my feet with her tears and dried them with her hair. ⁴⁵ You didn't greet me with a kiss, but from the time I came in, she has not stopped kissing my feet. ⁴⁶ You didn't even pour olive oil on my head, but she has poured expensive perfume on my feet. ⁴⁷ So I tell you that all her sins are forgiven, and that is why she has shown great love. But anyone who has been forgiven for only a little will show only a little love."

⁴⁸ Then Jesus said to the woman, "Your sins are forgiven."

⁴⁹ Some other guests started saying to one another, "Who is this who dares to forgive sins?"

⁵⁰ But Jesus told the woman, "Because of your faith, you are now saved.ʲ May God give you peace!"

Women Who Helped Jesus

8 Soon after this, Jesus was going through towns and villages, telling the good news about God's kingdom. His twelve apostles were with him, ² and so were some women who had been healed of evil spirits and all sorts of diseases. One of the women was Mary Magdalene, who once had seven demons in her. ³ Joanna, Susanna, and many others had also used what they owned to help Jesus and his disciples. Joanna's husband Chuza was one of Herod's officials.

A Story about a Farmer

⁴ When a large crowd from several towns had gathered around Jesus, he told them this story:

⁵ A farmer went out to scatter seed in a field. While the farmer was doing it, some of the seeds fell along the road and were stepped on or eaten by birds. ⁶ Other seeds fell on rocky ground and started growing. But the plants did not have enough water and soon dried up. ⁷ Some other seeds fell where thornbushes grew up and choked the plants. ⁸ The rest of the seeds fell on good ground where they grew and produced a hundred times as many seeds.

When Jesus had finished speaking, he said, "If you have ears, pay attention!"

Why Jesus Used Stories

⁹ Jesus' disciples asked him what the story meant. ¹⁰ So he answered:

I have explained the secrets about God's king-

ʲ7.50 saved: Or "healed." The Greek word may have either meaning.

dom to you, but for others I can only use stories. These people look, but they don't see, and they hear, but they don't understand.

Jesus Explains the Story about a Farmer

11 This is what the story means: The seed is God's message, 12 and the seeds that fell along the road are the people who hear the message. But the devil comes and snatches the message out of their hearts, so that they will not believe and be saved. 13 The seeds that fell on rocky ground are the people who gladly hear the message and accept it. But they don't have deep roots, and they believe only for a little while. As soon as life gets hard, they give up.

14 The seeds that fell among the thornbushes are also people who hear the message. But they are so eager for riches and pleasures that they never produce anything. 15 Those seeds that fell on good ground are the people who listen to the message and keep it in good and honest hearts. They last and produce a harvest.

Light

16 No one lights a lamp and puts it under a bowl or under a bed. A lamp is always put on a lampstand, so that people who come into a house will see the light. 17 There is nothing hidden that will not be found. There is no secret that will not be well known. 18 Pay attention to how you listen! Everyone who has something will be given more, but people who have nothing will lose what little they think they have.

Jesus' Mother and Brothers

19 Jesus' mother and brothers went to see him, but because of the crowd they could not get near him. 20 Someone told Jesus, "Your mother and brothers are standing outside and want to see you."

21 Jesus answered, "My mother and my brothers are those people who hear and obey God's message."

A Storm

22 One day, Jesus and his disciples got into a boat, and he said, "Let's cross the lake." They started out, 23 and while they were sailing across, he went to sleep.

Suddenly a windstorm struck the lake, and the boat started sinking. They were in danger. 24 So they went to Jesus and woke him up, "Master, Master! We are about to drown!"

Jesus got up and ordered the wind and waves to stop. They obeyed, and everything was calm. 25 Then Jesus asked the disciples, "Don't you have any faith?"

But they were frightened and amazed. They said to each other, "Who is this? He can give orders to the wind and the waves, and they obey him!"

A Man with Demons in Him

26 Jesus and his disciples sailed across Lake Galilee and came to shore near the town of Gerasa.*k* 27 As Jesus was getting out of the boat, he was met by a man from that town.

The man had demons in him. He had gone naked for a long time and no longer lived in a house, but in the graveyard. 28 The man saw Jesus and screamed. He knelt down in front of him and shouted, "Jesus, Son of God in heaven, what do you want with me? I beg you not to torture me!" 29 He said this because Jesus had already told the evil spirit to go out of him.

The man had often been attacked by the demon. And even though he had been bound with chains and leg irons and kept under guard, he smashed whatever bound him. Then the demon would force him out into lonely places.

30 Jesus asked the man, "What is your name?"

He answered, "My name is Lots." He said this because there were 'lots' of demons in him. 31 They begged Jesus not to send them to the deep pit, where they would be punished.

32 A large herd of pigs was feeding there on the hillside. So the demons begged Jesus to let them go into the pigs, and Jesus let them go. 33 Then the demons left the man and went into the pigs. The whole herd rushed down the steep bank into the lake and drowned.

34 When the men taking care of the pigs saw this, they ran to spread the news in the town and on the farms. 35 The people went out to see what had happened, and when they came to Jesus, they also found the man. The demons had gone out of him, and he was sitting there at the feet of Jesus. He had clothes on and was in his right mind. But the people were terrified.

36 Then all who had seen the man healed told about it. 37 Everyone from around Gerasa begged Jesus to leave, because they were so frightened.

When Jesus got into the boat to start back, 38 the man who had been healed begged to go with him. But Jesus sent him off and said, 39 "Go back home and tell everyone how much God has done for you." The man then went all over town, telling everything that Jesus had done for him.

A Dying Girl and a Sick Woman

40 Everyone had been waiting for Jesus, and when he came back, a crowd was there to welcome him. 41 Just then the man in charge of the Jewish meeting place came and knelt down in front of Jesus. His name was Jairus, and he begged Jesus to come to his home 42 because his twelve-year-old child was dying. She was his only daughter.

While Jesus was on his way, people were crowding all around him. 43 In the crowd was a woman who had been bleeding for twelve years. She had spent everything she had on doctors,*l* but none of them could make her well.

44 As soon as she came up behind Jesus and barely touched his clothes, her bleeding stopped.

45 "Who touched me?" Jesus asked.

While everyone was denying it, Peter said, "Master, people are crowding all around and pushing you from every side."*m*

46 But Jesus answered, "Someone touched me, because I felt power going out from me." 47 The woman knew that she could not hide, so she came trembling and knelt down in front of Jesus. She told everyone why she had touched him and that she had been healed right away.

---

k **8.26** *Gerasa*: Some manuscripts have "Gergesa."   *l* **8.43** *She had spent everything she had on doctors*: Some manuscripts do not have these words.   *m* **8.45** *from every side*: Some manuscripts add "and you ask, 'Who touched me?' "

48 Jesus said to the woman, "You are now well because of your faith. May God give you peace!"

49 While Jesus was speaking, someone came from Jairus' home and said, "Your daughter has died! Why bother the teacher anymore?"

50 When Jesus heard this, he told Jairus, "Don't worry! Have faith, and your daughter will get well."

51 Jesus went into the house, but he did not let anyone else go with him, except Peter, John, James, and the girl's father and mother. 52 Everyone was crying and weeping for the girl. But Jesus said, "The child isn't dead. She is just asleep." 53 The people laughed at him because they knew she was dead.

54 Jesus took hold of the girl's hand and said, "Child, get up!" 55 She came back to life and got right up. Jesus told them to give her something to eat. 56 Her parents were surprised, but Jesus ordered them not to tell anyone what had happened.

Instructions for the Twelve Apostles

9 Jesus called together his twelve apostles and gave them complete power over all demons and diseases. 2 Then he sent them to tell about God's kingdom and to heal the sick. 3 He told them, "Don't take anything with you! Don't take a walking stick or a traveling bag or food or money or even a change of clothes. 4 When you are welcomed into a home, stay there until you leave that town. 5 If people won't welcome you, leave the town and shake the dust from your feet as a warning to them."

6 The apostles left and went from village to village, telling the good news and healing people everywhere.

Herod Is Worried

7 Herod the ruler heard about all that was happening, and he was worried. Some people were saying that John the Baptist had come back to life. 8 Others were saying that Elijah had come or that one of the prophets from long ago had come back to life. 9 But Herod said, "I had John's head cut off! Who is this I hear so much about?" Herod was eager to meet Jesus.

Jesus Feeds Five Thousand

10 The apostles came back and told Jesus everything they had done. He then took them with him to the village of Bethsaida, where they could be alone. 11 But a lot of people found out about this and followed him. Jesus welcomed them. He spoke to them about God's kingdom and healed everyone who was sick.

12 Late in the afternoon the twelve apostles came to Jesus and said, "Send the crowd to the villages and farms around here. They need to find a place to stay and something to eat. There is nothing in this place. It is like a desert!"

13 Jesus answered, "You give them something to eat."

But they replied, "We have only five small loaves of bread and two fish. If we are going to feed all these people, we will have to go and buy food." 14 There were about five thousand men in the crowd.

Jesus said to his disciples, "Have the people sit in groups of fifty." 15 They did this, and all the people sat down. 16 Jesus took the five loaves and the two fish. He looked up toward heaven and blessed the food. Then he broke the bread and fish and handed them to his disciples to give to the people.

17 Everyone ate all they wanted. What was left over filled twelve baskets.

Who Is Jesus?

18 When Jesus was alone praying, his disciples came to him, and he asked them, "What do people say about me?"

19 They answered, "Some say that you are John the Baptist or Elijah or a prophet from long ago who has come back to life."

20 Jesus then asked them, "But who do you say I am?"

Peter answered, "You are the Messiah sent from God."

21 Jesus strictly warned his disciples not to tell anyone about this.

Jesus Speaks about His Suffering and Death

22 Jesus told his disciples, "The nation's leaders, the chief priests, and the teachers of the Law of Moses will make the Son of Man suffer terribly. They will reject him and kill him, but three days later he will rise to life."

23 Then Jesus said to all the people:

If any of you want to be my followers, you must forget about yourself. You must take up your cross each day and follow me. 24 If you want to save your life,[n] you will destroy it. But if you give up your life for me, you will save it. 25 What will you gain, if you own the whole world but destroy yourself or waste your life? 26 If you are ashamed of me and my message, the Son of Man will be ashamed of you when he comes in his glory and in the glory of his Father and the holy angels. 27 You can be sure that some of the people standing here will not die before they see God's kingdom.

The True Glory of Jesus

28 About eight days later Jesus took Peter, John, and James with him and went up on a mountain to pray. 29 While he was praying, his face changed, and his clothes became shining white. 30 Suddenly Moses and Elijah were there speaking with him. 31 They appeared in heavenly glory and talked about all that Jesus' death[o] in Jerusalem would mean.

32 Peter and the other two disciples had been sound asleep. All at once they woke up and saw how glorious Jesus was. They also saw the two men who were with him.

33 Moses and Elijah were about to leave, when Peter said to Jesus, "Master, it is good for us to be here! Let us make three shelters, one for you, one for Moses, and one for Elijah." But Peter did not know what he was talking about.

34 While Peter was still speaking, a shadow from a cloud passed over them, and they were frightened as the cloud covered them. 35 From the cloud a voice spoke, "This is my chosen Son. Listen to what he says!"

36 After the voice had spoken, Peter, John, and James saw only Jesus. For some time they kept quiet and did not say anything about what they had seen.

Jesus Heals a Boy

37 The next day Jesus and his three disciples came down from the mountain and were met by a large crowd. 38 Just

---

[n] 9.24 *life*: In verses 24,25 a Greek word which often means "soul" is translated "life" and "yourself."   [o] 9.31 *Jesus' death*: In Greek this is "his departure," which probably includes his rising to life and his return to heaven.

then someone in the crowd shouted, "Teacher, please do something for my son! He is my only child! 39 A demon often attacks him and makes him scream. It shakes him until he foams at the mouth, and it won't leave him until it has completely worn the boy out. 40 I begged your disciples to force out the demon, but they couldn't do it."

41 Jesus said to them, "You people are stubborn and don't have any faith! How much longer must I be with you? Why do I have to put up with you?"

Then Jesus said to the man, "Bring your son to me." 42 While the boy was being brought, the demon attacked him and made him shake all over. Jesus ordered the demon to stop. Then he healed the boy and gave him back to his father. 43 Everyone was amazed at God's great power.

Jesus Again Speaks about His Death

While everyone was still amazed at what Jesus was doing, he said to his disciples, 44 "Pay close attention to what I am telling you! The Son of Man will be handed over to his enemies." 45 But the disciples did not know what he meant. The meaning was hidden from them. They could not understand it, and they were afraid to ask.

Who Is the Greatest?

46 Jesus' disciples were arguing about which one of them was the greatest. 47 Jesus knew what they were thinking, and he had a child stand there beside him. 48 Then he said to his disciples, "When you welcome even a child because of me, you welcome me. And when you welcome me, you welcome the one who sent me. Whichever one of you is the most humble is the greatest."

For or against Jesus

49 John said, "Master, we saw a man using your name to force demons out of people. But we told him to stop, because he isn't one of us."

50 "Don't stop him!" Jesus said. "Anyone who isn't against you is for you."

A Samaritan Village Refuses To Receive Jesus

51 Not long before it was time for Jesus to be taken up to heaven, he made up his mind to go to Jerusalem. 52 He sent some messengers on ahead to a Samaritan village to get things ready for him. 53 But he was on his way to Jerusalem, so the people there refused to welcome him. 54 When the disciples James and John saw what was happening, they asked, "Lord, do you want us to call down fire from heaven to destroy these people?"[p]

55 But Jesus turned and corrected them for what they had said.[q] 56 Then they all went on to another village.

Three People Who Wanted To Be Followers

57 Along the way someone said to Jesus, "I'll go anywhere with you!"

58 Jesus said, "Foxes have dens, and birds have nests, but the Son of Man doesn't have a place to call his own."

59 Jesus told someone else to come with him. But the man said, "Lord, let me wait until I bury my father."

60 Jesus answered, "Let the dead take care of the dead, while you go and tell about God's kingdom."

61 Then someone said to Jesus, "I want to go with you, Lord, but first let me go back and take care of things at home."

62 Jesus answered, "Anyone who starts plowing and keeps looking back isn't worth a thing to God's kingdom!"

The Work of the Seventy-Two Followers

10 Later the Lord chose seventy-two[r] other followers and sent them out two by two to every town and village where he was about to go. 2 He said to them:

A large crop is in the fields, but there are only a few workers. Ask the Lord in charge of the harvest to send out workers to bring it in. 3 Now go, but remember, I am sending you like lambs into a pack of wolves. 4 Don't take along a moneybag or a traveling bag or sandals. And don't waste time greeting people on the road. 5 As soon as you enter a home, say, "God bless this home with peace." 6 If the people living there are peace-loving, your prayer for peace will bless them. But if they are not peace-loving, your prayer will return to you. 7 Stay with the same family, eating and drinking whatever they give you, because workers are worth what they earn. Don't move around from house to house.

8 If the people of a town welcome you, eat whatever they offer. 9 Heal their sick and say, "God's kingdom will soon be here!"[s]

10 But if the people of a town refuse to welcome you, go out into the street and say, 11 "We are shaking the dust from our feet as a warning to you. And you can be sure that God's kingdom will soon be here!"[s] 12 I tell you that on the day of judgment the people of Sodom will get off easier than the people of that town!

The Unbelieving Towns

13 You people of Chorazin are in for trouble! You people of Bethsaida are also in for trouble! If the miracles that took place in your towns had happened in Tyre and Sidon, the people there would have turned to God long ago. They would have dressed in sackcloth and put ashes on their heads. 14 On the day of judgment the people of Tyre and Sidon will get off easier than you will. 15 People of Capernaum, do you think you will be honored in heaven? Well, you will go down to hell!

16 My followers, whoever listens to you is listening to me. Anyone who says "No" to you is saying "No" to me. And anyone who says "No" to me is really saying "No" to the one who sent me.

The Return of the Seventy-Two

17 When the seventy-two followers returned, they were

---

[p] **9.54** *to destroy these people*: Some manuscripts add "as Elijah did." [q] **9.55** *what they had said*: Some manuscripts add, "and said, 'Don't you know what spirit you belong to? The Son of Man did not come to destroy people's lives, but to save them.' "

[r] **10.1** *seventy-two*: Some manuscripts have "seventy." According to Jewish tradition, there were seventy nations on earth. But the ancient Greek translation of the Old Testament has "seventy-two" in place of "seventy." Jesus probably chose this number of followers to show that his message was for everyone in the world. [s] **10.9,11** *will soon be here*: Or "is already here."

excited and said, "Lord, even the demons obeyed when we spoke in your name!"

¹⁸ Jesus told them:

I saw Satan fall from heaven like a flash of lightning. ¹⁹ I have given you the power to trample on snakes and scorpions and to defeat the power of your enemy Satan. Nothing can harm you. ²⁰ But don't be happy because evil spirits obey you. Be happy that your names are written in heaven!

Jesus Thanks His Father

²¹ At that same time, Jesus felt the joy that comes from the Holy Spirit,ᵗ and he said:

My Father, Lord of heaven and earth, I am grateful that you hid all this from wise and educated people and showed it to ordinary people. Yes, Father, that is what pleased you.

²² My Father has given me everything, and he is the only one who knows the Son. The only one who really knows the Father is the Son. But the Son wants to tell others about the Father, so that they can know him too.

²³ Jesus then turned to his disciples and said to them in private, "You are really blessed to see what you see! ²⁴ Many prophets and kings were eager to see what you see and to hear what you hear. But I tell you that they did not see or hear."

The Good Samaritan

²⁵ An expert in the Law of Moses stood up and asked Jesus a question to see what he would say. "Teacher," he asked, "what must I do to have eternal life?"

²⁶ Jesus answered, "What is written in the Scriptures? How do you understand them?"

²⁷ The man replied, "The Scriptures say, 'Love the Lord your God with all your heart, soul, strength, and mind.' They also say, 'Love your neighbors as much as you love yourself.' "

²⁸ Jesus said, "You have given the right answer. If you do this, you will have eternal life."

²⁹ But the man wanted to show that he knew what he was talking about. So he asked Jesus, "Who are my neighbors?"

³⁰ Jesus replied:

As a man was going down from Jerusalem to Jericho, robbers attacked him and grabbed everything he had. They beat him up and ran off, leaving him half dead.

³¹ A priest happened to be going down the same road. But when he saw the man, he walked by on the other side. ³² Later a temple helper came to the same place. But when he saw the man who had been beaten up, he also went by on the other side.

³³ A man from Samaria then came traveling along that road. When he saw the man, he felt sorry for him ³⁴ and went over to him. He treated his wounds with olive oil and wine and bandaged them. Then he put him on his own donkey and took him to an inn, where he took care of him. ³⁵ The next morning he gave the innkeeper two silver coins and said, "Please take care of the man. If you spend more

than this on him, I will pay you when I return."

³⁶ Then Jesus asked, "Which one of these three people was a real neighbor to the man who was beaten up by robbers?"

³⁷ The teacher answered, "The one who showed pity." Jesus said, "Go and do the same!"

Martha and Mary

³⁸ The Lord and his disciples were traveling along and came to a village. When they got there, a woman named Martha welcomed him into her home. ³⁹ She had a sister named Mary, who sat down in front of the Lord and was listening to what he said. ⁴⁰ Martha was worried about all that had to be done. Finally, she went to Jesus and said, "Lord, doesn't it bother you that my sister has left me to do all the work by myself? Tell her to come and help me!"

⁴¹ The Lord answered, "Martha, Martha! You are worried and upset about so many things, ⁴² but only one thing is necessary. Mary has chosen what is best, and it will not be taken away from her."

Prayer

11 When Jesus had finished praying, one of his disciples said to him, "Lord, teach us to pray, just as John taught his followers to pray."

² So Jesus told them, "Pray in this way:

'Father, help us
   to honor your name.
Come and set up
   your kingdom.
³ Give us each day
   the food we need.ᵘ
⁴ Forgive our sins,
   as we forgive everyone
   who has done wrong to us.
And keep us
   from being tempted.' "

⁵ Then Jesus went on to say:

Suppose one of you goes to a friend in the middle of the night and says, "Let me borrow three loaves of bread. ⁶ A friend of mine has dropped in, and I don't have a thing for him to eat." ⁷ And suppose your friend answers, "Don't bother me! The door is bolted, and my children and I are in bed. I cannot get up to give you something."

⁸ He may not get up and give you the bread, just because you are his friend. But he will get up and give you as much as you need, simply because you are not ashamed to keep on asking.

⁹ So I tell you to ask and you will receive, search and you will find, knock and the door will be opened for you. ¹⁰ Everyone who asks will receive, everyone who searches will find, and the door will be opened for everyone who knocks. ¹¹ Which one of you fathers would give your hungry child a snake if the child asked for a fish? ¹² Which one of you would give your child a scorpion if the child asked for an egg? ¹³ As bad as you are, you still know how

---

ᵗ **10.21** *the Holy Spirit:* Some manuscripts have "his spirit."   ᵘ **11.3** *the food we need:* Or "food for today" or "food for the coming day."

to give good gifts to your children. But your heavenly Father is even more ready to give the Holy Spirit to anyone who asks.

Jesus and the Ruler of Demons

14 Jesus forced a demon out of a man who could not talk. And after the demon had gone out, the man started speaking, and the crowds were amazed. 15 But some people said, "He forces out demons by the power of Beelzebul, the ruler of the demons!"

16 Others wanted to put Jesus to the test. So they asked him to show them a sign from God. 17 Jesus knew what they were thinking, and he said:

A kingdom where people fight each other will end up in ruin. And a family that fights will break up. 18 If Satan fights against himself, how can his kingdom last? Yet you say that I force out demons by the power of Beelzebul. 19 If I use his power to force out demons, whose power do your own followers use to force them out? They are the ones who will judge you. 20 But if I use God's power to force out demons, it proves that God's kingdom has already come to you.

21 When a strong man arms himself and guards his home, everything he owns is safe. 22 But if a stronger man comes and defeats him, he will carry off the weapons in which the strong man trusted. Then he will divide with others what he has taken. 23 If you are not on my side, you are against me. If you don't gather in the crop with me, you scatter it.

Return of an Evil Spirit

24 When an evil spirit leaves a person, it travels through the desert, looking for a place to rest. But when it doesn't find a place, it says, "I will go back to the home I left." 25 When it gets there and finds the place clean and fixed up, 26 it goes off and finds seven other evil spirits even worse than itself. They all come and make their home there, and that person ends up in worse shape than before.

Being Really Blessed

27 While Jesus was still talking, a woman in the crowd spoke up, "The woman who gave birth to you and nursed you is blessed!"

28 Jesus replied, "That's true, but the people who are really blessed are the ones who hear and obey God's message!"

A Sign from God

29 As crowds were gathering around Jesus, he said:

You people of today are evil! You keep looking for a sign from God. But what happened to Jonah is the only sign you will be given. 30 Just as Jonah was a sign to the people of Nineveh, the Son of Man will be a sign to the people of today. 31 When the judgment comes, the Queen of the South will stand there with you and condemn you. She traveled a long way to hear Solomon's wisdom, and yet here is something far greater than Solomon. 32 The people of Nineveh will also stand there with you and condemn you. They turned to God when Jonah preached, and yet here is something far greater than Jonah.

Light

33 No one lights a lamp and then hides it or puts it under a clay pot. A lamp is put on a lampstand, so that everyone who comes into the house can see the light. 34 Your eyes are the lamp for your body. When your eyes are good, you have all the light you need. But when your eyes are bad, everything is dark. 35 So be sure that your light isn't darkness. 36 If you have light, and nothing is dark, then light will be everywhere, as when a lamp shines brightly on you.

Jesus Condemns the Pharisees and Teachers of the Law of Moses

37 When Jesus finished speaking, a Pharisee invited him home for a meal. Jesus went and sat down to eat. 38 The Pharisee was surprised that he did not wash his hands before eating. 39 So the Lord said to him:

You Pharisees clean the outside of cups and dishes, but on the inside you are greedy and evil. 40 You fools! Didn't God make both the outside and the inside?ᵛ 41 If you would only give what you have to the poor, everything you do would please God.

42 You Pharisees are in for trouble! You give God a tenth of the spices from your gardens, such as mint and rue. But you cheat people, and you don't love God. You should be fair and kind to others and still give a tenth to God.

43 You Pharisees are in for trouble! You love the front seats in the meeting places, and you like to be greeted with honor in the market. 44 But you are in for trouble! You are like unmarked graves that people walk on without even knowing it.

45 A teacher of the Law of Moses spoke up, "Teacher, you said cruel things about us."

46 Jesus replied:

You teachers are also in for trouble! You load people down with heavy burdens, but you won't lift a finger to help them carry the loads. 47 Yes, you are really in for trouble. You build monuments to honor the prophets your own people murdered long ago. 48 You must think that was the right thing for your people to do, or else you would not have built monuments for the prophets they murdered.

49 Because of your evil deeds, the Wisdom of God said, "I will send prophets and apostles to you. But you will murder some and mistreat others." 50 You people living today will be punished for all the prophets who have been murdered since the beginning of the world. 51 This includes every prophet from the time of Abel to the time of Zechariah, who was murdered between the altar and the temple. You people will certainly be punished for all of this.

52 You teachers of the Law of Moses are really in for trouble! You carry the keys to the door of knowledge about God. But you never go in, and you keep others from going in.

ᵛ **11.40** *Didn't God make both the outside and the inside*: Or "Doesn't the person who washes the outside always wash the inside too?"

53 Jesus was about to leave, but the teachers and the Pharisees wanted to get even with him. They tried to make him say what he thought about other things, **54** so that they could catch him saying something wrong.

Warnings

12 As thousands of people crowded around Jesus and were stepping on each other, he told his disciples:

Be sure to guard against the dishonest teaching[w] of the Pharisees! It is their way of fooling people. **2** Everything that is hidden will be found out, and every secret will be known. **3** Whatever you say in the dark will be heard when it is day. Whatever you whisper in a closed room will be shouted from the housetops.

The One To Fear

4 My friends, don't be afraid of people. They can kill you, but after that, there is nothing else they can do. **5** God is the one you must fear. Not only can he take your life, but he can throw you into hell. God is certainly the one you should fear!

6 Five sparrows are sold for just two pennies, but God doesn't forget a one of them. **7** Even the hairs on your head are counted. So don't be afraid! You are worth much more than many sparrows.

Telling Others about Christ

8 If you tell others that you belong to me, the Son of Man will tell God's angels that you are my followers. **9** But if you reject me, you will be rejected in front of them. **10** If you speak against the Son of Man, you can be forgiven, but if you speak against the Holy Spirit, you cannot be forgiven.

11 When you are brought to trial in the Jewish meeting places or before rulers or officials, don't worry about how you will defend yourselves or what you will say. **12** At that time the Holy Spirit will tell you what to say.

A Rich Fool

13 A man in a crowd said to Jesus, "Teacher, tell my brother to give me my share of what our father left us when he died."

14 Jesus answered, "Who gave me the right to settle arguments between you and your brother?"

15 Then he said to the crowd, "Don't be greedy! Owning a lot of things won't make your life safe."

16 So Jesus told them this story:

A rich man's farm produced a big crop, **17** and he said to himself, "What can I do? I don't have a place large enough to store everything."

18 Later, he said, "Now I know what I'll do. I'll tear down my barns and build bigger ones, where I can store all my grain and other goods. **19** Then I'll say to myself, 'You have stored up enough good things to last for years to come. Live it up! Eat, drink, and enjoy yourself.'"

20 But God said to him, "You fool! Tonight you will die. Then who will get what you have stored up?"

21 "This is what happens to people who store up everything for themselves, but are poor in the sight of God."

Worry

22 Jesus said to his disciples:

I tell you not to worry about your life! Don't worry about having something to eat or wear. **23** Life is more than food and clothing. **24** Look at the crows! They don't plant or harvest, and they don't have storehouses or barns. But God takes care of them. You are much more important than any birds. **25** Can worry make you live longer?[x] **26** If you don't have power over small things, why worry about everything else?

27 Look how the wild flowers grow! They don't work hard to make their clothes. But I tell you that Solomon with all his wealth wasn't as well clothed as one of these flowers. **28** God gives such beauty to everything that grows in the fields, even though it is here today and thrown into a fire tomorrow. Won't he do even more for you? You have such little faith!

29 Don't keep worrying about having something to eat or drink. **30** Only people who don't know God are always worrying about such things. Your Father knows what you need. **31** But put God's work first, and these things will be yours as well.

Treasures in Heaven

32 My little group of disciples, don't be afraid! Your Father wants to give you the kingdom. **33** Sell what you have and give the money to the poor. Make yourselves moneybags that never wear out. Make sure your treasure is safe in heaven, where thieves cannot steal it and moths cannot destroy it. **34** Your heart will always be where your treasure is.

Faithful and Unfaithful Servants

35 Be ready and keep your lamps burning **36** just like those servants who wait up for their master to return from a wedding feast. As soon as he comes and knocks, they open the door for him. **37** Servants are fortunate if their master finds them awake and ready when he comes! I promise you that he will get ready and have his servants sit down so he can serve them. **38** Those servants are really fortunate if their master finds them ready, even though he comes late at night or early in the morning. **39** You would surely not let a thief break into your home, if you knew when the thief was coming. **40** So always be ready! You don't know when the Son of Man will come.

41 Peter asked Jesus, "Did you say this just for us or for everyone?"

42 The Lord answered:

Who are faithful and wise servants? Who are the ones the master will put in charge of giving the other servants their food supplies at the proper time? **43** Servants are fortunate if their master comes and finds them doing their job. **44** A servant who is

---

[w] **12.1** *dishonest teaching*: The Greek text has "yeast," which is used here of a teaching that is not true (see Matthew 16.6,12).
[x] **12.25** *live longer*: Or "grow taller."

always faithful will surely be put in charge of everything the master owns.

45 But suppose one of the servants thinks that the master won't return until late. Suppose that servant starts beating all the other servants and eats and drinks and gets drunk. 46 If that happens, the master will come on a day and at a time when the servant least expects him. That servant will then be punished and thrown out with the servants who cannot be trusted.

47 If servants are not ready or willing to do what their master wants them to do, they will be beaten hard. 48 But servants who don't know what their master wants them to do will not be beaten so hard for doing wrong. If God has been generous with you, he will expect you to serve him well. But if he has been more than generous, he will expect you to serve him even better.

Not Peace, but Trouble

49 I came to set fire to the earth, and I wish it were already on fire! 50 I am going to be put to a hard test. And I will have to suffer a lot of pain until it is over. 51 Do you think that I came to bring peace to earth? No indeed! I came to make people choose sides. 52 A family of five will be divided, with two of them against the other three. 53 Fathers and sons will turn against one another, and mothers and daughters will do the same. Mothers-in-law and daughters-in-law will also turn against each other.

Knowing What To Do

54 Jesus said to all the people:

As soon as you see a cloud coming up in the west, you say, "It's going to rain," and it does. 55 When the south wind blows, you say, "It's going to get hot," and it does. 56 Are you trying to fool someone? You can predict the weather by looking at the earth and sky, but you don't really know what's going on right now. 57 Why don't you understand the right thing to do? 58 When someone accuses you of something, try to settle things before you are taken to court. If you don't, you will be dragged before the judge. Then the judge will hand you over to the jailer, and you will be locked up. 59 You won't get out until you have paid the last cent you owe.

Turn Back to God

13 About this same time Jesus was told that Pilate had given orders for some people from Galilee to be killed while they were offering sacrifices. 2 Jesus replied:

Do you think that these people were worse sinners than everyone else in Galilee just because of what happened to them? 3 Not at all! But you can be sure that if you don't turn back to God, every one of you will also be killed. 4 What about those eighteen people who died when the tower in Siloam fell on them? Do you think they were worse than everyone else in Jerusalem? 5 Not at all! But you can be sure that if you don't turn back to God, every one of you will also die.

A Story about a Fig Tree

6 Jesus then told them this story:

A man had a fig tree growing in his vineyard. One day he went out to pick some figs, but he didn't find any. 7 So he said to the gardener, "For three years I have come looking for figs on this tree, and I haven't found any yet. Chop it down! Why should it take up space?"

8 The gardener answered, "Master, leave it for another year. I'll dig around it and put some manure on it to make it grow. 9 Maybe it will have figs on it next year. If it doesn't, you can have it cut down."

Healing a Woman on the Sabbath

10 One Sabbath, Jesus was teaching in a Jewish meeting place, 11 and a woman was there who had been crippled by an evil spirit for eighteen years. She was completely bent over and could not straighten up. 12 When Jesus saw the woman, he called her over and said, "You are now well." 13 He placed his hands on her, and right away she stood up straight and praised God.

14 The man in charge of the meeting place was angry because Jesus had healed someone on the Sabbath. So he said to the people, "Each week has six days when we can work. Come and be healed on one of those days, but not on the Sabbath."

15 The Lord replied, "Are you trying to fool someone? Won't any one of you untie your ox or donkey and lead it out to drink on a Sabbath? 16 This woman belongs to the family of Abraham, but Satan has kept her bound for eighteen years. Isn't it right to set her free on the Sabbath?" 17 Jesus' words made his enemies ashamed. But everyone else in the crowd was happy about the wonderful things he was doing.

A Mustard Seed and Yeast

18 Jesus said, "What is God's kingdom like? What can I compare it with? 19 It is like what happens when someone plants a mustard seed in a garden. The seed grows as big as a tree, and birds nest in its branches."

20 Then Jesus said, "What can I compare God's kingdom with? 21 It is like what happens when a woman mixes yeast into three batches of flour. Finally, all the dough rises."

The Narrow Door

22 As Jesus was on his way to Jerusalem, he taught the people in the towns and villages. 23 Someone asked him, "Lord, are only a few people going to be saved?" Jesus answered:

24 Do all you can to go in by the narrow door! A lot of people will try to get in, but will not be able to. 25 Once the owner of the house gets up and locks the door, you will be left standing outside. You will knock on the door and say, "Sir, open the door for us!"

But the owner will answer, "I don't know a thing about you!"

26 Then you will start saying, "We dined with you, and you taught in our streets."

27 But he will say, "I really don't know who you are! Get away from me, you evil people!"

28 Then when you have been thrown outside, you will weep and grit your teeth because you will

see Abraham, Isaac, Jacob, and all the prophets in God's kingdom. [29] People will come from all directions and sit down to feast in God's kingdom. [30] There the ones who are now least important will be the most important, and those who are now most important will be least important.

Jesus and Herod

[31] At that time some Pharisees came to Jesus and said, "You had better get away from here! Herod wants to kill you."

[32] Jesus said to them:

Go tell that fox, "I am going to force out demons and heal people today and tomorrow, and three days later I'll be through." [33] But I am going on my way today and tomorrow and the next day. After all, Jerusalem is the place where prophets are killed.

Jesus Loves Jerusalem

[34] Jerusalem, Jerusalem! Your people have killed the prophets and have stoned the messengers who were sent to you. I have often wanted to gather your people, as a hen gathers her chicks under her wings. But you wouldn't let me. [35] Now your temple will be deserted. You won't see me again until the time when you say,

"Blessed is the one who comes
in the name of the Lord."

Jesus Heals a Sick Man

14 One Sabbath, Jesus was having dinner in the home of an important Pharisee, and everyone was carefully watching Jesus. [2] All of a sudden a man with swollen legs stood up in front of him. [3] Jesus turned and asked the Pharisees and the teachers of the Law of Moses, "Is it right to heal on the Sabbath?" [4] But they did not say a word.

Jesus took hold of the man. Then he healed him and sent him away. [5] Afterwards, Jesus asked the people, "If your son or ox falls into a well, wouldn't you pull him out right away, even on the Sabbath?" [6] There was nothing they could say.

How To Be a Guest

[7] Jesus saw how the guests had tried to take the best seats. So he told them:

[8] When you are invited to a wedding feast, don't sit in the best place. Someone more important may have been invited. [9] Then the one who invited you will come and say, "Give your place to this other guest!" You will be embarrassed and will have to sit in the worst place.

[10] When you are invited to be a guest, go and sit in the worst place. Then the one who invited you may come and say, "My friend, take a better seat!" You will then be honored in front of all the other guests. [11] If you put yourself above others, you will be put down. But if you humble yourself, you will be honored.

[12] Then Jesus said to the man who had invited him: When you give a dinner or a banquet, don't invite your friends and family and relatives and rich neighbors. If you do, they will invite you in return, and you will be paid back. [13] When you give a feast, invite the poor, the crippled, the lame, and the blind. [14] They cannot pay you back. But God will bless you and reward you when his people rise from death.

The Great Banquet

[15] After Jesus had finished speaking, one of the guests said, "The greatest blessing of all is to be at the banquet in God's kingdom!"

[16] Jesus told him:

A man once gave a great banquet and invited a lot of guests. [17] When the banquet was ready, he sent a servant to tell the guests, "Everything is ready! Please come."

[18] One guest after another started making excuses. The first one said, "I bought some land, and I've got to look it over. Please excuse me."

[19] Another guest said, "I bought five teams of oxen, and I need to try them out. Please excuse me."

[20] Still another guest said, "I have just gotten married, and I can't be there."

[21] The servant told his master what happened, and the master became so angry that he said, "Go as fast as you can to every street and alley in town! Bring in everyone who is poor or crippled or blind or lame."

[22] When the servant returned, he said, "Master, I've done what you told me, and there is still plenty of room for more people."

[23] His master then told him, "Go out along the back roads and fence rows and make people come in, so that my house will be full. [24] Not one of the guests I first invited will get even a bite of my food!"

Being a Disciple

[25] Large crowds were walking along with Jesus, when he turned and said:

[26] You cannot be my disciple, unless you love me more than you love your father and mother, your wife and children, and your brothers and sisters. You cannot come with me unless you love me more than you love your own life.

[27] You cannot be my disciple unless you carry your own cross and come with me.

[28] Suppose one of you wants to build a tower. What is the first thing you will do? Won't you sit down and figure out how much it will cost and if you have enough money to pay for it? [29] Otherwise, you will start building the tower, but not be able to finish. Then everyone who sees what is happening will laugh at you. [30] They will say, "You started building, but could not finish the job."

[31] What will a king do if he has only ten thousand soldiers to defend himself against a king who is about to attack him with twenty thousand soldiers? Before he goes out to battle, won't he first sit down and decide if he can win? [32] If he thinks he

won't be able to defend himself, he will send messengers and ask for peace while the other king is still a long way off. ³³ So then, you cannot be my disciple unless you give away everything you own.

Salt and Light

³⁴ Salt is good, but if it no longer tastes like salt, how can it be made to taste salty again? ³⁵ It is no longer good for the soil or even for the manure pile. People simply throw it out. If you have ears, pay attention!

One Sheep

15 Tax collectors and sinners were all crowding around to listen to Jesus. ² So the Pharisees and the teachers of the Law of Moses started grumbling, "This man is friendly with sinners. He even eats with them."

³ Then Jesus told them this story:

⁴ If any of you has a hundred sheep, and one of them gets lost, what will you do? Won't you leave the ninety-nine in the field and go look for the lost sheep until you find it? ⁵ And when you find it, you will be so glad that you will put it on your shoulder ⁶ and carry it home. Then you will call in your friends and neighbors and say, "Let's celebrate! I've found my lost sheep."

⁷ Jesus said, "In the same way there is more happiness in heaven because of one sinner who turns to God than over ninety-nine good people who don't need to."

One Coin

⁸ Jesus told the people another story:

What will a woman do if she has ten silver coins and loses one of them? Won't she light a lamp, sweep the floor, and look carefully until she finds it? ⁹ Then she will call in her friends and neighbors and say, "Let's celebrate! I've found the coin I lost."

¹⁰ Jesus said, "In the same way God's angels are happy when even one person turns to him."

Two Sons

¹¹ Jesus also told them another story:

Once a man had two sons. ¹² The younger son said to his father, "Give me my share of the property." So the father divided his property between his two sons.

¹³ Not long after that, the younger son packed up everything he owned and left for a foreign country, where he wasted all his money in wild living. ¹⁴ He had spent everything, when a bad famine spread through that whole land. Soon he had nothing to eat.

¹⁵ He went to work for a man in that country, and the man sent him out to take care of his pigs. ¹⁶ He would have been glad to eat what the pigs were eating,ʸ but no one gave him a thing.

¹⁷ Finally, he came to his senses and said, "My father's workers have plenty to eat, and here I am, starving to death! ¹⁸ I will go to my father and say to him, 'Father, I have sinned against God in heaven and against you. ¹⁹ I am no longer good enough to be called your son. Treat me like one of your workers.'"

²⁰ The younger son got up and started back to his father. But when he was still a long way off, his father saw him and felt sorry for him. He ran to his son and hugged and kissed him.

²¹ The son said, "Father, I have sinned against God in heaven and against you. I am no longer good enough to be called your son."

²² But his father said to the servants, "Hurry and bring the best clothes and put them on him. Give him a ring for his finger and sandals for his feet. ²³ Get the best calf and prepare it, so we can eat and celebrate. ²⁴ This son of mine was dead, but has now come back to life. He was lost and has now been found." And they began to celebrate.

²⁵ The older son had been out in the field. But when he came near the house, he heard the music and dancing. ²⁶ So he called one of the servants over and asked, "What's going on here?"

²⁷ The servant answered, "Your brother has come home safe and sound, and your father ordered us to kill the best calf." ²⁸ The older brother got so angry that he would not even go into the house.

His father came out and begged him to go in. ²⁹ But he said to his father, "For years I have worked for you like a slave and have always obeyed you. But you have never even given me a little goat, so that I could give a dinner for my friends. ³⁰ This other son of yours wasted your money on prostitutes. And now that he has come home, you ordered the best calf to be killed for a feast."

³¹ His father replied, "My son, you are always with me, and everything I have is yours. ³² But we should be glad and celebrate! Your brother was dead, but he is now alive. He was lost and has now been found."

A Dishonest Manager

16 Jesus said to his disciples:

A rich man once had a manager to take care of his business. But he was told that his manager was wasting money. ² So the rich man called him in and said, "What is this I hear about you? Tell me what you have done! You are no longer going to work for me."

³ The manager said to himself, "What shall I do now that my master is going to fire me? I can't dig ditches, and I'm ashamed to beg. ⁴ I know what I'll do, so that people will welcome me into their homes after I've lost my job."

⁵ Then one by one he called in the people who were in debt to his master. He asked the first one, "How much do you owe my master?"

⁶ "A hundred barrels of olive oil," the man answered.

ʸ 15.16 *what the pigs were eating*: The Greek text has "(bean) pods," which came from a tree in Palestine. These were used to feed animals. Poor people sometimes ate them too.

So the manager said, "Take your bill and sit down and quickly write 'fifty'."

7 The manager asked someone else who was in debt to his master, "How much do you owe?"

"A thousand bushels[z] of wheat," the man replied.

The manager said, "Take your bill and write 'eight hundred'."

8 The master praised his dishonest manager for looking out for himself so well. That's how it is! The people of this world look out for themselves better than the people who belong to the light.

9 My disciples, I tell you to use wicked wealth to make friends for yourselves. Then when it is gone, you will be welcomed into an eternal home. 10 Anyone who can be trusted in little matters can also be trusted in important matters. But anyone who is dishonest in little matters will be dishonest in important matters. 11 If you cannot be trusted with this wicked wealth, who will trust you with true wealth? 12 And if you cannot be trusted with what belongs to someone else, who will give you something that will be your own? 13 You cannot be the slave of two masters. You will like one more than the other or be more loyal to one than to the other. You cannot serve God and money.

Some Sayings of Jesus

14 The Pharisees really loved money. So when they heard what Jesus said, they made fun of him. 15 But Jesus told them:

You are always making yourselves look good, but God sees what is in your heart. The things that most people think are important are worthless as far as God is concerned.

16 Until the time of John the Baptist, people had to obey the Law of Moses and the Books of the Prophets. But since God's kingdom has been preached, everyone is trying hard to get in. 17 Heaven and earth will disappear before the smallest letter of the Law does.

18 It is a terrible sin[a] for a man to divorce his wife and marry another woman. It is also a terrible sin for a man to marry a divorced woman.

Lazarus and the Rich Man

19 There was once a rich man who wore expensive clothes and every day ate the best food. 20 But a poor beggar named Lazarus was brought to the gate of the rich man's house. 21 He was happy just to eat the scraps that fell from the rich man's table. His body was covered with sores, and dogs kept coming up to lick them. 22 The poor man died, and angels took him to the place of honor next to Abraham.

The rich man also died and was buried. 23 He went to hell[b] and was suffering terribly. When he looked up and saw Abraham far off and Lazarus at his side, 24 he said to Abraham, "Have pity on me!

Send Lazarus to dip his finger in water and touch my tongue. I'm suffering terribly in this fire."

25 Abraham answered, "My friend, remember that while you lived, you had everything good, and Lazarus had everything bad. Now he is happy, and you are in pain. 26 And besides, there is a deep ditch between us, and no one from either side can cross over."

27 But the rich man said, "Abraham, then please send Lazarus to my father's home. 28 Let him warn my five brothers, so they won't come to this horrible place."

29 Abraham answered, "Your brothers can read what Moses and the prophets wrote. They should pay attention to that."

30 Then the rich man said, "No, that's not enough! If only someone from the dead would go to them, they would listen and turn to God."

31 So Abraham said, "If they won't pay attention to Moses and the prophets, they won't listen even to someone who comes back from the dead."

Faith and Service

17 Jesus said to his disciples:

There will always be something that causes people to sin. But anyone who causes them to sin is in for trouble. A person who causes even one of my little followers to sin 2 would be better off thrown into the ocean with a heavy stone tied around their neck. 3 So be careful what you do.

Correct any followers[c] of mine who sin, and forgive the ones who say they are sorry. 4 Even if one of them mistreats you seven times in one day and says, "I am sorry," you should still forgive that person.

5 The apostles said to the Lord, "Make our faith stronger!"

6 Jesus replied:

If you had faith no bigger than a tiny mustard seed, you could tell this mulberry tree to pull itself up, roots and all, and to plant itself in the ocean. And it would!

7 If your servant comes in from plowing or from taking care of the sheep, would you say, "Welcome! Come on in and have something to eat"? 8 No, you wouldn't say that. You would say, "Fix me something to eat. Get ready to serve me, so I can have my meal. Then later on you can eat and drink." 9 Servants don't deserve special thanks for doing what they are supposed to do. 10 And that's how it should be with you. When you've done all you should, then say, "We are merely servants, and we have simply done our duty."

Ten Men with Leprosy

11 On his way to Jerusalem, Jesus went along the border between Samaria and Galilee. 12 As he was going into a village, ten men with leprosy came toward him. They stood at a distance 13 and shouted, "Jesus, Master, have pity on us!"

---

z **16.7** *A thousand bushels*: The Greek text has "A hundred measures," and each measure is about ten or twelve bushels.

a **16.18** *a terrible sin*: The Greek text uses a word that means the sin of being unfaithful in marriage.   b **16.23** *hell*: The Greek text has "hades," which the Jewish people often thought of as the place where the dead wait for the final judgment.   c **17.3** *followers*: The Greek text has "brothers," which is often used in the New Testament for followers of Jesus.

14 Jesus looked at them and said, "Go show yourselves to the priests."

On their way they were healed. 15 When one of them discovered that he was healed, he came back, shouting praises to God. 16 He bowed down at the feet of Jesus and thanked him. The man was from the country of Samaria.

17 Jesus asked, "Weren't ten men healed? Where are the other nine? 18 Why was this foreigner the only one who came back to thank God?" 19 Then Jesus told the man, "You may get up and go. Your faith has made you well."

God's Kingdom

20 Some Pharisees asked Jesus when God's kingdom would come. He answered, "God's kingdom isn't something you can see. 21 There is no use saying, 'Look! Here it is' or 'Look! There it is.' God's kingdom is here with you."*d*

22 Jesus said to his disciples:

The time will come when you will long to see one of the days of the Son of Man, but you will not. 23 When people say to you, "Look there," or "Look here," don't go looking for him. 24 The day of the Son of Man will be like lightning flashing across the sky. 25 But first he must suffer terribly and be rejected by the people of today. 26 When the Son of Man comes, things will be just as they were when Noah lived. 27 People were eating, drinking, and getting married right up to the day when Noah went into the big boat. Then the flood came and drowned everyone on earth.

28 When Lot lived, people were also eating and drinking. They were buying, selling, planting, and building. 29 But on the very day Lot left Sodom, fiery flames poured down from the sky and killed everyone. 30 The same will happen on the day when the Son of Man appears.

31 At that time no one on a rooftop should go down into the house to get anything. No one in a field should go back to the house for anything. 32 Remember what happened to Lot's wife.

33 People who try to save their lives will lose them, and those who lose their lives will save them. 34 On that night two people will be sleeping in the same bed, but only one will be taken. The other will be left. 35-36 Two women will be together grinding wheat, but only one will be taken. The other will be left.*e*

37 Then Jesus' disciples spoke up, "But where will this happen, Lord?"

Jesus said, "Where there is a corpse, there will always be buzzards."

A Widow and a Judge

18 Jesus told his disciples a story about how they should keep on praying and never give up:

2 In a town there was once a judge who didn't fear God or care about people. 3 In that same town there was a widow who kept going to the judge and saying, "Make sure that I get fair treatment in court."

4 For a while the judge refused to do anything. Finally, he said to himself, "Even though I don't fear God or care about people, 5 I will help this widow because she keeps on bothering me. If I don't help her, she will wear me out."

6 The Lord said:

Think about what that crooked judge said. 7 Won't God protect his chosen ones who pray to him day and night? Won't he be concerned for them? 8 He will surely hurry and help them. But when the Son of Man comes, will he find on this earth anyone with faith?

A Pharisee and a Tax Collector

9 Jesus told a story to some people who thought they were better than others and who looked down on everyone else:

10 Two men went into the temple to pray. One was a Pharisee and the other a tax collector. 11 The Pharisee stood over by himself and prayed,*f* "God, I thank you that I am not greedy, dishonest, and unfaithful in marriage like other people. And I am really glad that I am not like that tax collector over there. 12 I go without eating for two days a week, and I give you one tenth of all I earn."

13 The tax collector stood off at a distance and did not think he was good enough even to look up toward heaven. He was so sorry for what he had done that he pounded his chest and prayed, "God, have pity on me! I am such a sinner."

14 Then Jesus said, "When the two men went home, it was the tax collector and not the Pharisee who was pleasing to God. If you put yourself above others, you will be put down. But if you humble yourself, you will be honored."

Jesus Blesses Little Children

15 Some people brought their little children for Jesus to bless. But when his disciples saw them doing this, they told the people to stop bothering him. 16 So Jesus called the children over to him and said, "Let the children come to me! Don't try to stop them. People who are like these children belong to God's kingdom.*g* 17 You will never get into God's kingdom unless you enter it like a child!"

A Rich and Important Man

18 An important man asked Jesus, "Good Teacher, what must I do to have eternal life?"

19 Jesus said, "Why do you call me good? Only God is good. 20 You know the commandments: 'Be faithful in marriage. Do not murder. Do not steal. Do not tell lies about others. Respect your father and mother.' "

21 He told Jesus, "I have obeyed all these commandments since I was a young man."

22 When Jesus heard this, he said, "There is one thing you still need to do. Go and sell everything you own! Give the

---

d **17.21** *here with you*: Or "in your hearts."   *e* **17.35,36** *will be left*: Some manuscripts add, "Two men will be in the same field, but only one will be taken. The other will be left."   *f* **18.11** *stood over by himself and prayed*: Some manuscripts have "stood up and prayed to himself."   *g* **18.16** *People who are like these children belong to God's kingdom*: Or "God's kingdom belongs to people who are like these children."

money to the poor, and you will have riches in heaven. Then come and be my follower." 23 When the man heard this, he was sad, because he was very rich.

24 Jesus saw how sad the man was. So he said, "It's terribly hard for rich people to get into God's kingdom! 25 In fact, it's easier for a camel to go through the eye of a needle than for a rich person to get into God's kingdom."

26 When the crowd heard this, they asked, "How can anyone ever be saved?"

27 Jesus replied, "There are some things that people cannot do, but God can do anything."

28 Peter said, "Remember, we left everything to be your followers!"

29 Jesus answered, "You can be sure that anyone who gives up home or wife or brothers or family or children because of God's kingdom 30 will be given much more in this life. And in the future world they will have eternal life."

Jesus Again Tells about His Death

31 Jesus took the twelve apostles aside and said:

We are now on our way to Jerusalem. Everything that the prophets wrote about the Son of Man will happen there. 32 He will be handed over to foreigners, who will make fun of him, mistreat him, and spit on him. 33 They will beat him and kill him, but three days later he will rise to life.

34 The apostles did not understand what Jesus was talking about. They could not understand, because the meaning of what he said was hidden from them.

Jesus Heals a Blind Beggar

35 When Jesus was coming close to Jericho, a blind man sat begging beside the road. 36 The man heard the crowd walking by and asked what was happening. 37 Some people told him that Jesus from Nazareth was passing by. 38 So the blind man shouted, "Jesus, Son of David, have pity on me!" 39 The people who were going along with Jesus told the man to be quiet. But he shouted even louder, "Son of David, have pity on me!"

40 Jesus stopped and told some people to bring the blind man over to him. When the blind man was getting near, Jesus asked, 41 "What do you want me to do for you?"

"Lord, I want to see!" he answered.

42 Jesus replied, "Look and you will see! Your eyes are healed because of your faith." 43 Right away the man could see, and he went with Jesus and started thanking God. When the crowds saw what happened, they praised God.

Zacchaeus

19 Jesus was going through Jericho, 2 where a man named Zacchaeus lived. He was in charge of collecting taxes and was very rich. 3-4 Jesus was heading his way, and Zacchaeus wanted to see what he was like. But Zacchaeus was a short man and could not see over the crowd. So he ran ahead and climbed up into a sycamore tree.

5 When Jesus got there, he looked up and said, "Zacchaeus, hurry down! I want to stay with you today." 6 Zacchaeus hurried down and gladly welcomed Jesus.

7 Everyone who saw this started grumbling, "This man Zacchaeus is a sinner! And Jesus is going home to eat with him."

8 Later that day Zacchaeus stood up and said to the Lord, "I will give half of my property to the poor. And I will now pay back four times as much to everyone I have ever cheated."

9 Jesus said to Zacchaeus, "Today you and your family have been saved, because you are a true son of Abraham. 10 The Son of Man came to look for and to save people who are lost."

A Story about Ten Servants

11 The crowd was still listening to Jesus as he was getting close to Jerusalem. Many of them thought that God's kingdom would soon appear, 12 and Jesus told them this story:

A prince once went to a foreign country to be crowned king and then to return. 13 But before leaving, he called in ten servants and gave each of them some money. He told them, "Use this to earn more money until I get back."

14 But the people of his country hated him, and they sent messengers to the foreign country to say, "We don't want this man to be our king."

15 After the prince had been made king, he returned and called in his servants. He asked them how much they had earned with the money they had been given.

16 The first servant came and said, "Sir, with the money you gave me I have earned ten times as much."

17 "That's fine, my good servant!" the king said. "Since you have shown that you can be trusted with a small amount, you will be given ten cities to rule."

18 The second one came and said, "Sir, with the money you gave me, I have earned five times as much."

19 The king said, "You will be given five cities."

20 Another servant came and said, "Sir, here is your money. I kept it safe in a handkerchief. 21 You are a hard man, and I was afraid of you. You take what isn't yours, and you harvest crops you didn't plant."

22 "You worthless servant!" the king told him. "You have condemned yourself by what you have just said. You knew that I am a hard man, taking what isn't mine and harvesting what I've not planted. 23 Why didn't you put my money in the bank? On my return, I could have had the money together with interest."

24 Then he said to some other servants standing there, "Take the money away from him and give it to the servant who earned ten times as much."

25 But they said, "Sir, he already has ten times as much!"

26 The king replied, "Those who have something will be given more. But everything will be taken away from those who don't have anything. 27 Now bring me the enemies who didn't want me to be their king. Kill them while I watch!"

Jesus Enters Jerusalem

28 When Jesus had finished saying all this, he went on toward Jerusalem. 29 As he was getting near Bethphage and Bethany on the Mount of Olives, he sent two of his disciples

on ahead. [30] He told them, "Go into the next village, where you will find a young donkey that has never been ridden. Untie the donkey and bring it here. [31] If anyone asks why you are doing that, just say, 'The Lord[h] needs it.' "

[32] They went off and found everything just as Jesus had said. [33] While they were untying the donkey, its owners asked, "Why are you doing that?"

[34] They answered, "The Lord[h] needs it."

[35] Then they led the donkey to Jesus. They put some of their clothes on its back and helped Jesus get on. [36] And as he rode along, the people spread clothes on the road in front of him. [37] When Jesus was starting down the Mount of Olives, his large crowd of disciples were happy and praised God because of all the miracles they had seen. [38] They shouted,

> "Blessed is the king who comes
>   in the name of the Lord!
> Peace in heaven
>   and glory to God."

[39] Some Pharisees in the crowd said to Jesus, "Teacher, make your disciples stop shouting!"

[40] But Jesus answered, "If they keep quiet, these stones will start shouting."

[41] When Jesus came closer and could see Jerusalem, he cried [42] and said:

It is too bad that today your people don't know what will bring them peace! Now it is hidden from them. [43] Jerusalem, the time will come when your enemies will build walls around you to attack you. Armies will surround you and close in on you from every side. [44] They will level you to the ground and kill your people. Not one stone in your buildings will be left on top of another. This will happen because you did not see that God had come to save you.

Jesus in the Temple

[45] When Jesus entered the temple, he started chasing out the people who were selling things. [46] He told them, "The Scriptures say, 'My house should be a place of worship.' But you have made it a place where robbers hide!"

[47] Each day, Jesus kept on teaching in the temple. So the chief priests, the teachers of the Law of Moses, and some other important people tried to have him killed. [48] But they could not find a way to do it, because everyone else was eager to listen to him.

A Question about Jesus' Authority

20 One day, Jesus was teaching in the temple and telling the good news. So the chief priests, the teachers, and the nation's leaders [2] asked him, "What right do you have to do these things? Who gave you this authority?"

[3] Jesus replied, "I want to ask you a question. [4] Who gave John the right to baptize? Was it God in heaven or merely some human being?"

[5] They talked this over and said to each other, "We can't say that God gave John this right. Jesus will ask us why we didn't believe John. [6] And we can't say that it was merely

some human who gave John the right to baptize. The crowd will stone us to death, because they think John was a prophet."

[7] So they told Jesus, "We don't know who gave John the right to baptize."

[8] Jesus replied, "Then I won't tell you who gave me the right to do what I do."

Renters of a Vineyard

[9] Jesus told the people this story:

A man once planted a vineyard and rented it out. Then he left the country for a long time. [10] When it was time to harvest the crop, he sent a servant to ask the renters for his share of the grapes. But they beat up the servant and sent him away without anything. [11] So the owner sent another servant. The renters also beat him up. They insulted him terribly and sent him away without a thing. [12] The owner sent a third servant. He was also beaten terribly and thrown out of the vineyard.

[13] The owner then said to himself, "What am I going to do? I know what. I'll send my son, the one I love so much. They will surely respect him!"

[14] When the renters saw the owner's son, they said to one another, "Someday he will own the vineyard. Let's kill him! Then we can have it all for ourselves." [15] So they threw him out of the vineyard and killed him.

Jesus asked, "What do you think the owner of the vineyard will do? [16] I'll tell you what. He will come and kill those renters and let someone else have his vineyard."

When the people heard this, they said, "This must never happen!"

[17] But Jesus looked straight at them and said, "Then what do the Scriptures mean when they say, 'The stone that the builders tossed aside is now the most important stone of all'? [18] Anyone who stumbles over this stone will get hurt, and anyone it falls on will be smashed to pieces."

[19] The chief priests and the teachers of the Law of Moses knew that Jesus was talking about them when he was telling this story. They wanted to arrest him right then, but they were afraid of the people.

Paying Taxes

[20] Jesus' enemies kept watching him closely, because they wanted to hand him over to the Roman governor. So they sent some men who pretended to be good. But they were really spies trying to catch Jesus saying something wrong. [21] The spies said to him, "Teacher, we know that you teach the truth about what God wants people to do. And you treat everyone with the same respect, no matter who they are. [22] Tell us, should we pay taxes to the Emperor or not?"

[23] Jesus knew that they were trying to trick him. So he told them, [24] "Show me a coin." Then he asked, "Whose picture and name are on it?"

"The Emperor's," they answered.

[25] Then he told them, "Give the Emperor what belongs to him and give God what belongs to God." [26] Jesus' enemies could not catch him saying anything wrong there in front of the people. They were amazed at his answer and kept quiet.

---

[h] 19.31,34 *The Lord*: Or "The master of the donkey."

Life in the Future World

27 The Sadducees did not believe that people would rise to life after death. So some of them came to Jesus 28 and said:

Teacher, Moses wrote that if a married man dies and has no children, his brother should marry the widow. Their first son would then be thought of as the son of the dead brother.

29 There were once seven brothers. The first one married, but died without having any children. 30 The second one married his brother's widow, and he also died without having any children. 31 The same thing happened to the third one. Finally, all seven brothers married that woman and died without having any children. 32 At last the woman died. 33 When God raises people from death, whose wife will this woman be? All seven brothers had married her.

34 Jesus answered:

The people in this world get married. 35 But in the future world no one who is worthy to rise from death will either marry 36 or die. They will be like the angels and will be God's children, because they have been raised to life.

37 In the story about the burning bush, Moses clearly shows that people will live again. He said, "The Lord is the God worshiped by Abraham, Isaac, and Jacob." 38 So the Lord isn't the God of the dead, but of the living. This means that everyone is alive as far as God is concerned.

39 Some of the teachers of the Law of Moses said, "Teacher, you have given a good answer!" 40 From then on, no one dared to ask Jesus any questions.

About David's Son

41 Jesus asked, "Why do people say that the Messiah will be the son of King David? 42 In the book of Psalms, David himself says,

'The Lord said to my Lord,
    Sit at my right side
43 until I make your enemies
    into a footstool for you.'

44 David spoke of the Messiah as his Lord, so how can the Messiah be his son?"

Jesus and the Teachers of the Law of Moses

45 While everyone was listening to Jesus, he said to his disciples:

46 Guard against the teachers of the Law of Moses! They love to walk around in long robes, and they like to be greeted in the market. They want the front seats in the meeting places and the best seats at banquets. 47 But they cheat widows out of their homes and then pray long prayers just to show off. These teachers will be punished most of all.

A Widow's Offering

21 Jesus looked up and saw some rich people tossing their gifts into the offering box. 2 He also saw a poor widow putting in two pennies. 3 And he said, "I tell you that this poor woman has put in more than all the others. 4 Everyone else gave what they didn't need. But she is very poor and gave everything she had."

The Temple Will Be Destroyed

5 Some people were talking about the beautiful stones used to build the temple and about the gifts that had been placed in it. Jesus said, 6 "Do you see these stones? The time is coming when not one of them will be left in place. They will all be knocked down."

Warning about Trouble

7 Some people asked, "Teacher, when will all this happen? How can we know when these things are about to take place?"

8 Jesus replied:

Don't be fooled by those who will come and claim to be me. They will say, "I am Christ!" and "Now is the time!" But don't follow them. 9 When you hear about wars and riots, don't be afraid. These things will have to happen first, but that isn't the end.

10 Nations will go to war against one another, and kingdoms will attack each other. 11 There will be great earthquakes, and in many places people will starve to death and suffer terrible diseases. All sorts of frightening things will be seen in the sky.

12 Before all this happens, you will be arrested and punished. You will be tried in your meeting places and put in jail. Because of me you will be placed on trial before kings and governors. 13 But this will be your chance to tell about your faith.

14 Don't worry about what you will say to defend yourselves. 15 I will give you the wisdom to know what to say. None of your enemies will be able to oppose you or to say that you are wrong. 16 You will be betrayed by your own parents, brothers, family, and friends. Some of you will even be killed. 17 Because of me, you will be hated by everyone. 18 But don't worry![i] 19 You will be saved by being faithful to me.

Jerusalem Will Be Destroyed

20 When you see Jerusalem surrounded by soldiers, you will know that it will soon be destroyed. 21 If you are living in Judea at that time, run to the mountains. If you are in the city, leave it. And if you are out in the country, don't go back into the city. 22 This time of punishment is what is written about in the Scriptures. 23 It will be an awful time for women who are expecting babies or nursing young children! Everywhere in the land people will suffer horribly and be punished. 24 Some of them will be killed by swords. Others will be carried off to foreign countries. Jerusalem will be overrun by foreign nations until their time comes to an end.

When the Son of Man Appears

25 Strange things will happen to the sun, moon, and stars. The nations on earth will be afraid of the

---

i 21.18 But don't worry: The Greek text has "Not a hair of your head will be lost," which means, "There's no need to worry."

roaring sea and tides, and they won't know what to do. 26 People will be so frightened that they will faint because of what is happening to the world. Every power in the sky will be shaken. 27 Then the Son of Man will be seen, coming in a cloud with great power and glory. 28 When all of this starts happening, stand up straight and be brave. You will soon be set free.

A Lesson from a Fig Tree

29 Then Jesus told them a story:

When you see a fig tree or any other tree 30 putting out leaves, you know that summer will soon come. 31 So, when you see these things happening, you know that God's kingdom will soon be here. 32 You can be sure that some of the people of this generation will still be alive when all of this takes place. 33 The sky and the earth won't last forever, but my words will.

A Warning

34 Don't spend all of your time thinking about eating or drinking or worrying about life. If you do, the final day will suddenly catch you 35 like a trap. That day will surprise everyone on earth. 36 Watch out and keep praying that you can escape all that is going to happen and that the Son of Man will be pleased with you.

37 Jesus taught in the temple each day, and he spent each night on the Mount of Olives. 38 Everyone got up early and came to the temple to hear him teach.

A Plot To Kill Jesus

22 The Festival of Thin Bread, also called Passover, was near. 2 The chief priests and the teachers of the Law of Moses were looking for a way to get rid of Jesus, because they were afraid of what the people might do. 3 Then Satan entered the heart of Judas Iscariot, who was one of the twelve apostles.

4 Judas went to talk with the chief priests and the officers of the temple police about how he could help them arrest Jesus. 5 They were very pleased and offered to pay Judas some money. 6 He agreed and started looking for a good chance to betray Jesus when the crowds were not around.

Jesus Eats with His Disciples

7 The day had come for the Festival of Thin Bread, and it was time to kill the Passover lambs. 8 So Jesus said to Peter and John, "Go and prepare the Passover meal for us to eat."

9 But they asked, "Where do you want us to prepare it?"

10 Jesus told them, "As you go into the city, you will meet a man carrying a jar of water. Follow him into the house 11 and say to the owner, 'Our teacher wants to know where he can eat the Passover meal with his disciples.' 12 The owner will take you upstairs and show you a large room ready for you to use. Prepare the meal there."

13 Peter and John left. They found everything just as Jesus had told them, and they prepared the Passover meal.

The Lord's Supper

14 When the time came for Jesus and the apostles to eat, 15 he said to them, "I have very much wanted to eat this Passover meal with you before I suffer. 16 I tell you that I will not eat another Passover meal until it is finally eaten in God's kingdom."

17 Jesus took a cup of wine in his hands and gave thanks to God. Then he told the apostles, "Take this wine and share it with each other. 18 I tell you that I will not drink any more wine until God's kingdom comes."

19 Jesus took some bread in his hands and gave thanks for it. He broke the bread and handed it to his apostles. Then he said, "This is my body, which is given for you. Eat this as a way of remembering me!"

20 After the meal he took another cup of wine in his hands. Then he said, "This is my blood. It is poured out for you, and with it God makes his new agreement. 21 The one who will betray me is here at the table with me! 22 The Son of Man will die in the way that has been decided for him, but it will be terrible for the one who betrays him!"

23 Then the apostles started arguing about who would ever do such a thing.

An Argument about Greatness

24 The apostles got into an argument about which one of them was the greatest. 25 So Jesus told them:

Foreign kings order their people around, and powerful rulers call themselves everyone's friends. 26 But don't be like them. The most important one of you should be like the least important, and your leader should be like a servant. 27 Who do people think is the greatest, a person who is served or one who serves? Isn't it the one who is served? But I have been with you as a servant.

28 You have stayed with me in all my troubles. 29 So I will give you the right to rule as kings, just as my Father has given me the right to rule as a king. 30 You will eat and drink with me in my kingdom, and you will each sit on a throne to judge the twelve tribes of Israel.

Jesus' Disciples Will Be Tested

31 Jesus said, "Simon, listen to me! Satan has demanded the right to test each one of you, as a farmer does when he separates wheat from the husks. 32 But Simon, I have prayed that your faith will be strong. And when you have come back to me, help the others."

33 Peter said, "Lord, I am ready to go with you to jail and even to die with you."

34 Jesus replied, "Peter, I tell you that before a rooster crows tomorrow morning, you will say three times that you don't know me."

Moneybags, Traveling Bags, and Swords

35 Jesus asked his disciples, "When I sent you out without a moneybag or a traveling bag or sandals, did you need anything?"

"No!" they answered.

36 Jesus told them, "But now, if you have a moneybag, take it with you. Also take a traveling bag, and if you don't have a sword, sell some of your clothes and buy one. 37 Do this because the Scriptures say, 'He was considered a criminal.' This was written about me, and it will soon come true."

38 The disciples said, "Lord, here are two swords!"

"Enough of that!" Jesus replied.

Jesus Prays

39 Jesus went out to the Mount of Olives, as he often did, and his disciples went with him. **40** When they got there, he told them, "Pray that you won't be tested."

41 Jesus walked on a little way before he knelt down and prayed, **42** "Father, if you will, please don't make me suffer by having me drink from this cup. But do what you want, and not what I want."

43 Then an angel from heaven came to help him. **44** Jesus was in great pain and prayed so sincerely that his sweat fell to the ground like drops of blood.

45 Jesus got up from praying and went over to his disciples. They were asleep and worn out from being so sad. **46** He said to them, "Why are you asleep? Wake up and pray that you won't be tested."

Jesus Is Arrested

47 While Jesus was still speaking, a crowd came up. It was led by Judas, one of the twelve apostles. He went over to Jesus and greeted him with a kiss.

48 Jesus asked Judas, "Are you betraying the Son of Man with a kiss?"

49 When Jesus' disciples saw what was about to happen, they asked, "Lord, should we attack them with a sword?" **50** One of the disciples even struck at the high priest's servant with his sword and cut off the servant's right ear.

51 "Enough of that!" Jesus said. Then he touched the servant's ear and healed it.

52 Jesus spoke to the chief priests, the temple police, and the leaders who had come to arrest him. He said, "Why do you come out with swords and clubs and treat me like a criminal? **53** I was with you every day in the temple, and you didn't arrest me. But this is your time, and darkness is in control."

Peter Says He Doesn't Know Jesus

54 Jesus was arrested and led away to the house of the high priest, while Peter followed at a distance. **55** Some people built a fire in the middle of the courtyard and were sitting around it. Peter sat there with them, **56** and a servant girl saw him. Then after she had looked at him carefully, she said, "This man was with Jesus!"

57 Peter said, "Woman, I don't even know that man!"

58 A little later someone else saw Peter and said, "You are one of them!"

"No, I'm not!" Peter replied.

59 About an hour later another man insisted, "This man must have been with Jesus. They both come from Galilee."

60 Peter replied, "I don't know what you are talking about!" Right then, while Peter was still speaking, a rooster crowed.

61 The Lord turned and looked at Peter. And Peter remembered that the Lord had said, "Before a rooster crows tomorrow morning, you will say three times that you don't know me." **62** Then Peter went out and cried hard.

63 The men who were guarding Jesus made fun of him and beat him. **64** They put a blindfold on him and said, "Tell us who struck you!" **65** They kept on insulting Jesus in many other ways.

Jesus Is Questioned by the Council

66 At daybreak the nation's leaders, the chief priests, and the teachers of the Law of Moses got together and brought Jesus before their council. **67** They said, "Tell us! Are you the Messiah?"

Jesus replied, "If I said so, you wouldn't believe me. **68** And if I asked you a question, you wouldn't answer. **69** But from now on, the Son of Man will be seated at the right side of God All-Powerful."

70 Then they asked, "Are you the Son of God?"

Jesus answered, "You say I am!"[/]

71 They replied, "Why do we need more witnesses? He said it himself!"

Pilate Questions Jesus

23 Everyone in the council got up and led Jesus off to Pilate. **2** They started accusing him and said, "We caught this man trying to get our people to riot and to stop paying taxes to the Emperor. He also claims that he is the Messiah, our king."

3 Pilate asked Jesus, "Are you the king of the Jews?"

"Those are your words," Jesus answered.

4 Pilate told the chief priests and the crowd, "I don't find him guilty of anything."

5 But they all kept on saying, "He has been teaching and causing trouble all over Judea. He started in Galilee and has now come all the way here."

Jesus Is Brought before Herod

6 When Pilate heard this, he asked, "Is this man from Galilee?" **7** After Pilate learned that Jesus came from the region ruled by Herod, he sent him to Herod, who was in Jerusalem at that time.

8 For a long time Herod had wanted to see Jesus and was very happy because he finally had this chance. He had heard many things about Jesus and hoped to see him work a miracle.

9 Herod asked him a lot of questions, but Jesus did not answer. **10** Then the chief priests and the teachers of the Law of Moses stood up and accused him of all kinds of bad things.

11 Herod and his soldiers made fun of Jesus and insulted him. They put a fine robe on him and sent him back to Pilate. **12** That same day Herod and Pilate became friends, even though they had been enemies before this.

The Death Sentence

13 Pilate called together the chief priests, the leaders, and the people. **14** He told them, "You brought Jesus to me and said he was a troublemaker. But I have questioned him here in front of you, and I have not found him guilty of anything that you say he has done. **15** Herod didn't find him guilty either and sent him back. This man doesn't deserve to be put to death! **16-17** I will just have him beaten with a whip and set free."[k]

18 But the whole crowd shouted, "Kill Jesus! Give us Barabbas!" **19** Now Barabbas was in jail because he had started a riot in the city and had murdered someone.

20 Pilate wanted to set Jesus free, so he spoke again to the crowds. **21** But they kept shouting, "Nail him to a cross! Nail him to a cross!"

---

l **22.70** *You say I am*: Or "That's what you say."

22 Pilate spoke to them a third time, "But what crime has he done? I have not found him guilty of anything for which he should be put to death. I will have him beaten with a whip and set free."

23 The people kept on shouting as loud as they could for Jesus to be put to death. **24** Finally, Pilate gave in. **25** He freed the man who was in jail for rioting and murder, because he was the one the crowd wanted to be set free. Then Pilate handed Jesus over for them to do what they wanted with him.

Jesus Is Nailed to a Cross

26 As Jesus was being led away, some soldiers grabbed hold of a man from Cyrene named Simon. He was coming in from the fields, but they put the cross on him and made him carry it behind Jesus.

27 A large crowd was following Jesus, and in the crowd a lot of women were crying and weeping for him. **28** Jesus turned to the women and said:

Women of Jerusalem, don't cry for me! Cry for yourselves and for your children. **29** Someday people will say, "Women who never had children are really fortunate!" **30** At that time everyone will say to the mountains, "Fall on us!" They will say to the hills, "Hide us!" **31** If this can happen when the wood is green, what do you think will happen when it is dry?

32 Two criminals were led out to be put to death with Jesus. **33** When the soldiers came to the place called "The Skull," they nailed Jesus to a cross. They also nailed the two criminals to crosses, one on each side of Jesus.

34-35 Jesus said, "Father, forgive these people! They don't know what they're doing."*l*

While the crowd stood there watching Jesus, the soldiers gambled for his clothes. The leaders insulted him by saying, "He saved others. Now he should save himself, if he really is God's chosen Messiah!"

36 The soldiers made fun of Jesus and brought him some wine. **37** They said, "If you are the king of the Jews, save yourself!"

38 Above him was a sign that said, "This is the King of the Jews."

39 One of the criminals hanging there also insulted Jesus by saying, "Aren't you the Messiah? Save yourself and save us!"

40 But the other criminal told the first one off, "Don't you fear God? Aren't you getting the same punishment as this man? **41** We got what was coming to us, but he didn't do anything wrong." **42** Then he said to Jesus, "Remember me when you come into power!"

43 Jesus replied, "I promise that today you will be with me in paradise."*m*

The Death of Jesus

44 Around noon the sky turned dark and stayed that way until the middle of the afternoon. **45** The sun stopped shining, and the curtain in the temple split down the middle.

46 Jesus shouted, "Father, I put myself in your hands!" Then he died.

47 When the Roman officer saw what had happened, he praised God and said, "Jesus must really have been a good man!"

48 A crowd had gathered to see the terrible sight. Then after they had seen it, they felt brokenhearted and went home. **49** All of Jesus' close friends and the women who had come with him from Galilee stood at a distance and watched.

Jesus Is Buried

50-51 There was a man named Joseph, who was from Arimathea in Judea. Joseph was a good and honest man, and he was eager for God's kingdom to come. He was also a member of the council, but he did not agree with what they had decided.

52 Joseph went to Pilate and asked for Jesus' body. **53** He took the body down from the cross and wrapped it in fine cloth. Then he put it in a tomb that had been cut out of solid rock and had never been used. **54** It was Friday, and the Sabbath was about to begin.

55 The women who had come with Jesus from Galilee followed Joseph and watched how Jesus' body was placed in the tomb. **56** Then they went to prepare some sweet-smelling spices for his burial. But on the Sabbath they rested, as the Law of Moses commands.

Jesus Is Alive

24 Very early on Sunday morning the women went to the tomb, carrying the spices that they had prepared. **2** When they found the stone rolled away from the entrance, **3** they went in. But they did not find the body of the Lord*n* Jesus, **4** and they did not know what to think.

Suddenly two men in shining white clothes stood beside them. **5** The women were afraid and bowed to the ground. But the men said, "Why are you looking in the place of the dead for someone who is alive? **6** Jesus isn't here! He has been raised from death. Remember that while he was still in Galilee, he told you, **7** 'The Son of Man will be handed over to sinners who will nail him to a cross. But three days later he will rise to life.' " **8** Then they remembered what Jesus had said.

9-10 Mary Magdalene, Joanna, Mary the mother of James, and some other women were the ones who had gone to the tomb. When they returned, they told the eleven apostles and the others what had happened. **11** The apostles thought it was all nonsense, and they would not believe.

12 But Peter ran to the tomb. And when he stooped down and looked in, he saw only the burial clothes. Then he returned, wondering what had happened.*o*

Jesus Appears to Two Disciples

13 That same day two of Jesus' disciples were going to the village of Emmaus, which was about seven miles from Jerusalem. **14** As they were talking and thinking about what had happened, **15** Jesus came near and started walking along beside them. **16** But they did not know who he was.

---

k **23.16,17** *set free*: Some manuscripts add, "Pilate said this, because at every Passover he was supposed to set one prisoner free for the Jewish people." *l* **23.34,35** *Jesus said, "Father, forgive these people! They don't know what they're doing."*: These words are not in some manuscripts. *m* **23.43** *paradise*: In the Greek translation of the Old Testament, this word is used for the Garden of Eden. In New Testament times it was sometimes used for the place where God's people are happy and at rest, as they wait for the final judgment. *n* **24.3** *the Lord*: These words are not in some manuscripts.

17 Jesus asked them, "What were you talking about as you walked along?"

The two of them stood there looking sad and gloomy. **18** Then the one named Cleopas asked Jesus, "Are you the only person from Jerusalem who didn't know what was happening there these last few days?"

19 "What do you mean?" Jesus asked.

They answered:

Those things that happened to Jesus from Nazareth. By what he did and said he showed that he was a powerful prophet, who pleased God and all the people. **20** Then the chief priests and our leaders had him arrested and sentenced to die on a cross. **21** We had hoped that he would be the one to set Israel free! But it has already been three days since all this happened.

22 Some women in our group surprised us. They had gone to the tomb early in the morning, **23** but did not find the body of Jesus. They came back, saying that they had seen a vision of angels who told them that he is alive. **24** Some men from our group went to the tomb and found it just as the women had said. But they didn't see Jesus either.

25 Then Jesus asked the two disciples, "Why can't you understand? How can you be so slow to believe all that the prophets said? **26** Didn't you know that the Messiah would have to suffer before he was given his glory?" **27** Jesus then explained everything written about himself in the Scriptures, beginning with the Law of Moses and the Books of the Prophets.

28 When the two of them came near the village where they were going, Jesus seemed to be going farther. **29** They begged him, "Stay with us! It's already late, and the sun is going down." So Jesus went into the house to stay with them.

30 After Jesus sat down to eat, he took some bread. He blessed it and broke it. Then he gave it to them. **31** At once they knew who he was, but he disappeared. **32** They said to each other, "When he talked with us along the road and explained the Scriptures to us, didn't it warm our hearts?" **33** So they got right up and returned to Jerusalem.

The two disciples found the eleven apostles and the others gathered together. **34** And they learned from the group that the Lord was really alive and had appeared to Peter. **35** Then the disciples from Emmaus told what happened on the road and how they knew he was the Lord when he broke the bread.

What Jesus' Followers Must Do

36 While Jesus' disciples were talking about what had happened, Jesus appeared and greeted them. **37** They were frightened and terrified because they thought they were seeing a ghost.

38 But Jesus said, "Why are you so frightened? Why do you doubt? **39** Look at my hands and my feet and see who I am! Touch me and find out for yourselves. Ghosts don't have flesh and bones as you see I have."

40 After Jesus said this, he showed them his hands and his feet. **41** The disciples were so glad and amazed that they could not believe it. Jesus then asked them, "Do you have something to eat?" **42** They gave him a piece of baked fish. **43** He took it and ate it as they watched.

44 Jesus said to them, "While I was still with you, I told you that everything written about me in the Law of Moses, the Books of the Prophets, and in the Psalms had to happen."

45 Then he helped them understand the Scriptures. **46** He told them:

The Scriptures say that the Messiah must suffer, then three days later he will rise from death. **47** They also say that all people of every nation must be told in my name to turn to God, in order to be forgiven. So beginning in Jerusalem, **48** you must tell everything that has happened. **49** I will send you the one my Father has promised, but you must stay in the city until you are given power from heaven.

Jesus Returns to Heaven

50 Jesus led his disciples out to Bethany, where he raised his hands and blessed them. **51** As he was doing this, he left and was taken up to heaven.*p* **52** After his disciples had worshiped him,*q* they returned to Jerusalem and were very happy. **53** They spent their time in the temple, praising God.

---

o **24.12** *what had happened*: Verse 12 is not in some manuscripts.   *p* **24.51** *and was taken up to heaven*: These words are not in some manuscripts.   *q* **24.52** *After his disciples had worshiped him*: These words are not in some manuscripts.

JOHN

The Word of Life

1 In the beginning was the one
who is called the Word.
The Word was with God
and was truly God.
² From the very beginning
the Word was with God.

³ And with this Word,
God created all things.
Nothing was made
without the Word.
Everything that was created
⁴ received its life from him,
and his life gave light
to everyone.
⁵ The light keeps shining
in the dark,
and darkness has never
put it out.ᵃ
⁶ God sent a man named John,
⁷ who came to tell
about the light
and to lead all people
to have faith.
⁸ John wasn't that light.
He came only to tell
about the light.

⁹ The true light that shines
on everyone
was coming into the world.
¹⁰ The Word was in the world,
but no one knew him,
though God had made the world
with his Word.
¹¹ He came into his own world,
but his own nation
did not welcome him.
¹² Yet some people accepted him
and put their faith in him.
So he gave them the right
to be the children of God.
¹³ They were not God's children
by nature or because
of any human desires.
God himself was the one
who made them his children.

¹⁴ The Word became
a human being
and lived here with us.
We saw his true glory,
the glory of the only Son
of the Father.
From him all the kindness
and all the truth of God
have come down to us.

¹⁵ John spoke about him and shouted, "This is the one I told you would come! He is greater than I am, because he was alive before I was born."
¹⁶ Because of all that the Son is, we have been given one blessing after another.ᵇ ¹⁷ The Law was given by Moses, but Jesus Christ brought us undeserved kindness and truth. ¹⁸ No one has ever seen God. The only Son, who is truly God and is closest to the Father, has shown us what God is like.

John the Baptist Tells about Jesus

¹⁹⁻²⁰ The Jewish leaders in Jerusalem sent priests and temple helpers to ask John who he was. He told them plainly, "I am not the Messiah." ²¹ Then when they asked him if he were Elijah, he said, "No, I am not!" And when they asked if he were the Prophet, he also said "No!"

²² Finally, they said, "Who are you then? We have to give an answer to the ones who sent us. Tell us who you are!"

²³ John answered in the words of the prophet Isaiah, "I am only someone shouting in the desert, 'Get the road ready for the Lord!' "

²⁴ Some Pharisees had also been sent to John. ²⁵ They asked him, "Why are you baptizing people, if you are not the Messiah or Elijah or the Prophet?"

²⁶ John told them, "I use water to baptize people. But here with you is someone you don't know. ²⁷ Even though I came first, I am not good enough to untie his sandals." ²⁸ John said this as he was baptizing east of the Jordan River in Bethany.

The Lamb of God

²⁹ The next day, John saw Jesus coming toward him and said:

Here is the Lamb of God who takes away the sin of the world! ³⁰ He is the one I told you about when I said, "Someone else will come. He is greater than I am, because he was alive before I was born." ³¹ I didn't know who he was. But I came to baptize you with water, so that everyone in Israel would see him.

³² I was there and saw the Spirit come down on him like a dove from heaven. And the Spirit stayed on him. ³³ Before this I didn't know who he was. But the one who sent me to baptize with water had told me, "You will see the Spirit come down and stay on someone. Then you will know

---

ᵃ **1.5** *put it out*: Or "understood it." ᵇ **1.16** *one blessing after another*: Or "one blessing in place of another."

that he is the one who will baptize with the Holy Spirit." [34] I saw this happen, and I tell you that he is the Son of God.

The First Disciples of Jesus

[35] The next day, John was there again, and two of his followers were with him. [36] When he saw Jesus walking by, he said, "Here is the Lamb of God!" [37] John's two followers heard him, and they went with Jesus.

[38] When Jesus turned and saw them, he asked, "What do you want?"

They answered, "Rabbi, where do you live?" The Hebrew word "Rabbi" means "Teacher."

[39] Jesus replied, "Come and see!" It was already about four o'clock in the afternoon when they went with him and saw where he lived. So they stayed on for the rest of the day.

[40] One of the two men who had heard John and had gone with Jesus was Andrew, the brother of Simon Peter. [41] The first thing Andrew did was to find his brother and tell him, "We have found the Messiah!" The Hebrew word "Messiah" means the same as the Greek word "Christ."

[42] Andrew brought his brother to Jesus. And when Jesus saw him, he said, "Simon son of John, you will be called Cephas." This name can be translated as "Peter."[c]

Jesus Chooses Philip and Nathanael

[43-44] The next day Jesus decided to go to Galilee. There he met Philip, who was from Bethsaida, the hometown of Andrew and Peter. Jesus said to Philip, "Come with me."

[45] Philip then found Nathanael and said, "We have found the one that Moses and the Prophets wrote about. He is Jesus, the son of Joseph from Nazareth."

[46] Nathanael asked, "Can anything good come from Nazareth?"

Philip answered, "Come and see."

[47] When Jesus saw Nathanael coming toward him, he said, "Here is a true descendant of our ancestor Israel. And he isn't deceitful."

[48] "How do you know me?" Nathanael asked.

Jesus answered, "Before Philip called you, I saw you under the fig tree."

[49] Nathanael said, "Rabbi, you are the Son of God and the King of Israel!"

[50] Jesus answered, "Did you believe me just because I said that I saw you under the fig tree? You will see something even greater. [51] I tell you for certain that you will see heaven open and God's angels going up and coming down on the Son of Man."

Jesus at a Wedding in Cana

2 Three days later Mary, the mother of Jesus, was at a wedding feast in the village of Cana in Galilee. [2] Jesus and his disciples had also been invited and were there.

[3] When the wine was all gone, Mary said to Jesus, "They don't have any more wine."

[4] Jesus replied, "Mother, my time hasn't yet come! You must not tell me what to do."

[5] Mary then said to the servants, "Do whatever Jesus tells you to do."

[6] At the feast there were six stone water jars that were used by the people for washing themselves in the way that their religion said they must. Each jar held about twenty or thirty gallons. [7] Jesus told the servants to fill them to the top with water. Then after the jars had been filled, [8] he said, "Now take some water and give it to the man in charge of the feast."

The servants did as Jesus told them, [9] and the man in charge drank some of the water that had now turned into wine. He did not know where the wine had come from, but the servants did. He called the bridegroom over [10] and said, "The best wine is always served first. Then after the guests have had plenty, the other wine is served. But you have kept the best until last!"

[11] This was Jesus' first miracle,[d] and he did it in the village of Cana in Galilee. There Jesus showed his glory, and his disciples put their faith in him. [12] After this, he went with his mother, his brothers, and his disciples to the town of Capernaum, where they stayed for a few days.

Jesus in the Temple

[13] Not long before the Jewish festival of Passover, Jesus went to Jerusalem. [14] There he found people selling cattle, sheep, and doves in the temple. He also saw moneychangers sitting at their tables. [15] So he took some rope and made a whip. Then he chased everyone out of the temple, together with their sheep and cattle. He turned over the tables of the moneychangers and scattered their coins.

[16] Jesus said to the people who had been selling doves, "Get those doves out of here! Don't make my Father's house a marketplace."

[17] The disciples then remembered that the Scriptures say, "My love for your house burns in me like a fire."

[18] The Jewish leaders asked Jesus, "What miracle[d] will you work to show us why you have done this?"

[19] "Destroy this temple," Jesus answered, "and in three days I will build it again!"

[20] The leaders replied, "It took forty-six years to build this temple. What makes you think you can rebuild it in three days?"

[21] But Jesus was talking about his body as a temple. [22] And when he was raised from death, his disciples remembered what he had told them. Then they believed the Scriptures and the words of Jesus.

Jesus Knows What People Are Like

[23] In Jerusalem during Passover many people put their faith in Jesus, because they saw him work miracles.[d] [24] But Jesus knew what was in their hearts, and he would not let them have power over him. [25] No one had to tell him what people were like. He already knew.

Jesus and Nicodemus

3 There was a man named Nicodemus who was a Pharisee and a Jewish leader. [2] One night he went to Jesus and said, "Sir, we know that God has sent you to teach us. You could not work these miracles, unless God were with you."

[3] Jesus replied, "I tell you for certain that you must be born from above[e] before you can see God's kingdom!"

---

[c] **1.42** *Peter*: The Aramaic name "Cephas" and the Greek name "Peter" each mean "rock." [d] **2.11,18,23** *miracle*: The Greek text has "sign." In the Gospel of John the word "sign" is used for the miracle itself and as a way of pointing to Jesus as the Son of God. [e] **3.3** *from above*: Or "in a new way." The same Greek word is used in verses 7, 31.

⁴ Nicodemus asked, "How can a grown man ever be born a second time?"

⁵ Jesus answered:

I tell you for certain that before you can get into God's kingdom, you must be born not only by water, but by the Spirit. ⁶ Humans give life to their children. Yet only God's Spirit can change you into a child of God. ⁷ Don't be surprised when I say that you must be born from above. ⁸ Only God's Spirit gives new life. The Spirit is like the wind that blows wherever it wants to. You can hear the wind, but you don't know where it comes from or where it is going.

⁹ "How can this be?" Nicodemus asked.

¹⁰ Jesus replied:

How can you be a teacher of Israel and not know these things? ¹¹ I tell you for certain that we know what we are talking about because we have seen it ourselves. But none of you will accept what we say. ¹² If you don't believe when I talk to you about things on earth, how can you possibly believe if I talk to you about things in heaven?

¹³ No one has gone up to heaven except the Son of Man, who came down from there. ¹⁴ And the Son of Man must be lifted up, just as that metal snake was lifted up by Moses in the desert. ¹⁵ Then everyone who has faith in the Son of Man will have eternal life.

¹⁶ God loved the people of this world so much that he gave his only Son, so that everyone who has faith in him will have eternal life and never really die. ¹⁷ God did not send his Son into the world to condemn its people. He sent him to save them! ¹⁸ No one who has faith in God's Son will be condemned. But everyone who doesn't have faith in him has already been condemned for not having faith in God's only Son.

¹⁹ The light has come into the world, and people who do evil things are judged guilty because they love the dark more than the light. ²⁰ People who do evil hate the light and won't come to the light, because it clearly shows what they have done. ²¹ But everyone who lives by the truth will come to the light, because they want others to know that God is really the one doing what they do.

Jesus and John the Baptist

²² Later, Jesus and his disciples went to Judea, where he stayed with them for a while and was baptizing people.

²³⁻²⁴ John had not yet been put in jail. He was at Aenon near Salim, where there was a lot of water, and people were coming there for John to baptize them.

²⁵ John's followers got into an argument with a Jewish man[f] about a ceremony of washing. ²⁶ They went to John and said, "Rabbi, you spoke about a man when you were with him east of the Jordan. He is now baptizing people, and everyone is going to him."

²⁷ John replied:

No one can do anything unless God in heaven allows it. ²⁸ You surely remember how I told you that I am not the Messiah. I am only the one sent ahead of him.

²⁹ At a wedding the groom is the one who gets married. The best man is glad just to be there and to hear the groom's voice. That's why I am so glad. ³⁰ Jesus must become more important, while I become less important.

The One Who Comes from Heaven

³¹ God's Son comes from heaven and is above all others. Everyone who comes from the earth belongs to the earth and speaks about earthly things. The one who comes from heaven is above all others. ³² He speaks about what he has seen and heard, and yet no one believes him. ³³ But everyone who does believe him has shown that God is truthful. ³⁴ The Son was sent to speak God's message, and he has been given the full power of God's Spirit.

³⁵ The Father loves the Son and has given him everything. ³⁶ Everyone who has faith in the Son has eternal life. But no one who rejects him will ever share in that life, and God will be angry with them forever.

4 Jesus knew that the Pharisees had heard that he was winning and baptizing more followers than John was. ² But Jesus' disciples were really the ones doing the baptizing, and not Jesus himself.

Jesus and the Samaritan Woman

³ Jesus left Judea and started for Galilee again. ⁴ This time he had to go through Samaria, ⁵ and on his way he came to the town of Sychar. It was near the field that Jacob had long ago given to his son Joseph. ⁶⁻⁸ The well that Jacob had dug was still there, and Jesus sat down beside it because he was tired from traveling. It was noon, and after Jesus' disciples had gone into town to buy some food, a Samaritan woman came to draw water from the well.

Jesus asked her, "Would you please give me a drink of water?"

⁹ "You are a Jew," she replied, "and I am a Samaritan woman. How can you ask me for a drink of water when Jews and Samaritans won't have anything to do with each other?"[g]

¹⁰ Jesus answered, "You don't know what God wants to give you, and you don't know who is asking you for a drink. If you did, you would ask me for the water that gives life."

¹¹ "Sir," the woman said, "you don't even have a bucket, and the well is deep. Where are you going to get this life-giving water? ¹² Our ancestor Jacob dug this well for us, and his family and animals got water from it. Are you greater than Jacob?"

¹³ Jesus answered, "Everyone who drinks this water will get thirsty again. ¹⁴ But no one who drinks the water I give will ever be thirsty again. The water I give is like a flowing fountain that gives eternal life."

¹⁵ The woman replied, "Sir, please give me a drink of

---

f **3.25** *a Jewish man*: Some manuscripts have "some Jewish men."   *g* **4.9** *won't have anything to do with each other*: Or "won't use the same cups." The Samaritans lived in the land between Judea and Galilee. They worshiped God differently from the Jews and did not get along with them.

that water! Then I won't get thirsty and have to come to this well again."

16 Jesus told her, "Go and bring your husband."

17-18 The woman answered, "I don't have a husband."

"That's right," Jesus replied, "you're telling the truth. You don't have a husband. You have already been married five times, and the man you are now living with isn't your husband."

19 The woman said, "Sir, I can see that you are a prophet. 20 My ancestors worshiped on this mountain, but you Jews say Jerusalem is the only place to worship."

21 Jesus said to her:

Believe me, the time is coming when you won't worship the Father either on this mountain or in Jerusalem. 22 You Samaritans don't really know the one you worship. But we Jews do know the God we worship, and by using us, God will save the world. 23 But a time is coming, and it is already here! Even now the true worshipers are being led by the Spirit to worship the Father according to the truth. These are the ones the Father is seeking to worship him. 24 God is Spirit, and those who worship God must be led by the Spirit to worship him according to the truth.

25 The woman said, "I know that the Messiah will come. He is the one we call Christ. When he comes, he will explain everything to us."

26 "I am that one," Jesus told her, "and I am speaking to you now."

27 The disciples returned about this time and were surprised to find Jesus talking with a woman. But none of them asked him what he wanted or why he was talking with her.

28 The woman left her water jar and ran back into town. She said to the people, 29 "Come and see a man who told me everything I have ever done! Could he be the Messiah?" 30 Everyone in town went out to see Jesus.

31 While this was happening, Jesus' disciples were saying to him, "Teacher, please eat something."

32 But Jesus told them, "I have food that you don't know anything about."

33 His disciples started asking each other, "Has someone brought him something to eat?"

34 Jesus said:

My food is to do what God wants! He is the one who sent me, and I must finish the work that he gave me to do. 35 You may say that there are still four months until harvest time. But I tell you to look, and you will see that the fields are ripe and ready to harvest. 36 Even now the harvest workers are receiving their reward by gathering a harvest that brings eternal life. Then everyone who planted the seed and everyone who harvests the crop will celebrate together. 37 So the saying proves true, "Some plant the seed, and others harvest the crop." 38 I am sending you to harvest crops in fields where others have done all the hard work.

39 A lot of Samaritans in that town put their faith in Jesus

because the woman had said, "This man told me everything I have ever done." 40 They came and asked him to stay in their town, and he stayed on for two days.

41 Many more Samaritans put their faith in Jesus because of what they heard him say. 42 They told the woman, "We no longer have faith in Jesus just because of what you told us. We have heard him ourselves, and we are certain that he is the Savior of the world!"

Jesus Heals an Official's Son

43-44 Jesus had said, "Prophets are honored everywhere, except in their own country." Then two days later he left 45 and went to Galilee. The people there welcomed him, because they had gone to the festival in Jerusalem and had seen everything he had done.

46 While Jesus was in Galilee, he returned to the village of Cana, where he had turned the water into wine. There was an official in Capernaum whose son was sick. 47 And when the man heard that Jesus had come from Judea, he went and begged him to keep his son from dying.

48 Jesus told the official, "You won't have faith unless you see miracles and wonders!"

49 The man replied, "Lord, please come before my son dies!"

50 Jesus then said, "Your son will live. Go on home to him." The man believed Jesus and started back home.

51 Some of the official's servants met him along the road and told him, "Your son is better!" 52 He asked them when the boy got better, and they answered, "The fever left him yesterday at one o'clock."

53 The boy's father realized that at one o'clock the day before, Jesus had told him, "Your son will live!" So the man and everyone in his family put their faith in Jesus.

54 This was the second miracle that Jesus worked after he left Judea and went to Galilee.

Jesus Heals a Sick Man

5 Later, Jesus went to Jerusalem for another Jewish festival. 2 In the city near the sheep gate was a pool with five porches, and its name in Hebrew was Bethzatha.h

3-4 Many sick, blind, lame, and crippled people were lying close to the pool.i

5 Beside the pool was a man who had been sick for thirty-eight years. 6 When Jesus saw the man and realized that he had been crippled for a long time, he asked him, "Do you want to be healed?"

7 The man answered, "Lord, I don't have anyone to put me in the pool when the water is stirred up. I try to get in, but someone else always gets there first."

8 Jesus told him, "Pick up your mat and walk!" 9 Right then the man was healed. He picked up his mat and started walking around. The day on which this happened was a Sabbath.

10 When the Jewish leaders saw the man carrying his mat, they said to him, "This is the Sabbath! No one is allowed to carry a mat on the Sabbath."

11 But he replied, "The man who healed me told me to pick up my mat and walk."

12 They asked him, "Who is this man that told you to

---

h 5.2 Bethzatha: Some manuscripts have "Bethesda" and others have "Bethsaida." i 5.3,4 pool: Some manuscripts add, "They were waiting for the water to be stirred, because an angel from the Lord would sometimes come down and stir it. The first person to get into the pool after that would be healed."

pick up your mat and walk?" [13] But he did not know who Jesus was, and Jesus had left because of the crowd.

[14] Later, Jesus met the man in the temple and told him, "You are now well. But don't sin anymore or something worse might happen to you." [15] The man left and told the leaders that Jesus was the one who had healed him. [16] They started making a lot of trouble for Jesus because he did things like this on the Sabbath.

[17] But Jesus said, "My Father has never stopped working, and that is why I keep on working." [18] Now the leaders wanted to kill Jesus for two reasons. First, he had broken the law of the Sabbath. But even worse, he had said that God was his Father, which made him equal with God.

The Son's Authority

[19] Jesus told the people:

I tell you for certain that the Son cannot do anything on his own. He can do only what he sees the Father doing, and he does exactly what he sees the Father do. [20] The Father loves the Son and has shown him everything he does. The Father will show him even greater things, and you will be amazed. [21] Just as the Father raises the dead and gives life, so the Son gives life to anyone he wants to.

[22] The Father doesn't judge anyone, but he has made his Son the judge of everyone. [23] The Father wants all people to honor the Son as much as they honor him. When anyone refuses to honor the Son, that is the same as refusing to honor the Father who sent him. [24] I tell you for certain that everyone who hears my message and has faith in the one who sent me has eternal life and will never be condemned. They have already gone from death to life.

[25] I tell you for certain that the time will come, and it is already here, when all of the dead will hear the voice of the Son of God. And those who listen to it will live! [26] The Father has the power to give life, and he has given that same power to the Son. [27] And he has given his Son the right to judge everyone, because he is the Son of Man.

[28] Don't be surprised! The time will come when all of the dead will hear the voice of the Son of Man, [29] and they will come out of their graves. Everyone who has done good things will rise to life, but everyone who has done evil things will rise and be condemned.

[30] I cannot do anything on my own. The Father sent me, and he is the one who told me how to judge. I judge with fairness, because I obey him, and I don't just try to please myself.

Witnesses to Jesus

[31] If I speak for myself, there is no way to prove I am telling the truth. [32] But there is someone else who speaks for me, and I know what he says is true. [33] You sent messengers to John, and he told them the truth. [34] I don't depend on what people say about me, but I tell you these things so that you may be saved. [35] John was a lamp that gave a lot of light, and you were glad to enjoy his light for a while.

[36] But something more important than John speaks for me. I mean the things that the Father has given me to do! All of these speak for me and prove that the Father sent me.

[37] The Father who sent me also speaks for me, but you have never heard his voice or seen him face to face. [38] You have not believed his message, because you refused to have faith in the one he sent.

[39] You search the Scriptures, because you think you will find eternal life in them. The Scriptures tell about me, [40] but you refuse to come to me for eternal life.

[41] I don't care about human praise, [42] but I do know that none of you love God. [43] I have come with my Father's authority, and you have not welcomed me. But you will welcome people who come on their own. [44] How could you possibly believe? You like to have your friends praise you, and you don't care about praise that the only God can give!

[45] Don't think that I will be the one to accuse you to the Father. You have put your hope in Moses, yet he is the very one who will accuse you. [46] Moses wrote about me, and if you had believed Moses, you would have believed me. [47] But if you don't believe what Moses wrote, how can you believe what I say?

Feeding Five Thousand

6 Jesus crossed Lake Galilee, which was also known as Lake Tiberias. [2] A large crowd had seen him work miracles to heal the sick, and those people went with him. [3-4] It was almost time for the Jewish festival of Passover, and Jesus went up on a mountain with his disciples and sat down.

[5] When Jesus saw the large crowd coming toward him, he asked Philip, "Where will we get enough food to feed all these people?" [6] He said this to test Philip, since he already knew what he was going to do.

[7] Philip answered, "Don't you know that it would take almost a year's wages/ just to buy only a little bread for each of these people?"

[8] Andrew, the brother of Simon Peter, was one of the disciples. He spoke up and said, [9] "There is a boy here who has five small loaves of barley bread and two fish. But what good is that with all these people?"

[10] The ground was covered with grass, and Jesus told his disciples to have everyone sit down. About five thousand men were in the crowd. [11] Jesus took the bread in his hands and gave thanks to God. Then he passed the bread to the people, and he did the same with the fish, until everyone had plenty to eat.

[12] The people ate all they wanted, and Jesus told his disciples to gather up the leftovers, so that nothing would be wasted. [13] The disciples gathered them up and filled twelve large baskets with what was left over from the five barley loaves.

[14] After the people had seen Jesus work this miracle, they began saying, "This must be the Prophet who is to come into the world!" [15] Jesus realized that they would try to force him to be their king. So he went up on a mountain, where he could be alone.

/ **6.7** *almost a year's wages*: The Greek text has "two hundred silver coins." Each coin was worth the average day's wages for a worker.

Jesus Walks on the Water

16 That evening, Jesus' disciples went down to the lake. 17 They got into a boat and started across for Capernaum. Later that evening Jesus had still not come to them, 18 and a strong wind was making the water rough.

19 When the disciples had rowed for three or four miles, they saw Jesus walking on the water. He kept coming closer to the boat, and they were terrified. 20 But he said, "I am Jesus!k Don't be afraid!" 21 The disciples wanted to take him into the boat, but suddenly the boat reached the shore where they were headed.

The Bread That Gives Life

22 The people who had stayed on the east side of the lake knew that only one boat had been there. They also knew that Jesus had not left in it with his disciples. But the next day 23 some boats from Tiberias sailed near the place where the crowd had eaten the bread for which the Lord had given thanks. 24 They saw that Jesus and his disciples had left. Then they got into the boats and went to Capernaum to look for Jesus. 25 They found him on the west side of the lake and asked, "Rabbi, when did you get here?"

26 Jesus answered, "I tell you for certain that you are not looking for me because you saw the miracles,l but because you ate all the food you wanted. 27 Don't work for food that spoils. Work for food that gives eternal life. The Son of Man will give you this food, because God the Father has given him the right to do so."

28 "What exactly does God want us to do?" the people asked.

29 Jesus answered, "God wants you to have faith in the one he sent."

30 They replied, "What miracle will you work, so that we can have faith in you? What will you do? 31 For example, when our ancestors were in the desert, they were given manna to eat. It happened just as the Scriptures say, 'God gave them bread from heaven to eat.' "

32 Jesus then told them, "I tell you for certain that Moses wasn't the one who gave you bread from heaven. My Father is the one who gives you the true bread from heaven. 33 And the bread that God gives is the one who came down from heaven to give life to the world."

34 The people said, "Lord, give us this bread and don't ever stop!"

35 Jesus replied:

I am the bread that gives life! No one who comes to me will ever be hungry. No one who has faith in me will ever be thirsty. 36 I have told you already that you have seen me and still do not have faith in me. 37 Everything and everyone that the Father has given me will come to me, and I won't turn any of them away.

38 I didn't come from heaven to do what I want! I came to do what the Father wants me to do. He sent me, 39 and he wants to make certain that none of the ones he has given me will be lost. Instead, he wants me to raise them to life on the last day. 40 My Father wants everyone who sees the Son to have faith in him and to have eternal life. Then I will raise them to life on the last day.

41 The people started grumbling because Jesus had said he was the bread that had come down from heaven. 42 They were asking each other, "Isn't he Jesus, the son of Joseph? Don't we know his father and mother? How can he say that he has come down from heaven?"

43 Jesus told them:

Stop grumbling! 44 No one can come to me, unless the Father who sent me makes them want to come. But if they do come, I will raise them to life on the last day. 45 One of the prophets wrote, "God will teach all of them." And so everyone who listens to the Father and learns from him will come to me.

46 The only one who has seen the Father is the one who has come from him. No one else has ever seen the Father. 47 I tell you for certain that everyone who has faith in me has eternal life.

48 I am the bread that gives life! 49 Your ancestors ate manna in the desert, and later they died. 50 But the bread from heaven has come down, so that no one who eats it will ever die. 51 I am that bread from heaven! Everyone who eats it will live forever. My flesh is the life-giving bread that I give to the people of this world.

52 They started arguing with each other and asked, "How can he give us his flesh to eat?"

53 Jesus answered:

I tell you for certain that you won't live unless you eat the flesh and drink the blood of the Son of Man. 54 But if you do eat my flesh and drink my blood, you will have eternal life, and I will raise you to life on the last day. 55 My flesh is the true food, and my blood is the true drink. 56 If you eat my flesh and drink my blood, you are one with me, and I am one with you.

57 The living Father sent me, and I have life because of him. Now everyone who eats my flesh will live because of me. 58 The bread that comes down from heaven isn't like what your ancestors ate. They died, but whoever eats this bread will live forever.

59 Jesus was teaching in a Jewish place of worship in Capernaum when he said these things.

The Words of Eternal Life

60 Many of Jesus' disciples heard him and said, "This is too hard for anyone to understand."

61 Jesus knew that his disciples were grumbling. So he asked, "Does this bother you? 62 What if you should see the Son of Man go up to heaven where he came from? 63 The Spirit is the one who gives life! Human strength can do nothing. The words that I have spoken to you are from that life-giving Spirit. 64 But some of you refuse to have faith in me." Jesus said this, because from the beginning he knew who would have faith in him. He also knew which one would betray him.

65 Then Jesus said, "You cannot come to me, unless the Father makes you want to come. That is why I have told these things to all of you."

66 Because of what Jesus said, many of his disciples

---

k 6.20 *I am Jesus*: The Greek text has "I am" (see the note at 8.24). l 6.26 *miracles*: The Greek text has "signs" here and "sign" in verse 30 (see the note at 2.11,18,23).

turned their backs on him and stopped following him. [67] Jesus then asked his twelve disciples if they were going to leave him. [68] Simon Peter answered, "Lord, there is no one else that we can go to! Your words give eternal life. [69] We have faith in you, and we are sure that you are God's Holy One."

[70] Jesus told his disciples, "I chose all twelve of you, but one of you is a demon!" [71] Jesus was talking about Judas, the son of Simon Iscariot.[m] He would later betray Jesus, even though he was one of the twelve disciples.

Jesus' Brothers Don't Have Faith in Him

7 Jesus decided to leave Judea and to start going through Galilee because the Jewish leaders wanted to kill him. [2] It was almost time for the Festival of Shelters, [3] and Jesus' brothers said to him, "Why don't you go to Judea? Then your disciples can see what you are doing. [4] No one does anything in secret, if they want others to know about them. So let the world know what you are doing!" [5] Even Jesus' own brothers had not yet become his followers.

[6] Jesus answered, "My time hasn't yet come, but your time is always here. [7] The people of this world cannot hate you. They hate me, because I tell them that they do evil things. [8] Go on to the festival. My time hasn't yet come, and I am not going." [9] Jesus said this and stayed on in Galilee.

Jesus at the Festival of Shelters

[10] After Jesus' brothers had gone to the festival, he went secretly, without telling anyone.

[11] During the festival the Jewish leaders looked for Jesus and asked, "Where is he?" [12] The crowds even got into an argument about him. Some were saying, "Jesus is a good man," while others were saying, "He is lying to everyone." [13] But the people were afraid of their leaders, and none of them talked in public about him.

[14] When the festival was about half over, Jesus went into the temple and started teaching. [15] The leaders were surprised and said, "How does this man know so much? He has never been taught!"

[16] Jesus replied:

I am not teaching something that I thought up. What I teach comes from the one who sent me. [17] If you really want to obey God, you will know if what I teach comes from God or from me. [18] If I wanted to bring honor to myself, I would speak for myself. But I want to honor the one who sent me. That is why I tell the truth and not a lie. [19] Didn't Moses give you the Law? Yet none of you obey it! So why do you want to kill me?

[20] The crowd replied, "You're crazy! What makes you think someone wants to kill you?"

[21] Jesus answered:

I worked one miracle, and it amazed you. [22] Moses commanded you to circumcise your sons. But it wasn't really Moses who gave you this command. It was your ancestors, and even on the Sabbath you circumcise your sons [23] in order to obey the Law of Moses. Why are you angry with me for making someone completely well on the Sabbath? [24] Don't judge by appearances. Judge by what is right.

[25] Some of the people from Jerusalem were saying, "Isn't this the man they want to kill? [26] Yet here he is, speaking for everyone to hear. And no one is arguing with him. Do you suppose the authorities know that he is the Messiah? [27] But how could that be? No one knows where the Messiah will come from, but we know where this man comes from."

[28] As Jesus was teaching in the temple, he shouted, "Do you really think you know me and where I came from? I didn't come on my own! The one who sent me is truthful, and you don't know him. [29] But I know the one who sent me, because I came from him."

[30] Some of the people wanted to arrest Jesus right then. But no one even laid a hand on him, because his time had not yet come. [31] A lot of people in the crowd put their faith in him and said, "When the Messiah comes, he surely won't perform more miracles than this man has done!"

Officers Sent To Arrest Jesus

[32] When the Pharisees heard the crowd arguing about Jesus, they got together with the chief priests and sent some temple police to arrest him. [33] But Jesus told them, "I will be with you a little while longer, and then I will return to the one who sent me. [34] You will look for me, but you won't find me. You cannot go where I am going."

[35] The Jewish leaders asked each other, "Where can he go to keep us from finding him? Is he going to some foreign country where our people live? Is he going there to teach the Greeks? [36] What did he mean by saying that we will look for him, but won't find him? Why can't we go where he is going?"

Streams of Life-Giving Water

[37] On the last and most important day of the festival, Jesus stood up and shouted, "If you are thirsty, come to me and drink! [38] Have faith in me, and you will have life-giving water flowing from deep inside you, just as the Scriptures say." [39] Jesus was talking about the Holy Spirit, who would be given to everyone that had faith in him. The Spirit had not yet been given to anyone, since Jesus had not yet been given his full glory.

The People Take Sides

[40] When the crowd heard Jesus say this, some of them said, "He must be the Prophet!" [41] Others said, "He is the Messiah!" Others even said, "Can the Messiah come from Galilee? [42] The Scriptures say that the Messiah will come from the family of King David. Doesn't this mean that he will be born in David's hometown of Bethlehem?" [43] The people started taking sides against each other because of Jesus. [44] Some of them wanted to arrest him, but no one laid a hand on him.

The Leaders Refuse To Have Faith in Jesus

[45] When the temple police returned to the chief priests and Pharisees, they were asked, "Why didn't you bring Jesus here?"

---

[m] 6.71 Iscariot: This may mean "a man from Kerioth" (a place in Judea). But more probably it means "a man who was a liar" or "a man who was a betrayer."

[46] They answered, "No one has ever spoken like that man!"

[47] The Pharisees said to them, "Have you also been fooled? [48] Not one of the chief priests or the Pharisees has faith in him. [49] And these people who don't know the Law are under God's curse anyway."

[50] Nicodemus was there at the time. He was a member of the council, and was the same one who had earlier come to see Jesus. He said, [51] "Our Law doesn't let us condemn people before we hear what they have to say. We cannot judge them before we know what they have done."

[52] Then they said, "Nicodemus, you must be from Galilee! Read the Scriptures, and you will find that no prophet is to come from Galilee."

A Woman Caught in Sin

8 [53] Everyone else went home, [1] but Jesus walked out to the Mount of Olives. [2] Then early the next morning he went to the temple. The people came to him, and he sat down and started teaching them.

[3] The Pharisees and the teachers of the Law of Moses brought in a woman who had been caught in bed with a man who wasn't her husband. They made her stand in the middle of the crowd. [4] Then they said, "Teacher, this woman was caught sleeping with a man who isn't her husband. [5] The Law of Moses teaches that a woman like this should be stoned to death! What do you say?"

[6] They asked Jesus this question, because they wanted to test him and bring some charge against him. But Jesus simply bent over and started writing on the ground with his finger.

[7] They kept on asking Jesus about the woman. Finally, he stood up and said, "If any of you have never sinned, then go ahead and throw the first stone at her!" [8] Once again he bent over and began writing on the ground. [9] The people left one by one, beginning with the oldest. Finally, Jesus and the woman were there alone.

[10] Jesus stood up and asked her, "Where is everyone? Isn't there anyone left to accuse you?"

[11] "No sir," the woman answered.

Then Jesus told her, "I am not going to accuse you either. You may go now, but don't sin anymore." [n]

Jesus Is the Light for the World

[12] Once again Jesus spoke to the people. This time he said, "I am the light for the world! Follow me, and you won't be walking in the dark. You will have the light that gives life."

[13] The Pharisees objected, "You are the only one speaking for yourself, and what you say isn't true!"

[14] Jesus replied:

Even if I do speak for myself, what I say is true! I know where I came from and where I am going. But you don't know where I am from or where I am going. [15] You judge in the same way that everyone else does, but I don't judge anyone. [16] If I did judge, I would judge fairly, because I would not be doing it alone. The Father who sent me is here with me. [17] Your Law requires two witnesses to prove that something is true. [18] I am one of my witnesses, and the Father who sent me is the other one.

[19] "Where is your Father?" they asked.

"You don't know me or my Father!" Jesus answered. "If you knew me, you would know my Father."

[20] Jesus said this while he was still teaching in the place where the temple treasures were stored. But no one arrested him, because his time had not yet come.

You Cannot Go Where I Am Going

[21] Jesus also told them, "I am going away, and you will look for me. But you cannot go where I am going, and you will die with your sins unforgiven."

[22] The Jewish leaders asked, "Does he intend to kill himself? Is that what he means by saying we cannot go where he is going?"

[23] Jesus answered, "You are from below, but I am from above. You belong to this world, but I don't . [24] That is why I said you will die with your sins unforgiven. If you don't have faith in me for who I am, you will die, and your sins will not be forgiven."

[25] "Who are you?" they asked Jesus.

Jesus answered, "I am exactly who I told you at the beginning. [26] There is a lot more I could say to condemn you. But the one who sent me is truthful, and I tell the people of this world only what I have heard from him."

[27] No one understood that Jesus was talking to them about the Father.

[28] Jesus went on to say, "When you have lifted up the Son of Man, you will know who I am. You will also know that I don't do anything on my own. I say only what my Father taught me. [29] The one who sent me is with me. I always do what pleases him, and he will never leave me."

[30] After Jesus said this, many of the people put their faith in him.

The Truth Will Set You Free

[31] Jesus told the people who had faith in him, "If you keep on obeying what I have said, you truly are my disciples. [32] You will know the truth, and the truth will set you free."

[33] They answered, "We are Abraham's children! We have never been anyone's slaves. How can you say we will be set free?"

[34] Jesus replied:

I tell you for certain that anyone who sins is a slave of sin! [35] And slaves don't stay in the family forever, though the Son will always remain in the family. [36] If the Son gives you freedom, you are free! [37] I know that you are from Abraham's family. Yet you want to kill me, because my message isn't really in your hearts. [38] I am telling you what my Father has shown me, just as you are doing what your father has taught you.

Your Father Is the Devil

[39] The people said to Jesus, "Abraham is our father!"

Jesus replied, "If you were Abraham's children, you would do what Abraham did. [40] Instead, you want to kill me for telling you the truth that God gave me. Abraham never did anything like that. [41] But you are doing exactly what your father does."

---

[n] **8.11** *don't sin anymore*: Verses 1-11 are not in some manuscripts. In other manuscripts these verses are placed after 7.36 or after 21.25 or after Luke 21.38, with some differences in the text.

"Don't accuse us of having someone else as our father!" they said. "We just have one father, and he is God."

42 Jesus answered:

If God were your Father, you would love me, because I came from God and only from him. He sent me. I did not come on my own. **43** Why can't you understand what I am talking about? Can't you stand to hear what I am saying? **44** Your father is the devil, and you do exactly what he wants. He has always been a murderer and a liar. There is nothing truthful about him. He speaks on his own, and everything he says is a lie. Not only is he a liar himself, but he is also the father of all lies.

45 Everything I have told you is true, and you still refuse to have faith in me. **46** Can any of you accuse me of sin? If you cannot, why won't you have faith in me? After all, I am telling you the truth. **47** Anyone who belongs to God will listen to his message. But you refuse to listen, because you don't belong to God.

Jesus and Abraham

48 The people told Jesus, "We were right to say that you are a Samaritan and that you have a demon in you!"

49 Jesus answered, "I don't have a demon in me. I honor my Father, and you refuse to honor me. **50** I don't want honor for myself. But there is one who wants me to be honored, and he is also the one who judges. **51** I tell you for certain that if you obey my words, you will never die."

52 Then the people said, "Now we are sure that you have a demon. Abraham is dead, and so are the prophets. How can you say that no one who obeys your words will ever die? **53** Are you greater than our father Abraham? He died, and so did the prophets. Who do you think you are?"

54 Jesus replied, "If I honored myself, it would mean nothing. My Father is the one who honors me. You claim that he is your God, **55** even though you don't really know him. If I said I didn't know him, I would be a liar, just like all of you. But I know him, and I do what he says. **56** Your father Abraham was really glad to see me."

57 "You are not even fifty years old!" they said. "How could you have seen Abraham?"

58 Jesus answered, "I tell you for certain that even before Abraham was, I was, and I am." **59** The people picked up stones to kill Jesus, but he hid and left the temple.

Jesus Heals a Man Born Blind

9 As Jesus walked along, he saw a man who had been blind since birth. **2** Jesus' disciples asked, "Teacher, why was this man born blind? Was it because he or his parents sinned?"

3 "No, it wasn't!" Jesus answered. "But because of his blindness, you will see God work a miracle for him. **4** As long as it is day, we must do what the one who sent me wants me to do. When night comes, no one can work. **5** While I am in the world, I am the light for the world."

6 After Jesus said this, he spit on the ground. He made some mud and smeared it on the man's eyes. **7** Then he said, "Go and wash off the mud in Siloam Pool." The man went and washed in Siloam, which means "One Who Is Sent." When he had washed off the mud, he could see.

8 The man's neighbors and the people who had seen him begging wondered if he really could be the same man. **9** Some of them said he was the same beggar, while others said he only looked like him. But he told them, "I am that man."

10 "Then how can you see?" they asked.

11 He answered, "Someone named Jesus made some mud and smeared it on my eyes. He told me to go and wash it off in Siloam Pool. When I did, I could see."

12 "Where is he now?" they asked.

"I don't know," he answered.

The Pharisees Try To Find Out What Happened

13-14 The day when Jesus made the mud and healed the man was a Sabbath. So the people took the man to the Pharisees. **15** They asked him how he was able to see, and he answered, "Jesus made some mud and smeared it on my eyes. Then after I washed it off, I could see."

16 Some of the Pharisees said, "This man Jesus doesn't come from God. If he did, he would not break the law of the Sabbath."

Others asked, "How could someone who is a sinner work such a miracle?"

Since the Pharisees could not agree among themselves, **17** they asked the man, "What do you say about this one who healed your eyes?"

"He is a prophet!" the man told them.

18 But the Jewish leaders would not believe that the man had once been blind. They sent for his parents **19** and asked them, "Is this the son that you said was born blind? How can he now see?"

20 The man's parents answered, "We are certain that he is our son, and we know that he was born blind. **21** But we don't know how he got his sight or who gave it to him. Ask him! He is old enough to speak for himself."

22-23 The man's parents said this because they were afraid of the Jewish leaders. The leaders had already agreed that no one was to have anything to do with anyone who said Jesus was the Messiah.

24 The leaders called the man back and said, "Swear by God to tell the truth! We know that Jesus is a sinner."

25 The man replied, "I don't know if he is a sinner or not. All I know is that I used to be blind, but now I can see!"

26 "What did he do to you?" the Jewish leaders asked. "How did he heal your eyes?"

27 The man answered, "I have already told you once, and you refused to listen. Why do you want me to tell you again? Do you also want to become his disciples?"

28 The leaders insulted the man and said, "You are his follower! We are followers of Moses. **29** We are sure that God spoke to Moses, but we don't even know where Jesus comes from."

30 "How strange!" the man replied. "He healed my eyes, and yet you don't know where he comes from. **31** We know that God listens only to people who love and obey him. God doesn't listen to sinners. **32** And this is the first time in history that anyone has ever given sight to someone born blind. **33** Jesus could not do anything unless he came from God."

34 The leaders told the man, "You have been a sinner since the day you were born! Do you think you can teach us anything?" Then they said, "You can never come back into any of our meeting places!"

35 When Jesus heard what had happened, he went and found the man. Then Jesus asked, "Do you have faith in the Son of Man?"

36 He replied, "Sir, if you will tell me who he is, I will put my faith in him."

37 "You have already seen him," Jesus answered, "and right now he is talking with you."

38 The man said, "Lord, I put my faith in you!" Then he worshiped Jesus.

39 Jesus told him, "I came to judge the people of this world. I am here to give sight to the blind and to make blind everyone who can see."

40 When the Pharisees heard Jesus say this, they asked, "Are we blind?"

41 Jesus answered, "If you were blind, you would not be guilty. But now that you claim to see, you will keep on being guilty."

A Story about Sheep

10 Jesus said:
I tell you for certain that only thieves and robbers climb over the fence instead of going in through the gate to the sheep pen. **2-3** But the gatekeeper opens the gate for the shepherd, and he goes in through it. The sheep know their shepherd's voice. He calls each of them by name and leads them out.

4 When he has led out all of his sheep, he walks in front of them, and they follow, because they know his voice. **5** The sheep will not follow strangers. They don't recognize a stranger's voice, and they run away.

6 Jesus told the people this story. But they did not understand what he was talking about.

Jesus Is the Good Shepherd

7 Jesus said:
I tell you for certain that I am the gate for the sheep. **8** Everyone who came before me was a thief or a robber, and the sheep did not listen to any of them. **9** I am the gate. All who come in through me will be saved. Through me they will come and go and find pasture.

10 A thief comes only to rob, kill, and destroy. I came so that everyone would have life, and have it in its fullest. **11** I am the good shepherd, and the good shepherd gives up his life for his sheep. **12** Hired workers are not like the shepherd. They don't own the sheep, and when they see a wolf coming, they run off and leave the sheep. Then the wolf attacks and scatters the flock. **13** Hired workers run away because they don't care about the sheep.

14 I am the good shepherd. I know my sheep, and they know me. **15** Just as the Father knows me, I know the Father, and I give up my life for my sheep. **16** I have other sheep that are not in this sheep pen. I must bring them together too, when they hear my voice. Then there will be one flock of sheep and one shepherd.

17 The Father loves me, because I give up my life, so that I may receive it back again. **18** No one takes my life from me. I give it up willingly! I have

the power to give it up and the power to receive it back again, just as my Father commanded me to do.

19 The people took sides because of what Jesus had told them. **20** Many of them said, "He has a demon in him! He is crazy! Why listen to him?"

21 But others said, "How could anyone with a demon in him say these things? No one like that could give sight to a blind person!"

Jesus Is Rejected

22 That winter, Jesus was in Jerusalem for the Temple Festival. **23** One day he was walking in that part of the temple known as Solomon's Porch, **24** and the people gathered all around him. They said, "How long are you going to keep us guessing? If you are the Messiah, tell us plainly!"

25 Jesus answered:

I have told you, and you refused to believe me. The things I do by my Father's authority show who I am. **26** But since you are not my sheep, you don't believe me. **27** My sheep know my voice, and I know them. They follow me, **28** and I give them eternal life, so that they will never be lost. No one can snatch them out of my hand. **29** My Father gave them to me, and he is greater than all others.*o* No one can snatch them from his hands, **30** and I am one with the Father.

31 Once again the Jewish leaders picked up stones in order to kill Jesus. **32** But he said, "I have shown you many good things that my Father sent me to do. Which one are you going to stone me for?"

33 They answered, "We are not stoning you because of any good thing you did. We are stoning you because you did a terrible thing. You are just a man, and here you are claiming to be God!"

34 Jesus replied:

In your Scriptures doesn't God say, "You are gods"? **35** You can't argue with the Scriptures, and God spoke to those people and called them gods. **36** So why do you accuse me of a terrible sin for saying that I am the Son of God? After all, it is the Father who prepared me for this work. He is also the one who sent me into the world. **37** If I don't do as my Father does, you should not believe me. **38** But if I do what my Father does, you should believe because of that, even if you don't have faith in me. Then you will know for certain that the Father is one with me, and I am one with the Father.

39 Again they wanted to arrest Jesus. But he escaped **40** and crossed the Jordan to the place where John had earlier been baptizing. While Jesus was there, **41** many people came to him. They were saying, "John didn't work any miracles, but everything he said about Jesus is true." **42** A lot of those people also put their faith in Jesus.

The Death of Lazarus

11 **1-2** A man by the name of Lazarus was sick in the village of Bethany. He had two sisters, Mary and Martha. This was the same Mary who later poured perfume on the Lord's head and wiped his feet with her hair. **3** The sisters sent a message to the Lord and told him that his good friend Lazarus was sick.

---

o **10.29** *he is greater than all others*: Some manuscripts have "they are greater than all others."

4 When Jesus heard this, he said, "His sickness won't end in death. It will bring glory to God and his Son."

5 Jesus loved Martha and her sister and brother. 6 But he stayed where he was for two more days. 7 Then he said to his disciples, "Now we will go back to Judea."

8 "Teacher," they said, "the people there want to stone you to death! Why do you want to go back?"

9 Jesus answered, "Aren't there twelve hours in each day? If you walk during the day, you will have light from the sun, and you won't stumble. 10 But if you walk during the night, you will stumble, because you don't have any light." 11 Then he told them, "Our friend Lazarus is asleep, and I am going there to wake him up."

12 They replied, "Lord, if he is asleep, he will get better." 13 Jesus really meant that Lazarus was dead, but they thought he was talking only about sleep.

14 Then Jesus told them plainly, "Lazarus is dead! 15 I am glad that I wasn't there, because now you will have a chance to put your faith in me. Let's go to him."

16 Thomas, whose nickname was "Twin," said to the other disciples, "Come on. Let's go, so we can die with him."

Jesus Brings Lazarus to Life

17 When Jesus got to Bethany, he found that Lazarus had already been in the tomb four days. 18 Bethany was only about two miles from Jerusalem, 19 and many people had come from the city to comfort Martha and Mary because their brother had died.

20 When Martha heard that Jesus had arrived, she went out to meet him, but Mary stayed in the house. 21 Martha said to Jesus, "Lord, if you had been here, my brother would not have died. 22 Yet even now I know that God will do anything you ask."

23 Jesus told her, "Your brother will live again!"

24 Martha answered, "I know that he will be raised to life on the last day, when all the dead are raised."

25 Jesus then said, "I am the one who raises the dead to life! Everyone who has faith in me will live, even if they die. 26 And everyone who lives because of faith in me will never really die. Do you believe this?"

27 "Yes, Lord!" she replied. "I believe that you are Christ, the Son of God. You are the one we hoped would come into the world."

28 After Martha said this, she went and privately said to her sister Mary, "The Teacher is here, and he wants to see you." 29 As soon as Mary heard this, she got up and went out to Jesus. 30 He was still outside the village where Martha had gone to meet him. 31 Many people had come to comfort Mary, and when they saw her quickly leave the house, they thought she was going out to the tomb to cry. So they followed her.

32 Mary went to where Jesus was. Then as soon as she saw him, she knelt at his feet and said, "Lord, if you had been here, my brother would not have died."

33 When Jesus saw that Mary and the people with her were crying, he was terribly upset 34 and asked, "Where have you put his body?"

They replied, "Lord, come and you will see."

35 Jesus started crying, 36 and the people said, "See how much he loved Lazarus."

37 Some of them said, "He gives sight to the blind. Why couldn't he have kept Lazarus from dying?"

38 Jesus was still terribly upset. So he went to the tomb, which was a cave with a stone rolled against the entrance. 39 Then he told the people to roll the stone away. But Martha said, "Lord, you know that Lazarus has been dead four days, and there will be a bad smell."

40 Jesus replied, "Didn't I tell you that if you had faith, you would see the glory of God?"

41 After the stone had been rolled aside, Jesus looked up toward heaven and prayed, "Father, I thank you for answering my prayer. 42 I know that you always answer my prayers. But I said this, so that the people here would believe that you sent me."

43 When Jesus had finished praying, he shouted, "Lazarus, come out!" 44 The man who had been dead came out. His hands and feet were wrapped with strips of burial cloth, and a cloth covered his face.

Jesus then told the people, "Untie him and let him go."

The Plot To Kill Jesus

45 Many of the people who had come to visit Mary saw the things that Jesus did, and they put their faith in him. 46 Others went to the Pharisees and told what Jesus had done. 47 Then the chief priests and the Pharisees called the council together and said, "What should we do? This man is working a lot of miracles. 48 If we don't stop him now, everyone will put their faith in him. Then the Romans will come and destroy our temple and our nation."

49 One of the council members was Caiaphas, who was also high priest that year. He spoke up and said, "You people don't have any sense at all! 50 Don't you know it is better for one person to die for the people than for the whole nation to be destroyed?" 51 Caiaphas did not say this on his own. As high priest that year, he was prophesying that Jesus would die for the nation. 52 Yet Jesus would not die just for the Jewish nation. He would die to bring together all of God's scattered people. 53 From that day on, the council started making plans to put Jesus to death.

54 Because of this plot against him, Jesus stopped going around in public. He went to the town of Ephraim, which was near the desert, and he stayed there with his disciples.

55 It was almost time for Passover. Many of the Jewish people who lived out in the country had come to Jerusalem to get themselves ready for the festival. 56 They looked around for Jesus. Then when they were in the temple, they asked each other, "You don't think he will come here for Passover, do you?"

57 The chief priests and the Pharisees told the people to let them know if any of them saw Jesus. That is how they hoped to arrest him.

At Bethany

12 Six days before Passover Jesus went back to Bethany, where he had raised Lazarus from death. 2 A meal had been prepared for Jesus. Martha was doing the serving, and Lazarus himself was there.

3 Mary took a very expensive bottle of perfume[p] and poured it on Jesus' feet. She wiped them with her hair, and the sweet smell of the perfume filled the house.

---

p 12.3 *very expensive bottle of perfume*: The Greek text has "expensive perfume made of pure spikenard," a plant used to make perfume.

4 A disciple named Judas Iscariot was there. He was the one who was going to betray Jesus, and he asked, 5 "Why wasn't this perfume sold for three hundred silver coins and the money given to the poor?" 6 Judas did not really care about the poor. He asked this because he carried the money-bag and sometimes would steal from it.

7 Jesus replied, "Leave her alone! She has kept this perfume for the day of my burial. 8 You will always have the poor with you, but you won't always have me."

A Plot To Kill Lazarus

9 A lot of people came when they heard that Jesus was there. They also wanted to see Lazarus, because Jesus had raised him from death. 10 So the chief priests made plans to kill Lazarus. 11 He was the reason that many of the Jewish people were turning from them and putting their faith in Jesus.

Jesus Enters Jerusalem

12 The next day a large crowd was in Jerusalem for Passover. When they heard that Jesus was coming for the festival, 13 they took palm branches and went out to greet him.*q* They shouted,

> "Hooray!
> God bless the one who comes
>   in the name of the Lord!
> God bless the King
>   of Israel!"

14 Jesus found a donkey and rode on it, just as the Scriptures say,

> 15 "People of Jerusalem,
>   don't be afraid!
> Your King is now coming,
> and he is riding
>   on a donkey."

16 At first, Jesus' disciples did not understand. But after he had been given his glory, they remembered all this. Everything had happened exactly as the Scriptures said it would.

17-18 A crowd had come to meet Jesus because they had seen him call Lazarus out of the tomb. They kept talking about him and this miracle. 19 But the Pharisees said to each other, "There is nothing that can be done! Everyone in the world is following Jesus."

Some Greeks Want To Meet Jesus

20 Some Greeks had gone to Jerusalem to worship during Passover. 21 Philip from Bethsaida in Galilee was there too. So they went to him and said, "Sir, we would like to meet Jesus." 22 Philip told Andrew. Then the two of them went to Jesus and told him.

The Son of Man Must Be Lifted Up

23 Jesus said:
> The time has come for the Son of Man to be given his glory. 24 I tell you for certain that a grain

of wheat that falls on the ground will never be more than one grain unless it dies. But if it dies, it will produce lots of wheat. 25 If you love your life, you will lose it. If you give it up in this world, you will be given eternal life. 26 If you serve me, you must go with me. My servants will be with me wherever I am. If you serve me, my Father will honor you.

27 Now I am deeply troubled, and I don't know what to say. But I must not ask my Father to keep me from this time of suffering. In fact, I came into the world to suffer. 28 So Father, bring glory to yourself.

A voice from heaven then said, "I have already brought glory to myself, and I will do it again!" 29 When the crowd heard the voice, some of them thought it was thunder. Others thought an angel had spoken to Jesus.

30 Then Jesus told the crowd, "That voice spoke to help you, not me. 31 This world's people are now being judged, and the ruler of this world is already being thrown out! 32 If I am lifted up above the earth, I will make everyone want to come to me." 33 Jesus was talking about the way he would be put to death.

34 The crowd said to Jesus, "The Scriptures teach that the Messiah will live forever. How can you say that the Son of Man must be lifted up? Who is this Son of Man?"

35 Jesus answered, "The light will be with you for only a little longer. Walk in the light while you can. Then you won't be caught walking blindly in the dark. 36 Have faith in the light while it is with you, and you will be children of the light."

The People Refuse To Have Faith in Jesus

After Jesus had said these things, he left and went into hiding. 37 He had worked a lot of miracles among the people, but they were still not willing to have faith in him. 38 This happened so that what the prophet Isaiah had said would come true,

> "Lord, who has believed
>   our message?
> And who has seen
>   your mighty strength?"

39 The people could not have faith in Jesus, because Isaiah had also said,

> 40 "The Lord has blinded
>   the eyes of the people,
> and he has made
>   the people stubborn.
> He did this so that they
> could not see
>   or understand,
> and so that they
> would not turn to the Lord
>   and be healed."

41 Isaiah said this, because he saw the glory of Jesus and spoke about him.*r* 42 Even then, many of the leaders put their faith in Jesus, but they did not tell anyone about it.

---

q **12.13** *took palm branches and went out to greet him:* This was one way that the Jewish people welcomed a famous person.
r **12.41** *he saw the glory of Jesus and spoke about him:* Or "he saw the glory of God and spoke about Jesus."

The Pharisees had already given orders for the people not to have anything to do with anyone who had faith in Jesus. 43 And besides, the leaders liked praise from others more than they liked praise from God.

Jesus Came To Save the World

44 In a loud voice Jesus said:

Everyone who has faith in me also has faith in the one who sent me. 45 And everyone who has seen me has seen the one who sent me. 46 I am the light that has come into the world. No one who has faith in me will stay in the dark.

47 I am not the one who will judge those who refuse to obey my teachings. I came to save the people of this world, not to be their judge. 48 But everyone who rejects me and my teachings will be judged on the last day by what I have said. 49 I don't speak on my own. I say only what the Father who sent me has told me to say. 50 I know that his commands will bring eternal life. That is why I tell you exactly what the Father has told me.

Jesus Washes the Feet of His Disciples

13 It was before Passover, and Jesus knew that the time had come for him to leave this world and to return to the Father. He had always loved his followers in this world, and he loved them to the very end.

2 Even before the evening meal started, the devil had made Judas, the son of Simon Iscariot, decide to betray Jesus.

3 Jesus knew that he had come from God and would go back to God. He also knew that the Father had given him complete power. 4 So during the meal Jesus got up, removed his outer garment, and wrapped a towel around his waist. 5 He put some water into a large bowl. Then he began washing his disciples' feet and drying them with the towel he was wearing.

6 But when he came to Simon Peter, that disciple asked, "Lord, are you going to wash my feet?"

7 Jesus answered, "You don't really know what I am doing, but later you will understand."

8 "You will never wash my feet!" Peter replied.

"If I don't wash you," Jesus told him, "you don't really belong to me."

9 Peter said, "Lord, don't wash just my feet. Wash my hands and my head."

10 Jesus answered, "People who have bathed and are clean all over need to wash just their feet. And you, my disciples, are clean, except for one of you." 11 Jesus knew who would betray him. That is why he said, "except for one of you."

12 After Jesus had washed his disciples' feet and had put his outer garment back on, he sat down again. Then he said:

Do you understand what I have done? 13 You call me your teacher and Lord, and you should, because that is who I am. 14 And if your Lord and teacher has washed your feet, you should do the same for each other. 15 I have set the example, and you should do for each other exactly what I have done for you. 16 I tell you for certain that servants are not greater than their master, and messengers are not greater than the one who sent them. 17 You know these things, and God will bless you, if you do them.

18 I am not talking about all of you. I know the ones I have chosen. But what the Scriptures say must come true. And they say, "The man who ate with me has turned against me!" 19 I am telling you this before it all happens. Then when it does happen, you will believe who I am. 20 I tell you for certain that anyone who welcomes my messengers also welcomes me, and anyone who welcomes me welcomes the one who sent me.

Jesus Tells What Will Happen to Him

21 After Jesus had said these things, he was deeply troubled and told his disciples, "I tell you for certain that one of you will betray me." 22 They were confused about what he meant. And they just stared at each other.

23 Jesus' favorite disciple was sitting next to him at the meal, 24 and Simon motioned for that disciple to find out which one Jesus meant. 25 So the disciple leaned toward Jesus and asked, "Lord, which one of us are you talking about?"

26 Jesus answered, "I will dip this piece of bread in the sauce and give it to the one I was talking about."

Then Jesus dipped the bread and gave it to Judas, the son of Simon Iscariot. 27 Right then Satan took control of Judas. Jesus said, "Judas, go quickly and do what you have to do." 28 No one at the meal understood what Jesus meant. 29 But because Judas was in charge of the money, some of them thought that Jesus had told him to buy something they needed for the festival. Others thought that Jesus had told him to give some money to the poor. 30 Judas took the piece of bread and went out.

It was already night.

The New Command

31 After Judas had gone, Jesus said:

Now the Son of Man will be given glory, and he will bring glory to God. 32 Then, after God is given glory because of him, God will bring glory to him, and God will do it very soon.

33 My children, I will be with you for a little while longer. Then you will look for me, but you won't find me. I tell you just as I told the people, "You cannot go where I am going." 34 But I am giving you a new command. You must love each other, just as I have loved you. 35 If you love each other, everyone will know that you are my disciples.

Peter's Promise

36 Simon Peter asked, "Lord, where are you going?"

Jesus answered, "You can't go with me now, but later on you will."

37 Peter asked, "Lord, why can't I go with you now? I would die for you!"

38 "Would you really die for me?" Jesus asked. "I tell you for certain that before a rooster crows, you will say three times that you don't even know me."

Jesus Is the Way to the Father

14 Jesus said to his disciples, "Don't be worried! Have faith in God and have faith in me.[s] ² There are many rooms in my Father's house. I wouldn't tell you this, unless it was true. I am going there to prepare a place for each of you. ³ After I have done this, I will come back and take you with me. Then we will be together. ⁴ You know the way to where I am going."

⁵ Thomas said, "Lord, we don't even know where you are going! How can we know the way?"

⁶ "I am the way, the truth, and the life!" Jesus answered. "Without me, no one can go to the Father. ⁷ If you had known me, you would have known the Father. But from now on, you do know him, and you have seen him."

⁸ Philip said, "Lord, show us the Father. That is all we need."

⁹ Jesus replied:

Philip, I have been with you for a long time. Don't you know who I am? If you have seen me, you have seen the Father. How can you ask me to show you the Father? ¹⁰ Don't you believe that I am one with the Father and that the Father is one with me? What I say isn't said on my own. The Father who lives in me does these things.

¹¹ Have faith in me when I say that the Father is one with me and that I am one with the Father. Or else have faith in me simply because of the things I do. ¹² I tell you for certain that if you have faith in me, you will do the same things that I am doing. You will do even greater things, now that I am going back to the Father. ¹³ Ask me, and I will do whatever you ask. This way the Son will bring honor to the Father. ¹⁴ I will do whatever you ask me to do.

The Holy Spirit Is Promised

¹⁵ Jesus said to his disciples:

If you love me, you will do as I command. ¹⁶ Then I will ask the Father to send you the Holy Spirit who will help[t] you and always be with you. ¹⁷ The Spirit will show you what is true. The people of this world cannot accept the Spirit, because they don't see or know him. But you know the Spirit, who is with you and will keep on living in you.

¹⁸ I won't leave you like orphans. I will come back to you. ¹⁹ In a little while the people of this world won't be able to see me, but you will see me. And because I live, you will live. ²⁰ Then you will know that I am one with the Father. You will know that you are one with me, and I am one with you. ²¹ If you love me, you will do what I have said, and my Father will love you. I will also love you and show you what I am like.

²² The other Judas, not Judas Iscariot, then spoke up and asked, "Lord, what do you mean by saying that you will show us what you are like, but you will not show the people of this world?"

²³ Jesus replied:

If anyone loves me, they will obey me. Then my Father will love them, and we will come to them and live in them. ²⁴ But anyone who doesn't love me, won't obey me. What they have heard me say doesn't really come from me, but from the Father who sent me.

²⁵ I have told you these things while I am still with you. ²⁶ But the Holy Spirit will come and help you, because the Father will send the Spirit to take my place. The Spirit will teach you everything and will remind you of what I said while I was with you.

²⁷ I give you peace, the kind of peace that only I can give. It isn't like the peace that this world can give. So don't be worried or afraid.

²⁸ You have already heard me say that I am going and that I will also come back to you. If you really love me, you should be glad that I am going back to the Father, because he is greater than I am.

²⁹ I am telling you this before I leave, so that when it does happen, you will have faith in me. ³⁰ I cannot speak with you much longer, because the ruler of this world is coming. But he has no power over me. ³¹ I obey my Father, so that everyone in the world might know that I love him.

It is time for us to go now.

Jesus Is the True Vine

15 Jesus said to his disciples:

I am the true vine, and my Father is the gardener. ² He cuts away every branch of mine that doesn't produce fruit. But he trims clean every branch that does produce fruit, so that it will produce even more fruit. ³ You are already clean because of what I have said to you.

⁴ Stay joined to me, and I will stay joined to you. Just as a branch cannot produce fruit unless it stays joined to the vine, you cannot produce fruit unless you stay joined to me. ⁵ I am the vine, and you are the branches. If you stay joined to me, and I stay joined to you, then you will produce lots of fruit. But you cannot do anything without me. ⁶ If you don't stay joined to me, you will be thrown away. You will be like dry branches that are gathered up and burned in a fire.

⁷ Stay joined to me and let my teachings become part of you. Then you can pray for whatever you want, and your prayer will be answered. ⁸ When you become fruitful disciples of mine, my Father will be honored. ⁹ I have loved you, just as my Father has loved me. So remain faithful to my love for you. ¹⁰ If you obey me, I will keep loving you, just as my Father keeps loving me, because I have obeyed him.

¹¹ I have told you this to make you as completely happy as I am. ¹² Now I tell you to love each other, as I have loved you. ¹³ The greatest way to show love for friends is to die for them. ¹⁴ And you are my friends, if you obey me. ¹⁵ Servants don't know what their master is doing, and so I don't speak to you as my servants. I speak to you as my

---

[s] **14.1** *Have faith in God and have faith in me*: Or "You have faith in God, so have faith in me."   [t] **14.16** *help*: The Greek word may mean "comfort," "encourage," or "defend."

friends, and I have told you everything that my Father has told me.

¹⁶ You did not choose me. I chose you and sent you out to produce fruit, the kind of fruit that will last. Then my Father will give you whatever you ask for in my name.ᵘ ¹⁷ So I command you to love each other.

The World's Hatred

¹⁸ If the people of this world hate you, just remember that they hated me first. ¹⁹ If you belonged to the world, its people would love you. But you don't belong to the world. I have chosen you to leave the world behind, and that is why its people hate you. ²⁰ Remember how I told you that servants are not greater than their master. So if people mistreat me, they will mistreat you. If they do what I say, they will do what you say.

²¹ People will do to you exactly what they did to me. They will do it because you belong to me, and they don't know the one who sent me. ²² If I had not come and spoken to them, they would not be guilty of sin. But now they have no excuse for their sin.

²³ Everyone who hates me also hates my Father. ²⁴ I have done things that no one else has ever done. If they had not seen me do these things, they would not be guilty. But they did see me do these things, and they still hate me and my Father too. ²⁵ That is why the Scriptures are true when they say, "People hated me for no reason."

²⁶ I will send you the Spirit who comes from the Father and shows what is true. The Spirit will help you and will tell you about me. ²⁷ Then you will also tell others about me, because you have been with me from the beginning.

16 I am telling you this to keep you from being afraid. ² You will be chased out of the Jewish meeting places. And the time will come when people will kill you and think they are doing God a favor. ³ They will do these things because they don't know either the Father or me. ⁴ I am saying this to you now, so that when the time comes, you will remember what I have said.

The Work of the Holy Spirit

I was with you at the first, and so I didn't tell you these things. ⁵ But now I am going back to the Father who sent me, and none of you asks me where I am going. ⁶ You are very sad from hearing all of this. ⁷ But I tell you that I am going to do what is best for you. That is why I am going away. The Holy Spirit cannot come to help you until I leave. But after I am gone, I will send the Spirit to you.

⁸ The Spirit will come and show the people of this world the truth about sin and God's justice and the judgment. ⁹ The Spirit will show them that they are wrong about sin, because they didn't have faith in me. ¹⁰ They are wrong about God's justice, because I am going to the Father, and you won't see

me again. ¹¹ And they are wrong about the judgment, because God has already judged the ruler of this world.

¹² I have much more to say to you, but right now it would be more than you could understand. ¹³ The Spirit shows what is true and will come and guide you into the full truth. The Spirit doesn't speak on his own. He will tell you only what he has heard from me, and he will let you know what is going to happen. ¹⁴ The Spirit will bring glory to me by taking my message and telling it to you. ¹⁵ Everything that the Father has is mine. That is why I have said that the Spirit takes my message and tells it to you.

Sorrow Will Turn into Joy

¹⁶ Jesus told his disciples, "For a little while you won't see me, but after a while you will see me."

¹⁷ They said to each other, "What does Jesus mean by saying that for a little while we won't see him, but after a while we will see him? What does he mean by saying that he is going to the Father? ¹⁸ What is this 'little while' that he is talking about? We don't know what he means."

¹⁹ Jesus knew that they had some questions, so he said:

You are wondering what I meant when I said that for a little while you won't see me, but after a while you will see me. ²⁰ I tell you for certain that you will cry and be sad, but the world will be happy. You will be sad, but later you will be happy.

²¹ When a woman is about to give birth, she is in great pain. But after it is all over, she forgets the pain and is happy, because she has brought a child into the world. ²² You are now very sad. But later I will see you, and you will be so happy that no one will be able to change the way you feel. ²³ When that time comes, you won't have to ask me about anything. I tell you for certain that the Father will give you whatever you ask for in my name. ²⁴ You have not asked for anything in this way before, but now you must ask in my name.ᵛ Then it will be given to you, so that you will be completely happy.

²⁵ I have used examples to explain to you what I have been talking about. But the time will come when I will speak to you plainly about the Father and will no longer use examples like these. ²⁶ You will ask the Father in my name,ʷ and I won't have to ask him for you. ²⁷ God the Father loves you because you love me, and you believe that I have come from him. ²⁸ I came from the Father into the world, but I am leaving the world and returning to the Father.

²⁹ The disciples said, "Now you are speaking plainly to us! You are not using examples. ³⁰ At last we know that you understand everything, and we don't have any more questions. Now we believe that you truly have come from God."

³¹ Jesus replied:

Do you really believe me? ³² The time will come and is already here when all of you will be scattered. Each of you will go back home and leave me by myself. But the Father will be with me, and I

ᵘ **15.16** *in my name:* Or "because you are my followers." ᵛ **16.23,24** *in my name . . . in my name:* Or "as my disciples . . . as my disciples." ʷ **16.26** *in my name:* Or "because you are my followers."

won't be alone. ³³ I have told you this, so that you might have peace in your hearts because of me. While you are in the world, you will have to suffer. But cheer up! I have defeated the world.

Jesus Prays

17 After Jesus had finished speaking to his disciples, he looked up toward heaven and prayed:

Father, the time has come for you to bring glory to your Son, in order that he may bring glory to you. ² And you gave him power over all people, so that he would give eternal life to everyone you give him. ³ Eternal life is to know you, the only true God, and to know Jesus Christ, the one you sent. ⁴ I have brought glory to you here on earth by doing everything you gave me to do. ⁵ Now, Father, give me back the glory that I had with you before the world was created.

⁶ You have given me some followers from this world, and I have shown them what you are like. They were yours, but you gave them to me, and they have obeyed you. ⁷ They know that you gave me everything I have. ⁸ I told my followers what you told me, and they accepted it. They know that I came from you, and they believe that you are the one who sent me. ⁹ I am praying for them, but not for those who belong to this world. My followers belong to you, and I am praying for them. ¹⁰ All that I have is yours, and all that you have is mine, and they will bring glory to me.

¹¹ Holy Father, I am no longer in the world. I am coming to you, but my followers are still in the world. So keep them safe by the power of the name that you have given me. Then they will be one with each other, just as you and I are one. ¹² While I was with them, I kept them safe by the power you have given me. I guarded them, and not one of them was lost, except the one who had to be lost. This happened so that what the Scriptures say would come true.

¹³ I am on my way to you. But I say these things while I am still in the world, so that my followers will have the same complete joy that I do. ¹⁴ I have told them your message. But the people of this world hate them, because they don't belong to this world, just as I don't.

¹⁵ Father, I don't ask you to take my followers out of the world, but keep them safe from the evil one. ¹⁶ They don't belong to this world, and neither do I. ¹⁷ Your word is the truth. So let this truth make them completely yours. ¹⁸ I am sending them into the world, just as you sent me. ¹⁹ I have given myself completely for their sake, so that they may belong completely to the truth.

²⁰ I am not praying just for these followers. I am also praying for everyone else who will have faith because of what my followers will say about me. ²¹ I want all of them to be one with each other, just as I am one with you and you are one with me. I also want them to be one with us. Then the people of this world will believe that you sent me.

²² I have honored my followers in the same way that you honored me, in order that they may be one with each other, just as we are one. ²³ I am one with them, and you are one with me, so that they may become completely one. Then this world's people will know that you sent me. They will know that you love my followers as much as you love me.

²⁴ Father, I want everyone you have given me to be with me, wherever I am. Then they will see the glory that you have given me, because you loved me before the world was created. ²⁵ Good Father, the people of this world don't know you. But I know you, and my followers know that you sent me. ²⁶ I told them what you are like, and I will tell them even more. Then the love that you have for me will become part of them, and I will be one with them.

Jesus Is Betrayed and Arrested

18 When Jesus had finished praying, he and his disciples crossed the Kidron Valley and went into a garden.ˣ ² Jesus had often met there with his disciples, and Judas knew where the place was.

³⁻⁵ Judas had promised to betray Jesus. So he went to the garden with some Roman soldiers and temple police, who had been sent by the chief priests and the Pharisees. They carried torches, lanterns, and weapons. Jesus already knew everything that was going to happen, but he asked, "Who are you looking for?"

They answered, "We are looking for Jesus from Nazareth!"

Jesus told them, "I am Jesus!"ʸ ⁶ At once they all backed away and fell to the ground.

⁷ Jesus again asked, "Who are you looking for?"

"We are looking for Jesus from Nazareth," they answered.

⁸ This time Jesus replied, "I have already told you that I am Jesus. If I am the one you are looking for, let these others go. ⁹ Then everything will happen, just as I said, 'I did not lose anyone you gave me.' "

¹⁰ Simon Peter had brought along a sword. He now pulled it out and struck at the servant of the high priest. The servant's name was Malchus, and Peter cut off his right ear. ¹¹ Jesus told Peter, "Put your sword away. I must drink from the cup that the Father has given me."

Jesus Is Brought to Annas

¹² The Roman officer and his men, together with the temple police, arrested Jesus and tied him up. ¹³ They took him first to Annas, who was the father-in-law of Caiaphas, the high priest that year. ¹⁴ This was the same Caiaphas who had told the Jewish leaders, "It is better if one person dies for the people."

Peter Says He Doesn't Know Jesus

¹⁵ Simon Peter and another disciple followed Jesus. That disciple knew the high priest, and he followed Jesus into the courtyard of the high priest's house. ¹⁶ Peter stayed outside near the gate. But the other disciple came back out

---

ˣ **18.1** *garden*: The Greek word is usually translated "garden," but probably referred to an olive orchard.   ʸ **18.3-5** *I am Jesus*: The Greek text has "I am".

and spoke to the girl at the gate. She let Peter go in, [17] but asked him, "Aren't you one of that man's followers?"

"No, I am not!" Peter answered.

[18] It was cold, and the servants and temple police had made a charcoal fire. They were warming themselves around it, when Peter went over and stood near the fire to warm himself.

Jesus Is Questioned by the High Priest

[19] The high priest questioned Jesus about his followers and his teaching. [20] But Jesus told him, "I have spoken freely in front of everyone. And I have always taught in our meeting places and in the temple, where all of our people come together. I have not said anything in secret. [21] Why are you questioning me? Why don't you ask the people who heard me? They know what I have said."

[22] As soon as Jesus said this, one of the temple police hit him and said, "That's no way to talk to the high priest!"

[23] Jesus answered, "If I have done something wrong, say so. But if not, why did you hit me?" [24] Jesus was still tied up, and Annas sent him to Caiaphas the high priest.

Peter Again Denies that He Knows Jesus

[25] While Simon Peter was standing there warming himself, someone asked him, "Aren't you one of Jesus' followers?"

Again Peter denied it and said, "No, I am not!"

[26] One of the high priest's servants was there. He was a relative of the servant whose ear Peter had cut off, and he asked, "Didn't I see you in the garden with that man?"

[27] Once more Peter denied it, and right then a rooster crowed.

Jesus Is Tried by Pilate

[28] It was early in the morning when Jesus was taken from Caiaphas to the building where the Roman governor stayed. But the crowd waited outside. Any of them who had gone inside would have become unclean and would not be allowed to eat the Passover meal.

[29] Pilate came out and asked, "What charges are you bringing against this man?"

[30] They answered, "He is a criminal! That's why we brought him to you."

[31] Pilate told them, "Take him and judge him by your own laws."

The crowd replied, "We are not allowed to put anyone to death." [32] And so what Jesus said about his death would soon come true.

[33] Pilate then went back inside. He called Jesus over and asked, "Are you the king of the Jews?"

[34] Jesus answered, "Are you asking this on your own or did someone tell you about me?"

[35] "You know I'm not a Jew!" Pilate said. "Your own people and the chief priests brought you to me. What have you done?"

[36] Jesus answered, "My kingdom doesn't belong to this world. If it did, my followers would have fought to keep me from being handed over to the Jewish leaders. No, my kingdom doesn't belong to this world."

[37] "So you are a king," Pilate replied.

"You are saying that I am a king," Jesus told him. "I was born into this world to tell about the truth. And everyone who belongs to the truth knows my voice."

[38] Pilate asked Jesus, "What is truth?"

Jesus Is Sentenced to Death

Pilate went back out and said, "I don't find this man guilty of anything! [39] And since I usually set a prisoner free for you at Passover, would you like for me to set free the king of the Jews?"

[40] They shouted, "No, not him! We want Barabbas." Now Barabbas was a terrorist.

19 Pilate gave orders for Jesus to be beaten with a whip. [2] The soldiers made a crown out of thorn branches and put it on Jesus. Then they put a purple robe on him. [3] They came up to him and said, "Hey, you king of the Jews!" They also hit him with their fists.

[4] Once again Pilate went out. This time he said, "I will have Jesus brought out to you again. Then you can see for yourselves that I have not found him guilty."

[5] Jesus came out, wearing the crown of thorns and the purple robe. Pilate said, "Here is the man!" [z]

[6] When the chief priests and the temple police saw him, they yelled, "Nail him to a cross! Nail him to a cross!"

Pilate told them, "You take him and nail him to a cross! I don't find him guilty of anything."

[7] The crowd replied, "He claimed to be the Son of God! Our Jewish Law says that he must be put to death."

[8] When Pilate heard this, he was terrified. [9] He went back inside and asked Jesus, "Where are you from?" But Jesus did not answer.

[10] "Why won't you answer my question?" Pilate asked. "Don't you know that I have the power to let you go free or to nail you to a cross?"

[11] Jesus replied, "If God had not given you the power, you couldn't do anything at all to me. But the one who handed me over to you did something even worse."

[12] Then Pilate wanted to set Jesus free. But the crowd again yelled, "If you set this man free, you are no friend of the Emperor! Anyone who claims to be a king is an enemy of the Emperor."

[13] When Pilate heard this, he brought Jesus out. Then he sat down on the judge's bench at the place known as "The Stone Pavement." In Aramaic this pavement is called "Gabbatha." [14] It was about noon on the day before Passover, and Pilate said to the crowd, "Look at your king!"

[15] "Kill him! Kill him!" they yelled. "Nail him to a cross!"

"So you want me to nail your king to a cross?" Pilate asked.

The chief priests replied, "The Emperor is our king!" [16] Then Pilate handed Jesus over to be nailed to a cross.

Jesus Is Nailed to a Cross

Jesus was taken away, [17] and he carried his cross to a place known as "The Skull." In Aramaic this place is called "Golgotha." [18] There Jesus was nailed to the cross, and on each side of him a man was also nailed to a cross.

[19] Pilate ordered the charge against Jesus to be written on a board and put above the cross. It read, "Jesus of Nazareth, King of the Jews." [20] The words were written in Hebrew, Latin, and Greek.

---

[z] **19.5** "*Here is the man!*": Or "Look at the man!"

The place where Jesus was taken wasn't far from the city, and many of the Jewish people read the charge against him. [21] So the chief priests went to Pilate and said, "Why did you write that he is King of the Jews? You should have written, 'He claimed to be King of the Jews.'"

[22] But Pilate told them, "What is written will not be changed!"

[23] After the soldiers had nailed Jesus to the cross, they divided up his clothes into four parts, one for each of them. But his outer garment was made from a single piece of cloth, and it did not have any seams. [24] The soldiers said to each other, "Let's not rip it apart. We will gamble to see who gets it." This happened so that the Scriptures would come true, which say,

> "They divided up my clothes
> and gambled
>   for my garments."

The soldiers then did what they had decided.

[25] Jesus' mother stood beside his cross with her sister and Mary the wife of Clopas. Mary Magdalene was standing there too.[a] [26] When Jesus saw his mother and his favorite disciple with her, he said to his mother, "This man is now your son." [27] Then he said to the disciple, "She is now your mother." From then on, that disciple took her into his own home.

The Death of Jesus

[28] Jesus knew that he had now finished his work. And in order to make the Scriptures come true, he said, "I am thirsty!" [29] A jar of cheap wine was there. Someone then soaked a sponge with the wine and held it up to Jesus' mouth on the stem of a hyssop plant. [30] After Jesus drank the wine, he said, "Everything is done!" He bowed his head and died.

A Spear Is Stuck in Jesus' Side

[31] The next day would be both a Sabbath and the Passover. It was a special day for the Jewish people, and they did not want the bodies to stay on the crosses during that day. So they asked Pilate to break the men's legs and take their bodies down. [32] The soldiers first broke the legs of the other two men who were nailed there. [33] But when they came to Jesus, they saw that he was already dead, and they did not break his legs.

[34] One of the soldiers stuck his spear into Jesus' side, and blood and water came out. [35] We know this is true, because it was told by someone who saw it happen. Now you can have faith too. [36] All this happened so that the Scriptures would come true, which say, "No bone of his body will be broken" [37] and, "They will see the one in whose side they stuck a spear."

Jesus Is Buried

[38] Joseph from Arimathea was one of Jesus' disciples. He had kept it secret though, because he was afraid of the Jewish leaders. But now he asked Pilate to let him have Jesus'

body. Pilate gave him permission, and Joseph took it down from the cross.

[39] Nicodemus also came with about seventy-five pounds of spices made from myrrh and aloes. This was the same Nicodemus who had visited Jesus one night. [40] The two men wrapped the body in a linen cloth, together with the spices, which was how the Jewish people buried their dead. [41] In the place where Jesus had been nailed to a cross, there was a garden with a tomb that had never been used. [42] The tomb was nearby, and since it was the time to prepare for the Sabbath, they were in a hurry to put Jesus' body there.

Jesus Is Alive

20 On Sunday morning while it was still dark, Mary Magdalene went to the tomb and saw that the stone had been rolled away from the entrance. [2] She ran to Simon Peter and to Jesus' favorite disciple and said, "They have taken the Lord from the tomb! We don't know where they have put him."

[3] Peter and the other disciple started for the tomb. [4] They ran side by side, until the other disciple ran faster than Peter and got there first. [5] He bent over and saw the strips of linen cloth lying inside the tomb, but he did not go in.

[6] When Simon Peter got there, he went into the tomb and saw the strips of cloth. [7] He also saw the piece of cloth that had been used to cover Jesus' face. It was rolled up and in a place by itself. [8] The disciple who got there first then went into the tomb, and when he saw it, he believed. [9] At that time Peter and the other disciple did not know that the Scriptures said Jesus would rise to life. [10] So the two of them went back to the other disciples.

Jesus Appears to Mary Magdalene

[11] Mary Magdalene stood crying outside the tomb. She was still weeping, when she stooped down [12] and saw two angels inside. They were dressed in white and were sitting where Jesus' body had been. One was at the head and the other was at the foot. [13] The angels asked Mary, "Why are you crying?"

She answered, "They have taken away my Lord's body! I don't know where they have put him."

[14] As soon as Mary said this, she turned around and saw Jesus standing there. But she did not know who he was. [15] Jesus asked her, "Why are you crying? Who are you looking for?"

She thought he was the gardener and said, "Sir, if you have taken his body away, please tell me, so I can go and get him."

[16] Then Jesus said to her, "Mary!"

She turned and said to him, "Rabboni." The Aramaic word "Rabboni" means "Teacher."

[17] Jesus told her, "Don't hold on to me! I have not yet gone to the Father. But tell my disciples that I am going to the one who is my Father and my God, as well as your Father and your God." [18] Mary Magdalene then went and told the disciples that she had seen the Lord. She also told them what he had said to her.

---

[a] **19.25** *Jesus' mother stood beside his cross with her sister and Mary the wife of Clopas. Mary Magdalene was standing there too*: The Greek text may also be understood to include only three women ("Jesus' mother stood beside the cross with her sister, Mary the mother of Clopas. Mary Magdalene was standing there too.") or merely two women ("Jesus' mother was standing there with her sister Mary of Clopas, that is, Mary Magdalene."). "Of Clopas" may mean "daughter of" or "mother of."

Jesus Appears to His Disciples

19 The disciples were afraid of the Jewish leaders, and on the evening of that same Sunday they locked themselves in a room. Suddenly, Jesus appeared in the middle of the group. He greeted them **20** and showed them his hands and his side. When the disciples saw the Lord, they became very happy.

21 After Jesus had greeted them again, he said, "I am sending you, just as the Father has sent me." **22** Then he breathed on them and said, "Receive the Holy Spirit. **23** If you forgive anyone's sins, they will be forgiven. But if you don't forgive their sins, they will not be forgiven."

Jesus and Thomas

24 Although Thomas the Twin was one of the twelve disciples, he wasn't with the others when Jesus appeared to them. **25** So they told him, "We have seen the Lord!"

But Thomas said, "First, I must see the nail scars in his hands and touch them with my finger. I must put my hand where the spear went into his side. I won't believe unless I do this!"

26 A week later the disciples were together again. This time, Thomas was with them. Jesus came in while the doors were still locked and stood in the middle of the group. He greeted his disciples **27** and said to Thomas, "Put your finger here and look at my hands! Put your hand into my side. Stop doubting and have faith!"

28 Thomas replied, "You are my Lord and my God!"

29 Jesus said, "Thomas, do you have faith because you have seen me? The people who have faith in me without seeing me are the ones who are really blessed!"

Why John Wrote His Book

30 Jesus worked many other miracles for his disciples, and not all of them are written in this book. **31** But these are written so that you will put your faith in Jesus as the Messiah and the Son of God. If you have faith in him, you will have true life.

Jesus Appears to Seven Disciples

21 Jesus later appeared to his disciples along the shore of Lake Tiberias. **2** Simon Peter, Thomas the Twin, Nathanael from Cana in Galilee, and the brothers James and John,[a] were there, together with two other disciples. **3** Simon Peter said, "I'm going fishing!"

The others said, "We will go with you." They went out in their boat. But they didn't catch a thing that night.

4 Early the next morning Jesus stood on the shore, but the disciples did not realize who he was. **5** Jesus shouted, "Friends, have you caught anything?"

"No!" they answered.

6 So he told them, "Let your net down on the right side of your boat, and you will catch some fish."

They did, and the net was so full of fish that they could not drag it up into the boat.

7 Jesus' favorite disciple told Peter, "It's the Lord!" When Simon heard that it was the Lord, he put on the clothes that he had taken off while he was working. Then he jumped into the water. **8** The boat was only about a hundred yards from shore. So the other disciples stayed in the boat and dragged in the net full of fish.

9 When the disciples got out of the boat, they saw some bread and a charcoal fire with fish on it. **10** Jesus told his disciples, "Bring some of the fish you just caught." **11** Simon Peter got back into the boat and dragged the net to shore. In it were one hundred fifty-three large fish, but still the net did not rip.

12 Jesus said, "Come and eat!" But none of the disciples dared ask who he was. They knew he was the Lord. **13** Jesus took the bread in his hands and gave some of it to his disciples. He did the same with the fish. **14** This was the third time that Jesus appeared to his disciples after he was raised from death.

Jesus and Peter

15 When Jesus and his disciples had finished eating, he asked, "Simon son of John, do you love me more than the others do?"[c]

Simon Peter answered, "Yes, Lord, you know I do!"

"Then feed my lambs," Jesus said.

16 Jesus asked a second time, "Simon son of John, do you love me?"

Peter answered, "Yes, Lord, you know I love you!"

"Then take care of my sheep," Jesus told him.

17 Jesus asked a third time, "Simon son of John, do you love me?"

Peter was hurt because Jesus had asked him three times if he loved him. So he told Jesus, "Lord, you know everything. You know I love you."

Jesus replied, "Feed my sheep. **18** I tell you for certain that when you were a young man, you dressed yourself and went wherever you wanted to go. But when you are old, you will hold out your hands. Then others will wrap your belt around you and lead you where you don't want to go."

19 Jesus said this to tell how Peter would die and bring honor to God. Then he said to Peter, "Follow me!"

Jesus and His Favorite Disciple

20 Peter turned and saw Jesus' favorite disciple following them. He was the same one who had sat next to Jesus at the meal and had asked, "Lord, who is going to betray you?" **21** When Peter saw that disciple, he asked Jesus, "Lord, what about him?"

22 Jesus answered, "What is it to you, if I want him to live until I return? You must follow me. " **23** So the rumor spread among the other disciples that this disciple would not die. But Jesus did not say he would not die. He simply said, "What is it to you, if I want him to live until I return?"

24 This disciple is the one who told all of this. He wrote it, and we know he is telling the truth.

25 Jesus did many other things. If they were all written in books, I don't suppose there would be room enough in the whole world for all the books.

---

b **21.2** *the brothers James and John*: Greek "the two sons of Zebedee."   *c* **21.15** *more than the others do*: Or "more than you love these things?"

ACTS

1 Theophilus, I first wrote to you about all that Jesus did and taught from the very first [2] until he was taken up to heaven. But before he was taken up, he gave orders to the apostles he had chosen with the help of the Holy Spirit.

[3] For forty days after Jesus had suffered and died, he proved in many ways that he had been raised from death. He appeared to his apostles and spoke to them about God's kingdom. [4] While he was still with them, he said:

Don't leave Jerusalem yet. Wait here for the Father to give you the Holy Spirit, just as I told you he has promised to do. [5] John baptized with water, but in a few days you will be baptized with the Holy Spirit.

Jesus Is Taken to Heaven

[6] While the apostles were still with Jesus, they asked him, "Lord, are you now going to give Israel its own king again?"[a]

[7] Jesus said to them, "You don't need to know the time of those events that only the Father controls. [8] But the Holy Spirit will come upon you and give you power. Then you will tell everyone about me in Jerusalem, in all Judea, in Samaria, and everywhere in the world." [9] After Jesus had said this and while they were watching, he was taken up into a cloud. They could not see him, [10] but as he went up, they kept looking up into the sky.

Suddenly two men dressed in white clothes were standing there beside them. [11] They said, "Why are you men from Galilee standing here and looking up into the sky? Jesus has been taken to heaven. But he will come back in the same way that you have seen him go."

Someone To Take the Place of Judas

[12-13] The Mount of Olives was about half a mile from Jerusalem. The apostles who had gone there were Peter, John, James, Andrew, Philip, Thomas, Bartholomew, Matthew, James the son of Alphaeus, Simon, known as the Eager One,[b] and Judas the son of James.

After the apostles returned to the city, they went upstairs to the room where they had been staying.

[14] The apostles often met together and prayed with a single purpose in mind.[c] The women and Mary the mother of Jesus would meet with them, and so would his brothers. [15] One day there were about one hundred twenty of the Lord's followers meeting together, and Peter stood up to speak to them. [16-17] He said:

My friends, long ago by the power of the Holy Spirit, David said something about Judas, and what he said has now happened. Judas was one of us and had worked with us, but he brought the mob to arrest Jesus. [18] Then Judas bought some land with the money he was given for doing that

evil thing. He fell headfirst into the field. His body burst open, and all his insides came out. [19] When the people of Jerusalem found out about this, they called the place Akeldama, which in the local language means "Field of Blood."

[20] In the book of Psalms it says,

"Leave his house empty,
and don't let anyone
live there."

It also says,

"Let someone else
have his job."

[21-22] So we need someone else to help us tell others that Jesus has been raised from death. He must also be one of the men who was with us from the very beginning. He must have been with us from the time the Lord Jesus was baptized by John until the day he was taken to heaven.

[23] Two men were suggested: One of them was Joseph Barsabbas, known as Justus, and the other was Matthias. [24] Then they all prayed, "Lord, you know what everyone is like! Show us the one you have chosen [25] to be an apostle and to serve in place of Judas, who got what he deserved." [26] They drew names, and Matthias was chosen to join the group of the eleven apostles.

The Coming of the Holy Spirit

2 On the day of Pentecost all the Lord's followers were together in one place. [2] Suddenly there was a noise from heaven like the sound of a mighty wind! It filled the house where they were meeting. [3] Then they saw what looked like fiery tongues moving in all directions, and a tongue came and settled on each person there. [4] The Holy Spirit took control of everyone, and they began speaking whatever languages the Spirit let them speak.

[5] Many religious Jews from every country in the world were living in Jerusalem. [6] And when they heard this noise, a crowd gathered. But they were surprised, because they were hearing everything in their own languages. [7] They were excited and amazed, and said:

Don't all these who are speaking come from Galilee? [8] Then why do we hear them speaking our very own languages? [9] Some of us are from Parthia, Media, and Elam. Others are from Mesopotamia, Judea, Cappadocia, Pontus, Asia, [10] Phrygia, Pamphylia, Egypt, parts of Libya near Cyrene, Rome, [11] Crete, and Arabia. Some of us were born Jews, and others of us have chosen to be Jews. Yet

---

[a] **1.6** *are you now going to give Israel its own king again*: Or "Are you now going to rule Israel as its king?"   [b] **1.12,13** *known as the Eager One*: The Greek text has "Zealot," a name later given to the members of a Jewish group that resisted and fought against the Romans.   [c] **1.14** *met together and prayed with a single purpose in mind*: Or "met together in a special place for prayer."

we all hear them using our own languages to tell the wonderful things God has done.

12 Everyone was excited and confused. Some of them even kept asking each other, "What does all this mean?"

13 Others made fun of the Lord's followers and said, "They are drunk."

Peter Speaks to the Crowd

14 Peter stood with the eleven apostles and spoke in a loud and clear voice to the crowd:

Friends and everyone else living in Jerusalem, listen carefully to what I have to say! **15** You are wrong to think that these people are drunk. After all, it is only nine o'clock in the morning. **16** But this is what God had the prophet Joel say,

17 "When the last days come,
I will give my Spirit
to everyone.
Your sons and daughters
will prophesy.
Your young men
will see visions,
and your old men
will have dreams.
18 In those days I will give
my Spirit to my servants,
both men and women,
and they will prophesy.

19 I will work miracles
in the sky above
and wonders
on the earth below.
There will be blood and fire
and clouds of smoke.
20 The sun will turn dark,
and the moon
will be as red as blood
before the great
and wonderful day
of the Lord appears.
21 Then the Lord
will save everyone
who asks for his help."

22 Now, listen to what I have to say about Jesus from Nazareth. God proved that he sent Jesus to you by having him work miracles, wonders, and signs. All of you know this. **23** God had already planned and decided that Jesus would be handed over to you. So you took him and had evil men put him to death on a cross. **24** But God set him free from death and raised him to life. Death could not hold him in its power. **25** What David said are really the words of Jesus,

"I always see the Lord
near me,
and I will not be afraid
with him at my right side.
26 Because of this,
my heart will be glad,

my words will be joyful,
and I will live in hope.
27 The Lord won't leave me
in the grave.
I am his holy one,
and he won't let
my body decay.
28 He has shown me
the path to life,
and he makes me glad
by being near me."

29 My friends, it is right for me to speak to you about our ancestor David. He died and was buried, and his tomb is still here. **30** But David was a prophet, and he knew that God had made a promise he would not break. He had told David that someone from his own family would someday be king.

31 David knew this would happen, and so he told us that Christ would be raised to life. He said that God would not leave him in the grave or let his body decay. **32** All of us can tell you that God has raised Jesus to life!

33 Jesus was taken up to sit at the right side of God, and he was given the Holy Spirit, just as the Father had promised. Jesus is also the one who has given the Spirit to us, and that is what you are now seeing and hearing.

34 David didn't go up to heaven. So he wasn't talking about himself when he said, "The Lord told my Lord to sit at his right side, **35** until he made my Lord's enemies into a footstool for him." **36** Everyone in Israel should then know for certain that God has made Jesus both Lord and Christ, even though you put him to death on a cross.

37 When the people heard this, they were very upset. They asked Peter and the other apostles, "Friends, what shall we do?"

38 Peter said, "Turn back to God! Be baptized in the name of Jesus Christ, so that your sins will be forgiven. Then you will be given the Holy Spirit. **39** This promise is for you and your children. It is for everyone our Lord God will choose, no matter where they live."

40 Peter told them many other things as well. Then he said, "I beg you to save yourselves from what will happen to all these evil people." **41** On that day about three thousand believed his message and were baptized. **42** They spent their time learning from the apostles, and they were like family to each other. They also broke bread and prayed together.

Life among the Lord's Followers

43 Everyone was amazed by the many miracles and wonders that the apostles worked. **44** All the Lord's followers often met together, and they shared everything they had. **45** They would sell their property and possessions and give the money to whoever needed it. **46** Day after day they met together in the temple. They broke bread together in different homes and shared their food happily and freely, **47** while praising God. Everyone liked them, and each day the Lord added to their group others who were being saved.

Peter and John Heal a Lame Man

3 The time of prayer was about three o'clock in the afternoon, and Peter and John were going into the temple. 2 A man who had been born lame was being carried to the temple door. Each day he was placed beside this door, known as the Beautiful Gate. He sat there and begged from the people who were going in.

3 The man saw Peter and John entering the temple, and he asked them for money. 4 But they looked straight at him and said, "Look up at us!"

5 The man stared at them and thought he was going to get something. 6 But Peter said, "I don't have any silver or gold! But I will give you what I do have. In the name of Jesus Christ from Nazareth, get up and start walking." 7 Peter then took him by the right hand and helped him up.

At once the man's feet and ankles became strong, 8 and he jumped up and started walking. He went with Peter and John into the temple, walking and jumping and praising God. 9 Everyone saw him walking around and praising God. 10 They knew that he was the beggar who had been lying beside the Beautiful Gate, and they were completely surprised. They could not imagine what had happened to the man.

Peter Speaks in the Temple

11 While the man kept holding on to Peter and John, the whole crowd ran to them in amazement at the place known as Solomon's Porch. 12 Peter saw that a crowd had gathered, and he said:

Friends, why are you surprised at what has happened? Why are you staring at us? Do you think we have some power of our own? Do you think we were able to make this man walk because we are so religious? 13 The God that Abraham, Isaac, Jacob, and our other ancestors worshiped has brought honor to his Servant*d* Jesus. He is the one you betrayed. You turned against him when he was being tried by Pilate, even though Pilate wanted to set him free.

14 You rejected Jesus, who was holy and good. You asked for a murderer to be set free, 15 and you killed the one who leads people to life. But God raised him from death, and all of us can tell you what he has done. 16 You see this man, and you know him. He put his faith in the name of Jesus and was made strong. Faith in Jesus made this man completely well while everyone was watching.

17 My friends, I am sure that you and your leaders didn't know what you were doing. 18 But God had his prophets tell that his Messiah would suffer, and now he has kept that promise. 19 So turn to God! Give up your sins, and you will be forgiven. 20 Then that time will come when the Lord will give you fresh strength. He will send you Jesus, his chosen Messiah. 21 But Jesus must stay in heaven until God makes all things new, just as his holy prophets promised long ago.

22 Moses said, "The Lord your God will choose one of your own people to be a prophet, just as he chose me. Listen to everything he tells you. 23 No one who disobeys that prophet will be one of God's people any longer."

24 Samuel and all the other prophets who came later also spoke about what is now happening. 25 You are really the ones God told his prophets to speak to. And you were given the promise that God made to your ancestors. He said to Abraham, "All nations on earth will be blessed because of someone from your family." 26 God sent his chosen Son*e* to you first, because God wanted to bless you and make each one of you turn away from your sins.

Peter and John Are Brought in Front of the Council

4 The apostles were still talking to the people, when some priests, the captain of the temple guard, and some Sadducees arrived. 2 These men were angry because the apostles were teaching the people that the dead would be raised from death, just as Jesus had been raised from death. 3 It was already late in the afternoon, and they arrested Peter and John and put them in jail for the night. 4 But a lot of people who had heard the message believed it. So by now there were about five thousand followers of the Lord.

5 The next morning the leaders, the elders, and the teachers of the Law of Moses met in Jerusalem. 6 The high priest Annas was there, as well as Caiaphas, John, Alexander, and other members of the high priest's family. 7 They brought in Peter and John and made them stand in the middle while they questioned them. They asked, "By what power and in whose name have you done this?"

8 Peter was filled with the Holy Spirit and told the nation's leaders and the elders:

9 You are questioning us today about a kind deed in which a crippled man was healed. 10 But there is something we must tell you and everyone else in Israel. This man is standing here completely well because of the power of Jesus Christ from Nazareth. You put Jesus to death on a cross, but God raised him to life. 11 He is the stone that you builders thought was worthless, and now he is the most important stone of all. 12 Only Jesus has the power to save! His name is the only one in all the world that can save anyone.

13 The officials were amazed to see how brave Peter and John were, and they knew that these two apostles were only ordinary men and not well educated. The officials were certain that these men had been with Jesus. 14 But they could not deny what had happened. The man who had been healed was standing there with the apostles.

15 The officials commanded them to leave the council room. Then the officials said to each other, 16 "What can we do with these men? Everyone in Jerusalem knows about this miracle, and we cannot say it didn't happen. 17 But to keep this thing from spreading, we will warn them never again to speak to anyone about the name of Jesus." 18 So they called the two apostles back in and told them that they must never, for any reason, teach anything about the name of Jesus.

19 Peter and John answered, "Do you think God wants us to obey you or to obey him? 20 We cannot keep quiet about what we have seen and heard."

21-22 The officials could not find any reason to punish Peter and John. So they threatened them and let them go. The man who was healed by this miracle was more than

---

*d*3.13 *Servant*: Or "Son."   *e*3.26 *Son*: Or "Servant."

forty years old, and everyone was praising God for what had happened.

Peter and Others Pray for Courage

23 As soon as Peter and John had been set free, they went back and told the others everything that the chief priests and the leaders had said to them. **24** When the rest of the Lord's followers heard this, they prayed together and said:

Master, you created heaven and earth, the sea, and everything in them. **25** And by the Holy Spirit you spoke to our ancestor David. He was your servant, and you told him to say:

"Why are all the Gentiles
so furious?
Why do people
make foolish plans?
26 The kings of earth
prepare for war,
and the rulers
join together
against the Lord
and his Messiah."

27 Here in Jerusalem, Herod and Pontius Pilate got together with the Gentiles and the people of Israel. Then they turned against your holy Servant*f* Jesus, your chosen Messiah. **28** They did what you in your power and wisdom had already decided would happen.

29 Lord, listen to their threats! We are your servants. So make us brave enough to speak your message. **30** Show your mighty power, as we heal people and work miracles and wonders in the name of your holy Servant*f* Jesus.

31 After they had prayed, the meeting place shook. They were all filled with the Holy Spirit and bravely spoke God's message.

Sharing Possessions

32 The group of followers all felt the same way about everything. None of them claimed that their possessions were their own, and they shared everything they had with each other. **33** In a powerful way the apostles told everyone that the Lord Jesus was now alive. God greatly blessed his followers,*g* **34** and no one went in need of anything. Everyone who owned land or houses would sell them and bring the money **35** to the apostles. Then they would give the money to anyone who needed it.

36-37 Joseph was one of the followers who had sold a piece of property and brought the money to the apostles. He was a Levite from Cyprus, and the apostles called him Barnabas, which means "one who encourages others."

Peter Condemns Ananias and Sapphira

5 Ananias and his wife Sapphira also sold a piece of property. **2** But they agreed to cheat and keep some of the money for themselves.

So when Ananias took the rest of the money to the apostles, **3** Peter said, "Why has Satan made you keep back some of the money from the sale of the property? Why have you lied to the Holy Spirit? **4** The property was yours before you sold it, and even after you sold it, the money was still yours. What made you do such a thing? You didn't lie to people. You lied to God!"

5 As soon as Ananias heard this, he dropped dead, and everyone who heard about it was frightened. **6** Some young men came in and wrapped up his body. Then they took it out and buried it.

7 Three hours later Sapphira came in, but she did not know what had happened to her husband. **8** Peter asked her, "Tell me, did you sell the property for this amount?"

"Yes," she answered, "that's the amount."

9 Then Peter said, "Why did the two of you agree to test the Lord's Spirit? The men who buried Ananias are by the door, and they will carry you out!" **10** At once she fell at Peter's feet and died.

When the young men came back in, they found Sapphira lying there dead. So they carried her out and buried her beside her husband. **11** The church members were afraid, and so was everyone else who heard what had happened.

Peter's Unusual Power

12 The apostles worked many miracles and wonders among the people. All of the Lord's followers often met in the part of the temple known as Solomon's Porch. **13** No one outside their group dared join them, even though everyone liked them very much.

14 Many men and women started having faith in the Lord. **15** Then sick people were brought out to the road and placed on cots and mats. It was hoped that Peter would walk by, and his shadow would fall on them and heal them. **16** A lot of people living in the towns near Jerusalem brought those who were sick or troubled by evil spirits, and they were all healed.

Trouble for the Apostles

17 The high priest and all the other Sadducees who were with him became jealous. **18** They arrested the apostles and put them in the city jail. **19** But that night an angel from the Lord opened the doors of the jail and led the apostles out. The angel said, **20** "Go to the temple and tell the people everything about this new life." **21** So they went into the temple before sunrise and started teaching.

The high priest and his men called together their council, which included all of Israel's leaders. Then they ordered the apostles to be brought to them from the jail. **22** The temple police who were sent to the jail did not find the apostles. They returned and said, **23** "We found the jail locked tight and the guards standing at the doors. But when we opened the doors and went in, we didn't find anyone there." **24** The captain of the temple police and the chief priests listened to their report, but they did not know what to think about it.

25 Just then someone came in and said, "Right now those men you put in jail are in the temple, teaching the people!" **26** The captain went with some of the temple police and brought the apostles back. But they did not use force. They were afraid that the people might start throwing stones at them.

27 When the apostles were brought before the council, the high priest said to them, **28** "We told you plainly not to

---

f **4.27,30** *Servant*: See the note at 3.13.   *g* **4.33** *God greatly blessed his followers*: Or "Everyone highly respected his followers."

teach in the name of Jesus. But look what you have done! You have been teaching all over Jerusalem, and you are trying to blame us for his death."

²⁹ Peter and the apostles replied:

We don't obey people. We obey God. ³⁰ You killed Jesus by nailing him to a cross. But the God our ancestors worshiped raised him to life ³¹ and made him our Leader and Savior. Then God gave him a place at his right side, so that the people of Israel would turn back to him and be forgiven. ³² We are here to tell you about all this, and so is the Holy Spirit, who is God's gift to everyone who obeys God.

³³ When the council members heard this, they became so angry that they wanted to kill the apostles. ³⁴ But one of the members was the Pharisee Gamaliel, a highly respected teacher. He ordered the apostles to be taken out of the room for a little while. ³⁵ Then he said to the council:

People of Israel, be careful what you do with these men. ³⁶ Not long ago Theudas claimed to be someone important, and about four hundred men joined him. But he was killed. All his followers were scattered, and that was the end of that.

³⁷ Later, when the people of our nation were being counted, Judas from Galilee showed up. A lot of people followed him, but he was killed, and all his followers were scattered.

³⁸ So I advise you to stay away from these men. Leave them alone. If what they are planning is something of their own doing, it will fail. ³⁹ But if God is behind it, you cannot stop it anyway, unless you want to fight against God.

The council members agreed with what he said, ⁴⁰ and they called the apostles back in. They had them beaten with a whip and warned them not to speak in the name of Jesus. Then they let them go.

⁴¹ The apostles left the council and were happy, because God had considered them worthy to suffer for the sake of Jesus. ⁴² Every day they spent time in the temple and in one home after another. They never stopped teaching and telling the good news that Jesus is the Messiah.

Seven Leaders for the Church

6 A lot of people were now becoming followers of the Lord. But some of the ones who spoke Greek started complaining about the ones who spoke Aramaic. They complained that the Greek-speaking widows were not given their share when the food supplies were handed out each day.

² The twelve apostles called the whole group of followers together and said, "We should not give up preaching God's message in order to serve at tables. ³ My friends, choose seven men who are respected and wise and filled with God's Spirit. We will put them in charge of these things. ⁴ We can spend our time praying and serving God by preaching."

⁵ This suggestion pleased everyone, and they began by choosing Stephen. He had great faith and was filled with the Holy Spirit. Then they chose Philip, Prochorus, Nicanor, Timon, Parmenas, and also Nicolaus, who worshiped with the Jewish people*ʰ* in Antioch. ⁶ These men were brought to the apostles. Then the apostles prayed and placed their hands on the men to show that they had been chosen to do this work. ⁷ God's message spread, and many more people in Jerusalem became followers. Even a large number of priests put their faith in the Lord.

Stephen Is Arrested

⁸ God gave Stephen the power to work great miracles and wonders among the people. ⁹ But some Jews from Cyrene and Alexandria were members of a group who called themselves "Free Men." They started arguing with Stephen. Some others from Cilicia and Asia also argued with him. ¹⁰ But they were no match for Stephen, who spoke with the great wisdom that the Spirit gave him. ¹¹ So they talked some men into saying, "We heard Stephen say terrible things against Moses and God!"

¹² They turned the people and their leaders and the teachers of the Law of Moses against Stephen. Then they all grabbed Stephen and dragged him in front of the council.

¹³ Some men agreed to tell lies about Stephen, and they said, "This man keeps on saying terrible things about this holy temple and the Law of Moses. ¹⁴ We have heard him claim that Jesus from Nazareth will destroy this place and change the customs that Moses gave us." ¹⁵ Then all the council members stared at Stephen. They saw that his face looked like the face of an angel.

Stephen's Speech

7 The high priest asked Stephen, "Are they telling the truth about you?"

² Stephen answered:

Friends, listen to me. Our glorious God appeared to our ancestor Abraham while he was still in Mesopotamia, before he had moved to Haran. ³ God told him, "Leave your country and your relatives and go to a land that I will show you." ⁴ Then Abraham left the land of the Chaldeans and settled in Haran.

After his father died, Abraham came and settled in this land where you now live. ⁵ God didn't give him any part of it, not even a square foot. But God did promise to give it to him and his family forever, even though Abraham didn't have any children. ⁶ God said that Abraham's descendants would live for a while in a foreign land. There they would be slaves and would be mistreated four hundred years. ⁷ But he also said, "I will punish the nation that makes them slaves. Then later they will come and worship me in this place."

⁸ God said to Abraham, "Every son in each family must be circumcised to show that you have kept your agreement with me." So when Isaac was eight days old, Abraham circumcised him. Later, Isaac circumcised his son Jacob, and Jacob circumcised his twelve sons. ⁹ These men were our ancestors.

Joseph was also one of our famous ancestors. His brothers were jealous of him and sold him as a slave to be taken to Egypt. But God was with him ¹⁰ and rescued him from all his troubles. God made

---

ʰ **6.5** *worshiped with the Jewish people:* This translates the Greek word "proselyte" that means a Gentile who had accepted the Jewish religion.

him so wise that the Egyptian king Pharaoh[i] thought highly of him. The king even made Joseph governor over Egypt and put him in charge of everything he owned.

11 Everywhere in Egypt and Canaan the grain crops failed. There was terrible suffering, and our ancestors could not find enough to eat. **12** But when Jacob heard that there was grain in Egypt, he sent our ancestors there for the first time. **13** It was on their second trip that Joseph told his brothers who he was, and Pharaoh learned about Joseph's family.

14 Joseph sent for his father and his relatives. In all, there were seventy-five of them. **15** His father went to Egypt and died there, just as our ancestors did. **16** Later their bodies were taken back to Shechem and placed in the tomb that Abraham had bought from the sons of Hamor.

17 Finally, the time came for God to do what he had promised Abraham. By then the number of our people in Egypt had greatly increased. **18** Another king was ruling Egypt, and he didn't know anything about Joseph. **19** He tricked our ancestors and was cruel to them. He even made them leave their babies outside, so they would die.

20 During this time Moses was born. He was a very beautiful child, and for three months his parents took care of him in their home. **21** Then when they were forced to leave him outside, the king's daughter found him and raised him as her own son. **22** Moses was given the best education in Egypt. He was a strong man and a powerful speaker.

23 When Moses was forty years old, he wanted to help the Israelites because they were his own people. **24** One day he saw an Egyptian mistreating one of them. So he rescued the man and killed the Egyptian. **25** Moses thought the rest of his people would realize that God was going to use him to set them free. But they didn't understand.

26 The next day Moses saw two of his own people fighting, and he tried to make them stop. He said, "Men, you are both Israelites. Why are you so cruel to each other?"

27 But the man who had started the fight pushed Moses aside and asked, "Who made you our ruler and judge? **28** Are you going to kill me, just as you killed that Egyptian yesterday?" **29** When Moses heard this, he ran away to live in the country of Midian. His two sons were born there.

30 Forty years later, an angel appeared to Moses from a burning bush in the desert near Mount Sinai. **31** Moses was surprised by what he saw. He went closer to get a better look, and the Lord said, **32** "I am the God who was worshiped by your ancestors, Abraham, Isaac, and Jacob." Moses started shaking all over and didn't dare to look at the bush.

33 The Lord said to him, "Take off your sandals. The place where you are standing is holy. **34** With my own eyes I have seen the suffering of my people in Egypt. I have heard their groans and have come down to rescue them. Now I am sending you back to Egypt."

35 This was the same Moses that the people rejected by saying, "Who made you our leader and judge?" God's angel had spoken to Moses from the bush. And God had even sent the angel to help Moses rescue the people and be their leader.

36 In Egypt and at the Red Sea and in the desert, Moses rescued the people by working miracles and wonders for forty years. **37** Moses is the one who told the people of Israel, "God will choose one of your people to be a prophet, just as he chose me." **38** Moses brought our people together in the desert, and the angel spoke to him on Mount Sinai. There he was given these life-giving words to pass on to us. **39** But our ancestors refused to obey Moses. They rejected him and wanted to go back to Egypt.

40 The people said to Aaron, "Make some gods to lead us! Moses led us out of Egypt, but we don't know what's happened to him now." **41** Then they made an idol in the shape of a calf. They offered sacrifices to the idol and were pleased with what they had done.

42 God turned his back on his people and left them. Then they worshiped the stars in the sky, just as it says in the Book of the Prophets, "People of Israel, you didn't offer sacrifices and offerings to me during those forty years in the desert. **43** Instead, you carried the tent where the god Molech is worshiped, and you took along the star of your god Rephan. You made those idols and worshiped them. So now I will have you carried off beyond Babylonia."

44 The tent where our ancestors worshiped God was with them in the desert. This was the same tent that God had commanded Moses to make. And it was made like the model that Moses had seen. **45** Later it was given to our ancestors, and they took it with them when they went with Joshua. They carried the tent along as they took over the land from those people that God had chased out for them. Our ancestors used this tent until the time of King David. **46** He pleased God and asked him if he could build a house of worship for the people[j] of Israel. **47** And it was finally King Solomon who built a house for God.[k]

48 But the Most High God doesn't live in houses made by humans. It is just as the prophet said, when he spoke for the Lord,

49 "Heaven is my throne,
and the earth
   is my footstool.
What kind of house
   will you build for me?
In what place will I rest?
50 I have made everything."

51 You stubborn and hardheaded people! You are always fighting against the Holy Spirit, just as

[i]**7.10** *Pharaoh*: A Hebrew word sometimes used for the title of the King of Egypt. [j]**7.46** *the people*: Some manuscripts have "God." [k]**7.47** *God*: Or "the people."

your ancestors did. 52 Is there one prophet that your ancestors didn't mistreat? They killed the prophets who told about the coming of the One Who Obeys God. And now you have turned against him and killed him. 53 Angels gave you God's Law, but you still don't obey it.

Stephen Is Stoned to Death

54 When the council members heard Stephen's speech, they were angry and furious. 55 But Stephen was filled with the Holy Spirit. He looked toward heaven, where he saw our glorious God and Jesus standing at his right side. 56 Then Stephen said, "I see heaven open and the Son of Man standing at the right side of God!"

57 The council members shouted and covered their ears. At once they all attacked Stephen 58 and dragged him out of the city. Then they started throwing stones at him. The men who had brought charges against him put their coats at the feet of a young man named Saul.

59 As Stephen was being stoned to death, he called out, "Lord Jesus, please welcome me!" 60 He knelt down and shouted, "Lord, don't blame them for what they have done." Then he died.

8 1-2 Saul approved the stoning of Stephen. Some faithful followers of the Lord buried Stephen and mourned very much for him.

Saul Makes Trouble for the Church

At that time the church in Jerusalem suffered terribly. All of the Lord's followers, except the apostles, were scattered everywhere in Judea and Samaria. 3 Saul started making a lot of trouble for the church. He went from house to house, arresting men and women and putting them in jail.

The Good News Is Preached in Samaria

4 The Lord's followers who had been scattered went from place to place, telling the good news. 5 Philip went to the city of Samaria and told the people about Christ. 6 They crowded around Philip because they were eager to hear what he was saying and to see him work miracles. 7 Many people with evil spirits were healed, and the spirits went out of them with a shout. A lot of crippled and lame people were also healed. 8 Everyone in that city was very glad because of what was happening.

9 For some time a man named Simon had lived in the city of Samaria and had amazed the people. He practiced witchcraft and claimed to be somebody great. 10 Everyone, rich and poor, crowded around him. They said, "This man is the power of God called 'The Great Power.' "

11 For a long time, Simon had used witchcraft to amaze the people, and they kept crowding around him. 12 But when they believed what Philip was saying about God's kingdom and about the name of Jesus Christ, they were all baptized. 13 Even Simon believed and was baptized. He stayed close to Philip, because he marveled at all the miracles and wonders.

14 The apostles in Jerusalem heard that some people in Samaria had accepted God's message, and they sent Peter and John. 15 When the two apostles arrived, they prayed that the people would be given the Holy Spirit. 16 Before this, the Holy Spirit had not been given to anyone in Samaria, though some of them had been baptized in the name of the Lord Jesus. 17 Peter and John then placed their hands on everyone who had faith in the Lord, and they were given the Holy Spirit.

18 Simon noticed that the Spirit was given only when the apostles placed their hands on the people. So he brought money 19 and said to Peter and John, "Let me have this power too! Then anyone I place my hands on will also be given the Holy Spirit."

20 Peter said to him, "You and your money will both end up in hell if you think you can buy God's gift! 21 You don't have any part in this, and God sees that your heart isn't right. 22 Get rid of these evil thoughts and ask God to forgive you. 23 I can see that you are jealous and bound by your evil ways."

24 Simon said, "Please pray to the Lord, so that what you said won't happen to me."

25 After Peter and John had preached about the Lord, they returned to Jerusalem. On their way they told the good news in many villages of Samaria.

Philip and an Ethiopian Official

26 The Lord's angel said to Philip, "Go south[l] along the desert road that leads from Jerusalem to Gaza."[m] 27 So Philip left.

An important Ethiopian official happened to be going along that road in his chariot. He was the chief treasurer for Candace, the Queen of Ethiopia. The official had gone to Jerusalem to worship 28 and was now on his way home. He was sitting in his chariot, reading the book of the prophet Isaiah.

29 The Spirit told Philip to catch up with the chariot. 30 Philip ran up close and heard the man reading aloud from the book of Isaiah. Philip asked him, "Do you understand what you are reading?"

31 The official answered, "How can I understand unless someone helps me?" He then invited Philip to come up and sit beside him.

32 The man was reading the passage that said,

"He was led like a sheep
　　on its way to be killed.
He was silent as a lamb
　whose wool
　　is being cut off,
and he did not say
　a word.
33 He was treated like a nobody
　and did not receive
　　a fair trial.
How can he have children,
　if his life
　　is snatched away?"

34 The official said to Philip, "Tell me, was the prophet talking about himself or about someone else?" 35 So Philip began at this place in the Scriptures and explained the good news about Jesus.

36-37 As they were going along the road, they came to a place where there was some water. The official said, "Look!

---

[l] 8.26 Go south: Or "About noon go."   [m] 8.26 the desert road that leads from Jerusalem to Gaza: Or "the road that leads from Jerusalem to Gaza in the desert."

Here is some water. Why can't I be baptized?"[n] 38 He ordered the chariot to stop. Then they both went down into the water, and Philip baptized him.

39 After they had come out of the water, the Lord's Spirit took Philip away. The official never saw him again, but he was very happy as he went on his way.

40 Philip later appeared in Azotus. He went from town to town, all the way to Caesarea, telling people about Jesus.

Saul Becomes a Follower of the Lord

9 Saul kept on threatening to kill the Lord's followers. He even went to the high priest 2 and asked for letters to the Jewish leaders in Damascus. He did this because he wanted to arrest and take to Jerusalem any man or woman who had accepted the Lord's Way. 3 When Saul had almost reached Damascus, a bright light from heaven suddenly flashed around him. 4 He fell to the ground and heard a voice that said, "Saul! Saul! Why are you so cruel to me?"

5 "Who are you?" Saul asked.

"I am Jesus," the Lord answered. "I am the one you are so cruel to. 6 Now get up and go into the city, where you will be told what to do."

7 The men with Saul stood there speechless. They had heard the voice, but they had not seen anyone. 8 Saul got up from the ground, and when he opened his eyes, he could not see a thing. Someone then led him by the hand to Damascus, 9 and for three days he was blind and did not eat or drink.

10 A follower named Ananias lived in Damascus, and the Lord spoke to him in a vision. Ananias answered, "Lord, here I am."

11 The Lord said to him, "Get up and go to the house of Judas on Straight Street. When you get there, you will find a man named Saul from the city of Tarsus. Saul is praying, 12 and he has seen a vision. He saw a man named Ananias coming to him and putting his hands on him, so that he could see again."

13 Ananias replied, "Lord, a lot of people have told me about the terrible things this man has done to your followers in Jerusalem. 14 Now the chief priests have given him the power to come here and arrest anyone who worships in your name."

15 The Lord said to Ananias, "Go! I have chosen him to tell foreigners, kings, and the people of Israel about me. 16 I will show him how much he must suffer for worshiping in my name."

17 Ananias left and went into the house where Saul was staying. Ananias placed his hands on him and said, "Saul, the Lord Jesus has sent me. He is the same one who appeared to you along the road. He wants you to be able to see and to be filled with the Holy Spirit."

18 Suddenly something like fish scales fell from Saul's eyes, and he could see. He got up and was baptized. 19 Then he ate and felt much better.

Saul Preaches in Damascus

For several days Saul stayed with the Lord's followers in Damascus. 20 Soon he went to the Jewish meeting places and started telling people that Jesus is the Son of God. 21 Everyone who heard Saul was amazed and said, "Isn't this the man who caused so much trouble for those people in Jerusalem who worship in the name of Jesus? Didn't he come here to arrest them and take them to the chief priests?"

22 Saul preached with such power that he completely confused the Jewish people in Damascus, as he tried to show them that Jesus is the Messiah.

23 Later some of them made plans to kill Saul, 24 but he found out about it. He learned that they were guarding the gates of the city day and night in order to kill him. 25 Then one night his followers let him down over the city wall in a large basket.

Saul in Jerusalem

26 When Saul arrived in Jerusalem, he tried to join the followers. But they were all afraid of him, because they did not believe he was a true follower. 27 Then Barnabas helped him by taking him to the apostles. He explained how Saul had seen the Lord and how the Lord had spoken to him. Barnabas also said that when Saul was in Damascus, he had spoken bravely in the name of Jesus.

28 Saul moved about freely with the followers in Jerusalem and told everyone about the Lord. 29 He was always arguing with the Jews who spoke Greek, and so they tried to kill him. 30 But the followers found out about this and took Saul to Caesarea. From there they sent him to the city of Tarsus.

31 The church in Judea, Galilee, and Samaria now had a time of peace and kept on worshiping the Lord. The church became stronger, as the Holy Spirit encouraged it and helped it grow.

Peter Heals Aeneas

32 While Peter was traveling from place to place, he visited the Lord's followers who lived in the town of Lydda. 33 There he met a man named Aeneas, who for eight years had been sick in bed and could not move. 34 Peter said to Aeneas, "Jesus Christ has healed you! Get up and make up your bed."[o] Right away he stood up.

35 Many people in the towns of Lydda and Sharon saw Aeneas and became followers of the Lord.

Peter Brings Dorcas Back to Life

36 In Joppa there was a follower named Tabitha. Her Greek name was Dorcas, which means "deer." She was always doing good things for people and had given much to the poor. 37 But she got sick and died, and her body was washed and placed in an upstairs room. 38 Joppa wasn't far from Lydda, and the followers heard that Peter was there. They sent two men to say to him, "Please come with us as quickly as you can!" 39 Right away, Peter went with them.

The men took Peter upstairs into the room. Many widows were there crying. They showed him the coats and clothes that Dorcas had made while she was still alive.

40 After Peter had sent everyone out of the room, he knelt down and prayed. Then he turned to the body of Dorcas and said, "Tabitha, get up!" The woman opened her eyes, and when she saw Peter, she sat up. 41 He took her by the hand and helped her to her feet.

Peter called in the widows and the other followers and showed them that Dorcas had been raised from death.

---

[n] 8.36,37 Why can't I be baptized: Some manuscripts add, "Philip replied, 'You can, if you believe with all your heart.' The official answered, 'I believe that Jesus Christ is the Son of God.'"   [o] 9.34 and make up your bed: Or "and fix something to eat."

42 Everyone in Joppa heard what had happened, and many of them put their faith in the Lord. 43 Peter stayed on for a while in Joppa in the house of a man named Simon, who made leather.

Peter and Cornelius

10 In Caesarea there was a man named Cornelius, who was the captain of a group of soldiers called "The Italian Unit." 2 Cornelius was a very religious man. He worshiped God, and so did everyone else who lived in his house. He had given a lot of money to the poor and was always praying to God.

3 One afternoon at about three o'clock, Cornelius had a vision. He saw an angel from God coming to him and calling him by name. 4 Cornelius was surprised and stared at the angel. Then he asked, "What is this all about?"

The angel answered, "God has heard your prayers and knows about your gifts to the poor. 5 Now send some men to Joppa for a man named Simon Peter. 6 He is visiting with Simon the leather maker, who lives in a house near the sea." 7 After saying this, the angel left.

Cornelius called in two of his servants and one of his soldiers who worshiped God. 8 He explained everything to them and sent them off to Joppa.

9 The next day about noon these men were coming near Joppa. Peter went up on the roof of the house to pray 10 and became very hungry. While the food was being prepared, he fell sound asleep and had a vision. 11 He saw heaven open, and something came down like a huge sheet held up by its four corners. 12 In it were all kinds of animals, snakes, and birds. 13 A voice said to him, "Peter, get up! Kill these and eat them."

14 But Peter said, "Lord, I can't do that! I've never eaten anything that is unclean and not fit to eat."

15 The voice spoke to him again, "When God says that something can be used for food, don't say it isn't fit to eat."

16 This happened three times before the sheet was suddenly taken back to heaven.

17 Peter was still wondering what all of this meant, when the men sent by Cornelius came and stood at the gate. They had found their way to Simon's house 18 and were asking if Simon Peter was staying there.

19 While Peter was still thinking about the vision, the Holy Spirit said to him, "Three[p] men are here looking for you. 20 Hurry down and go with them. Don't worry, I sent them."

21 Peter went down and said to the men, "I am the one you are looking for. Why have you come?"

22 They answered, "Captain Cornelius sent us. He is a good man who worships God and is liked by the Jewish people. One of God's holy angels told Cornelius to send for you, so he could hear what you have to say." 23 Peter invited them to spend the night.

The next morning, Peter and some of the Lord's followers in Joppa left with the men who had come from Cornelius. 24 The next day they arrived in Caesarea where Cornelius was waiting for them. He had also invited his relatives and close friends.

25 When Peter arrived, Cornelius greeted him. Then he knelt at Peter's feet and started worshiping him. 26 But Peter took hold of him and said, "Stand up! I am nothing more than a human."

27 As Peter entered the house, he was still talking with Cornelius. Many people were there, 28 and Peter said to them, "You know that we Jews are not allowed to have anything to do with other people. But God has shown me that he doesn't think anyone is unclean or unfit. 29 I agreed to come here, but I want to know why you sent for me."

30 Cornelius answered:

> Four days ago at about three o'clock in the afternoon I was praying at home. Suddenly a man in bright clothes stood in front of me. 31 He said, "Cornelius, God has heard your prayers, and he knows about your gifts to the poor. 32 Now send to Joppa for Simon Peter. He is visiting in the home of Simon the leather maker, who lives near the sea."
>
> 33 I sent for you right away, and you have been good enough to come. All of us are here in the presence of the Lord God, so that we can hear what he has to say.

34 Peter then said:

> Now I am certain that God treats all people alike. 35 God is pleased with everyone who worships him and does right, no matter what nation they come from. 36 This is the same message that God gave to the people of Israel, when he sent Jesus Christ, the Lord of all, to offer peace to them.
>
> 37 You surely know what happened[q] everywhere in Judea. It all began in Galilee after John had told everyone to be baptized. 38 God gave the Holy Spirit and power to Jesus from Nazareth. He was with Jesus, as he went around doing good and healing everyone who was under the power of the devil. 39 We all saw what Jesus did both in Israel and in the city of Jerusalem.
>
> Jesus was put to death on a cross. 40 But three days later, God raised him to life and let him be seen. 41 Not everyone saw him. He was seen only by us, who ate and drank with him after he was raised from death. We were the ones God chose to tell others about him.
>
> 42 God told us to announce clearly to the people that Jesus is the one he has chosen to judge the living and the dead. 43 Every one of the prophets has said that all who have faith in Jesus will have their sins forgiven in his name.

44 While Peter was still speaking, the Holy Spirit took control of everyone who was listening. 45 Some Jewish followers of the Lord had come with Peter, and they were surprised that the Holy Spirit had been given to Gentiles. 46 Now they were hearing Gentiles speaking unknown languages and praising God.

Peter said, 47 "These Gentiles have been given the Holy Spirit, just as we have! I am certain that no one would dare stop us from baptizing them." 48 Peter ordered them to be baptized in the name of Jesus Christ, and they asked him to stay on for a few days.

Peter Reports to the Church in Jerusalem

11 The apostles and the followers in Judea heard that Gentiles had accepted God's message. 2 So when Peter came to Jerusalem, some of the Jewish followers started

---

[p] **10.19** *Three*: One manuscript has "two;" some manuscripts have "some." [q] **10.37** *what happened*: Or "the message that went."

arguing with him. They wanted Gentile followers to be circumcised, and [3] they said, "You stayed in the homes of Gentiles, and you even ate with them!"

[4] Then Peter told them exactly what had happened: [5] I was in the town of Joppa and was praying when I fell sound asleep and had a vision. I saw heaven open, and something like a huge sheet held by its four corners came down to me. [6] When I looked in it, I saw animals, wild beasts, snakes, and birds. [7] I heard a voice saying to me, "Peter, get up! Kill these and eat them."

[8] But I said, "Lord, I can't do that! I've never taken a bite of anything that is unclean and not fit to eat."

[9] The voice from heaven spoke to me again, "When God says that something can be used for food, don't say it isn't fit to eat." [10] This happened three times before it was all taken back into heaven.

[11] Suddenly three men from Caesarea stood in front of the house where I was staying. [12] The Holy Spirit told me to go with them and not to worry. Then six of the Lord's followers went with me to the home of a man [13] who told us that an angel had appeared to him. The angel had ordered him to send to Joppa for someone named Simon Peter. [14] Then Peter would tell him how he and everyone in his house could be saved.

[15] After I started speaking, the Holy Spirit was given to them, just as the Spirit had been given to us at the beginning. [16] I remembered that the Lord had said, "John baptized with water, but you will be baptized with the Holy Spirit." [17] God gave those Gentiles the same gift that he gave us when we put our faith in the Lord Jesus Christ. So how could I have gone against God?

[18] When they heard Peter say this, they stopped arguing and started praising God. They said, "God has now let Gentiles turn to him, and he has given life to them!"

The Church in Antioch

[19] Some of the Lord's followers had been scattered because of the terrible trouble that started when Stephen was killed. They went as far as Phoenicia, Cyprus, and Antioch, but they told the message only to the Jews.

[20] Some of the followers from Cyprus and Cyrene went to Antioch and started telling Gentiles[r] the good news about the Lord Jesus. [21] The Lord's power was with them, and many people turned to the Lord and put their faith in him. [22] News of what was happening reached the church in Jerusalem. Then they sent Barnabas to Antioch.

[23] When Barnabas got there and saw what God had been kind enough to do for them, he was very glad. So he begged them to remain faithful to the Lord with all their hearts. [24] Barnabas was a good man of great faith, and he was filled with the Holy Spirit. Many more people turned to the Lord.

[25] Barnabas went to Tarsus to look for Saul. [26] He found Saul and brought him to Antioch, where they met with the church for a whole year and taught many of its people.

There in Antioch the Lord's followers were first called Christians.

[27] During this time some prophets from Jerusalem came to Antioch. [28] One of them was Agabus. Then with the help of the Spirit, he told that there would be a terrible famine everywhere in the world. And it happened when Claudius was Emperor. [29] The followers in Antioch decided to send whatever help they could to the followers in Judea. [30] So they had Barnabas and Saul take their gifts to the church leaders in Jerusalem.

Herod Causes Trouble for the Church

12 At that time King Herod caused terrible suffering for some members of the church. [2] He ordered soldiers to cut off the head of James, the brother of John. [3] When Herod saw that this pleased the Jewish people, he had Peter arrested during the Festival of Thin Bread. [4] He put Peter in jail and ordered four squads of soldiers to guard him. Herod planned to put him on trial in public after the festival.

[5] While Peter was being kept in jail, the church never stopped praying to God for him.

Peter Is Rescued

[6] The night before Peter was to be put on trial, he was asleep and bound by two chains. A soldier was guarding him on each side, and two other soldiers were guarding the entrance to the jail. [7] Suddenly an angel from the Lord appeared, and light flashed around in the cell. The angel poked Peter in the side and woke him up. Then he said, "Quick! Get up!"

The chains fell off his hands, [8] and the angel said, "Get dressed and put on your sandals." Peter did what he was told. Then the angel said, "Now put on your coat and follow me." [9] Peter left with the angel, but he thought everything was only a dream. [10] They went past the two groups of soldiers, and when they came to the iron gate to the city, it opened by itself. They went out and were going along the street, when all at once the angel disappeared.

[11] Peter now realized what had happened, and he said, "I am certain that the Lord sent his angel to rescue me from Herod and from everything the Jewish leaders planned to do to me." [12] Then Peter went to the house of Mary the mother of John whose other name was Mark. Many of the Lord's followers had come together there and were praying.

[13] Peter knocked on the gate, and a servant named Rhoda came to answer. [14] When she heard Peter's voice, she was too excited to open the gate. She ran back into the house and said that Peter was standing there.

[15] "You are crazy!" everyone told her. But she kept saying that it was Peter. Then they said, "It must be his angel."[s] [16] But Peter kept on knocking, until finally they opened the gate. They saw him and were completely amazed.

[17] Peter motioned for them to keep quiet. Then he told how the Lord had led him out of jail. He also said, "Tell James and the others what has happened." After that, he left and went somewhere else.

[18] The next morning the soldiers who had been on

---

[r] **11.20** *Gentiles:* This translates a Greek word that may mean "people who speak Greek" or "people who live as Greeks do." Here the word seems to mean "people who are not Jews." Some manuscripts have "Greeks," which also seems to mean "people who are not Jews."
[s] **12.15** *his angel:* Probably meaning "his guardian angel."

guard were terribly worried and wondered what had happened to Peter. [19] Herod ordered his own soldiers to search for him, but they could not find him. Then he questioned the guards and had them put to death. After this, Herod left Judea to stay in Caesarea for a while.

Herod Dies

[20] Herod and the people of Tyre and Sidon were very angry with each other. But their country got its food supply from the region that he ruled. So a group of them went to see Blastus, who was one of Herod's high officials. They convinced Blastus that they wanted to make peace between their cities and Herod, [21] and a day was set for them to meet with him.

Herod came dressed in his royal robes. He sat down on his throne and made a speech. [22] The people shouted, "You speak more like a god than a man!" [23] At once an angel from the Lord struck him down because he took the honor that belonged to God. Later, Herod was eaten by worms and died.

[24] God's message kept spreading. [25] And after Barnabas and Saul had done the work they were sent to do, they went back to Jerusalem[t] with John, whose other name was Mark.

Barnabas and Saul Are Chosen and Sent

13 The church at Antioch had several prophets and teachers. They were Barnabas, Simeon, also called Niger, Lucius from Cyrene, Manaen, who was Herod's close friend, and Saul. [2] While they were worshiping the Lord and going without eating, the Holy Spirit told them, "Appoint Barnabas and Saul to do the work for which I have chosen them." [3] Everyone prayed and went without eating for a while longer. Next, they placed their hands on Barnabas and Saul to show that they had been appointed to do this work. Then everyone sent them on their way.

Barnabas and Saul in Cyprus

[4] After Barnabas and Saul had been sent by the Holy Spirit, they went to Seleucia. From there they sailed to the island of Cyprus. [5] They arrived at Salamis and began to preach God's message in the Jewish meeting places. They also had John as a helper.

[6] Barnabas and Saul went all the way to the city of Paphos on the other end of the island, where they met a Jewish man named Bar-Jesus. He practiced witchcraft and was a false prophet. [7] He also worked for Sergius Paulus, who was very smart and was the governor of the island. Sergius Paulus wanted to hear God's message, and he sent for Barnabas and Saul. [8] But Bar-Jesus, whose other name was Elymas, was against them. He even tried to keep the governor from having faith in the Lord.

[9] Then Saul, better known as Paul, was filled with the Holy Spirit. He looked straight at Elymas [10] and said, "You son of the devil! You are a liar, a crook, and an enemy of everything that is right. When will you stop speaking against the true ways of the Lord? [11] The Lord is going to punish you by making you completely blind for a while."

Suddenly the man's eyes were covered by a dark mist, and he went around trying to get someone to lead him by the hand. [12] When the governor saw what had happened, he was amazed at this teaching about the Lord. So he put his faith in the Lord.

Paul and Barnabas in Antioch of Pisidia

[13] Paul and the others left Paphos and sailed to Perga in Pamphylia. But John left them and went back to Jerusalem. [14] The rest of them went on from Perga to Antioch in Pisidia. Then on the Sabbath they went to the Jewish meeting place and sat down.

[15] After the reading of the Law and the Prophets, the leaders sent someone over to tell Paul and Barnabas, "Friends, if you have anything to say that will help the people, please say it."

[16] Paul got up. He motioned with his hand and said:

People of Israel, and everyone else who worships God, listen! [17] The God of Israel chose our ancestors, and he let our people prosper while they were living in Egypt. Then with his mighty power he led them out, [18] and for about forty years he took care of[u] them in the desert. [19] He destroyed seven nations in the land of Canaan and gave their land to our people. [20] All this happened in about 450 years.

Then God gave our people judges until the time of the prophet Samuel, [21] but the people demanded a king. So for forty years God gave them King Saul, the son of Kish from the tribe of Benjamin. [22] Later, God removed Saul and let David rule in his place. God said about him, "David the son of Jesse is the kind of person who pleases me most! He does everything I want him to do."

[23] God promised that someone from David's family would come to save the people of Israel, and that one is Jesus. [24] But before Jesus came, John was telling everyone in Israel to turn back to God and be baptized. [25] Then, when John's work was almost done, he said, "Who do you people think I am? Do you think I am the Promised One? He will come later, and I am not good enough to untie his sandals."

[26] Now listen, you descendants of Abraham! Pay attention, all of you Gentiles who are here to worship God! Listen to this message about how to be saved, because it is for everyone. [27] The people of Jerusalem and their leaders didn't realize who Jesus was. And they didn't understand the words of the prophets that they read each Sabbath. So they condemned Jesus just as the prophets had said.

[28-29] They did exactly what the Scriptures said they would. Even though they couldn't find any reason to put Jesus to death, they still asked Pilate to have him killed.

After Jesus had been put to death, he was taken down from the cross[v] and placed in a tomb. [30] But God raised him from death! [31] Then for many days Jesus appeared to his followers who had gone with him from Galilee to Jerusalem. Now they are telling our people about him.

---

[t] **12.25** *went back to Jerusalem:* Some manuscripts have "left Jerusalem," and others have "went to Antioch."   [u] **13.18** *took care of:* Some manuscripts have "put up with."

32 God made a promise to our ancestors. And we are here to tell you the good news 33 that he has kept this promise to us. It is just as the second Psalm says about Jesus,

"You are my son because today
I have become your Father."

34 God raised Jesus from death and will never let his body decay. It is just as God said,

"I will make to you
the same holy promise
that I made to David."

35 And in another psalm it says, "God will never let the body of his Holy One decay."
36 When David was alive, he obeyed God. Then after he died, he was buried in the family grave, and his body decayed. 37 But God raised Jesus from death, and his body did not decay.
38 My friends, the message is that Jesus can forgive your sins! The Law of Moses could not set you free from all your sins. 39 But everyone who has faith in Jesus is set free. 40 Make sure that what the prophets have said doesn't happen to you. They said,

41 "Look, you people
who make fun of God!
Be amazed
and disappear.
I will do something today
that you won't believe,
even if someone
tells you about it!"

42 As Paul and Barnabas were leaving the meeting, the people begged them to say more about these same things on the next Sabbath. 43 After the service, many Jews and a lot of Gentiles who worshiped God went with them. Paul and Barnabas begged them all to remain faithful to God, who had been so kind to them.
44 The next Sabbath almost everyone in town came to hear the message about the Lord.w 45 When the Jewish people saw the crowds, they were very jealous. They insulted Paul and spoke against everything he said.
46 But Paul and Barnabas bravely said:
We had to tell God's message to you before we told it to anyone else. But you rejected the message! This proves that you don't deserve eternal life. Now we are going to the Gentiles. 47 The Lord has given us this command,

"I have placed you here
as a light
for the Gentiles.
You are to take
the saving power of God
to people everywhere on earth."

48 This message made the Gentiles glad, and they praised what they had heard about the Lord.w Everyone who had been chosen for eternal life then put their faith in the Lord.
49 The message about the Lord spread all over that region. 50 But the Jewish leaders went to some of the important men in the town and to some respected women who were religious. They turned them against Paul and Barnabas and started making trouble for them. They even chased them out of that part of the country.
51 Paul and Barnabas shook the dust from that place off their feet and went on to the city of Iconium.
52 But the Lord's followers in Antioch were very happy and were filled with the Holy Spirit.

Paul and Barnabas in Iconium

14 Paul and Barnabas spoke in the Jewish meeting place in Iconium, just as they had done at Antioch, and many Jews and Gentilesx put their faith in the Lord. 2 But the Jews who did not have faith in him made the other Gentiles angry and turned them against the Lord's followers.
3 Paul and Barnabas stayed there for a while, having faith in the Lord and bravely speaking his message. The Lord gave them the power to work miracles and wonders, and he showed that their message about his great kindness was true.
4 The people of Iconium did not know what to think. Some of them believed the Jewish group, and others believed the apostles. 5 Finally, some Gentiles and Jews, together with their leaders, decided to make trouble for Paul and Barnabas and to stone them to death.
6-7 But when the two apostles found out what was happening, they escaped to the region of Lycaonia. They preached the good news there in the towns of Lystra and Derbe and in the nearby countryside.

Paul and Barnabas in Lystra

8 In Lystra there was a man who had been born with crippled feet and had never been able to walk. 9 The man was listening to Paul speak, when Paul saw that he had faith in Jesus and could be healed. So he looked straight at the man 10 and shouted, "Stand up!" The man jumped up and started walking around.
11 When the crowd saw what Paul had done, they yelled out in the language of Lycaonia, "The gods have turned into humans and have come down to us!" 12 The people then gave Barnabas the name Zeus, and they gave Paul the name Hermes, because he did the talking.
13 The temple of Zeus was near the entrance to the city. Its priest and the crowds wanted to offer a sacrifice to Barnabas and Paul. So the priest brought some bulls and flowers to the city gates. 14 When the two apostles found out about this, they tore their clothes in horror and ran to the crowd, shouting:
15 Why are you doing this? We are humans just like you. Please give up all this foolishness. Turn to the living God, who made the sky, the earth, the sea, and everything in them. 16 In times past, God let each nation go its own way. 17 But he

---

v 13.28,29 cross: This translates a Greek word that means "wood," "pole," or "tree."   w 13.44,48 the Lord: Some manuscripts have "God."   x 14.1 Gentiles: The Greek text has "Greeks," which probably means people who were not Jews. But it may mean Gentiles who worshiped with the Jews.

showed that he was there by the good things he did. God sends rain from heaven and makes your crops grow. He gives food to you and makes your hearts glad.

18 Even after Paul and Barnabas had said all this, they could hardly keep the people from offering a sacrifice to them.

19 Some Jewish leaders from Antioch and Iconium came and turned the crowds against Paul. They hit him with stones and dragged him out of the city, thinking he was dead. 20 But when the Lord's followers gathered around Paul, he stood up and went back into the city. The next day he and Barnabas went to Derbe.

Paul and Barnabas Return to Antioch in Syria

21 Paul and Barnabas preached the good news in Derbe and won some people to the Lord. Then they went back to Lystra, Iconium, and Antioch in Pisidia. 22 They encouraged the followers and begged them to remain faithful. They told them, "We have to suffer a lot before we can get into God's kingdom." 23 Paul and Barnabas chose some leaders for each of the churches. Then they went without eating and prayed that the Lord would take good care of these leaders.

24 Paul and Barnabas went on through Pisidia to Pamphylia, 25 where they preached in the town of Perga. Then they went down to Attalia 26 and sailed to Antioch in Syria. It was there that they had been placed in God's care for the work they had now completed.

27 After arriving in Antioch, they called the church together. They told the people what God had helped them do and how he had made it possible for the Gentiles to believe. 28 Then they stayed there with the followers for a long time.

15 Some people came from Judea and started teaching the Lord's followers that they could not be saved, unless they were circumcised as Moses had taught. 2 This caused trouble, and Paul and Barnabas argued with them about this teaching. So it was decided to send Paul and Barnabas and a few others to Jerusalem to discuss this problem with the apostles and the church leaders.

The Church Leaders Meet in Jerusalem

3 The men who were sent by the church went through Phoenicia and Samaria, telling how the Gentiles had turned to God. This news made the Lord's followers very happy. 4 When the men arrived in Jerusalem, they were welcomed by the church, including the apostles and the leaders. They told them everything God had helped them do. 5 But some Pharisees had become followers of the Lord. They stood up and said, "Gentiles who have faith in the Lord must be circumcised and told to obey the Law of Moses."

6 The apostles and church leaders met to discuss this problem about Gentiles. 7 They had talked it over for a long time, when Peter got up and said:

My friends, you know that God decided long ago to let me be the one from your group to preach the good news to the Gentiles. God did this so that they would hear and obey him. 8 He knows what is in everyone's heart. And he showed that he had chosen the Gentiles, when he gave them the Holy Spirit, just as he had given his Spirit to us. 9 God

treated them in the same way that he treated us. They put their faith in him, and he made their hearts pure.

10 Now why are you trying to make God angry by placing a heavy burden on these followers? This burden was too heavy for us or our ancestors. 11 But our Lord Jesus was kind to us, and we are saved by faith in him, just as the Gentiles are.

12 Everyone kept quiet and listened as Barnabas and Paul told how God had given them the power to work a lot of miracles and wonders for the Gentiles.

13 After they had finished speaking, James said:

My friends, listen to me! 14 Simon Peter[y] has told how God first came to the Gentiles and made some of them his own people. 15 This agrees with what the prophets wrote,

16 "I, the Lord, will return
    and rebuild
        David's fallen house.
I will build it from its ruins
    and set it up again.
17 Then other nations
    will turn to me
        and be my chosen ones.
I, the Lord, say this.
18   I promised it long ago."

19 And so, my friends, I don't think we should place burdens on the Gentiles who are turning to God. 20 We should simply write and tell them not to eat anything that has been offered to idols. They should be told not to eat the meat of any animal that has been strangled or that still has blood in it. They must also not commit any terrible sexual sins.

21 We must remember that the Law of Moses has been preached in city after city for many years, and every Sabbath it is read when we Jews meet.

A Letter to Gentiles Who Had Faith in the Lord

22 The apostles, the leaders, and all the church members decided to send some men to Antioch along with Paul and Barnabas. They chose Silas and Judas Barsabbas, who were two leaders of the Lord's followers. 23 They wrote a letter that said:

We apostles and leaders send friendly greetings to all of you Gentiles who are followers of the Lord in Antioch, Syria, and Cilicia.

24 We have heard that some people from here have terribly upset you by what they said. But we did not send them! 25 So we met together and decided to choose some men and to send them to you along with our good friends Barnabas and Paul. 26 These men have risked their lives for our Lord Jesus Christ. 27 We are also sending Judas and Silas, who will tell you in person the same things that we are writing.

28 The Holy Spirit has shown us that we should not place any extra burden on you. 29 But you should not eat anything offered to idols. You should not eat any meat that still has the blood in it

---

y 15.14 Simon Peter: The Greek text has "Simeon," which is another form of the name "Simon." The apostle Peter is meant.

or any meat of any animal that has been strangled. You must also not commit any terrible sexual sins. If you follow these instructions, you will do well.

We send our best wishes.

30 The four men left Jerusalem and went to Antioch. Then they called the church members together and gave them the letter. 31 When the letter was read, everyone was pleased and greatly encouraged. 32 Judas and Silas were prophets, and they spoke a long time, encouraging and helping the Lord's followers.

33 The men from Jerusalem stayed on in Antioch for a while. And when they left to return to the ones who had sent them, the followers wished them well. 34-35 But Paul and Barnabas stayed on in Antioch, where they and many others taught and preached about the Lord.

Paul and Barnabas Go Their Separate Ways

36 Sometime later Paul said to Barnabas, "Let's go back and visit the Lord's followers in the cities where we preached his message. Then we will know how they are doing." 37 Barnabas wanted to take along John, whose other name was Mark. 38 But Paul did not want to, because Mark had left them in Pamphylia and had stopped working with them.

39 Paul and Barnabas argued, then each of them went his own way. Barnabas took Mark and sailed to Cyprus, 40 but Paul took Silas and left after the followers had placed them in God's care. 41 They traveled through Syria and Cilicia, encouraging the churches.

Timothy Works with Paul and Silas

16 Paul and Silas went back to Derbe and Lystra, where there was a follower named Timothy. His mother was also a follower. She was Jewish, and his father was Greek. 2 The Lord's followers in Lystra and Iconium said good things about Timothy, 3 and Paul wanted him to go with them. But Paul first had him circumcised, because all the Jewish people around there knew that Timothy's father was Greek.

4 As Paul and the others went from city to city, they told the followers what the apostles and leaders in Jerusalem had decided, and they urged them to follow these instructions. 5 The churches became stronger in their faith, and each day more people put their faith in the Lord.

Paul's Vision in Troas

6 Paul and his friends went through Phrygia and Galatia, but the Holy Spirit would not let them preach in Asia. 7 After they arrived in Mysia, they tried to go into Bithynia, but the Spirit of Jesus would not let them. 8 So they went on through [z] Mysia until they came to Troas.

9 During the night, Paul had a vision of someone from Macedonia who was standing there and begging him, "Come over to Macedonia and help us!" 10 After Paul had seen the vision, we began looking for a way to go to Macedonia. We were sure that God had called us to preach the good news there.

Lydia Becomes a Follower of the Lord

11 We sailed straight from Troas to Samothrace, and the next day we arrived in Neapolis. 12 From there we went to Philippi, which is a Roman colony in the first district of Macedonia.[a]

We spent several days in Philippi. 13 Then on the Sabbath we went outside the city gate to a place by the river, where we thought there would be a Jewish meeting place for prayer. We sat down and talked with the women who came. 14 One of them was Lydia, who was from the city of Thyatira and sold expensive purple cloth. She was a worshiper of the Lord God, and he made her willing to accept what Paul was saying. 15 Then after she and her family were baptized, she kept on begging us, "If you think I really do have faith in the Lord, come stay in my home." Finally, we accepted her invitation.

Paul and Silas Are Put in Jail

16 One day on our way to the place of prayer, we were met by a slave girl. She had a spirit in her that gave her the power to tell the future. By doing this she made a lot of money for her owners. 17 The girl followed Paul and the rest of us and kept yelling, "These men are servants of the Most High God! They are telling you how to be saved."

18 This went on for several days. Finally, Paul got so upset that he turned and said to the spirit, "In the name of Jesus Christ, I order you to leave this girl alone!" At once the evil spirit left her.

19 When the girl's owners realized that they had lost all chances for making more money, they grabbed Paul and Silas and dragged them into court. 20 They told the officials, "These Jews are upsetting our city! 21 They are telling us to do things we Romans are not allowed to do."

22 The crowd joined in the attack on Paul and Silas. Then the officials tore the clothes off the two men and ordered them to be beaten with a whip. 23 After they had been badly beaten, they were put in jail, and the jailer was told to guard them carefully. 24 The jailer did as he was told. He put them deep inside the jail and chained their feet to heavy blocks of wood.

25 About midnight Paul and Silas were praying and singing praises to God, while the other prisoners listened. 26 Suddenly a strong earthquake shook the jail to its foundations. The doors opened, and the chains fell from all the prisoners.

27 When the jailer woke up and saw that the doors were open, he thought that the prisoners had escaped. He pulled out his sword and was about to kill himself. 28 But Paul shouted, "Don't harm yourself! No one has escaped."

29 The jailer asked for a torch and went into the jail. He was shaking all over as he knelt down in front of Paul and Silas. 30 After he had led them out of the jail, he asked, "What must I do to be saved?"

31 They replied, "Have faith in the Lord Jesus and you will be saved! This is also true for everyone who lives in your home."

32 Then Paul and Silas told him and everyone else in his house about the Lord. 33 While it was still night, the jailer took them to a place where he could wash their cuts and bruises. Then he and everyone in his home were baptized. 34 They were very glad that they had put their faith in God. After this, the jailer took Paul and Silas to his home and gave them something to eat.

---

[z] 16.8 went on through: Or "passed by."   [a] 16.12 in the first district of Macedonia: Some manuscripts have "and the leading city of Macedonia."

35 The next morning the officials sent some police with orders for the jailer to let Paul and Silas go. **36** The jailer told Paul, "The officials have ordered me to set you free. Now you can leave in peace."

37 But Paul told the police, "We are Roman citizens, and the Roman officials had us beaten in public without giving us a trial. They threw us into jail. Now do they think they can secretly send us away? No, they cannot! They will have to come here themselves and let us out."

38 When the police told the officials that Paul and Silas were Roman citizens, the officials were afraid. **39** So they came and apologized. They led them out of the jail and asked them to please leave town. **40** But Paul and Silas went straight to the home of Lydia, where they saw the Lord's followers and encouraged them. Then they left.

Trouble in Thessalonica

17 After Paul and his friends had traveled through Amphipolis and Apollonia, they went on to Thessalonica. A Jewish meeting place was in that city. **2** So as usual, Paul went there to worship, and on three Sabbaths he spoke to the people. He used the Scriptures **3** to show them that the Messiah had to suffer, but that he would rise from death. Paul also told them that Jesus is the Messiah he was preaching about. **4** Some of them believed what Paul had said, and they became followers with Paul and Silas. Some Gentiles and many important women also believed the message.

5 The Jewish leaders were jealous and got some worthless bums who hung around the marketplace to start a riot in the city. They wanted to drag Paul and Silas out to the mob, and so they went straight to Jason's home. **6** But when they did not find them there, they dragged out Jason and some of the Lord's followers. They took them to the city authorities and shouted, "Paul and Silas have been upsetting things everywhere. Now they have come here, **7** and Jason has welcomed them into his home. All of them break the laws of the Roman Emperor by claiming that someone named Jesus is king."

8 The officials and the people were upset when they heard this. **9** So they made Jason and the other followers pay bail before letting them go.

People in Berea Welcome the Message

10 That same night the Lord's followers sent Paul and Silas on to Berea, and after they arrived, they went to the Jewish meeting place. **11** The people in Berea were much nicer than those in Thessalonica, and they gladly accepted the message. Day after day they studied the Scriptures to see if these things were true. **12** Many of them put their faith in the Lord, including some important Greek women and several men.

13 When the Jewish leaders in Thessalonica heard that Paul had been preaching God's message in Berea, they went there and caused trouble by turning the crowds against Paul.

14 Right away the followers sent Paul down to the coast, but Silas and Timothy stayed in Berea. **15** Some men went with Paul as far as Athens, and then returned with instructions for Silas and Timothy to join him as soon as possible.

Paul in Athens

16 While Paul was waiting in Athens, he was upset to see all the idols in the city. **17** He went to the Jewish meeting place to speak to the Jews and to anyone who worshiped with them. Day after day he also spoke to everyone he met in the market. **18** Some of them were Epicureans and some were Stoics, and they started arguing with him.

People were asking, "What is this know-it-all trying to say?"

Some even said, "Paul must be preaching about foreign gods! That's what he means when he talks about Jesus and about people rising from death." *b*

19 They brought Paul before a council called the Areopagus, and said, "Tell us what your new teaching is all about. **20** We have heard you say some strange things, and we want to know what you mean."

21 More than anything else the people of Athens and the foreigners living there loved to hear and to talk about anything new. **22** So Paul stood up in front of the council and said:

People of Athens, I see that you are very religious. **23** As I was going through your city and looking at the things you worship, I found an altar with the words, "To an Unknown God." You worship this God, but you don't really know him. So I want to tell you about him. **24** This God made the world and everything in it. He is Lord of heaven and earth, and he doesn't live in temples built by human hands. **25** He doesn't need help from anyone. He gives life, breath, and everything else to all people. **26** From one person God made all nations who live on earth, and he decided when and where every nation would be.

27 God has done all this, so that we will look for him and reach out and find him. He isn't far from any of us, **28** and he gives us the power to live, to move, and to be who we are. "We are his children," just as some of your poets have said.

29 Since we are God's children, we must not think that he is like an idol made out of gold or silver or stone. He isn't like anything that humans have thought up and made. **30** In the past, God forgave all this because people did not know what they were doing. But now he says that everyone everywhere must turn to him. **31** He has set a day when he will judge the world's people with fairness. And he has chosen the man Jesus to do the judging for him. God has given proof of this to all of us by raising Jesus from death.

32 As soon as the people heard Paul say that a man had been raised from death, some of them started laughing. Others said, "We will hear you talk about this some other time." **33** When Paul left the council meeting, **34** some of the men put their faith in the Lord and went with Paul. One of them was a council member named Dionysius. A woman named Damaris and several others also put their faith in the Lord.

Paul in Corinth

18 Paul left Athens and went to Corinth, **2** where he met Aquila, a Jewish man from Pontus. Not long before this, Aquila had come from Italy with his wife Priscilla, because Emperor Claudius had ordered the Jewish people to leave Rome. Paul went to see Aquila and

---

b **17.18** *people rising from death*: Or "a goddess named 'Rising from Death.' "

Priscilla [3] and found out that they were tent makers. Paul was a tent maker too. So he stayed with them, and they worked together.

[4] Every Sabbath, Paul went to the Jewish meeting place. He spoke to Jews and Gentiles[c] and tried to win them over. [5] But after Silas and Timothy came from Macedonia, he spent all his time preaching to the Jews about Jesus the Messiah. [6] Finally, they turned against him and insulted him. So he shook the dust from his clothes and told them, "Whatever happens to you will be your own fault! I am not to blame. From now on I am going to preach to the Gentiles."

[7] Paul then moved into the house of a man named Titius Justus, who worshiped God and lived next door to the Jewish meeting place. [8] Crispus was the leader of the meeting place. He and everyone in his family put their faith in the Lord. Many others in Corinth also heard the message, and all the people who had faith in the Lord were baptized.

[9] One night, Paul had a vision, and in it the Lord said, ' 'Don't be afraid to keep on preaching. Don't stop! [10] I am with you, and you won't be harmed. Many people in this city belong to me." [11] Paul stayed on in Corinth for a year and a half, teaching God's message to the people.

[12] While Gallio was governor of Achaia, some of the Jewish leaders got together and grabbed Paul. They brought him into court [13] and said, "This man is trying to make our people worship God in a way that is against our Law!"

[14] Even before Paul could speak, Gallio said, "If you were charging this man with a crime or some other wrong, I would have to listen to you. [15] But since this concerns only words, names, and your own law, you will have to take care of it. I refuse to judge such matters." [16] Then he sent them out of the court. [17] The crowd grabbed Sosthenes, the Jewish leader, and beat him up in front of the court. But none of this mattered to Gallio.

Paul Returns to Antioch in Syria

[18] After Paul had stayed for a while with the Lord's followers in Corinth, he told them good-by and sailed on to Syria with Aquila and Priscilla. But before he left, he had his head shaved at Cenchreae because he had made a promise to God.

[19] The three of them arrived in Ephesus, where Paul left Priscilla and Aquila. He then went into the Jewish meeting place to talk with the people there. [20] They asked him to stay longer, but he refused. [21] He told them good-by and said, "If God lets me, I will come back."

[22] Paul sailed to Caesarea, where he greeted the church. Then he went on to Antioch. [23] After staying there for a while, he left and visited several places in Galatia and Phrygia. He helped the followers there to become stronger in their faith.

Apollos in Ephesus

[24] A Jewish man named Apollos came to Ephesus. Apollos had been born in the city of Alexandria. He was a very good speaker and knew a lot about the Scriptures. [25] He also knew much about the Lord's Way, and he spoke about it with great excitement. What he taught about Jesus was right, but all he knew was John's message about baptism. [26] Apollos started speaking bravely in the Jewish meeting place. But when Priscilla and Aquila heard him, they took him to their home and helped him understand God's Way even better.

[27] Apollos decided to travel through Achaia. So the Lord's followers wrote letters, encouraging the followers there to welcome him. After Apollos arrived in Achaia, he was a great help to everyone who had put their faith in the Lord Jesus because of God's kindness. [28] He got into fierce arguments with the Jewish people, and in public he used the Scriptures to prove that Jesus is the Messiah.

Paul in Ephesus

19 While Apollos was in Corinth, Paul traveled across the hill country to Ephesus, where he met some of the Lord's followers. [2] He asked them, "When you put your faith in Jesus, were you given the Holy Spirit?"

"No!" they answered. "We have never even heard of the Holy Spirit."

[3] "Then why were you baptized?" Paul asked.

They answered, "Because of what John taught."[d]

[4] Paul replied, "John baptized people so that they would turn to God. But he also told them that someone else was coming, and that they should put their faith in him. Jesus is the one that John was talking about." [5] After the people heard Paul say this, they were baptized in the name of the Lord Jesus. [6] Then Paul placed his hands on them. The Holy Spirit was given to them, and they spoke unknown languages and prophesied. [7] There were about twelve men in this group.

[8] For three months Paul went to the Jewish meeting place and talked bravely with the people about God's kingdom. He tried to win them over, [9] but some of them were stubborn and refused to believe. In front of everyone they said terrible things about God's Way. Paul left and took the followers with him to the lecture hall of Tyrannus. He spoke there every day [10] for two years, until every Jew and Gentile[e] in Asia had heard the Lord's message.

The Sons of Sceva

[11] God gave Paul the power to work great miracles. [12] People even took handkerchiefs and aprons that had touched Paul's body, and they carried them to everyone who was sick. All of the sick people were healed, and the evil spirits went out.

[13] Some Jewish men started going around trying to force out evil spirits by using the name of the Lord Jesus. They said to the spirits, "Come out in the name of that same Jesus that Paul preaches about!"

[14] Seven sons of a Jewish high priest named Sceva were doing this, [15] when an evil spirit said to them, "I know Jesus! And I have heard about Paul. But who are you?" [16] Then the man with the evil spirit jumped on them and beat them up. They ran out of the house, naked and bruised.

[17] When the Jews and Gentiles[e] in Ephesus heard about this, they were so frightened that they praised the name of the Lord Jesus. [18] Many who were followers now started

---

[c] **18.4** *Gentiles*: Here the word is "Greeks." But see the note at 14.1.   [d] **19.3** *Then why were you baptized? . . . Because of what John taught*: Or "In whose name were you baptized? . . . We were baptized in John's name."   [e] **19.10,17** *Gentile*(s): The text has "Greek(s)" (see the note at 14.1).

telling everyone about the evil things they had been doing. [19] Some who had been practicing witchcraft even brought their books and burned them in public. These books were worth about fifty thousand silver coins. [20] So the Lord's message spread and became even more powerful.

The Riot in Ephesus

[21] After all of this had happened, Paul decided[f] to visit Macedonia and Achaia on his way to Jerusalem. Paul had said, "From there I will go on to Rome." [22] So he sent his two helpers, Timothy and Erastus, to Macedonia. But he stayed on in Asia for a while.

[23] At that time there was serious trouble because of the Lord's Way. [24] A silversmith named Demetrius had a business that made silver models of the temple of the goddess Artemis. Those who worked for him earned a lot of money. [25] Demetrius brought together everyone who was in the same business and said:

Friends, you know that we make a good living at this. [26] But you have surely seen and heard how this man Paul is upsetting a lot of people, not only in Ephesus, but almost everywhere in Asia. He claims that the gods we humans make are not really gods at all. [27] Everyone will start saying terrible things about our business. They will stop respecting the temple of the goddess Artemis, who is worshiped in Asia and all over the world. Our great goddess will be forgotten!

[28] When the workers heard this, they got angry and started shouting, "Great is Artemis, the goddess of the Ephesians!" [29] Soon the whole city was in a riot, and some men grabbed Gaius and Aristarchus, who had come from Macedonia with Paul. Then everyone in the crowd rushed to the place where the town meetings were held.

[30] Paul wanted to go out and speak to the people, but the Lord's followers would not let him. [31] A few of the local officials were friendly to Paul, and they sent someone to warn him not to go.

[32] Some of the people in the meeting were shouting one thing, and others were shouting something else. Everyone was completely confused, and most of them did not even know why they were there.

[33] Several of the Jewish leaders pushed a man named Alexander to the front of the crowd and started telling him what to say. He motioned with his hand and tried to explain what was going on. [34] But when the crowd saw that he was Jewish, they all shouted for two hours, "Great is Artemis, the goddess of the Ephesians!"

[35] Finally, a town official made the crowd be quiet. Then he said:

People of Ephesus, who in the world doesn't know that our city is the center for worshiping the great goddess Artemis? Who doesn't know that her image which fell from heaven is right here? [36] No one can deny this, and so you should calm down and not do anything foolish. [37] You have brought men in here who have not robbed temples or spoken against our goddess. [38] If Demetrius and his workers have a case against these men, we have courts and judges. Let them take their complaints there. [39] But if you

want to do more than that, the matter will have to be brought before the city council. [40] We could easily be accused of starting a riot today. There is no excuse for it! We cannot even give a reason for this uproar.

[41] After saying this, he told the people to leave.

Paul Goes through Macedonia and Greece

20 When the riot was over, Paul sent for the followers and encouraged them. He then told them good-by and left for Macedonia. [2] As he traveled from place to place, he encouraged the followers with many messages. Finally, he went to Greece [3] and stayed there for three months.

Paul was about to sail to Syria. But some of the Jewish leaders plotted against him, so he decided to return by way of Macedonia. [4] With him were Sopater, son of Pyrrhus from Berea, and Aristarchus and Secundus from Thessalonica. Gaius from Derbe was also with him, and so were Timothy and the two Asians, Tychicus and Trophimus. [5] They went on ahead to Troas and waited for us there. [6] After the Festival of Thin Bread, we sailed from Philippi. Five days later we met them in Troas and stayed there for a week.

Paul's Last Visit to Troas

[7] On the first day of the week we met to break bread together. Paul spoke to the people until midnight because he was leaving the next morning. [8] In the upstairs room where we were meeting, there were a lot of lamps. [9] A young man by the name of Eutychus was sitting on a window sill. While Paul was speaking, the young man got very sleepy. Finally, he went to sleep and fell three floors all the way down to the ground. When they picked him up, he was dead.

[10] Paul went down and bent over Eutychus. He took him in his arms and said, "Don't worry! He's alive." [11] After Paul had gone back upstairs, he broke bread, and ate with us. He then spoke until dawn and left. [12] Then the followers took the young man home alive and were very happy.

The Voyage from Troas to Miletus

[13] Paul decided to travel by land to Assos. The rest of us went on ahead by ship, and we were to take him aboard there. [14] When he met us in Assos, he came aboard, and we sailed on to Mitylene. [15] The next day we came to a place near Chios, and the following day we reached Samos. The day after that we sailed to Miletus. [16] Paul had decided to sail on past Ephesus, because he did not want to spend too much time in Asia. He was in a hurry and wanted to be in Jerusalem in time for Pentecost.

Paul Says Good-By to the Church Leaders of Ephesus

[17] From Miletus, Paul sent a message for the church leaders at Ephesus to come and meet with him. [18] When they got there, he said:

You know everything I did during the time I was with you when I first came to Asia. [19] Some of the Jews plotted against me and caused me a lot of sorrow and trouble. But I served the Lord and was humble. [20] When I preached in public or taught in your homes, I didn't hold back from telling anything that would help you. [21] I told Jews and

---

Gentiles to turn to God and have faith in our Lord Jesus.

²² I don't know what will happen to me in Jerusalem, but I must obey God's Spirit and go there. ²³ In every city I visit, I am told by the Holy Spirit that I will be put in jail and will be in trouble in Jerusalem. ²⁴ But I don't care what happens to me, as long as I finish the work that the Lord Jesus gave me to do. And that work is to tell the good news about God's great kindness.

²⁵ I have gone from place to place, preaching to you about God's kingdom, but now I know that none of you will ever see me again. ²⁶ I tell you today that I am no longer responsible for any of you! ²⁷ I have told you everything God wants you to know. ²⁸ Look after yourselves and everyone the Holy Spirit has placed in your care. Be like shepherds to God's church. It is the flock that he bought with the blood of his own Son.*g*

²⁹ I know that after I am gone, others will come like fierce wolves to attack you. ³⁰ Some of your own people will tell lies to win over the Lord's followers. ³¹ Be on your guard! Remember how day and night for three years I kept warning you with tears in my eyes.

³² I now place you in God's care. Remember the message about his great kindness! This message can help you and give you what belongs to you as God's people. ³³ I have never wanted anyone's money or clothes. ³⁴ You know how I have worked with my own hands to make a living for myself and my friends. ³⁵ By everything I did, I showed how you should work to help everyone who is weak. Remember that our Lord Jesus said, "More blessings come from giving than from receiving."

³⁶ After Paul had finished speaking, he knelt down with all of them and prayed. ³⁷ Everyone cried and hugged and kissed him. ³⁸ They were especially sad because Paul had told them, "You will never see me again."

Then they went with him to the ship.

Paul Goes to Jerusalem

21 After saying good-by, we sailed straight to Cos. The next day we reached Rhodes and from there sailed on to Patara. ² We found a ship going to Phoenicia, so we got on board and sailed off.

³ We came within sight of Cyprus and then sailed south of it on to the port of Tyre in Syria, where the ship was going to unload its cargo. ⁴ We looked up the Lord's followers and stayed with them for a week. The Holy Spirit had told them to warn Paul not to go on to Jerusalem. ⁵ But when the week was over, we started on our way again. All the men, together with their wives and children, walked with us from the town to the seashore. We knelt on the beach and prayed. ⁶ Then after saying good-by to each other, we got into the ship, and they went back home.

⁷ We sailed from Tyre to Ptolemais, where we greeted the followers and stayed with them for a day. ⁸ The next day we went to Caesarea and stayed with Philip, the preacher.

He was one of the seven men who helped the apostles, ⁹ and he had four unmarried*h* daughters who prophesied.

¹⁰ We had been in Caesarea for several days, when the prophet Agabus came to us from Judea. ¹¹ He took Paul's belt, and with it he tied up his own hands and feet. Then he told us, "The Holy Spirit says that some of the Jewish leaders in Jerusalem will tie up the man who owns this belt. They will also hand him over to the Gentiles." ¹² After Agabus said this, we and the followers living there begged Paul not to go to Jerusalem.

¹³ But Paul answered, "Why are you crying and breaking my heart? I am not only willing to be put in jail for the Lord Jesus. I am even willing to die for him in Jerusalem!"

¹⁴ Since we could not get Paul to change his mind, we gave up and prayed, "Lord, please make us willing to do what you want."

¹⁵ Then we got ready to go to Jerusalem. ¹⁶ Some of the followers from Caesarea went with us and took us to stay in the home of Mnason. He was from Cyprus and had been a follower from the beginning.

Paul Visits James

¹⁷ When we arrived in Jerusalem, the Lord's followers gladly welcomed us. ¹⁸ Paul went with us to see James the next day, and all the church leaders were present. ¹⁹ Paul greeted them and told how God had used him to help the Gentiles. ²⁰ Everyone who heard this praised God and said to Paul:

My friend, you can see how many tens of thousands of the Jewish people have become followers! And all of them are eager to obey the Law of Moses. ²¹ But they have been told that you are teaching those who live among the Gentiles to disobey this Law. They claim that you are telling them not to circumcise their sons or to follow Jewish customs.

²² What should we do now that our people have heard that you are here? ²³ Please do what we ask, because four of our men have made special promises to God. ²⁴ Join with them and prepare yourself for the ceremony that goes with the promises. Pay the cost for their heads to be shaved. Then everyone will learn that the reports about you are not true. They will know that you do obey the Law of Moses.

²⁵ Some while ago we told the Gentile followers what we think they should do. We instructed them not to eat anything offered to idols. They were told not to eat any meat with blood still in it or the meat of an animal that has been strangled. They were also told not to commit any terrible sexual sins.

²⁶ The next day Paul took the four men with him and got himself ready at the same time they did. Then he went into the temple and told when the final ceremony would take place and when an offering would be made for each of them.

Paul Is Arrested

²⁷ When the period of seven days for the ceremony was

---

g **20.28** *the blood of his own Son*: Or "his own blood."   *h* **21.9** *unmarried*: Or "virgin."

almost over, some of the Jewish people from Asia saw Paul in the temple. They got a large crowd together and started attacking him. 28 They were shouting, "Friends, help us! This man goes around everywhere, saying bad things about our nation and about the Law of Moses and about this temple. He has even brought shame to this holy temple by bringing in Gentiles." 29 Some of them thought that Paul had brought Trophimus from Ephesus into the temple, because they had seen them together in the city.

30 The whole city was in an uproar, and the people turned into a mob. They grabbed Paul and dragged him out of the temple. Then suddenly the doors were shut. 31 The people were about to kill Paul when the Roman army commander heard that all Jerusalem was starting to riot. 32 So he quickly took some soldiers and officers and ran to where the crowd had gathered.

As soon as the mob saw the commander and soldiers, they stopped beating Paul. 33 The army commander went over and arrested him and had him bound with two chains. Then he tried to find out who Paul was and what he had done. 34 Part of the crowd shouted one thing, and part of them shouted something else. But they were making so much noise that the commander could not find out a thing. Then he ordered Paul to be taken into the fortress. 35 As they reached the steps, the crowd became so wild that the soldiers had to lift Paul up and carry him. 36 The crowd followed and kept shouting, "Kill him! Kill him!"

Paul Speaks to the Crowd

37 When Paul was about to be taken into the fortress, he asked the commander, "Can I say something to you?"

"How do you know Greek?" the commander asked. 38 "Aren't you that Egyptian who started a riot not long ago and led four thousand terrorists into the desert?"

39 "No!" Paul replied. "I am a Jew from Tarsus, an important city in Cilicia. Please let me speak to the crowd."

40 The commander told him he could speak, so Paul stood on the steps and motioned to the people. When they were quiet, he spoke to them in Aramaic:

22 "My friends and leaders of our nation, listen as I explain what happened!" 2 When the crowd heard Paul speak to them in Aramaic, they became even quieter. Then Paul said:

3 I am a Jew, born and raised in the city of Tarsus in Cilicia. I was a student of Gamaliel and was taught to follow every single law of our ancestors. In fact, I was just as eager to obey God as any of you are today.

4 I made trouble for everyone who followed the Lord's Way, and I even had some of them killed. I had others arrested and put in jail. I didn't care if they were men or women. 5 The high priest and all the council members can tell you that this is true. They even gave me letters to the Jewish leaders in Damascus, so that I could arrest people there and bring them to Jerusalem to be punished.

6 One day about noon I was getting close to Damascus, when a bright light from heaven suddenly flashed around me. 7 I fell to the ground and heard a voice asking, "Saul, Saul, why are you so cruel to me?"

8 "Who are you?" I answered.

The Lord replied, "I am Jesus from Nazareth! I am the one you are so cruel to." 9 The men who were traveling with me saw the light, but did not hear the voice.

10 I asked, "Lord, what do you want me to do?"

Then he told me, "Get up and go to Damascus. When you get there, you will be told what to do." 11 The light had been so bright that I couldn't see. And the other men had to lead me by the hand to Damascus.

12 In that city there was a man named Ananias, who faithfully obeyed the Law of Moses and was well liked by all the Jewish people living there. 13 He came to me and said, "Saul, my friend, you can now see again!"

At once I could see. 14 Then Ananias told me, "The God that our ancestors worshiped has chosen you to know what he wants done. He has chosen you to see the One Who Obeys God and to hear his voice. 15 You must tell everyone what you have seen and heard. 16 What are you waiting for? Get up! Be baptized, and wash away your sins by praying to the Lord."

17 After this I returned to Jerusalem and went to the temple to pray. There I had a vision 18 of the Lord who said to me, "Hurry and leave Jerusalem! The people won't listen to what you say about me."

19 I replied, "Lord, they know that in many of our meeting places I arrested and beat people who had faith in you. 20 Stephen was killed because he spoke for you, and I stood there and cheered them on. I even guarded the clothes of the men who murdered him."

21 But the Lord told me to go, and he promised to send me far away to the Gentiles.

22 The crowd listened until Paul said this. Then they started shouting, "Get rid of this man! He doesn't deserve to live." 23 They kept shouting. They waved their clothes around and threw dust into the air.

Paul and the Roman Army Commander

24 The Roman commander ordered Paul to be taken into the fortress and beaten with a whip. He did this to find out why the people were screaming at Paul.

25 While the soldiers were tying Paul up to be beaten, he asked the officer standing there, "Is it legal to beat a Roman citizen before he has been tried in court?"

26 When the officer heard this, he went to the commander and said, "What are you doing? This man is a Roman citizen!"

27 The commander went to Paul and asked, "Tell me, are you a Roman citizen?"

"Yes," Paul answered.

28 The commander then said, "I paid a lot of money to become a Roman citizen."

But Paul replied, "I was born a Roman citizen."

29 The men who were about to beat and question Paul quickly backed off. And the commander himself was frightened when he realized that he had put a Roman citizen in chains.

Paul Is Tried by the Council

30 The next day the commander wanted to know the real reason why the Jewish leaders had brought charges against Paul. So he had Paul's chains removed, and he ordered the chief priests and the whole council to meet. Then he had Paul led in and made him stand in front of them.

23 Paul looked straight at the council members and said, "My friends, to this day I have served God with a clear conscience!"

2 Then Ananias the high priest ordered the men standing beside Paul to hit him on the mouth. **3** Paul turned to the high priest and said, "You whitewashed wall! God will hit you. You sit there to judge me by the Law of Moses. But at the same time you order men to break the Law by hitting me."

4 The men standing beside Paul asked, "Don't you know you are insulting God's high priest?"

5 Paul replied, "Oh! I didn't know he was the high priest. The Scriptures do tell us not to speak evil about a leader of our people."

6 When Paul saw that some of the council members were Sadducees and others were Pharisees, he shouted, "My friends, I am a Pharisee and the son of a Pharisee. I am on trial simply because I believe that the dead will be raised to life."

7 As soon as Paul said this, the Pharisees and the Sadducees got into a big argument, and the council members started taking sides. **8** The Sadducees do not believe in angels or spirits or that the dead will rise to life. But the Pharisees believe in all of these, **9** and so there was a lot of shouting. Some of the teachers of the Law of Moses were Pharisees. Finally, they became angry and said, "We don't find anything wrong with this man. Maybe a spirit or an angel really did speak to him."

10 The argument became fierce, and the commander was afraid that Paul would be pulled apart. So he ordered the soldiers to go in and rescue Paul. Then they took him back into the fortress.

11 That night the Lord stood beside Paul and said, "Don't worry! Just as you have told others about me in Jerusalem, you must also tell about me in Rome."

A Plot To Kill Paul

12-13 The next morning more than forty Jewish men got together and vowed that they would not eat or drink anything until they had killed Paul. **14** Then some of them went to the chief priests and the nation's leaders and said, "We have promised God that we would not eat a thing until we have killed Paul. **15** You and everyone in the council must go to the commander and pretend that you want to find out more about the charges against Paul. Ask for him to be brought before your court. Meanwhile, we will be waiting to kill him before he gets there."

16 When Paul's nephew heard about the plot, he went to the fortress and told Paul about it. **17** So Paul said to one of the army officers, "Take this young man to the commander. He has something to tell him."

18 The officer took him to the commander and said, "The prisoner named Paul asked me to bring this young man to you, because he has something to tell you."

19 The commander took the young man aside and asked him in private, "What do you want to tell me?"

20 He answered, "Some men are planning to ask you to bring Paul down to the Jewish council tomorrow. They will claim that they want to find out more about him. **21** But please don't do what they say. More than forty men are going to attack Paul. They have made a vow not to eat or drink anything until they have killed him. Even now they are waiting to hear what you decide."

22 The commander sent the young man away after saying to him, "Don't let anyone know that you told me this."

Paul Is Sent to Felix the Governor

23 The commander called in two of his officers and told them, "By nine o'clock tonight have two hundred soldiers ready to go to Caesarea. Take along seventy men on horseback and two hundred foot soldiers with spears. **24** Get a horse ready for Paul and make sure that he gets safely through to Felix the governor."

25 The commander wrote a letter that said:

26 Greetings from Claudius Lysias to the Honorable Governor Felix:

27 Some Jews grabbed this man and were about to kill him. But when I found out that he was a Roman citizen, I took some soldiers and rescued him.

28 I wanted to find out what they had against him. So I brought him before their council **29** and learned that the charges concern only their religious laws. This man isn't guilty of anything for which he should die or even be put in jail.

30 As soon as I learned that there was a plot against him, I sent him to you and told their leaders to bring charges against him in your court.

31 The soldiers obeyed the commander's orders, and that same night they took Paul to the city of Antipatris. **32** The next day the foot soldiers returned to the fortress and let the soldiers on horseback take him the rest of the way. **33** When they came to Caesarea, they gave the letter to the governor and handed Paul over to him.

34 The governor read the letter. Then he asked Paul and found out that he was from Cilicia. **35** The governor said, "I will listen to your case as soon as the people come to bring their charges against you." After saying this, he gave orders for Paul to be kept as a prisoner in Herod's palace.

Paul Is Accused in the Court of Felix

24 Five days later Ananias the high priest, together with some of their leaders and a lawyer named Tertullus, went to the governor to present their case against Paul. **2** So Paul was called in, and Tertullus stated the case against him:[i]

Honorable Felix, you have brought our people a long period of peace, and because of your concern our nation is much better off. **3** All of us are always grateful for what you have done. **4** I don't want to bother you, but please be patient with us and listen to me for just a few minutes.

5 This man has been found to be a real pest and troublemaker for Jews all over the world. He is also

---

[i] **24.2** *Paul was called in, and Tertullus stated the case against him*: Or "Tertullus was called in and stated the case against Paul."

a leader of a group called Nazarenes. 6-8 When he tried to disgrace the temple, we arrested him./ If you question him, you will find out for yourself that our charges are true.

9 The Jewish crowd spoke up and agreed with what Tertullus had said.

Paul Defends Himself

10 The governor motioned for Paul to speak, and he began:

I know that you have judged the people of our nation for many years, and I am glad to defend myself in your court.

11 It was no more than twelve days ago that I went to worship in Jerusalem. You can find this out easily enough. 12 Never once did the Jews find me arguing with anyone in the temple. I didn't cause trouble in the Jewish meeting places or in the city itself. 13 There is no way that they can prove these charges that they are now bringing against me.

14 I admit that their leaders think that the Lord's Way which I follow is based on wrong beliefs. But I still worship the same God that my ancestors worshiped. And I believe everything written in the Law of Moses and in the Prophets. 15 I am just as sure as these people are that God will raise from death everyone who is good or evil. 16 And because I am sure, I try my best to have a clear conscience in whatever I do for God or for people.

17 After being away for several years, I returned here to bring gifts for the poor people of my nation and to offer sacrifices. 18 This is what I was doing when I was found going through a ceremony in the temple. I wasn't with a crowd, and there was no uproar.

19 Some Jews from Asia were there at that time, and if they have anything to say against me, they should be here now. 20 Or ask the ones who are here. They can tell you that they didn't find me guilty of anything when I was tried by their own council. 21 The only charge they can bring against me is what I shouted out in court, when I said, "I am on trial today because I believe that the dead will be raised to life!"

22 Felix knew a lot about the Lord's Way. But he brought the trial to an end and said, "I will make my decision after Lysias the commander arrives." 23 He then ordered the army officer to keep Paul under guard, but not to lock him up or to stop his friends from helping him.

Paul Is Kept under Guard

24 Several days later Felix and his wife Drusilla, who was Jewish, went to the place where Paul was kept under guard. They sent for Paul and listened while he spoke to them about having faith in Christ Jesus. 25 But Felix was frightened when Paul started talking to them about doing right, about self-control, and about the coming judgment. So he said to Paul, "That's enough for now. You may go. But when I have time I will send for you." 26 After this, Felix often sent for Paul and talked with him, because he hoped that Paul would offer him a bribe.

27 Two years later Porcius Festus became governor in place of Felix. But since Felix wanted to do the Jewish leaders a favor, he kept Paul in jail.

Paul Asks To Be Tried by the Roman Emperor

25 Three days after Festus had become governor, he went from Caesarea to Jerusalem. 2 There the chief priests and some Jewish leaders told him about their charges against Paul. They also asked Festus 3 if he would be willing to bring Paul to Jerusalem. They begged him to do this because they were planning to attack and kill Paul on the way. 4 But Festus told them, "Paul will be kept in Caesarea, and I am soon going there myself. 5 If he has done anything wrong, let your leaders go with me and bring charges against him there." .

6 Festus stayed in Jerusalem for eight or ten more days before going to Caesarea. Then the next day he took his place as judge and had Paul brought into court. 7 As soon as Paul came in, the Jewish leaders from Jerusalem crowded around him and said he was guilty of many serious crimes. But they could not prove anything. 8 Then Paul spoke in his own defense, "I have not broken the Law of my people. And I have not done anything against either the temple or the Emperor."

9 Festus wanted to please the leaders. So he asked Paul, "Are you willing to go to Jerusalem and be tried by me on these charges?"

10 Paul replied, "I am on trial in the Emperor's court, and that's where I should be tried. You know very well that I have not done anything to harm the Jewish nation. 11 If I had done something deserving death, I would not ask to escape the death penalty. But I am not guilty of any of these crimes, and no one has the right to hand me over to these people. I now ask to be tried by the Emperor himself."

12 After Festus had talked this over with members of his council, he told Paul, "You have asked to be tried by the Emperor, and to the Emperor you will go!"

Paul Speaks to Agrippa and Bernice

13 A few days later King Agrippa and Bernice came to Caesarea to visit Festus. 14 They had been there for several days, when Festus told the king about the charges against Paul. He said:

Felix left a man here in jail, 15 and when I went to Jerusalem, the chief priests and the Jewish leaders came and asked me to find him guilty. 16 I told them that it isn't the Roman custom to hand a man over to people who are bringing charges against him. He must first have the chance to meet them face to face and to defend himself against their charges.

17 So when they came here with me, I wasted no time. On the very next day I took my place on the judge's bench and ordered him to be brought in. 18 But when the men stood up to make their charges against him, they did not accuse him of any of the crimes that I thought they would. 19 Instead, they argued with him about some of their beliefs and about a dead man named Jesus, who Paul said was alive.

/ 24.6-8 *we arrested him*: Some manuscripts add, "We wanted to judge him by our own laws. But Lysias the commander took him away from us by force. Then Lysias ordered us to bring our charges against this man in your court."

20 Since I did not know how to find out the truth about all this, I asked Paul if he would be willing to go to Jerusalem and be put on trial there. 21 But Paul asked to be kept in jail until the Emperor could decide his case. So I ordered him to be kept here until I could send him to the Emperor. 22 Then Agrippa said to Festus, "I would also like to hear what this man has to say."

Festus answered, "You can hear him tomorrow."

23 The next day Agrippa and Bernice made a big show as they came into the meeting room. High ranking army officers and leading citizens of the town were also there. Festus then ordered Paul to be brought in 24 and said:

King Agrippa and other guests, look at this man! Every Jew from Jerusalem and Caesarea has come to me, demanding for him to be put to death. 25 I have not found him guilty of any crime deserving death. But because he has asked to be judged by the Emperor, I have decided to send him to Rome.

26 I have to write some facts about this man to the Emperor. So I have brought him before all of you, but especially before you, King Agrippa. After we have talked about his case, I will then have something to write. 27 It makes no sense to send a prisoner to the Emperor without stating the charges against him.

Paul's Defense before Agrippa

26 Agrippa told Paul, "You may now speak for yourself."

Paul stretched out his hand and said:

2 King Agrippa, I am glad for this chance to defend myself before you today on all these charges that my own people have brought against me. 3 You know a lot about our religious customs and the beliefs that divide us. So I ask you to listen patiently to me.

4-5 All the Jews have known me since I was a child. They know what kind of life I have lived in my own country and in Jerusalem. And if they were willing, they could tell you that I was a Pharisee, a member of a group that is stricter than any other. 6 Now I am on trial because I believe the promise God made to our people long ago.

7 Day and night our twelve tribes have earnestly served God, waiting for his promised blessings. King Agrippa, because of this hope, the Jewish leaders have brought charges against me. 8 Why should any of you doubt that God raises the dead to life?

9 I once thought that I should do everything I could to oppose Jesus from Nazareth. 10 I did this first in Jerusalem, and with the authority of the chief priests I put many of God's people in jail. I even voted for them to be killed. 11 I often had them punished in our meeting places, and I tried to make them give up their faith. In fact, I was so angry with them, that I went looking for them in foreign cities.

12 King Agrippa, one day I was on my way to Damascus with the authority and permission of the chief priests. 13 About noon I saw a light brighter than the sun. It flashed from heaven on me and on everyone traveling with me. 14 We all fell to the ground. Then I heard a voice say to me in Aramaic, "Saul, Saul, why are you so cruel to me? It's foolish to fight against me!"

15 "Who are you?" I asked.

Then the Lord answered, "I am Jesus! I am the one you are so cruel to. 16 Now stand up. I have appeared to you, because I have chosen you to be my servant. You are to tell others what you have learned about me and what I will show you later."

17 The Lord also said, "I will protect you from the Jews and from the Gentiles that I am sending you to. 18 I want you to open their eyes, so that they will turn from darkness to light and from the power of Satan to God. Then their sins will be forgiven, and by faith in me they will become part of God's holy people."

19 King Agrippa, I obeyed this vision from heaven. 20 First I preached to the people in Damascus, and then I went to Jerusalem and all over Judea. Finally, I went to the Gentiles and said, "Stop sinning and turn to God! Then prove what you have done by the way you live."

21 That is why some men grabbed me in the temple and tried to kill me. 22 But all this time God has helped me, and I have preached both to the rich and to the poor. I have told them only what the prophets and Moses said would happen. 23 I told them how the Messiah would suffer and be the first to be raised from death, so that he could bring light to his own people and to the Gentiles.

24 Before Paul finished defending himself, Festus shouted, "Paul, you're crazy! Too much learning has driven you out of your mind."

25 But Paul replied, "Honorable Festus, I am not crazy. What I am saying is true, and it makes sense. 26 None of these things happened off in a corner somewhere. I am sure that King Agrippa knows what I am talking about. That's why I can speak so plainly to him."

27 Then Paul said to Agrippa, "Do you believe what the prophets said? I know you do."

28 Agrippa asked Paul, "In such a short time do you think you can talk me into being a Christian?"

29 Paul answered, "Whether it takes a short time or a long time, I wish you and everyone else who hears me today would become just like me! Except, of course, for these chains."

30 Then King Agrippa, Governor Festus, Bernice, and everyone who was with them got up. 31 But before they left, they said, "This man isn't guilty of anything. He doesn't deserve to die or to be put in jail."

32 Agrippa told Festus, "Paul could have been set free, if he had not asked to be tried by the Roman Emperor."

Paul Is Taken to Rome

27 When it was time for us to sail to Rome, Captain Julius from the Emperor's special troops was put in charge of Paul and the other prisoners. 2 We went aboard a ship from Adramyttium that was about to sail to some ports along the coast of Asia. Aristarchus from Thessalonica in Macedonia sailed on the ship with us.

³ The next day we came to shore at Sidon. Captain Julius was very kind to Paul. He even let him visit his friends, so they could give him whatever he needed. ⁴ When we left Sidon, the winds were blowing against us, and we sailed close to the island of Cyprus to be safe from the wind. ⁵ Then we sailed south of Cilicia and Pamphylia until we came to the port of Myra in Lycia. ⁶ There the army captain found a ship from Alexandria that was going to Italy. So he ordered us to board that ship.

⁷ We sailed along slowly for several days and had a hard time reaching Cnidus. The wind would not let us go any farther in that direction, so we sailed past Cape Salmone, where the island of Crete would protect us from the wind. ⁸ We went slowly along the coast and finally reached a place called Fair Havens, not far from the town of Lasea.

⁹ By now we had already lost a lot of time, and sailing was no longer safe. In fact, even the Great Day of Forgiveness was past. ¹⁰ Then Paul spoke to the crew of the ship, "Men, listen to me! If we sail now, our ship and its cargo will be badly damaged, and many lives will be lost." ¹¹ But Julius listened to the captain of the ship and its owner, rather than to Paul.

¹² The harbor at Fair Havens wasn't a good place to spend the winter. Because of this, almost everyone agreed that we should at least try to sail along the coast of Crete as far as Phoenix. It had a harbor that opened toward the southwest and northwest,ᵏ and we could spend the winter there.

The Storm at Sea

¹³ When a gentle wind from the south started blowing, the men thought it was a good time to do what they had planned. So they pulled up the anchor, and we sailed along the coast of Crete. ¹⁴ But soon a strong wind called "The Northeaster" blew against us from the island. ¹⁵ The wind struck the ship, and we could not sail against it. So we let the wind carry the ship.

¹⁶ We went along the island of Cauda on the side that was protected from the wind. We had a hard time holding the lifeboat in place, ¹⁷ but finally we got it where it belonged. Then the sailors wrapped ropes around the ship to hold it together. They lowered the sail and let the ship drift along, because they were afraid it might hit the sandbanks in the gulf of Syrtis.

¹⁸ The storm was so fierce that the next day they threw some of the ship's cargo overboard. ¹⁹ Then on the third day, with their bare hands they threw overboard some of the ship's gear. ²⁰ For several days we could not see either the sun or the stars. A strong wind kept blowing, and we finally gave up all hope of being saved.

²¹ Since none of us had eaten anything for a long time, Paul stood up and told the men:

You should have listened to me! If you had stayed on in Crete, you would not have had this damage and loss. ²² But now I beg you to cheer up, because you will be safe. Only the ship will be lost.

²³ I belong to God, and I worship him. Last night he sent an angel ²⁴ to tell me, "Paul, don't be afraid! You will stand trial before the Emperor. And because of you, God will save the lives of everyone on the ship." ²⁵ Cheer up! I am sure that God will

do exactly what he promised. ²⁶ But we will first be shipwrecked on some island.

²⁷ For fourteen days and nights we had been blown around over the Mediterranean Sea. But about midnight the sailors realized that we were getting near land. ²⁸ They measured and found that the water was about one hundred twenty feet deep. A little later they measured again and found it was only about ninety feet. ²⁹ The sailors were afraid that we might hit some rocks, and they let down four anchors from the back of the ship. Then they prayed for daylight.

³⁰ The sailors wanted to escape from the ship. So they lowered the lifeboat into the water, pretending that they were letting down an anchor from the front of the ship. ³¹ But Paul said to Captain Julius and the soldiers, "If the sailors don't stay on the ship, you won't have any chance to save your lives." ³² The soldiers then cut the ropes that held the lifeboat and let it fall into the sea.

³³ Just before daylight Paul begged the people to eat something. He told them, "For fourteen days you have been so worried that you haven't eaten a thing. ³⁴ I beg you to eat something. Your lives depend on it. Do this and not one of you will be hurt."

³⁵ After Paul had said this, he took a piece of bread and gave thanks to God. Then in front of everyone, he broke the bread and ate some. ³⁶ They all felt encouraged, and each of them ate something. ³⁷ There were 276 people on the ship, ³⁸ and after everyone had eaten, they threw the cargo of wheat into the sea to make the ship lighter.

The Shipwreck

³⁹ Morning came, and the ship's crew saw a coast that they did not recognize. But they did see a cove with a beach. So they decided to try to run the ship aground on the beach. ⁴⁰ They cut the anchors loose and let them sink into the sea. At the same time they untied the ropes that were holding the rudders. Next, they raised the sail at the front of the ship and let the wind carry the ship toward the beach. ⁴¹ But it ran aground on a sandbank. The front of the ship stuck firmly in the sand, and the rear was being smashed by the force of the waves.

⁴² The soldiers decided to kill the prisoners to keep them from swimming away and escaping. ⁴³ But Captain Julius wanted to save Paul's life, and he did not let the soldiers do what they had planned. Instead, he ordered everyone who could swim to dive into the water and head for shore. ⁴⁴ Then he told the others to hold on to planks of wood or parts of the ship. At last, everyone safely reached shore.

On the Island of Malta

28 When we came ashore, we learned that the island was called Malta. ² The local people were very friendly, and they welcomed us by building a fire, because it was rainy and cold.

³ After Paul had gathered some wood and had put it on the fire, the heat caused a snake to crawl out, and it bit him on the hand. ⁴ When the local people saw the snake hanging from Paul's hand, they said to each other, "This man must be a murderer! He didn't drown in the sea, but the goddess of justice will kill him anyway."

ᵏ **27.12** *southwest and northwest*: Or "northeast and southeast."

5 Paul shook the snake off into the fire and wasn't harmed. 6 The people kept thinking that Paul would either swell up or suddenly drop dead. They watched him for a long time, and when nothing happened to him, they changed their minds and said, "This man is a god."

7 The governor of the island was named Publius, and he owned some of the land around there. Publius was very friendly and welcomed us into his home for three days. 8 His father was in bed, sick with fever and stomach trouble, and Paul went to visit him. Paul healed the man by praying and placing his hands on him.

9 After this happened, everyone on the island brought their sick people to Paul, and they were all healed. 10 The people were very respectful to us, and when we sailed, they gave us everything we needed.

From Malta to Rome

11 Three months later we sailed in a ship that had been docked at Malta for the winter. The ship was from Alexandria in Egypt and was known as "The Twin Gods."[l] 12 We arrived in Syracuse and stayed for three days. 13 From there we sailed to Rhegium. The next day a south wind began to blow, and two days later we arrived in Puteoli. 14 There we found some of the Lord's followers, who begged us to stay with them. A week later we left for the city of Rome.

15 Some of the followers in Rome heard about us and came to meet us at the Market of Appius and at the Three Inns. When Paul saw them, he thanked God and was encouraged.

Paul in Rome

16 We arrived in Rome, and Paul was allowed to live in a house by himself with a soldier to guard him.

17 Three days after we got there, Paul called together some of the Jewish leaders and said:

My friends, I have never done anything to hurt our people, and I have never gone against the customs of our ancestors. But in Jerusalem I was handed over as a prisoner to the Romans. 18 They looked into the charges against me and wanted to release me. They found that I had not done anything deserving death. 19 The Jewish leaders disagreed, so I asked to be tried by the Emperor.

But I don't have anything to say against my own nation. 20 I am bound by these chains because of what we people of Israel hope for. That's why I have called you here to talk about this hope of ours.

21 The leaders replied, "No one from Judea has written us a letter about you. And not one of them has come here to report on you or to say anything against you. 22 But we would like to hear what you have to say. We understand that people everywhere are against this new group."

23 They agreed on a time to meet with Paul, and many of them came to his house. From early morning until late in the afternoon, Paul talked to them about God's kingdom. He used the Law of Moses and the Books of the Prophets to try to win them over to Jesus.

24 Some of the leaders agreed with what Paul said, but others did not. 25 Since they could not agree among themselves, they started leaving. But Paul said, "The Holy Spirit said the right thing when he sent Isaiah the prophet 26 to tell our ancestors,

'Go to these people
    and tell them:
You will listen and listen,
    but never understand.
You will look and look,
    but never see.
27 All of you
    have stubborn hearts.
Your ears are stopped up,
    and your eyes are covered.
You cannot see or hear
    or understand.
If you could,
    you would turn to me,
    and I would heal you.' "

28-29 Paul said, "You may be sure that God wants to save the Gentiles! And they will listen."[m]

30 For two years Paul stayed in a rented house and welcomed everyone who came to see him. 31 He bravely preached about God's kingdom and taught about the Lord Jesus Christ, and no one tried to stop him.

---

[l] 28.11 *known as "The Twin Gods"*: Or "carried on its bow a wooden carving of the Twin Gods." These gods were Castor and Pollux, two of the favorite gods among sailors.   [m] 28.28,29 *And they will listen*: Some manuscripts add, "After Paul said this, the people left, but they got into a fierce argument among themselves."

ROMANS

1 From Paul, a servant of Christ Jesus.

God chose me to be an apostle, and he appointed me to preach the good news [2] that he promised long ago by what his prophets said in the holy Scriptures. [3-4] This good news is about his Son, our Lord Jesus Christ! As a human, he was from the family of David. But the Holy Spirit[a] proved that Jesus is the powerful Son of God,[b] because he was raised from death.

[5] Jesus was kind to me and chose me to be an apostle,[c] so that people of all nations would obey and have faith. [6] You are some of those people chosen by Jesus Christ.

[7] This letter is to all of you in Rome. God loves you and has chosen you to be his very own people.

I pray that God our Father and our Lord Jesus Christ will be kind to you and will bless you with peace!

A Prayer of Thanks

[8] First, I thank God in the name of Jesus Christ for all of you. I do this because people everywhere in the world are talking about your faith. [9] God has seen how I never stop praying for you, while I serve him with all my heart and tell the good news about his Son.

[10] In all my prayers, I ask God to make it possible for me to visit you. [11] I want to see you and share with you the same blessings that God's Spirit has given me. Then you will grow stronger in your faith. [12] What I am saying is that we can encourage each other by the faith that is ours.

[13] My friends, I want you to know that I have often planned to come for a visit. But something has always kept me from doing it. I want to win followers to Christ in Rome, as I have done in many other places. [14-15] It doesn't matter if people are civilized and educated, or if they are uncivilized and uneducated. I must tell the good news to everyone. That's why I am eager to visit all of you in Rome.

The Power of the Good News

[16] I am proud of the good news! It is God's powerful way of saving all people who have faith, whether they are Jews or Gentiles. [17] The good news tells how God accepts everyone who has faith, but only those who have faith.[d] It is just as the Scriptures say, "The people God accepts because of their faith will live."[e]

Everyone Is Guilty

[18] From heaven God shows how angry he is with all the wicked and evil things that sinful people do to crush the truth. [19] They know everything that can be known about God, because God has shown it all to them. [20] God's eternal power and character cannot be seen. But from the beginning of creation, God has shown what these are like by all he has made. That's why those people don't have any excuse. [21] They know about God, but they don't honor him or even thank him. Their thoughts are useless, and their stupid minds are in the dark. [22] They claim to be wise, but they are fools. [23] They don't worship the glorious and eternal God. Instead, they worship idols that are made to look like humans who cannot live forever, and like birds, animals, and reptiles.

[24] So God let these people go their own way. They did what they wanted to do, and their filthy thoughts made them do shameful things with their bodies. [25] They gave up the truth about God for a lie, and they worshiped God's creation instead of God, who will be praised forever. Amen.

[26] God let them follow their own evil desires. Women no longer wanted to have sex in a natural way, and they did things with each other that were not natural. [27] Men behaved in the same way. They stopped wanting to have sex with women and had strong desires for sex with other men. They did shameful things with each other, and what has happened to them is punishment for their foolish deeds.

[28] Since these people refused even to think about God, he let their useless minds rule over them. That's why they do all sorts of indecent things. [29] They are evil, wicked, and greedy, as well as mean in every possible way. They want what others have, and they murder, argue, cheat, and are hard to get along with. They gossip, [30] say cruel things about others, and hate God. They are proud, conceited, and boastful, always thinking up new ways to do evil.

These people don't respect their parents. [31] They are stupid, unreliable, and don't have any love or pity for others. [32] They know God has said that anyone who acts this way deserves to die. But they keep on doing evil things, and they even encourage others to do them.

God's Judgment Is Fair

2 Some of you accuse others of doing wrong. But there is no excuse for what you do. When you judge others, you condemn yourselves, because you are guilty of doing the very same things. [2] We know that God is right to judge everyone who behaves in this way. [3] Do you really think God won't punish you, when you behave exactly like the people you accuse? [4] You surely don't think much of God's wonderful goodness or of his patience and willingness to put up with you. Don't you know that the reason God is good to you is because he wants you to turn to him?

[5] But you are stubborn and refuse to turn to God. So you are making things even worse for yourselves on that day when he will show how angry he is and will judge the world with fairness. [6] God will reward each of us for what we have done. [7] He will give eternal life to everyone who has patiently done what is good in the hope of receiving glory, honor, and life that lasts forever. [8] But he will show how angry and furious he can be with every selfish person

---

who rejects the truth and wants to do evil. ⁹ All who are wicked will be punished with trouble and suffering. It doesn't matter if they are Jews or Gentiles. ¹⁰ But all who do right will be rewarded with glory, honor, and peace, whether they are Jews or Gentiles. ¹¹ God doesn't have any favorites!

¹² Those people who don't know about God's Law will still be punished for what they do wrong. And the Law will be used to judge everyone who knows what it says. ¹³ God accepts those who obey his Law, but not those who simply hear it.

¹⁴ Some people naturally obey the Law's commands, even though they don't have the Law. ¹⁵ This proves that the conscience is like a law written in the human heart. And it will show whether we are forgiven or condemned, ¹⁶ when God appoints Jesus Christ to judge everyone's secret thoughts, just as my message says.

The Jews and the Law

¹⁷ Some of you call yourselves Jews. You trust in the Law and take pride in God. ¹⁸ By reading the Scriptures you learn how God wants you to behave, and you discover what is right. ¹⁹ You are sure that you are a guide for the blind and a light for all who are in the dark. ²⁰ And since there is knowledge and truth in God's Law, you think you can instruct fools and teach young people.

²¹ But how can you teach others when you refuse to learn? You preach that it is wrong to steal. But do you steal? ²² You say people should be faithful in marriage. But are you faithful? You hate idols, yet you rob their temples. ²³ You take pride in the Law, but you disobey the Law and bring shame to God. ²⁴ It is just as the Scriptures tell us, "You have made foreigners say insulting things about God."

²⁵ Being circumcised is worthwhile, if you obey the Law. But if you don't obey the Law, you are no better off than people who are not circumcised. ²⁶ In fact, if they obey the Law, they are as good as anyone who is circumcised. ²⁷ So everyone who obeys the Law, but has never been circumcised, will condemn you. Even though you are circumcised and have the Law, you still don't obey its teachings.

²⁸ Just because you live like a Jew and are circumcised doesn't make you a real Jew. ²⁹ To be a real Jew you must obey the Law. True circumcision is something that happens deep in your heart, not something done to your body. And besides, you should want praise from God and not from humans.

3 What good is it to be a Jew? What good is it to be circumcised? ² It is good in a lot of ways! First of all, God's messages were spoken to the Jews. ³ It is true that some of them did not believe the message. But does this mean that God cannot be trusted, just because they did not have faith? ⁴ No, indeed! God tells the truth, even if everyone else is a liar. The Scriptures say about God,

"Your words
    will be proven true,
and in court
    ·you will win your case."

⁵ If our evil deeds show how right God is, then what can we say? Is it wrong for God to become angry and punish us?

What a foolish thing to ask. ⁶ But the answer is, "No." Otherwise, how could God judge the world? ⁷ Since your lies bring great honor to God by showing how truthful he is, you may ask why God still says you are a sinner. ⁸ You might as well say, "Let's do something evil, so that something good will come of it!" Some people even claim that we are saying this. But God is fair and will judge them as well.

No One Is Good

⁹ What does all this mean? Does it mean that we Jews are better off ᶠ than the Gentiles? No, it doesn't! Jews, as well as Gentiles, are ruled by sin, just as I have said. ¹⁰ The Scriptures tell us,

"No one is acceptable to God!
¹¹ Not one of them understands
    or even searches for God.
¹² They have all turned away
    and are worthless.
There isn't one person
    who does right.
¹³ Their words are like
    an open pit,
and their tongues are good
    only for telling lies.
Each word is as deadly
    as the fangs of a snake,
¹⁴ and they say nothing
    but bitter curses.
¹⁵ These people quickly
    become violent.
¹⁶ Wherever they go,
    they leave ruin
    and destruction.
¹⁷ They don't know how
    to live in peace.
¹⁸   They don't even fear God."

¹⁹ We know that everything in the Law was written for those who are under its power. The Law says these things to stop anyone from making excuses and to let God show that the whole world is guilty. ²⁰ God doesn't accept people simply because they obey the Law. No, indeed! All the Law does is to point out our sin.

God's Way of Accepting People

²¹ Now we see how God does make us acceptable to him. The Law and the Prophets tell how we become acceptable, and it isn't by obeying the Law of Moses. ²² God treats everyone alike. He accepts people only because they have faith in Jesus Christ. ²³ All of us have sinned and fallen short of God's glory. ²⁴ But God treats us much better than we deserve, and because of Christ Jesus, he freely accepts us and sets us free from our sins. ²⁵⁻²⁶ God sent Christ to be our sacrifice. Christ offered his life's blood, so that by faith in him we could come to God. And God did this to show that in the past he was right to be patient and forgive sinners. This also shows that God is right when he accepts people who have faith in Jesus.

²⁷ What is left for us to brag about? Not a thing! Is it because we obeyed some law? No! It is because of faith. ²⁸ We

ᶠ **3.9** *better off*: Or "worse off."

see that people are acceptable to God because they have faith, and not because they obey the Law. 29 Does God belong only to the Jews? Isn't he also the God of the Gentiles? Yes, he is! 30 There is only one God, and he accepts Gentiles as well as Jews, simply because of their faith. 31 Do we destroy the Law by our faith? Not at all! We make it even more powerful.

The Example of Abraham

4 Well then, what can we say about our ancestor Abraham? 2 If he became acceptable to God because of what he did, then he would have something to brag about. But he would never be able to brag about it to God. 3 The Scriptures say, "God accepted Abraham because Abraham had faith in him."

4 Money paid to workers isn't a gift. It is something they earn by working. 5 But you cannot make God accept you because of something you do. God accepts sinners only because they have faith in him. 6 In the Scriptures David talks about the blessings that come to people who are acceptable to God, even though they don't do anything to deserve these blessings. David says,

7 "God blesses people
  whose sins are forgiven
and whose evil deeds
  are forgotten.
8 The Lord blesses people
  whose sins are erased
  from his book."

9 Are these blessings meant for circumcised people or for those who are not circumcised? Well, the Scriptures say that God accepted Abraham because Abraham had faith in him. 10 But when did this happen? Was it before or after Abraham was circumcised? Of course, it was before.

11 Abraham let himself be circumcised to show that he had been accepted because of his faith even before he was circumcised. This makes Abraham the father of all who are acceptable to God because of their faith, even though they are not circumcised. 12 This also makes Abraham the father of everyone who is circumcised and has faith in God, as Abraham did before he was circumcised.

The Promise Is for All Who Have Faith

13 God promised Abraham and his descendants that he would give them the world. This promise wasn't made because Abraham had obeyed a law, but because his faith in God made him acceptable. 14 If Abraham and his descendants were given this promise because they had obeyed a law, then faith would mean nothing, and the promise would be worthless.

15 God becomes angry when his Law is broken. But where there isn't a law, it cannot be broken. 16 Everything depends on having faith in God, so that God's promise is assured by his great kindness. This promise isn't only for Abraham's descendants who have the Law. It is for all who are Abraham's descendants because they have faith, just as he did. Abraham is the ancestor of us all. 17 The Scriptures say that Abraham would become the ancestor of many nations. This promise was made to Abraham because he had faith in God, who raises the dead to life and creates new things.

18 God promised Abraham a lot of descendants. And when it all seemed hopeless, Abraham still had faith in God and became the ancestor of many nations. 19 Abraham's faith never became weak, not even when he was nearly a hundred years old. He knew that he was almost dead and that his wife Sarah could not have children. 20 But Abraham never doubted or questioned God's promise. His faith made him strong, and he gave all the credit to God.

21 Abraham was certain that God could do what he had promised. 22 So God accepted him, 23 just as we read in the Scriptures. But these words were not written only for Abraham. 24 They were written for us, since we will also be accepted because of our faith in God, who raised our Lord Jesus to life. 25 God gave Jesus to die for our sins, and he raised him to life, so that we would be made acceptable to God.

What It Means To Be Acceptable to God

5 By faith we have been made acceptable to God. And now, because of our Lord Jesus Christ, we live at peace8 with God. 2 Christ has also introduced us8 to God's undeserved kindness on which we take our stand. So we are happy, as we look forward to sharing in the glory of God. 3 But that's not all! We gladly suffer,[i] because we know that suffering helps us to endure. 4 And endurance builds character, which gives us a hope 5 that will never disappoint us. All of this happens because God has given us the Holy Spirit, who fills our hearts with his love.

6 Christ died for us at a time when we were helpless and sinful. 7 No one is really willing to die for an honest person, though someone might be willing to die for a truly good person. 8 But God showed how much he loved us by having Christ die for us, even though we were sinful.

9 But there is more! Now that God has accepted us because Christ sacrificed his life's blood, we will also be kept safe from God's anger. 10 Even when we were God's enemies, he made peace with us, because his Son died for us. Yet something even greater than friendship is ours. Now that we are at peace with God, we will be saved by his Son's life. 11 And in addition to everything else, we are happy because God sent our Lord Jesus Christ to make peace with us.

Adam and Christ

12 Adam sinned, and that sin brought death into the world. Now everyone has sinned, and so everyone must die. 13 Sin was in the world before the Law came. But no record of sin was kept, because there was no Law. 14 Yet death still had power over all who lived from the time of Adam to the time of Moses. This happened, though not everyone disobeyed a direct command from God, as Adam did.

In some ways Adam is like Christ who came later. 15 But the gift that God was kind enough to give was very different from Adam's sin. That one sin brought death to many others. Yet in an even greater way, Jesus Christ alone brought God's gift of kindness to many people.

16 There is a lot of difference between Adam's sin and God's gift. That one sin led to punishment. But God's gift

---

g 5.1 we live at peace: Some manuscripts have "let us live at peace."   h 5.2 introduced us: Some manuscripts add "by faith."
i 5.3 We gladly suffer: Or "Let us gladly suffer."

made it possible for us to be acceptable to him, even though we have sinned many times. [17] Death ruled like a king because Adam had sinned. But that cannot compare with what Jesus Christ has done. God has been so kind to us, and he has accepted us because of Jesus. And so we will live and rule like kings.

[18] Everyone was going to be punished because Adam sinned. But because of the good thing that Christ has done, God accepts us and gives us the gift of life. [19] Adam disobeyed God and caused many others to be sinners. But Jesus obeyed him and will make many people acceptable to God.

[20] The Law came, so that the full power of sin could be seen. Yet where sin was powerful, God's kindness was even more powerful. [21] Sin ruled by means of death. But God's kindness now rules, and God has accepted us because of Jesus Christ our Lord. This means that we will have eternal life.

Dead to Sin but Alive because of Christ

6 What should we say? Should we keep on sinning, so that God's wonderful kindness will show up even better? [2] No, we should not! If we are dead to sin, how can we go on sinning? [3] Don't you know that all who share in Christ Jesus by being baptized also share in his death? [4] When we were baptized, we died and were buried with Christ. We were baptized, so that we would live a new life, as Christ was raised to life by the glory of God the Father.

[5] If we shared in Jesus' death by being baptized, we will be raised to life with him. [6] We know that the persons we used to be were nailed to the cross with Jesus. This was done, so that our sinful bodies would no longer be the slaves of sin. [7] We know that sin doesn't have power over dead people.

[8] As surely as we died with Christ, we believe we will also live with him. [9] We know that death no longer has any power over Christ. He died and was raised to life, never again to die. [10] When Christ died, he died for sin once and for all. But now he is alive, and he lives only for God. [11] In the same way, you must think of yourselves as dead to the power of sin. But Christ Jesus has given life to you, and you live for God.

[12] Don't let sin rule your body. After all, your body is bound to die, so don't obey its desires [13] or let any part of it become a slave of evil. Give yourselves to God, as people who have been raised from death to life. Make every part of your body a slave that pleases God. [14] Don't let sin keep ruling your lives. You are ruled by God's kindness and not by the Law.

Slaves Who Do What Pleases God

[15] What does all this mean? Does it mean we are free to sin, because we are ruled by God's wonderful kindness and not by the Law? Certainly not! [16] Don't you know that you are slaves of anyone you obey? You can be slaves of sin and die, or you can be obedient slaves of God and be acceptable to him. [17] You used to be slaves of sin. But I thank God that with all your heart you obeyed the teaching you received from me. [18] Now you are set free from sin and are slaves who please God.

[19] I am using these everyday examples, because in some ways you are still weak. You used to let the different parts of your body be slaves of your evil thoughts. But now you must make every part of your body serve God, so that you will belong completely to him.

[20] When you were slaves of sin, you didn't have to please God. [21] But what good did you receive from the things you did? All you have to show for them is your shame, and they lead to death. [22] Now you have been set free from sin, and you are God's slaves. This will make you holy and will lead you to eternal life. [23] Sin pays off with death. But God's gift is eternal life given by Jesus Christ our Lord.

An Example from Marriage

7 My friends, you surely understand enough about law to know that laws only have power over people who are alive. [2] For example, the Law says that a man's wife must remain his wife as long as he lives. But once her husband is dead, she is free [3] to marry someone else. However, if she goes off with another man while her husband is still alive, she is said to be unfaithful.

[4] That is how it is with you, my friends. You are now part of the body of Christ and are dead to the power of the Law. You are free to belong to Christ, who was raised to life so that we could serve God. [5] When we thought only of ourselves, the Law made us have sinful desires. It made every part of our bodies into slaves who are doomed to die. [6] But the Law no longer rules over us. We are like dead people, and it cannot have any power over us. Now we can serve God in a new way by obeying his Spirit, and not in the old way by obeying the written Law.

The Battle with Sin

[7] Does this mean that the Law is sinful? Certainly not! But if it had not been for the Law, I would not have known what sin is really like. For example, I would not have known what it means to want something that belongs to someone else, unless the Law had told me not to do that. [8] It was sin that used this command as a way of making me have all kinds of desires. But without the Law, sin is dead.

[9] Before I knew about the Law, I was alive. But as soon as I heard that command, sin came to life, [10] and I died. The very command that was supposed to bring life to me, instead brought death. [11] Sin used this command to trick me, and because of it I died. [12] Still, the Law and its commands are holy and correct and good.

[13] Am I saying that something good caused my death? Certainly not! It was sin that killed me by using something good. Now we can see how terrible and evil sin really is. [14] We know that the Law is spiritual. But I am merely a human, and I have been sold as a slave to sin. [15] In fact, I don't understand why I act the way I do. I don't do what I know is right. I do the things I hate. [16] Although I don't do what I know is right, I agree that the Law is good. [17] So I am not the one doing these evil things. The sin that lives in me is what does them.

[18] I know that my selfish desires won't let me do anything that is good. Even when I want to do right, I cannot. [19] Instead of doing what I know is right, I do wrong. [20] And so, if I don't do what I know is right, I am no longer the one doing these evil things. The sin that lives in me is what does them.

[21] The Law has shown me that something in me keeps me from doing what I know is right. [22] With my whole heart

I agree with the Law of God. ²³ But in every part of me I discover something fighting against my mind, and it makes me a prisoner of sin that controls everything I do. ²⁴ What a miserable person I am. Who will rescue me from this body that is doomed to die? ²⁵ Thank God! Jesus Christ will rescue me.

So with my mind I serve the Law of God, although my selfish desires make me serve the law of sin.

Living by the Power of God's Spirit

8 If you belong to Christ Jesus, you won't be punished. ² The Holy Spirit will give you life that comes from Christ Jesus and will set you*ʲ* free from sin and death. ³ The Law of Moses cannot do this, because our selfish desires make the Law weak. But God set you free when he sent his own Son to be like us sinners and to be a sacrifice for our sin. God used Christ's body to condemn sin. ⁴ He did this, so that we would do what the Law commands by obeying the Spirit instead of our own desires.

⁵ People who are ruled by their desires think only of themselves. Everyone who is ruled by the Holy Spirit thinks about spiritual things. ⁶ If our minds are ruled by our desires, we will die. But if our minds are ruled by the Spirit, we will have life and peace. ⁷ Our desires fight against God, because they do not and cannot obey God's laws. ⁸ If we follow our desires, we cannot please God.

⁹ You are no longer ruled by your desires, but by God's Spirit, who lives in you. People who don't have the Spirit of Christ in them don't belong to him. ¹⁰ But Christ lives in you. So you are alive because God has accepted you, even though your bodies must die because of your sins. ¹¹ Yet God raised Jesus to life! God's Spirit now lives in you, and he will raise you to life by his Spirit.

¹² My dear friends, we must not live to satisfy our desires. ¹³ If you do, you will die. But you will live, if by the help of God's Spirit you say "No" to your desires. ¹⁴ Only those people who are led by God's Spirit are his children. ¹⁵ God's Spirit doesn't make us slaves who are afraid of him. Instead, we become his children and call him our Father.ᵏ ¹⁶ God's Spirit makes us sure that we are his children. ¹⁷ His Spirit lets us know that together with Christ we will be given what God has promised. We will also share in the glory of Christ, because we have suffered with him.

A Wonderful Future for God's People

¹⁸ I am sure that what we are suffering now cannot compare with the glory that will be shown to us. ¹⁹ In fact, all creation is eagerly waiting for God to show who his children are. ²⁰ Meanwhile, creation is confused, but not because it wants to be confused. God made it this way in the hope ²¹ that creation would be set free from decay and would share in the glorious freedom of his children. ²² We know that all creation is still groaning and is in pain, like a woman about to give birth.

²³ The Spirit makes us sure about what we will be in the future. But now we groan silently, while we wait for God to show that we are his children.ˡ This means that our bodies will also be set free. ²⁴ And this hope is what saves us. But if we already have what we hope for, there is no need to keep on hoping. ²⁵ However, we hope for something we have not yet seen, and we patiently wait for it.

²⁶ In certain ways we are weak, but the Spirit is here to help us. For example, when we don't know what to pray for, the Spirit prays for us in ways that cannot be put into words. ²⁷ All of our thoughts are known to God. He can understand what is in the mind of the Spirit, as the Spirit prays for God's people. ²⁸ We know that God is always at work for the good of everyone who loves him.ᵐ They are the ones God has chosen for his purpose, ²⁹ and he has always known who his chosen ones would be. He had decided to let them become like his own Son, so that his Son would be the first of many children. ³⁰ God then accepted the people he had already decided to choose, and he has shared his glory with them.

God's Love

³¹ What can we say about all this? If God is on our side, can anyone be against us? ³² God did not keep back his own Son, but he gave him for us. If God did this, won't he freely give us everything else? ³³ If God says his chosen ones are acceptable to him, can anyone bring charges against them? ³⁴ Or can anyone condemn them? No indeed! Christ died and was raised to life, and now he is at God's right side, speaking to him for us. ³⁵ Can anything separate us from the love of Christ? Can trouble, suffering, and hard times, or hunger and nakedness, or danger and death? ³⁶ It is exactly as the Scriptures say,

> "For you we face death
> all day long.
> We are like sheep
> on their way
> to be butchered."

³⁷ In everything we have won more than a victory because of Christ who loves us. ³⁸ I am sure that nothing can separate us from God's love—not life or death, not angels or spirits, not the present or the future, ³⁹ and not powers above or powers below. Nothing in all creation can separate us from God's love for us in Christ Jesus our Lord!

God's Choice of Israel

9 I am a follower of Christ, and the Holy Spirit is a witness to my conscience. So I tell the truth and I am not lying when I say ² my heart is broken and I am in great sorrow. ³ I would gladly be placed under God's curse and be separated from Christ for the good of my own people. ⁴ They are the descendants of Israel, and they are also God's chosen people. God showed them his glory. He made agreements with them and gave them his Law. The temple is theirs and so are the promises that God made to them. ⁵ They have those famous ancestors, who were also the an-

---

ʲ **8.2** *you*: Some manuscripts have "me."   ᵏ **8.15** *our Father*: The Greek text uses the Aramaic word "Abba" (meaning "father"), which shows the close relation between the children and their father.   ˡ **8.23** *to show that we are his children*: These words are not in some manuscripts. The translation of the remainder of the verse would then read, "while we wait for God to set our bodies free."

ᵐ **8.28** *God is always at work for the good of everyone who loves him*: Or "All things work for the good of everyone who loves God" or "God's Spirit always works for the good of everyone who loves God."

cestors of Jesus Christ. I pray that God, who rules over all, will be praised forever![n] Amen.

6 It cannot be said that God broke his promise. After all, not all of the people of Israel are the true people of God. [7-8] In fact, when God made the promise to Abraham, he meant only Abraham's descendants by his son Isaac. God was talking only about Isaac when he promised **9** Sarah, "At this time next year I will return, and you will already have a son."

10 Don't forget what happened to the twin sons of Isaac and Rebekah. [11-12] Even before they were born or had done anything good or bad, the Lord told Rebekah that her older son would serve the younger one. The Lord said this to show that he makes his own choices and that it wasn't because of anything either of them had done. [13] That's why the Scriptures say that the Lord liked Jacob more than Esau.

14 Are we saying that God is unfair? Certainly not! [15] The Lord told Moses that he has pity and mercy on anyone he wants to. [16] Everything then depends on God's mercy and not on what people want or do. [17] In the Scriptures the Lord says to Pharaoh of Egypt, "I let you become king, so that I could show you my power and be praised by all people on earth." [18] Everything depends on what God decides to do, and he can either have pity on people or make them stubborn.

God's Anger and Mercy

19 Someone may ask, "How can God blame us, if he makes us behave in the way he wants us to?" **20** But, my friend, I ask, "Who do you think you are to question God? Does the clay have the right to ask the potter why he shaped it the way he did? [21] Doesn't a potter have the right to make a fancy bowl and a plain bowl out of the same lump of clay?"

22 God wanted to show his anger and reveal his power against everyone who deserved to be destroyed. But instead, he patiently put up with them. [23] He did this by showing how glorious he is when he has pity on the people he has chosen to share in his glory. [24] Whether Jews or Gentiles, we are those chosen ones, [25] just as the Lord says in the book of Hosea,

> "Although they are not
> my people,
>   I will make them my people.
> I will treat with love
> those nations
>   that have never been loved.

26 "Once they were told,
>   'You are not my people.'
> But in that very place
> they will be called
>   children of the living God."

27 And this is what the prophet Isaiah said about the people of Israel,

> "The people of Israel
> are as many

as the grains of sand
>   along the beach.
> But only a few who are left
>   will be saved.
28 The Lord will be quick
>   and sure to do on earth
> what he has warned
>   he will do."

29 Isaiah also said,

> "If the Lord All-Powerful
> had not spared some
>   of our descendants,
> we would have been destroyed
> like the cities of Sodom
>   and Gomorrah."

Israel and the Good News

30 What does all of this mean? It means that the Gentiles were not trying to be acceptable to God, but they found that he would accept them if they had faith. [31-32] It also means that the people of Israel were not acceptable to God. And why not? It was because they were trying[o] to be acceptable by obeying the Law instead of by having faith in God. The people of Israel fell over the stone that makes people stumble, [33] just as God says in the Scriptures,

> "Look! I am placing in Zion
> a stone to make people
>   stumble and fall.
> But those who have faith
> in that one will never
>   be disappointed."

10 Dear friends, my greatest wish and my prayer to God is for the people of Israel to be saved. **2** I know they love God, but they don't understand **3** what makes people acceptable to him. So they refuse to trust God, and they try to be acceptable by obeying the Law. **4** But Christ makes the Law no longer necessary[p] for those who become acceptable to God by faith.

Anyone Can Be Saved

5 Moses said that a person could become acceptable to God by obeying the Law. He did this when he wrote, "If you want to live, you must do all that the Law commands."

6 But people whose faith makes them acceptable to God will never ask, "Who will go up to heaven to bring Christ down?" **7** Neither will they ask, "Who will go down into the world of the dead to raise him to life?"

8 All who are acceptable because of their faith simply say, "The message is as near as your mouth or your heart." And this is the same message we preach about faith. **9** So you will be saved, if you honestly say, "Jesus is Lord," and if you believe with all your heart that God raised him from death. **10** God will accept you and save you, if you truly believe this and tell it to others.

---

[n] **9.5** *Christ. I pray that God, who rules over all, will be praised forever*: Or "Christ, who rules over all. I pray that God will be praised forever" or "Christ. And I pray that Christ, who is God and rules over all, will be praised forever."   [o] **9.31, 32** *because they were trying*: Or "while they were trying" or "even though they were trying."   [p] **10.4** *But Christ makes the Law no longer necessary*: Or "But Christ gives the full meaning to the Law."

[11] The Scriptures say that no one who has faith will be disappointed, [12] no matter if that person is a Jew or a Gentile. There is only one Lord, and he is generous to everyone who asks for his help. [13] All who call out to the Lord will be saved.

[14] How can people have faith in the Lord and ask him to save them, if they have never heard about him? And how can they hear, unless someone tells them? [15] And how can anyone tell them without being sent by the Lord? The Scriptures say it is a beautiful sight to see even the feet of someone coming to preach the good news. [16] Yet not everyone has believed the message. For example, the prophet Isaiah asked, "Lord, has anyone believed what we said?"

[17] No one can have faith without hearing the message about Christ. [18] But am I saying that the people of Israel did not hear? No, I am not! The Scriptures say,

> "The message was told
>   everywhere on earth.
> It was announced
>   all over the world."

[19] Did the people of Israel understand or not? Moses answered this question when he told that the Lord had said,

> "I will make Israel jealous
>   of people
> who are a nation
>   of nobodies.
> I will make them angry
>   at people
> who don't understand
>   a thing."

[20] Isaiah was fearless enough to tell that the Lord had said,

> "I was found by people
> who were not looking
>   for me.
> I appeared to the ones
> who were not asking
>   about me."

[21] And Isaiah said about the people of Israel,

> "All day long the Lord
>   has reached out
> to people who are stubborn
>   and refuse to obey."

God Has Not Rejected His People

11 Am I saying that God has turned his back on his people? Certainly not! I am one of the people of Israel, and I myself am a descendant of Abraham from the tribe of Benjamin. [2] God did not turn his back on his chosen people. Don't you remember reading in the Scriptures how Elijah complained to God about the people of Israel? [3] He said, "Lord, they killed your prophets and destroyed your altars. I am the only one left, and now they want to kill me." [4] But the Lord told Elijah, "I still have seven thousand followers who have not worshiped Baal." [5] It is the same

way now. God was kind to the people of Israel, and so a few of them are still his followers. [6] This happened because of God's undeserved kindness and not because of anything they have done. It could not have happened except for God's kindness.

[7] This means that only a chosen few of the people of Israel found what all of them were searching for. And the rest of them were stubborn, [8] just as the Scriptures say,

> "God made them so stupid
>   that their eyes are blind,
> and their ears
>   are still deaf."

[9] Then David said,

> "Turn their meals
>   into bait for a trap,
> so that they will stumble
> and be given
>   what they deserve.
> [10] Blindfold their eyes!
>   Don't let them see.
> Bend their backs
> beneath a burden
>   that will never be lifted."

Gentiles Will Be Saved

[11] Do I mean that the people of Israel fell, never to get up again? Certainly not! Their failure made it possible for the Gentiles to be saved, and this will make the people of Israel jealous. [12] But if the rest of the world's people were helped so much by Israel's sin and loss, they will be helped even more by their full return.

[13] I am now speaking to you Gentiles, and as long as I am an apostle to you, I will take pride in my work. [14] I hope in this way to make some of my own people jealous enough to be saved. [15] When Israel rejected God,[q] the rest of the people in the world were able to turn to him. So when God makes friends with Israel, it will be like bringing the dead back to life. [16] If part of a batch of dough is made holy by being offered to God, then all of the dough is holy. If the roots of a tree are holy, the rest of the tree is holy too.

[17] You Gentiles are like branches of a wild olive tree that were made to be part of a cultivated olive tree. You have taken the place of some branches that were cut away from it. And because of this, you enjoy the blessings that come from being part of that cultivated tree. [18] But don't think you are better than the branches that were cut away. Just remember that you are not supporting the roots of that tree. Its roots are supporting you.

[19] Maybe you think those branches were cut away, so that you could be put in their place. [20] That's true enough. But they were cut away because they did not have faith, and you are where you are because you do have faith. So don't be proud, but be afraid. [21] If God cut away those natural branches, couldn't he do the same to you?

[22] Now you see both how kind and how hard God can be. He was hard on those who fell, but he was kind to you. And he will keep on being kind to you, if you keep on trusting in his kindness. Otherwise, you will be cut away too.

---

[q] **11.15** *When Israel rejected God*: Or "When Israel was rejected."

23 If those other branches will start having faith, they will be made a part of that tree again. God has the power to put them back. **24** After all, it wasn't natural for branches to be cut from a wild olive tree and to be made part of a cultivated olive tree. So it is much more likely that God will join the natural branches back to the cultivated olive tree.

The People of Israel Will Be Brought Back

25 My friends, I don't want you Gentiles to be too proud of yourselves. So I will explain the mystery of what has happened to the people of Israel. Some of them have become stubborn, and they will stay like that until the complete number of you Gentiles has come in. **26** In this way all of Israel will be saved, as the Scriptures say,

> "From Zion someone will come
>   to rescue us.
> Then Jacob's descendants
>   will stop being evil.
> **27** This is what the Lord
>   has promised to do
> when he forgives their sins."

28 The people of Israel are treated as God's enemies, so that the good news can come to you Gentiles. But they are still the chosen ones, and God loves them because of their famous ancestors. **29** God doesn't take back the gifts he has given or forget about the people he has chosen.

30 At one time you Gentiles rejected God. But now Israel has rejected God, and you have been shown mercy. **31** And because of the mercy shown to you, they will also be shown mercy. **32** All people have disobeyed God, and that's why he treats them as prisoners. But he does this, so that he can have mercy on all of them.

33 Who can measure the wealth and wisdom and knowledge of God? Who can understand his decisions or explain what he does?

> **34** "Has anyone known
>   the thoughts of the Lord
>   or given him advice?
> **35** Has anyone loaned
>   something to the Lord
>   that must be repaid?"

36 Everything comes from the Lord. All things were made because of him and will return to him. Praise the Lord forever! Amen.

Christ Brings New Life

12 Dear friends, God is good. So I beg you to offer your bodies to him as a living sacrifice, pure and pleasing. That's the most sensible way to serve God. **2** Don't be like the people of this world, but let God change the way you think. Then you will know how to do everything that is good and pleasing to him.

3 I realize how kind God has been to me, and so I tell each of you not to think you are better than you really are. Use good sense and measure yourself by the amount of faith that God has given you. **4** A body is made up of many parts, and each of them has its own use. **5** That's how it is

with us. There are many of us, but we each are part of the body of Christ, as well as part of one another.

6 God has also given each of us different gifts to use. If we can prophesy, we should do it according to the amount of faith we have. **7** If we can serve others, we should serve. If we can teach, we should teach. **8** If we can encourage others, we should encourage them. If we can give, we should be generous. If we are leaders, we should do our best. If we are good to others, we should do it cheerfully.

Rules for Christian Living

9 Be sincere in your love for others. Hate everything that is evil and hold tight to everything that is good. **10** Love each other as brothers and sisters and honor others more than you do yourself. **11** Never give up. Eagerly follow the Holy Spirit and serve the Lord. **12** Let your hope make you glad. Be patient in time of trouble and never stop praying. **13** Take care of God's needy people and welcome strangers into your home.

14 Ask God to bless everyone who mistreats you. Ask him to bless them and not to curse them. **15** When others are happy, be happy with them, and when they are sad, be sad. **16** Be friendly with everyone. Don't be proud and feel that you are smarter than others. Make friends with ordinary people.[r] **17** Don't mistreat someone who has mistreated you. But try to earn the respect of others, **18** and do your best to live at peace with everyone.

19 Dear friends, don't try to get even. Let God take revenge. In the Scriptures the Lord says,

> "I am the one to take revenge
>   and pay them back."

20 The Scriptures also say,

> "If your enemies are hungry,
>   give them something to eat.
> And if they are thirsty,
> give them something
>   to drink.
> This will be the same
> as piling burning coals
>   on their heads."

21 Don't let evil defeat you, but defeat evil with good.

Obey Rulers

13 Obey the rulers who have authority over you. Only God can give authority to anyone, and he puts these rulers in their places of power. **2** People who oppose the authorities are opposing what God has done, and they will be punished. **3** Rulers are a threat to evil people, not to good people. There is no need to be afraid of the authorities. Just do right, and they will praise you for it. **4** After all, they are God's servants, and it is their duty to help you.

If you do something wrong, you ought to be afraid, because these rulers have the right to punish you. They are God's servants who punish criminals to show how angry God is. **5** But you should obey the rulers because you know it is the right thing to do, and not just because of God's anger.

---

r **12.16** *Make friends with ordinary people*: Or "Do ordinary jobs."

6 You must also pay your taxes. The authorities are God's servants, and it is their duty to take care of these matters. **7** Pay all that you owe, whether it is taxes and fees or respect and honor.

Love

8 Let love be your only debt! If you love others, you have done all that the Law demands. **9** In the Law there are many commands, such as, "Be faithful in marriage. Do not murder. Do not steal. Do not want what belongs to others." But all of these are summed up in the command that says, "Love others as much as you love yourself." **10** No one who loves others will harm them. So love is all that the Law demands.

The Day When Christ Returns

11 You know what sort of times we live in, and so you should live properly. It is time to wake up. You know that the day when we will be saved is nearer now than when we first put our faith in the Lord. **12** Night is almost over, and day will soon appear. We must stop behaving as people do in the dark and be ready to live in the light. **13** So behave properly, as people do in the day. Don't go to wild parties or get drunk or be vulgar or indecent. Don't quarrel or be jealous. **14** Let the Lord Jesus Christ be as near to you as the clothes you wear. Then you won't try to satisfy your selfish desires.

Don't Criticize Others

14 Welcome all the Lord's followers, even those whose faith is weak. Don't criticize them for having beliefs that are different from yours. **2** Some think it is all right to eat anything, while those whose faith is weak will eat only vegetables. **3** But you should not criticize others for eating or for not eating. After all, God welcomes everyone. **4** What right do you have to criticize someone else's servants? Only their Lord can decide if they are doing right, and the Lord will make sure that they do right.

5 Some of the Lord's followers think one day is more important than another. Others think all days are the same. But each of you should make up your own mind. **6** Any followers who count one day more important than another day do it to honor their Lord. And any followers who eat meat give thanks to God, just like the ones who don't eat meat.

7 Whether we live or die, it must be for God, rather than for ourselves. **8** Whether we live or die, it must be for the Lord. Alive or dead, we still belong to the Lord. **9** This is because Christ died and rose to life, so that he would be the Lord of the dead and of the living. **10** Why do you criticize other followers of the Lord? Why do you look down on them? The day is coming when God will judge all of us. **11** In the Scriptures God says,

"I swear by my very life
　　that everyone will kneel down
　　　　and praise my name!"

12 And so, each of us must give an account to God for what we do.

Don't Cause Problems for Others

13 We must stop judging others. We must also make up our minds not to upset anyone's faith. **14** The Lord Jesus has made it clear to me that God considers all foods fit to eat. But if you think some foods are unfit to eat, then for you they are not fit.

15 If you are hurting others by the foods you eat, you are not guided by love. Don't let your appetite destroy someone Christ died for. **16** Don't let your right to eat bring shame to Christ. **17** God's kingdom isn't about eating and drinking. It is about pleasing God, about living in peace, and about true happiness. All this comes from the Holy Spirit. **18** If you serve Christ in this way, you will please God and be respected by people. **19** We should try^s to live at peace and help each other have a strong faith.

20 Don't let your appetite destroy what God has done. All foods are fit to eat, but it is wrong to cause problems for others by what you eat. **21** It is best not to eat meat or drink wine or do anything else that causes problems for other followers of the Lord. **22** What you believe about these things should be kept between you and God. You are fortunate, if your actions don't make you have doubts. **23** But if you do have doubts about what you eat, you are going against your beliefs. And you know that is wrong, because anything you do against your beliefs is sin.

Please Others and Not Yourself

15 If our faith is strong, we should be patient with the Lord's followers whose faith is weak. We should try to please them instead of ourselves. **2** We should think of their good and try to help them by doing what pleases them. **3** Even Christ did not try to please himself. But as the Scriptures say, "The people who insulted you also insulted me." **4** And the Scriptures were written to teach and encourage us by giving us hope. **5** God is the one who makes us patient and cheerful. I pray that he will help you live at peace with each other, as you follow Christ. **6** Then all of you together will praise God, the Father of our Lord Jesus Christ.

The Good News Is for Jews and Gentiles

7 Honor God by accepting each other, as Christ has accepted you. **8** I tell you that Christ came as a servant of the Jews to show that God has kept the promises he made to their famous ancestors. Christ also came, **9** so that the Gentiles would praise God for being kind to them. It is just as the Scriptures say,

"I will tell the nations
　　about you,
　　and I will sing praises
　　　　to your name."

10 The Scriptures also say to the Gentiles, "Come and celebrate with God's people."
11 Again the Scriptures say,

"Praise the Lord,
　　all you Gentiles.
All you nations, come
　　and worship him."

12 Isaiah says,

"Someone from David's family
　　will come to power.

He will rule the nations,
and they will put their hope
  in him."

13 I pray that God, who gives hope, will bless you with complete happiness and peace because of your faith. And may the power of the Holy Spirit fill you with hope.

Paul's Work as a Missionary

14 My friends, I am sure that you are very good and that you have all the knowledge you need to teach each other. 15 But I have spoken to you plainly and have tried to remind you of some things. God was so kind to me! 16 He chose me to be a servant of Christ Jesus for the Gentiles and to do the work of a priest in the service of his good news. God did this so that the Holy Spirit could make the Gentiles into a holy offering, pleasing to him.

17 Because of Christ Jesus, I can take pride in my service for God. 18 In fact, all I will talk about is how Christ let me speak and work, so that the Gentiles would obey him. 19 Indeed, I will tell how Christ worked miracles and wonders by the power of the Holy Spirit. I have preached the good news about him all the way from Jerusalem to Illyricum. 20 But I have always tried to preach where people have never heard about Christ. I am like a builder who doesn't build on anyone else's foundation. 21 It is just as the Scriptures say,

"All who haven't been told
about him
    will see him,
and those who haven't heard
about him
    will understand."

Paul's Plan To Visit Rome

22 My work has always kept me from coming to see you. 23 Now there is nothing left for me to do in this part of the world, and for years I have wanted to visit you. 24 So I plan to stop off on my way to Spain. Then after a short, but refreshing, visit with you, I hope you will quickly send me on.

25-26 I am now on my way to Jerusalem to deliver the money that the Lord's followers in Macedonia and Achaia collected for God's needy people. 27 This is something they really wanted to do. But sharing their money with the Jews was also like paying back a debt, because the Jews had already shared their spiritual blessings with the Gentiles. 28 After I have safely delivered this money, I will visit you and then go on to Spain. 29 And when I do arrive in Rome, I know it will be with the full blessings of Christ.

30 My friends, by the power of the Lord Jesus Christ and by the love that comes from the Holy Spirit, I beg you to pray sincerely with me and for me. 31 Pray that God will protect me from the unbelievers in Judea, and that his people in Jerusalem will be pleased with what I am doing. 32 Ask God to let me come to you and have a pleasant and refreshing visit. 33 I pray that God, who gives peace, will be with all of you. Amen.

Personal Greetings

16 I have good things to say about Phoebe, who is a leader in the church at Cenchreae. 2 Welcome her in a way that is proper for someone who has faith in the Lord and is one of God's own people. Help her in any way you can. After all, she has proved to be a respected leader for many others, including me.

3 Give my greetings to Priscilla and Aquila. They have not only served Christ Jesus together with me, 4 but they have even risked their lives for me. I am grateful for them and so are all the Gentile churches. 5 Greet the church that meets in their home.

Greet my dear friend Epaenetus, who was the first person in Asia to have faith in Christ.

6 Greet Mary, who has worked so hard for you.

7 Greet my relatives[t] Andronicus and Junias,[u] who were in jail with me. They are highly respected by the apostles and were followers of Christ before I was.

8 Greet Ampliatus, my dear friend whose faith is in the Lord.

9 Greet Urbanus, who serves Christ along with us. Greet my dear friend Stachys.

10 Greet Apelles, a faithful servant of Christ. Greet Aristobulus and his family.

11 Greet Herodion, who is a relative[v] of mine.

Greet Narcissus and the others in his family, who have faith in the Lord.

12 Greet Tryphaena and Tryphosa, who work hard for the Lord.

Greet my dear friend Persis. She also works hard for the Lord.

13 Greet Rufus, that special servant of the Lord, and greet his mother, who has been like a mother to me.

14 Greet Asyncritus, Phlegon, Hermes, Patrobas, and Hermas, as well as our friends who are with them.

15 Greet Philologus, Julia, Nereus and his sister, and Olympas, and all of God's people who are with them.

16 Be sure to give each other a warm greeting.

All of Christ's churches greet you.

17 My friends, I beg you to watch out for anyone who causes trouble and divides the church by refusing to do what all of you were taught. Stay away from them! 18 They want to serve themselves and not Christ the Lord. Their flattery and fancy talk fool people who don't know any better. 19 I am glad that everyone knows how well you obey the Lord. But still, I want you to understand what is good and not have anything to do with evil. 20 Then God, who gives peace, will soon crush Satan under your feet. I pray that our Lord Jesus will be kind to you.

21 Timothy, who works with me, sends his greetings, and so do my relatives,[v] Lucius, Jason, and Sosipater.

22 I, Tertius, also send my greetings. I am a follower of the Lord, and I wrote this letter.

23-24 Gaius welcomes me and the whole church into his home, and he sends his greetings.

Erastus, the city treasurer, and our dear friend Quartus send their greetings too.[w]

---

t 16.7 *relatives*: Or "Jewish friends."   u 16.7 *Junias*: Or "Junia". Some manuscripts have "Julia".   v 16.11,21 *relative(s)*: See the note at verse 7.   w 16.23,24 *send their greetings too*: Some manuscripts add, "I pray that our Lord Jesus Christ will always be kind to you. Amen."

Paul's Closing Prayer

25 Praise God! He can make you strong by means of my good news, which is the message about[x] Jesus Christ. For ages and ages this message was kept secret, **26** but now at last it has been told. The eternal God commanded his prophets to write about the good news, so that all nations would obey and have faith. **27** And now, because of Jesus Christ, we can praise the only wise God forever! Amen.[y]

---

[x]**16.25** *about*: Or "from."   [y]**16.27** *Amen*: Some manuscripts have verses 25-27 after 14.23. Others have the verses here and after 14.23, and one manuscript has them after 15.33.

---

1 CORINTHIANS

1 From Paul, chosen by God to be an apostle of Christ Jesus, and from Sosthenes, who is also a follower. **2** To God's church in Corinth. Christ Jesus chose you to be his very own people, and you worship in his name, as we and all others do who call him Lord.

3 My prayer is that God our Father and the Lord Jesus Christ will be kind to you and will bless you with peace!

4 I never stop thanking my God for being kind enough to give you Christ Jesus, **5** who helps you speak and understand so well. **6** Now you are certain that everything we told you about our Lord Christ Jesus is true. **7** You are not missing out on any blessings, as you wait for him to return. **8** And until the day Christ does return, he will keep you completely innocent. **9** God can be trusted, and he chose you to be partners with his Son, our Lord Jesus Christ.

Taking Sides

10 My dear friends, as a follower of our Lord Jesus Christ, I beg you to get along with each other. Don't take sides. Always try to agree in what you think. **11** Several people from Chloe's family have already reported to me that you keep arguing with each other. **12** They have said that some of you claim to follow me, while others claim to follow Apollos or Peter[a] or Christ.

13 Has Christ been divided up? Was I nailed to a cross for you? Were you baptized in my name? **14** I thank God[b] that I didn't baptize any of you except Crispus and Gaius. **15** Not one of you can say that you were baptized in my name. **16** I did baptize the family of Stephanas, but I don't remember if I baptized anyone else. **17** Christ did not send me to baptize. He sent me to tell the good news without using big words that would make the cross of Christ lose its power.

Christ Is God's Power and Wisdom

18 The message about the cross doesn't make any sense to lost people. But for those of us who are being saved, it is God's power at work. **19** As God says in the Scriptures,

"I will destroy the wisdom
of all who claim
to be wise.

I will confuse those
who think they know
so much."

20 What happened to those wise people? What happened to those experts in the Scriptures? What happened to the ones who think they have all the answers? Didn't God show that the wisdom of this world is foolish? **21** God was wise and decided not to let the people of this world use their wisdom to learn about him.

Instead, God chose to save only those who believe the foolish message we preach. **22** Jews ask for miracles, and Greeks want something that sounds wise. **23** But we preach that Christ was nailed to a cross. Most Jews have problems with this, and most Gentiles think it is foolish. **24** Our message is God's power and wisdom for the Jews and the Greeks that he has chosen. **25** Even when God is foolish, he is wiser than everyone else, and even when God is weak, he is stronger than everyone else.

26 My dear friends, remember what you were when God chose you. The people of this world didn't think that many of you were wise. Only a few of you were in places of power, and not many of you came from important families. **27** But God chose the foolish things of this world to put the wise to shame. He chose the weak things of this world to put the powerful to shame. **28** What the world thinks is worthless, useless, and nothing at all is what God has used to destroy what the world considers important. **29** God did all this to keep anyone from bragging to him. **30** You are God's children. He sent Christ Jesus to save us and to make us wise; acceptable, and holy. **31** So if you want to brag, do what the Scriptures say and brag about the Lord.

Telling about Christ and the Cross

2 Friends, when I came and told you the mystery[c] that God had shared with us, I didn't use big words or try to sound wise. **2** In fact, while I was with you, I made up my mind to speak only about Jesus Christ, who had been nailed to a cross.

3 At first, I was weak and trembling with fear. **4** When I talked with you or preached, I didn't try to prove anything

---

[a]**1.12** *Peter*: The Greek text has "Cephas," which is an Aramaic name meaning "rock." Peter is the Greek name with the same meaning.   [b]**1.14** *I thank God*: Some manuscripts have "I thank my God."   [c]**2.1** *mystery*: Some manuscripts have "testimony."

by sounding wise. I simply let God's Spirit show his power. [5] That way you would have faith because of God's power and not because of human wisdom.

[6] We do use wisdom when speaking to people who are mature in their faith. But it isn't the wisdom of this world or of its rulers, who will soon disappear. [7] We speak of God's hidden and mysterious wisdom that God decided to use for our glory long before the world began. [8] The rulers of this world didn't know anything about this wisdom. If they had known about it, they would not have nailed the glorious Lord to a cross. [9] But it is just as the Scriptures say,

"What God has planned
    for people who love him
is more than eyes have seen
    or ears have heard.
It has never even
    entered our minds!"

[10] God's Spirit has shown you everything. His Spirit finds out everything, even what is deep in the mind of God. [11] You are the only one who knows what is in your own mind, and God's Spirit is the only one who knows what is in God's mind. [12] But God has given us his Spirit. That's why we don't think the same way that the people of this world think. That's also why we can recognize the blessings that God has given us.

[13] Every word we speak was taught to us by God's Spirit, not by human wisdom. And this same Spirit helps us teach spiritual things to spiritual people.[d] [14] That's why only someone who has God's Spirit can understand spiritual blessings. Anyone who doesn't have God's Spirit thinks these blessings are foolish. [15] People who are guided by the Spirit can make all kinds of judgments, but they cannot be judged by others. [16] The Scriptures ask,

"Has anyone ever known
    the thoughts of the Lord
    or given him advice?"

But we understand what Christ is thinking.[e]

Working Together for God

3 My friends, you are acting like the people of this world. That's why I could not speak to you as spiritual people. You are like babies as far as your faith in Christ is concerned. [2] So I had to treat you like babies and feed you milk. You could not take solid food, and you still cannot, [3] because you are not yet spiritual. You are jealous and argue with each other. This proves that you are not spiritual and that you are acting like the people of this world.

[4] Some of you say that you follow me, and others claim to follow Apollos. Isn't that how ordinary people behave? [5] Apollos and I are merely servants who helped you to have faith. It was the Lord who made it all happen. [6] I planted the seeds, Apollos watered them, but God made them sprout and grow. [7] What matters isn't those who planted or watered, but God who made the plants grow. [8] The one who plants is just as important as the one who waters. And each one will be paid for what they do. [9] Apollos and I

work together for God, and you are God's garden and God's building.

Only One Foundation

[10] God was kind and let me become an expert builder. I laid a foundation on which others have built. But we must each be careful how we build, [11] because Christ is the only foundation. [12-13] Whatever we build on that foundation will be tested by fire on the day of judgment. Then everyone will find out if we have used gold, silver, and precious stones, or wood, hay, and straw. [14] We will be rewarded if our building is left standing. [15] But if it is destroyed by the fire, we will lose everything. Yet we ourselves will be saved, like someone escaping from flames.

[16] All of you surely know that you are God's temple and that his Spirit lives in you. [17] Together you are God's holy temple, and God will destroy anyone who destroys his temple.

[18] Don't fool yourselves! If any of you think you are wise in the things of this world, you will have to become foolish before you can be truly wise. [19] This is because God considers the wisdom of this world to be foolish. It is just as the Scriptures say, "God catches the wise when they try to outsmart him." [20] The Scriptures also say, "The Lord knows that the plans made by wise people are useless." [21-22] So stop bragging about what anyone has done. Paul and Apollos and Peter[f] all belong to you. In fact, everything is yours, including the world, life, death, the present, and the future. Everything belongs to you, [23] and you belong to Christ, and Christ belongs to God.

The Work of the Apostles

4 Think of us as servants of Christ who have been given the work of explaining God's mysterious ways. [2] And since our first duty is to be faithful to the one we work for, [3] it doesn't matter to me if I am judged by you or even by a court of law. In fact, I don't judge myself. [4] I don't know of anything against me, but that doesn't prove that I am right. The Lord is my judge. [5] So don't judge anyone until the Lord returns. He will show what is hidden in the dark and what is in everyone's heart. Then God will be the one who praises each of us.

[6] Friends, I have used Apollos and myself as examples to teach you the meaning of the saying, "Follow the rules." I want you to stop saying that one of us is better than the other. [7] What is so special about you? What do you have that you were not given? And if it was given to you, how can you brag? [8] Are you already satisfied? Are you now rich? Have you become kings while we are still nobodies? I wish you were kings. Then we could have a share in your kingdom.

[9] It seems to me that God has put us apostles in the worst possible place. We are like prisoners on their way to death. Angels and the people of this world just laugh at us. [10] Because of Christ we are thought of as fools, but Christ has made you wise. We are weak and hated, but you are powerful and respected. [11] Even today we go hungry and thirsty and don't have anything to wear except rags. We are mistreated and don't have a place to live. [12] We work hard with our own hands, and when people abuse us, we wish

---

[d] **2.13** *teach spiritual things to spiritual people*: Or "compare spiritual things with spiritual things."   [e] **2.16** *we understand what Christ is thinking*: Or "we think as Christ does."   [f] **3.21,22** *Peter*: See the note at 1.12.

them well. When we suffer, we are patient. [13] When someone curses us, we answer with kind words. Until now we are thought of as nothing more than the trash and garbage of this world.

[14] I am not writing to embarrass you. I want to help you, just as parents help their own dear children. [15] Ten thousand people may teach you about Christ, but I am your only father. You became my children when I told you about Christ Jesus, [16] and I want you to be like me. [17] That's why I sent Timothy to you. I love him like a son, and he is a faithful servant of the Lord. Timothy will tell you what I do to follow Christ and how it agrees with what I always teach about Christ in every church.

[18] Some of you think I am not coming for a visit, and so you are bragging. [19] But if the Lord lets me come, I will soon be there. Then I will find out if the ones who are doing all this bragging really have any power. [20] God's kingdom isn't just a lot of words. It is power. [21] What do you want me to do when I arrive? Do you want me to be hard on you or to be kind and gentle?

Immoral Followers

5 I have heard terrible things about some of you. In fact, you are behaving worse than the Gentiles. A man is even sleeping with his own stepmother.[g] [2] You are proud, when you ought to feel bad enough to chase away anyone who acts like that.

[3-4] I am with you only in my thoughts. But in the name of our Lord Jesus I have already judged this man, as though I were with you in person. So when you meet together and the power of the Lord Jesus is with you, I will be there too. [5] You must then hand that man over to Satan. His body will be destroyed, but his spirit will be saved when the Lord Jesus returns.

[6] Stop being proud! Don't you know how a little yeast can spread through the whole batch of dough? [7] Get rid of the old yeast! Then you will be like fresh bread made without yeast, and that is what you are. Our Passover lamb is Christ, who has already been sacrificed. [8] So don't celebrate the festival by being evil and sinful, which is like serving bread made with yeast. Be pure and truthful and celebrate by using bread made without yeast.

[9] In my other letter I told you not to have anything to do with immoral people. [10] But I wasn't talking about the people of this world. You would have to leave this world to get away from everyone who is immoral or greedy or who cheats or worships idols. [11] I was talking about your own people who are immoral or greedy or worship idols or curse others or get drunk or cheat. Don't even eat with them! [12] Why should I judge outsiders? Aren't we supposed to judge only church members? [13] God judges everyone else. The Scriptures say, "Chase away any of your own people who are evil."

Taking Each Other to Court

6 When one of you has a complaint against another, do you take your complaint to a court of sinners? Or do you take it to God's people? [2] Don't you know that God's people will judge the world? And if you are going to judge the world, can't you settle small problems? [3] Don't you

know that we will judge angels? And if that is so, we can surely judge everyday matters. [4] Why do you take everyday complaints to judges who are not respected by the church? [5] I say this to your shame. Aren't any of you wise enough to act as a judge between one follower and another? [6] Why should one of you take another to be tried by unbelievers?

[7] When one of you takes another to court, all of you lose. It would be better to let yourselves be cheated and robbed. [8] But instead, you cheat and rob other followers.

[9] Don't you know that evil people won't have a share in the blessings of God's kingdom? Don't fool yourselves! No one who is immoral or worships idols or is unfaithful in marriage or is a pervert or behaves like a homosexual [10] will share in God's kingdom. Neither will any thief or greedy person or drunkard or anyone who curses and cheats others. [11] Some of you used to be like that. But now the name of our Lord Jesus Christ and the power of God's Spirit have washed you and made you holy and acceptable to God.

Honor God with Your Body

[12] Some of you say, "We can do anything we want to." But I tell you that not everything is good for us. So I refuse to let anything have power over me. [13] You also say, "Food is meant for our bodies, and our bodies are meant for food." But I tell you that God will destroy them both. We are not supposed to do indecent things with our bodies. We are to use them for the Lord who is in charge of our bodies. [14] God will raise us from death by the same power that he used when he raised our Lord to life.

[15] Don't you know that your bodies are part of the body of Christ? Is it right for me to join part of the body of Christ to a prostitute? No, it isn't! [16] Don't you know that a man who does that becomes part of her body? The Scriptures say, "The two of them will be one person." [17] But anyone who is joined to the Lord is one in spirit with him.

[18] Don't be immoral in matters of sex. That is a sin against your own body in a way that no other sin is. [19] You surely know that your body is a temple where the Holy Spirit lives. The Spirit is in you and is a gift from God. You are no longer your own. [20] God paid a great price for you. So use your body to honor God.

Questions about Marriage

7 Now I will answer the questions that you asked in your letter. You asked, "Is it best for people not to marry?"[h] [2] Well, having your own husband or wife should keep you from doing something immoral. [3] Husbands and wives should be fair with each other about having sex. [4] A wife belongs to her husband instead of to herself, and a husband belongs to his wife instead of to himself. [5] So don't refuse sex to each other, unless you agree not to have sex for a little while, in order to spend time in prayer. Then Satan won't be able to tempt you because of your lack of self-control. [6] In my opinion that is what should be done, though I don't know of anything the Lord said about this matter. [7] I wish that all of you were like me, but God has given different gifts to each of us.

[8] Here is my advice for people who have never been married and for widows. You should stay single, just as I am. [9] But if you don't have enough self-control, then go

---

[g] 5.1 *is even sleeping with his own stepmother*: Or "has even married his own stepmother."   [h] 7.1 *people not to marry*: Or "married couples not to have sex."

ahead and get married. After all, it is better to marry than to burn with desire.*i*

10 I instruct married couples to stay together, and this is exactly what the Lord himself taught. A wife who leaves her husband 11 should either stay single or go back to her husband. And a husband should not leave his wife.

12 I don't know of anything else the Lord said about marriage. All I can do is to give you my own advice. If your wife isn't a follower of the Lord, but is willing to stay with you, don't divorce her. 13 If your husband isn't a follower, but is willing to stay with you, don't divorce him. 14 Your husband or wife who isn't a follower is made holy by having you as a mate. This also makes your children holy and keeps them from being unclean in God's sight.

15 If your husband or wife isn't a follower of the Lord and decides to divorce you, then you should agree to it. You are no longer bound to that person. After all, God chose you and wants you to live at peace. 16 And besides, how do you know if you will be able to save your husband or wife who isn't a follower?

Obeying the Lord at All Times

17 In every church I tell the people to stay as they were when the Lord Jesus chose them and God called them to be his own. Now I say the same thing to you. 18 If you are already circumcised, don't try to change it. If you are not circumcised, don't get circumcised. 19 Being circumcised or uncircumcised isn't really what matters. The important thing is to obey God's commands. 20 So don't try to change what you were when God chose you. 21 Are you a slave? Don't let that bother you. But if you can win your freedom, you should. 22 When the Lord chooses slaves, they become his free people. And when he chooses free people, they become slaves of Christ. 23 God paid a great price for you. So don't become slaves of anyone else. 24 Stay what you were when God chose you.

Unmarried People

25 I don't know of anything that the Lord said about people who have never been married.*j* But I will tell you what I think. And you can trust me, because the Lord has treated me with kindness. 26 We are now going through hard times, and I think it is best for you to stay as you are. 27 If you are married, stay married. If you are not married, don't try to get married. 28 It isn't wrong to marry, even if you have never been married before. But those who marry will have a lot of trouble, and I want to protect you from that.

29 My friends, what I mean is that the Lord will soon come,*k* and it won't matter if you are married or not. 30 It will be all the same if you are crying or laughing, or if you are buying or are completely broke. 31 It won't make any difference how much good you are getting from this world or how much you like it. This world as we know it is now passing away.

32 I want all of you to be free from worry. An unmarried man worries about how to please the Lord. 33 But a married man has more worries. He must worry about the things of this world, because he wants to please his wife. 34 So he is pulled in two directions. Unmarried women and women who have never been married*l* worry only about pleasing the Lord, and they keep their bodies and minds pure. But a married woman worries about the things of this world, because she wants to please her husband. 35 What I am saying is for your own good—it isn't to limit your freedom. I want to help you to live right and to love the Lord above all else.

36 But suppose you are engaged to someone old enough to be married, and you want her so much that all you can think about is getting married. Then go ahead and marry.*m* There is nothing wrong with that. 37 But it is better to have self-control and to make up your mind not to marry. 38 It is perfectly all right to marry, but it is better not to get married at all.

39 A wife should stay married to her husband until he dies. Then she is free to marry again, but only to a man who is a follower of the Lord. 40 However, I think I am obeying God's Spirit when I say she would be happier to stay single.

Food Offered to Idols

8 In your letter you asked me about food offered to idols. All of us know something about this subject. But knowledge makes us proud of ourselves, while love makes us helpful to others. 2 In fact, people who think they know so much don't know anything at all. 3 But God has no doubts about who loves him.

4 Even though food is offered to idols, we know that none of the idols in this world are alive. After all, there is only one God. 5 Many things in heaven and on earth are called gods and lords, but none of them really are gods or lords. 6 We have only one God, and he is the Father. He created everything, and we live for him. Jesus Christ is our only Lord. Everything was made by him, and by him life was given to us.

7 Not everyone knows these things. In fact, many people have grown up with the belief that idols have life in them. So when they eat meat offered to idols, they are bothered by a weak conscience. 8 But food doesn't bring us any closer to God. We are no worse off if we don't eat, and we are no better off if we do.

9 Don't cause problems for someone with a weak conscience, just because you have the right to eat anything. 10 You know all this, and so it doesn't bother you to eat in the temple of an idol. But suppose a person with a weak conscience sees you and decides to eat food that has been offered to idols. 11 Then what you know has destroyed someone Christ died for. 12 When you sin by hurting a follower with a weak conscience, you sin against Christ. 13 So if I hurt one of the Lord's followers by what I eat, I will never eat meat as long as I live.

The Rights of an Apostle

9 I am free. I am an apostle. I have seen the Lord Jesus and have led you to have faith in him. 2 Others may think that I am not an apostle, but you are proof that I am an apostle to you.

---

i **7.9** *with desire*: Or "in the flames of hell."   *j* **7.25** *people who have never been married*: Or "virgins."   *k* **7.29** *the Lord will soon come*: Or "there's not much time left" or "the time for decision comes quickly."   *l* **7.34** *women who have never been married*: Or "virgins."   *m* **7.36** *But suppose you are engaged . . . go ahead and marry*: Verses 36-38 may also be translated: 36"If you feel that you are not treating your grown daughter right by keeping her from getting married, then let her marry. You won't be doing anything wrong. 37But it is better to have self-control and make up your mind not to let your daughter get married. 38It is all right for you to let her marry. But it is better if you don't let her marry at all."

3 When people question me, I tell them 4 that Barnabas and I have the right to our food and drink. 5 We each have the right to marry one of the Lord's followers and to take her along with us, just as the other apostles and the Lord's brothers and Peter[n] do. 6 Are we the only ones who have to support ourselves by working at another job? 7 Do soldiers pay their own salaries? Don't people who raise grapes eat some of what they grow? Don't shepherds get milk from their own goats?

8-9 I am not saying this on my own authority. The Law of Moses tells us not to muzzle an ox when it is grinding grain. But was God concerned only about an ox? 10 No, he wasn't! He was talking about us. This was written in the Scriptures so that all who plow and all who grind the grain will look forward to sharing in the harvest.

11 When we told the message to you, it was like planting spiritual seed. So we have the right to accept material things as our harvest from you. 12 If others have the right to do this, we have an even greater right. But we haven't used this right of ours. We are willing to put up with anything to keep from causing trouble for the message about Christ.

13 Don't you know that people who work in the temple make their living from what is brought to the temple? Don't you know that a person who serves at the altar is given part of what is offered? 14 In the same way, the Lord wants everyone who preaches the good news to make a living from preaching this message.

15 But I have never used these privileges of mine, and I am not writing this because I want to start now. I would rather die than have someone rob me of the right to take pride in this. 16 I don't have any reason to brag about preaching the good news. Preaching is something God told me to do, and if I don't do it, I am doomed. 17 If I preach because I want to, I will be paid. But even if I don't want to, it is still something God has sent me to do. 18 What pay am I given? It is the chance to preach the good news free of charge and not to use the privileges that are mine because I am a preacher.

19 I am not anyone's slave. But I have become a slave to everyone, so that I can win as many people as possible. 20 When I am with the Jews, I live like a Jew to win Jews. They are ruled by the Law of Moses, and I am not. But I live by the Law to win them. 21 And when I am with people who are not ruled by the Law, I forget about the Law to win them. Of course, I never really forget about the law of God. In fact, I am ruled by the law of Christ. 22 When I am with people whose faith is weak, I live as they do to win them. I do everything I can to win everyone I possibly can. 23 I do all this for the good news, because I want to share in its blessings.

A Race and a Fight

24 You know that many runners enter a race, and only one of them wins the prize. So run to win! 25 Athletes work hard to win a crown that cannot last, but we do it for a crown that will last forever. 26 I don't run without a goal. And I don't box by beating my fists in the air. 27 I keep my body under control and make it my slave, so I won't lose out after telling the good news to others.

Don't Worship Idols

10 Friends, I want to remind you that all of our ancestors walked under the cloud and went through the sea. 2 This was like being baptized and becoming followers of Moses. 3 All of them also ate the same spiritual food 4 and drank the same spiritual drink, which flowed from the spiritual rock that followed them. That rock was Christ. 5 But most of them did not please God. So they died, and their bodies were scattered all over the desert.

6 What happened to them is a warning to keep us from wanting to do the same evil things. 7 They worshiped idols, just as the Scriptures say, "The people sat down to eat and drink. Then they got up to dance around." So don't worship idols. 8 Some of those people did shameful things, and in a single day about twenty-three thousand of them died. Don't do shameful things as they did. 9 And don't try to test Christ,[o] as some of them did and were later bitten by poisonous snakes. 10 Don't even grumble, as some of them did and were killed by the destroying angel. 11 These things happened to them as a warning to us. All this was written in the Scriptures to teach us who live in these last days.

12 Even if you think you can stand up to temptation, be careful not to fall. 13 You are tempted in the same way that everyone else is tempted. But God can be trusted not to let you be tempted too much, and he will show you how to escape from your temptations.

14 My friends, you must keep away from idols. 15 I am speaking to you as people who have enough sense to know what I am talking about. 16 When we drink from the cup that we ask God to bless, isn't that sharing in the blood of Christ? When we eat the bread that we break, isn't that sharing in the body of Christ? 17 By sharing in the same loaf of bread, we become one body, even though there are many of us.

18 Aren't the people of Israel sharing in the worship when they gather around the altar and eat the sacrifices offered there? 19 Am I saying that either the idols or the food sacrificed to them is anything at all? 20 No, I am not! That food is really sacrificed to demons and not to God. I don't want you to have anything to do with demons. 21 You cannot drink from the cup of demons and still drink from the Lord's cup. You cannot eat at the table of demons and still eat at the Lord's table. 22 We would make the Lord jealous if we did that. And we are not stronger than the Lord.

Always Honor God

23 Some of you say, "We can do whatever we want to!" But I tell you that not everything may be good or helpful. 24 We should think about others and not about ourselves. 25 However, when you buy meat in the market, go ahead and eat it. Keep your conscience clear by not asking where the meat came from. 26 The Scriptures say, "The earth and everything in it belong to the Lord."

27 If an unbeliever invites you to dinner, and you want to go, then go. Eat whatever you are served. Don't cause a problem for someone's conscience by asking where the food came from. 28-29 But if you are told that it has been sacrificed to idols, don't cause a problem by eating it. I don't mean a problem for yourself, but for the one who told you. Why should my freedom be limited by someone else's conscience? 30 If I give thanks for what I eat, why should anyone accuse me of doing wrong?

31 When you eat or drink or do anything else, always do it to honor God. 32 Don't cause problems for Jews or Greeks or

---

[n] 9.5 *Peter*: See the note at 1.12.   [o] 10.9 *Christ*: Some manuscripts have "the Lord."

anyone else who belongs to God's church. 33 I always try to please others instead of myself, in the hope that many of them will be saved. 11 1 You must follow my example, as I follow the example of Christ.

Rules for Worship

2 I am proud of you, because you always remember me and obey the teachings I gave you. 3 Now I want you to know that Christ is the head over all men, and a man is the head over a woman. But God is the head over Christ. 4 This means that any man who prays or prophesies with something on his head brings shame to his head.

5 But any woman who prays or prophesies without something on her head brings shame to her head. In fact, she may as well shave her head. 6 A woman should wear something on her head. It is a disgrace for a woman to shave her head or cut her hair. But if she refuses to wear something on her head, let her cut off her hair.

7 Men were created to be like God and to bring honor to God. This means that a man should not wear anything on his head. Women were created to bring honor to men. 8 It was the woman who was made from a man, and not the man who was made from a woman. 9 He wasn't created for her. She was created for him. 10 And so, because of this, and also because of the angels, a woman ought to wear something on her head, as a sign of her authority.[p]

11 As far as the Lord is concerned, men and women need each other. 12 It is true that the first woman came from a man, but all other men have been given birth by women. Yet God is the one who created everything. 13 Ask yourselves if it is proper for a woman to pray without something on her head. 14 Isn't it unnatural and disgraceful for men to have long hair? 15 But long hair is a beautiful way for a woman to cover her head. 16 This is how things are done in all of God's churches,[q] and that's why none of you should argue about what I have said.

Rules for the Lord's Supper

17 Your worship services do you more harm than good. I am certainly not going to praise you for this. 18 I am told that you can't get along with each other when you worship, and I am sure that some of what I have heard is true. 19 You are bound to argue with each other, but it is easy to see which of you have God's approval.

20 When you meet together, you don't really celebrate the Lord's Supper. 21 You even start eating before everyone gets to the meeting, and some of you go hungry, while others get drunk. 22 Don't you have homes where you can eat and drink? Do you hate God's church? Do you want to embarrass people who don't have anything? What can I say to you? I certainly cannot praise you.

The Lord's Supper

23 I have already told you what the Lord Jesus did on the night he was betrayed. And it came from the Lord himself.

He took some bread in his hands. 24 Then after he had given thanks, he broke it and said, "This is my body, which is given for you. Eat this and remember me."

25 After the meal, Jesus took a cup of wine in his hands and said, "This is my blood, and with it God makes his new agreement with you. Drink this and remember me."

26 The Lord meant that when you eat this bread and drink from this cup, you tell about his death until he comes.

27 But if you eat the bread and drink the wine in a way that isn't worthy of the Lord, you sin against his body and blood. 28 That's why you must examine the way you eat and drink. 29 If you fail to understand that you are the body of the Lord, you will condemn yourselves by the way you eat and drink. 30 That's why many of you are sick and weak and why a lot of others have died. 31 If we carefully judge ourselves, we won't be punished. 32 But when the Lord judges and punishes us, he does it to keep us from being condemned with the rest of the world.

33 My dear friends, you should wait until everyone gets there before you start eating. 34 If you really are hungry, you can eat at home. Then you won't condemn yourselves when you meet together.

After I arrive, I will instruct you about the other matters.

Spiritual Gifts

12 My friends, you asked me about spiritual gifts. 2 I want you to remember that before you became followers of the Lord, you were led in all the wrong ways by idols that cannot even talk. 3 Now I want you to know that if you are led by God's Spirit, you will say that Jesus is Lord, and you will never curse Jesus.

4 There are different kinds of spiritual gifts, but they all come from the same Spirit. 5 There are different ways to serve the same Lord, 6 and we can each do different things. Yet the same God works in all of us and helps us in everything we do.

7 The Spirit has given each of us a special way of serving others. 8 Some of us can speak with wisdom, while others can speak with knowledge, but these gifts come from the same Spirit. 9 To others the Spirit has given great faith or the power to heal the sick 10 or the power to work mighty miracles. Some of us are prophets, and some of us recognize when God's Spirit is present.[r] Others can speak different kinds of languages, and still others can tell what these languages mean. 11 But it is the Spirit who does all this and decides which gifts to give to each of us.

One Body with Many Parts

12 The body of Christ has many different parts, just as any other body does. 13 Some of us are Jews, and others are Gentiles. Some of us are slaves, and others are free. But God's Spirit baptized each of us and made us part of the body of Christ. Now we each drink from that same Spirit.[s]

14 Our bodies don't have just one part. They have many parts. 15 Suppose a foot says, "I'm not a hand, and so I'm not part of the body." Wouldn't the foot still belong to the body? 16 Or suppose an ear says, "I'm not an eye, and so I'm

---

[p] **11.10** *as a sign of her authority*: Or "as a sign that she is under someone's authority." [q] **11.16** *This is how things are done in all of God's churches*: Or "There is no set rule for this in any of God's churches." [r] **12.10** *and some of us ... present*: Or "and some of us recognize the difference between God's Spirit and other spirits." [s] **12.13** *Some of us are Jews ... that same Spirit*: Verse 13 may also be translated, "God's Spirit is inside each of us, and all around us as well. So it doesn't matter that some of us are Jews and others are Gentiles and that some are slaves and others are free. Together we are one body."

not part of the body." Wouldn't the ear still belong to the body? [17] If our bodies were only an eye, we couldn't hear a thing. And if they were only an ear, we couldn't smell a thing. [18] But God has put all parts of our body together in the way that he decided is best.

[19] A body isn't really a body, unless there is more than one part. [20] It takes many parts to make a single body. [21] That's why the eyes cannot say they don't need the hands. That's also why the head cannot say it doesn't need the feet. [22] In fact, we cannot get along without the parts of the body that seem to be the weakest. [23] We take special care to dress up some parts of our bodies. We are modest about our personal parts, [24] but we don't have to be modest about other parts.

God put our bodies together in such a way that even the parts that seem the least important are valuable. [25] He did this to make all parts of the body work together smoothly, with each part caring about the others. [26] If one part of our body hurts, we hurt all over. If one part of our body is honored, the whole body will be happy.

[27] Together you are the body of Christ. Each one of you is part of his body. [28] First, God chose some people to be apostles and prophets and teachers for the church. But he also chose some to work miracles or heal the sick or help others or be leaders or speak different kinds of languages. [29] Not everyone is an apostle. Not everyone is a prophet. Not everyone is a teacher. Not everyone can work miracles. [30] Not everyone can heal the sick. Not everyone can speak different kinds of languages. Not everyone can tell what these languages mean. [31] I want you to desire the best gifts.[t] So I will show you a much better way.

Love

13

What if I could speak
all languages of humans
and of angels?
If I did not love others,
I would be nothing more
than a noisy gong
or a clanging cymbal.
[2] What if I could prophesy
and understand all secrets
and all knowledge?
And what if I had faith
that moved mountains?
I would be nothing,
unless I loved others.
[3] What if I gave away all
that I owned
and let myself
be burned alive?[u]
I would gain nothing,
unless I loved others.
[4] Love is kind and patient,
never jealous, boastful,
proud, or [5] rude.
Love isn't selfish
or quick tempered.
It doesn't keep a record
of wrongs that others do.

[6] Love rejoices in the truth,
but not in evil.
[7] Love is always supportive,
loyal, hopeful,
and trusting.
[8] Love never fails!

Everyone who prophesies
will stop,
and unknown languages
will no longer
be spoken.
All that we know
will be forgotten.
[9] We don't know everything,
and our prophecies
are not complete.
[10] But what is perfect
will someday appear,
and what isn't perfect
will then disappear.

[11] When we were children,
we thought and reasoned
as children do.
But when we grew up,
we quit our childish ways.
[12] Now all we can see of God
is like a cloudy picture
in a mirror.
Later we will see him
face to face.
We don't know everything,
but then we will,
just as God completely
understands us.
[13] For now there are faith,
hope, and love.
But of these three,
the greatest is love.

Speaking Unknown Languages and Prophesying

14

Love should be your guide. Be eager to have the gifts that come from the Holy Spirit, especially the gift of prophecy. [2] If you speak languages that others don't know, God will understand what you are saying, though no one else will know what you mean. You will be talking about mysteries that only the Spirit understands. [3] But when you prophesy, you will be understood, and others will be helped. They will be encouraged and made to feel better.

[4] By speaking languages that others don't know, you help only yourself. But by prophesying you help everyone in the church. [5] I am glad for you to speak unknown languages, although I had rather for you to prophesy. In fact, prophesying does much more good than speaking unknown languages, unless someone can help the church by explaining what you mean.

[6] My friends, what good would it do, if I came and spoke unknown languages to you and didn't explain what I meant?

---

[t] **12.31** *I want you to desire the best gifts*: Or "You desire the best gifts."   [u] **13.3** *and let myself be burned alive*: Some manuscripts have "so that I could brag."

How would I help you, unless I told you what God had shown me or gave you some knowledge or prophecy or teaching? [7] If all musical instruments sounded alike, how would you know the difference between a flute and a harp? [8] If a bugle call isn't clear, how would you know to get ready for battle?

[9] That's how it is when you speak unknown languages. If no one can understand what you are talking about, you will only be talking to the wind. [10] There are many different languages in this world, and all of them make sense. [11] But if I don't understand the language that someone is using, we will be like foreigners to each other. [12] If you really want spiritual gifts, choose the ones that will be most helpful to the church.

[13] When we speak languages that others don't know, we should pray for the power to explain what we mean. [14] For example, if I use an unknown language in my prayers, my spirit prays but my mind is useless. [15] Then what should I do? There are times when I should pray with my spirit, and times when I should pray with my mind. Sometimes I should sing with my spirit, and at other times I should sing with my mind.

[16] Suppose some strangers are in your worship service, when you are praising God with your spirit. If they don't understand you, how will they know to say, "Amen"? [17] You may be worshiping God in a wonderful way, but no one else will be helped. [18] I thank God that I speak unknown languages more than any of you. [19] But words that make sense can help the church. That's why in church I had rather speak five words that make sense than to speak ten thousand words in a language that others don't know.

[20] My friends, stop thinking like children. Think like mature people and be as innocent as tiny babies. [21] In the Scriptures the Lord says,

"I will use strangers
   who speak unknown languages
      to talk to my people.
They will speak to them
      in foreign languages,
but still my people
      won't listen to me."

[22] Languages that others don't know may mean something to unbelievers, but not to the Lord's followers. Prophecy, on the other hand, is for followers, not for unbelievers. [23] Suppose everyone in your worship service started speaking unknown languages, and some outsiders or some unbelievers come in. Won't they think you are crazy? [24] But suppose all of you are prophesying when those unbelievers and outsiders come in. They will realize that they are sinners, and they will want to change their ways because of what you are saying. [25] They will tell what is hidden in their hearts. Then they will kneel down and say to God, "We are certain that you are with these people."

Worship Must Be Orderly

[26] My friends, when you meet to worship, you must do everything for the good of everyone there. That's how it should be when someone sings or teaches or tells what God has said or speaks an unknown language or explains what the language means. [27] No more than two or three of you

should speak unknown languages during the meeting. You must take turns, and someone should always be there to explain what you mean. [28] If no one can explain, you must keep silent in church and speak only to yourself and to God.

[29] Two or three persons may prophesy, and everyone else must listen carefully. [30] If someone sitting there receives a message from God, the speaker must stop and let the other person speak. [31] Let only one person speak at a time, then all of you will learn something and be encouraged. [32] A prophet should be willing to stop and let someone else speak. [33] God wants everything to be done peacefully and in order.

When God's people meet in church, [34] the women must not be allowed to speak. They must keep quiet and listen, as the Law of Moses teaches. [35] If there is something they want to know, they can ask their husbands when they get home. It is disgraceful for women to speak in church. [36] God's message did not start with you people, and you are not the only ones it has reached.

[37] If you think of yourself as a prophet or a spiritual person, you will know that I am writing only what the Lord has commanded. [38] So don't pay attention to anyone who ignores what I am writing. [39] My friends, be eager to prophesy and don't stop anyone from speaking languages that others don't know. [40] But do everything properly and in order.

Christ Was Raised to Life

15 My friends, I want you to remember the message that I preached and that you believed and trusted. [2] You will be saved by this message, if you hold firmly to it. But if you don't, your faith was all for nothing.

[3] I told you the most important part of the message exactly as it was told to me. That part is:

Christ died for our sins,
      as the Scriptures say.
[4] He was buried,
      and three days later
he was raised to life,
      as the Scriptures say.
[5] Christ appeared to Peter,[v]
      then to the twelve.
[6] After this, he appeared
      to more than five hundred
         other followers.
Most of them are still alive,
      but some have died.
[7] He also appeared to James,
      and then to all
         of the apostles.

[8] Finally, he appeared to me, even though I am like someone who was born at the wrong time.[w]

[9] I am the least important of all the apostles. In fact, I caused so much trouble for God's church that I don't even deserve to be called an apostle. [10] But God was kind! He made me what I am, and his wonderful kindness wasn't wasted. I worked much harder than any of the other apostles, although it was really God's kindness at work and not me. [11] But it doesn't matter if I preached or if they preached. All of you believed the message just the same.

---

[v] **15.5** *Peter*: See the note at 1.12.   [w] **15.8** *who was born at the wrong time*: The meaning of these words in Greek is not clear.

God's People Will Be Raised to Life

12 If we preach that Christ was raised from death, how can some of you say that the dead will not be raised to life? **13** If they won't be raised to life, Christ himself wasn't raised to life. **14** And if Christ wasn't raised to life, our message is worthless, and so is your faith. **15** If the dead won't be raised to life, we have told lies about God by saying that he raised Christ to life, when he really did not.

16 So if the dead won't be raised to life, Christ wasn't raised to life. **17** Unless Christ was raised to life, your faith is useless, and you are still living in your sins. **18** And those people who died after putting their faith in him are completely lost. **19** If our hope in Christ is good only for this life, we are worse off than anyone else.

20 But Christ has been raised to life! And he makes us certain that others will also be raised to life. **21** Just as we will die because of Adam, we will be raised to life because of Christ. **22** Adam brought death to all of us, and Christ will bring life to all of us. **23** But we must each wait our turn. Christ was the first to be raised to life, and his people will be raised to life when he returns. **24** Then after Christ has destroyed all powers and forces, the end will come, and he will give the kingdom to God the Father.

25 Christ will rule until he puts all his enemies under his power, **26** and the last enemy he destroys will be death. **27** When the Scriptures say that he will put everything under his power, they don't include God. It was God who put everything under the power of Christ. **28** After everything is under the power of God's Son, he will put himself under the power of God, who put everything under his Son's power. Then God will mean everything to everyone.

29 If the dead are not going to be raised to life, what will people do who are being baptized for them? Why are they being baptized for those dead people? **30** And why do we always risk our lives **31** and face death every day? The pride that I have in you because of Christ Jesus our Lord is what makes me say this. **32** What do you think I gained by fighting wild animals in Ephesus? If the dead are not raised to life,

"Let's eat and drink.
    Tomorrow we die."

33 Don't fool yourselves. Bad friends will destroy you. **34** Be sensible and stop sinning. You should be embarrassed that some people still don't know about God.

What Our Bodies Will Be Like

35 Some of you have asked, "How will the dead be raised to life? What kind of bodies will they have?" **36** Don't be foolish. A seed must die before it can sprout from the ground. **37** Wheat seeds and all other seeds look different from the sprouts that come up. **38** This is because God gives everything the kind of body he wants it to have. **39** People, animals, birds, and fish are each made of flesh, but none of them are alike. **40** Everything in the heavens has a body, and so does everything on earth. But each one is very different from all the others. **41** The sun isn't like the moon, the moon isn't like the stars, and star is different.

42 That's how it will be when our bodies are raised to life. These bodies will die, but the bodies that are raised will live forever. **43** These ugly and weak bodies will become beautiful and strong. **44** As surely as there are physical bod-

ies, there are spiritual bodies. And our physical bodies will be changed into spiritual bodies.

45 The first man was named Adam, and the Scriptures tell us that he was a living person. But Jesus, who may be called the last Adam, is a life-giving spirit. **46** We see that the one with a spiritual body did not come first. He came after the one who had a physical body. **47** The first man was made from the dust of the earth, but the second man came from heaven. **48** Everyone on earth has a body like the body of the one who was made from the dust of the earth. And everyone in heaven has a body like the body of the one who came from heaven. **49** Just as we are like the one who was made out of earth, we will be like the one who came from heaven.

50 My friends, I want you to know that our bodies of flesh and blood will decay. This means that they cannot share in God's kingdom, which lasts forever. **51** I will explain a mystery to you. Not every one of us will die, but we will all be changed. **52** It will happen suddenly, quicker than the blink of an eye. At the sound of the last trumpet the dead will be raised. We will all be changed, so that we will never die again. **53** Our dead and decaying bodies will be changed into bodies that won't die or decay. **54** The bodies we now have are weak and can die. But they will be changed into bodies that are eternal. Then the Scriptures will come true,

"Death has lost the battle!
55 Where is its victory?
      Where is its sting?"

56 Sin is what gives death its sting, and the Law is the power behind sin. **57** But thank God for letting our Lord Jesus Christ give us the victory!

58 My dear friends, stand firm and don't be shaken. Always keep busy working for the Lord. You know that everything you do for him is worthwhile.

A Collection for God's People

16 When you collect money for God's people, I want you to do exactly what I told the churches in Galatia to do. **2** That is, each Sunday each of you must put aside part of what you have earned. If you do this, you won't have to take up a collection when I come. **3** Choose some followers to take the money to Jerusalem. I will send them on with the money and with letters which show that you approve of them. **4** If you think I should go along, they can go with me.

Paul's Travel Plans

5 After I have gone through Macedonia, I hope to see you **6** and visit with you for a while. I may even stay all winter, so that you can help me on my way to wherever I will be going next. **7** If the Lord lets me, I would rather come later for a longer visit than to stop off now for only a short visit. **8** I will stay in Ephesus until Pentecost, **9** because there is a wonderful opportunity for me to do some work here. But there are also many people who are against me.

10 When Timothy arrives, give him a friendly welcome. He is doing the Lord's work, just as I am. **11** Don't let anyone mistreat him. I am looking for him to return to me together with the other followers. So when he leaves, send him off with your blessings.

12 I have tried hard to get our friend Apollos to visit you with the other followers. He doesn't want to come just now, but he will come when he can.

Personal Concerns and Greetings

13 Keep alert. Be firm in your faith. Stay brave and strong. **14** Show love in everything you do.

15 You know that Stephanas and his family were the first in Achaia to have faith in the Lord. They have done all they can for God's people. My friends, I ask you **16** to obey leaders like them and to do the same for all others who work hard with you.

17 I was glad to see Stephanas and Fortunatus and Achai-cus. Having them here was like having you. **18** They made me feel much better, just as they made you feel better. You should appreciate people like them.

19 Greetings from the churches in Asia.

Aquila and Priscilla, together with the church that meets in their house, send greetings in the name of the Lord.

20 All of the Lord's followers send their greetings.

Give each other a warm greeting.

21 I am signing this letter myself: PAUL.

22 I pray that God will put a curse on everyone who doesn't love the Lord. And may the Lord come soon.

23 I pray that the Lord Jesus will be kind to you.

24 I love everyone who belongs to Christ Jesus.

2 CORINTHIANS

1 From Paul, chosen by God to be an apostle of Jesus Christ, and from Timothy, who is also a follower.

To God's church in Corinth and to all of God's people in Achaia.

2 I pray that God our Father and the Lord Jesus Christ will be kind to you and will bless you with peace!

Paul Gives Thanks

3 Praise God, the Father of our Lord Jesus Christ! The Father is a merciful God, who always gives us comfort. **4** He comforts us when we are in trouble, so that we can share that same comfort with others in trouble. **5** We share in the terrible sufferings of Christ, but also in the wonderful comfort he gives. **6** We suffer in the hope that you will be comforted and saved. And because we are comforted, you will also be comforted, as you patiently endure suffering like ours. **7** You never disappoint us. You suffered as much as we did, and we know that you will be comforted as we were.

8 My friends, I want you to know what a hard time we had in Asia. Our sufferings were so horrible and so unbearable that death seemed certain. **9** In fact, we felt sure that we were going to die. But this made us stop trusting in ourselves and start trusting God, who raises the dead to life. **10** God saved us from the threat of death,[a] and we are sure that he will do it again and again. **11** Please help us by praying for us. Then many people will give thanks for the blessings we receive in answer to all these prayers.

Paul's Change of Plans

12 We can be proud of our clear conscience. We have always lived honestly and sincerely, especially when we were with you. And we were guided by God's wonderful kindness instead of by the wisdom of this world. **13** I am not writing anything you cannot read and understand. I hope you will understand it completely, **14** just as you already partly understand us. Then when our Lord Jesus returns, you can be as proud of us as we are of you.

15 I was so sure of your pride in us that I had planned to visit you first of all. In this way you would have the blessing of two visits from me. **16** Once on my way to Macedonia and again on my return from there. Then you could send me on to Judea. **17** Do you think I couldn't make up my mind about what to do? Or do I seem like someone who says "Yes" or "Nó" simply to please others? **18** God can be trusted, and so can I, when I say that our answer to you has always been "Yes" and never "No." **19** This is because Jesus Christ the Son of God is always "Yes" and never "No." And he is the one that Silas,[b] Timothy, and I told you about.

20 Christ says "Yes" to all of God's promises. That's why we have Christ to say "Amen" for us to the glory of God. **21** And so God makes it possible for you and us to stand firmly together with Christ. God is also the one who chose us **22** and put his Spirit in our hearts to show that we belong only to him.

23 God is my witness that I stayed away from Corinth, just to keep from being hard on you. **24** We are not bosses who tell you what to believe. We are working with you to make you glad, because your faith is strong.

2 I have decided not to make my next visit with you so painful. **2** If I make you feel bad, who would be left to cheer me up, except the people I had made to feel bad? **3** The reason I want to be happy is to make you happy. I wrote as I did because I didn't want to visit you and be made to feel bad, when you should make me feel happy. **4** At the time I wrote, I was suffering terribly. My eyes were full of tears, and my heart was broken. But I didn't want to make you feel bad. I only wanted to let you know how much I cared for you.

---

[a] **1.10** *the threat of death*: Some manuscripts have "many threats of death."   [b] **1.19** *Silas*: The Greek text has "Silvanus," which is another form of the name Silas.

Forgiveness

5 I don't want to be hard on you. But if one of you has made someone feel bad, I am not really the one who has been made to feel bad. Some of you are the ones. **6** Most of you have already pointed out the wrong that person did, and that is punishment enough for what was done.

7 When people sin, you should forgive and comfort them, so they won't give up in despair. **8** You should make them sure of your love for them.

9 I also wrote because I wanted to test you and find out if you would follow my instructions. **10** I will forgive anyone you forgive. Yes, for your sake and with Christ as my witness, I have forgiven whatever needed to be forgiven. **11** I have done this to keep Satan from getting the better of us. We all know what goes on in his mind.

12 When I went to Troas to preach the good news about Christ, I found that the Lord had already prepared the way. **13** But I was worried when I didn't find my friend Titus there. So I left the other followers and went on to Macedonia.

14 I am grateful that God always makes it possible for Christ to lead us to victory. God also helps us spread the knowledge about Christ everywhere, and this knowledge is like the smell of perfume. **15-16** In fact, God thinks of us as a perfume that brings Christ to everyone. For people who are being saved, this perfume has a sweet smell and leads them to a better life. But for people who are lost, it has a bad smell and leads them to a horrible death.

No one really has what it takes to do this work. **17** A lot of people try to get rich from preaching God's message. But we are God's sincere messengers, and by the power of Christ we speak our message with God as our witness.

God's New Agreement

3 Are we once again bragging about ourselves? Do we need letters to you or from you to tell others about us? Some people do need letters that tell about them. **2** But you are our letter, and you are in our*c* hearts for everyone to read and understand. **3** You are like a letter written by Christ and delivered by us. But you are not written with pen and ink or on tablets made of stone. You are written in our hearts by the Spirit of the living God.

4 We are sure about all this. Christ makes us sure in the very presence of God. **5** We don't have the right to claim that we have done anything on our own. God gives us what it takes to do all that we do. **6** He makes us worthy to be the servants of his new agreement that comes from the Holy Spirit and not from a written Law. After all, the Law brings death, but the Spirit brings life.

7 The Law of Moses brought only the promise of death, even though it was carved on stones and given in a wonderful way. Still the Law made Moses' face shine so brightly that the people of Israel could not look at it, even though it was a fading glory. **8** So won't the agreement that the Spirit brings to us be even more wonderful? **9** If something that brings the death sentence is glorious, won't something that makes us acceptable to God be even more glorious? **10** In fact, the new agreement is so wonderful that the Law is no longer glorious at all. **11** The Law was given with a glory that faded away. But the glory of the new agreement is much greater, because it will never fade away.

12 This wonderful hope makes us feel like speaking freely. **13** We are not like Moses. His face was shining, but he covered it to keep the people of Israel from seeing the brightness fade away. **14** The people were stubborn, and something still keeps them from seeing the truth when the Law is read. Only Christ can take away the covering that keeps them from seeing.

15 When the Law of Moses is read, they have their minds covered over **16** with a covering that is removed only for those who turn to the Lord. **17** The Lord and the Spirit are one and the same, and the Lord's Spirit sets us free. **18** So our faces are not covered. They show the bright glory of the Lord, as the Lord's Spirit makes us more and more like our glorious Lord.

Treasure in Clay Jars

4 God has been kind enough to trust us with this work. That's why we never give up. **2** We don't do shameful things that must be kept secret. And we don't try to fool anyone or twist God's message around. God is our witness that we speak only the truth, so others will be sure that we can be trusted. **3** If there is anything hidden about our message, it is hidden only to someone who is lost.

4 The god who rules this world has blinded the minds of unbelievers. They cannot see the light, which is the good news about our glorious Christ, who shows what God is like. **5** We are not preaching about ourselves. Our message is that Jesus Christ is Lord. He also sent us to be your servants. **6** The Scriptures say, "God commanded light to shine in the dark." Now God is shining in our hearts to let you know that his glory is seen in Jesus Christ.

7 We are like clay jars in which this treasure is stored. The real power comes from God and not from us. **8** We often suffer, but we are never crushed. Even when we don't know what to do, we never give up. **9** In times of trouble, God is with us, and when we are knocked down, we get up again. **10-11** We face death every day because of Jesus. Our bodies show what his death was like, so that his life can also be seen in us. **12** This means that death is working in us, but life is working in you.

13 In the Scriptures it says, "I spoke because I had faith." We have that same kind of faith. So we speak **14** because we know that God raised the Lord Jesus to life. And just as God raised Jesus, he will also raise us to life. Then he will bring us into his presence together with you. **15** All of this has been done for you, so that more and more people will know how kind God is and will praise and honor him.

Faith in the Lord

16 We never give up. Our bodies are gradually dying, but we ourselves are being made stronger each day. **17** These little troubles are getting us ready for an eternal glory that will make all our troubles seem like nothing. **18** Things that are seen don't last forever, but things that are not seen are eternal. That's why we keep our minds on the things that cannot be seen.

5 Our bodies are like tents that we live in here on earth. But when these tents are destroyed, we know that God will give each of us a place to live. These homes will not be buildings that someone has made, but they are in heaven and will last forever. **2** While we are here on earth, we sigh because we want to live in that heavenly home. **3** We want to put it on like clothes and not be naked.

---

c **3.2** *our*: Some manuscripts have "your."

4 These tents we now live in are like a heavy burden, and we groan. But we don't do this just because we want to leave these bodies that will die. It is because we want to change them for bodies that will never die. 5 God is the one who makes all of this possible. He has given us his Spirit to make us certain that he will do it. 6 So always be cheerful!

As long as we are in these bodies, we are away from the Lord. 7 But we live by faith, not by what we see. 8 We should be cheerful, because we would rather leave these bodies and be at home with the Lord. 9 But whether we are at home with the Lord or away from him, we still try our best to please him. 10 After all, Christ will judge each of us for the good or the bad that we do while living in these bodies.

Bringing People to God

11 We know what it means to respect the Lord, and we encourage everyone to turn to him. God himself knows what we are like, and I hope you also know what kind of people we are. 12 We are not trying once more to brag about ourselves. But we want you to be proud of us, when you are with those who are not sincere and brag about what others think of them.

13 If we seem out of our minds, it is between God and us. But if we are in our right minds, it is for your good. 14 We are ruled by Christ's love for us. We are certain that if one person died for everyone else, then all of us have died. 15 And Christ did die for all of us. He died so we would no longer live for ourselves, but for the one who died and was raised to life for us.

16 We are careful not to judge people by what they seem to be, though we once judged Christ in that way. 17 Anyone who belongs to Christ is a new person. The past is forgotten, and everything is new. 18 God has done it all! He sent Christ to make peace between himself and us, and he has given us the work of making peace between himself and others.

19 What we mean is that God was in Christ, offering peace and forgiveness to the people of this world. And he has given us the work of sharing his message about peace. 20 We were sent to speak for Christ, and God is begging you to listen to our message. We speak for Christ and sincerely ask you to make peace with God. 21 Christ never sinned! But God treated him as a sinner, so that Christ could make us acceptable to God.

6 We work together with God, and we beg you to make good use of God's kindness to you. 2 In the Scriptures God says,

> "When the time came,
>   I listened to you,
> and when you needed help,
>   I came to save you."

That time has come. This is the day for you to be saved.

3 We don't want anyone to find fault with our work, and so we try hard not to cause problems. 4 But in everything and in every way we show that we truly are God's servants. We have always been patient, though we have had a lot of trouble, suffering, and hard times. 5 We have been beaten, put in jail, and hurt in riots. We have worked hard and have gone without sleep or food. 6 But we have kept ourselves pure and have been understanding, patient, and kind. The Holy Spirit has been with us, and our love has been real. 7 We have spoken the truth, and God's power has worked in us. In all our struggles we have said and done only what is right.

8 Whether we were honored or dishonored or praised or cursed, we always told the truth about ourselves. But some people said we did not. 9 We are unknown to others, but well known to you. We seem to be dying, and yet we are still alive. We have been punished, but never killed, 10 and we are always happy, even in times of suffering. Although we are poor, we have made many people rich. And though we own nothing, everything is ours.

11 Friends in Corinth, we are telling the truth when we say that there is room in our hearts for you. 12 We are not holding back on our love for you, but you are holding back on your love for us. 13 I speak to you as I would speak to my own children. Please make room in your hearts for us.

The Temple of the Living God

14 Stay away from people who are not followers of the Lord! Can someone who is good get along with someone who is evil? Are light and darkness the same? 15 Is Christ a friend of Satan?*d* Can people who follow the Lord have anything in common with those who don't? 16 Do idols belong in the temple of God? We are the temple of the living God, as God himself says,

> "I will live with these people
>   and walk among them.
> I will be their God,
> and they will be
>   my people."

17 The Lord also says,

> "Leave them and stay away!
> Don't touch anything
>   that isn't clean.
> Then I will welcome you
> 18   and be your Father.
> You will be my sons
>   and my daughters,
> as surely as I am God,
>   the All-Powerful."

7 My friends, God has made us these promises. So we should stay away from everything that keeps our bodies and spirits from being clean. We should honor God and try to be completely like him.

The Church Makes Paul Happy

2 Make a place for us in your hearts! We haven't mistreated or hurt anyone. We haven't cheated anyone. 3 I am not saying this to be hard on you. But, as I have said before, you will always be in our thoughts, whether we live or die. 4 I trust you completely.*e* I am always proud of you, and I am greatly encouraged. In all my trouble I am still very happy.

---

d 6.15 *Satan*: The Greek text has "Beliar," which is another form of the Hebrew word "Belial," meaning "wicked" or "useless." The Jewish people sometimes used this as a name for Satan.   *e* 7.4 *I trust you completely*: Or "I have always spoken the truth to you" or "I can speak freely to you."

5 After we came to Macedonia, we didn't have any chance to rest. We were faced with all kinds of problems. We were troubled by enemies and troubled by fears. 6 But God cheers up people in need, and that is what he did when he sent Titus to us. 7 Of course, we were glad to see Titus, but what really made us glad is the way you cheered him up. He told how sorry you were and how concerned you were about me. And this made me even happier.

8 I don't feel bad anymore, even though my letter hurt your feelings. I did feel bad at first, but I don't now. I know that the letter hurt you for a while. 9 Now I am happy, but not because I hurt your feelings. It is because God used your hurt feelings to make you turn back to him, and none of you were harmed by us. 10 When God makes you feel sorry enough to turn to him and be saved, you don't have anything to feel bad about. But when this world makes you feel sorry, it can cause your death.

11 Just look what God has done by making you feel sorry! You sincerely want to prove that you are innocent. You are angry. You are shocked. You are eager to see that justice is done. You have proved that you were completely right in this matter. 12 When I wrote you, it wasn't to accuse the one who was wrong or to take up for the one who was hurt. I wrote, so that God would show you how much you do care for us. 13 And we were greatly encouraged.

Although we were encouraged, we felt even better when we saw how happy Titus was, because you had shown that he had nothing to worry about. 14 We had told him how much we thought of you, and you did not disappoint us. Just as we have always told you the truth, so everything we told him about you has also proved to be true. 15 Titus loves all of you very much, especially when he remembers how you obeyed him and how you trembled with fear when you welcomed him. 16 It makes me really glad to know that I can depend on you.

Generous Giving

8 My friends, we want you to know that the churches in Macedonia have shown others how kind God is. 2 Although they were going through hard times and were very poor, they were glad to give generously. 3 They gave as much as they could afford and even more, simply because they wanted to. 4 They even asked and begged us to let them have the joy of giving their money for God's people. 5 And they did more than we had hoped. They gave themselves first to the Lord and then to us, just as God wanted them to do.

6 Titus was the one who got you started doing this good thing, so we begged him to have you finish what you had begun. 7 You do everything better than anyone else. You have stronger faith. You speak better and know more. You are eager to give, and you love us better.*f* Now you must give more generously than anyone else.

8 I am not ordering you to do this. I am simply testing how real your love is by comparing it with the concern that others have shown. 9 You know that our Lord Jesus Christ was kind enough to give up all his riches and become poor, so that you could become rich.

10 A year ago you were the first ones to give, and you gave because you wanted to. So listen to my advice. 11 I think you should finish what you started. If you give according to what you have, you will prove that you are as eager to give

as you were to think about giving. 12 It doesn't matter how much you have. What matters is how much you are willing to give from what you have.

13 I am not trying to make life easier for others by making life harder for you. But it is only fair 14 for you to share with them when you have so much, and they have so little. Later, when they have more than enough, and you are in need, they can share with you. Then everyone will have a fair share, 15 just as the Scriptures say,

"Those who gathered
too much
      had nothing left.
Those who gathered
only a little
      had all they needed."

Titus and His Friends

16 I am grateful that God made Titus care as much about you as we do. 17 When we begged Titus to visit you, he said he would. He wanted to because he cared so much for you. 18 With Titus we are also sending one of the Lord's followers who is well known in every church for spreading the good news. 19 The churches chose this follower to travel with us while we carry this gift that will bring praise to the Lord and show how much we hope to help. 20 We don't want anyone to find fault with the way we handle your generous gift. 21 But we want to do what pleases the Lord and what people think is right.

22 We are also sending someone else with Titus and the other follower. We approve of this man. In fact, he has already shown us many times that he wants to help. And now he wants to help even more than ever, because he trusts you so much. 23 Titus is my partner, who works with me to serve you. The other two followers are sent by the churches, and they bring honor to Christ. 24 Treat them in such a way that the churches will see your love and will know why we bragged about you.

The Money for God's People

9 I don't need to write you about the money you plan to give for God's people. 2 I know how eager you are to give. And I have proudly told the Lord's followers in Macedonia that you people in Achaia have been ready for a whole year. Now your desire to give has made them want to give. 3 That's why I am sending Titus and the two others to you. I want you to be ready, just as I promised. This will prove that we were not wrong to brag about you.

4 Some followers from Macedonia may come with me, and I want them to find that you have the money ready. If you don't, I would be embarrassed for trusting you to do this. But you would be embarrassed even more. 5 So I have decided to ask Titus and the others to spend some time with you before I arrive. This way they can arrange to collect the money you have promised. Then you will have the chance to give because you want to, and not because you feel forced to.

6 Remember this saying,

"A few seeds make
      a small harvest,

f 8.7 *you love us better*: Some manuscripts have "we love you better."

but a lot of seeds make
a big harvest."

7 Each of you must make up your own mind about how much to give. But don't feel sorry that you must give and don't feel that you are forced to give. God loves people who love to give. **8** God can bless you with everything you need, and you will always have more than enough to do all kinds of good things for others. **9** The Scriptures say,

"God freely gives his gifts
to the poor,
and always does right."

10 God gives seed to farmers and provides everyone with food. He will increase what you have, so that you can give even more to those in need. **11** You will be blessed in every way, and you will be able to keep on being generous. Then many people will thank God when we deliver your gift.

12 What you are doing is much more than a service that supplies God's people with what they need. It is something that will make many others thank God. **13** The way in which you have proved yourselves by this service will bring honor and praise to God. You believed the message about Christ, and you obeyed it by sharing generously with God's people and with everyone else. **14** Now they are praying for you and want to see you, because God used you to bless them so very much. **15** Thank God for his gift that is too wonderful for words!

Paul Defends His Work for Christ

10 Do you think I am a coward when I am with you and brave when I am far away? Well, I ask you to listen, because Christ himself was humble and gentle. **2** Some people have said that we act like the people of this world. So when I arrive, I expect I will have to be firm and forceful in what I say to them. Please don't make me treat you that way. **3** We live in this world, but we don't act like its people **4** or fight our battles with the weapons of this world. Instead, we use God's power that can destroy fortresses. We destroy arguments **5** and every bit of pride that keeps anyone from knowing God. We capture people's thoughts and make them obey Christ. **6** And when you completely obey him, we will punish anyone who refuses to obey.

7 You judge by appearances.*g* If any of you think you are the only ones who belong to Christ, then think again. We belong to Christ as much as you do. **8** Maybe I brag a little too much about the authority that the Lord gave me to help you and not to hurt you. Yet I am not embarrassed to brag. **9** And I am not trying to scare you with my letters. **10** Some of you are saying, "Paul's letters are harsh and powerful. But in person, he is a weakling and has nothing worth saying." **11** Those people had better understand that when I am with you, I will do exactly what I say in my letters.

12 We won't dare compare ourselves with those who think so much of themselves. But they are foolish to compare themselves with themselves. **13** We won't brag about something we don't have a right to brag about. We will only brag about the work that God has sent us to do, and you are part of

that work. **14** We are not bragging more than we should. After all, we did bring the message about Christ to you.

15 We don't brag about what others have done, as if we had done those things ourselves. But I hope that as you become stronger in your faith, we will be able to reach many more of the people around you.*h* That has always been our goal. **16** Then we will be able to preach the good news in other lands where we cannot take credit for work someone else has already done. **17** The Scriptures say, "If you want to brag, then brag about the Lord." **18** You may brag about yourself, but the only approval that counts is the Lord's approval.

Paul and the False Apostles

11 Please put up with a little of my foolishness. **2** I am as concerned about you as God is. You were like a virgin bride I had chosen only for Christ. **3** But now I fear that you will be tricked, just as Eve was tricked by that lying snake. I am afraid that you might stop thinking about Christ in an honest and sincere way. **4** We told you about Jesus, and you received the Holy Spirit and accepted our message. But you let some people tell you about another Jesus. Now you are ready to receive another spirit and accept a different message. **5** I think I am as good as any of those super apostles. **6** I may not speak as well as they do, but I know as much. And this has already been made perfectly clear to you.

7 Was it wrong for me to lower myself and honor you by preaching God's message free of charge? **8** I robbed other churches by taking money from them to serve you. **9** Even when I was in need, I still didn't bother you. In fact, some of the Lord's followers from Macedonia brought me what I needed. I have not been a burden to you in the past, and I will never be a burden. **10** As surely as I speak the truth about Christ, no one in Achaia can stop me from bragging about this. **11** And it isn't because I don't love you. God himself knows how much I do love you.

12 I plan to go on doing just what I have always done. Then those people won't be able to brag about doing the same things we are doing. **13** Anyway, they are no more than false apostles and dishonest workers. They only pretend to be apostles of Christ. **14** And it is no wonder. Even Satan tries to make himself look like an angel of light. **15** So why does it seem strange for Satan's servants to pretend to do what is right? Someday they will get exactly what they deserve.

Paul's Sufferings for Christ

16 I don't want any of you to think that I am a fool. But if you do, then let me be a fool and brag a little. **17** When I do all this bragging, I do it as a fool and not for the Lord. **18** Yet if others want to brag about what they have done, so will I. **19** And since you are so smart, you will gladly put up with a fool. **20** In fact, you let people make slaves of you and cheat you and steal from you. Why, you even let them strut around and slap you in the face. **21** I am ashamed to say that we are too weak to behave in such a way.

If they can brag, so can I, but it is a foolish thing to do. **22** Are they Hebrews? So am I. Are they Jews? So am I. Are they from the family of Abraham? Well, so am I. **23** Are they servants of Christ? I am a fool to talk this way, but I serve him better than they do. I have worked harder and have

---

g **10.7** *You judge by appearances*: Or "Take a close look at yourselves."   *h* **10.15** *we will be able to reach many more of the people around you*: Or "you will praise us even more because of our work among you."

been put in jail more times. I have been beaten with whips more and more and been in danger of death more often.

²⁴ Five times the Jews gave me thirty-nine lashes with a whip. ²⁵ Three times the Romans beat me with a big stick, and once my enemies stoned me. I have been shipwrecked three times, and I even had to spend a night and a day in the sea. ²⁶ During my many travels, I have been in danger from rivers, robbers, my own people, and foreigners. My life has been in danger in cities, in deserts, at sea, and with people who only pretended to be the Lord's followers.

²⁷ I have worked and struggled and spent many sleepless nights. I have gone hungry and thirsty and often had nothing to eat. I have been cold from not having enough clothes to keep me warm. ²⁸ Besides everything else, each day I am burdened down, worrying about all the churches. ²⁹ When others are weak, I am weak too. When others are tricked into sin, I get angry.ⁱ

³⁰ If I have to brag, I will brag about how weak I am. ³¹ God, the Father of our Lord Jesus, knows I am not lying, And God is to be praised forever! ³² The governor of Damascus at the time of King Aretas had the city gates guarded, so that he could capture me. ³³ But I escaped by being let down in a basket through a window in the city wall.

Visions from the Lord

12 I have to brag. There is nothing to be gained by it, but I must brag about the visions and other things that the Lord has shown me. ² I know about one of Christ's followers who was taken up into the third heaven fourteen years ago. I don't know if the man was still in his body when it happened, but God certainly knows.

³ As I said, only God really knows if this man was in his body at the time. ⁴ But he was taken up into paradise, where he heard things that are too wonderful to tell. ⁵ I will brag about that man, but not about myself, except to say how weak I am.

⁶ Yet even if I did brag, I would not be foolish. I would simply be speaking the truth. But I will try not to say too much. That way, none of you will think more highly of me than you should because of what you have seen me do and say. ⁷ Of course, I am now referring to the wonderful things I saw. One of Satan's angels was sent to make me suffer terribly, so that I would not feel too proud.ʲ

⁸ Three times I begged the Lord to make this suffering go away. ⁹ But he replied, "My kindness is all you need. My power is strongest when you are weak." So if Christ keeps giving me his power, I will gladly brag about how weak I am. ¹⁰ Yes, I am glad to be weak or insulted or mistreated or to have troubles and sufferings, if it is for Christ. Because when I am weak, I am strong.

Paul's Concern for the Lord's Followers at Corinth

¹¹ I have been making a fool of myself. But you forced me to do it, when you should have been speaking up for me. I may be nothing at all, but I am as good as those super apostles. ¹² When I was with you, I was patient and worked all the powerful miracles and signs and wonders of a true apostle. ¹³ You missed out on only one blessing that the other churches received. That is, you didn't have to support me. Forgive me for doing you wrong.

¹⁴ I am planning to visit you for the third time. But I still won't make a burden of myself. What I really want is you, and not what you have. Children are not supposed to save up for their parents, but parents are supposed to take care of their children. ¹⁵ So I will gladly give all that I have and all that I am. Will you love me less for loving you too much? ¹⁶ You agree that I wasn't a burden to you. Maybe that's because I was trying to catch you off guard and trick you. ¹⁷ Were you cheated by any of those I sent to you? ¹⁸ I urged Titus to visit you, and I sent another follower with him. But Titus didn't cheat you, and we felt and behaved the same way he did.

¹⁹ Have you been thinking all along that we have been defending ourselves to you? Actually, we have been speaking to God as followers of Christ. But, my friends, we did it all for your good.

²⁰ I am afraid that when I come, we won't be pleased with each other. I fear that some of you may be arguing or jealous or angry or selfish or gossiping or insulting each other. I even fear that you may be proud and acting like a mob. ²¹ I am afraid God will make me ashamed when I visit you again. I will feel like crying because many of you have never given up your old sins. You are still doing things that are immoral, indecent, and shameful.

Final Warnings and Greetings

13 I am on my way to visit you for the third time. And as the Scriptures say, "Any charges must be proved true by at least two or three witnesses." ² During my second visit I warned you that I would punish you and anyone else who doesn't stop sinning. I am far away from you now, but I give you the same warning. ³ This should prove to you that I am speaking for Christ. When he corrects you, he won't be weak. He will be powerful! ⁴ Although he was weak when he was nailed to the cross, he now lives by the power of God. We are weak, just as Christ was. But you will see that we will live by the power of God, just as Christ does.

⁵ Test yourselves and find out if you really are true to your faith. If you pass the test, you will discover that Christ is living in you. But if Christ isn't living in you, you have failed. ⁶ I hope you will discover that we have not failed. ⁷ We pray that you will stop doing evil things. We don't pray like this to make ourselves look good, but to get you to do right, even if we are failures.

⁸ All we can do is to follow the truth and not fight against it. ⁹ Even though we are weak, we are glad that you are strong, and we pray that you will do even better. ¹⁰ I am writing these things to you before I arrive. This way I won't have to be hard on you when I use the authority that the Lord has given me. I was given this authority, so that I could help you and not destroy you.

¹¹ Good-by, my friends. Do better and pay attention to what I have said. Try to get along and live peacefully with each other.

Now I pray that God, who gives love and peace, will be with you. ¹² Give each other a warm greeting. All of God's people send their greetings.

¹³ I pray that the Lord Jesus Christ will bless you and be kind to you! May God bless you with his love, and may the Holy Spirit join all your hearts together.

ⁱ**11.29** *When others are tricked into sin, I get angry*: Or "When others stumble into sin, I hurt for them." ʲ**12.7** *Of course . . . too proud*: Or "Because of the wonderful things that I saw, one of Satan's angels was sent to make me suffer terribly, so that I would not feel too proud."

GALATIANS

1 ¹⁻² From the apostle Paul and from all the Lord's followers with me.

I was chosen to be an apostle by Jesus Christ and by God the Father, who raised him from death. No mere human chose or appointed me to this work.

To the churches in Galatia.

³ I pray that God the Father and our Lord Jesus Christ will be kind to you and will bless you with peace! ⁴ Christ obeyed God our Father and gave himself as a sacrifice for our sins to rescue us from this evil world. ⁵ God will be given glory forever and ever. Amen.

The Only True Message

⁶ I am shocked that you have so quickly turned from God, who chose you because of his wonderful kindness.*ᵃ* You have believed another message, ⁷ when there is really only one true message. But some people are causing you trouble and want to make you turn away from the good news about Christ. ⁸ I pray that God will punish anyone who preaches anything different from our message to you! It doesn't matter if that person is one of us or an angel from heaven. ⁹ I have said it before, and I will say it again. I hope God will punish anyone who preaches anything different from what you have already believed.

¹⁰ I am not trying to please people. I want to please God. Do you think I am trying to please people? If I were doing that, I would not be a servant of Christ.

How Paul Became an Apostle

¹¹ My friends, I want you to know that no one made up the message I preach. ¹² It wasn't given or taught to me by some mere human. My message came directly from Jesus Christ when he appeared to me.

¹³ You know how I used to live as a Jew. I was cruel to God's church and even tried to destroy it. ¹⁴ I was a much better Jew than anyone else my own age, and I obeyed every law that our ancestors had given us. ¹⁵ But even before I was born, God had chosen me. He was kind and had decided ¹⁶ to show me his Son, so that I would announce his message to the Gentiles. I didn't talk this over with anyone. ¹⁷ I didn't say a word, not even to the men in Jerusalem who were apostles before I was. Instead, I went at once to Arabia, and afterwards I returned to Damascus.

¹⁸ Three years later I went to visit Peterᵇ in Jerusalem and stayed with him for fifteen days. ¹⁹ The only other apostle I saw was James, the Lord's brother. ²⁰ And in the presence of God I swear I am telling the truth.

²¹ Later, I went to the regions of Syria and Cilicia. ²² But no one who belonged to Christ's churches in Judea had ever seen me in person. ²³ They had only heard that the one who had been cruel to them was now preaching the message that he had once tried to destroy. ²⁴ And because of me, they praised God.

2 Fourteen years later I went to Jerusalem with Barnabas. I also took along Titus. ² But I went there because God had told me to go, and I explained the good news that I had been preaching to the Gentiles. Then I met privately with the ones who seemed to be the most important leaders. I wanted to make sure that my work in the past and my future work would not be for nothing.

³ Titus went to Jerusalem with me. He was a Greek, but still he wasn't forced to be circumcised. ⁴ We went there because of those who pretended to be followers and had sneaked in among us as spies. They had come to take away the freedom that Christ Jesus had given us, and they were trying to make us their slaves. ⁵ But we wanted you to have the true message. That's why we didn't give in to them, not even for a second.

⁶ Some of them were supposed to be important leaders, but I didn't care who they were. God doesn't have any favorites! None of these so-called special leaders added anything to my message. ⁷ They realized that God had sent me with the good news for Gentiles, and that he had sent Peter with the same message for Jews. ⁸ God, who had sent Peter on a mission to the Jews, was now using me to preach to the Gentiles.

⁹ James, Peter,ᵇ and John realized that God had given me the message about his undeserved kindness. And these men are supposed to be the backbone of the church. They even gave Barnabas and me a friendly handshake. This was to show that we would work with Gentiles and that they would work with Jews. ¹⁰ They only asked us to remember the poor, and that was something I had always been eager to do.

Paul Corrects Peter at Antioch

¹¹ When Peter came to Antioch, I told him face to face that he was wrong. ¹² He used to eat with Gentile followers of the Lord, until James sent some Jewish followers. Peter was afraid of the Jews and soon stopped eating with Gentiles. ¹³ He and the other Jews hid their true feelings so well that even Barnabas was fooled. ¹⁴ But when I saw that they were not really obeying the truth that is in the good news, I corrected Peter in front of everyone and said:

Peter, you are a Jew, but you live like a Gentile. So how can you force Gentiles to live like Jews?

¹⁵ We are Jews by birth and are not sinners like Gentiles. ¹⁶ But we know that God accepts only those who have faith in Jesus Christ. No one can please God by simply obeying the Law. So we put our faith in Christ Jesus, and God accepted us because of our faith.

¹⁷ When we Jews started looking for a way to please God, we discovered that we are sinners too. Does this mean that Christ is the one who makes

---

ᵃ **1.6** *his wonderful kindness*: Some manuscripts have "the wonderful kindness of Christ."   *ᵇ* **1.18; 2.9** *Peter*: The Greek text has "Cephas," which is an Aramaic name meaning "rock." Peter is the Greek name with the same meaning.

us sinners? No, it doesn't! ¹⁸ But if I tear down something and then build it again, I prove that I was wrong at first. ¹⁹ It was the Law itself that killed me and freed me from its power, so that I could live for God.

I have been nailed to the cross with Christ. ²⁰ I have died, but Christ lives in me. And I now live by faith in the Son of God, who loved me and gave his life for me. ²¹ I don't turn my back on God's undeserved kindness. If we can be acceptable to God by obeying the Law, it was useless for Christ to die.

Faith Is the Only Way

3 You stupid Galatians! I told you exactly how Jesus Christ was nailed to a cross. Has someone now put an evil spell on you? ² I want to know only one thing. How were you given God's Spirit? Was it by obeying the Law of Moses or by hearing about Christ and having faith in him? ³ How can you be so stupid? Do you think that by yourself you can complete what God's Spirit started in you? ⁴ Have you gone through all of this for nothing? Is it all really for nothing? ⁵ God gives you his Spirit and works miracles in you. But does he do this because you obey the Law of Moses or because you have heard about Christ and have faith in him?

⁶ The Scriptures say that God accepted Abraham because Abraham had faith. ⁷ And so, you should understand that everyone who has faith is a child of Abraham. ⁸ Long ago the Scriptures said that God would accept the Gentiles because of their faith. That's why God told Abraham the good news that all nations would be blessed because of him. ⁹ This means that everyone who has faith will share in the blessings that were given to Abraham because of his faith.

¹⁰ Anyone who tries to please God by obeying the Law is under a curse. The Scriptures say, "Everyone who doesn't obey everything in the Law is under a curse." ¹¹ No one can please God by obeying the Law. The Scriptures also say, "The people God accepts because of their faith will live."ᶜ

¹² The Law isn't based on faith. It promises life only to people who obey its commands. ¹³ But Christ rescued us from the Law's curse, when he became a curse in our place. This is because the Scriptures say that anyone who is nailed to a tree is under a curse. ¹⁴ And because of what Jesus Christ has done, the blessing that was promised to Abraham was taken to the Gentiles. This happened so that by faith we would be given the promised Holy Spirit.

The Law and the Promise

¹⁵ My friends, I will use an everyday example to explain what I mean. Once someone agrees to something, no one else can change or cancel the agreement.ᵈ ¹⁶ That is how it is with the promises God made to Abraham and his descendant.ᵉ The promises were not made to many descendants, but only to one, and that one is Christ. ¹⁷ What I am saying is that the Law cannot change or cancel God's promise that was made 430 years before the Law was given. ¹⁸ If we have to obey the Law in order to receive God's blessings, those blessings don't really come to us because of God's promise. But God was kind to Abraham and made him a promise.

¹⁹ What is the use of the Law? It was given later to show that we sin. But it was only supposed to last until the coming of that descendant who was given the promise. In fact, angels gave the Law to Moses, and he gave it to the people. ²⁰ There is only one God, and the Law did not come directly from him.

Slaves and Children

²¹ Does the Law disagree with God's promises? No, it doesn't! If any law could give life to us, we could become acceptable to God by obeying that law. ²² But the Scriptures say that sin controls everyone, so that God's promises will be for anyone who has faith in Jesus Christ.

²³ The Law controlled us and kept us under its power until the time came when we would have faith. ²⁴ In fact, the Law was our teacher. It was supposed to teach us until we had faith and were acceptable to God. ²⁵ But once a person has learned to have faith, there is no more need to have the Law as a teacher.

²⁶ All of you are God's children because of your faith in Christ Jesus. ²⁷ And when you were baptized, it was as though you had put on Christ in the same way you put on new clothes. ²⁸ Faith in Christ Jesus is what makes each of you equal with each other, whether you are a Jew or a Greek, a slave or a free person, a man or a woman. ²⁹ So if you belong to Christ, you are now part of Abraham's family, and you will be 4 given what God has promised. ¹ Children who are under age are no better off than slaves, even though everything their parents own will someday be theirs. ² This is because children are placed in the care of guardians and teachers until the time their parents have set. ³ That is how it was with us. We were like children ruled by the powers of this world.

⁴ But when the time was right, God sent his Son, and a woman gave birth to him. His Son obeyed the Law, ⁵ so he could set us free from the Law, and we could become God's children. ⁶ Now that we are his children, God has sent the Spirit of his Son into our hearts. And his Spirit tells us that God is our Father. ⁷ You are no longer slaves. You are God's children, and you will be given what he has promised.

Paul's Concern for the Galatians

⁸ Before you knew God, you were slaves of gods that are not real. ⁹ But now you know God, or better still, God knows you. How can you turn back and become the slaves of those weak and pitiful powers? ¹⁰ You even celebrate certain days, months, seasons, and years. ¹¹ I am afraid I have wasted my time working with you.

¹² My friends, I beg you to be like me, just as I once tried to be like you. Did you mistreat me ¹³ when I first preached to you? No you didn't, even though you knew I had come there because I was sick. ¹⁴ My illness must have caused you some trouble, but you didn't hate me or turn me away because of it. You welcomed me as though I were one of God's angels or even Christ Jesus himself. ¹⁵ Where is that good feeling now? I am sure that if it had been possible, you would have taken out your own eyes and given them to me. ¹⁶ Am I now your enemy, just because I told you the truth?

ᶜ**3.11** *The people God accepts because of their faith will live*: Or "The people God accepts will live because of their faith."
ᵈ**3.15** *Once someone . . . cancel the agreement*: Or "Once a person makes out a will, no one can change or cancel it."
ᵉ**3.16** *descendant*: The Greek text has "seed," which may mean one or many descendants. In this verse Paul says it means Christ.

¹⁷ Those people may be paying you a lot of attention, but it isn't for your good. They only want to keep you away from me, so you will pay them a lot of attention. ¹⁸ It is always good to give your attention to something worthwhile, even when I am not with you. ¹⁹ My children, I am in terrible pain until Christ may be seen living in you. ²⁰ I wish I were with you now. Then I would not have to talk this way. You really have me puzzled.

Hagar and Sarah

²¹ Some of you would like to be under the rule of the Law of Moses. But do you know what the Law says? ²² In the Scriptures we learn that Abraham had two sons. The mother of one of them was a slave, while the mother of the other one had always been free. ²³ The son of the slave woman was born in the usual way. But the son of the free woman was born because of God's promise.

²⁴ All of this has another meaning as well. Each of the two women stands for one of the agreements God made with his people. Hagar, the slave woman, stands for the agreement that was made at Mount Sinai. Everyone born into her family is a slave. ²⁵ Hagar also stands for Mount Sinai in Arabia*f* and for the present city of Jerusalem. She*g* and her children are slaves. ²⁶ But our mother is the city of Jerusalem in heaven above, and she isn't a slave. ²⁷ The Scriptures say about her,

"You have never had children,
    but now you can be glad.
You have never given birth,
    but now you can shout.
Once you had no children,
    but now you will have
more children than a woman
who has been married
    for a long time."

²⁸ My friends, you were born because of this promise, just as Isaac was. ²⁹ But the child who was born in the natural way made trouble for the child who was born because of the Spirit. The same thing is happening today. ³⁰ The Scriptures say, "Get rid of the slave woman and her son! He won't be given anything. The son of the free woman will receive everything." ³¹ My friends, we are children of the free woman and not of the slave.

Christ Gives Freedom

5 Christ has set us free! This means we are really free. Now hold on to your freedom and don't ever become slaves of the Law again.

² I, Paul, promise you that Christ won't do you any good if you get circumcised. ³ If you do, you must obey the whole Law. ⁴ And if you try to please God by obeying the Law, you have cut yourself off from Christ and his wonderful kindness. ⁵ But the Spirit makes us sure that God will accept us because of our faith in Christ. ⁶ If you are a follower of Christ Jesus, it makes no difference whether you are circumcised or not. All that matters is your faith that makes you love others.

⁷ You were doing so well until someone made you turn from the truth. ⁸ And that person was certainly not sent by the one who chose you. ⁹ A little yeast can change a whole batch of dough, ¹⁰ but you belong to the Lord. That makes me certain that you will do what I say, instead of what someone else tells you to do. Whoever is causing trouble for you will be punished.

¹¹ My friends, if I still preach that people need to be circumcised, why am I in so much trouble? The message about the cross would no longer be a problem, if I told people to be circumcised. ¹² I wish that everyone who is upsetting you would not only get circumcised, but would cut off much more!

¹³ My friends, you were chosen to be free. So don't use your freedom as an excuse to do anything you want. Use it as an opportunity to serve each other with love. ¹⁴ All that the Law says can be summed up in the command to love others as much as you love yourself. ¹⁵ But if you keep attacking each other like wild animals, you had better watch out or you will destroy yourselves.

God's Spirit and Our Own Desires

¹⁶ If you are guided by the Spirit, you won't obey your selfish desires. ¹⁷ The Spirit and your desires are enemies of each other. They are always fighting each other and keeping you from doing what you feel you should. ¹⁸ But if you obey the Spirit, the Law of Moses has no control over you.

¹⁹ People's desires make them give in to immoral ways, filthy thoughts, and shameful deeds. ²⁰ They worship idols, practice witchcraft, hate others, and are hard to get along with. People become jealous, angry, and selfish. They not only argue and cause trouble, but they are ²¹ envious. They get drunk, carry on at wild parties, and do other evil things as well. I told you before, and I am telling you again: No one who does these things will share in the blessings of God's kingdom.

²² God's Spirit makes us loving, happy, peaceful, patient, kind, good, faithful, ²³ gentle, and self-controlled. There is no law against behaving in any of these ways. ²⁴ And because we belong to Christ Jesus, we have killed our selfish feelings and desires. ²⁵ God's Spirit has given us life, and so we should follow the Spirit. ²⁶ But don't be conceited or make others jealous by claiming to be better than they are.

Help Each Other

6 My friends, you are spiritual. So if someone is trapped in sin, you should gently lead that person back to the right path. But watch out, and don't be tempted yourself. ² You obey the law of Christ when you offer each other a helping hand.

³ If you think you are better than others, when you really aren't, you are wrong. ⁴ Do your own work well, and then you will have something to be proud of. But don't compare yourself with others. ⁵ We each must carry our own load.

⁶ Share every good thing you have with anyone who teaches you what God has said.

⁷ You cannot fool God, so don't make a fool of yourself! You will harvest what you plant. ⁸ If you follow your selfish desires, you will harvest destruction, but if you follow the Spirit, you will harvest eternal life. ⁹ Don't get tired of helping others. You will be rewarded when the time is right, if you don't give up. ¹⁰ We should help people whenever we can, especially if they are followers of the Lord.

---

f **4.25** *Hagar also stands for Mount Sinai in Arabia*: Some manuscripts have "Sinai is a mountain in Arabia." This sentence would then be translated: "Sinai is a mountain in Arabia, and Hagar stands for the present city of Jerusalem."   *g* **4.25** *She*: "Hagar" or "Jerusalem."

Final Warnings

11 You can see what big letters I make when I write with my own hand.

12 Those people who are telling you to get circumcised are only trying to show how important they are. And they don't want to get into trouble for preaching about the cross of Christ. **13** They are circumcised, but they don't obey the Law of Moses. All they want is to brag about having you circumcised. **14** But I will never brag about anything except the cross of our Lord Jesus Christ. Because of his cross, the world is dead as far as I am concerned, and I am dead as far as the world is concerned.

15 It doesn't matter if you are circumcised or not. All that matters is that you are a new person.

16 If you follow this rule, you will belong to God's true people. God will treat you with undeserved kindness and will bless you with peace.

17 On my own body are scars that prove I belong to Christ Jesus. So I don't want anyone to bother me anymore.

18 My friends, I pray that the Lord Jesus Christ will be kind to you! Amen.

EPHESIANS

1 From Paul, chosen by God to be an apostle of Christ Jesus.

To God's people who live in Ephesus and*a* are faithful followers of Christ Jesus.

2 I pray that God our Father and our Lord Jesus Christ will be kind to you and will bless you with peace!

Christ Brings Spiritual Blessings

3 Praise the God and Father of our Lord Jesus Christ for the spiritual blessings that Christ has brought us from heaven! **4** Before the world was created, God had Christ choose us to live with him and to be his holy and innocent and loving people. **5** God was kind*b* and decided that Christ would choose us to be God's own adopted children. **6** God was very kind to us because of the Son he dearly loves, and so we should praise God.

7-8 Christ sacrificed his life's blood to set us free, which means that our sins are now forgiven. Christ did this because God was so kind to us. God has great wisdom and understanding, **9** and by what Christ has done, God has shown us his own mysterious ways. **10** Then when the time is right, God will do all that he has planned, and Christ will bring together everything in heaven and on earth.

11 God always does what he plans, and that's why he appointed Christ to choose us. **12** He did this so that we Jews would bring honor to him and be the first ones to have hope because of him. **13** Christ also brought you the truth, which is the good news about how you can be saved. You put your faith in Christ and were given the promised Holy Spirit to show that you belong to God. **14** The Spirit also makes us sure that we will be given what God has stored up for his people. Then we will be set free, and God will be honored and praised.

Paul's Prayer

15 I have heard about your faith in the Lord Jesus and your love for all of God's people. **16** So I never stop being grateful for you, as I mention you in my prayers. **17** I ask the glorious Father and God of our Lord Jesus Christ to give you his Spirit. The Spirit will make you wise and let you understand what it means to know God. **18** My prayer is that light will flood your hearts and that you will understand the hope that was given to you when God chose you. Then you will discover the glorious blessings that will be yours together with all of God's people.

19 I want you to know about the great and mighty power that God has for us followers. It is the same wonderful power he used **20** when he raised Christ from death and let him sit at his right side in heaven. **21** There Christ rules over all forces, authorities, powers, and rulers. He rules over all beings in this world and will rule in the future world as well. **22** God has put all things under the power of Christ, and for the good of the church he has made him the head of everything. **23** The church is Christ's body and is filled with Christ who completely fills everything.*c*

From Death to Life

2 In the past you were dead because you sinned and fought against God. **2** You followed the ways of this world and obeyed the devil. He rules the world, and his spirit has power over everyone who doesn't obey God. **3** Once we were also ruled by the selfish desires of our bodies and minds. We had made God angry, and we were going to be punished like everyone else.

4-5 But God was merciful! We were dead because of our sins, but God loved us so much that he made us alive with Christ, and God's wonderful kindness is what saves you. **6** God raised us from death to life with Christ Jesus, and he has given us a place beside Christ in heaven. **7** God did this so that in the future world he could show how truly good and kind he is to us because of what Christ Jesus has done. **8** You were saved by faith in God, who treats us much better than we deserve. This is God's gift to you, and not anything you have done on your own. **9** It isn't something

a **1.1** *live in Ephesus and*: Some manuscripts do not have these words.   *b* **1.4,5** *holy and innocent and loving people.*[5] *God was kind*: Or "holy and innocent people. God was loving[5] and kind."   *c* **1.23** *and is filled with Christ who completely fills everything*: Or "which completely fills Christ and fully completes his work."

you have earned, so there is nothing you can brag about. [10] God planned for us to do good things and to live as he has always wanted us to live. That's why he sent Christ to make us what we are.

United by Christ

[11] Don't forget that you are Gentiles. In fact, you used to be called "uncircumcised" by those who take pride in being circumcised. [12] At that time you did not know about Christ. You were foreigners to the people of Israel, and you had no part in the promises that God had made to them. You were living in this world without hope and without God, [13] and you were far from God. But Christ offered his life's blood as a sacrifice and brought you near God.

[14] Christ has made peace between Jews and Gentiles, and he has united us by breaking down the wall of hatred that separated us. Christ gave his own body [15] to destroy the Law of Moses with all its rules and commands. He even brought Jews and Gentiles together as though we were only one person, when he united us in peace. [16] On the cross Christ did away with our hatred for each other. He also made peace[d] between us and God by uniting Jews and Gentiles in one body. [17] Christ came and preached peace to you Gentiles, who were far from God, and peace to us Jews, who were near God. [18] And because of Christ, all of us can come to the Father by the same Spirit.

[19] You Gentiles are no longer strangers and foreigners. You are citizens with everyone else who belongs to the family of God. [20] You are like a building with the apostles and prophets as the foundation and with Christ as the most important stone. [21] Christ is the one who holds the building together and makes it grow into a holy temple for the Lord. [22] And you are part of that building Christ has built as a place for God's own Spirit to live.

Paul's Mission to the Gentiles

3 Christ Jesus made me his prisoner, so that I could help you Gentiles. [2] You have surely heard about God's kindness in choosing me to help you. [3] In fact, this letter tells you a little about how God has shown me his mysterious ways. [4] As you read the letter, you will also find out how well I really do understand the mystery about Christ. [5] No one knew about this mystery until God's Spirit told it to his holy apostles and prophets. [6] And the mystery is this: Because of Christ Jesus, the good news has given the Gentiles a share in the promises that God gave to the Jews. God has also let the Gentiles be part of the same body.

[7] God treated me with kindness. His power worked in me, and it became my job to spread the good news. [8] I am the least important of all God's people. But God was kind and chose me to tell the Gentiles that because of Christ there are blessings that cannot be measured. [9] God, who created everything, wanted me to let everyone understand the mysterious plan that had always been hidden in his mind. [10] Then God would use the church to show the powers and authorities in the spiritual world that he has many different kinds of wisdom.

[11] God did this according to his eternal plan. And he was able to do what he had planned because of all that Christ Jesus our Lord had done. [12] Christ now gives us courage and con-

fidence, so that we can come to God by faith. [13] That's why you should not be discouraged when I suffer for you. After all, it will bring honor to you.

Christ's Love for Us

[14] I kneel in prayer to the Father. [15] All beings in heaven and on earth receive their life from him.[e] [16] God is wonderful and glorious. I pray that his Spirit will make you become strong followers [17] and that Christ will live in your hearts because of your faith. Stand firm and be deeply rooted in his love. [18] I pray that you and all of God's people will understand what is called wide or long or high or deep. [19] I want you to know all about Christ's love, although it is too wonderful to be measured. Then your lives will be filled with all that God is.

[20-21] I pray that Christ Jesus and the church will forever bring praise to God. His power at work in us can do far more than we dare ask or imagine. Amen.

Unity with Christ

4 As a prisoner of the Lord, I beg you to live in a way that is worthy of the people God has chosen to be his own. [2] Always be humble and gentle. Patiently put up with each other and love each other. [3] Try your best to let God's Spirit keep your hearts united. Do this by living at peace. [4] All of you are part of the same body. There is only one Spirit of God, just as you were given one hope when you were chosen to be God's people. [5] We have only one Lord, one faith, and one baptism. [6] There is one God who is the Father of all people. Not only is God above all others, but he works by using all of us, and he lives in all of us.

[7] Christ has generously divided out his gifts to us. [8] As the Scriptures say,

> "When he went up
>   to the highest place,
>   he led away many prisoners
>   and gave gifts to people."

[9] When it says, "he went up," it means that Christ had been deep in the earth. [10] This also means that the one who went deep into the earth is the same one who went into the highest heaven, so that he would fill the whole universe.

[11] Christ chose some of us to be apostles, prophets, missionaries, pastors, and teachers, [12] so that his people would learn to serve and his body would grow strong. [13] This will continue until we are united by our faith and by our understanding of the Son of God. Then we will be mature, just as Christ is, and we will be completely like him.[f]

[14] We must stop acting like children. We must not let deceitful people trick us by their false teachings, which are like winds that toss us around from place to place. [15] Love should always make us tell the truth. Then we will grow in every way and be more like Christ, the head [16] of the body. Christ holds it together and makes all of its parts work perfectly, as it grows and becomes strong because of love.

The Old Life and the New Life

[17] As a follower of the Lord, I order you to stop living like stupid, godless people. [18] Their minds are in the dark,

---

[d] **2.16** *He also made peace*: Or "The cross also made peace."   [e] **3.15** *receive their life from him*: Or "know who they really are because of him."   [f] **4.13** *and we will be completely like him*: Or "and he is completely perfect."

and they are stubborn and ignorant and have missed out on the life that comes from God. They no longer have any feelings about what is right, [19] and they are so greedy that they do all kinds of indecent things.

[20-21] But that isn't what you were taught about Jesus Christ. He is the truth, and you heard about him and learned about him. [22] You were told that your foolish desires will destroy you and that you must give up your old way of life with all its bad habits. [23] Let the Spirit change your way of thinking [24] and make you into a new person. You were created to be like God, and so you must please him and be truly holy.

Rules for the New Life

[25] We are part of the same body. Stop lying and start telling each other the truth. [26] Don't get so angry that you sin. Don't go to bed angry [27] and don't give the devil a chance.

[28] If you are a thief, quit stealing. Be honest and work hard, so you will have something to give to people in need.

[29] Stop all your dirty talk. Say the right thing at the right time and help others by what you say.

[30] Don't make God's Spirit sad. The Spirit makes you sure that someday you will be free from your sins.

[31] Stop being bitter and angry and mad at others. Don't yell at one another or curse each other or ever be rude. [32] Instead, be kind and merciful, and forgive others, just as God forgave you because of Christ.

5 Do as God does. After all, you are his dear children. [2] Let love be your guide. Christ loved us[g] and offered his life for us as a sacrifice that pleases God.

[3] You are God's people, so don't let it be said that any of you are immoral or indecent or greedy. [4] Don't use dirty or foolish or filthy words. Instead, say how thankful you are. [5] Being greedy, indecent, or immoral is just another way of worshiping idols. You can be sure that people who behave in this way will never be part of the kingdom that belongs to Christ and to God.

Living as People of Light

[6] Don't let anyone trick you with foolish talk. God punishes everyone who disobeys him and says[h] foolish things. [7] So don't have anything to do with anyone like that.

[8] You used to be like people living in the dark, but now you are people of the light because you belong to the Lord. So act like people of the light [9] and make your light shine. Be good and honest and truthful, [10] as you try to please the Lord. [11] Don't take part in doing those worthless things that are done in the dark. Instead, show how wrong they are. [12] It is disgusting even to talk about what is done in the dark. [13] But the light will show what these things are really like. [14] Light shows up everything,[i] just as the Scriptures say,

"Wake up from your sleep
and rise from death.
Then Christ will shine on you."

[15] Act like people with good sense and not like fools. [16] These are evil times, so make every minute count. [17] Don't be stupid. Instead, find out what the Lord wants you to do. [18] Don't destroy yourself by getting drunk, but let the Spirit fill your life. [19] When you meet together, sing psalms, hymns, and spiritual songs, as you praise the Lord with all your heart. [20] Always use the name of our Lord Jesus Christ to thank God the Father for everything.

Wives and Husbands

[21] Honor Christ and put others first. [22] A wife should put her husband first, as she does the Lord. [23] A husband is the head of his wife, as Christ is the head and the Savior of the church, which is his own body. [24] Wives should always put their husbands first, as the church puts Christ first.

[25] A husband should love his wife as much as Christ loved the church and gave his life for it. [26] He made the church holy by the power of his word, and he made it pure by washing it with water. [27] Christ did this, so that he would have a glorious and holy church, without faults or spots or wrinkles or any other flaws.

[28] In the same way, a husband should love his wife as much as he loves himself. A husband who loves his wife shows that he loves himself. [29] None of us hate our own bodies. We provide for them and take good care of them, just as Christ does for the church, [30] because we are each part of his body. [31] As the Scriptures say, "A man leaves his father and mother to get married, and he becomes like one person with his wife." [32] This is a great mystery, but I understand it to mean Christ and his church. [33] So each husband should love his wife as much as he loves himself, and each wife should respect her husband.

Children and Parents

6 Children, you belong to the Lord, and you do the right thing when you obey your parents. The first commandment with a promise says, [2] "Obey your father and your mother, [3] and you will have a long and happy life."

[4] Parents, don't be hard on your children. Raise them properly. Teach them and instruct them about the Lord.

Slaves and Masters

[5] Slaves, you must obey your earthly masters. Show them great respect and be as loyal to them as you are to Christ. [6] Try to please them at all times, and not just when you think they are watching. You are slaves of Christ, so with your whole heart you must do what God wants you to do. [7] Gladly serve your masters, as though they were the Lord himself, and not simply people. [8] You know that you will be rewarded for any good things you do, whether you are slaves or free.

[9] Slave owners, you must treat your slaves with this same respect. Don't threaten them. They have the same Master in heaven that you do, and he doesn't have any favorites.

The Fight against Evil

[10] Finally, let the mighty strength of the Lord make you strong. [11] Put on all the armor that God gives, so you can defend yourself against the devil's tricks. [12] We are not fighting against humans. We are fighting against forces and authorities and against rulers of darkness and powers in the spiritual world. [13] So put on all the armor that God gives. Then when that evil day comes, you will be able to defend yourself. And when the battle is over, you will still be standing firm.

---

g **5.2** *us*: Some manuscripts have "you."   h **5.6** *says*: Or "does."   i **5.14** *Light shows up everything*: Or "Everything that is seen in the light becomes light itself."

14 Be ready! Let the truth be like a belt around your waist, and let God's justice protect you like armor. 15 Your desire to tell the good news about peace should be like shoes on your feet. 16 Let your faith be like a shield, and you will be able to stop all the flaming arrows of the evil one. 17 Let God's saving power be like a helmet, and for a sword use God's message that comes from the Spirit.

18 Never stop praying, especially for others. Always pray by the power of the Spirit. Stay alert and keep praying for God's people. 19 Pray that I will be given the message to speak and that I may fearlessly explain the mystery about the good news. 20 I was sent to do this work, and that's the reason I am in jail. So pray that I will be brave and will speak as I should.

Final Greetings

21-22 I want you to know how I am getting along and what I am doing. That's why I am sending Tychicus to you. He is a dear friend, as well as a faithful servant of the Lord. He will tell you how I am doing, and he will cheer you up.

23 I pray that God the Father and the Lord Jesus Christ will give peace, love, and faith to every follower! 24 May God be kind to everyone who keeps on loving our Lord Jesus Christ.

PHILIPPIANS

1 From Paul and Timothy, servants of Christ Jesus.
To all of God's people who belong to Christ Jesus at Philippi and to all of your church officials and officers.[a]

2 I pray that God our Father and the Lord Jesus Christ will be kind to you and will bless you with peace!

Paul's Prayer for the Church in Philippi

3 Every time I think of you, I thank my God. 4 And whenever I mention you in my prayers, it makes me happy. 5 This is because you have taken part with me in spreading the good news from the first day you heard about it. 6 God is the one who began this good work in you, and I am certain that he won't stop before it is complete on the day that Christ Jesus returns.

7 You have a special place in my heart. So it is only natural for me to feel the way I do. All of you have helped in the work that God has given me, as I defend the good news and tell about it here in jail. 8 God himself knows how much I want to see you. He knows that I care for you in the same way that Christ Jesus does.

9 I pray that your love will keep on growing and that you will fully know and understand 10 how to make the right choices. Then you will still be pure and innocent when Christ returns. And until that day, 11 Jesus Christ will keep you busy doing good deeds that bring glory and praise to God.

What Life Means to Paul

12 My dear friends, I want you to know that what has happened to me has helped to spread the good news. 13 The Roman guards and all the others know that I am here in jail because I serve Christ. 14 Now most of the Lord's followers have become brave and are fearlessly telling the message.[b]

15 Some are preaching about Christ because they are jealous and envious of us. Others are preaching because they want to help. 16 They love Christ and know that I am here to defend the good news about him. 17 But the ones who are jealous of us are not sincere. They just want to cause trouble for me while I am in jail. 18 But that doesn't matter. All that matters is that people are telling about Christ, whether they are sincere or not. That is what makes me glad.

I will keep on being glad, 19 because I know that your prayers and the help that comes from the Spirit of Christ Jesus will keep me safe. 20 I honestly expect and hope that I will never do anything to be ashamed of. Whether I live or die, I always want to be as brave as I am now and bring honor to Christ.

21 If I live, it will be for Christ, and if I die, I will gain even more. 22 I don't know what to choose. I could keep on living and doing something useful. 23 It is a hard choice to make. I want to die and be with Christ, because that would be much better. 24-25 But I know that all of you still need me. That's why I am sure I will stay on to help you grow and be happy in your faith. 26 Then, when I visit you again, you will have good reason to take great pride in Christ Jesus because of me.[c]

27 Above all else, you must live in a way that brings honor to the good news about Christ. Then, whether I visit you or not, I will hear that all of you think alike. I will know that you are working together and that you are struggling side by side to get others to believe the good news.

28 Be brave when you face your enemies. Your courage will show them that they are going to be destroyed, and it will show you that you will be saved. God will make all of this happen, 29 and he has blessed you. Not only do you have faith in Christ, but you suffer for him. 30 You saw me suffer, and you still hear about my troubles. Now you must suffer in the same way.

True Humility

2 Christ encourages you, and his love comforts you. God's Spirit unites you, and you are concerned for others. 2 Now make me completely happy! Live in harmony by showing love for each other. Be united in what you think, as if you were only one person. 3 Don't be jealous or proud,

---

[a] **1.1** *church officials and officers*: Or "bishops and deacons."   [b] **1.14** *the message*: Some manuscripts have "the Lord's message," and others have "God's message."   [c] **1.26** *take great pride in Christ Jesus because of me*: Or "take great pride in me because of Christ Jesus."

but be humble and consider others more important than yourselves. [4] Care about them as much as you care about yourselves [5] and think the same way that Christ Jesus thought:[d]

[6] Christ was truly God.
But he did not try to remain[e]
equal with God.
[7] Instead he gave up everything[f]
and became a slave,
when he became
like one of us.

[8] Christ was humble.
He obeyed God and even died
on a cross.
[9] Then God gave Christ
the highest place
and honored his name
above all others.

[10] So at the name of Jesus
everyone will bow down,
those in heaven, on earth,
and under the earth.
[11] And to the glory
of God the Father
everyone will openly agree,
"Jesus Christ is Lord!"

Lights in the World

[12] My dear friends, you always obeyed when I was with you. Now that I am away, you should obey even more. So work with fear and trembling to discover what it really means to be saved. [13] God is working in you to make you willing and able to obey him.

[14] Do everything without grumbling or arguing. [15] Then you will be the pure and innocent children of God. You live among people who are crooked and evil, but you must not do anything that they can say is wrong. Try to shine as lights among the people of this world, [16] as you hold firmly to[g] the message that gives life. Then on the day when Christ returns, I can take pride in you. I can also know that my work and efforts were not useless.

[17] Your faith in the Lord and your service are like a sacrifice offered to him. And my own blood may have to be poured out with the sacrifice. If this happens, I will be glad and rejoice with you. [18] In the same way, you should be glad and rejoice with me.

Timothy and Epaphroditus

[19] I want to be encouraged by news about you. So I hope the Lord Jesus will soon let me send Timothy to you. [20] I don't have anyone else who cares about you as much as he does. [21] The others think only about what interests them and not about what concerns Christ Jesus. [22] But you know what kind of person Timothy is. He has worked with me like a son in spreading the good news. [23] I hope to send him

to you, as soon as I find out what is going to happen to me. [24] And I feel sure that the Lord will also let me come soon.

[25] I think I ought to send my dear friend Epaphroditus back to you. He is a follower and a worker and a soldier of the Lord, just as I am. You sent him to look after me, [26] but now he is eager to see you. He is worried, because you heard he was sick. [27] In fact, he was very sick and almost died. But God was kind to him, and also to me, and he kept me from being burdened down with sorrow.

[28] Now I am more eager than ever to send Epaphroditus back again. You will be glad to see him, and I won't have to worry any longer. [29] Be sure to give him a cheerful welcome, just as people who serve the Lord deserve. [30] He almost died working for Christ, and he risked his own life to do for me what you could not.

Being Acceptable to God

3 Finally, my dear friends, be glad that you belong to the Lord. It doesn't bother me to write the same things to you that I have written before. In fact, it is for your own good.

[2] Watch out for those people who behave like dogs! They are evil and want to do more than just circumcise you. [3] But we are the ones who are truly circumcised, because we worship by the power of God's Spirit[h] and take pride in Christ Jesus. We don't brag about what we have done, [4] although I could. Others may brag about themselves, but I have more reason to brag than anyone else. [5] I was circumcised when I was eight days old, and I am from the nation of Israel and the tribe of Benjamin. I am a true Hebrew. As a Pharisee, I strictly obeyed the Law of Moses. [6] And I was so eager that I even made trouble for the church. I did everything the Law demands in order to please God.

[7] But Christ has shown me that what I once thought was valuable is worthless. [8] Nothing is as wonderful as knowing Christ Jesus my Lord. I have given up everything else and count it all as garbage. All I want is Christ [9] and to know that I belong to him. I could not make myself acceptable to God by obeying the Law of Moses. God accepted me simply because of my faith in Christ. [10] All I want is to know Christ and the power that raised him to life. I want to suffer and die as he did, [11] so that somehow I also may be raised to life.

Running toward the Goal

[12] I have not yet reached my goal, and I am not perfect. But Christ has taken hold of me. So I keep on running and struggling to take hold of the prize. [13] My friends, I don't feel that I have already arrived. But I forget what is behind, and I struggle for what is ahead. [14] I run toward the goal, so that I can win the prize of being called to heaven. This is the prize that God offers because of what Christ Jesus has done. [15] All of us who are mature should think in this same way. And if any of you think differently, God will make it clear to you. [16] But we must keep going in the direction that we are now headed.

[17] My friends, I want you to follow my example and learn from others who closely follow the example we set for you. [18] I often warned you that many people are living as enemies of the cross of Christ. And now with tears in my eyes, I warn

---

[d] **2.5** *think the same way that Christ Jesus thought*: Or "think the way you should because you belong to Christ Jesus."
[e] **2.6** *remain*: Or "become." [f] **2.7** *he gave up everything*: Greek, "He emptied himself." [g] **2.16** *hold firmly to*: Or "offer them."
[h] **3.3** *by the power of God's Spirit*: Some manuscripts have "sincerely."

you again ¹⁹ that they are headed for hell! They worship their stomachs and brag about the disgusting things they do. All they can think about are the things of this world.

²⁰ But we are citizens of heaven and are eagerly waiting for our Savior to come from there. Our Lord Jesus Christ ²¹ has power over everything, and he will make these poor bodies of ours like his own glorious body.

4 Dear friends, I love you and long to see you. Please keep on being faithful to the Lord. You are my pride and joy.

Paul Encourages the Lord's Followers

² Euodia and Syntyche, you belong to the Lord, so I beg you to stop arguing with each other. ³ And, my true partner,ⁱ I ask you to help them. These women have worked together with me and with Clement and with the others in spreading the good news. Their names are now written in the book of life.

⁴ Always be glad because of the Lord! I will say it again: Be glad. ⁵ Always be gentle with others. The Lord will soon be here. ⁶ Don't worry about anything, but pray about everything. With thankful hearts offer up your prayers and requests to God. ⁷ Then, because you belong to Christ Jesus, God will bless you with peace that no one can completely understand. And this peace will control the way you think and feel.

⁸ Finally, my friends, keep your minds on whatever is true, pure, right, holy, friendly, and proper. Don't ever stop thinking about what is truly worthwhile and worthy of praise. ⁹ You know the teachings I gave you, and you know what you heard me say and saw me do. So follow my example. And God, who gives peace, will be with you.

Paul Gives Thanks for the Gifts He Was Given

¹⁰ The Lord has made me very grateful that at last you have thought about me once again. Actually, you were thinking about me all along, but you didn't have any chance to show it. ¹¹ I am not complaining about having too little. I have learned to be satisfied with/ whatever I have. ¹² I know what it is to be poor or to have plenty, and I have lived under all kinds of conditions. I know what it means to be full or to be hungry, to have too much or too little. ¹³ Christ gives me the strength to face anything.

¹⁴ It was good of you to help me when I was having such a hard time. ¹⁵ My friends at Philippi, you remember what it was like when I started preaching the good news in Macedonia. After I left there, you were the only church that became my partner by giving blessings and by receiving them in return. ¹⁶ Even when I was in Thessalonica, you helped me more than once. ¹⁷ I am not trying to get something from you, but I want you to receive the blessings that come from giving.

¹⁸ I have been paid back everything, and with interest. I am completely satisfied with the gifts that you had Epaphroditus bring me. They are like a sweet-smelling offering or like the right kind of sacrifice that pleases God. ¹⁹ I pray that God will take care of all your needs with the wonderful blessings that come from Christ Jesus! ²⁰ May God our Father be praised forever and ever. Amen.

Final Greetings

²¹ Give my greetings to all who are God's people because of Christ Jesus.

The Lord's followers here with me send you their greetings.

²² All of God's people send their greetings, especially those in the service of the Emperor.

²³ I pray that our Lord Jesus Christ will be kind to you and will bless your life!

ⁱ **4.3** *partner*: Or "Syzygus," a person's name.   ʲ **4.11** *be satisfied with*: Or "get by on."

COLOSSIANS

1 From Paul, chosen by God to be an apostle of Christ Jesus, and from Timothy, who is also a follower.

² To God's people who live in Colossae and are faithful followers of Christ.

I pray that God our Father will be kind to you and will bless you with peace!

A Prayer of Thanks

³ Each time we pray for you, we thank God, the Father of our Lord Jesus Christ. ⁴ We have heard of your faith in Christ and of your love for all of God's people, ⁵ because what you hope for is kept safe for you in heaven. You first heard about this hope when you believed the true message, which is the good news.

⁶ The good news is spreading all over the world with great success. It has spread in that same way among you, ever since the first day you learned the truth about God's wonderful kindness ⁷ from our good friend Epaphras. He works together with us for Christ and is a faithful worker for you.ᵃ ⁸ He is also the one who told us about the love that God's Spirit has given you.

The Person and Work of Christ

⁹ We have not stopped praying for you since the first day we heard about you. In fact, we always pray that God will show you everything he wants you to do and that you may have all the wisdom and understanding that his Spirit gives. ¹⁰ Then you will live a life that honors the Lord, and

---

ᵃ **1.7,12** *you*: Some manuscripts have "us."

you will always please him by doing good deeds. You will come to know God even better. [11] His glorious power will make you patient and strong enough to endure anything, and you will be truly happy.

[12] I pray that you will be grateful to God for letting you[a] have part in what he has promised his people in the kingdom of light. [13] God rescued us from the dark power of Satan and brought us into the kingdom of his dear Son, [14] who forgives our sins and sets us free.

[15] Christ is exactly like God,
 who cannot be seen.
He is the first-born Son,
 superior to all creation.
[16] Everything was created by him,
 everything in heaven
  and on earth,
 everything seen and unseen,
 including all forces
  and powers,
 and all rulers
  and authorities.
All things were created
 by God's Son,
and everything was made
 for him.

[17] God's Son was before all else,
 and by him everything
  is held together.
[18] He is the head of his body,
 which is the church.
He is the very beginning,
 the first to be raised
  from death,
so that he would be
 above all others.

[19] God himself was pleased
 to live fully in his Son.
[20] And God was pleased
 for him to make peace
 by sacrificing his blood
  on the cross,
so that all beings in heaven
 and on earth
would be brought back to God.

[21] You used to be far from God. Your thoughts made you his enemies, and you did evil things. [22] But his Son became a human and died. So God made peace with you, and now he lets you stand in his presence as people who are holy and faultless and innocent. [23] But you must stay deeply rooted and firm in your faith. You must not give up the hope you received when you heard the good news. It was preached to everyone on earth, and I myself have become a servant of this message.

Paul's Service to the Church

[24] I am glad that I can suffer for you. I am pleased also that in my own body I can continue[b] the suffering of Christ for his body, the church. [25] God's plan was to make me a servant of his church and to send me to preach his complete message to you. [26] For ages and ages this message was kept secret from everyone, but now it has been explained to God's people. [27] God did this because he wanted you Gentiles to understand his wonderful and glorious mystery. And the mystery is that Christ lives in you, and he is your hope of sharing in God's glory.

[28] We announce the message about Christ, and we use all our wisdom to warn and teach everyone, so that all of Christ's followers will grow and become mature. [29] That's why I work so hard and use the mighty power he gives me.

2 I want you to know what a struggle I am going through for you, for God's people at Laodicea, and for all of those followers who have never met me. [2] I do it to encourage them. Then as their hearts are joined together in love, they will be wonderfully blessed with complete understanding. And they will truly know Christ. Not only is he the key to God's mystery, [3] but all wisdom and knowledge are hidden away in him. [4] I tell you these things to keep you from being fooled by fancy talk. [5] Even though I am not with you, I keep thinking about you. I am glad to know that you are living as you should and that your faith in Christ is strong.

Christ Brings Real Life

[6] You have accepted Christ Jesus as your Lord. Now keep on following him. [7] Plant your roots in Christ and let him be the foundation for your life. Be strong in your faith, just as you were taught. And be grateful.

[8] Don't let anyone fool you by using senseless arguments. These arguments may sound wise, but they are only human teachings. They come from the powers of this world and not from Christ.

[9] God lives fully in Christ. [10] And you are fully grown because you belong to Christ, who is over every power and authority. [11] Christ has also taken away your selfish desires, just as circumcision removes flesh from the body. [12] And when you were baptized, it was the same as being buried with Christ. Then you were raised to life because you had faith in the power of God, who raised Christ from death. [13] You were dead, because you were sinful and were not God's people. But God let Christ make you[c] alive, when he forgave all our sins.

[14] God wiped out the charges that were against us for disobeying the Law of Moses. He took them away and nailed them to the cross. [15] There Christ defeated all powers and forces. He let the whole world see them being led away as prisoners when he celebrated his victory.

[16] Don't let anyone tell you what you must eat or drink. Don't let them say that you must celebrate the New Moon festival, the Sabbath, or any other festival. [17] These things are only a shadow of what was to come. But Christ is real!

[18] Don't be cheated by people who make a show of acting humble and who worship angels.[d] They brag about seeing visions. But it is all nonsense, because their minds are filled with selfish desires. [19] They are no longer part of Christ, who is the head of the whole body. Christ gives the body its strength, and he uses its joints and muscles to hold it together, as it grows by the power of God.

---

[a] 1.7,12 *you*: Some manuscripts have "us."   [b] 1.24 *continue*: Or "complete."   [c] 2.13 *you*: See the note at 1.7, 12.
[d] 2.18 *worship angels*: Or "worship with angels (in visions of heaven)."

Christ Brings New Life

20 You died with Christ. Now the forces of the universe don't have any power over you. Why do you live as if you had to obey such rules as, **21** "Don't handle this. Don't taste that. Don't touch this."? **22** After these things are used, they are no longer good for anything. So why be bothered with the rules that humans have made up? **23** Obeying these rules may seem to be the smart thing to do. They appear to make you love God more and to be very humble and to have control over your body. But they don't really have any power over our desires.

3 You have been raised to life with Christ. Now set your heart on what is in heaven, where Christ rules at God's right side. **2** Think about what is up there, not about what is here on earth. **3** You died, which means that your life is hidden with Christ, who sits beside God. **4** Christ gives meaning to your*e* life, and when he appears, you will also appear with him in glory.

5 Don't be controlled by your body. Kill every desire for the wrong kind of sex. Don't be immoral or indecent or have evil thoughts. Don't be greedy, which is the same as worshiping idols. **6** God is angry with people who disobey him by doing*f* these things. **7** And that is exactly what you did, when you lived among people who behaved in this way. **8** But now you must stop doing such things. You must quit being angry, hateful, and evil. You must no longer say insulting or cruel things about others. **9** And stop lying to each other. You have given up your old way of life with its habits. **10** Each of you is now a new person. You are becoming more and more like your Creator, and you will understand him better. **11** It doesn't matter if you are a Greek or a Jew, or if you are circumcised or not. You may even be a barbarian or a Scythian, and you may be a slave or a free person. Yet Christ is all that matters, and he lives in all of us.

12 God loves you and has chosen you as his own special people. So be gentle, kind, humble, meek, and patient. **13** Put up with each other, and forgive anyone who does you wrong, just as Christ has forgiven you. **14** Love is more important than anything else. It is what ties everything completely together.

15 Each one of you is part of the body of Christ, and you were chosen to live together in peace. So let the peace that comes from Christ control your thoughts. And be grateful. **16** Let the message about Christ completely fill your lives, while you use all your wisdom to teach and instruct each other. With thankful hearts, sing psalms, hymns, and spiritual songs to God. **17** Whatever you say or do should be done in the name of the Lord Jesus, as you give thanks to God the Father because of him.

Some Rules for Christian Living

18 A wife must put her husband first. This is her duty as a follower of the Lord.

19 A husband must love his wife and not abuse her.

20 Children must always obey their parents. This pleases the Lord.

21 Parents, don't be hard on your children. If you are, they might give up.

22 Slaves, you must always obey your earthly masters. Try to please them at all times, and not just when you think they are watching. Honor the Lord and serve your masters with your whole heart. **23** Do your work willingly, as though you were serving the Lord himself, and not just your earthly master. **24** In fact, the Lord Christ is the one you are really serving, and you know that he will reward you. **25** But Christ has no favorites! He will punish evil people, just as they deserve.

4 Slave owners, be fair and honest with your slaves. Don't forget that you have a Master in heaven.

2 Never give up praying. And when you pray, keep alert and be thankful. **3** Be sure to pray that God will make a way for us to spread his message and explain the mystery about Christ, even though I am in jail for doing this. **4** Please pray that I will make the message as clear as possible.

5 When you are with unbelievers, always make good use of the time. **6** Be pleasant and hold their interest when you speak the message. Choose your words carefully and be ready to give answers to anyone who asks questions.

Final Greetings

7 Tychicus is the dear friend, who faithfully works and serves the Lord with us, and he will give you the news about me. **8** I am sending him to cheer you up by telling you how we are getting along. **9** Onesimus, that dear and faithful follower from your own group, is coming with him. The two of them will tell you everything that has happened here.

10 Aristarchus is in jail with me. He sends greetings to you, and so does Mark, the cousin of Barnabas. You have already been told to welcome Mark, if he visits you. **11** Jesus, who is known as Justus, sends his greetings. These three men are the only Jewish followers who have worked with me for the kingdom of God. They have given me much comfort.

12 Your own Epaphras, who serves Christ Jesus, sends his greetings. He always prays hard that you may fully know what the Lord wants you to do and that you may do it completely. **13** I have seen how much trouble he has gone through for you and for the followers in Laodicea and Hierapolis.

14 Our dear doctor Luke sends you his greetings, and so does Demas.

15 Give my greetings to the followers at Laodicea, especially to Nympha and the church that meets in her home. **16** After this letter has been read to your people, be sure to have it read in the church at Laodicea. And you should read the letter that I have sent to them.

17 Remind Archippus to do the work that the Lord has given him to do.

18 I am signing this letter myself: PAUL.
Don't forget that I am in jail.
I pray that God will be kind to you.

---

e **3.4** *your*: Some manuscripts have "our."   *f* **3.6** *people who disobey him by doing*: Some manuscripts do not have these words.

1 THESSALONIANS

1 From Paul, Silas,[a] and Timothy.
  To the church in Thessalonica, the people of God the Father and of the Lord Jesus Christ.

I pray that God will be kind to you and will bless you with peace!

2 We thank God for you and always mention you in our prayers. Each time we pray, 3 we tell God our Father about your faith and loving work and about your firm hope in our Lord Jesus Christ.

The Thessalonians' Faith and Example

4 My dear friends, God loves you, and we know he has chosen you to be his people. 5 When we told you the good news, it was with the power and assurance that come from the Holy Spirit, and not simply with words. You knew what kind of people we were and how we helped you. 6 So, when you accepted the message, you followed our example and the example of the Lord. You suffered, but the Holy Spirit made you glad.

7 You became an example for all the Lord's followers in Macedonia and Achaia. 8 And because of you, the Lord's message has spread everywhere in those regions. Now the news of your faith in God is known all over the world, and we don't have to say a thing about it. 9 Everyone is talking about how you welcomed us and how you turned away from idols to serve the true and living God. 10 They also tell how you are waiting for his Son Jesus to come from heaven. God raised him from death, and on the day of judgment Jesus will save us from God's anger.

Paul's Work in Thessalonica

2 My friends, you know that our time with you wasn't wasted. 2 As you remember, we had been mistreated and insulted at Philippi. But God gave us the courage to tell you the good news about him, even though many people caused us trouble. 3 We didn't have any hidden motives when we won you over, and we didn't try to fool or trick anyone. 4 God was pleased to trust us with his message. We didn't speak to please people, but to please God who knows our motives.

5 You also know that we didn't try to flatter anyone. God himself knows that what we did wasn't a cover-up for greed. 6 We were not trying to get you or anyone else to praise us. 7 But as apostles, we could have demanded help from you. After all, Christ is the one who sent us. We chose to be like children or like a mother[b] nursing her baby. 8 We cared so much for you, and you became so dear to us, that we were willing to give our lives for you when we gave you God's message.

9 My dear friends, you surely haven't forgotten our hard work and hardships. You remember how night and day we struggled to make a living, so that we could tell you God's message without being a burden to anyone. 10 Both you and

God are witnesses that we were pure and honest and innocent in our dealings with you followers of the Lord. 11 You also know we did everything for you that parents would do for their own children. 12 We begged, encouraged, and urged each of you to live in a way that would honor God. He is the one who chose you to share in his own kingdom and glory.

13 We always thank God that you believed the message we preached. It came from him, and it isn't something made up by humans. You accepted it as God's message, and now he is working in you. 14 My friends, you did just like God's churches in Judea and like the other followers of Christ Jesus there. And so, you were mistreated by your own people, in the same way they were mistreated by their people.

15 Those Jews killed the Lord Jesus and the prophets, and they even chased us away. God doesn't like what they do and neither does anyone else. 16 They keep us from speaking his message to the Gentiles and from leading them to be saved. The Jews have always gone too far with their sins. Now God has finally become angry and will punish them.

Paul Wants To Visit the Church Again

17 My friends, we were kept from coming to you for a while, but we never stopped thinking about you. We were eager to see you and tried our best to visit you in person. 18 We really wanted to come. I myself tried several times, but Satan always stopped us. 19 After all, when the Lord Jesus appears, who else but you will give us hope and joy and be like a glorious crown for us? 20 You alone are our glory and joy!

3 Finally, we couldn't stand it any longer. We decided to stay in Athens by ourselves 2 and send our friend Timothy to you. He works with us as God's servant and preaches the good news about Christ. We wanted him to make you strong in your faith and to encourage you. 3 We didn't want any of you to be discouraged by all these troubles. You knew we would have to suffer, 4 because when we were with you, we told you this would happen. And we did suffer, as you well know. 5 At last, when I could not wait any longer, I sent Timothy to find out about your faith. I hoped that Satan had not tempted you and made all our work useless.

6 Timothy has come back from his visit with you and has told us about your faith and love. He also said that you always have happy memories of us and that you want to see us as much as we want to see you.

7 My friends, even though we have a lot of trouble and suffering, your faith makes us feel better about you. 8 Your strong faith in the Lord is like a breath of new life. 9 How can we possibly thank God enough for all the happiness you have brought us? 10 Day and night we sincerely pray that we will see you again and help you to have an even stronger faith.

11 We pray that God our Father and our Lord Jesus will let us visit you. 12 May the Lord make your love for each other

---

[a] 1.1 *Silas*: The Greek text has "Silvanus," another form of the name Silas.   [b] 2.7 *like children or like a mother*: Some manuscripts have "as gentle as a mother."

and for everyone else grow by leaps and bounds. That's how our love for you has grown. 13 And when our Lord comes with all of his people, I pray that he will make your hearts pure and innocent in the sight of God the Father.

A Life That Pleases God

4 Finally, my dear friends, since you belong to the Lord Jesus, we beg and urge you to live as we taught you. Then you will please God. You are already living that way, but try even harder. 2 Remember the instructions we gave you as followers of the Lord Jesus. 3 God wants you to be holy, so don't be immoral in matters of sex. 4 Respect and honor your wife.c 5 Don't be a slave of your desires or live like people who don't know God. 6 You must not cheat any of the Lord's followers in matters of sex.d Remember, we warned you that he punishes everyone who does such things. 7 God didn't choose you to be filthy, but to be pure. 8 So if you don't obey these rules, you are not really disobeying us. You are disobeying God, who gives you his Holy Spirit.

9 We don't have to write you about the need to love each other. God has taught you to do this, 10 and you already have shown your love for all of his people in Macedonia. But, my dear friends, we ask you to do even more. 11 Try your best to live quietly, to mind your own business, and to work hard, just as we taught you to do. 12 Then you will be respected by people who are not followers of the Lord, and you won't have to depend on anyone.

The Lord's Coming

13 My friends, we want you to understand how it will be for those followers who have already died. Then you won't grieve over them and be like people who don't have any hope. 14 We believe that Jesus died and was raised to life. We also believe that when God brings Jesus back again, he will bring with him all who had faith in Jesus before they died. 15 Our Lord Jesus told us that when he comes, we won't go up to meet him ahead of his followers who have already died.

16 With a loud command and with the shout of the chief angel and a blast of God's trumpet, the Lord will return from heaven. Then those who had faith in Christ before they died will be raised to life. 17 Next, all of us who are still alive will be taken up into the clouds together with them to meet the Lord in the sky. From that time on we will all be with the Lord forever. 18 Encourage each other with these words.

5 I don't need to write you about the time or date when all this will happen. 2 You surely know that the Lord's returne will be as a thief coming at night. 3 People will think they are safe and secure. But destruction will suddenly strike them like the pains of a woman about to give birth. And they won't escape.

4 My dear friends, you don't live in darkness, and so that day won't surprise you like a thief. 5 You belong to the light and live in the day. We don't live in the night or belong to the dark. 6 Others may sleep, but we should stay awake and be alert. 7 People sleep during the night, and some even get drunk. 8 But we belong to the day. So we must stay sober and let our faith and love be like a suit of armor. Our firm hope that we will be saved is our helmet.

9 God doesn't intend to punish us, but wants us to be saved by our Lord Jesus Christ. 10 Christ died for us, so that we could live with him, whether we are alive or dead when he comes. 11 That's why you must encourage and help each other, just as you are already doing.

Final Instructions and Greetings

12 My friends, we ask you to be thoughtful of your leaders who work hard and tell you how to live for the Lord. 13 Show them great respect and love because of their work. Try to get along with each other. 14 My friends, we beg you to warn anyone who isn't living right. Encourage anyone who feels left out, help all who are weak, and be patient with everyone. 15 Don't be hateful to people, just because they are hateful to you. Rather, be good to each other and to everyone else.

16 Always be joyful 17 and never stop praying. 18 Whatever happens, keep thanking God because of Jesus Christ. This is what God wants you to do.

19 Don't turn away God's Spirit 20 or ignore prophecies. 21 Put everything to the test. Accept what is good 22 and don't have anything to do with evil.

23 I pray that God, who gives peace, will make you completely holy. And may your spirit, soul, and body be kept healthy and faultless until our Lord Jesus Christ returns. 24 The one who chose you can be trusted, and he will do this.

25 Friends, please pray for us.

26 Give the Lord's followers a warm greeting.

27 In the name of the Lord I beg you to read this letter to all his followers.

28 I pray that our Lord Jesus Christ will be kind to you!

---

c 4.4 your wife: Or "your body."   d 4.6 in matters of sex: Or "in business."   e 5.2 the Lord's return: The Greek text has "the day of the Lord."

2 THESSALONIANS

1 From Paul, Silas,[a] and Timothy.
To the church in Thessalonica, the people of God our Father and of the Lord Jesus Christ.

[2] I pray that God our Father and the Lord Jesus Christ will be kind to you and will bless you with peace!

When Christ Returns

[3] My dear friends, we always have good reason to thank God for you, because your faith in God and your love for each other keep growing all the time. [4] That's why we brag about you to all of God's churches. We tell them how patient you are and how you keep on having faith, even though you are going through a lot of trouble and suffering.

[5] All of this shows that God judges fairly and that he is making you fit to share in his kingdom for which you are suffering. [6] It is only right for God to punish everyone who is causing you trouble, [7] but he will give you relief from your troubles. He will do the same for us, when the Lord Jesus comes from heaven with his powerful angels [8] and with a flaming fire.

Our Lord Jesus will punish anyone who doesn't know God and won't obey his message. [9] Their punishment will be eternal destruction, and they will be kept far from the presence of our Lord and his glorious strength. [10] This will happen on that day when the Lord returns to be praised and honored by all who have faith in him and belong to him. This includes you, because you believed what we said.

[11] God chose you, and we keep praying that God will make you worthy of being his people. We pray for God's power to help you do all the good things that you hope to do and that your faith makes you want to do. [12] Then, because God and our Lord Jesus Christ are so kind, you will bring honor to the name of our Lord Jesus, and he will bring honor to you.

The Lord's Return

2 When our Lord Jesus returns, we will be gathered up to meet him. So I ask you, my friends, [2] not to be easily upset or disturbed by people who claim that the Lord[b] has already come. They may say that they heard this directly from the Holy Spirit, or from someone else, or even that they read it in one of our letters. [3] But don't be fooled! People will rebel against God. Then before the Lord returns, the wicked[c] one who is doomed to be destroyed will appear. [4] He will brag and oppose everything that is holy or sacred. He will even sit in God's temple and claim to be God. [5] Don't you remember that I told you this while I was still with you?

[6] You already know what is holding this wicked one back until it is time for him to come. [7] His mysterious power is already at work, but someone is holding him back. And the wicked one won't appear until that someone is out of the way. [8] Then he will appear, but the Lord Jesus will kill him simply by breathing on him. He will be completely destroyed by the Lord's glorious return.

[9] When the wicked one appears, Satan will pretend to work all kinds of miracles, wonders, and signs. [10] Lost people will be fooled by his evil deeds. They could be saved, but they will refuse to love the truth and accept it. [11] So God will make sure that they are fooled into believing a lie. [12] All of them will be punished, because they would rather do evil than believe the truth.

Be Faithful

[13] My friends, the Lord loves you, and it is only natural for us to thank God for you. God chose you to be the first ones to be saved.[d] His Spirit made you holy, and you put your faith in the truth. [14] God used our preaching as his way of inviting you to share in the glory of our Lord Jesus Christ. [15] My friends, that's why you must remain faithful and follow closely what we taught you in person and by our letters.

[16] God our Father loves us. He is kind and has given us eternal comfort and a wonderful hope. We pray that our Lord Jesus Christ and God our Father [17] will encourage you and help you always to do and say the right thing.

Pray for Us

3 Finally, our friends, please pray for us. This will help the message about the Lord to spread quickly, and others will respect it, just as you do. [2] Pray that we may be kept safe from worthless and evil people. After all, not everyone has faith. [3] But the Lord can be trusted to make you strong and protect you from harm. [4] He has made us sure that you are obeying what we taught you and that you will keep on obeying. [5] I pray that the Lord will guide you to be as loving as God and as patient as Christ.

Warnings against Laziness

[6] My dear friends, in the name of[e] the Lord Jesus, I beg you not to have anything to do with any of your people who loaf around and refuse to obey the instructions we gave you. [7] You surely know that you should follow our example. We didn't waste our time loafing, [8] and we didn't accept food from anyone without paying for it. We didn't want to be a burden to any of you, so night and day we worked as hard as we could.

[9] We had the right not to work, but we wanted to set an example for you. [10] We also gave you the rule that if you don't work, you don't eat. [11] Now we learn that some of you just loaf around and won't do any work, except the work of a busybody. [12] So, for the sake of our Lord Jesus Christ, we ask and beg these people to settle down and start working for a living. [13] Dear friends, you must never become tired of doing right.

---

[a] 1.1 *Silas*: The Greek text has "Silvanus," which is another form of the name Silas. [b] 2.2 *Lord*: The Greek text has "day of the Lord."
[c] 2.3 *wicked*: Some manuscripts have "sinful." [d] 2.13 *God chose you to be the first ones to be saved*: Some manuscripts have "From the beginning God chose you to be saved." [e] 3.6 *in the name of*: Or "as a follower of."

14 Be on your guard against any followers who refuse to obey what we have written in this letter. Put them to shame by not having anything to do with them. 15 Don't consider them your enemies, but speak kindly to them as you would to any other follower.

Final Prayer

16 I pray that the Lord, who gives peace, will always bless you with peace. May the Lord be with all of you.

17 I always sign my letters as I am now doing: PAUL.

18 I pray that our Lord Jesus Christ will be kind to all of you.

1 TIMOTHY

1 From Paul.
God our Savior and Christ Jesus commanded me to be an apostle of Christ Jesus, who gives us hope.

2 Timothy, because of our faith, you are like a son to me. I pray that God our Father and our Lord Jesus Christ will be kind and merciful to you. May they bless you with peace!

Warning against False Teaching

3 When I was leaving for Macedonia, I asked you to stay on in Ephesus and warn certain people there to stop spreading their false teachings. 4 You needed to warn them to stop wasting their time on senseless stories and endless lists of ancestors. Such things only cause arguments. They don't help anyone to do God's work that can only be done by faith.

5 You must teach people to have genuine love, as well as a good conscience and true faith. 6 There are some who have given up these for nothing but empty talk. 7 They want to be teachers of the Law of Moses. But they don't know what they are talking about, even though they think they do.

8 We know that the Law is good, if it is used in the right way. 9 We also understand that it wasn't given to control people who please God, but to control lawbreakers, criminals, godless people, and sinners. It is for wicked and evil people, and for murderers, who would even kill their own parents. 10 The Law was written for people who are sexual perverts or who live as homosexuals or are kidnappers or liars or won't tell the truth in court. It is for anything else that opposes the correct teaching 11 of the good news that the glorious and wonderful God has given me.

Being Thankful for God's Kindness

12 I thank Christ Jesus our Lord. He has given me the strength for my work because he knew that he could trust me. 13 I used to say terrible and insulting things about him, and I was cruel. But he had mercy on me because I didn't know what I was doing, and I had not yet put my faith in him. 14 Christ Jesus our Lord was very kind to me. He has greatly blessed my life with faith and love just like his own.

15 "Christ Jesus came into the world to save sinners." This saying is true, and it can be trusted. I was the worst sinner of all! 16 But since I was worse than anyone else, God had mercy on me and let me be an example of the endless patience of Christ Jesus. He did this so that others would put their faith in Christ and have eternal life. 17 I pray that

honor and glory will always be given to the only God, who lives forever and is the invisible and eternal King! Amen.

18 Timothy, my son, the instructions I am giving you are based on what some prophets once said about you. If you follow these instructions, you will fight like a good soldier. 19 You will be faithful and have a clear conscience. Some people have made a mess of their faith because they didn't listen to their consciences. 20 Two of them are Hymenaeus and Alexander. I have given these men over to the power of Satan, so they will learn not to oppose God.

How To Pray

2 First of all, I ask you to pray for everyone. Ask God to help and bless them all, and tell God how thankful you are for each of them. 2 Pray for kings and others in power, so that we may live quiet and peaceful lives as we worship and honor God. 3 This kind of prayer is good, and it pleases God our Savior. 4 God wants everyone to be saved and to know the whole truth, which is,

5 There is only one God,
and Christ Jesus
is the only one
who can bring us
to God.
Jesus was truly human,
and he gave himself
to rescue all of us.
6 God showed us this
at the right time.

7 This is why God chose me to be a preacher and an apostle of the good news. I am telling the truth. I am not lying. God sent me to teach the Gentiles about faith and truth.

8 I want everyone everywhere to lift innocent hands toward heaven and pray, without being angry or arguing with each other.

9 I would like for women to wear modest and sensible clothes. They should not have fancy hairdos, or wear expensive clothes, or put on jewelry made of gold or pearls. 10 Women who claim to love God should do helpful things for others, 11 and they should learn by being quiet and paying attention. 12 They should be silent and not be allowed to teach or to tell men what to do. 13 After all, Adam was cre-

ated before Eve, [14] and the man Adam wasn't the one who was fooled. It was the woman Eve who was completely fooled and sinned. [15] But women will be saved by having children,[a] if they stay faithful, loving, holy, and modest.

Church Officials

3 It is true that anyone who desires to be a church official[b] wants to be something worthwhile. [2] That's why officials must have a good reputation and be faithful in marriage.[c] They must be self-controlled, sensible, well-behaved, friendly to strangers, and able to teach. [3] They must not be heavy drinkers or troublemakers. Instead, they must be kind and gentle and not love money.

[4] Church officials must be in control of their own families, and they must see that their children are obedient and always respectful. [5] If they don't know how to control their own families, how can they look after God's people?

[6] They must not be new followers of the Lord. If they are, they might become proud and be doomed along with the devil. [7] Finally, they must be well-respected by people who are not followers. Then they won't be trapped and disgraced by the devil.

Church Officers

[8] Church officers[d] should be serious. They must not be liars, heavy drinkers, or greedy for money. [9] And they must have a clear conscience and hold firmly to what God has shown us about our faith. [10] They must first prove themselves. Then if no one has anything against them, they can serve as officers.

[11] Women must also be serious. They must not gossip or be heavy drinkers, and they must be faithful in everything they do.

[12] Church officers must be faithful in marriage.[e] They must be in full control of their children and everyone else in their home. [13] Those who serve well as officers will earn a good reputation and will be highly respected for their faith in Christ Jesus.

The Mystery of Our Religion

[14] I hope to visit you soon. But I am writing these instructions, [15] so that if I am delayed, you will know how everyone who belongs to God's family ought to behave. After all, the church of the living God is the strong foundation of truth.

[16] Here is the great mystery of our religion:

Christ[f] came as a human.
The Spirit proved
    that he pleased God,
and he was seen by angels.

Christ was preached
    to the nations.
People in this world
    put their faith in him,
and he was taken up to glory.

People Will Turn from Their Faith

4 God's Spirit clearly says that in the last days many people will turn from their faith. They will be fooled by evil spirits and by teachings that come from demons. [2] They will also be fooled by the false claims of liars whose consciences have lost all feeling. These liars [3] will forbid people to marry or to eat certain foods. But God created these foods to be eaten with thankful hearts by his followers who know the truth. [4] Everything God created is good. And if you give thanks, you may eat anything. [5] What God has said and your prayer will make it fit to eat.

Paul's Advice to Timothy

[6] If you teach these things to other followers, you will be a good servant of Christ Jesus. You will show that you have grown up on the teachings about our faith and on the good instructions you have obeyed. [7] Don't have anything to do with worthless, senseless stories. Work hard to be truly religious. [8-9] As the saying goes,

"Exercise is good
    for your body,
but religion helps you
    in every way.
It promises life
    now and forever."

These words are worthwhile and should not be forgotten. [10] We have put our hope in the living God, who is the Savior of everyone, but especially of those who have faith. That's why we work and struggle so hard.[g]

[11] Teach these things and tell everyone to do what you say. [12] Don't let anyone make fun of you, just because you are young. Set an example for other followers by what you say and do, as well as by your love, faith, and purity.

[13] Until I arrive, be sure to keep on reading the Scriptures in worship, and don't stop preaching and teaching. [14] Use the gift you were given when the prophets spoke and the group of church leaders[h] blessed you by placing their hands on you. [15] Remember these things and think about them, so everyone can see how well you are doing. [16] Be careful about the way you live and about what you teach. Keep on doing this, and you will save not only yourself, but the people who hear you.

How To Act toward Others

5 Don't correct an older man. Encourage him, as you would your own father. Treat younger men as you would your own brother, [2] and treat older women as you would your own mother. Show the same respect to younger women that you would to your sister.

[3] Take care of any widow who is really in need. [4] But if a widow has children or grandchildren, they should learn to serve God by taking care of her, as she once took care of them. This is what God wants them to do. [5] A widow who is really in need is one who doesn't have any relatives. She

---

[a] **2.15** *saved by having children*: Or "brought safely through childbirth" or "saved by the birth of a child" (that is, by the birth of Jesus) or "saved by being good mothers."   [b] **3.1** *church official*: Or "bishop."   [c] **3.2** *be faithful in marriage*: Or "be the husband of only one wife" or "have never been divorced."   [d] **3.8** *Church officers*: Or "Deacons."   [e] **3.12** *be faithful in marriage*: See the note at 3.2.   [f] **3.16** *Christ*: The Greek text has "he," probably meaning "Christ." Some manuscripts have "God."   [g] **4.10** *struggle so hard*: Some manuscripts have "are treated so badly."   [h] **4.14** *group of church leaders*: Or "group of elders" or "group of presbyters" or "group of priests." This translates one Greek word, and it is related to the one used in 5.17,19.

has faith in God, and she keeps praying to him night and day, asking for his help.

⁶ A widow who thinks only about having a good time is already dead, even though she is still alive.

⁷ Tell all of this to everyone, so they will do the right thing. ⁸ People who don't take care of their relatives, and especially their own families, have given up their faith. They are worse than someone who doesn't have faith in the Lord.

⁹ For a widow to be put on the list of widows, she must be at least sixty years old, and she must have been faithful in marriage.ⁱ ¹⁰ She must also be well-known for doing all sorts of good things, such as raising children, giving food to strangers, welcoming God's people into her home,ʲ helping people in need, and always making herself useful.

¹¹ Don't put young widows on the list. They may later have a strong desire to get married. Then they will turn away from Christ ¹² and become guilty of breaking their promise to him. ¹³ Besides, they will become lazy and get into the habit of going from house to house. Next, they will start gossiping and become busybodies, talking about things that are none of their business.

¹⁴ I would prefer that young widows get married, have children, and look after their families. Then the enemy won't have any reason to say insulting things about us. ¹⁵ Look what's already happened to some of the young widows! They have turned away to follow Satan.

¹⁶ If a woman who is a follower has any widows in her family, sheᵏ should help them. This will keep the church from having that burden, and then the church can help widows who are really in need.

Church Leaders

¹⁷ Church leadersˡ who do their job well deserve to be paidᵐ twice as much, especially if they work hard at preaching and teaching. ¹⁸ It is just as the Scriptures say, "Don't muzzle an ox when you are using it to grind grain." You also know the saying, "Workers are worth their pay."

¹⁹ Don't listen to any charge against a church leader, unless at least two or three people bring the same charges. ²⁰ But if any of the leaders should keep on sinning, they must be corrected in front of the whole group, as a warning to everyone else.

²¹ In the presence of God and Christ Jesus and their chosen angels, I order you to follow my instructions! Be fair with everyone, and don't have any favorites.

²² Don't be too quick to accept people into the service of the Lordⁿ by placing your hands on them.

Don't sin because others do, but stay close to God.

²³ Stop drinking only water. Take a little wine to help your stomach trouble and the other illnesses you always have.

²⁴ Some people get caught in their sins right away, even before the time of judgment. But other people's sins don't show up until later. ²⁵ It is the same with good deeds. Some are easily seen, but none of them can be hidden.

6 If you are a slave, you should respect and honor your owner. This will keep people from saying bad things about God and about our teaching. ² If any of you slaves have owners who are followers, you should show them respect. After all, they are also followers of Christ, and he loves them. So you should serve and help them the best you can.

False Teaching and True Wealth

These are the things you must teach and tell the people to do. ³ Anyone who teaches something different disagrees with the correct and godly teaching of our Lord Jesus Christ. ⁴ Those people who disagree are proud of themselves, but they don't really know a thing. Their minds are sick, and they like to argue over words. They cause jealousy, disagreements, unkind words, evil suspicions, ⁵ and nasty quarrels. They have wicked minds and have missed out on the truth.

These people think religion is supposed to make you rich. ⁶ And religion does make your life rich, by making you content with what you have. ⁷ We didn't bring anything into this world, and we won'tᵒ take anything with us when we leave. ⁸ So we should be satisfied just to have food and clothes. ⁹ People who want to be rich fall into all sorts of temptations and traps. They are caught by foolish and harmful desires that drag them down and destroy them. ¹⁰ The love of money causes all kinds of trouble. Some people want money so much that they have given up their faith and caused themselves a lot of pain.

Fighting a Good Fight for the Faith

¹¹ Timothy, you belong to God, so keep away from all these evil things. Try your best to please God and to be like him. Be faithful, loving, dependable, and gentle. ¹² Fight a good fight for the faith and claim eternal life. God offered it to you when you clearly told about your faith, while so many people listened. ¹³ Now I ask you to make a promise. Make it in the presence of God, who gives life to all, and in the presence of Jesus Christ, who openly told Pontius Pilate about his faith. ¹⁴ Promise to obey completely and fully all that you have been told until our Lord Jesus Christ returns.

¹⁵ The glorious God
　is the only Ruler,
　the King of kings
　and Lord of lords.
At the time that God
　has already decided,
he will send Jesus Christ
　back again.

¹⁶ Only God lives forever!
And he lives in light
　that no one can come near.
No human has ever seen God
　or ever can see him.
God will be honored,
and his power
　will last forever. Amen.

ⁱ **5.9** *been faithful in marriage:* Or "been the wife of only one husband" or "never been divorced."　ʲ **5.10** *welcoming God's people into her home:* The Greek text has "washing the feet of God's people." In New Testament times most people either went barefoot or wore sandals, and a host would often wash the feet of special guests.　ᵏ **5.16** *woman . . . she:* Some manuscripts have "man or woman . . . that person."　ˡ **5.17** *leaders:* Or "elders" or "presbyters" or "priests."　ᵐ **5.17** *paid:* Or "honored" or "respected."　ⁿ **5.22** *to accept people into the service of the Lord:* Or "to forgive people."　ᵒ **6.7** *we won't:* Some manuscripts have "we surely won't."

17 Warn the rich people of this world not to be proud or to trust in wealth that is easily lost. Tell them to have faith in God, who is rich and blesses us with everything we need to enjoy life. **18** Instruct them to do as many good deeds as they can and to help everyone. Remind the rich to be generous and share what they have. **19** This will lay a solid foundation for the future, so that they will know what true life is like.

20 Timothy, guard what God has placed in your care! Don't pay any attention to that godless and stupid talk that sounds smart but really isn't. **21** Some people have even lost their faith by believing this talk.

I pray that the Lord will be kind to all of you!

2 TIMOTHY

1 From Paul, an apostle of Christ Jesus.
God himself chose me to be an apostle, and he gave me the promised life that Jesus Christ makes possible.

2 Timothy, you are like a dear child to me. I pray that God our Father and our Lord Christ Jesus will be kind and merciful to you and will bless you with peace!

Do Not Be Ashamed of the Lord

3 Night and day I mention you in my prayers. I am always grateful for you, as I pray to the God my ancestors and I have served with a clear conscience. **4** I remember how you cried, and I want to see you, because that will make us truly happy. **5** I also remember the genuine faith of your mother Eunice. Your grandmother Lois had the same sort of faith, and I am sure that you have it as well. **6** So I ask you to make full use of the gift that God gave you when I placed my hands on you. Use it well. **7** God's Spirit*ᵃ* doesn't make cowards out of us. The Spirit gives us power, love, and self-control.

8 Don't be ashamed to speak for our Lord. And don't be ashamed of me, just because I am in jail for serving him. Use the power that comes from God and join with me in suffering for telling the good news.

9 God saved us and chose us
  to be his holy people.
We did nothing
  to deserve this,
but God planned it
  because he is so kind.
Even before time began
God planned for Christ Jesus
  to show kindness to us.

10 Now Christ Jesus has come
to show us the kindness
  of God.
Christ our Savior defeated death
and brought us
  the good news.
It shines like a light

and offers life
  that never ends.

11 My work is to be a preacher, an apostle, and a teacher.*ᵇ* **12** That's why I am suffering now. But I am not ashamed! I know the one I have faith in, and I am sure that he can guard until the last day what he has trusted me with.*ᶜ* **13** Now follow the example of the correct teaching I gave you, and let the faith and love of Christ Jesus be your model. **14** You have been trusted with a wonderful treasure. Guard it with the help of the Holy Spirit, who lives within you.

15 You know that everyone in Asia has turned against me, especially Phygelus and Hermogenes. **16** I pray that the Lord will be kind to the family of Onesiphorus. He often cheered me up and wasn't ashamed of me when I was put in jail. **17** Then after he arrived in Rome, he searched everywhere until he found me. **18** I pray that the Lord Jesus will ask God to show mercy to Onesiphorus on the day of judgment. You know how much he helped me in Ephesus.

A Good Soldier of Christ Jesus

2 Timothy, my child, Christ Jesus is kind, and you must let him make you strong. **2** You have often heard me teach. Now I want you to tell these same things to followers who can be trusted to tell others.

3 As a good soldier of Christ Jesus you must endure your share of suffering. **4** Soldiers on duty don't work at outside jobs. They try only to please their commanding officer. **5** No one wins an athletic contest without obeying the rules. **6** And farmers who work hard are the first to eat what grows in their field. **7** If you keep in mind what I have told you, the Lord will help you understand completely.

8 Keep your mind on Jesus Christ! He was from the family of David and was raised from death, just as my good news says. **9** And because of this message, I am locked up in jail and treated like a criminal. But God's good news isn't locked in jail, **10** and so I am willing to put up with anything. Then God's special people will be saved. They will be given eternal glory because they belong to Christ Jesus. **11** Here is a true message:

ᵃ **1.7** *God's Spirit*: Or "God."   *ᵇ* **1.11** *teacher*: Some manuscripts add "of the Gentiles."   *ᶜ* **1.12** *what he has trusted me with*: Or "what I have trusted him with."

"If we died with Christ,
  we will live with him.
[12] If we don't give up,
  we will rule with him.
If we deny
  that we know him,
he will deny
  that he knows us.
[13] If we are not faithful,
  he will still be faithful.
Christ cannot deny
  who he is."

An Approved Worker

[14] Don't let anyone forget these things. And with God[d] as your witness, you must warn them not to argue about words. These arguments don't help anyone. In fact, they ruin everyone who listens to them. [15] Do your best to win God's approval as a worker who doesn't need to be ashamed and who teaches only the true message.

[16] Keep away from worthless and useless talk. It only leads people farther away from God. [17] That sort of talk is like a sore that won't heal. And Hymenaeus and Philetus have been talking this way [18] by teaching that the dead have already been raised to life. This is far from the truth, and it is destroying the faith of some people.

[19] But the foundation that God has laid is solid. On it is written, "The Lord knows who his people are. So everyone who worships the Lord must turn away from evil."

[20] In a large house some dishes are made of gold or silver, while others are made of wood or clay. Some of these are special, and others are not. [21] That's also how it is with people. The ones who stop doing evil and make themselves pure will become special. Their lives will be holy and pleasing to their Master, and they will be able to do all kinds of good deeds.

[22] Run from temptations that capture young people. Always do the right thing. Be faithful, loving, and easy to get along with. Worship with people whose hearts are pure. [23] Stay away from stupid and senseless arguments. These only lead to trouble, [24] and God's servants must not be troublemakers. They must be kind to everyone, and they must be good teachers and very patient.

[25] Be humble when you correct people who oppose you. Maybe God will lead them to turn to him and learn the truth. [26] They have been trapped by the devil, and he makes them obey him, but God may help them escape.

What People Will Be Like in the Last Days

3 You can be certain that in the last days there will be some very hard times. [2] People will love only themselves and money. They will be proud, stuck-up, rude, and disobedient to their parents. They will also be ungrateful, godless, [3] heartless, and hateful. Their words will be cruel, and they will have no self-control or pity. These people will hate everything that is good. [4] They will be sneaky, reckless, and puffed up with pride. Instead of loving God, they will love pleasure. [5] Even though they will make a show of being religious, their religion won't be real. Don't have anything to do with such people.

[6] Some men fool whole families, just to get power over those women who are slaves of sin and are controlled by all sorts of desires. [7] These women always want to learn something new, but they never can discover the truth. [8] Just as Jannes and Jambres opposed Moses, these people are enemies of the truth. Their minds are sick, and their faith isn't real. [9] But they won't get very far with their foolishness. Soon everyone will know the truth about them, just as Jannes and Jambres were found out.

Paul's Last Instructions to Timothy

[10] Timothy, you know what I teach and how I live. You know what I want to do and what I believe. You have seen how patient and loving I am, and how in the past I put up with [11] trouble and suffering in the cities of Antioch, Iconium, and Lystra. Yet the Lord rescued me from all those terrible troubles. [12] Anyone who belongs to Christ Jesus and wants to live right will have trouble from others. [13] But evil people who pretend to be what they are not will become worse than ever, as they fool others and are fooled themselves.

[14] Keep on being faithful to what you were taught and to what you believed. After all, you know who taught you these things. [15] Since childhood, you have known the Holy Scriptures that are able to make you wise enough to have faith in Christ Jesus and be saved. [16] Everything in the Scriptures is God's Word. All of it is useful for teaching and helping people and for correcting them and showing them how to live. [17] The Scriptures train God's servants to do all kinds of good deeds.

4 When Christ Jesus comes as king, he will be the judge of everyone, whether they are living or dead. So with God and Christ as witnesses, I command you [2] to preach God's message. Do it willingly, even if it isn't the popular thing to do. You must correct people and point out their sins. But also cheer them up, and when you instruct them, always be patient. [3] The time is coming when people won't listen to good teaching. Instead, they will look for teachers who will please them by telling them only what they are itching to hear. [4] They will turn from the truth and eagerly listen to senseless stories. [5] But you must stay calm and be willing to suffer. You must work hard to tell the good news and to do your job well.

[6] Now the time has come for me to die. My life is like a drink offering being poured out on the altar. [7] I have fought well. I have finished the race, and I have been faithful. [8] So a crown will be given to me for pleasing the Lord. He judges fairly, and on the day of judgment he will give a crown to me and to everyone else who wants him to appear with power.

Personal Instructions

[9] Come to see me as soon as you can. [10] Demas loves the things of this world so much that he left me and went to Thessalonica. Crescens has gone to Galatia, and Titus has gone to Dalmatia. [11] Only Luke has stayed with me.

Mark can be very helpful to me, so please find him and bring him with you. [12] I sent Tychicus to Ephesus.

[13] When you come, bring the coat I left at Troas with Carpus. Don't forget to bring the scrolls, especially the ones made of leather.

[14] Alexander, the metalworker, has hurt me in many ways. But the Lord will pay him back for what he has done.

---

[d] 2.14 *God*: Some manuscripts have "the Lord," and others have "Christ."

15 Alexander opposes what we preach. You had better watch out for him.

16 When I was first put on trial, no one helped me. In fact, everyone deserted me. I hope it won't be held against them. 17 But the Lord stood beside me. He gave me the strength to tell his full message, so that all Gentiles would hear it. And I was kept safe from hungry lions. 18 The Lord will always keep me from being harmed by evil, and he will bring me safely into his heavenly kingdom. Praise him forever and ever! Amen.

Final Greetings

19 Give my greetings to Priscilla and Aquila and to the family of Onesiphorus.

20 Erastus stayed at Corinth.

Trophimus was sick when I left him at Miletus.

21 Do your best to come before winter.

Eubulus, Pudens, Linus, and Claudia send you their greetings, and so do the rest of the Lord's followers.

22 I pray that the Lord will bless your life and will be kind to you.

TITUS

1 From Paul, a servant of God and an apostle of Jesus Christ.

I encourage God's own people to have more faith and to understand the truth about religion. 2 Then they will have the hope of eternal life that God promised long ago. And God never tells a lie! 3 So, at the proper time, God our Savior gave this message and told me to announce what he had said.

4 Titus, because of our faith, you are like a son to me. I pray that God our Father and Christ Jesus our Savior will be kind to you and will bless you with peace!

What Titus Was To Do in Crete

5 I left you in Crete to do what had been left undone and to appoint leaders[a] for the churches in each town. As I told you, 6 they must have a good reputation and be faithful in marriage.[b] Their children must be followers of the Lord and not have a reputation for being wild and disobedient.

7 Church officials[c] are in charge of God's work, and so they must also have a good reputation. They must not be bossy, quick-tempered, heavy drinkers, bullies, or dishonest in business. 8 Instead, they must be friendly to strangers and enjoy doing good things. They must also be sensible, fair, pure, and self-controlled. 9 They must stick to the true message they were taught, so that their good teaching can help others and correct everyone who opposes it.

10 There are many who don't respect authority, and they fool others by talking nonsense. This is especially true of some Jewish followers. 11 But you must make them be quiet. They are after money, and they upset whole families by teaching what they should not. 12 It is like one of their own prophets once said,

"The people of Crete
    always tell lies.
They are greedy and lazy
    like wild animals."

13 That surely is a true saying. And you should be hard on such people, so you can help them grow stronger in their faith. 14 Don't pay any attention to any of those senseless Jewish stories and human commands. These are made up by people who won't obey the truth.

15 Everything is pure for someone whose heart is pure. But nothing is pure for an unbeliever with a dirty mind. That person's mind and conscience are destroyed. 16 Such people claim to know God, but their actions prove that they really don't. They are disgusting. They won't obey God, and they are too worthless to do anything good.

Instructions for Different Groups of People

2 Titus, you must teach only what is correct. 2 Tell the older men to have self-control and to be serious and sensible. Their faith, love, and patience must never fail.

3 Tell the older women to behave as those who love the Lord should. They must not gossip about others or be slaves of wine. They must teach what is proper, 4 so the younger women will be loving wives and mothers. 5 Each of the younger women must be sensible and kind, as well as a good homemaker, who puts her own husband first. Then no one can say insulting things about God's message.

6 Tell the young men to have self-control in everything.

7 Always set a good example for others. Be sincere and serious when you teach. 8 Use clean language that no one can criticize. Do this, and your enemies will be too ashamed to say anything against you.

9 Tell slaves always to please their owners by obeying them in everything. Slaves must not talk back to their owners 10 or steal from them. They must be completely honest and trustworthy. Then everyone will show great respect for what is taught about God our Savior.

God's Kindness and the New Life

11 God has shown us how kind he is by coming to save all people. 12 He taught us to give up our wicked ways and our worldly desires and to live decent and honest lives in

---

a 1.5 leaders: Or "elders" or "presbyters" or "priests." b 1.6 be faithful in marriage: Or "be the husband of only one wife" or "have never been divorced." c 1.7 Church officials: Or "Bishops."

this world. [13] We are filled with hope, as we wait for the glorious return of our great God and Savior Jesus Christ.[d] [14] He gave himself to rescue us from everything that is evil and to make our hearts pure. He wanted us to be his own people and to be eager to do right.

[15] Teach these things, as you use your full authority to encourage and correct people. Make sure you earn everyone's respect.

Doing Helpful Things

3 Remind your people to obey the rulers and authorities and not to be rebellious. They must always be ready to do something helpful [2] and not say cruel things or argue. They should be gentle and kind to everyone. [3] We used to be stupid, disobedient, and foolish, as well as slaves of all sorts of desires and pleasures. We were evil and jealous. Everyone hated us, and we hated everyone.

[4] God our Savior showed us
how good and kind he is.
[5] He saved us because
of his mercy,
and not because
of any good things
that we have done.

God washed us by the power
of the Holy Spirit.
He gave us new birth
and a fresh beginning.
[6] God sent Jesus Christ

our Savior
to give us his Spirit.

[7] Jesus treated us much better
than we deserve.
He made us acceptable to God
and gave us the hope
of eternal life.

[8] This message is certainly true.

These teachings are useful and helpful for everyone. I want you to insist that the people follow them, so that all who have faith in God will be sure to do good deeds. [9] But don't have anything to do with stupid arguments about ancestors. And stay away from disagreements and quarrels about the Law of Moses. Such arguments are useless and senseless.

[10] Warn troublemakers once or twice. Then don't have anything else to do with them. [11] You know that their minds are twisted, and their own sins show how guilty they are.

Personal Instructions and Greetings

[12] I plan to send Artemas or Tychicus to you. After he arrives, please try your best to meet me at Nicopolis. I have decided to spend the winter there.

[13] When Zenas the lawyer and Apollos get ready to leave, help them as much as you can, so they won't have need of anything.

[14] Our people should learn to spend their time doing something useful and worthwhile.

[15] Greetings to you from everyone here. Greet all of our friends who share in our faith.

I pray that the Lord will be kind to all of you!

---

[d] **2.13** *the glorious return of our great God and Savior Jesus Christ*: Or "the glorious return of our great God and our Savior Jesus Christ" or "the return of Jesus Christ, who is the glory of our great God and Savior."

PHILEMON

[1] From Paul, who is in jail for serving Christ Jesus, and from Timothy, who is like a brother because of our faith.

Philemon, you work with us and are very dear to us. This letter is to you [2] and to the church that meets in your home. It is also to our dear friend Apphia and to Archippus, who serves the Lord as we do.

[3] I pray that God our Father and our Lord Jesus Christ will be kind to you and will bless you with peace!

Philemon's Love and Faith

[4] Philemon, each time I mention you in my prayers, I thank God. [5] I hear about your faith in our Lord Jesus and about your love for all of God's people. [6] As you share your faith with others, I pray that they may come to know all the

blessings Christ has given us. [7] My friend, your love has made me happy and has greatly encouraged me. It has also cheered the hearts of God's people.

Paul Speaks to Philemon about Onesimus

[8] Christ gives me the courage to tell you what to do. [9] But I would rather ask you to do it simply because of love. Yes, as someone[a] in jail for Christ, [10] I beg you to help Onesimus! He is like a son to me because I led him to Christ here in jail. [11] Before this, he was useless to you, but now he is useful both to you and to me.

[12] Sending Onesimus back to you makes me very sad. [13] I would like to keep him here with me, where he could take your place in helping me while I am here in prison for

---

[a] **1.9** *someone*: Greek "a messenger" or "an old man."

preaching the good news. [14] But I won't do anything unless you agree to it first. I want your act of kindness to come from your heart, and not be something you feel forced to do.

[15] Perhaps Onesimus was taken from you for a little while so that you could have him back for good, [16] but not as a slave. Onesimus is much more than a slave. To me he is a dear friend, but to you he is even more, both as a person and as a follower of the Lord.

[17] If you consider me a friend because of Christ, then welcome Onesimus as you would welcome me. [18] If he has cheated you or owes you anything, charge it to my account.

[19] With my own hand I write: I, PAUL, WILL PAY YOU BACK. But don't forget that you owe me your life. [20] My dear friend and follower of Christ our Lord, please cheer me up by doing this for me.

[21] I am sure you will do all I have asked, and even more. [22] Please get a room ready for me. I hope your prayers will be answered, and I can visit you.

[23] Epaphras is also here in jail for being a follower of Christ Jesus. He sends his greetings, [24] and so do Mark, Aristarchus, Demas, and Luke, who work together with me.

[25] I pray that the Lord Jesus Christ will be kind to you!

HEBREWS

1 Long ago in many ways and at many times God's prophets spoke his message to our ancestors. [2] But now at last, God sent his Son to bring his message to us. God created the universe by his Son, and everything will someday belong to the Son. [3] God's Son has all the brightness of God's own glory and is like him in every way. By his own mighty word, he holds the universe together.

After the Son had washed away our sins, he sat down at the right side of the glorious God in heaven. [4] He had become much greater than the angels, and the name he was given is far greater than any of theirs.

God's Son Is Greater than Angels

[5] God has never said
    to any of the angels,
"You are my Son, because today
    I have become your Father!"
Neither has God said
    to any of them,
"I will be his Father,
    and he will be my Son!"

[6] When God brings his first-born Son into the world, he commands all of his angels to worship him. [7] And when God speaks about the angels, he says,

"I change my angels into wind
and my servants
    into flaming fire."

[8] But God says about his Son,

"You are God,
    and you will rule
        as King forever!
Your[a] royal power
    brings about justice.

[9] You loved justice
    and hated evil,
and so I, your God,
    have chosen you.
I appointed you
and made you happier
    than any of your friends."

[10] The Scriptures also say,

"In the beginning, Lord,
    you were the one
who laid the foundation
of the earth
    and created the heavens.
[11] They will all disappear
    and wear out like clothes,
        but you will last forever.
[12] You will roll them up
    like a robe
and change them
    like a garment.
But you are always the same,
    and you will live forever."

[13] God never said to any
        of the angels,
"Sit at my right side
until I make your enemies
    into a footstool for you!"

[14] Angels are merely spirits sent to serve people who are going to be saved.

This Great Way of Being Saved

2 We must give our full attention to what we were told, so that we won't drift away. [2] The message spoken by

---

[a] **1.8** *Your*: Some manuscripts have "His."

angels proved to be true, and all who disobeyed or rejected it were punished as they deserved. ³ So if we refuse this great way of being saved, how can we hope to escape? The Lord himself was the first to tell about it, and people who heard the message proved to us that it was true. ⁴ God himself showed that his message was true by working all kinds of powerful miracles and wonders. He also gave his Holy Spirit to anyone he chose to.

The One Who Leads Us To Be Saved

⁵ We know that God did not put the future world under the power of angels. ⁶ Somewhere in the Scriptures someone says to God,

> "What makes you care
>   about us humans?
> Why are you concerned
>   for weaklings such as we?
> ⁷ You made us lower
>   than the angels
>   for a while.
> Yet you have crowned us
>   with glory and honor.ᵇ
> ⁸ And you have put everything
>   under our power!"

God has put everything under our power and has not left anything out of our power. But we still don't see it all under our power. ⁹ What we do see is Jesus, who for a little while was made lower than the angels. Because of God's wonderful kindness, Jesus died for everyone. And now that Jesus has suffered and died, he is crowned with glory and honor!

¹⁰ Everything belongs to God, and all things were created by his power. So God did the right thing when he made Jesus perfect by suffering, as Jesus led many of God's children to be saved and to share in his glory. ¹¹ Jesus and the people he makes holy all belong to the same family. That is why he isn't ashamed to call them his brothers and sisters. ¹² He even said to God,

> "I will tell them your name
>   and sing your praises
> when they come together
>   to worship."

¹³ He also said,

> "I will trust God."

Then he said,

> "Here I am with the children
>   God has given me."

¹⁴ We are people of flesh and blood. That is why Jesus became one of us. He died to destroy the devil, who had power over death. ¹⁵ But he also died to rescue all of us who live each day in fear of dying. ¹⁶ Jesus clearly did not come to help angels, but he did come to help Abraham's descend-

ants. ¹⁷ He had to be one of us, so that he could serve God as our merciful and faithful high priest and sacrifice himself for the forgiveness of our sins. ¹⁸ And now that Jesus has suffered and was tempted, he can help anyone else who is tempted.

Jesus Is Greater than Moses

3 My friends, God has chosen you to be his holy people. So think about Jesus, the one we call our apostle and high priest! ² Jesus was faithful to God, who appointed him, just as Moses was faithful in serving all ofᶜ God's people. ³ But Jesus deserves more honor than Moses, just as the builder of a house deserves more honor than the house. ⁴ Of course, every house is built by someone, and God is really the one who built everything.

⁵ Moses was a faithful servant and told God's people what would be said in the future. ⁶ But Christ is the Son in charge of God's people. And we are those people, if we keep on being brave and don't lose hope.

A Rest for God's People

⁷ It is just as the Holy Spirit says,

> "If you hear God's voice today,
> ⁸   don't be stubborn!
> Don't rebel like those people
>   who were tested
>   in the desert.
> *⁹ For forty years your ancestors
>   tested God and saw
>   the things he did.
>
> ¹⁰ "Then God got tired of them
>   and said,
> 'You people never
>   show good sense,
> and you don't understand
>   what I want you to do.'
> ¹¹ God became angry
>   and told the people,
> 'You will never enter
>   my place of rest!' "

¹² My friends, watch out! Don't let evil thoughts or doubts make any of you turn from the living God. ¹³ You must encourage one another each day. And you must keep on while there is still a time that can be called "today." If you don't, then sin may fool some of you and make you stubborn. ¹⁴ We were sure about Christ when we first became his people. So let's hold tightly to our faith until the end. ¹⁵ The Scriptures say,

> "If you hear his voice today,
>   don't be stubborn
>   like those who rebelled."

¹⁶ Who were those people that heard God's voice and rebelled? Weren't they the same ones that came out of Egypt with Moses? ¹⁷ Who were the people that made God angry for forty years? Weren't they the ones that sinned and

---

ᵇ 2.7 *and honor*: Some manuscripts add "and you have placed us in charge of all you created."   ᶜ 3.2 *all of*: Some manuscripts do not have these words.

died in the desert? 18 And who did God say would never enter his place of rest? Weren't they the ones that disobeyed him? 19 We see that those people did not enter the place of rest because they did not have faith.

4 The promise to enter the place of rest is still good, and we must take care that none of you miss out. 2 We have heard the message, just as they did. But they failed to believe what they heard, and the message did not do them any good. 3 Only people who have faith will enter the place of rest. It is just as the Scriptures say,

"God became angry
    and told the people,
'You will never enter
    my place of rest!' "

God said this, even though everything has been ready from the time of creation. 4 In fact, somewhere the Scriptures say that by the seventh day, God had finished his work, and so he rested. 5 We also read that he later said, "You people will never enter my place of rest!" 6 This means that the promise to enter is still good, because those who first heard about it disobeyed and did not enter. 7 Much later God told David to make the promise again, just as I have already said,

"If you hear his voice today,
    don't be stubborn!"

8 If Joshua had really given the people rest, there would not be any need for God to talk about another day of rest. 9 But God has promised us a Sabbath when we will rest, even though it has not yet come. 10 On that day God's people will rest from their work, just as God rested from his work.

11 We should do our best to enter that place of rest, so that none of us will disobey and miss going there, as they did. 12 What God has said isn't only alive and active! It is sharper than any double-edged sword. His word can cut through our spirits and souls and through our joints and marrow, until it discovers the desires and thoughts of our hearts. 13 Nothing is hidden from God! He sees through everything, and we will have to tell him the truth.

Jesus Is the Great High Priest

14 We have a great high priest, who has gone into heaven, and he is Jesus the Son of God. That is why we must hold on to what we have said about him. 15 Jesus understands every weakness of ours, because he was tempted in every way that we are. But he did not sin! 16 So whenever we are in need, we should come bravely before the throne of our merciful God. There we will be treated with undeserved kindness, and we will find help.

5 Every high priest is appointed to help others by offering gifts and sacrifices to God because of their sins. 2 A high priest has weaknesses of his own, and he feels sorry for foolish and sinful people. 3 That is why he must offer sacrifices for his own sins and for the sins of others. 4 But no one can have the honor of being a high priest simply by wanting to be one. Only God can choose a priest, and God is the one who chose Aaron.

5 That is how it was with Christ. He became a high priest, but not just because he wanted the honor of being one. It was God who told him,

"You are my Son, because today
    I have become your Father!"

6 In another place, God says,

"You are a priest forever
    just like Melchizedek."

7 God had the power to save Jesus from death. And while Jesus was on earth, he begged God with loud crying and tears to save him. He truly worshiped God, and God listened to his prayers. 8 Jesus is God's own Son, but still he had to suffer before he could learn what it really means to obey God. 9 Suffering made Jesus perfect, and now he can save forever all who obey him. 10 This is because God chose him to be a high priest like Melchizedek.

Warning against Turning Away

11 Much more could be said about this subject. But it is hard to explain, and all of you are slow to understand. 12 By now you should have been teachers, but once again you need to be taught the simplest things about what God has said. You need milk instead of solid food. 13 People who live on milk are like babies who don't really know what is right. 14 Solid food is for mature people who have been trained to know right from wrong.

6 We must try to become mature and start thinking about more than just the basic things we were taught about Christ. We shouldn't need to keep talking about why we ought to turn from deeds that bring death and why we ought to have faith in God. 2 And we shouldn't need to keep teaching about baptisms*d* or about the laying on of hands or about people being raised from death and the future judgment. 3 Let's grow up, if God is willing.

4-6 But what about people who turn away after they have already seen the light and have received the gift from heaven and have shared in the Holy Spirit? What about those who turn away after *t*hey have received the good message of God and the powers of the future world? There is no way to bring them back. What they are doing is the same as nailing the Son of God to a cross and insulting him in public!

7 A field is useful to farmers, if there is enough rain to make good crops grow. In fact, God will bless that field. 8 But land that produces only thornbushes is worthless. It is likely to fall under God's curse, and in the end it will be set on fire.

9 My friends, we are talking this way. But we are sure that you are doing those really good things that people do when they are being saved. 10 God is always fair. He will remember how you helped his people in the past and how you are still helping them. You belong to God, and he won't forget the love you have shown his people. 11 We wish that each of you would always be eager to show how strong and lasting your hope really is. 12 Then you would never be lazy. You would be following the example of those who had faith and were patient until God kept his promise to them.

d **6.2** *baptisms*: Or "ceremonies of washing."

God's Promise Is Sure

13 No one is greater than God. So he made a promise in his own name when he said to Abraham, **14** "I, the Lord, will bless you with many descendants!" **15** Then after Abraham had been very patient, he was given what God had promised. **16** When anyone wants to settle an argument, they make a vow by using the name of someone or something greater than themselves. **17** So when God wanted to prove for certain that his promise to his people could not be broken, he made a vow. **18** God cannot tell lies! And so his promises and vows are two things that can never be changed.

We have run to God for safety. Now his promises should greatly encourage us to take hold of the hope that is right in front of us. **19** This hope is like a firm and steady anchor for our souls. In fact, hope reaches behind the curtain and into the most holy place. **20** Jesus has gone there ahead of us, and he is our high priest forever, just like Melchizedek.

The Priestly Family of Melchizedek

7 Melchizedek was both king of Salem and priest of God Most High. He was the one who went out and gave Abraham his blessing, when Abraham returned from killing the kings. **2** Then Abraham gave him a tenth of everything he had.

The meaning of the name Melchizedek is "King of Justice." But since Salem means "peace," he is also "King of Peace." **3** We are not told that he had a father or mother or ancestors or beginning or end. He is like the Son of God and will be a priest forever.

4 Notice how great Melchizedek is! Our famous ancestor Abraham gave him a tenth of what he had taken from his enemies. **5** The Law teaches that even Abraham's descendants must give a tenth of what they possess. And they are to give this to their own relatives, who are the descendants of Levi and are priests. **6** Although Melchizedek wasn't a descendant of Levi, Abraham gave him a tenth of what he had. Then Melchizedek blessed Abraham, who had been given God's promise. **7** Everyone agrees that a person who gives a blessing is greater than the one who receives the blessing.

8 Priests are given a tenth of what people earn. But all priests die, except Melchizedek, and the Scriptures teach that he is alive. **9** Levi's descendants are now the ones who receive a tenth from people. We could even say that when Abraham gave Melchizedek a tenth, Levi also gave him a tenth. **10** This is because Levi was born later into the family of Abraham, who gave a tenth to Melchizedek.

11 Even though the Law of Moses says that the priests must be descendants of Levi, those priests cannot make anyone perfect. So there needs to be a priest like Melchizedek, rather than one from the priestly family of Aaron. **12** And when the rules for selecting a priest are changed, the Law must also be changed.

13 The person we are talking about is our Lord, who came from a tribe that had never had anyone to serve as a priest at the altar. **14** Everyone knows he came from the tribe of Judah, and Moses never said that priests would come from that tribe.

15 All of this becomes clearer, when someone who is like Melchizedek is appointed to be a priest. **16** That person wasn't appointed because of his ancestors, but because his life can never end. **17** The Scriptures say about him,

"You are a priest forever,
just like Melchizedek."

18 In this way a weak and useless command was put aside, **19** because the Law cannot make anything perfect. At the same time, we are given a much better hope, and it can bring us close to God.

20-21 God himself made a promise when this priest was appointed. But he did not make a promise like this when the other priests were appointed. The promise he made is,

"I, the Lord, promise that you
will be a priest forever!
And I will never
change my mind!"

22 This means that Jesus guarantees us a better agreement with God. **23** There have been a lot of other priests, and all of them have died. **24** But Jesus will never die, and so he will be a priest forever! **25** He is forever able to save[e] the people he leads to God, because he always lives to speak to God for them.

26 Jesus is the high priest we need. He is holy and innocent and faultless, and not at all like us sinners. Jesus is honored above all beings in heaven, **27** and he is better than any other high priest. Jesus doesn't need to offer sacrifices each day for his own sins and then for the sins of the people. He offered a sacrifice once for all, when he gave himself. **28** The Law appoints priests who have weaknesses. But God's promise, which came later than the Law, appoints his Son. And he is the perfect high priest forever.

A Better Promise

8 What I mean is that we have a high priest who sits at the right side of God's great throne in heaven. **2** He also serves as the priest in the most holy place inside the real tent there in heaven. This tent of worship was set up by the Lord, not by humans.

3 Since all priests must offer gifts and sacrifices, Christ also needed to have something to offer. **4** If he were here on earth, he would not be a priest at all, because here the Law appoints other priests to offer sacrifices. **5** But the tent where they serve is just a copy and a shadow of the real one in heaven. Before Moses made the tent, he was told, "Be sure to make it exactly like the pattern you were shown on the mountain!" **6** Now Christ has been appointed to serve as a priest in a much better way, and he has given us much assurance of a better agreement.

7 If the first agreement with God had been all right, there would not have been any need for another one. **8** But the Lord found fault with it and said,

"I tell you the time will come,
when I will make
a new agreement
with the people of Israel
and the people of Judah.
9 It won't be like the agreement
that I made
with their ancestors,

---

e **7.25** *forever able to save*: Or "able to save forever."

when I took them by the hand
and led them out of Egypt.
They broke their agreement
with me,
and I stopped caring
about them!

10 "But now I tell the people
of Israel
this is my new agreement:
'The time will come
when I, the Lord,
will write my laws
on their minds and hearts.
I will be their God,
and they will be
my people.
11 Not one of them
will have to teach another
to know me, their Lord.'

"All of them will know me,
no matter who they are.
12 I will treat them with kindness,
even though they are wicked.
I will forget their sins."

13 When the Lord talks about a new agreement, he means that the first one is out of date. And anything that is old and useless will soon disappear.

The Tent in Heaven

9 The first promise that was made included rules for worship and a tent for worship here on earth. 2 The first part of the tent was called the holy place, and a lampstand, a table, and the sacred loaves of bread were kept there.

3 Behind the curtain was the most holy place. 4 The gold altar that was used for burning incense was in this holy place. The gold-covered sacred chest was also there, and inside it were three things. First, there was a gold jar filled with manna. Then there was Aaron's walking stick that sprouted. Finally, there were the flat stones with the Ten Commandments written on them. 5 On top of the chest were the glorious creatures with wings opened out above the place of mercy.

Now isn't the time to go into detail about these things. 6 But this is how everything was when the priests went each day into the first part of the tent to do their duties. 7 However, only the high priest could go into the second part of the tent, and he went in only once a year. Each time he carried blood to offer for his sins and for any sins that the people had committed without meaning to.

8 All of this is the Holy Spirit's way of saying that no one could enter the most holy place while the tent was still the place of worship. 9 This also has a meaning for today. It shows that we cannot make our consciences clear by offering gifts and sacrifices. 10 These rules are merely about such things as eating and drinking and ceremonies for washing ourselves. And rules about physical things will last only until the time comes to change them for something better.

11 Christ came as the high priest of the good things that are now here.*f* He also went into a much better tent that wasn't made by humans and that doesn't belong to this world. 12 Then Christ went once for all into the most holy place and freed us from sin forever. He did this by offering his own blood instead of the blood of goats and bulls.

13 According to the Law of Moses, those people who become unclean are not fit to worship God. Yet they will be considered clean, if they are sprinkled with the blood of goats and bulls and with the ashes of a sacrificed calf. 14 But Christ was sinless, and he offered himself as an eternal and spiritual sacrifice to God. That's why his blood is much more powerful and makes our*g* consciences clear. Now we can serve the living God and no longer do things that lead to death.

15 Christ died to rescue those who had sinned and broken the old agreement. Now he brings his chosen ones a new agreement with its guarantee of God's eternal blessings! 16 In fact, making an agreement of this kind is like writing a will. This is because the one who makes the will must die before it is of any use. 17 In other words, a will doesn't go into effect as long as the one who made it is still alive.

18 Blood was also used*h* to put the first agreement into effect. 19 Moses told the people all that the Law said they must do. Then he used red wool and a hyssop plant to sprinkle the people and the book of the Law with the blood of bulls and goats*i* and with water. 20 He told the people, "With this blood God makes his agreement with you." 21 Moses also sprinkled blood on the tent and on everything else that was used in worship. 22 The Law says that almost everything must be sprinkled with blood, and no sins can be forgiven unless blood is offered.

Christ's Great Sacrifice

23 These things are only copies of what is in heaven, and so they had to be made holy by these ceremonies. But the real things in heaven must be made holy by something better. 24 This is why Christ did not go into a tent that had been made by humans and was only a copy of the real one. Instead, he went into heaven and is now there with God to help us.

25 Christ did not have to offer himself many times. He wasn't like a high priest who goes into the most holy place each year to offer the blood of an animal. 26 If he had offered himself every year, he would have suffered many times since the creation of the world. But instead, near the end of time he offered himself once and for all, so that he could be a sacrifice that does away with sin.

27 We die only once, and then we are judged. 28 So Christ died only once to take away the sins of many people. But when he comes again, it will not be to take away sin. He will come to save everyone who is waiting for him.

10 The Law of Moses is like a shadow of the good things to come. This shadow isn't the good things themselves, because it cannot free people from sin by the sacrifices that are offered year after year. 2 If there were worshipers who already have their sins washed away and their consciences made clear, there would not be any need to go on offering sacrifices. 3-4 But the blood of bulls and goats cannot take away sins. It only reminds people of their sins from one year to the next.

---

f 9.11 *that are now here:* Some manuscripts have "that were coming." "their." *h* 9.18 *Blood was also used:* Or "There also had to be a death." *g* 9.14 *our:* Some manuscripts have "your," and others have *i* 9.19 *blood of bulls and goats:* Some manuscripts do not have "and goats."

5 When Christ came into the world, he said to God,

> "Sacrifices and offerings
>   are not what you want,
> but you have given me
>   my body.
> 6 No, you are not pleased
>   with animal sacrifices
>   and offerings for sin."

7 Then Christ said,

> "And so, my God,
>   I have come to do
> what you want,
>   as the Scriptures say."

8 The Law teaches that offerings and sacrifices must be made because of sin. But why did Christ mention these things and say that God did not want them? 9 Well, it was to do away with offerings and sacrifices and to replace them. That is what he meant by saying to God, "I have come to do what you want." 10 So we are made holy because Christ obeyed God and offered himself once for all.

11 The priests do their work each day, and they keep on offering sacrifices that can never take away sins. 12 But Christ offered himself as a sacrifice that is good forever. Now he is sitting at God's right side, 13 and he will stay there until his enemies are put under his power. 14 By his one sacrifice he has forever set free from sin the people he brings to God.

15 The Holy Spirit also speaks of this by telling us that the Lord said,

> 16 "When the time comes,
>   I will make an agreement
>   with them.
> I will write my laws
>   on their minds and hearts.
> 17 Then I will forget
>   about their sins
> and no longer remember
>   their evil deeds."

18 When sins are forgiven, there is no more need to offer sacrifices.

Encouragement and Warning

19 My friends, the blood of Jesus gives us courage to enter the most holy place 20 by a new way that leads to life! And this way takes us through the curtain that is Christ himself. 21 We have a great high priest who is in charge of God's house. 22 So let's come near God with pure hearts and a confidence that comes from having faith. Let's keep our hearts pure, our consciences free from evil, and our bodies washed with clean water. 23 We must hold tightly to the hope that we say is ours. After all, we can trust the one who made the agreement with us. 24 We should keep on encouraging each other to be thoughtful and to do helpful things. 25 Some people have gotten out of the habit of meeting for worship, but we must not do that. We should keep on encouraging each other, especially since you know that the day of the Lord's coming is getting closer.

26 No sacrifices can be made for people who decide to sin after they find out about the truth. 27 They are God's enemies, and all they can look forward to is a terrible judgment and a furious fire. 28 If two or more witnesses accused someone of breaking the Law of Moses, that person could be put to death. 29 But it is much worse to dishonor God's Son and to disgrace the blood of the promise that made us holy. And it is just as bad to insult the Holy Spirit, who shows us mercy. 30 We know that God has said he will punish and take revenge. We also know that the Scriptures say the Lord will judge his people. 31 It is a terrible thing to fall into the hands of the living God!

32 Don't forget all the hard times you went through when you first received the light. 33 Sometimes you were abused and mistreated in public, and at other times you shared in the sufferings of others. 34 You were kind to people in jail. And you gladly let your possessions be taken away, because you knew you had something better, something that would last forever.

35 Keep on being brave! It will bring you great rewards. 36 Learn to be patient, so that you will please God and be given what he has promised. 37 As the Scriptures say,

> "God is coming soon!
>   It won't be very long.
> 38 The people God accepts
>   will live because
>   of their faith./
> But he isn't pleased
>   with anyone
>   who turns back."

39 We are not like those people who turn back and get destroyed. We will keep on having faith until we are saved.

The Great Faith of God's People

11 Faith makes us sure of what we hope for and gives us proof of what we cannot see. 2 It was their faith that made our ancestors pleasing to God.

3 Because of our faith, we know that the world was made at God's command. We also know that what can be seen was made out of what cannot be seen.

4 Because Abel had faith, he offered God a better sacrifice than Cain did. God was pleased with him and his gift, and even though Abel is now dead, his faith still speaks for him.

5 Enoch had faith and did not die. He pleased God, and God took him up to heaven. That's why his body was never found. 6 But without faith no one can please God. We must believe that God is real and that he rewards everyone who searches for him.

7 Because Noah had faith, he was warned about something that had not yet happened. He obeyed and built a boat that saved him and his family. In this way the people of the world were judged, and Noah was given the blessings that come to everyone who pleases God.

8 Abraham had faith and obeyed God. He was told to go to the land that God had said would be his, and he left for a country he had never seen. 9 Because Abraham had faith, he lived as a stranger in the promised land. He lived there in

---

/ **10.38** *The people God accepts will live because of their faith:* Or "The people God accepts because of their faith will live."

a tent, and so did Isaac and Jacob, who were later given the same promise. 10 Abraham did this, because he was waiting for the eternal city that God had planned and built.

11 Even when Sarah was too old to have children, she had faith that God would do what he had promised, and she had a son. 12 Her husband Abraham was almost dead, but he became the ancestor of many people. In fact, there are as many of them as there are stars in the sky or grains of sand along the beach.

13 Every one of those people died. But they still had faith, even though they had not received what they had been promised. They were glad just to see these things from far away, and they agreed that they were only strangers and foreigners on this earth. 14 When people talk this way, it is clear that they are looking for a place to call their own. 15 If they had been talking about the land where they had once lived, they could have gone back at any time. 16 But they were looking forward to a better home in heaven. That's why God wasn't ashamed for them to call him their God. He even built a city for them.

17-18 Abraham had been promised that Isaac, his only son, would continue his family. But when Abraham was tested, he had faith and was willing to sacrifice Isaac, 19 because he was sure that God could raise people to life. This was just like getting Isaac back from death.

20 Isaac had faith, and he promised blessings to Jacob and Esau. 21 Later, when Jacob was about to die, he leaned on his walking stick and worshiped. Then because of his faith he blessed each of Joseph's sons. 22 And right before Joseph died, he had faith that God would lead the people of Israel out of Egypt. So he told them to take his bones with them.

23 Because Moses' parents had faith, they kept him hidden until he was three months old. They saw that he was a beautiful child, and they were not afraid to disobey the king's orders. 24 Then after Moses grew up, his faith made him refuse to be called Pharaoh's grandson. 25 He chose to be mistreated with God's people instead of having the good time that sin could bring for a little while. 26 Moses knew that the treasures of Egypt were not as wonderful as what he would receive from suffering for the Messiah,^{k} and he looked forward to his reward.

27 Because of his faith, Moses left Egypt. Moses had seen the invisible God and wasn't afraid of the king's anger. 28 His faith also made him celebrate Passover. He sprinkled the blood of animals on the doorposts, so that the first-born sons of the people of Israel would not be killed by the destroying angel.

29 Because of their faith, the people walked through the Red Sea on dry land. But when the Egyptians tried to do it, they were drowned.

30 God's people had faith, and when they had walked around the city of Jericho for seven days, its walls fell down.

31 Rahab had been a prostitute, but she had faith and welcomed the spies. So she wasn't killed with the people who disobeyed.

32 What else can I say? There isn't enough time to tell about Gideon, Barak, Samson, Jephthah, David, Samuel, and the prophets. 33 Their faith helped them conquer kingdoms, and because they did right, God made promises to them. They closed the jaws of lions 34 and put out raging fires and escaped from the swords of their enemies. Although they were weak, they were given the strength and power to chase foreign armies away.

35 Some women received their loved ones back from death. Many of these people were tortured, but they refused to be released. They were sure that they would get a better reward when the dead are raised to life. 36 Others were made fun of and beaten with whips, and some were chained in jail. 37 Still others were stoned to death or sawed in two^l or killed with swords. Some had nothing but sheep skins or goat skins to wear. They were poor, mistreated, and tortured. 38 The world did not deserve these good people, who had to wander in deserts and on mountains and had to live in caves and holes in the ground.

39 All of them pleased God because of their faith! But still they died without being given what had been promised. 40 This was because God had something better in store for us. And he did not want them to reach the goal of their faith without us.

A Large Crowd of Witnesses

12 Such a large crowd of witnesses is all around us! So we must get rid of everything that slows us down, especially the sin that just won't let go. And we must be determined to run the race that is ahead of us. 2 We must keep our eyes on Jesus, who leads us and makes our faith complete. He endured the shame of being nailed to a cross, because he knew that later on he would be glad he did. Now he is seated at the right side of God's throne! 3 So keep your mind on Jesus, who put up with many insults from sinners. Then you won't get discouraged and give up.

4 None of you have yet been hurt^m in your battle against sin. 5 But you have forgotten that the Scriptures say to God's children,

"When the Lord punishes you,
   don't make light of it,
and when he corrects you,
   don't be discouraged.
6 The Lord corrects the people
   he loves
and disciplines those
   he calls his own."

7 Be patient when you are being corrected! This is how God treats his children. Don't all parents correct their children? 8 God corrects all of his children, and if he doesn't correct you, then you don't really belong to him. 9 Our earthly fathers correct us, and we still respect them. Isn't it even better to be given true life by letting our spiritual Father correct us?

10 Our human fathers correct us for a short time, and they do it as they think best. But God corrects us for our own good, because he wants us to be holy, as he is. 11 It is never fun to be corrected. In fact, at the time it is always painful. But if we learn to obey by being corrected, we will do right and live at peace.

12 Now stand up straight! Stop your knees from shaking 13 and walk a straight path. Then lame people will be healed, instead of getting worse.

---

^{k} 11.26 the Messiah: Or "Christ." ^{l} 11.37 sawed in two: Some manuscripts have "tested" or "tempted." ^{m} 12.4 hurt: Or "killed."

Warning against Turning from God

14 Try to live at peace with everyone! Live a clean life. If you don't, you will never see the Lord. **15** Make sure that no one misses out on God's wonderful kindness. Don't let anyone become bitter and cause trouble for the rest of you. **16** Watch out for immoral and ungodly people like Esau, who sold his future blessing for only one meal. **17** You know how he later wanted it back. But there was nothing he could do to change things, even though he begged his father and cried.

18 You have not come to a place like Mount Sinai[n] that can be seen and touched. There is no flaming fire or dark cloud or storm **19** or trumpet sound. The people of Israel heard a voice speak. But they begged it to stop, **20** because they could not obey its commands. They were even told to kill any animal that touched the mountain. **21** The sight was so frightening that Moses said he shook with fear.

22 You have now come to Mount Zion and to the heavenly Jerusalem. This is the city of the living God, where thousands and thousands of angels have come to celebrate. **23** Here you will find all of God's dearest children,[o] whose names are written in heaven. And you will find God himself, who judges everyone. Here also are the spirits of those good people who have been made perfect. **24** And Jesus is here! He is the one who makes God's new agreement with us, and his sprinkled blood says much better things than the blood of Abel.

25 Make sure that you obey the one who speaks to you. The people did not escape, when they refused to obey the one who spoke to them at Mount Sinai. Do you think you can possibly escape, if you refuse to obey the one who speaks to you from heaven? **26** When God spoke the first time, his voice shook only the earth. This time he has promised to shake the earth once again, and heaven too. **27** The words "once again" mean that these created things will someday be shaken and removed. Then what cannot be shaken will last. **28** We should be grateful that we were given a kingdom that cannot be shaken. And in this kingdom we please God by worshiping him and by showing him great honor and respect. **29** Our God is like a destructive fire!

Service That Pleases God

13 Keep being concerned about each other as the Lord's followers should.

2 Be sure to welcome strangers into your home. By doing this, some people have welcomed angels as guests, without even knowing it.

3 Remember the Lord's people who are in jail and be concerned for them. Don't forget those who are suffering, but imagine that you are there with them.

4 Have respect for marriage. Always be faithful to your partner, because God will punish anyone who is immoral or unfaithful in marriage.

5 Don't fall in love with money. Be satisfied with what you have. The Lord has promised that he will not leave us or desert us. **6** That should make you feel like saying,

> "The Lord helps me!
> Why should I be afraid
>   of what people
>   can do to me?"

7 Don't forget about your leaders who taught you God's message. Remember what kind of lives they lived and try to have faith like theirs.

8 Jesus Christ never changes! He is the same yesterday, today, and forever. **9** Don't be fooled by any kind of strange teachings. It is better to receive strength from God's undeserved kindness than to depend on certain foods. After all, these foods don't really help the people who eat them. **10** But we have an altar where even the priests who serve in the place of worship have no right to eat.

11 After the high priest offers the blood of animals as a sin offering, the bodies of those animals are burned outside the camp. **12** Jesus himself suffered outside the city gate, so that his blood would make people holy. **13** That's why we should go outside the camp to Jesus and share in his disgrace. **14** On this earth we don't have a city that lasts forever, but we are waiting for such a city.

15 Our sacrifice is to keep offering praise to God in the name of Jesus. **16** But don't forget to help others and to share your possessions with them. This too is like offering a sacrifice that pleases God.

17 Obey your leaders and do what they say. They are watching over you, and they must answer to God. So don't make them sad as they do their work. Make them happy. Otherwise, they won't be able to help you at all.

18 Pray for us. Our consciences are clear, and we always try to live right. **19** I especially want you to pray that I can visit you again soon.

Final Prayers and Greetings

20 God gives peace, and he raised our Lord Jesus Christ from death. Now Jesus is like a Great Shepherd whose blood was used to make God's eternal agreement with his flock. **21** I pray that God will make you ready to obey him and that you will always be eager to do right. May Jesus help you do what pleases God. To Jesus Christ be glory forever and ever! Amen.

22 My friends, I have written only a short letter to encourage you, and I beg you to pay close attention to what I have said.

23 By now you surely must know that our friend Timothy is out of jail. If he gets here in time, I will bring him with me when I come to visit you.

24 Please give my greetings to your leaders and to the rest of the Lord's people.

His followers from Italy send you their greetings.

25 I pray that God will be kind to all of you![p]

---

[n] **12.18** *a place like Mount Sinai*: The Greek text has "a place," but the writer is referring to the time that the Lord spoke to the people of Israel from Mount Sinai (see Exodus 19.16-25). [o] **12.23** *all of God's dearest children*: The Greek text has "the gathering of the first-born children" (see the note at 1.6). [p] **13.25** *to all of you*: Some manuscripts add "Amen."

JAMES

1 From James, a servant of God and of our Lord Jesus Christ.

Greetings to the twelve tribes scattered all over the world.

Faith and Wisdom

² My friends, be glad, even if you have a lot of trouble. ³ You know that you learn to endure by having your faith tested. ⁴ But you must learn to endure everything, so that you will be completely mature and not lacking in anything.

⁵ If any of you need wisdom, you should ask God, and it will be given to you. God is generous and won't correct you for asking. ⁶ But when you ask for something, you must have faith and not doubt. Anyone who doubts is like an ocean wave tossed around in a storm. ⁷⁻⁸ If you are that kind of person, you can't make up your mind, and you surely can't be trusted. So don't expect the Lord to give you anything at all.

Poor People and Rich People

⁹ Any of God's people who are poor should be glad that he thinks so highly of them. ¹⁰ But any who are rich should be glad when God makes them humble. Rich people will disappear like wild flowers ¹¹ scorched by the burning heat of the sun. The flowers lose their blossoms, and their beauty is destroyed. That is how the rich will disappear, as they go about their business.

Trials and Temptations

¹² God will bless you, if you don't give up when your faith is being tested. He will reward you with a glorious life,[a] just as he rewards everyone who loves him.

¹³ Don't blame God when you are tempted! God cannot be tempted by evil, and he doesn't use evil to tempt others. ¹⁴ We are tempted by our own desires that drag us off and trap us. ¹⁵ Our desires make us sin, and when sin is finished with us, it leaves us dead.

¹⁶ Don't be fooled, my dear friends. ¹⁷ Every good and perfect gift comes down from the Father who created all the lights in the heavens. He is always the same and never makes dark shadows by changing. ¹⁸ He wanted us to be his own special people,[b] and so he sent the true message to give us new birth.

Hearing and Obeying

¹⁹ My dear friends, you should be quick to listen and slow to speak or to get angry. ²⁰ If you are angry, you cannot do any of the good things that God wants done. ²¹ You must stop doing anything immoral or evil. Instead be humble and accept the message that is planted in you to save you.

²² Obey God's message! Don't fool yourselves by just listening to it. ²³ If you hear the message and don't obey it, you are like people who stare at themselves in a mirror ²⁴ and forget what they look like as soon as they leave. ²⁵ But you must never stop looking at the perfect law that sets you free. God will bless you in everything you do, if you listen and obey, and don't just hear and forget.

²⁶ If you think you are being religious, but can't control your tongue, you are fooling yourself, and everything you do is useless. ²⁷ Religion that pleases God the Father must be pure and spotless. You must help needy orphans and widows and not let this world make you evil.

Warning against Having Favorites

2 My friends, if you have faith in our glorious Lord Jesus Christ, you won't treat some people better than others. ² Suppose a rich person wearing fancy clothes and a gold ring comes to one of your meetings. And suppose a poor person dressed in worn-out clothes also comes. ³ You must not give the best seat to the one in fancy clothes and tell the one who is poor to stand at the side or sit on the floor. ⁴ That is the same as saying that some people are better than others, and you would be acting like a crooked judge.

⁵ My dear friends, pay attention. God has given a lot of faith to the poor people in this world. He has also promised them a share in his kingdom that he will give to everyone who loves him. ⁶ You mistreat the poor. But isn't it the rich who boss you around and drag you off to court? ⁷ Aren't they the ones who make fun of your Lord?

⁸ You will do all right, if you obey the most important law[c] in the Scriptures. It is the law that commands us to love others as much as we love ourselves. ⁹ But if you treat some people better than others, you have done wrong, and the Scriptures teach that you have sinned.

¹⁰ If you obey every law except one, you are still guilty of breaking them all. ¹¹ The same God who told us to be faithful in marriage also told us not to murder. So even if you are faithful in marriage, but murder someone, you still have broken God's Law.

¹² Speak and act like people who will be judged by the law that sets us free. ¹³ Do this, because on the day of judgment there will be no pity for those who have not had pity on others. But even in judgment, God is merciful![d]

Faith and Works

¹⁴ My friends, what good is it to say you have faith, when you don't do anything to show that you really do have faith? Can that kind of faith save you? ¹⁵ If you know someone who doesn't have any clothes or food, ¹⁶ you shouldn't just say, "I hope all goes well for you. I hope you will be warm and have plenty to eat." What good is it to say

---

[a] **1.12** *a glorious life*: The Greek text has "the crown of life." In ancient times an athlete who had won a contest was rewarded with a crown of flowers as a sign of victory. [b] **1.18** *his own special people*: The Greek text has "the first of his creatures." The Law of Moses taught that the first-born of all animals and the first part of the harvest were special and belonged to the Lord. [c] **2.8** *most important law*: The Greek text has "royal law," meaning the one given by the king (that is, God). [d] **2.13** *But even in judgment, God is merciful*: Or "So be merciful, and you will be shown mercy on the day of judgment."

this, unless you do something to help? 17 Faith that doesn't lead us to do good deeds is all alone and dead!

18 Suppose someone disagrees and says, "It is possible to have faith without doing kind deeds."

I would answer, "Prove that you have faith without doing kind deeds, and I will prove that I have faith by doing them." 19 You surely believe there is only one God. That's fine. Even demons believe this, and it makes them shake with fear.

20 Does some stupid person want proof that faith without deeds is useless? 21 Well, our ancestor Abraham pleased God by putting his son Isaac on the altar to sacrifice him. 22 Now you see how Abraham's faith and deeds worked together. He proved that his faith was real by what he did. 23 This is what the Scriptures mean by saying, "Abraham had faith in God, and God was pleased with him." That's how Abraham became God's friend.

24 You can now see that we please God by what we do and not only by what we believe. 25 For example, Rahab had been a prostitute. But she pleased God when she welcomed the spies and sent them home by another way.

26 Anyone who doesn't breathe is dead, and faith that doesn't do anything is just as dead!

The Tongue

3 My friends, we should not all try to become teachers. In fact, teachers will be judged more strictly than others. 2 All of us do many wrong things. But if you can control your tongue, you are mature and able to control your whole body.

3 By putting a bit into the mouth of a horse, we can turn the horse in different directions. 4 It takes strong winds to move a large sailing ship, but the captain uses only a small rudder to make it go in any direction. 5 Our tongues are small too, and yet they brag about big things.

It takes only a spark to start a forest fire! 6 The tongue is like a spark. It is an evil power that dirties the rest of the body and sets a person's entire life on fire with flames that come from hell itself. 7 All kinds of animals, birds, reptiles, and sea creatures can be tamed and have been tamed. 8 But our tongues get out of control. They are restless and evil, and always spreading deadly poison.

9-10 My dear friends, with our tongues we speak both praises and curses. We praise our Lord and Father, and we curse people who were created to be like God, and this isn't right. 11 Can clean water and dirty water both flow from the same spring? 12 Can a fig tree produce olives or a grapevine produce figs? Does fresh water come from a well full of salt water?

Wisdom from Above

13 Are any of you wise or sensible? Then show it by living right and by being humble and wise in everything you do. 14 But if your heart is full of bitter jealousy and selfishness, don't brag or lie to cover up the truth. 15 That kind of wisdom doesn't come from above. It is earthly and selfish and comes from the devil himself. 16 Whenever people are jealous or selfish, they cause trouble and do all sorts of cruel things. 17 But the wisdom that comes from above leads us to be pure, friendly, gentle, sensible, kind, helpful, genuine, and sincere. 18 When peacemakers plant seeds of peace, they will harvest justice.

Friendship with the World

4 Why do you fight and argue with each other? Isn't it because you are full of selfish desires that fight to control your body? 2 You want something you don't have, and you will do anything to get it. You will even kill! But you still cannot get what you want, and you won't get it by fighting and arguing. You should pray for it. 3 Yet even when you do pray, your prayers are not answered, because you pray just for selfish reasons.

4 You people aren't faithful to God! Don't you know that if you love the world, you are God's enemies? And if you decide to be a friend of the world, you make yourself an enemy of God. 5 Do you doubt the Scriptures that say, "God truly cares about the Spirit he has put in us"?e 6 In fact, God treats us with even greater kindness, just as the Scriptures say,

"God opposes everyone
who is proud,
but he is kind to everyone
who is humble."

7 Surrender to God! Resist the devil, and he will run from you. 8 Come near to God, and he will come near to you. Clean up your lives, you sinners. Purify your hearts, you people who can't make up your mind. 9 Be sad and sorry and weep. Stop laughing and start crying. Be gloomy instead of glad. 10 Be humble in the Lord's presence, and he will honor you.

Saying Cruel Things about Others

11 My friends, don't say cruel things about others! If you do, or if you condemn others, you are condemning God's Law. And if you condemn the Law, you put yourself above the Law and refuse to obey either it 12 or God who gave it. God is our judge, and he can save or destroy us. What right do you have to condemn anyone?

Warning against Bragging

13 You should know better than to say, "Today or tomorrow we will go to the city. We will do business there for a year and make a lot of money!" 14 What do you know about tomorrow? How can you be so sure about your life? It is nothing more than mist that appears for only a little while before it disappears. 15 You should say, "If the Lord lets us live, we will do these things." 16 Yet you are stupid enough to brag, and it is wrong to be so proud. 17 If you don't do what you know is right, you have sinned.

Warning to the Rich

5 You rich people should cry and weep! Terrible things are going to happen to you. 2 Your treasures have already rotted, and moths have eaten your clothes. 3 Your money has rusted, and the rust will be evidence against you, as it burns your body like fire. Yet you keep on storing up wealth in these last days. 4 You refused to pay the people who worked in your fields, and now their unpaid wages are shouting out against you. The Lord All-Powerful has surely heard the cries of the workers who harvested your crops.

5 While here on earth, you have thought only of filling your own stomachs and having a good time. But now you

---

e 4.5 *God truly cares about the Spirit he has put in us*: One possible meaning for the difficult Greek text; other translations are possible, such as, "the Spirit that God put in us truly cares."

are like fat cattle on their way to be butchered. 6 You have condemned and murdered innocent people, who couldn't even fight back.

Be Patient and Kind

7 My friends, be patient until the Lord returns. Think of farmers who wait patiently for the spring and summer rains to make their valuable crops grow. 8 Be patient like those farmers and don't give up. The Lord will soon be here! 9 Don't grumble about each other or you will be judged, and the judge is right outside the door.

10 My friends, follow the example of the prophets who spoke for the Lord. They were patient, even when they had to suffer. 11 In fact, we praise the ones who endured the most. You remember how patient Job was and how the Lord finally helped him. The Lord did this because he is so merciful and kind.

12 My friends, above all else, don't take an oath. You must not swear by heaven or by earth or by anything else.

"Yes" or "No" is all you need to say. If you say anything more, you will be condemned.

13 If you are having trouble, you should pray. And if you are feeling good, you should sing praises. 14 If you are sick, ask the church leaders[f] to come and pray for you. Ask them to put olive oil on you in the name of the Lord. 15 If you have faith when you pray for sick people, they will get well. The Lord will heal them, and if they have sinned, he will forgive them.

16 If you have sinned, you should tell each other what you have done. Then you can pray for one another and be healed. The prayer of an innocent person is powerful, and it can help a lot. 17 Elijah was just as human as we are, and for three and a half years his prayers kept the rain from falling. 18 But when he did pray for rain, it fell from the skies and made the crops grow.

19 My friends, if any followers have wandered away from the truth, you should try to lead them back. 20 If you turn sinners from the wrong way, you will save them from death, and many of their sins will be forgiven.

---

[f] 5.14 church leaders: Or "elders" or "presbyters" or "priests."

1 PETER

1 From Peter, an apostle of Jesus Christ.
To God's people who are scattered like foreigners in Pontus, Galatia, Cappadocia, Asia, and Bithynia.

2 God the Father decided to choose you as his people, and his Spirit has made you holy. You have obeyed Jesus Christ and are sprinkled with his blood.

I pray that God will be kind to you and will keep on giving you peace!

A Real Reason for Hope

3 Praise God, the Father of our Lord Jesus Christ. God is so good, and by raising Jesus from death, he has given us new life and a hope that lives on. 4 God has something stored up for you in heaven, where it will never decay or be ruined or disappear.

5 You have faith in God, whose power will protect you until the last day. Then he will save you, just as he has always planned to do. 6 On that day you will be glad, even if you have to go through many hard trials for a while. 7 Your faith will be like gold that has been tested in a fire. And these trials will prove that your faith is worth much more than gold that can be destroyed. They will show that you will be given praise and honor and glory when Jesus Christ returns.

8 You have never seen Jesus, and you don't see him now. But still you love him and have faith in him, and no words can tell how glad and happy 9 you are to be saved. That's why you have faith.

10 Some prophets told how kind God would be to you, and they searched hard to find out more about the way you

would be saved. 11 The Spirit of Christ was in them and was telling them how Christ would suffer and would then be given great honor. So they searched to find out exactly who Christ would be and when this would happen. 12 But they were told that they were serving you and not themselves. They preached to you by the power of the Holy Spirit, who was sent from heaven. And their message was only for you, even though angels would like to know more about it.

Chosen To Live a Holy Life

13 Be alert and think straight. Put all your hope in how kind God will be to you when Jesus Christ appears. 14 Behave like obedient children. Don't let your lives be controlled by your desires, as they used to be. 15 Always live as God's holy people should, because God is the one who chose you, and he is holy. 16 That's why the Scriptures say, "I am the holy God, and you must be holy too."

17 You say that God is your Father, but God doesn't have favorites! He judges all people by what they do. So you must honor God while you live as strangers here on earth. 18 You were rescued from the useless way of life that you learned from your ancestors. But you know that you were not rescued by such things as silver or gold that don't last forever. 19 You were rescued by the precious blood of Christ, that spotless and innocent lamb. 20 Christ was chosen even before the world was created, but because of you, he did not come until these last days. 21 And when he did come, it was to lead you to have faith in God, who raised him from death and honored him in a glorious way. That's why you have put your faith and hope in God.

22 You obeyed the truth,*a* and your souls were made pure. Now you sincerely love each other. But you must keep on loving with all your heart. 23 Do this because God has given you new birth by his message that lives on forever. 24 The Scriptures say,

> "Humans wither like grass,
>   and their glory fades
>   like wild flowers.
> Grass dries up,
>   and flowers fall
>   to the ground.
> 25 But what the Lord has said
>   will stand forever."

Our good news to you is what the Lord has said.

A Living Stone and a Holy Nation

2 Stop being hateful! Quit trying to fool people, and start being sincere. Don't be jealous or say cruel things about others. 2 Be like newborn babies who are thirsty for the pure spiritual milk that will help you grow and be saved. 3 You have already found out how good the Lord really is.

4 Come to Jesus Christ. He is the living stone that people have rejected, but which God has chosen and highly honored. 5 And now you are living stones that are being used to build a spiritual house. You are also a group of holy priests, and with the help of Jesus Christ you will offer sacrifices that please God. 6 It is just as God says in the Scriptures,

> "Look! I am placing in Zion
>   a choice and precious
>   cornerstone.
> No one who has faith
>   in that one
>   will be disappointed."

7 You are followers of the Lord, and that stone is precious to you. But it isn't precious to those who refuse to follow him. They are the builders who tossed aside the stone that turned out to be the most important one of all. 8 They disobeyed the message and stumbled and fell over that stone, because they were doomed.

9 But you are God's chosen and special people. You are a group of royal priests and a holy nation. God has brought you out of darkness into his marvelous light. Now you must tell all the wonderful things that he has done. The Scriptures say,

> 10 "Once you were nobody.
>   Now you are God's people.
> At one time no one
>   had pity on you.
> Now God has treated you
>   with kindness.

Live as God's Servants Should

11 Dear friends, you are foreigners and strangers on this earth. So I beg you not to surrender to those desires that fight against you. 12 Always let others see you behaving properly, even though they may still accuse you of doing wrong.

Then on the day of judgment, they will honor God by telling the good things they saw you do.

13 The Lord wants you to obey all human authorities, especially the Emperor, who rules over everyone. 14 You must also obey governors, because they are sent by the Emperor to punish criminals and to praise good citizens. 15 God wants you to silence stupid and ignorant people by doing right. 16 You are free, but still you are God's servants, and you must not use your freedom as an excuse for doing wrong. 17 Respect everyone and show special love for God's people. Honor God and respect the Emperor.

The Example of Christ's Suffering

18 Servants, you must obey your masters and always show respect to them. Do this, not only to those who are kind and thoughtful, but also to those who are cruel. 19 God will bless you, even if others treat you unfairly for being loyal to him. 20 You don't gain anything by being punished for some wrong you have done. But God will bless you, if you have to suffer for doing something good. 21 After all, God chose you to suffer as you follow in the footsteps of Christ, who set an example by suffering for you.

> 22 Christ did not sin
>   or ever tell a lie.
> 23 Although he was abused,
>   he never tried to get even.
> And when he suffered,
>   he made no threats.
> Instead, he had faith in God,
>   who judges fairly.
> 24 Christ carried the burden
>   of our sins.
> He was nailed to the cross,
>   so that we would stop sinning
>   and start living right.
> By his cuts and bruises
>   you are healed.
> 25 You had wandered away
>   like sheep.
> Now you have returned
>   to the one
> who is your shepherd
>   and protector.

Wives and Husbands

3 If you are a wife, you must put your husband first. Even if he opposes our message, you will win him over by what you do. No one else will have to say anything to him, 2 because he will see how you honor God and live a pure life. 3 Don't depend on things like fancy hairdos or gold jewelry or expensive clothes to make you look beautiful. 4 Be beautiful in your heart by being gentle and quiet. This kind of beauty will last, and God considers it very special.

5 Long ago those women who worshiped God and put their hope in him made themselves beautiful by putting their husbands first. 6 For example, Sarah obeyed Abraham and called him her master. You are her true children, if you do right and don't let anything frighten you.

7 If you are a husband, you should be thoughtful of your

---

a 1.22 *You obeyed the truth*: Some manuscripts add "by the power of the Spirit."

wife. Treat her with honor, because she isn't as strong as you are, and she shares with you in the gift of life. Then nothing will stand in the way of your prayers.

Suffering for Doing Right

8 Finally, all of you should agree and have concern and love for each other. You should also be kind and humble. 9 Don't be hateful and insult people just because they are hateful and insult you. Instead, treat everyone with kindness. You are God's chosen ones, and he will bless you. The Scriptures say,

> 10 "Do you really love life?
>   Do you want to be happy?
> Then stop saying cruel things
>   and quit telling lies.
> 11 Give up your evil ways
>   and do right,
> as you find and follow
>   the road that leads
>   to peace.
> 12 The Lord watches over
>   everyone who obeys him,
> and he listens
>   to their prayers.
> But he opposes everyone
>   who does evil."

13 Can anyone really harm you for being eager to do good deeds? 14 Even if you have to suffer for doing good things, God will bless you. So stop being afraid and don't worry about what people might do. 15 Honor Christ and let him be the Lord of your life.

Always be ready to give an answer when someone asks you about your hope. 16 Give a kind and respectful answer and keep your conscience clear. This way you will make people ashamed for saying bad things about your good conduct as a follower of Christ. 17 You are better off to obey God and suffer for doing right than to suffer for doing wrong.

> 18 Christ died once for our sins.
> An innocent person died
>   for those who are guilty.
> Christ did this
>   to bring you to God,
>   when his body
>   was put to death
> and his spirit
>   was made alive.

19 Christ then preached to the spirits that were being kept in prison. 20 They had disobeyed God while Noah was building the boat, but God had been patient with them. Eight people went into that boat and were brought safely through the flood. 21 Those flood waters were like baptism that now saves you. But baptism is more than just washing your body. It means turning to God with a clear conscience, because Jesus Christ was raised from death. 22 Christ is now in heaven, where he sits at the right side of God. All angels, authorities, and powers are under his control.

Being Faithful to God

4 Christ suffered here on earth. Now you must be ready to suffer as he did, because suffering shows that you have stopped sinning. 2 It means you have turned from your own desires and want to obey God for the rest of your life. 3 You have already lived long enough like people who don't know God. You were immoral and followed your evil desires. You went around drinking and partying and carrying on. In fact, you even worshiped disgusting idols. 4 Now your former friends wonder why you have stopped running around with them, and they curse you for it. 5 But they will have to answer to God, who judges the living and the dead. 6 The good news has even been preached to the dead, so that after they have been judged for what they have done in this life, their spirits will live with God.

7 Everything will soon come to an end. So be serious and be sensible enough to pray. 8 Most important of all, you must sincerely love each other, because love wipes away many sins. 9 Welcome people into your home and don't grumble about it. 10 Each of you has been blessed with one of God's many wonderful gifts to be used in the service of others. So use your gift well. 11 If you have the gift of speaking, preach God's message. If you have the gift of helping others, do it with the strength that God supplies. Everything should be done in a way that will bring honor to God because of Jesus Christ, who is glorious and powerful forever. Amen.

Suffering for Being a Christian

12 Dear friends, don't be surprised or shocked that you are going through testing that is like walking through fire. 13 Be glad for the chance to suffer as Christ suffered. It will prepare you for even greater happiness when he makes his glorious return.

14 Count it a blessing when you suffer for being a Christian. This shows that God's glorious Spirit is with you. 15 But you deserve to suffer if you are a murderer, a thief, a crook, or a busybody. 16 Don't be ashamed to suffer for being a Christian. Praise God that you belong to him. 17 God has already begun judging his own people. And if his judgment begins with us, imagine how terrible it will be for those who refuse to obey his message. The Scriptures say,

> 18 "If good people barely escape,
>   what will happen to sinners
> and to others
>   who don't respect God?"

19 If you suffer for obeying God, you must have complete faith in your faithful Creator and keep on doing right.

Helping Christian Leaders

5 Church leaders,b I am writing to encourage you. I too am a leader, as well as a witness to Christ's suffering, and I will share in his glory when it is shown to us.

2 Just as shepherds watch over their sheep, you must

---

b 5.1 Church leaders: Or "Elders" or "Presbyters" or "Priests."

watch over everyone God has placed in your care. Do it willingly in order to please God, and not simply because you think you must. Let it be something you want to do, instead of something you do merely to make money. ³ Don't be bossy to those people who are in your care, but set an example for them. ⁴ Then when Christ the Chief Shepherd returns, you will be given a crown that will never lose its glory.

⁵ All of you young people should obey your elders. In fact, everyone should be humble toward everyone else. The Scriptures say,

> "God opposes proud people,
>   but he helps everyone
>   who is humble."

⁶ Be humble in the presence of God's mighty power, and he will honor you when the time comes. ⁷ God cares for you, so turn all your worries over to him.

⁸ Be on your guard and stay awake. Your enemy, the devil, is like a roaring lion, sneaking around to find someone to attack. ⁹ But you must resist the devil and stay strong in your faith. You know that all over the world the Lord's followers are suffering just as you are. ¹⁰ But God shows undeserved kindness to everyone. That's why he appointed Christ Jesus to choose you to share in his eternal glory. You will suffer for a while, but God will make you complete, steady, strong, and firm. ¹¹ God will be in control forever! Amen.

Final Greetings

¹² Silvanus helped me write this short letter, and I consider him a faithful follower of the Lord. I wanted to encourage you and tell you how kind God really is, so that you will keep on having faith in him.

¹³ Greetings from the Lord's followers in Babylon. They are God's chosen ones.

Mark, who is like a son to me, sends his greetings too.

¹⁴ Give each other a warm greeting. I pray that God will give peace to everyone who belongs to Christ.ᶜ

ᶜ **5.14** *Christ*: Some manuscripts add "Amen."

2 PETER

1 From Simon Peter, a servant and an apostle of Jesus Christ.

To everyone who shares with us in the privilege of believing that our God and Savior Jesus Christ will do what is just and fair.ᵃ

² I pray that God will be kind to you and will let you live in perfect peace! May you keep learning more and more about God and our Lord Jesus.

Living as the Lord's Followers

³ We have everything we need to live a life that pleases God. It was all given to us by God's own power, when we learned that he had invited us to share in his wonderful goodness. ⁴ God made great and marvelous promises, so that his nature would become part of us. Then we could escape our evil desires and the corrupt influences of this world.

⁵ Do your best to improve your faith. You can do this by adding goodness, understanding, ⁶ self-control, patience, devotion to God, ⁷ concern for others, and love. ⁸ If you keep growing in this way, it will show that what you know about our Lord Jesus Christ has made your lives useful and meaningful. ⁹ But if you don't grow, you are like someone who is nearsighted or blind, and you have forgotten that your past sins are forgiven.

¹⁰ My friends, you must do all you can to show that God has really chosen and selected you. If you keep on doing this, you won't stumble and fall. ¹¹ Then our Lord and Savior Jesus Christ will give you a glorious welcome into his kingdom that will last forever.

¹² You are holding firmly to the truth that you were given. But I am still going to remind you of these things. ¹³ In fact, I think I should keep on reminding you until I leave this body. ¹⁴ And our Lord Jesus Christ has already told me that I will soon leave it behind. ¹⁵ That is why I am doing my best to make sure that each of you remembers all of this after I am gone.

The Message about the Glory of Christ

¹⁶ When we told you about the power and the return of our Lord Jesus Christ, we were not telling clever stories that someone had made up. But with our own eyes we saw his true greatness. ¹⁷ God, our great and wonderful Father, truly honored him by saying, "This is my own dear Son, and I am pleased with him." ¹⁸ We were there with Jesus on the holy mountain and heard this voice speak from heaven.

¹⁹ All of this makes us even more certain that what the prophets said is true. So you should pay close attention to their message, as you would to a lamp shining in some dark place. You must keep on paying attention until daylight comes and the morning star rises in your hearts. ²⁰ But you need to realize that no one alone can understand any of the prophecies in the Scriptures. ²¹ The prophets did not think these things up on their own, but they were guided by the Spirit of God.

ᵃ **1.1** *To everyone who . . . just and fair*: Or "To everyone whose faith in the justice and fairness of our God and Savior Jesus Christ is as precious as our own faith."

False Prophets and Teachers

2 Sometimes false prophets spoke to the people of Israel. False teachers will also sneak in and speak harmful lies to you. But these teachers don't really belong to the Master who paid a great price for them, and they will quickly destroy themselves. [2] Many people will follow their evil ways and cause others to tell lies about the true way. [3] They will be greedy and cheat you with smooth talk. But long ago God decided to punish them, and God doesn't sleep.

[4] God did not have pity on the angels that sinned. He had them tied up and thrown into the dark pits of hell until the time of judgment. [5] And during Noah's time, God did not have pity on the ungodly people of the world. He destroyed them with a flood, though he did save eight people, including Noah, who preached the truth.

[6] God punished the cities of Sodom and Gomorrah by burning them to ashes, and this is a warning to anyone else who wants to sin.

[7-8] Lot lived right and was greatly troubled by the terrible way those wicked people were living. He was a good man, and day after day he suffered because of the evil things he saw and heard. So the Lord rescued him. [9] This shows that the Lord knows how to rescue godly people from their sufferings and to punish evil people while they wait for the day of judgment.

[10] The Lord is especially hard on people who disobey him and don't think of anything except their own filthy desires. They are reckless and proud and are not afraid of cursing the glorious beings in heaven. [11] Although angels are more powerful than these evil beings,[b] even the angels don't dare to accuse them to the Lord.

[12] These people are no better than senseless animals that live by their feelings and are born to be caught and killed. They speak evil of things they don't know anything about. But their own corrupt deeds will destroy them. [13] They have done evil, and they will be rewarded with evil.

They think it is fun to have wild parties during the day. They are immoral, and the meals they eat with you are spoiled by the shameful and selfish way they carry on.[c] [14] All they think about is having sex with someone else's husband or wife. There is no end to their wicked deeds. They trick people who are easily fooled, and their minds are filled with greedy thoughts. But they are headed for trouble!

[15] They have left the true road and have gone down the wrong path by following the example of the prophet Balaam. He was the son of Beor and loved what he got from being a crook. [16] But a donkey corrected him for this evil deed. It spoke to him with a human voice and made him stop his foolishness.

[17] These people are like dried up water holes and clouds blown by a windstorm. The darkest part of hell is waiting for them. [18] They brag out loud about their stupid nonsense. And by being vulgar and crude, they trap people who have barely escaped from living the wrong kind of life. [19] They promise freedom to everyone. But they are merely slaves of filthy living, because people are slaves of whatever controls them.

[20] When they learned about our Lord and Savior Jesus Christ, they escaped from the filthy things of this world. But they are again caught up and controlled by these filthy things, and now they are in worse shape than they were at first. [21] They would have been better off if they had never known about the right way. Even after they knew what was right, they turned their backs on the holy commandments that they were given. [22] What happened to them is just like the true saying,

"A dog will come back
    to lick up its own vomit.
A pig that has been washed
    will roll in the mud."

The Lord Will Return

3 My dear friends, this is the second letter I have written to encourage you to do some honest thinking. I don't want you to forget [2] what God's prophets said would happen. You must never forget what the holy prophets taught in the past. And you must remember what the apostles told you our Lord and Savior has commanded us to do.

[3] But first you must realize that in the last days some people won't think about anything except their own selfish desires. They will make fun of you [4] and say, "Didn't your Lord promise to come back? Yet the first leaders have already died, and the world hasn't changed a bit."

[5] They will say this because they want to forget that long ago the heavens and the earth were made at God's command. The earth came out of water and was made from water. [6] Later it was destroyed by the waters of a mighty flood. [7] But God has commanded the present heavens and earth to remain until the day of judgment. Then they will be set on fire, and ungodly people will be destroyed.

[8] Dear friends, don't forget that for the Lord one day is the same as a thousand years, and a thousand years is the same as one day. [9] The Lord isn't slow about keeping his promises, as some people think he is. In fact, God is patient, because he wants everyone to turn from sin and no one to be lost.

[10] The day of the Lord's return will surprise us like a thief. The heavens will disappear with a loud noise, and the heat will melt the whole universe. Then the earth and everything on it will be seen for what they are.[d]

[11] Everything will be destroyed. So you should serve and honor God by the way you live. [12] You should look forward to the day when God judges everyone, and you should try to make it come soon.[e] On that day the heavens will be destroyed by fire, and everything else will melt in the heat. [13] But God has promised us a new heaven and a new earth, where justice will rule. We are really looking forward to that!

[14] My friends, while you are waiting, you should make certain that the Lord finds you pure, spotless, and living at peace. [15] Don't forget that the Lord is patient because he wants people to be saved. This is also what our dear friend Paul said when he wrote you with the wisdom that God had given him. [16] Paul talks about these same things in all his letters, but part of what he says is hard to understand. Some ignorant and unsteady people even destroy them-

---

[b]2.11 evil beings: Or "evil teachers."   [c]2.13 and the meals they eat with you are spoiled by the shameful and selfish way they carry on: Some manuscripts have "and the meals they eat with you are spoiled by the shameful way they carry on during your feasts of Christian love."   [d]3.10 will be seen for what they are: Some manuscripts have "will go up in flames."   [e]3.12 and you should try to make it come soon: Or "and you should eagerly desire for that day to come."

selves by twisting what he said. They do the same thing with other Scriptures too.

17 My dear friends, you have been warned ahead of time! So don't let the errors of evil people lead you down the wrong path and make you lose your balance. **18** Let the wonderful kindness and the understanding that come from our Lord and Savior Jesus Christ help you to keep on growing. Praise Jesus now and forever! Amen.*f*

---

f **3.18** *Amen*: Some manuscripts do not have "Amen."

1 JOHN

1   The Word that gives life
　　　was from the beginning,
　and this is the one
　　　our message is about.

　Our ears have heard,
　　　our own eyes have seen,
　and our hands touched
　　　this Word.

2 The one who gives life appeared! We saw it happen, and we are witnesses to what we have seen. Now we are telling you about this eternal life that was with the Father and appeared to us. **3** We are telling you what we have seen and heard, so that you may share in this life with us. And we share in it with the Father and with his Son Jesus Christ. **4** We are writing to tell you these things, because this makes us*a* truly happy.

God Is Light

5 Jesus told us that God is light and doesn't have any darkness in him. Now we are telling you. **6** If we say that we share in life with God and keep on living in the dark, we are lying and are not living by the truth. **7** But if we live in the light, as God does, we share in life with each other. And the blood of his Son Jesus washes all our sins away. **8** If we say that we have not sinned, we are fooling ourselves, and the truth isn't in our hearts. **9** But if we confess our sins to God, he can always be trusted to forgive us and take our sins away.

10 If we say that we have not sinned, we make God a liar, and his message isn't in our hearts.*b*

Christ Helps Us

2   My children, I am writing this so that you won't sin. But if you do sin, Jesus Christ always does the right thing, and he will speak to the Father for us. **2** Christ is the sacrifice that takes away our sins and the sins of all the world's people.

3 When we obey God, we are sure that we know him. **4** But if we claim to know him and don't obey him, we are lying and the truth isn't in our hearts. **5** We truly love God only when we obey him as we should, and then we know

that we belong to him. **6** If we say we are his, we must follow the example of Christ.

The New Commandment

7 My dear friends, I am not writing to give you a new commandment. It is the same one that you were first given, and it is the message you heard. **8** But it really is a new commandment, and you know its true meaning, just as Christ does. You can see the darkness fading away and the true light already shining.

9 If we claim to be in the light and hate someone, we are still in the dark. **10** But if we love others, we are in the light, and we don't cause problems for them.*c* **11** If we hate others, we are living and walking in the dark. We don't know where we are going, because we can't see in the dark.

12 Children, I am writing you,
　　　because your sins
　have been forgiven
　　　in the name of Christ.
13 Parents, I am writing you,
　　　because you have known
　the one who was there
　　　from the beginning.
　Young people, I am writing you,
　because you have defeated
　　　the evil one.
14 Children, I am writing you,
　because you have known
　　　the Father.
　Parents, I am writing you,
　　　because you have known
　the one who was there
　　　from the beginning.
　Young people, I am writing you,
　　　because you are strong.
　God's message is firm
　　　in your hearts,
　and you have defeated
　　　the evil one.

15 Don't love the world or anything that belongs to the world. If you love the world, you cannot love the Father.

---

a **1.4** *us*: Some manuscripts have "you."　 *b* **1.10** *and his message isn't in our hearts*: Or "because we have not accepted his message."
c **2.10** *and we don't cause problems for them*: Or "and we can see anything that might make us fall."

16 Our foolish pride comes from this world, and so do our selfish desires and our desire to have everything we see. None of this comes from the Father. 17 The world and the desires it causes are disappearing. But if we obey God, we will live forever.

The Enemy of Christ

18 Children, this is the last hour. You heard that the enemy of Christ would appear at this time, and many of Christ's enemies have already appeared. So we know that the last hour is here. 19 These people came from our own group, yet they were not part of us. If they had been part of us, they would have stayed with us. But they left, which proves that they did not belong to our group.

20 Christ, the Holy One,*d* has blessed you, and now all of you understand.*e* 21 I did not need to write you about the truth, since you already know it. You also know that liars do not belong to the truth. 22 And a liar is anyone who says that Jesus isn't truly Christ. Anyone who says this is an enemy of Christ and rejects both the Father and the Son. 23 If we reject the Son, we reject the Father. But if we say that we accept the Son, we have the Father. 24 Keep thinking about the message you first heard, and you will always be one in your heart with the Son and with the Father. 25 The Son*f* has promised us*g* eternal life.

26 I am writing to warn you about those people who are misleading you. 27 But Christ has blessed you with the Holy Spirit.*h* Now the Spirit stays in you, and you don't need any teachers. The Spirit is truthful and teaches you everything. So stay one in your heart with Christ, just as the Spirit has taught you to do.

Children of God

28 Children, stay one in your hearts with Christ. Then when he returns, we will have confidence and won't have to hide in shame. 29 You know that Christ always does right and that everyone who does right is a child of God.

3 Think how much the Father loves us. He loves us so much that he lets us be called his children, as we truly are. But since the people of this world did not know who Christ*i* is, they don't know who we are. 2 My dear friends, we are already God's children, though what we will be hasn't yet been seen. But we do know that when Christ returns, we will be like him, because we will see him as he truly is. 3 This hope makes us keep ourselves holy, just as Christ*i* is holy.

4 Everyone who sins breaks God's law, because sin is the same as breaking God's law. 5 You know that Christ came to take away sins. He isn't sinful, 6 and people who stay one in their hearts with him won't keep on sinning. If they do keep on sinning, they don't know Christ, and they have never seen him.

7 Children, don't be fooled. Anyone who does right is good, just like Christ himself. 8 Anyone who keeps on sinning belongs to the devil. He has sinned from the beginning, but the Son of God came to destroy all that he has done.

9 God's children cannot keep on being sinful. His life-giving power*k* lives in them and makes them his children, so that they cannot keep on sinning. 10 You can tell God's children from the devil's children, because those who belong to the devil refuse to do right or to love each other.

Love Each Other

11 From the beginning you were told that we must love each other. 12 Don't be like Cain, who belonged to the devil and murdered his own brother. Why did he murder him? He did it because his brother was good, and he was evil. 13 My friends, don't be surprised if the people of this world hate you. 14 Our love for each other proves that we have gone from death to life. But if you don't love each other, you are still under the power of death.

15 If you hate each other, you are murderers, and we know that murderers do not have eternal life. 16 We know what love is because Jesus gave his life for us. That's why we must give our lives for each other. 17 If we have all we need and see one of our own people in need, we must have pity on that person, or else we cannot say we love God. 18 Children, you show love for others by truly helping them, and not merely by talking about it.

19 When we love others, we know that we belong to the truth, and we feel at ease in the presence of God. 20 But even if we don't feel at ease, God is greater than our feelings, and he knows everything. 21 Dear friends, if we feel at ease in the presence of God, we will have the courage to come near him. 22 He will give us whatever we ask, because we obey him and do what pleases him. 23 God wants us to have faith in his Son Jesus Christ and to love each other. This is also what Jesus taught us to do. 24 If we obey God's commandments, we will stay one in our hearts with him, and he will stay one with us. The Spirit that he has given us is proof that we are one with him.

God Is Love

4 Dear friends, don't believe everyone who claims to have the Spirit of God. Test them all to find out if they really do come from God. Many false prophets have already gone out into the world, 2 and you can know which ones come from God. His Spirit says that Jesus Christ had a truly human body. 3 But when someone doesn't say this about Jesus, you know that person has a spirit that doesn't come from God and is the enemy of Christ. You knew that this enemy was coming into the world and now is already here.

4 Children, you belong to God, and you have defeated these enemies. God's Spirit*i* is in you and is more powerful than the one that is in the world. 5 These enemies belong to this world, and the world listens to them, because they speak its language. 6 We belong to God, and everyone who knows God will listen to us. But the people who don't know God won't listen to us. That is how we can tell the Spirit that speaks the truth from the one that tells lies.

7 My dear friends, we must love each other. Love comes from God, and when we love each other, it shows that we

---

d **2.20** *Christ, the Holy One*: The Greek text has "the Holy One" which may refer either to Christ or to God the Father.
e **2.20** *now all of you understand*: Some manuscripts have "you understand all things."   *f* **2.25** *The Son*: The Greek text has "he" and may refer to God the Father.   *g* **2.25** *us*: Some manuscripts have "you."   *h* **2.27** *Christ has blessed you with the Holy Spirit*: The Greek text has "You received a pouring on of olive oil from him" (see verse 20). The "pouring on of olive oil" is here taken to refer to the gift of the Holy Spirit, and "he" may refer either to Christ or to the Father.   *i* **3.1** *Christ*: The Greek text has "he" and may refer to God.
j **3.3** *Christ*: The Greek text has "that one" and may refer to God.   *k* **3.9** *His life-giving power*: The Greek text has "his seed."
l **4.4** *God's Spirit*: The Greek text has "he" and may refer to the Spirit or to God or to Jesus.

have been given new life. We are now God's children, and we know him. 8 God is love, and anyone who doesn't love others has never known him. 9 God showed his love for us when he sent his only Son into the world to give us life. 10 Real love isn't our love for God, but his love for us. God sent his Son to be the sacrifice by which our sins are forgiven. 11 Dear friends, since God loved us this much, we must love each other.

12 No one has ever seen God. But if we love each other, God lives in us, and his love is truly in our hearts.

13 God has given us his Spirit. That is how we know that we are one with him, just as he is one with us. 14 God sent his Son to be the Savior of the world. We saw his Son and are now telling others about him. 15 God stays one with everyone who openly says that Jesus is the Son of God. That's how we stay one with God 16 and are sure that God loves us.

God is love. If we keep on loving others, we will stay one in our hearts with God, and he will stay one with us. 17 If we truly love others and live as Christ did in this world, we won't be worried about the day of judgment. 18 A real love for others will chase those worries away. The thought of being punished is what makes us afraid. It shows that we have not really learned to love.

19 We love because God loved us first. 20 But if we say we love God and don't love each other, we are liars. We cannot see God. So how can we love God, if we don't love the people we can see? 21 The commandment that God has given us is: "Love God and love each other!"

Victory over the World

5 If we believe that Jesus is truly Christ, we are God's children. Everyone who loves the Father will also love his children. 2 If we love and obey God, we know that we will love his children. 3 We show our love for God by obeying his commandments, and they are not hard to follow.

4 Every child of God can defeat the world, and our faith is what gives us this victory. 5 No one can defeat the world without having faith in Jesus as the Son of God.

Who Jesus Is

6 Water and blood came out from the side of Jesus Christ. It wasn't just water, but water and blood. The Spirit tells about this, because the Spirit is truthful. 7 In fact, there are three who tell about it. 8 They are the Spirit, the water, and the blood, and they all agree.

9 We believe what people tell us. But we can trust what God says even more, and God is the one who has spoken about his Son. 10 If we have faith in God's Son, we have believed what God has said. But if we don't believe what God has said about his Son, it is the same as calling God a liar. 11 God has also said that he gave us eternal life and that this life comes to us from his Son. 12 And so, if we have God's Son, we have this life. But if we don't have the Son, we don't have this life.

Knowing about Eternal Life

13 All of you have faith in the Son of God, and I have written to let you know that you have eternal life. 14 We are certain that God will hear our prayers when we ask for what pleases him. 15 And if we know that God listens when we pray, we are sure that our prayers have already been answered.

16 Suppose you see one of our people commit a sin that isn't a deadly sin. You can pray, and that person will be given eternal life. But the sin must not be one that is deadly. 17 Everything that is wrong is sin, but not all sins are deadly.

18 We are sure that God's children do not keep on sinning. God's own Son protects them, and the devil cannot harm them.

19 We are certain that we come from God and that the rest of the world is under the power of the devil.

20 We know that Jesus Christ the Son of God has come and has shown us the true God. And because of Jesus, we now belong to the true God who gives eternal life.

21 Children, you must stay away from idols.

2 JOHN

1 From the church leader.[a]

To a very special woman and her children. I truly love all of you, and so does everyone else who knows the truth. 2 We love you because the truth is now in our hearts, and it will be there forever.

3 I pray that God the Father and Jesus Christ his Son will be kind and merciful to us! May they give us peace and truth and love.

Truth and Love

4 I was very glad to learn that some of your children are obeying the truth, as the Father told us to do. 5 Dear friend, I am not writing to tell you and your children to do something you have not done before. I am writing to tell you to love each other, which is the first thing you were told to do. 6 Love means that we do what God tells us. And from the beginning, he told you to love him.

7 Many liars have gone out into the world. These deceitful liars are saying that Jesus Christ did not have a truly human body. But they are liars and the enemies of Christ. 8 So be sure not to lose what we[b] have worked for. If you do, you won't be given your full reward. 9 Don't keep changing what you were taught about Christ, or else God will no longer be with you. But if you hold

---

[a] 1 church leader: Or "elder" or "presbyter" or "priest."   [b] 8 we: Some manuscripts have "you."

firmly to what you were taught, both the Father and the Son will be with you. [10] If people won't agree to this teaching, don't welcome them into your home or even greet them. [11] Greeting them is the same as taking part in their evil deeds.

Final Greetings

[12] I have much more to tell you, but I don't want to write it with pen and ink. I want to come and talk to you in person, because that will make us[c] really happy.

[13] Greetings from the children of your very special sister.[d]

---

[c] **12** *us*: Some manuscripts have "you."

3 JOHN

[1] From the church leader.[a]
To my dear friend Gaius.

I love you because we follow the truth, [2] dear friend, and I pray that all goes well for you. I hope that you are as strong in body, as I know you are in spirit. [3] It makes me very happy when the Lord's followers come by and speak openly of how you obey the truth. [4] Nothing brings me greater happiness than to hear that my children are obeying the truth.

Working Together

[5] Dear friend, you have always been faithful in helping other followers of the Lord, even the ones you didn't know before. [6] They have told the church about your love. They say you were good enough to welcome them and to send them on their mission in a way that God's servants deserve. [7] When they left to tell others about the Lord, they decided not to accept help from anyone who wasn't a follower. [8] We must support people like them, so that we can take part in what they are doing to spread the truth.

[9] I wrote to the church. But Diotrephes likes to be the number-one leader, and he won't pay any attention to us.

[10] So if I come, I will remind him of how he has been attacking us with gossip. Not only has he been doing this, but he refuses to welcome any of the Lord's followers who come by. And when other church members want to welcome them, he puts them out of the church.

[11] Dear friend, don't copy the evil deeds of others! Follow the example of people who do kind deeds. They are God's children, but those who are always doing evil have never seen God.

[12] Everyone speaks well of Demetrius, and so does the true message that he teaches. I also speak well of him, and you know what I say is true.

Final Greetings

[13] I have much more to say to you, but I don't want to write it with pen and ink. [14] I hope to see you soon, and then we can talk in person.

[15] I pray that God will bless you with peace! Your friends send their greetings. Please give a personal greeting to each of our friends.

---

[a] **1** *church leader*: Or "elder" or "presbyter" or "priest."

JUDE

From Jude, a servant of Jesus Christ and the brother of James.

To all who are chosen and loved by God the Father and are kept safe by Jesus Christ.

2 I pray that God will greatly bless you with kindness, peace, and love!

False Teachers

3 My dear friends, I really wanted to write you about God's saving power at work in our lives. But instead, I must write and ask you to defend the faith that God has once for all given to his people. 4 Some godless people have sneaked in among us and are saying, "God treats us much better than we deserve, and so it is all right to be immoral." They even deny that we must obey Jesus Christ as our only Master and Lord. But long ago the Scriptures warned that these godless people were doomed.

5 Don't forget what happened to those people that the Lord rescued from Egypt. Some of them did not have faith, and he later destroyed them. 6 You also know about the angels who didn't do their work and left their proper places. God chained them with everlasting chains and is now keeping them in dark pits until the great day of judgment. 7 We should also be warned by what happened to the cities of Sodom and Gomorrah and the nearby towns. Their people became immoral and did all sorts of sexual sins. Then God made an example of them and punished them with eternal fire.

8 The people I am talking about are behaving just like those dreamers who destroyed their own bodies. They reject all authority and insult angels. 9 Even Michael, the chief angel, didn't dare to insult the devil, when the two of them were arguing about the body of Moses. All Michael said was, "The Lord will punish you!"

10 But these people insult powers they don't know anything about. They are like senseless animals that end up getting destroyed, because they live only by their feelings. 11 Now they are in for real trouble. They have followed Cain's example and have made the same mistake that Balaam did by caring only for money. They have also rebelled against God, just as Korah did. Because of all this, they will be destroyed.

12 These people are filthy minded, and by their shameful and selfish actions they spoil the meals you eat together. They are like clouds blown along by the wind, but never bringing any rain. They are like leafless trees, uprooted and dead, and unable to produce fruit. 13 Their shameful deeds show up like foam on wild ocean waves. They are like wandering stars forever doomed to the darkest pits of hell.

14 Enoch was the seventh person after Adam, and he was talking about these people when he said:

Look! The Lord is coming with thousands and thousands of holy angels 15 to judge everyone. He will punish all those ungodly people for all the evil things they have done. The Lord will surely punish those ungodly sinners for every evil thing they have ever said about him.

16 These people grumble and complain and live by their own selfish desires. They brag about themselves and flatter others to get what they want.

More Warnings

17 My dear friends, remember the warning you were given by the apostles of our Lord Jesus Christ. 18 They told you that near the end of time, selfish and godless people would start making fun of God. 19 And now these people are already making you turn against each other. They think only about this life, and they don't have God's Spirit.

20 Dear friends, keep building on the foundation of your most holy faith, as the Holy Spirit helps you to pray. 21 And keep in step with God's love, as you wait for our Lord Jesus Christ to show how kind he is by giving you eternal life. 22 Be helpful to*a* all who may have doubts. 23 Rescue any who need to be saved, as you would rescue someone from a fire. Then with fear in your own hearts, have mercy on everyone who needs it. But hate even the clothes of those who have been made dirty by their filthy deeds.

Final Prayer

24-25 Offer praise to God our Savior because of our Lord Jesus Christ! Only God can keep you from falling and make you pure and joyful in his glorious presence. Before time began and now and forevermore, God is worthy of glory, honor, power, and authority. Amen.

---

a **22** *Be helpful to*: Some manuscripts have "Correct."

REVELATION

1 This is what God showed to Jesus Christ, so that he could tell his servants what must happen soon. Christ then sent his angel with the message to his servant John. [2] And John told everything that he had seen about God's message and about what Jesus Christ had said and done.

[3] God will bless everyone who reads this prophecy to others, and he will bless everyone who hears and obeys it. The time is almost here.

[4] From John to the seven churches in Asia.

I pray that you
   will be blessed
with kindness and peace
from God, who is and was
   and is coming.
May you receive
   kindness and peace
from the seven spirits
   before the throne of God.
[5] May kindness and peace
   be yours
from Jesus Christ,
   the faithful witness.

Jesus was the first
   to conquer death,
and he is the ruler
   of all earthly kings.
Christ loves us,
   and by his blood
he set us free
   from our sins.
[6] He lets us rule as kings
and serve God his Father
   as priests.
To him be glory and power
   forever and ever! Amen.
[7] Look! He is coming
   with the clouds.
Everyone will see him,
even the ones who stuck
   a sword through him.
All people on earth
will weep because of him.
   Yes, it will happen! Amen.

[8] The Lord God says, "I am Alpha and Omega, the one who is and was and is coming. I am God All-Powerful!"

A Vision of the Risen Lord

[9] I am John, a follower together with all of you. We suffer because Jesus is our king, but he gives us the strength to endure. I was sent to Patmos Island, because I had preached God's message and had told about Jesus. [10] On the Lord's day the Spirit took control of me, and behind me I heard a loud voice that sounded like a trumpet. [11] The voice said, "Write in a book what you see. Then send it to the seven churches in Ephesus, Smyrna, Pergamum, Thyatira, Sardis, Philadelphia, and Laodicea."

[12] When I turned to see who was speaking to me, I saw seven gold lampstands. [13] There with the lampstands was someone who seemed to be the Son of Man. He was wearing a robe that reached down to his feet, and a gold cloth was wrapped around his chest. [14] His head and his hair were white as wool or snow, and his eyes looked like flames of fire. [15] His feet were glowing like bronze being heated in a furnace, and his voice sounded like the roar of a waterfall. [16] He held seven stars in his right hand, and a sharp double-edged sword was coming from his mouth. His face was shining as bright as the sun at noon.

[17] When I saw him, I fell at his feet like a dead person. But he put his right hand on me and said:

Don't be afraid! I am the first, the last, [18] and the living one. I died, but now I am alive forevermore, and I have the keys to death and the world of the dead. [19] Write what you have seen and what is and what will happen after these things. [20] I will explain the mystery of the seven stars that you saw at my right side and the seven gold lampstands. The seven stars are the angels of the seven churches, and the lampstands are the seven churches.

The Letter to Ephesus

2 This is what you must write to the angel of the church in Ephesus:

I am the one who holds the seven stars in my right hand, and I walk among the seven gold lampstands. Listen to what I say.

[2] I know everything you have done, including your hard work and how you have endured. I know you won't put up with anyone who is evil. When some people pretended to be apostles, you tested them and found out that they were liars. [3] You have endured and gone through hard times because of me, and you have not given up.

[4] But I do have something against you! And it is this: You don't have as much love as you used to. [5] Think about where you have fallen from, and then turn back and do as you did at first. If you don't turn back, I will come and take away your lampstand. [6] But there is one thing you are doing right. You hate what the Nicolaitans are doing, and so do I.

[7] If you have ears, listen to what the Spirit says to the churches. I will let everyone who wins the victory eat from the life-giving tree in God's wonderful garden.

The Letter to Smyrna

[8] This is what you must write to the angel of the church in Smyrna:

I am the first and the last. I died, but now I am alive! Listen to what I say.

9 I know how much you suffer and how poor you are, but you are rich. I also know the cruel things being said about you by people who claim to be Jews. But they are not really Jews. They are a group that belongs to Satan.

10 Don't worry about what you will suffer. The devil will throw some of you into jail, and you will be tested and made to suffer for ten days. But if you are faithful until you die, I will reward you with a glorious life.*a*

11 If you have ears, listen to what the Spirit says to the churches. Whoever wins the victory will not be hurt by the second death.

The Letter to Pergamum

12 This is what you must write to the angel of the church in Pergamum:

I am the one who has the sharp double-edged sword! Listen to what I say.

13 I know that you live where Satan has his throne. But you have kept true to my name. Right there where Satan lives, my faithful witness Antipas was taken from you and put to death. Even then you did not give up your faith in me.

14 I do have a few things against you. Some of you are following the teaching of Balaam. Long ago he told Balak to teach the people of Israel to eat food that had been offered to idols and to be immoral. 15 Now some of you are following the teaching of the Nicolaitans. 16 Turn back! If you don't, I will come quickly and fight against these people. And my words will cut like a sword.

17 If you have ears, listen to what the Spirit says to the churches. To everyone who wins the victory, I will give some of the hidden food. I will also give each one a white stone with a new name written on it. No one will know that name except the one who is given the stone.

The Letter to Thyatira

18 This is what you must write to the angel of the church in Thyatira:

I am the Son of God! My eyes are like flames of fire, and my feet are like bronze. Listen to what I say.

19 I know everything about you, including your love, your faith, your service, and how you have endured. I know that you are doing more now than you have ever done before. 20 But I still have something against you because of that woman Jezebel. She calls herself a prophet, and you let her teach and mislead my servants to do immoral things and to eat food offered to idols. 21 I gave her a chance to turn from her sins, but she did not want to stop doing these immoral things.

22 I am going to strike down Jezebel. Everyone who does these immoral things with her will also be punished, if they don't stop. 23 I will even kill her followers.*b* Then all the churches will see that I know everyone's thoughts and feelings. I will treat each of you as you deserve.

24 Some of you in Thyatira don't follow Jezebel's teaching. You don't know anything about what her followers call the "deep secrets of Satan." So I won't burden you down with any other commands. 25 But until I come, you must hold firmly to the teaching you have.

26 I will give power over the nations to everyone who wins the victory and keeps on obeying me until the end. 27-28 I will give each of them the same power that my Father has given me. They will rule the nations with an iron rod and smash those nations to pieces like clay pots. I will also give them the morning star.

29 If you have ears, listen to what the Spirit says to the churches.

The Letter to Sardis

3 This is what you must write to the angel of the church in Sardis:

I have the seven spirits of God and the seven stars. Listen to what I say.

I know what you are doing. Everyone may think you are alive, but you are dead. 2 Wake up! You have only a little strength left, and it is almost gone. So try to become stronger. I have found that you are not completely obeying God. 3 Remember the teaching that you were given and that you heard. Hold firmly to it and turn from your sins. If you don't wake up, I will come when you least expect it, just as a thief does.

4 A few of you in Sardis have not dirtied your clothes with sin. You will walk with me in white clothes, because you are worthy. 5 Everyone who wins the victory will wear white clothes. Their names will not be erased from the book of life, and I will tell my Father and his angels that they are my followers.

6 If you have ears, listen to what the Spirit says to the churches.

The Letter to Philadelphia

7 This is what you must write to the angel of the church in Philadelphia:

I am the one who is holy and true, and I have the keys that belonged to David. When I open a door, no one can close it. And when I close a door, no one can open it. Listen to what I say.

8 I know everything you have done. And I have placed before you an open door that no one can close. You were not very strong, but you obeyed my message and did not deny that you are my followers.*c* 9 Now you will see what I will do with those people who belong to Satan's group. They claim to be Jews, but they are liars. I will make them come and kneel down at your feet. Then they will know that I love you.

10 You obeyed my message and endured. So I will protect you from the time of testing that everyone in all the world must go through. 11 I am com-

---

a **2.10** *a glorious life*: The Greek text has "a crown of life." In ancient times an athlete who had won a contest was rewarded with a crown of flowers as a sign of victory. *b* **2.23** *her followers*: Or "her children." *c* **3.8** *did not deny that you are my followers*: Or "did not say evil things about me."

ing soon. So hold firmly to what you have, and no one will take away the crown that you will be given as your reward.

12 Everyone who wins the victory will be made into a pillar in the temple of my God, and they will stay there forever. I will write on each of them the name of my God and the name of his city. It is the new Jerusalem that my God will send down from heaven. I will also write on them my own new name.

13 If you have ears, listen to what the Spirit says to the churches.

The Letter to Laodicea

14 This is what you must write to the angel of the church in Laodicea:

I am the one called Amen! I am the faithful and true witness and the source[d] of God's creation. Listen to what I say.

15 I know everything you have done, and you are not cold or hot. I wish you were either one or the other. **16** But since you are lukewarm and neither cold nor hot, I will spit you out of my mouth. **17** You claim to be rich and successful and to have everything you need. But you don't know how bad off you are. You are pitiful, poor, blind, and naked.

18 Buy your gold from me. It has been refined in a fire, and it will make you rich. Buy white clothes from me. Wear them and you can cover up your shameful nakedness. Buy medicine for your eyes, so that you will be able to see.

19 I correct and punish everyone I love. So make up your minds to turn away from your sins. **20** Listen! I am standing and knocking at your door. If you hear my voice and open the door, I will come in and we will eat together. **21** Everyone who wins the victory will sit with me on my throne, just as I won the victory and sat with my Father on his throne.

22 If you have ears, listen to what the Spirit says to the churches.

Worship in Heaven

4 After this, I looked and saw a door that opened into heaven. Then the voice that had spoken to me at first and that sounded like a trumpet said, "Come up here! I will show you what must happen next." **2** Right then the Spirit took control of me, and there in heaven I saw a throne and someone sitting on it. **3** The one who was sitting there sparkled like precious stones of jasper and carnelian. A rainbow that looked like an emerald surrounded the throne.

4 Twenty-four other thrones were in a circle around that throne. And on each of these thrones there was an elder dressed in white clothes and wearing a gold crown. **5** Flashes of lightning and roars of thunder came out from the throne in the center of the circle. Seven torches, which are the seven spirits of God, were burning in front of the throne. **6** Also in front of the throne was something that looked like a glass sea, clear as crystal.

Around the throne in the center were four living creatures covered front and back with eyes. **7** The first creature was like a lion, the second one was like a bull, the third one had the face of a human, and the fourth was like a flying eagle. **8** Each of the four living creatures had six wings, and their bodies were covered with eyes. Day and night they never stopped singing,

"Holy, holy, holy is the Lord,
    the all-powerful God,
who was and is
    and is coming!"

9 The living creatures kept praising, honoring, and thanking the one who sits on the throne and who lives forever and ever. **10** At the same time the twenty-four elders knelt down before the one sitting on the throne. And as they worshiped the one who lives forever, they placed their crowns in front of the throne and said,

11 "Our Lord and God,
    you are worthy
to receive glory,
    honor, and power.
You created all things,
    and by your decision they are
        and were created."

The Scroll and the Lamb

5 In the right hand of the one sitting on the throne I saw a scroll that had writing on the inside and on the outside. And it was sealed in seven places. **2** I saw a mighty angel ask with a loud voice, "Who is worthy to open the scroll and break its seals?" **3** No one in heaven or on earth or under the earth was able to open the scroll or see inside it.

4 I cried hard because no one was found worthy to open the scroll or see inside it. **5** Then one of the elders said to me, "Stop crying and look! The one who is called both the 'Lion from the Tribe of Judah' and 'King David's Great Descendant'[e] has won the victory. He will open the book and its seven seals."

6 Then I looked and saw a Lamb standing in the center of the throne that was surrounded by the four living creatures and the elders. The Lamb looked as if it had once been killed. It had seven horns and seven eyes, which are the seven spirits[f] of God, sent out to all the earth.

7 The Lamb went over and took the scroll from the right hand of the one who sat on the throne. **8** After he had taken it, the four living creatures and the twenty-four elders knelt down before him. Each of them had a harp and a gold bowl full of incense, which are the prayers of God's people. **9** Then they sang a new song,

"You are worthy
    to receive the scroll
and open its seals,
    because you were killed.
And with your own blood
    you bought for God

---

d 3.14 source: Or "beginning."   **e 5.5** 'King David's Great Descendant': The Greek text has "the root of David" which is a title for the Messiah based on Isaiah 11.1,10.   **f 5.6** the seven spirits: Some manuscripts have "the spirits."

people from every tribe,
language, nation, and race.
10 You let them become kings
and serve God as priests,
and they will rule on earth."

11 As I looked, I heard the voices of a lot of angels around the throne and the voices of the living creatures and of the elders. There were millions and millions of them, 12 and they were saying in a loud voice,

"The Lamb who was killed
is worthy to receive power,
riches, wisdom, strength,
honor, glory, and praise."

13 Then I heard all beings in heaven and on the earth and under the earth and in the sea offer praise. Together, all of them were saying,

"Praise, honor, glory,
and strength
forever and ever
to the one who sits
on the throne
and to the Lamb!"

14 The four living creatures said "Amen," while the elders knelt down and worshiped.

Opening the Seven Seals

6 At the same time that I saw the Lamb open the first of the seven seals, I heard one of the four living creatures shout with a voice like thunder. It said, "Come out!" 2 Then I saw a white horse. Its rider carried a bow and was given a crown. He had already won some victories, and he went out to win more.

3 When the Lamb opened the second seal, I heard the second living creature say, "Come out!" 4 Then another horse came out. It was fiery red. And its rider was given the power to take away all peace from the earth, so that people would slaughter one another. He was also given a big sword.

5 When the Lamb opened the third seal, I heard the third living creature say, "Come out!" Then I saw a black horse, and its rider had a balance scale in one hand. 6 I heard what sounded like a voice from somewhere among the four living creatures. It said, "A quart of wheat will cost you a whole day's wages! Three quarts of barley will cost you a day's wages too. But don't ruin the olive oil or the wine."

7 When the Lamb opened the fourth seal, I heard the voice of the fourth living creature say, "Come out!" 8 Then I saw a pale green horse. Its rider was named Death, and Death's Kingdom followed behind. They were given power over one fourth of the earth, and they could kill its people with swords, famines, diseases, and wild animals.

9 When the Lamb opened the fifth seal, I saw under the altar the souls of everyone who had been killed for speaking God's message and telling about their faith. 10 They shouted, "Master, you are holy and faithful! How long will it be before you judge and punish the people of this earth who killed us?"

11 Then each of those who had been killed was given a white robe and told to rest for a little while. They had to wait until the complete number of the Lord's other servants and followers would be killed.

12 When I saw the Lamb open the sixth seal, I looked and saw a great earthquake. The sun turned as dark as sackcloth, and the moon became as red as blood. 13 The stars in the sky fell to earth, just like figs shaken loose by a windstorm. 14 Then the sky was rolled up like a scroll, and all mountains and islands were moved from their places.

15 The kings of the earth, its famous people, and its military leaders hid in caves or behind rocks on the mountains. They hid there together with the rich and the powerful and with all the slaves and free people. 16 Then they shouted to the mountains and the rocks, "Fall on us! Hide us from the one who sits on the throne and from the anger of the Lamb. 17 That terrible day has come! God and the Lamb will show their anger, and who can face it?"

The 144,000 Are Marked for God

7 1-2 After this I saw four angels. Each one was standing on one of the earth's four corners. The angels held back the four winds, so that no wind would blow on the earth or on the sea or on any tree. These angels had also been given the power to harm the earth and the sea. Then I saw another angel come up from where the sun rises in the east, and he was ready to put the mark of the living God on people. He shouted to the four angels, 3 "Don't harm the earth or the sea or any tree! Wait until I have marked the foreheads of the servants of our God."

4 Then I heard how many people had been marked on the forehead. There were one hundred forty-four thousand, and they came from every tribe of Israel:

5 12,000 from Judah,
12,000 from Reuben,
12,000 from Gad,
6 12,000 from Asher,
12,000 from Naphtali,
12,000 from Manasseh,
7 12,000 from Simeon,
12,000 from Levi,
12,000 from Issachar,
8 12,000 from Zebulun,
12,000 from Joseph, and
12,000 from Benjamin.

People from Every Nation

9 After this, I saw a large crowd with more people than could be counted. They were from every race, tribe, nation, and language, and they stood before the throne and before the Lamb. They wore white robes and held palm branches in their hands, 10 as they shouted,

"Our God, who sits
upon the throne,
has the power
to save his people,
and so does the Lamb."

11 The angels who stood around the throne knelt in front of it with their faces to the ground. The elders and the four living creatures knelt there with them. Then they all worshiped God 12 and said,

"Amen! Praise, glory, wisdom,
    thanks, honor, power,
and strength belong to our God
    forever and ever! Amen!"

13 One of the elders asked me, "Do you know who these people are that are dressed in white robes? Do you know where they come from?"

14 "Sir," I answered, "you must know."

Then he told me:

"These are the ones
who have gone through
    the great suffering.
They have washed their robes
in the blood of the Lamb
    and have made them white.
15 And so they stand
    before the throne of God
and worship him in his temple
    day and night.
The one who sits on the throne
will spread his tent
    over them.
16 They will never hunger
    or thirst again,
and they won't be troubled
by the sun
    or any scorching heat.

17 The Lamb in the center
    of the throne
    will be their shepherd.
He will lead them to streams
    of life-giving water,
and God will wipe all tears
    from their eyes."

The Seventh Seal Is Opened

8 When the Lamb opened the seventh seal, there was silence in heaven for about half an hour. 2 I noticed that the seven angels who stood before God were each given a trumpet.

3 Another angel, who had a gold container for incense, came and stood at the altar. This one was given a lot of incense to offer with the prayers of God's people on the gold altar in front of the throne. 4 Then the smoke of the incense, together with the prayers of God's people, went up to God from the hand of the angel.

5 After this, the angel filled the incense container with fire from the altar and threw it on the earth. Thunder roared, lightning flashed, and the earth shook.

The Trumpets

6 The seven angels now got ready to blow their trumpets.

7 When the first angel blew his trumpet, hail and fire mixed with blood were thrown down on the earth. A third of the earth, a third of the trees, and a third of all green plants were burned.

8 When the second angel blew his trumpet, something like a great fiery mountain was thrown into the sea. A third of the sea turned to blood, 9 a third of the living creatures in the sea died, and a third of the ships were destroyed.

10 When the third angel blew his trumpet, a great star fell from heaven. It was burning like a torch, and it fell on a third of the rivers and on a third of the springs of water. 11 The name of the star was Bitter, and a third of the water turned bitter. Many people died because the water was so bitter.

12 When the fourth angel blew his trumpet, a third of the sun, a third of the moon, and a third of the stars were struck. They each lost a third of their light. So during a third of the day there was no light, and a third of the night was also without light.

13 Then I looked and saw a lone eagle flying across the sky. It was shouting, "Trouble, trouble, trouble to everyone who lives on earth! The other three angels are now going to blow their trumpets."

9 When the fifth angel blew his trumpet, I saw a star fall from the sky to earth. It was given the key to the tunnel that leads down to the deep pit. 2 As it opened the tunnel, smoke poured out like the smoke of a great furnace. The sun and the air turned dark because of the smoke. 3 Locusts came out of the smoke and covered the earth. They were given the same power that scorpions have.

4 The locusts were told not to harm the grass on the earth or any plant or any tree. They were to punish only those people who did not have God's mark on their foreheads. 5 The locusts were allowed to make them suffer for five months, but not to kill them. The suffering they caused was like the sting of a scorpion. 6 In those days people will want to die, but they will not be able to. They will hope for death, but it will escape from them.

7 These locusts looked like horses ready for battle. On their heads they wore something like gold crowns, and they had human faces. 8 Their hair was like a woman's long hair, and their teeth were like those of a lion. 9 On their chests they wore armor made of iron. Their wings roared like an army of horse-drawn chariots rushing into battle. 10 Their tails were like a scorpion's tail with a stinger that had the power to hurt someone for five months. 11 Their king was the angel in charge of the deep pit. In Hebrew his name was Abaddon, and in Greek it was Apollyon.ᵍ

12 The first horrible thing has now happened! But wait. Two more horrible things will happen soon.

13 Then the sixth angel blew his trumpet. I heard a voice speak from the four corners of the gold altar that stands in the presence of God. 14 The voice spoke to this angel and said, "Release the four angels who are tied up beside the great Euphrates River." 15 The four angels had been prepared for this very hour and day and month and year. Now they were set free to kill a third of all people.

16 By listening, I could tell there were more than two hundred million of these war horses. 17 In my vision their riders wore fiery-red, dark-blue, and yellow armor on their chests. The heads of the horses looked like lions, with fire and smoke and sulfur coming out of their mouths. 18 One-third of all people were killed by the three terrible troubles caused by the fire, the smoke, and the sulfur. 19 The horses had powerful mouths, and their tails were like poisonous snakes that bite and hurt.

20 The people who lived through these terrible troubles did not turn away from the idols they had made, and

---

ᵍ 9.11 *Abaddon . . . Apollyon*: The Hebrew word "Abaddon" and the Greek word "Apollyon" each mean "destruction."

they did not stop worshiping demons. They kept on worshiping idols that were made of gold, silver, bronze, stone,
and wood. Not one of these idols could see, hear, or walk.
21 No one stopped murdering or practicing witchcraft or
being immoral or stealing.

The Angel and the Little Scroll

10 I saw another powerful angel come down from
heaven. This one was covered with a cloud, and a
rainbow was over his head. His face was like the sun, his
legs were like columns of fire, 2 and with his hand he held a
little scroll that had been unrolled. He stood there with his
right foot on the sea and his left foot on the land. 3 Then he
shouted with a voice that sounded like a growling lion.
Thunder roared seven times.

4 After the thunder stopped, I was about to write what
it had said. But a voice from heaven shouted, "Keep it secret! Don't write these things."

5 The angel I had seen standing on the sea and the land
then held his right hand up toward heaven. 6 He made a
promise in the name of God who lives forever and who created heaven, earth, the sea, and every living creature. The
angel said, "You won't have to wait any longer. 7 God told
his secret plans to his servants the prophets, and it will all
happen by the time the seventh angel sounds his trumpet."

8 Once again the voice from heaven spoke to me. It
said, "Go and take the open scroll from the hand of the angel standing on the sea and the land."

9 When I went over to ask the angel for the little scroll,
the angel said, "Take the scroll and eat it! Your stomach will
turn sour, but the taste in your mouth will be as sweet as
honey." 10 I took the little scroll from the hand of the angel
and ate it. The taste was as sweet as honey, but my stomach
turned sour.

11 Then some voices said, "Keep on telling what will
happen to the people of many nations, races, and languages, and also to kings."

The Two Witnesses

11 An angel gave me a measuring stick and said:
Measure around God's temple. Be sure to include the altar and everyone worshiping there.
2 But don't measure the courtyard outside the temple building. Leave it out. It has been given to those
people who don't know God, and they will trample all
over the holy city for forty-two months. 3 My two witnesses will wear sackcloth, while I let them preach
for one thousand two hundred sixty days.

4 These two witnesses are the two olive trees and the
two lampstands that stand in the presence of the Lord who
rules the earth. 5 Any enemy who tries to harm them will
be destroyed by the fire that comes out of their mouths.
6 They have the power to lock up the sky and to keep rain
from falling while they are prophesying. And whenever
they want to, they can turn water to blood and cause all
kinds of terrible troubles on earth.

7 After the two witnesses have finished preaching
God's message, the beast that lives in the deep pit will come
up and fight against them. It will win the battle and kill them.
8 Their bodies will be left lying in the streets of the same great
city where their Lord was nailed to a cross. And that city is
spiritually like the city of Sodom or the country of Egypt.

9 For three and a half days the people of every nation,
tribe, language, and race will stare at the bodies of these
two witnesses and refuse to let them be buried. 10 Everyone on earth will celebrate and be happy. They will give
gifts to each other, because of what happened to the two
prophets who caused them so much trouble. 11 But three
and a half days later, God will breathe life into their bodies.
They will stand up, and everyone who sees them will be
terrified.

12 The witnesses then heard a loud voice from heaven,
saying, "Come up here." And while their enemies were
watching, they were taken up to heaven in a cloud. 13 At
that same moment there was a terrible earthquake that destroyed a tenth of the city. Seven thousand people were
killed, and the rest were frightened and praised the God
who rules in heaven.

14 The second horrible thing has now happened! But
the third one will be here soon.

The Seventh Trumpet

15 At the sound of the seventh trumpet, loud voices
were heard in heaven. They said,

"Now the kingdom
of this world
belongs to our Lord
and to his Chosen One!
And he will rule
forever and ever!"

16 Then the twenty-four elders, who were seated on
thrones in God's presence, knelt down and worshiped him.
17 They said,

"Lord God All-Powerful,
you are and you were,
and we thank you.
You used your great power
and started ruling.
18 When the nations got angry,
you became angry too!
Now the time has come
for the dead
to be judged.
It is time for you to reward
your servants the prophets
and all of your people
who honor your name,
no matter who they are.
It is time to destroy everyone
who has destroyed
the earth."

19 The door to God's temple in heaven was then
opened, and the sacred chest could be seen inside the temple. I saw lightning and heard roars of thunder. The earth
trembled and huge hailstones fell to the ground.

The Woman and the Dragon

12 Something important appeared in the sky. It was a
woman whose clothes were the sun. The moon
was under her feet, and a crown made of twelve stars was

on her head. ² She was about to give birth, and she was crying because of the great pain.

³ Something else appeared in the sky. It was a huge red dragon with seven heads and ten horns, and a crown on each of its seven heads. ⁴ With its tail, it dragged a third of the stars from the sky and threw them down to the earth. Then the dragon turned toward the woman, because it wanted to eat her child as soon as it was born.

⁵ The woman gave birth to a son, who would rule all nations with an iron rod. The boy was snatched away. He was taken to God and placed on his throne. ⁶ The woman ran into the desert to a place that God had prepared for her. There she would be taken care of for one thousand two hundred sixty days.

Michael Fights the Dragon

⁷ A war broke out in heaven. Michael and his angels were fighting against the dragon and its angels. ⁸ But the dragon lost the battle. It and its angels were forced out of their places in heaven ⁹ and were thrown down to the earth. Yes, that old snake and his angels were thrown out of heaven! That snake, who fools everyone on earth, is known as the devil and Satan. ¹⁰ Then I heard a voice from heaven shout,

> "Our God has shown
> his saving power,
>   and his kingdom has come!
> God's own Chosen One
>   has shown his authority.
> Satan accused our people
> in the presence of God
>   day and night.
> Now he has been thrown out!
>
> ¹¹ Our people defeated Satan
>   because of the blood ʰ
> of the Lamb
>   and the message of God.
> They were willing
>   to give up their lives.
>
> ¹² The heavens should rejoice,
>   together with everyone
>   who lives there.
> But pity the earth
>   and the sea,
> because the devil
> was thrown down
>   to the earth.
> He knows his time is short,
>   and he is very angry."

¹³ When the dragon realized that it had been thrown down to the earth, it tried to make trouble for the woman who had given birth to a son. ¹⁴ But the woman was given two wings like those of a huge eagle, so that she could fly into the desert. There she would escape from the snake and be taken care of for a time, two times, and half a time.

¹⁵ The snake then spewed out water like a river to sweep the woman away. ¹⁶ But the earth helped her and swallowed the water that had come from the dragon's mouth. ¹⁷ This made the dragon terribly angry with the woman. So it started a war against the rest of her children. They are the people who obey God and are faithful to what Jesus did and taught. ¹⁸ The dragon ⁱ stood on the beach beside the sea.

The Two Beasts

13 I looked and saw a beast coming up from the sea. This one had ten horns and seven heads, and a crown was on each of its ten horns. On each of its heads were names that were an insult to God. ² The beast that I saw had the body of a leopard, the feet of a bear, and the mouth of a lion. The dragon handed over its own power and throne and great authority to this beast. ³ One of its heads seemed to have been fatally wounded, but now it was well. Everyone on earth marveled at this beast, ⁴ and they worshiped the dragon who had given its authority to the beast. They also worshiped the beast and said, "No one is like this beast! No one can fight against it."

⁵ The beast was allowed to brag and claim to be God, and for forty-two months it was allowed to rule. ⁶ The beast cursed God, and it cursed the name of God. It even cursed the place where God lives, as well as everyone who lives in heaven with God. ⁷ It was allowed to fight against God's people and defeat them. It was also given authority over the people of every tribe, nation, language, and race. ⁸ The beast was worshiped by everyone whose name wasn't written before the time of creation in the book of the Lamb who was killed.ʲ

> ⁹ If you have ears,
>   then listen!
> ¹⁰ If you are doomed
>   to be captured,
>   you will be captured.
> If you are doomed
>   to be killed by a sword,
> you will be killed
>   by a sword.

This means that God's people must learn to endure and be faithful!

¹¹ I now saw another beast. This one came out of the ground. It had two horns like a lamb, but spoke like a dragon. ¹² It worked for the beast whose fatal wound had been healed. And it used all its authority to force the earth and its people to worship that beast. ¹³ It worked mighty miracles, and while people watched, it even made fire come down from the sky.

¹⁴ This second beast fooled people on earth by working miracles for the first one. Then it talked them into making an idol in the form of the beast that did not die after being wounded by a sword. ¹⁵ It was allowed to put breath into the idol, so that it could speak. Everyone who refused to worship the idol of the beast was put to death. ¹⁶ All people were forced to put a mark on their right hand or forehead. Whether they were powerful or weak, rich or poor, free

---

ʰ **12.11** *blood*: Or "death."   ⁱ **12.18** *The dragon*: The text has "he," and some manuscripts have "I."
ʲ **13.8** *wasn't written . . . was killed*: Or "not written in the book of the Lamb who was killed before the time of creation."

people or slaves, 17 they all had to have this mark, or else they could not buy or sell anything. This mark stood for the name of the beast and for the number of its name.

18 You need wisdom to understand the number of the beast! But if you are smart enough, you can figure this out. Its number is six hundred sixty-six, and it stands for a person.

The Lamb and His 144,000 Followers

14 I looked and saw the Lamb standing on Mount Zion! With him were a hundred forty-four thousand, who had his name and his Father's name written on their foreheads. 2 Then I heard a sound from heaven that was like a roaring flood or loud thunder or even like the music of harps. 3 And a new song was being sung in front of God's throne and in front of the four living creatures and the elders. No one could learn that song, except the one hundred forty-four thousand who had been rescued from the earth. 4 All of these are pure virgins, and they follow the Lamb wherever he leads. They have been rescued to be presented to God and the Lamb as the most precious people*k* on earth. 5 They never tell lies, and they are innocent.

The Messages of the Three Angels

6 I saw another angel. This one was flying across the sky and had the eternal good news to announce to the people of every race, tribe, language, and nation on earth. 7 The angel shouted, "Worship and honor God! The time has come for him to judge everyone. Kneel down before the one who created heaven and earth, the oceans, and every stream."

8 A second angel followed and said, "The great city of Babylon has fallen! This is the city that made all nations drunk and immoral. Now God is angry, and Babylon has fallen."

9 Finally, a third angel came and shouted:

Here is what will happen if you worship the beast and the idol and have the mark of the beast on your hand or forehead. 10 You will have to drink the wine that God gives to everyone who makes him angry. You will feel his mighty anger, and you will be tortured with fire and burning sulfur, while the holy angels and the Lamb look on.

11 If you worship the beast and the idol and accept the mark of its name, you will be tortured day and night. The smoke from your torture will go up forever and ever, and you will never be able to rest.

12 God's people must learn to endure. They must also obey his commands and have faith in Jesus.

13 Then I heard a voice from heaven say, "Put this in writing. From now on, the Lord will bless everyone who has faith in him when they die."

The Spirit answered, "Yes, they will rest from their hard work, and they will be rewarded for what they have done."

The Earth Is Harvested

14 I looked and saw a bright cloud, and someone who seemed to be the Son of Man was sitting on the cloud. He wore a gold crown on his head and held a sharp sickle in his hand. 15 An angel came out of the temple and shouted, "Start cutting with your sickle! Harvest season is here, and all crops on earth are ripe." 16 The one on the cloud swung his sickle and harvested the crops.

17 Another angel with a sharp sickle then came out of the temple in heaven. 18 After this, an angel with power over fire came from the altar and shouted to the angel who had the sickle. He said, "All grapes on earth are ripe! Harvest them with your sharp sickle." 19 The angel swung his sickle on earth and cut off its grapes. He threw them into a pit where they were trampled on as a sign of God's anger. 20 The pit was outside the city, and when the grapes were mashed, blood flowed out. The blood turned into a river that was about two hundred miles long and almost deep enough to cover a horse.

The Last of the Terrible Troubles

15 After this, I looked at the sky and saw something else that was strange and important. Seven angels were bringing the last seven terrible troubles. When these are ended, God will no longer be angry.

2 Then I saw something that looked like a glass sea mixed with fire, and people were standing on it. They were the ones who had defeated the beast and the idol and the number that tells the name of the beast. God had given them harps, 3 and they were singing the song that his servant Moses and the Lamb had sung. They were singing,

"Lord God All-Powerful,
you have done great
    and marvelous things.
You are the ruler
    of all nations,
and you do what is
    right and fair.
4 Lord, who doesn't honor
    and praise your name?
You alone are holy,
and all nations will come
    and worship you,
because you have shown
that you judge
    with fairness."

5 After this, I noticed something else in heaven. The sacred tent used for a temple was open. 6 And the seven angels who were bringing the terrible troubles were coming out of it. They were dressed in robes of pure white linen and wore belts made of pure gold. 7 One of the four living creatures gave each of the seven angels a bowl made of gold. These bowls were filled with the anger of God who lives forever and ever. 8 The temple quickly filled with smoke from the glory and power of God. No one could enter it until the seven angels had finished pouring out the seven last troubles.

The Bowls of God's Anger

16 From the temple I heard a voice shout to the seven angels, "Go and empty the seven bowls of God's anger on the earth."

---

k **14.4** *the most precious people*: The Greek text has "the first people." The Law of Moses taught that the first-born of all animals and the first part of the harvest were special and belonged to the Lord.

² The first angel emptied his bowl on the earth. At once ugly and painful sores broke out on everyone who had the mark of the beast and worshiped the idol.

³ The second angel emptied his bowl on the sea. Right away the sea turned into blood like that of a dead person, and every living thing in the sea died.

⁴ The third angel emptied his bowl into the rivers and streams. At once they turned to blood. ⁵ Then I heard the angel, who has power over water, say,

> "You have always been,
> and you always will be
>   the holy God.
> You had the right
>   to judge in this way.
> ⁶ They poured out the blood
> of your people
>   and your prophets.
> So you gave them blood
>   to drink, as they deserve!"
> ⁷ After this, I heard
>   the altar shout,
> "Yes, Lord God All-Powerful,
> your judgments are honest
>   and fair."

⁸ The fourth angel emptied his bowl on the sun, and it began to scorch people like fire. ⁹ Everyone was scorched by its great heat, and all of them cursed the name of God who had power over these terrible troubles. But no one turned to God and praised him.

¹⁰ The fifth angel emptied his bowl on the throne of the beast. At once darkness covered its kingdom, and its people began biting their tongues in pain. ¹¹ And because of their painful sores, they cursed the God who rules in heaven. But still they did not stop doing evil things.

¹² The sixth angel emptied his bowl on the great Euphrates River, and it completely dried up to make a road for the kings from the east. ¹³ An evil spirit that looked like a frog came out of the mouth of the dragon. One also came out of the mouth of the beast, and another out of the mouth of the false prophet. ¹⁴ These evil spirits had the power to work miracles. They went to every king on earth, to bring them together for a war against God All-Powerful. But that will be the day of God's great victory.

¹⁵ Remember that Christ says, "When I come, it will surprise you like a thief! But God will bless you, if you are awake and ready. Then you won't have to walk around naked and be ashamed."

¹⁶ Those armies came together in a place that in Hebrew is called Armagedon.ᶦ

¹⁷ As soon as the seventh angel emptied his bowl in the air, a loud voice from the throne in the temple shouted, "It's done!" ¹⁸ There were flashes of lightning, roars of thunder, and the worst earthquake in all history. ¹⁹ The great city of Babylon split into three parts, and the cities of other nations fell. So God made Babylon drink from the wine cup that was filled with his anger. ²⁰ Every island ran away, and the mountains disappeared. ²¹ Hailstones, weighing about a hundred pounds each, fell from the sky on people. Finally, the people cursed God, because the hail was so terrible.

The Prostitute and the Beast

17 One of the seven angels who had emptied the bowls came over and said to me, "Come on! I will show you how God will punish that shameless prostitute who sits on many oceans. ² Every king on earth has slept with her, and her shameless ways are like wine that has made everyone on earth drunk."

³ With the help of the Spirit, the angel took me into the desert, where I saw a woman sitting on a red beast. The beast was covered with names that were an insult to God, and it had seven heads and ten horns. ⁴ The woman was dressed in purple and scarlet robes, and she wore jewelry made of gold, precious stones, and pearls. In her hand she held a gold cup filled with the filthy and nasty things she had done. ⁵ On her forehead a mysterious name was written:

I AM THE GREAT CITY OF BABYLON,
THE MOTHER OF EVERY IMMORAL
AND FILTHY THING ON EARTH.

⁶ I could tell that the woman was drunk on the blood of God's people who had given their lives for Jesus. This surprising sight amazed me, ⁷ and the angel said:

Why are you so amazed? I will explain the mystery about this woman and about the beast she is sitting on, with its seven heads and ten horns. ⁸ The beast you saw is one that used to be and no longer is. It will come back from the deep pit, but only to be destroyed. Everyone on earth whose names were not written in the book of life before the time of creation will be amazed. They will see this beast that used to be and no longer is, but will be once more.

⁹ Anyone with wisdom can figure this out. The seven heads that the woman is sitting on stand for seven hills. These heads are also seven kings. ¹⁰ Five of the kings are dead. One is ruling now, and the other one has not yet come. But when he does, he will rule for only a little while.

¹¹ You also saw a beast that used to be and no longer is. That beast is one of the seven kings who will return as the eighth king, but only to be destroyed.

¹² The ten horns that you saw are ten more kings, who have not yet come into power, and they will rule with the beast for only a short time. ¹³ They all think alike and will give their power and authority to the beast. ¹⁴ These kings will go to war against the Lamb. But he will defeat them, because he is Lord over all lords and King over all kings. His followers are chosen and special and faithful.

¹⁵ The oceans that you saw the prostitute sitting on are crowds of people from all races and languages. ¹⁶ The ten horns and the beast will start hating the shameless woman. They will strip off her clothes and leave her naked. Then they will eat her flesh and throw the rest of her body into a fire. ¹⁷ God is the one who made these kings all think alike and decide to give their power to the beast. And they will do this until what God has said comes true.

ᶦ**16.16** *Armagedon*: The Hebrew form of the name would be "Har Megiddo," meaning "Hill of Megiddo," where many battles were fought in ancient times (see Judges 5.19; 2 Kings 23.29,30).

18 The woman you saw is the great city that rules over all kings on earth.

The Fall of Babylon

18 I saw another angel come from heaven. This one had great power, and the earth was bright because of his glory. 2 The angel shouted,

"Fallen! Powerful Babylon
has fallen
and is now the home
of demons.
It is the den
of every filthy spirit
and of all unclean birds,
and every dirty
and hated animal.
3 Babylon's evil and immoral wine
has made all nations drunk.
Every king on earth
has slept with her,
and every merchant on earth
is rich because of
her evil desires."

4 Then I heard another voice
from heaven shout,
"My people, you must escape
from Babylon.
Don't take part in her sins
and share her punishment.
5 Her sins are piled
as high as heaven.
God has remembered the evil
she has done.
6 Treat her as she
has treated others.
Make her pay double
for what she has done.
Make her drink twice as much
of what she mixed
for others.
7 That woman honored herself
with a life of luxury.
Reward her now
with suffering and pain.

"Deep in her heart
Babylon said,
'I am the queen!
Never will I be a widow
or know what it means
to be sad.'
8 And so, in a single day
she will suffer the pain
of sorrow, hunger, and death.
Fire will destroy
her dead body,
because her judge
is the powerful Lord God."

9 Every king on earth who slept with her and shared in her luxury will mourn. They will weep, when they see the smoke from that fire. 10 Her sufferings will frighten them, and they will stand at a distance and say,

"Pity that great
and powerful city!
Pity Babylon!
In a single hour
her judgment has come."

11 Every merchant on earth will mourn, because there is no one to buy their goods. 12 There won't be anyone to buy their gold, silver, jewels, pearls, fine linen, purple cloth, silk, scarlet cloth, sweet-smelling wood, fancy carvings of ivory and wood, as well as things made of bronze, iron, or marble. 13 No one will buy their cinnamon, spices, incense, myrrh, frankincense, wine, olive oil, fine flour, wheat, cattle, sheep, horses, chariots, slaves, and other humans.

14 Babylon, the things
your heart desired
have all escaped
from you.
Every luxury
and all your glory
will be lost forever.
You will never
get them back.

15 The merchants had become rich because of her. But when they saw her sufferings, they were terrified. They stood at a distance, crying and mourning. 16 Then they shouted,

"Pity the great city
of Babylon!
She dressed in fine linen
and wore purple
and scarlet cloth.
She had jewelry
made of gold
and precious stones
and pearls.
17 Yet in a single hour
her riches disappeared."

Every ship captain and passenger and sailor stood at a distance, together with everyone who does business by traveling on the sea. 18 When they saw the smoke from her fire, they shouted, "This was the greatest city ever!"
19 They cried loudly, and in their sorrow they threw dust on their heads, as they said,

"Pity the great city
of Babylon!
Everyone who sailed the seas
became rich
from her treasures.
But in a single hour
the city was destroyed.
20 The heavens should be happy
with God's people
and apostles and prophets.

God has punished her
for them."

²¹ A powerful angel then picked up a huge stone and threw it into the sea. The angel said,

"This is how the great city
of Babylon
will be thrown down,
never to rise again.
²² The music of harps and singers
and of flutes and trumpets
will no longer be heard.
No workers will ever
set up shop in that city,
and the sound
of grinding grain
will be silenced forever.
²³ Lamps will no longer shine
anywhere in Babylon,
and couples will never again
say wedding vows there.
Her merchants ruled
the earth,
and by her witchcraft
she fooled all nations.
²⁴ On the streets of Babylon
is found the blood
of God's people
and of his prophets,
and everyone else."

19

After this, I heard what sounded like a lot of voices in heaven, and they were shouting,

"Praise the Lord!
To our God belongs
the glorious power to save,
² because his judgments
are honest and fair.
That filthy prostitute
ruined the earth
with shameful deeds.
But God has judged her
and made her pay
the price for murdering
his servants."

³ Then the crowd shouted,

"Praise the Lord!
Smoke will never stop rising
from her burning body."

⁴ After this, the twenty-four elders and the four living creatures all knelt before the throne of God and worshiped him. They said, "Amen! Praise the Lord!"

The Marriage Supper of the Lamb
⁵ From the throne a voice said,

"If you worship
and fear our God,
give praise to him,
no matter who you are."

⁶ Then I heard what seemed to be a large crowd that sounded like a roaring flood and loud thunder all mixed together. They were saying,

"Praise the Lord!
Our Lord God All-Powerful
now rules as king.
⁷ So we will be glad and happy
and give him praise.
The wedding day of the Lamb
is here,
and his bride is ready.
⁸ She will be given
a wedding dress
made of pure
and shining linen.
This linen stands for
the good things
God's people have done."

⁹ Then the angel told me, "Put this in writing. God will bless everyone who is invited to the wedding feast of the Lamb." The angel also said, "These things that God has said are true."

¹⁰ I knelt at the feet of the angel and began to worship him. But the angel said, "Don't do that! I am a servant, just like you and everyone else who tells about Jesus. Don't worship anyone but God. Everyone who tells about Jesus does it by the power of the Spirit."

The Rider on the White Horse
¹¹ I looked and saw that heaven was open, and a white horse was there. Its rider was called Faithful and True, and he is always fair when he judges or goes to war. ¹² He had eyes like flames of fire, and he was wearing a lot of crowns. His name was written on him, but he was the only one who knew what the name meant. ¹³ The rider wore a robe that was covered with*ᵐ* blood, and he was known as "The Word of God." ¹⁴ He was followed by armies from heaven that rode on horses and were dressed in pure white linen. ¹⁵ From his mouth a sharp sword went out to attack the nations. He will rule them with an iron rod and will show the fierce anger of God All-Powerful by trampling the grapes in the pit where wine is made. ¹⁶ On the part of the robe that covered his thigh was written, "KING OF KINGS AND LORD OF LORDS."

¹⁷ I then saw an angel standing on the sun, and he shouted to all the birds flying in the sky, "Come and join in God's great feast! ¹⁸ You can eat the flesh of kings, rulers, leaders, horses, riders, free people, slaves, important people, and everyone else."

¹⁹ I also saw the beast and all kings of the earth come together. They fought against the rider on the white horse and against his army. ²⁰ But the beast was captured and so was the false prophet. This is the same prophet who had worked

---

ᵐ **19.13** *covered with*: Some manuscripts have "sprinkled with."

miracles for the beast, so that he could fool everyone who had the mark of the beast and worshiped the idol. The beast and the false prophet were thrown alive into a lake of burning sulfur. 21 But the rest of their army was killed by the sword that came from the mouth of the rider on the horse. Then birds stuffed themselves on the dead bodies.

The Thousand Years

20 I saw an angel come down from heaven, carrying the key to the deep pit and a big chain. 2 He chained the dragon for a thousand years. It is that old snake, who is also known as the devil and Satan. 3 Then the angel threw the dragon into the pit. He locked and sealed it, so that a thousand years would go by before the dragon could fool the nations again. But after that, it would have to be set free for a little while.

4 I saw thrones, and sitting on those thrones were the ones who had been given the right to judge. I also saw the souls of the people who had their heads cut off because they had told about Jesus and preached God's message. They were the same ones who had not worshiped the beast or the idol, and they had refused to let its mark be put on their hands or foreheads. They will come to life and rule with Christ for a thousand years.

5-6 These people are the first to be raised to life, and they are especially blessed and holy. The second death has no power over them. They will be priests for God and Christ and will rule with them for a thousand years.

No other dead people were raised to life until a thousand years later.

Satan Is Defeated

7 At the end of the thousand years, Satan will be set free. 8 He will fool the countries of Gog and Magog, which are at the far ends of the earth, and their people will follow him into battle. They will have as many followers as there are grains of sand along the beach, 9 and they will march all the way across the earth. They will surround the camp of God's people and the city that his people love. But fire will come down from heaven and destroy the whole army. 10 Then the devil who fooled them will be thrown into the lake of fire and burning sulfur. He will be there with the beast and the false prophet, and they will be in pain day and night forever and ever.

The Judgment at the Great White Throne

11 I saw a great white throne with someone sitting on it. Earth and heaven tried to run away, but there was no place for them to go. 12 I also saw all the dead people standing in front of that throne. Every one of them was there, no matter who they had once been. Several books were opened, and then the book of life was opened. The dead were judged by what those books said they had done. 13 The sea gave up the dead people who were in it, and death and its kingdom also gave up their dead. Then everyone was judged by what they had done. 14 Afterwards, death and its kingdom were thrown into the lake of fire. This is the second death. 15 Anyone whose name wasn't written in the book of life was thrown into the lake of fire.

The New Heaven and the New Earth

21 I saw a new heaven and a new earth. The first heaven and the first earth had disappeared, and so had the sea. 2 Then I saw New Jerusalem, that holy city, coming down from God in heaven. It was like a bride dressed in her wedding gown and ready to meet her husband. 3 I heard a loud voice shout from the throne:

God's home is now with his people. He will live with them, and they will be his own. Yes, God will make his home among his people. 4 He will wipe all tears from their eyes, and there will be no more death, suffering, crying, or pain. These things of the past are gone forever.

5 Then the one sitting on the throne said:

I am making everything new. Write down what I have said. My words are true and can be trusted. 6 Everything is finished! I am Alpha and Omega, the beginning and the end. I will freely give water from the life-giving fountain to everyone who is thirsty. 7 All who win the victory will be given these blessings. I will be their God, and they will be my people.

8 But I will tell you what will happen to cowards and to everyone who is unfaithful or dirty-minded or who murders or is sexually immoral or uses witchcraft or worships idols or tells lies. They will be thrown into that lake of fire and burning sulfur. This is the second death.

The New Jerusalem

9 I saw one of the seven angels who had the bowls filled with the seven last terrible troubles. The angel came to me and said, "Come on! I will show you the one who will be the bride and wife of the Lamb." 10 Then with the help of the Spirit, he took me to the top of a very high mountain. There he showed me the holy city of Jerusalem coming down from God in heaven.

11 The glory of God made the city bright. It was dazzling and crystal clear like a precious jasper stone. 12 The city had a high and thick wall with twelve gates, and each one of them was guarded by an angel. On each of the gates was written the name of one of the twelve tribes of Israel. 13 Three of these gates were on the east, three were on the north, three more were on the south, and the other three were on the west. 14 The city was built on twelve foundation stones. On each of the stones was written the name of one of the Lamb's twelve apostles.

15 The angel who spoke to me had a gold measuring stick to measure the city and its gates and its walls. 16 The city was shaped like a cube, because it was just as high as it was wide. When the angel measured the city, it was about fifteen hundred miles high and fifteen hundred miles wide. 17 Then the angel measured the wall, and by our measurements it was about two hundred sixteen feet high.

18 The wall was built of jasper, and the city was made of pure gold, clear as crystal. 19 Each of the twelve foundations was a precious stone. The first was jasper, the second was sapphire, the third was agate, the fourth was emerald, 20 the fifth was onyx, the sixth was carnelian, the seventh was chrysolite, the eighth was beryl, the ninth was topaz, the tenth was chrysoprase, the eleventh was jacinth, and the twelfth was amethyst. 21 Each of the twelve gates was a solid pearl. The streets of the city were made of pure gold, clear as crystal.

22 I did not see a temple there. The Lord God All-Powerful

and the Lamb were its temple. 23 And the city did not need the sun or the moon. The glory of God was shining on it, and the Lamb was its light.

24 Nations will walk by the light of that city, and kings will bring their riches there. 25 Its gates are always open during the day, and night never comes. 26 The glorious treasures of nations will be brought into the city. 27 But nothing unworthy will be allowed to enter. No one who is dirty-minded or who tells lies will be there. Only those whose names are written in the Lamb's book of life will be in the city.

22 The angel showed me a river that was crystal clear, and its waters gave life. The river came from the throne where God and the Lamb were seated. 2 Then it flowed down the middle of the city's main street. On each side of the river are trees[n] that grow a different kind of fruit each month of the year. The fruit gives life, and the leaves are used as medicine to heal the nations.

3 God's curse will no longer be on the people of that city. He and the Lamb will be seated there on their thrones, and its people will worship God 4 and will see him face to face. God's name will be written on the foreheads of the people. 5 Never again will night appear, and no one who lives there will ever need a lamp or the sun. The Lord God will be their light, and they will rule forever.

The Coming of Christ

6 Then I was told:

These words are true and can be trusted. The Lord God controls the spirits of his prophets, and he is the one who sent his angel to show his servants what must happen right away. 7 Remember, I am coming soon! God will bless everyone who pays attention to the message of this book.

8 My name is John, and I am the one who heard and saw these things. Then after I had heard and seen all this, I knelt down and began to worship at the feet of the angel who had shown it to me.

9 But the angel said,

Don't do that! I am a servant, just like you. I am the same as a follower or a prophet or anyone else who obeys what is written in this book. God is the one you should worship.

10 Don't keep the prophecies in this book a secret. These things will happen soon.

11 Evil people will keep on being evil, and everyone who is dirty-minded will still be dirty-minded. But good people will keep on doing right, and God's people will always be holy.

12 Then I was told:

I am coming soon! And when I come, I will reward everyone for what they have done. 13 I am Alpha and Omega, the first and the last, the beginning and the end.

14 God will bless all who have washed their robes. They will each have the right to eat fruit from the tree that gives life, and they can enter the gates of the city. 15 But outside the city will be dogs, witches, immoral people, murderers, idol worshipers, and everyone who loves to tell lies and do wrong.

16 I am Jesus! And I am the one who sent my angel to tell all of you these things for the churches. I am David's Great Descendant, and I am also the bright morning star.

17 The Spirit and the bride say, "Come!"

Everyone who hears this should say, "Come!"

If you are thirsty, come! If you want life-giving water, come and take it. It's free!

18 Here is my warning for everyone who hears the prophecies in this book:

If you add anything to them, God will make you suffer all the terrible troubles written in this book. 19 If you take anything away from these prophecies, God will not let you have part in the life-giving tree and in the holy city described in this book.

20 The one who has spoken these things says, "I am coming soon!"

So, Lord Jesus, please come soon!

21 I pray that the Lord Jesus will be kind to all of you.

---

[n] **22.2** *trees*: The Greek has "tree," which is used in a collective sense of trees on both sides of the heavenly river.

WHAT'S IN THE NEW TESTAMENT

The following brief descriptions are intended to give readers a general idea of what each book of the New Testament is about, to identify some of the key figures and themes, and to help readers get a sense of how one book of the Bible relates to the rest of the biblical literature. They cannot provide the depth of detail typically found in a Bible dictionary article or study Bible introduction.

NEW TESTAMENT

MATTHEW, MARK, LUKE, and JOHN: These four books together make up about half of the New Testament. They are called "Gospels," an Old English word meaning "Good News," because they tell the Good News about Jesus Christ and the kingdom of God. Although each Gospel is told from a different point of view, Matthew, Mark, and Luke's Gospels have clearly drawn upon some of the same oral and written sources. Mark is the shortest Gospel and provides a good overview of Jesus' ministry. Matthew and Luke cover much of the same material, but also provide details about Jesus' birth and include additional examples of Jesus' teachings. John's Gospel stands apart from the other three. It is organized around seven signs (miracles) that point to Jesus as the Son of God. This Gospel also reproduces a number of long conversations Jesus had in which he revealed to people who he was.

ACTS: Written by the author of Luke as a sequel to that Gospel, Acts tells the story of the early church. It begins with a description of Jesus being taken into heaven and the coming of the Holy Spirit to Jesus' disciples on the Day of Pentecost. Empowered by the Holy Spirit, the apostles take the Good News of Jesus Christ throughout the Mediterranean World. The apostle Peter is the dominant figure at the beginning of Acts; Paul, a Pharisee who had persecuted Jesus' disciples but later became a follower himself, is the key figure in the second half the book.

ROMANS: The letters that Paul wrote to churches and individuals to better explain the Good News of Jesus Christ are some of the earliest writings in the New Testament. The letter Paul wrote to the church in Rome is his longest, and perhaps his best effort to explain how people can be made acceptable to God because of the sacrifice Jesus Christ made for their sins.

1 and 2 CORINTHIANS: Paul had personally helped found the church in Corinth, a bustling Greek port city. The letters Paul wrote to this church are evidence that Paul cared deeply about the way the Christians there lived out their faith. In these letters, he tries to resolve a number of disputes on religious and ethical matters. In addition, he explains doctrinal issues, encourages unity among the believers, defends his right to be considered an apostle, warns against the teachings of false apostles, and asks the Corinthians to give money to support the struggling church in Jerusalem.

GALATIANS: This letter is addressed to unnamed churches in a region of central Asia Minor called Galatia. In it Paul asserts that he is a true apostle of Christ, that he received his message directly from Jesus Christ, and that the church leaders in Jerusalem, including Peter, agreed that Paul should take the Good News about Jesus to the Gentiles. Paul discusses the importance of faith and the wonderful freedom that people receive when they put their trust in Christ.

EPHESIANS: This short book summarizes many of the teachings found in the letters of Paul. A strong emphasis is placed on the unity that Christians have because of the sacrifice Christ made for all and because of the new life God's Spirit gives them.

PHILIPPIANS: Paul wrote this letter from prison. In it he expresses his affection for the Christians at the church in the Macedonian city Philippi and encourages them to remain faithful to Christ and to rejoice in whatever circumstance they find themselves.

COLOSSIANS: This letter, written to a Gentile church in Asia Minor, challenges the Christians there to avoid the false teachings of a group of people who were encouraging them to give up certain physical desires and to worship angels and spiritual powers. Instead, they are to set their hearts on Christ who is enthroned in heaven.

1 and 2 THESSALONIANS: First Thessalonians may be the oldest document in the New Testament. Here Paul gives advice to the people of Thessalonica concerning Christ's return and encourages them to make themselves ready. Second Thessalonians discusses the same topics.

1 and 2 TIMOTHY, and TITUS: These three letters have been called "Pastoral Letters," because they give advice about what local church leaders should do to look after the spiritual needs of the people in their care.

PHILEMON: In this letter, Paul urges a wealthy Christian named Philemon to forgive Onesimus, a slave who had run away. Onesimus had become a follower of

Christ and a friend to Paul. Paul urges Philemon to accept Onesimus as a brother in Christ.

HEBREWS: This book, written in the form of a letter, is a sermon about the superiority of Jesus Christ. He is shown to be superior to the angels, to the priesthood of Moses, and to the sacrifices that were made in the temple. Jesus is described as both the high priest and the sacrifice that takes away the sins of many. Written at a time when the church was being persecuted by Roman authorities, this letter encourages Christians to remain faithful to Christ and to learn from his example of self-sacrifice.

JAMES: This short book is a collection of teachings on a wide range of topics. The author advises Christians to learn to control what they say, to avoid showing favoritism to wealthy people, to care for the sick and needy, and to make a point of putting their faith into action.

1 and 2 PETER: The first letter was written to bring comfort and strength to Christians who were being persecuted for their faith. The second letter, which bears some similarities to the Letter of Jude, warns Christians about false teachers who will try to lure Christians away from the truth. The author urges Christians to remain loyal to God and to keep themselves pure because the Lord will return one day to judge the world.

1, 2, and 3 JOHN: First John was written to affirm that Jesus is the Christ, warn Christians about false prophets, and to explain basic truths about the Christian life. A special emphasis is placed on the command to love one another. Second John is a letter addressed to a church identified as "the elect lady and her children." It warns against false teachers. Third John is about a conflict between the author and a church leader named Diotrephes. It speaks about the importance of helping other followers to spread the truth about Christ.

JUDE: This letter warns against the influence of ungodly (immoral) people who claimed to have spiritual authority based on visions they received. These evil people were trying to encourage believers to disobey Jesus Christ. The author encourages his readers to keep their faith in God and to help any among them who may have doubts.

REVELATION: This book was written to encourage persecuted believers and to affirm their faith that God will care for them. Using visions and symbols, the writer announces that in the end Christ will defeat all the forces of evil and that those who have remained faithful to Christ will be welcomed into a new heaven and new earth.

WORD LIST

Aaron The brother of Moses. Only he and his descendants were to serve as priests and offer sacrifices for the people of Israel.

Abel The second son of Adam and Eve and the younger brother of Cain. Abel was killed by Cain after God accepted Abel's offering and refused to accept Cain's.

Abraham The first of the three great ancestors of the people of Israel. Abraham was the husband of Sarah and the father of Isaac. At first Abraham's name was Abram, meaning "Great Father." Then, when Abram was ninety-nine years old, God changed Abram's name to Abraham, which means "Father of a Crowd." Abraham trusted God, and so God promised that Abraham and his wife Sarah would have a son and more descendants than could be counted. God also promised that Abraham would be a blessing to everyone on earth.

Adam The first man and the husband of Eve.

Agrippa (1) Herod Agrippa was king of Judea A.D. 41-44 and mistreated Christians (see Acts 12.1-5) (2) Agrippa II was the son of Herod Agrippa and ruled parts of Palestine from A.D. 53 to A.D. 93 or later. He and his sister Bernice listened to Paul defend himself (see Acts 25.13-26,32).

Aloes A sweet-smelling spice that was mixed with myrrh and used as a perfume.

Altar A raised structure where sacrifices and offerings were presented to God or to pagan gods. Altars could be made of rocks, packed earth, metal, or pottery.

Amen A Hebrew word used after a prayer or a blessing and meaning that what had been said was right and true.

Ancestor Someone born earlier in a family line, especially several generations earlier.

Angel A supernatural being who tells God's messages to people or protects those who belong to God.

Antipas (1) Herod Antipas, son of Herod the Great (see "Herod"). (2) An otherwise unknown Christian at Pergamum, who was killed because he was a follower of Christ (see Revelation 2.13).

Apostle A person chosen and sent by Christ to take his message to others. Lists of the names of Christ's twelve apostles can be found in Matthew 10.2-4; Mark 3.16-19; Luke 6.14-16; Acts 1.12,13. Later, others such as Paul and James the brother of Jesus also became known as apostles.

Aramaic A language closely related to Hebrew. In New Testament times Aramaic was spoken by many Jews including Jesus.

Asia A Roman province in what is today the nation of Turkey.

Augustus A title meaning "honored," which was given to Octavian by the Romans when he began ruling the Roman world in 27 B.C. He was the Roman Emperor when Jesus was born.

Babylonia A large empire of Old Testament times, whose capital city Babylon was located in south-central Mesopotamia. The Babylonians defeated the southern kingdom of Judah in 586 B.C. and forced many of its people to live in Babylonia.

Barley A grain that was used to make bread.

Bashan The flat highlands and wooded hills of southern Syria. Bashan was just north of the region of Gilead and was known for its fat cattle and fine grain.

Benjamin Occupied land between Bethel and Jerusalem. When the northern tribes of Israel broke away following the death of Solomon, only the tribes of Benjamin and Judah were left to form the southern kingdom.

Cain The first son of Adam and Eve; Cain killed his brother Abel after God accepted Abel's offering and refused to accept Cain's.

Christ A Greek word meaning "the Chosen One" and used to translate the Hebrew word "Messiah." In New Testament times, many of the Jews believed that God was going to send the Messiah to set them free from the power of their enemies. The term "Christ" is used in the New Testament both as a title and as a name for Jesus.

Circumcise To cut off the foreskin from the male organ. This was done for Israelite boys eight days after they were born. God commanded that all newborn Israelite boys be circumcised to show that they belonged to his people.

Citizen A person who is given special rights and privileges by a nation or state. In return, a citizen was expected to be loyal to that nation or state.

Commandments God's rules for his people to live by. The most famous are the Ten Commandments.

Council (1) A group of leaders who meet and make decisions for their people. (2) The Old Testament refers to God's council as a group of angels who meet and talk with God in heaven.

Cumin A plant with small seeds used for seasoning food.

David King of Israel from about 1010-970 B.C. David was the most famous king Israel ever had, and many of the people of Israel hoped that one of his descendants would always be their king.

Demons and **Evil Spirits** Supernatural beings that do harmful things to people and sometimes cause them to do bad things. In the New Testament they are sometimes called "unclean spirits," because people under their power were thought to be unclean and unfit to worship God.

Descendant Someone born one or more generations later in a family line.

Devil The chief of the demons and evil spirits, also known as "Satan."

Disciples Those who were followers of Jesus and learned from him. The term often refers to his twelve apostles.

Edomites A nation living in Edom or Seir, an area south and southeast of the Dead Sea. The Edomites descended from Esau, Jacob's brother.

Elijah A prophet who spoke for God in the early ninth century B.C. and who opposed the evil King Ahab and Queen Jezebel of the northern kingdom. Many Jews in later centuries thought Elijah would return to get everything ready for the day of judgment or for the coming of the Messiah (see Matthew 17.10,11; Mark 9.11,12).

Elders Men whose age and wisdom made them respected leaders.

Emperor The person who ruled an empire.

Ephraim One of the largest tribes. Ephraim occupied the land north of Benjamin and south of West Manasseh.

Epicureans People who followed the teachings of a man named Epicurus, who taught that happiness should be the main goal in life.

Eternal Life Life that is the gift of God and that never ends.

Ethiopia A region south of Egypt that included parts of the present countries of Ethiopia and Sudan.

Evil Spirits See "Demons."

Exile The time in Israel's history (597-539 B.C.) when the Babylonians took away many of the people of Jerusalem and Judah as prisoners of war and made them live in Babylonia. The northern tribes had been taken away by Assyria in 722 B.C.

Felix The Roman governor of Palestine A.D. 52-60, who listened to Paul speak and kept him in jail (see Acts 23.24-24.27).

Festival of Shelters A festival in the early fall celebrating the period of forty years when the people of Israel walked through the desert and lived in small shelters. This happy celebration began on the fifteenth day of Tishri; and for the next seven days, the people lived in small shelters made of tree branches. The name of this festival in Hebrew is "Sukkoth."

Festival of Thin Bread A seven-day festival right after Passover. During this festival the Israelites ate a thin, flat bread made without yeast to remind themselves how God freed the people of Israel from slavery in Egypt and made them into a nation. The name of this festival in Hebrew is "Mazzoth."

Festus The Roman governor after Felix, who sent Paul to stand trial in Rome (see Acts 24.27-26.32).

Generation One way of describing a group of people who live during the same period of time. In the Bible the time of one generation is often understood to be about forty years.

Gentiles Those people who are not Jews.

Glory Something seen, heard, or felt that shows a person or thing is important, wonderful, or powerful. When God appeared to people, his glory was often seen as a bright light or as fire and smoke. Jesus' glory was seen when he performed miracles, when he was lifted up on the cross, and when he was raised from death.

God's Tent See "Sacred Tent."

Greek The language used throughout the Mediterranean world in New Testament times, and _the language in which the New Testament was written.

Hagar A slave of Sarah, the wife of Abraham. When Sarah could not have any children, she followed the ancient custom of letting her husband have a child by Hagar, her slave. The boy's name was Ishmael.

Hebrew The language used by most of the people of Israel until the Exile. But after the people returned, more and more people spoke Aramaic instead. Most of the Old Testament was written in Hebrew.

Hermes The Greek god of skillful speaking and the messenger of the other Greek gods.

Herod (1) Herod the Great was the king of all Palestine 37-4 B.C., and so he was king at the time Jesus was born (see the note at "A.D."). _(2) Herod Antipas was the son of Herod the Great and was the ruler of Galilee 4 B.C.-A.D. 39. (3) Herod Agrippa I, the grandson of Herod the Great, ruled Palestine A.D. 41-44.

High Priest See "priest."

Holy One A name for the Savior that God had promised to send (see "Savior").

Hyssop A bush with clusters of small branches. In religious ceremonies, hyssop was sometimes dipped in a liquid and then used to sprinkle people or objects.

Incense A material that makes a sweet smell when burned. It was used in the worship of God.

Isaac The second of the three great ancestors of the people of Israel. He was the son of Abraham and Sarah, and he was the father of Esau and Jacob.

Israel See "Jacob."

Jacob The third great ancestor of the people of Israel. Jacob was the son of Isaac and Rebekah, and his name was changed to Israel when he struggled with God at Peniel near the Jabbok River.

Joseph A son of Jacob and Rachel. Joseph was sold as a slave by his brothers, but later he became governor of Egypt.

Judah Occupied the hill country west of the Dead Sea. When the ten northern tribes of Israel broke away following the death of Solomon, only the tribes of Judah and Benjamin were left to form the southern kingdom, and it was also called "Judah."

Judges Leaders chosen by the Lord for the people of Israel after the time of Joshua and before the time of the kings.

Kadesh A town in the desert of Paran southwest of the Dead Sea, near the southern border of Israel and the western border of Edom. Israel camped at Kadesh while the twelve tribal leaders explored Canaan.

Law and the Prophets A term used in New Testament times to refer to the sacred writings of the Jews. The Law and the Prophets were two of the three sections of the Old Testament, but the expression sometimes refers to the entire Old Testament.

Law of Moses and Law of the Lord Usually refers to the first five books of the Old Testament, but sometimes to the entire Old Testament.

Leviathan A legendary sea monster representing revolt and evil, also known from Canaanite writings.

Levites Those Israelites who belonged to the tribe of Levi. God chose the men of one Levite family, the descendants of Aaron, to be Israel's priests. The other men from this tribe helped with the work in the sacred tent and later in the temple.

LORD In the Old Testament the word "LORD" in capital letters stands for the Hebrew consonants YHWH, the personal name of God. Ancient Hebrew did not have vowel letters, and so anyone reading Hebrew would have to know what vowels to put with the consonants. It is not known for certain what vowel sounds were originally used with the consonants YHWH. The word "Lord" represents the Hebrew term Adonai, the usual word for "lord." By late Old Testament times, Jews considered God's personal name too holy to be pronounced. So they said Adonai, "Lord," whenever they read YHWH. When the Jewish scribes first translated the Hebrew Scriptures into ancient Greek, they translated the personal name of God as Kurios, "Lord." Since that time, most translations, including the Contemporary English Version, have followed their example and have avoided using the personal name of God.

Manasseh Occupied two areas of land: (1) East Manasseh lived east of the Jordan River and north of the Jabbok River in the areas of Bashan and northern Gilead. (2) West Manasseh lived west of the Jordan River and to the north of Ephraim.

Messiah See "Christ."

Mint A garden plant used for seasoning and medicine.

Moab A nation that lived east of the Dead Sea. The people of Moab descended from Lot, the nephew of Abraham.

Moses The prophet who led the people of Israel when God rescued them from slavery in Egypt. Moses also received laws from God and gave them to Israel.

Myrrh A valuable sweet-smelling powder used in perfume.

Naphtali Occupied land north and west of Lake Galilee.

Nazarenes A name that was sometimes used for the followers of Jesus, who came from the small town of Nazareth (see Acts 24.5).

Noah When God destroyed the world by a flood, Noah and his family were kept safe in a big boat that God had told him to build.

Passover A festival held on the fourteenth day of Abib in the early spring. At Passover the Israelites celebrated the time God rescued them from slavery in Egypt. The name of this festival in Hebrew is "Pesach."

Pentecost A Jewish festival held in mid-spring, fifty days after Passover. At this festival Israelites celebrated the wheat harvest. Pentecost was also known as "the Harvest Festival" and has traditionally been called "the Feast of Weeks"; in Hebrew, its name is "Shavuoth."

Pharisees A group of Jews who thought they could best serve God by strictly obeying the laws of the Old Testament as well as their own rules, traditions, and teachings.

Phoenicia The territory along the Mediterranean Sea controlled by the cities of Tyre, Sidon,

Arvad, and Byblos. The coast of modern Lebanon covers about the same area.

Priest A man who led the worship in the sacred tent or in the temple and who offered sacrifices. Some of the more important priests were called "chief priests," and the most important priest was called the "high priest."

Promised One A title for the Savior that God promised to send (see "Savior").

Prophesy See "prophet."

Prophet Someone who speaks God's message, which at times included telling what would happen in the future. Sometimes when the Spirit of God took control of prophets, they lost some or all control over their speech and actions or were not aware of what was happening around them.

Proverb A wise saying that is short and easy to remember.

Psalm A Hebrew poem. Psalms were often written in such a way that they could be prayed or sung by an individual or a group. Some of the psalms thank and praise God, while others ask God to take away sins or to give protection, comfort, vengeance, or mercy.

Rue A garden plant used for seasoning and medicine.

Sabbath The seventh day of the week, from sunset on Friday to sunset on Saturday. Israelites worshiped on the Sabbath and rested from their work.

Sacred Tent The tent where the people of Israel worshiped God before the temple was built. It has traditionally been called "the tabernacle."

Sacrifices These gifts to God included certain animals, grains, fruits, and sweet-smelling spices. Israelites offered sacrifices to give thanks to God, to ask for his forgiveness and his blessing, and to make a payment for a wrong. Some sacrifices were completely burned on the altar. In the case of other sacrifices, a portion was given to the Lord and burned on the altar, then the rest was eaten by the priests or the worshipers who had offered the sacrifice.

Sadducees A small and powerful group of Jews in New Testament times. They were closely connected with the high priests and accepted only the first five books of the Old Testament as their Bible. They also did not believe in life after death.

Samaria (1) The capital city of the northern kingdom of Israel beginning with the rule of King Omri (ruled 885-874 B.C.). (2) In New Testament times, a district between Judea and Galilee, named for the city of Samaria. The people of this district, called "Samaritans," worshiped God differently from the Jews, and these two groups refused to have anything to do with one another.

Sarah The wife of Abraham and the mother of Isaac. At first her name was Sarai, but when she was old, God promised her that she would have a son, and he changed her name to Sarah. Both names mean "princess."

Satan See "devil."

Save To rescue people from the power of their enemies or from the power of evil, and to give them new life and place them under God's care (see also "Savior").

Savior The one that God has chosen to rescue or save his people (see also "Save").

Scriptures Although this term now refers to the whole Bible, in the New Testament it refers to the Old Testament.

Sin Turning away from God and disobeying the teachings or commandments of God.

Solomon A son of King David and Bathsheba. After David's death, Solomon ruled Israel about 970-931 B.C. Solomon built the temple in Jerusalem and was widely known for his wisdom. The Hebrew text indicates that he wrote many of the proverbs and two of the psalms.

Son of Man A title often used by Jesus to refer to himself. This title is also found in the Hebrew text of Daniel and Psalms and God uses it numerous times in the book of Ezekiel to refer to Ezekiel.

Stoics Followers of a man named Zeno, who taught that people should learn self-control and be guided by their consciences.

Taxes and **Tax Collectors** Special fees collected by rulers. Taxes are usually part of the value of crops, property, or income. Taxes were collected at markets, city gates, ports, and border crossings. In New Testament times, Jews were hired by the Roman government to collect taxes from other Jews, and these tax collectors were hated by their own people.

Temple A building used as a place of worship. The god that was worshiped in a particular temple was believed to be present there in a special way. The LORD's temple was in Jerusalem.

Temple Festival In 165 B.C. the Jewish people recaptured the temple in Jerusalem from their enemies and made it fit for worship again. They celebrated this event each year by an eight-day festival that began on the twenty-fifth day of the month of Chislev in the late fall. This festival is traditionally called "the Festival of Dedication," or in Hebrew, "Hanukkah."

Way In the book of Acts the Christian life is sometimes called "the Way" or "the Way of the Lord" or "God's Way."

Wisdom Often refers to the common sense and practical skill needed to solve everyday problems, but sometimes involves trying to find answers to the hard questions about the meaning of life.

Zebulun Occupied land north of Manasseh from the eastern end of Mount Carmel to Mount Tabor.

Zeus The chief god of the Greeks.

Zion Another name for Jerusalem. Zion can also refer to the hill in Jerusalem where the temple was built.

PALESTINE IN NEW TESTAMENT TIMES

MILES 0 — 40

KMS 0 — 40

MEDITERRANEAN SEA

Sidon

Zarephath

LEBANON MTS.

Tyre

PHOENICIA

SYRIA

Abila

ABILENE

Damascus

▲ MT. HERMON

Caesarea Philippi

Ptolemais

GALILEE

Chorazin

Capernaum ● Bethsaida

Magadan

Lake

▲ MT. CARMEL

Cana

Tiberias

Galilee

Nazareth

Nain ● ▲MT. TABOR

Gadara

Caesarea

SAMARIA

Salim

Aenon

TEN TOWNS

Samaria

▲MT. EBAL

MT. GERIZIM ▲● Sychar

Gerasa

Joppa

Arimathea?

Jordan River

Ephraim

PEREA

Jericho

Emmaus

Bethany

Azotus

Jerusalem

Qumran

Ascalon

Bethlehem

JUDEA

Dead

Sea

Gaza

Hebron

IDUMEA

NABATEA

© United Bible Societies, 1976

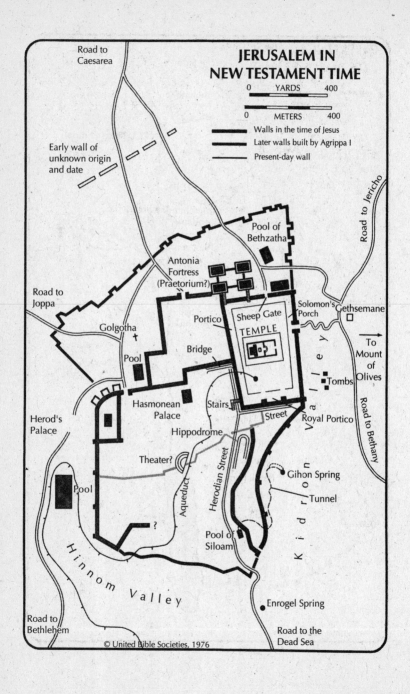

JERUSALEM IN NEW TESTAMENT TIME

Road to Caesarea

YARDS
0   400

METERS
0   400

━━━ Walls in the time of Jesus
═══ Later walls built by Agrippa I
─── Present-day wall

Early wall of unknown origin and date

Road to Jericho

Pool of Bethzatha

Antonia Fortress (Praetorium?)

Road to Joppa

Golgotha

Portico

Sheep Gate

Solomon's Porch

Gethsemane

TEMPLE

Pool

Bridge

Street

To Mount of Olives

Hasmonean Palace

Stairs

Royal Portico

Tombs

Herod's Palace

Hippodrome

Road to Bethany

Theater?

Gihon Spring

Tunnel

Pool

Aqueduct

Herodian Street

?

Pool of Siloam

Kidron Valley

Hinnom Valley

Enrogel Spring

Road to Bethlehem

Road to the Dead Sea